Wiley CIAexcel® Exam Review 2022

Wiley CIAexcel® Exam Review 2022

Part 1: Essentials of Internal Auditing

S. Rao Vallabhaneni

Wiley Efficient Learning™

For general information about our other products and services, please contact our Customer Care Department within the United States at (800) 762-2974, outside the United States at (317) 572-3993 or fax (317) 572-4002.

Wiley publishes in a variety of print and electronic formats and by print-on-demand. Some material included with standard print versions of this book may not be included in e-books or in print-on-demand. If this book refers to media such as a CD or DVD that is not included in the version you purchased, you may download this material at http://booksupport.wiley.com. For more information about Wiley products, visit www.wiley.com.

Library of Congress Cataloging-in-Publication Data:

ISBN 978-1-119-84628-4; ISBN 978-1-119-84627-7 (ePDF); ISBN 978-1-119-84619-2 (ePub)

Printed in the United States of America

SKY10029280_082021

Contents

Preface

The Certified Internal Auditor (CIA) Examination is a program of the Institute of Internal Auditors (IIA), Inc. The CIA examination certifies a person as a professional internal auditor and is intended to measure the knowledge, skills, and competency required in the field of internal auditing. The Certified Internal Auditor designation is the hallmark of an expert in internal auditing. Wiley's CIA Exam Review Products are developed to help prepare a CIA Exam candidate for the CIA Exam by reflecting the exam syllabus and by reflecting the new International Professional Practices Framework of 2017 (new IPPF of 2017) issued in January 2017 consisting of professional standards.

The CIA Exam syllabus tests a CIA Exam candidate's knowledge at two cognitive levels—the proficient level and the basic level—as indicated in the IIA's content specifications outlines (www.theiia.org). These cognitive levels suggest allocating more time and effort to prepare for the proficient-level topics and comparatively less time and effort to prepare for the basic-level topics. The scope of the CIA Exam consists of three parts:

Part 1: Essentials of Internal Auditing

Part 2: Practice of Internal Auditing

Part 3: Business Knowledge for Internal Auditing

This Review Book covers Part 1 of the CIA Exam.

For each part of the exam, Wiley has developed a comprehensive suite of review products to study and prepare for the CIA Exam. This suite includes (1) Review Book (Study Guide), (2) Focus Notes, and (3) Web-Based Online Test Bank Software.

1. The **Review Book** provides a thorough presentation of theoretical coverage of the subject matter as required in the exam syllabus.

2. The **Focus Notes** (index cards) provide a quick review of the same subject matter presented in the Review Book but in a condensed manner to reinforce key concepts. Wiley's theme in the Focus Notes is Remember, Reinforce, and Recall key concepts.

3. The **Web-based online test bank software** provides hundreds of sample multiple-choice questions to practice. We suggest repeating the test bank several times for reinforcement before taking the actual exam. The actual CIA Exam questions will be harder than these sample questions. However, practicing the sample questions yields several benefits to students, such as (1) providing a knowledge base of the subject matter; (2) conditioning

students to the exam mode; (3) using sample questions close to the actual exam questions; and (4) above all, building student confidence in taking the real CIA Exam.

Wiley's goal is to provide all the required study materials for CIA Exam study and preparation in one place with one source for either self-study or a group study effort. Visit www.wileyCIA.com for product details and order placement.

We suggest students use a sequential, four-step study approach for each part of the exam:

1. Study the theory domains from each part of the Review Book.

2. Practice the multiple-choice questions from the online test bank for each part.

3. Read the Focus Notes for each part for a quick review at any time and especially before taking the actual exam.

Administrative Matters

We encourage new, prospective CIA Exam candidates to contact the Institute of Internal Auditors directly for exam application forms, exam eligibility requirements, online exam-taking sites and fees, and general information about the exam.

Institute of Internal Auditors

1035 Greenwood Boulevard, Suite 401

Lake Mary, FL, 32746, USA

Phone: +1-407-937-1100, Fax: +1-407-937-1108

Website: www.theiia.org

Acknowledgments

The author is indebted to a number of people and organizations that helped to improve the content and quality of this book. Thanks to the Director of Certifications and the CIA certification team at the Institute of Internal Auditors, Lake Mary, Florida, for providing great assistance during the writing of these books. Special thanks to the IIA for providing previous CIA Exam questions, answers, and explanations, IIA's International Professional Practices Framework (IPPF) *Standards, Implementation Guidance, Code of Ethics, Practice Guides,* and *CIA's Model Exam* questions. Many thanks also go to Wiley's editorial content management and marketing teams for their capable assistance in completing the CIA Exam Review Products.

Specifically, the author wants to thank the following for using or adapting their materials.

- U.S. Government Accountability Office, Washington, DC, www.gao.gov
- Federal Trade Commission, Washington, DC, www.ftc.gov
- Securities and Exchange Commission, Washington, DC, www.sec.gov
- U.S. Federal Reserve System, Washington, DC, www.federalreserve.gov
- U.S. Business Roundtable. Washington, DC, www.brt.org
- U.S. Office of Management and Budget, Washington, DC, www.omb.gov
- U.S. Committee of Sponsoring Organizations of the Treadway Commission (COSO), New York, NY, www.coso.org
- France's Organisation for Economic Co-operation and Development, Paris, France, www.oecd.org
- Risk Management Society (RIMS), New York, NY, www.rims.org
- U.S. National Association of Corporate Directors, Arlington, VA, www.nacdonline.org
- Switzerland's International Organization for Standardization, Geneva, Switzerland, www.iso.org

CIA Exam Content Syllabus and Specifications

Part 1 of the CIA Exam syllabus is called **Essentials of Internal Auditing** and includes six domains containing several topics. These six domains cover:

1. The foundation of internal auditing

2. Independence and objectivity

3. Proficiency and due professional care

4. Quality assurance and improvement program

5. Governance, risk management, and control

6. Fraud risks

Part 1 tests a CIA Exam candidate's knowledge, skills, and abilities related to the *International Standards for the Professional Practice of Internal Auditing*, particularly the Attribute Standards (i.e., Series 1000, 1100, 1200, and 1300) as well as Performance Standard 2100. In other words, the Part 1 syllabus is greatly aligned with the IIA's *Attribute Standards*.

Each domain is assigned with a relative weight of its importance to each part, expressed as a percentage of study time and effort required (i.e., higher weights require larger amounts of study time and effort). Each topic within a domain will be tested at the cognitive level of proficient (P) or basic (B). Here, "proficient" means CIA Exam candidates are required to demonstrate a proficiency in their KSAs. "Basic" means the candidates are required to demonstrate a basic comprehension of concepts. Greater amounts of study time and effort are required for topics tested at the proficient level. Note that the combination of higher weight and proficient level requires a greater amount of study time and effort to earn success in the exam than the combination of lower weight and basic level.

The exam duration for Part 1 is 2.5 hours (150 minutes) with 125 multiple-choice questions. The following is a breakdown of domains and topics in Part 1.

Domain I: Foundations of Internal Auditing (15%)

A Interpret the IIA's Mission of Internal Audit, Definition of Internal Auditing, and Core Principles for the Professional Practice of Internal Auditing, and the purpose, authority, and responsibility of the internal audit activity. (P)

B Explain the requirements of an internal audit charter (e.g., required components, board approval, and communication of the charter). (B)

C Interpret the difference between assurance and consulting services provided by the internal audit activity. (P)

D Demonstrate conformance with the IIA Code of Ethics. (P)

Domain II: Independence and Objectivity (15%)

A Interpret organizational independence of the internal audit activity (e.g., importance of independence and functional reporting). (B)

B Identify whether the internal audit activity has any impairments to its independence. (B)

C Assess and maintain an individual internal auditor's objectivity, including determining whether an individual internal auditor has any impairments to his/her objectivity. (P)

D Analyze policies that promote objectivity. (P)

Domain III: Proficiency and Due professional Care (18%)

A Recognize the knowledge, skills, and competencies required (i.e., whether developed or procured) to fulfill the responsibilities of the internal audit activity. (B)

B Demonstrate the knowledge and competencies that an internal auditor needs to possess to perform his/her individual responsibilities, including technical skills and soft skills (e.g., communication skills, critical thinking skills, persuasion/negotiation skills, and collaboration skills). (P)

C Demonstrate due professional care. (P)

D Demonstrate an individual internal auditor's competency through continuing professional development. (P)

Domain IV: Quality Assurance and Improvement Program (7%)

A Describe the required elements of the quality assurance and improvement program (e.g., internal assessments and external assessments). (B)

B Describe the requirement of reporting the results of the quality assurance and improvement program to the board or other governing body. (B)

C Identify appropriate disclosure of conformance versus nonconformance with the IIA's *International Standards for the Professional Practice of Internal Auditing*. (B)

Domain V: Governance, Risk Management, and Control (35%)

A Describe the concept of organizational governance. (B)

B Recognize the impact of organizational culture on the overall control environment and individual engagement risks and controls. (B)

C Recognize and interpret the organization's ethics and compliance-related issues, alleged violations, and dispositions. (B)

D Describe corporate social responsibility. (B)

E Interpret fundamental concepts of risk and the risk management process. (P)

F Describe globally accepted risk management frameworks appropriate to the organization (e.g., COSO, ERM, and ISO 31000). (B)

G Examine the effectiveness of risk management within processes and functions. (P)

H Recognize the appropriateness of the internal audit activity's role in the organization's risk management process. (B)

I Interpret internal control concepts and types of controls. (P)

J Apply globally accepted internal control frameworks appropriate to the organization (e.g., COSO). (P)

K Examine the effectiveness and efficiency of internal controls. (P)

Domain VI: Fraud Risks (10%)

A Interpret fraud risks and types of frauds and determine whether fraud risks require special consideration when conducting an engagement. (P)

B Evaluate the potential for occurrence of fraud (e.g., red flags) and how the organization detects and manages fraud risks. (P)

C Recommend controls to prevent and detect fraud and education to improve the organization's fraud awareness. (P)

D Recognize techniques and internal audit roles related to forensic auditing (e.g., interview, investigation, and testing). (B)

CIA Exam-Taking Tips

The types of questions a candidate can expect to see in the CIA Exam are fact-based, concept-based, application-based, objective-based, and scenario-based multiple-choice (M/C) questions with four choices of A, B, C, and D or a, b, c, and d. A systematic method in reading, interpreting, and answering the M/C questions can make the difference between a pass or fail in the exam. Moreover, answering the M/C questions requires a good amount of practice and effort.

These tips and techniques will be helpful in answering the CIA Exam questions:

- Stay with your first impression of the correct choice.

- Know the subject area or topic. Don't read too much into the question.

- Remember that questions are independent of specific country, products, practices, vendors, hardware, software, or industry.

- Read the last sentence of the question first followed by all choices and then the body (stem) of the question paragraph containing the last sentence. This is a reversal of the normal reading to highlight the key points quickly.

- Read the question twice, read the keywords twice, and watch for tip-off words that denote absolute conditions. Examples of keywords are *most, least, major, minor, all, not,* and *except.* Examples of tip-off words are *always, never,* and *every.*

- Do not project the question into your own organizational environment, practices, policies, procedures, standards, and guidelines. The examination focuses on the IIA's Professional Standards and Publications and on the CIA Exam syllabus (i.e., content specifications). Also, questions require a universal answer and knowledge of best practices.

- Try to eliminate wrong choices as quickly as possible. When you get down to two semifinal choices, take a big-picture approach. For example, if choices A and D are semifinalists, and choice D could be a part of choice A, then select choice A; or if choice D could be a more complete answer, then select choice D.

- Don't spend too much time on one question. If you are not sure of an answer, move on, and go back to it if time permits. The last resort is to guess the answer. There is no penalty for guessing the wrong answer.

Remember that success in any professional certification examination depends on several factors required of any student, such as time management skills, preparation time and effort levels, education and experience levels, memory recall of the subject matter in a timely manner, calm and collected state of mind before or during the exam, and decision-making skills. Good luck on the exam!

Professional *Standards*

This section defines the new International Professional Practices Framework – 2017 (new IPPF of 2017) issued in January 2017 and serves as a strong orientation to the new CIA Exam's Professional *Standards*, all of which are effective in January 2019.

It presents a detailed discussion of four Attribute *Standards*, such as 1000, 1100, 1200, and 1300 series, and one Performance *Standard*, such as 2100 series. The only reason for putting all the relevant Professional *Standards* in one place in this section is to provide a solid mind-print of the *Standards* in the first reading. Later, study the specific *Standards* in this section as they apply to each domain for an in-depth understanding of the *Standards*. In addition to the *Standards*, three important topics, Risks to Internal Audit Activity, Auditing Metrics and Key Performance Indicators, and Three Lines of Defense, are presented. Listing all the relevant *Standards* in one place is a great convenience to students in serving as a memory jogger.

Note that the *Standards* should be studied together with the theoretical subject matter presented in Domains 1 through 6, as follows.

> *Standards*: 1000 and 1010 ⟶ Domain 1
>
> *Standards*: 1100, 1110, 1111, 1112, 1120, and 1130 ⟶ Domain 2
>
> *Standards*: 1200, 1210, 1220, and 1230 ⟶ Domain 3
>
> *Standards*: 1300, 1310, 1311, 1312, 1320, 1321, and 1322 ⟶ Domain 4
>
> *Standards*: 2100, 2110, 2120, and 2130 ⟶ Domain 5
>
> *Standards*: 1220 ⟶ Domain 6

Note that this section does not contain any sample practice questions at the end because such questions are included in their respective domains in this book (i.e., Domains 1 through 6). With respect to the CIA Exam, cognitive levels are labeled as proficient level and basic level. These cognitive levels suggest that more time and effort should be spent in studying and mastering the subject matter covered in the topics labeled as the proficient level. Comparatively less time and effort should be spent on the topics labeled as the basic level.

i.1 New IPPF Defined

The new International Professional Practices Framework – 2017 (new IPPF of 2017) is the conceptual framework that organizes the authoritative guidance promulgated by The Institute of Internal Auditors (IIA). Authoritative guidance is composed of two categories: mandatory guidance and recommended guidance.

The mission of internal audit describes internal audit's primary purpose and overarching goal. Achievement of the mission is supported by the new IPPF of 2017, including the mandatory guidance elements of the Core Principles for the Professional Practice of Internal Auditing (Core Principles), the Definition of Internal Auditing (Definition), the Code of Ethics, and the *International Standards for the Professional Practice of Internal Auditing* (*Standards*). The IPPF also includes recommended guidance with elements of implementation guidance and supplemental guidance.

Mission = Purpose + Goals + Objectives

Authoritative Guidance = Mandatory Guidance + Recommended Guidance

Mandatory Guidance = Core Principles + Definition + Code of Ethics + *Standards*

Recommended Guidance = Implementation Guidance + Supplemental Guidance.

New IPPF = Mission + Mandatory Guidance + Recommended Guidance

i.2 Introduction to the IIA's *Standards*

A **Standard** is a professional pronouncement promulgated by the IIA's Internal Audit Standards Board (IASB) that delineates the requirements for performing a broad range of internal audit activities and for evaluating internal audit performance.

Internal auditing is conducted in diverse legal and cultural environments; for organizations that vary in purpose, size, complexity, and structure; and by persons within or outside the organization. Examples of these environments where audits are conducted include private sector, public sector, for-profit organizations, and not-for-profit organizations operating at the local, city, state, regional, province, national, and continent level. While differences may affect the practice of internal auditing in each environment, conformance with the Institute of Internal Auditor's (IIA's) *International Standards for the Professional Practice of Internal Auditing – 2017* (*Standards – 2017*) is essential in meeting the responsibilities of internal auditors and the internal audit activity.

The purpose of the *Standards* is to:

- Guide adherence with the mandatory elements of the International Professional Practices Framework (IPPF-2017).

- Provide a framework for performing and promoting a broad range of value-added internal auditing service.

- Establish the basis for the evaluation of internal audit performance.

- Foster improved organizational processes and operations.

The *Standards* are a set of principles-based, mandatory requirements consisting of:

- Statements of core requirements for the professional practice of internal auditing and for evaluating the effectiveness of performance that is internationally applicable at organizational and individual levels.

- Interpretations clarifying terms or concepts within the *Standards*.

The *Standards*, together with the Code of Ethics, encompass all mandatory elements of the IPPF; therefore, conformance with the Code of Ethics and the *Standards* demonstrates conformance with all mandatory elements of the IPPF.

The *Standards* use the word "must" to specify an unconditional requirement and the word "should" where conformance is expected unless, when applying professional judgment, circumstances justify deviation.

The *Standards* comprise two main categories: Attribute *Standards* and Performance *Standards*. Implementation *Standards* expand on the Attribute *Standards* and Performance *Standards* by providing the requirements applicable to assurance services or consulting services.

- **Attribute *Standards*** address the characteristics of organizations and parties performing internal audit activities.

- **Performance *Standards*** describe the nature of internal audit activities and provide criteria against which the performance of these services can be evaluated.

Both Attribute *Standards* and Performance *Standards* apply to all internal audit services.

The *Standards* apply to individual internal auditors and the internal audit activity. All internal auditors are accountable for conforming with the *Standards* related to individual objectivity, proficiency, and due professional care and the *Standards* relevant to the performance of their job responsibilities. Chief audit executives (CAEs) are additionally accountable for the internal audit activity's overall conformance with the *Standards*.

If internal auditors or the internal audit activity is prohibited by law or regulation from conformance with certain parts of the *Standards*, conformance with all other parts of the *Standards* and appropriate disclosures are needed.

If the *Standards* are used in conjunction with requirements issued by other authoritative bodies, internal audit communications may also cite the use of other requirements, as appropriate. In such a case, if the internal audit activity indicates conformance with the *Standards* and inconsistencies exist between the *Standards* and other requirements, internal auditors and the internal audit activity must conform to the *Standards* and may conform with the other requirements if such requirements are more restrictive.

Mandatory Guidance versus Recommended Guidance

The IIA offers two major types of guidance to the internal auditing profession—mandatory guidance and recommended guidance—which are the scope of authoritative guidance.

Mandatory guidance is developed following an established due diligence process, which includes a period of public exposure for stakeholder input. The ultimate goal is to have a framework where conformance with the Code of Ethics and the *Standards* achieves conformance with the Core Principles. Conformance with the principles set forth in mandatory guidance is required and essential for the professional practice of internal auditing.

Specifically, mandatory guidance covers attribute standards and performance standards. Attribute *Standards* address the characteristics of organizations and parties performing internal audit activities. Performance *Standards* describe the nature of internal audit activities and provide criteria against which the performance of these services can be evaluated.

Recommended guidance (nonmandatory guidance) addresses implementation guidance and supplemental guidance. These guides are endorsed by the IIA through a formal approval process. It describes practices for effective implementation of the IIA's Core Principles, Definition of Internal Auditing, Code of Ethics, and *Standards*.

Implementation guidance is designed to assist both internal auditors and internal audit activities to enhance their ability to achieve conformance with the *Standards*. Specifically, implementation guides assist internal auditors in applying the *Standards*, and they expand on the Attribute *Standards* and Performance *Standards*. They collectively address internal audit's approach, methodologies, and consideration, but do not detail processes or procedures.

Supplemental guidance provides detailed guidance for conducting internal audit activities. These include topical areas, sector-specific issues, as well as processes and procedures, tools and techniques, programs, step-by-step approaches, and examples of deliverables. Specifically, supplemental guides include several types of practice guides, such as global technology audit guides, guides to the assessment of information technology (IT) risks, and general-purpose practice guides.

Mandatory Guidance = Attribute *Standards* + Performance *Standards*

Recommended Guidance = Implementation Guidance + Supplemental Guidance

i.3 IIA's International *Standards*

This section presents four Attribute *Standards*, the 1000, 1100, 1200, and 1300 series, and one Performance *Standard*, the 2100 series. These *Standards* and their substandards include the following.

   ✱ 1000—Purpose, Authority, and Responsibility

      1010—Recognizing Mandatory Guidance in the Internal Audit Charter

   ✱ 1100—Independence and Objectivity

      1110—Organizational Independence

      1111—Direct Interaction with the Board

      1112—Chief Audit Executive Roles Beyond Internal Auditing

      1120—Individual Objectivity

      1130—Impairment to Independence or Objectivity

   ✱ 1200—Proficiency and Due Professional Care

Note that *Standard* 1112—Chief Audit Executive Roles Beyond Internal Auditing—is a new *Standard* added in 2017 to recognize the evolving nature of the CAE's roles and responsibilities. While *Standard* 1112 does not promote multiple roles for the CAE, it suggests situations where an organization's board may require a CAE to undertake new roles or additional responsibilities that fall outside of internal audit (i.e., nonaudit work). *Standard* 1112 was added to ensure that there are safeguards in place when this situation occurs.

1000—Purpose, Authority, and Responsibility

The purpose, authority, and responsibility of the internal audit activity must be formally defined in an internal audit charter, consistent with the Mission of Internal Audit and the mandatory elements of the International Professional Practices Framework (the Core Principles for the Professional Practice of Internal Auditing, the Code of Ethics, the *Standards*, and the Definition of Internal Auditing). The chief audit executive (CAE) must periodically review the internal audit charter and present it to senior management and the board for approval.

Interpretation: *The internal audit charter is a formal document that defines the internal audit activity's purpose, authority, and responsibility. The internal audit charter establishes the internal audit activity's position within the organization, including the nature of the CAE's functional reporting relationship with the board; authorizes access to records, personnel, and physical properties relevant to the performance of engagements; and defines the scope of internal audit activities. Final approval of the internal audit charter resides with the board.*

1000.A1—The nature of assurance services provided to the organization must be defined in the internal audit charter. If assurances are to be provided to parties outside the organization, the nature of these assurances must also be defined in the internal audit charter.

1000.C1—The nature of consulting services must be defined in the internal audit charter.

1000—Implementation Guide

Establishing a scope for implementation work consists of developing an audit charter, including coordination and consultation between the CAE, internal legal counsel, external consulting counsel, board of directors (board), and senior management (senior managers). Note that the board and senior management together can set the **tone at the top** for others to follow and can express the **voice of the top** for others to hear. The CAE can use the IIA's model charter or the industry format (e.g., retail or healthcare) as a template to create an initial (draft) and a final audit charter document.

Initial Draft ⟶ Board Review ⟶ Final Draft ⟶ Board Approval ⟶ Final Document

Considerations for implementation include developing an internal audit charter with a standard format and using essential elements. A draft version of the charter document can contain these sections:

- Introduction
- Authority
- Organization and reporting structure (functional reporting to the board and administrative reporting to the chief executive officer (CEO)
- Independence and objectivity (either in fact or appearance)
- Responsibilities (audit work and nonaudit work)
- Quality assurance and improvement
- Approval signatures

The board needs to confirm that the draft accurately describes the agreed-upon role and expectations and later accepts it. Then the CAE presents the charter document during a board meeting for discussion and approval, including future (periodic) review and reaffirmation schedule going forward.

Considerations for demonstrating conformance require the following output documents:

- Minutes of the board meetings listing the initial discussions and final presentations of the audit charter
- The board's meeting minutes showing a standby annual agenda item to discuss, update, and approve the charter document as needed

Requiring a familiarity with the related Standards includes:

- Recognizing mandatory guidance in the internal audit charter (*Standard* 1010)

1010—Recognizing Mandatory Guidance in the Internal Audit Charter

The mandatory nature of the Core Principles for the Professional Practice of Internal Auditing, the Code of Ethics, the *Standards*, and the Definition of Internal Auditing must be recognized in the internal audit charter. The chief audit executive should discuss the Mission of Internal Audit and the mandatory elements of the International Professional Practices Framework with senior management and the board.

1010—Implementation Guide

Establishing a scope for implementation work includes determining all the input documents required and understanding their purpose before developing or revising the internal audit charter document. These input documents include:

- Mission of internal audit
- Core Principles
- Code of Ethics
- *Standards*
- Definition of internal auditing

The Core Principles, Code of Ethics, *Standards*, and definition are part of mandatory guidance, which in turn, when combined with the mission, become the mandatory elements of the new IIA's International Professional Practices Framework (new IPPF).

Mission = Purpose + Goals + Objectives

Mandatory Guidance = Core Principles + Code of Ethics + *Standards* + Definition

New IPPF = Mission + Mandatory Guidance

Considerations for implementation include the CAE discussing the internal audit charter with senior management and the board and how the audit charter recognizes the mandatory elements. After the charter has been adopted, the CAE monitors the charter for any changes that may require updates during the next charter review.

Considerations for demonstrating conformance are evidenced in the written and approved charter that recognizes the mandatory elements of the IPPF. In addition, board's meeting minutes documented during the initial review and periodic reviews are considered adequate.

Requiring a familiarity with the related Standards includes:

- Purpose, authority, and responsibility (*Standard* 1000)

1100—Independence and Objectivity

The internal audit activity must be independent, and internal auditors must be objective in performing their work.

Interpretation: *Independence is the freedom from conditions that threaten the ability of the internal audit activity to carry out internal audit responsibilities in an unbiased manner. To achieve the degree of independence necessary to effectively carry out the responsibilities of the internal audit activity, the chief audit executive has direct and unrestricted access to senior management and the board.*

This can be achieved through a dual-reporting relationship. Threats to independence must be managed at the individual auditor, engagement, functional, and organizational levels.

Objectivity is an unbiased mental attitude that allows internal auditors to perform engagements in such a manner that they believe in their work product and that no quality compromises are made. Objectivity requires that internal auditors do not subordinate their judgment on audit matters to others. Threats to objectivity must be managed at the individual auditor, engagement, functional, and organizational levels.

1100—Implementation Guide

Establishing a scope for implementation work requires defining terms such as *independence* and *objectivity*. Because there is confusion between these two terms, some individuals may treat independence as a proxy for objectivity, which is not right within the context of the *Standards*. **Independence** is the freedom from conditions that threaten the ability of the internal audit activity to carry out internal audit responsibilities in an unbiased manner. **Objectivity** requires that internal auditors do not subordinate their judgment on audit matters to others.

Considerations for implementation include how the CAE's reporting lines and responsibilities are established. Several approaches follow to ensure independence and to curb objectivity impairment.

- A direct **functional reporting** line to the board (i.e., audit committee) is good because it provides the CAE a direct access to the board for sensitive matters and elevates the CAE's organizational status in the company. The board members in the audit committee can establish safeguards (i.e., oversight activities) when they feel that the CAE's objectivity is impaired.

- An **administrative reporting** to a senior manager or the CEO is good because it provides authority to perform audit work without impediments. The IIA recommends that the CAE report to the CEO. This approach implies that the CAE should not report to an accounting controller, an IT manager, a business division head, or a mid-level manager because the CAE would perform audit work in their business functions. Senior managers can establish safeguards (i.e., oversight activities) when they feel that the CAE's objectivity is impaired.

- Preferred reporting lines are:
  - CAE's functional reporting to the board
  - CAE's administrative reporting to a senior manager or the CEO

Many CAEs have issued an internal audit policy manual or handbook to describe expectations and requirements for an internal auditor's unbiased mindsets. The contents of the policy manual can include:

- A list of objectivity-impairing or threat-creating situations and scenarios with approaches to avoid or address them. These situations include self-interest, self-review, conflict, familiarity, bias, and undue influence.

- A requirement that internal auditors discuss their objectivity concerns with their audit manager or the CAE for advice.

- A requirement where each internal auditor periodically reports and discloses conflict-of-interest situations.

- A requirement that all internal auditors go through training classes or workshops to understand the objectivity-impairing or threat-creating scenarios in order to avoid conflicts.

Many CAEs are conducting client-satisfaction feedback surveys from audit clients after audit work is completed. These surveys have advantages and disadvantages. An advantage is that the survey results build a stronger relationship between auditors and audit clients, which represents a good business practice.

A disadvantage is that the survey results could negatively affect an auditor's performance evaluation ratings and compensation benefits. This means that reporting negative audit findings could result in low satisfaction ratings, which in turn lower the auditor's compensation benefits. The reverse is also true, requiring a balancing act on the part of the CAE.

Considerations for demonstrating conformance include internal audit charter, organization chart, internal audit policy manual, training records, and conflict-of-interest disclosure forms.

Requiring a familiarity with the related Standards includes:

- Organizational independence (*Standard* 1110)
- Direct interaction with the board (*Standard* 1111)
- CAE roles beyond internal auditing (*Standard* 1112)
- Individual objectivity (*Standard* 1120)
- Impairment to independence and objectivity (*Standard* 1130)

Risks to Internal Audit Activity—*Standard* 1100

Similar to other functions, the internal audit function is a risk-prone activity, as there is no function in an organization that is risk resistant. Risks to internal audit activities fall into three broad categories: audit failure risks, false assurance risks, and reputation risks.

Audit Failure Risks

In addition to control breakdowns and fraud occurrences, the internal audit activity itself could be a contributing factor to audit failures due to auditors' own doing. This means auditors showing negligence in performing their professional work, not following their professional standards, not identifying high-risk auditable areas during the planning of individual audits, not paying attention to fraud alerts and red flags, not doing the right audits at the right time, wasting resources on doing the wrong audits at the wrong time, and not delivering a quality audit product.

Seven *specific causes leading to audit failure risks* include failure to:

1. Design effective internal audit procedures to test the "real" risks and the right controls.
2. Evaluate both the design adequacy and the control effectiveness as part of internal audit procedures.
3. Provide adequate internal audit supervision.
4. Exercise professional skepticism and judgment.
5. Undertake extended internal audit procedures related to negative findings or control deficiencies.
6. Communicate fraud suspicions to the right people at the right time.
7. Assign competent auditors to perform complex audit engagements.

Six *remedies to address audit failure risks* include:

1. Periodic review of the audit universe and audit plan.
2. Effective audit planning process and audit design of the system of internal controls.

Risks to Internal Audit Activity— *Standard* 1100 *(Continued)*

3. Escalation procedures within the internal audit activity indicating when and what types of issues to escalate to which level of the audit management hierarchy.

4. Ensuring that high-risk audit engagements are staffed with auditors possessing a combination of right experience, knowledge, skills, competencies, or talents (i.e., right mix of audit resources with a blend of hard skills and soft skills).

5. Ensuring that lead auditors have strong project management skills to complete an audit engagement on time and within the budget.

6. Implementing an effective quality assurance and improvement program (QAIP) to conduct internal assessments and external assessments.

False Assurance Risks

False assurance is a level of confidence or assurance based on perceptions or assumptions, not based on facts. False assurance risks result when auditors are unknowingly overselling or underperforming themselves and making empty promises to audit clients who take those promises very seriously and who make auditors accountable for what they promised. Simply put, false assurances result from what was said, when it was said, and how it was said. Examples of empty promises or false assurances that could raise an **expectation gap** include: "We will take care of it," "We will help you, don't worry about it," "I will talk to my audit management and let me see what I can do for you."

Four *specific causes leading to false assurance risks* include:

1. Not keeping the proper mental distance between auditors and audit clients.

2. Not monitoring an auditor's independence and objectivity issues.

3. Not clearly defining and documenting the auditor's roles and responsibilities (**role gap**) when business units request the audit staff's help in implementing a new computer system project in the accounting department or analyzing the customer service department's problems with product warranty and guarantee claims (**loaned audit resources**).

4. Not communicating scope inclusions (what is covered, in scope) and scope exclusions (what is not covered, out of scope) in the auditor's work when conducting risk assessments, developing internal audit plans, and performing internal audit engagements (**expectation gap**).

Auditors need to realize that a role gap and an expectation gap may exist in the minds of audit clients.

Auditors' Role Gap = Audit Clients' Perceived Role of Auditors − Auditors' Actual Role

Auditors' Expectation Gap = Audit Clients' Expected Deliverables − Auditors' Actual Deliverables

Loaned audit resources can create false assurance risks, in part due to the expectation gap.

Four *remedies to address the false assurance risks* include:

1. Communicating frequently and clearly to all affected parties about the auditor's role, professional mission and mandate, and adherence to the professional *Standards*.

2. Communicating scope inclusions and exclusions in every audit engagement project.

3. Documenting "project risk" information at the beginning of a project by describing the types and sources of risks a project is facing, including its risk immunity levels (risk resistant or risk prone) and risk sensitivity levels (sensitive or insensitive).

4. Installing a "project acceptance" process at the beginning of a project where auditors document their specific roles and project outcomes and deliverables, the types of project risks being handled, the types of audit talent and competencies required or available, and auditor independence.

Reputation Risks

Reputation risks primarily deal with positive or negative impressions or images of auditors in the eyes of audit clients. A positive image can take many years to earn, whereas it takes very little time to earn a negative image due to one high-profile and high-impact adverse event. Both audit failure risks and false assurance risks in combination can result in reputation risks, as they are interconnected.

Reputation Risks = Audit Failure Risks + False Assurance Risks

For example, when auditors are assigned to a business function to assist its day-to-day work due to that function's staff shortages or to participate in a special project taking considerable duration (say three to six months), these **loaned resources** of auditors can create false assurance situations and reputation risks. This is because nonauditors think that auditors are highly experienced and highly knowledgeable people who carry a strong "brand" name for perfection and excellence and that they never make mistakes or have mishaps. When something goes wrong in auditor-assisted work, auditors are the first ones to be blamed for problems because they are outsiders and are assumed to do perfect work, and to know everything (or should know everything). Loaned audit resources can be found in accounting, finance, treasury, corporate tax, insurance, and loss prevention departments.

Three *specific causes leading to reputation risks* include:

1. Using auditors as loaned resources to other business functions, whether short term or long term.
2. Auditors' behavior and performance as loaned resources in other business functions and the impressions and images they leave on employees and managers of those business functions.
3. The inability of auditors to understand, protect, and maintain their own strong audit "brand" name (goodwill), leading to credibility issues (**credibility gaps**). A clear connection among the reputation, role, expectation, and credibility gap can be seen:

Reputation Gap = Role Gap + Expectation Gap + Credibility Gap

Eight *remedies to address the reputation risks* include:

1. Training all internal auditors about the scope and nature of false assurances, reputation risks, and brand-name protections.
2. Educating auditors in that each auditor is a source for creating audit failures, false assurances, and reputation risks. The same auditor can be a source for eliminating such failures and risks.
3. Conducting an assessment of the internal audit department by outsiders, similar to what internal auditors do at an internal audit client location.
4. Maintaining an **audit incident log** describing all the audit failures, false assurances, and reputation issues and not revealing the auditors' names and locations.
5. Posting, publicizing, and notifying every internal auditor about the **lessons learned** from recent observations and experiences regarding audit failures, false assurances, and reputation risks.
6. Installing a **suggestion box** system within the internal audit department for improving or removing audit failures, false assurances, and reputation risks.
7. Selecting internal auditors for job rotational assignments in nonaudit functions (job rotations) based on a careful blend of **hard skills** and **soft skills** they possess and those auditors that can protect internal audit's brand reputation.

Note that CAEs must be open-minded (transparent), forward-thinking, and proactive in nature to maintain an audit incident log, similar to a security incident log maintained in the IT function. Security incident logs document all data security breaches and cyberattacks that occur on data files and websites respectively.

Audit Risk Components

Audit risk is the overall risk of audit work and is composed of five individual risks: inherent risk, control risk, materiality risk, detection risk, and fraud risk. We added other terms related to audit risk such as systemic risk, sampling risk, nonsampling risk, and evidence risk, and internal audit risk to provide a comprehensive list of risks. Exhibit i.1 summarizes a number of audit-related risk types with brief descriptions.

Risks to Internal Audit Activity— *Standard* 1100 *(Continued)*

EXHIBIT i.1 A Summary of Audit-Related Risk Types

Risk Type	Description
Audit risk	Audit risk is the risk that the auditor may unknowingly fail to appropriately modify his or her opinion on financial statements that are materially misstated. It is also defined as the risk that an auditor may fail to detect a significant error or weakness during an examination.
	Audit risk = Inherent risk × Control risk × Materiality risk × Detection risk × Fraud risk
Inherent risk	Inherent risk is the susceptibility of a management assertion to a material misstatement, assuming that there are no related internal control structure policies or procedures.
	Inherent risk – Materiality risk + Control risk (i.e., lack of controls)
Systemic risk	Systemic risk is same as the inherent risk. Systemic risk is a built-in risk and is common to and natural in most activities.
Control risk	Control risk is the risk that a material misstatement in a management assertion will not be prevented or detected on a timely basis by the entity's internal control structure policies or procedures.
	Control risk = Design effectiveness + Control operational efficiency
Materiality risk	Materiality risk is the risk of material misstatement of financial statements where the risk is significant. An auditor using judgment assesses the inherent risk and control risk either individually or collectively. The higher the management's assertion levels, the greater the need for extended audit procedures.
	Materiality risk = Inherent risk + Control risk
	Note that materiality risk and detection risk together are used in determining substantive audit procedures.
Detection risk	Detection risk is the risk that the auditor will not detect a material misstatement present in a management assertion.
	Detection risk = Effectiveness of audit procedures + Application of audit procedures
	Note that detection risk and materiality risk together are used in determining substantive audit procedures.
Fraud risk	The auditor determines the risks of material fraud occurring concurrently with the consideration of inherent risk and control risk. The scope of fraud includes fraudulent financial reporting, misappropriation of assets, and material misstatement of financial statements.
	Fraud risk = Inherent risk + Control risk
Audit assurance risk	Audit assurance equals 100% minus the percentage of allowable audit risk. Audit assurance risk is the complement of audit risk. The auditor determines the level of assurance to use based on judgment. For example, when an auditor states that he has 95% audit assurance that the financial statements are not materially misstated, he means that he allowed for a 5% audit risk (100 – 95 = 5). Audit assurance of 95% = 100% – 5%. Note that the audit assurance level is not the same as the confidence level because the former is related to an auditor's judgment and the latter is related to an individual sample.

Risk Type	Description
Sampling risk	The risk that the auditor's conclusion based on a sample might differ from the conclusion that would be reached by applying the test in the same way to the entire population. For tests of controls, sampling risk is the risk of assessing control risk either too low or too high. For substantive testing, sampling risk is the risk of incorrect acceptance or the risk of incorrect rejection. Usually the smaller the sample size, the larger the sampling risk will be.
Nonsampling risk	Nonsampling risk occurs even if the entire population is tested and is due to errors in auditor judgment, such as (1) use of inappropriate audit procedures, (2) incorrectly applying appropriate audit procedures, (3) misreading of sampling test results, and (4) not recognizing errors during sampling. This risk can be controlled with better audit planning and supervision. Auditors can use nonsampling selections to test controls through inquiry, observation, and walk-through procedures.
Evidence risk	Evidence risk occurs when an auditor collects incorrect, insufficient, irrelevant, inappropriate, and unreliable evidence that does not fit the audit scope and objectives. Evidence can be physical and/or digital. Moreover, the auditor-collected evidence could be rejected in a court of law when it does not meet the court's requirements.
Audit failure risk (internal audit)	Audit failure risk means that auditors show negligence in performing their professional work; do not follow their Professional *Standards*; do not identify high-risk auditable areas during the planning of individual audits; do not pay attention to fraud alerts and red flags; do not do the right audits at the right time; waste resources on doing the wrong audits at the wrong time; and do not deliver a quality audit product.
Audit false assurance risk (internal audit)	Audit false assurance risk results from what was said, when it was said, and how it was said by auditors to audit clients.
Audit reputation risk (internal audit)	Audit reputation risk is a combined audit failure risk and audit false assurance risk resulting in the reputation risk.
Total internal audit risk	Total internal audit risk = Audit failure risk + Audit false assurance risk + Audit reputation risk

1110—Organizational Independence

The chief audit executive (CAE) must report to a level within the organization that allows the internal audit activity to fulfill its responsibilities. The CAE must confirm to the board, at least annually, the organizational independence of the internal audit activity.

Interpretation: *Organizational independence is effectively achieved when the CAE reports functionally to the board. Examples of functional reporting to the board involve the board:*

- Approving the internal audit charter.
- Approving the risk-based internal audit plan.
- Approving the internal audit budget and resource plan.

- Receiving communications from the CAE on the internal audit activity's performance relative to its plan and other matters.

- Approving decisions regarding the appointment and removal of the CAE.

- Approving the remuneration of the CAE.

- Making appropriate inquiries of management and the CAE to determine whether there is inappropriate scope or resource limitations.

> **1110.A1**—The internal audit activity must be free from interference in determining the scope of internal auditing, performing work, and communicating results. The chief audit executive must disclose such interference to the board and discuss the implications.

1110—Implementation Guide

Establishing a scope for implementation work includes considering the organizational placement, supervisory oversight, regulatory requirements, and reporting lines of internal audit activity to ensure organizational independence. The internal audit charter shows the organizational placement and reporting lines. Assuring organizational independence is a shared understanding of internal audit's responsibility, authority, and expectations among the CAE, senior managers, and board members.

Considerations for implementation include determining the correct organizational placement and reporting lines for the internal audit activity. It consists of two types of reporting structures: functional and administrative.

1. A **functional reporting** line to the board (i.e., audit committee) provides direct access for sensitive matters and enables sufficient organizational status to conduct internal audit work. The board provides functional oversight because it approves the audit charter, audit plan, audit budget and resource plan, and hiring and removal of the CAE, including performance evaluation and compensation benefits for the CAE. In return, the CAE is required to provide periodic performance updates and quarterly meetings with the board with agreed-upon agenda. The CAE also discusses key audit findings, impairments to audit independence, and other matters of concern to the board.

2. An **administrative reporting** line to senior management or the CEO provides authority and status to fulfill audit responsibilities. The CAE would not report to an accounting controller, an accounting manager, or a mid-level functional manager because they are not senior-level positions. Audit independence cannot be assured with low-level positions.

   Functional Reporting ⟶ Board of Directors ⟶ "Solid" Line of Reporting

   Administrative Reporting ⟶ Senior Managers or the CEO ⟶ "Dotted" Line of Reporting

Considerations for demonstrating conformance include several documents such as the internal audit charter, the audit committee charter, the CAE's job description and his performance evaluation results, the internal audit policy manual, board's periodic reports, and the board's meeting minutes and agenda. In addition, documentation showing who interviewed the CAE when hiring indicates the final person making the CAE's hiring decision. External auditors should not make such a final decision in hiring the CAE. Only the internal management and the board should make that final decision.

Requiring a familiarity with the related Standards includes:

- Independence and objectivity (*Standard* 1100)
- Direct interaction with the board (*Standard* 1111)
- CAE roles beyond internal auditing (*Standard* 1112)
- Individual objectivity (*Standard* 1120)
- Impairment to independence and objectivity (*Standard* 1130)

1111—Direct Interaction with the Board

The chief audit executive (CAE) must communicate and interact directly with the board.

1111—Implementation Guide

Establishing a scope for implementation work highlights the need for a functional reporting relationship with the board to ensure a direct and open communication with the entire board or individual members of the board.

Considerations for implementation require the CAE to participate in audit committee meetings and/or the full board meetings. The CAE can contact the chair or any member of the board through in-person meetings or by phone calls either prior to scheduled meetings or routinely during the year to ensure a direct and open communication. If the CAE does not have direct access to or functional reporting to the board, the CAE can show the related IIA's *Standards* entitled Independence and Objectivity and Organizational Independence to the board as external evidence and authority requiring a direct access.

Considerations for demonstrating conformance can be shown with board meeting agendas and minutes and the CAE's calendar listing the scheduled meetings. In addition, a policy requiring the CAE to meet privately with the board periodically should be documented in the board's charter or the audit committee's charter.

Requiring a familiarity with the related Standards includes:

- Independence and objectivity (*Standard* 1100)
- Organizational independence (*Standard* 1110)
- Chief audit executive roles beyond internal auditing (*Standard* 1112)
- Individual objectivity (*Standard* 1120)
- Impairment to independence and objectivity (*Standard* 1130)

1112—Chief Audit Executive Roles Beyond Internal Auditing

Where the chief audit executive (CAE) has or is expected to have roles and/or responsibilities that fall outside of internal auditing, safeguards must be in place to limit impairments to independence or objectivity.

Interpretation: *The CAE may be asked to take on additional roles and responsibilities outside of internal auditing, such as responsibility for compliance or risk management activities. These roles and responsibilities may impair, or appear to impair, the organizational independence of the* *internal audit activity or the individual objectivity of the internal auditor. Safeguards are those oversight activities, often undertaken by the board, to address these potential impairments, and may include such activities as periodically evaluating reporting lines and responsibilities and developing alternative processes to obtain assurance related to the areas of additional responsibility.*

1112—Implementation Guide

Usually the scope of internal audit work is confined to conducting routine and planned internal audits within the organization where audit independence and objectivity can be maintained and assured. However, there will be occasions where the board can ask the CAE to perform specific roles in nonaudit work for which management is normally responsible which could impair audit independence and objectivity because the work is not routine internal audit work. The reason for the board asking the CAE to perform nonaudit work is due to lack of resources (employees and budgets) in other functional departments to perform such roles or due to presence of special skills, talent, and expertise only available in the audit department.

Nonaudit Work ⟶ Management ⟶ CAE (before the work is performed)

Nonaudit Work ⟶ CAE ⟶ Management (after the work is performed)

Five examples of these unusual, specific roles in nonaudit work assigned to the internal audit include:

1. Fulfilling new regulatory compliance requirements with needed policies, procedures, controls, and risk management activities, which cannot be fulfilled today.

2. Performing risk management processes and activities for acquisition of new businesses.

3. Assuming greater responsibilities for designing, developing, and implementing risk management controls and compliance with them.

4. Working in loss prevention, insurance, accounting, corporate taxes, finance, and treasury departments.

5. Fulfilling (filling in) sudden changes that occurred in key management positions (e.g., promotion, demotion, termination, resignation, or death).

Establishing a scope for implementation work requires the IIA's Mission Statement, Code of Ethics, Core Principles, *Standards* (dealing with audit independence and auditor objectivity), internal audit charter, audit committee charter, and organization's general policies. If the CAE's specific role falls outside of internal auditing, the CAE should report to senior management and the board about potential impairments to independence and objectivity, risks associated with the proposed role, and control safeguards needed to mitigate those risks.

Considerations for implementation include establishing safeguards such as board oversight activities to protect the CAE's independence and objectivity and hiring an outsourced assurance provider when the CAE's objectivity is impaired due to previous duties performed beyond internal auditing.

The scope and nature of nonaudit roles and responsibilities assigned to the internal auditing could be short term (temporary) or long term (ongoing). A transition plan is required when the CAE is transferring the temporary (short-term) nonaudit work back to management showing timelines and resources needed. Ongoing (long-term) nonaudit work requires changes to the audit charter and safeguards to control the CAE's independence and objectivity.

Short Term ⟶ Transition Plan Required ⟶ No Change to Audit Charter Required

Long Term ⟶ No Transition Plan Required ⟶ Change to Audit Charter Required with Safeguards Established to Protect Independence and Objectivity

Considerations for demonstrating conformance include proper documentation of safeguards to protect the CAE's independence and objectivity. The type of documentation can include organization's general policies, code of ethics, audit committee charter, audit mission statement, audit charter, transition plans, minutes of board meetings, reports from outsourced assurance providers, surveys of audit clients, and reports of external assessments performed by an independent assessor.

Requiring a familiarity with the related Standards includes:

- Independence and objectivity (*Standard* 1100)
- Organizational independence (*Standard* 1110)
- Direct interaction with the board (*Standard* 1111)
- Individual objectivity (*Standard* 1120)
- Impairment to independence and objectivity (*Standard* 1130)
- Purpose, authority, and responsibility (*Standard* 1000)
- External assessments (*Standard* 1312)

1120—Individual Objectivity

Internal auditors must have an impartial, unbiased attitude and avoid any conflict of interest.

Interpretation: *Conflict of interest* *is a situation in which an internal auditor, who is in a position of trust, has a competing professional or personal interest. Such competing interests can make it difficult to fulfill his or her duties impartially. A conflict of interest exists even if no unethical or improper act results. A conflict of interest can create an appearance of impropriety that can undermine confidence in the internal auditor, the internal audit activity, and the profession. A conflict of interest could impair an individual's ability to perform his or her duties and responsibilities objectively.*

1120—Implementation Guide

An internal auditor's objectivity is recognized or enhanced when he or she avoids conflict-of-interest situations and is related to whether the auditor has an impartial and unbiased mind-set. Objectivity is personal to the auditor based on trust and confidence placed on him or her by others. A conflict-of-interest situation can arise based on the appearance of impropriety, and it can occur even when the auditor did not commit unethical or illegal acts.

Presence of Objectivity ⟶ Showing Impartiality and Exhibiting Unbiased Mind-set

Lack of Objectivity ⟶ Showing Partiality and Exhibiting Biased Mind-set

Establishing a scope for implementation work requires a review of an organization's general policies related to employee performance evaluation and compensation, internal audit's policies, conflict-of-interest policies, and auditor training policies. All these policies taken as a whole can provide a working environment where conflict-of-interest situations can arise or hinder.

Considerations for implementation require an understanding of conflict-of-interest situations that could undermine an auditor's objectivity and avoiding those situations. Examples of such situations include auditing (1) a business function where an auditor previously and recently worked as an employee, (2) a family member or a close friend who is in charge of or working in a business function, and (3) a business function with prior positive experiences (i.e., auditor friendly). Situations also include not auditing a business function with prior negative experiences (i.e., auditor unfriendly).

Internal auditors are required to discuss, report, or disclose to an internal audit manager or the CAE (1) current objectivity concerns, (2) potential objectivity concerns, and (3) potential conflicts or threats that can occur. A common practice is to require that all auditors sign an annual statement indicating that no potential threats exist and acknowledging any known potential threats.

Disclosure Requirements = No Known Current Conflicts + No Known Future Threats

Considerations for demonstrating conformance include internal audit policies, auditor training records, examples of conflict-of-interest situations, signed acknowledgment forms disclosing existence and nonexistence of conflicts, and engagement workpapers showing the audit team assigned to an audit. These workpapers can be compared to auditor employment records and auditor-signed acknowledgment forms to determine the presence or absence of conflict-of-interest conditions.

Requiring a familiarity with the related Standards includes:

- Independence and objectivity (*Standard* 1100)
- Organizational independence (*Standard* 1110)
- Direct interaction with the board (*Standard* 1111)
- Chief audit executive roles beyond internal auditing (*Standard* 1112)
- Impairment to independence and objectivity (*Standard* 1130)

1130—Impairment to Independence or Objectivity

If independence or objectivity is impaired in fact or appearance, the details of the impairment must be disclosed to appropriate parties. The nature of the disclosure will depend upon the impairment.

Interpretation: *Impairment to organizational independence and individual objectivity may include, but is not limited to, personal conflict of interest, scope limitations, restrictions on access to records, personnel, and properties, and resource limitations, such as funding.*

The determination of appropriate parties to whom the details of an impairment to independence or objectivity must be disclosed is dependent upon the expectations of the internal audit activity's and the CAE's responsibilities to senior management and the board as described in the internal audit charter, as well as the nature of the impairment.

> **1130.A1**—Internal auditors must refrain from assessing specific operations for which they were previously responsible. Objectivity is presumed to be impaired if an internal auditor provides assurance services for an activity for which the internal auditor had responsibility within the previous year.
>
> **1130.A2**—Assurance engagements for functions over which the CAE has responsibility must be overseen by a party outside the internal audit activity.

1130.A3—The internal audit activity may provide assurance services where it had previously performed consulting services, provided the nature of the consulting did not impair objectivity and provided individual objectivity is managed when assigning resources to the engagement.

1130.C1—Internal auditors may provide consulting services relating to operations for which they had previous responsibilities.

1130.C2—If internal auditors have potential impairments to independence or objectivity relating to proposed consulting services, disclosure must be made to the engagement client prior to accepting the engagement.

1130—Implementation Guide

Establishing a scope for implementation work includes an internal audit policy manual or handbook describing a discussion of organizational independence and internal auditor objectivity, the nature of impairments (real or perceived), and how internal auditors should handle potential impairments. The CAE will discuss these impairments with the board and senior management.

Considerations for implementation include understanding of various impairment situations, such as self-imposed, self-interest, self-review, self-bias, familiarity, or undue influence—all leading to conflicts of interest, scope limitations, resource limitations, or placing unnecessary and deliberate restrictions on access to records, personnel, or properties. The CAE needs to disclose the real impairments (now) or after-the-fact (later) impairments to the board and senior management for resolution.

Examples leading to an internal audit activity's (organizational) independence impairments include:

- The internal audit's annual budget is insufficient to fulfill its responsibilities.

- The CAE does not report functionally to the board or does not communicate or interact directly with the board.

- The CAE reports administratively to the chief financial officer (CFO), chief accounting officer (CAO), or lower-level management in finance and accounting functions and when the CAE audits those functions.

- The CAE manages more than the internal audit function, such as risk management, loss prevention, or insurance functions, and the CAE audits those functions.

Examples leading to an internal auditor's objectivity impairments include:

- The auditor is assigned to audit a business function that employs the auditor's relative or a close friend, or the auditor has previously worked in the same business function.

- The auditor does not apply professional skepticism and assumes that a business function must have mitigated risks because this function has received a positive audit opinion in previous audits or this function is being managed by a good manager who happens to be the auditor's friend.

- The auditor is influenced by a supervisor or manager during audit scope establishment and audit engagement instead of using his own judgment and experience and without proper justification (say *Standards* or best practices).

Considerations for demonstrating conformance include the following output documents:

- Internal audit's policy and procedure manual describing how to handle conflicts and impairment situations and how to report or communicate them
- Board meeting minutes discussing impairments
- Memos to files, emails, or reports documenting the discussions of impairments

Requiring a familiarity with the related Standards includes:

- Independence and objectivity (*Standard* 1100)
- Organizational independence (*Standard* 1110)
- Direct interaction with the board (*Standard* 1111)
- Chief audit executive roles beyond internal auditing (*Standard* 1112)
- Individual objectivity (*Standard* 1120)
- Communication and approval (*Standard* 2020)
- Errors and omissions (*Standard* 2421)

1200—Proficiency and Due Professional Care

Engagements must be performed with proficiency and due professional care.

1200—Implementation Guide

All professionals, such as doctors, lawyers, and accountants, need to be proficient (expert) in what work they do for a society or for a business entity with utmost care and attention. *Proficiency* refers to knowledge, skills, abilities (KSAs), experiences, talents, or competencies. Proficiency or professionalism asks a basic question: Is he or she qualified to do the assigned job? Due professional care is a legal concept referring to discipline without gross negligence. Due care asks a basic question: Can he or she show diligence and exercise professional judgment similar to peers? The same requirements of professionalism and due care that are used during audit planning, staffing, and supervising specific audit engagements apply to internal auditors.

Establishing a scope for implementation work includes the following input documents:

- Internal audit charter
- Internal audit plan
- Internal audit's policies and procedures, which incorporate the IIA's Mandatory Guidance of the IPPF, signed and acknowledged by auditors

Considerations for implementation include:

- Compliance with the IIA's Code of Ethics by signing an annual declaration document
- Compliance with the organization's Code of Conduct by signing an annual declaration document
- Compliance with the IIA's Global Internal Audit Competency Framework
- Adherence to benchmarks and best practices established in the industry

The CAE can use the above criteria and others when creating job descriptions, developing skills inventory, and when recruiting, training, and assigning auditors to an audit engagement. Here, the CAE's goal is to keep the competencies of internal auditors current and sufficient, thus making them competent at all times and for all audit engagements.

Considerations for demonstrating conformance include the following output documents:

- Internal audit plan and individual audit engagement plans are matched to determine the competencies required with the competencies available. Any **competency gaps** must be addressed in a timely manner prior to assigning auditors to specific and individual audits.

  Competency Gap = Competencies Required − Competencies Available

- Internal audit's policies and procedures by signing an annual declaration document.

- The IIA's Code of Ethics and the organization's Code of Conduct by signing an annual declaration document.

- Audit engagement workpapers showing an individual auditor's professionalism and due care and showing an audit supervisor's professionalism and due care.

- Feedback and survey results from audit client showing the proficiency and due professional care exhibited by individual internal auditors assigned to audit engagements.

- Reports from independent external assessors indicating that internal audit engagements are performed with proficiency and due professional care. These assessors perform a review of the internal audit activity's quality assurance and improvement program. Here, the key point is to determine whether individual audit engagements were conducted with greater proficiency and due professional care.

Requiring a familiarity with the related Standards includes:

- Proficiency (*Standard* 1210)
- Due professional care (*Standard* 1220)
- Continuing professional development (*Standard* 1230)
- Policies and procedures (*Standard* 2040)

1210—Proficiency

Internal auditors must possess the knowledge, skills, and other competencies needed to perform their individual responsibilities. The internal audit activity collectively must possess or obtain the knowledge, skills, and other competencies needed to perform its responsibilities.

Interpretation: Proficiency *is a collective term that refers to the knowledge, skills, and other competencies required of internal auditors to effectively carry out their professional responsibilities. It encompasses consideration of current activities, trends, and emerging issues, to provide relevant advice and recommendations. Internal auditors are encouraged to demonstrate their proficiency by obtaining appropriate professional certifications and qualifications, such as the Certified Internal Auditor designation and other designations offered by the IIA and other appropriate professional organizations.*

> **1210.A1**—The CAE must obtain competent advice and assistance if the internal auditors lack the knowledge, skills, or other competencies needed to perform all or part of the engagement.

1210.A2—Internal auditors must have sufficient knowledge to evaluate the risk of fraud and the manner in which it is managed by the organization, but are not expected to have the expertise of a person whose primary responsibility is detecting and investigating fraud.

1210.A3—Internal auditors must have sufficient knowledge of key information technology risks and controls and available technology-based audit techniques to perform their assigned work. However, not all internal auditors are expected to have the expertise of an internal auditor whose primary responsibility is IT auditing.

1210.C1—The CAE must decline the consulting engagement or obtain competent advice and assistance if the internal auditors lack the knowledge, skills, or other competencies needed to perform all or part of the engagement.

1210—Implementation Guide

Establishing a scope for implementation work requires that the CAE is responsible for ensuring the **collective proficiency** of the internal audit activity after understanding the core competencies required by the IIA's Global Internal Audit Competency Framework. This framework defines the core competencies. Here, *collective audit proficiency* means:

Proficiency of Auditor 1 + Proficiency of Auditor 2 + Proficiency of Auditor N

Considerations for implementation include:

- Developing competency assessments tools or skills assessment tools based on the IIA's Global Internal Audit Competency Framework as input into auditors' job descriptions and recruitment materials.

- Identifying skills gaps or competency gaps lacking proper mix of KSAs to fulfill the internal audit plan.

  Competency Gaps = Competencies Required − Competencies Available

- Knowing that competency gaps lead to audit coverage gaps, which can be removed through proper hiring, training, and outsourcing.

  Audit Coverage Gaps = Coverage Required − Coverage Completed

- Encouraging professional development of auditors through on-the-job training, attending seminars and conferences, and acquiring professional certifications, which require continuing professional development programs.

- Requiring all auditors to keep abreast of current trends and emerging issues in the industry in which they work and their impact on the internal audit profession. This proficiency can be acquired through reading whitepapers and research studies, subscribing to the industry's newsletters and services, attending in-person seminars, and participating in online seminars (webinars).

- Supervising each audit engagement to ensure quality of audit work, achievement of audit objectives, and audit staff development. There is a direct relationship between the proficiency of auditors and the extent of supervision required, meaning highly proficient and competent auditors require less supervision and vice versa.

- Surveying or interviewing the audit client after an audit engagement is completed to assess the level of proficiencies and competencies exhibited by the engagement audit staff in order to determine whether current audit objectives have been achieved. This input can be used to tailor future audit engagements.

Considerations for demonstrating conformance include the following output documents:

- An auditor's proficiency is evidenced through resumes or curriculum vitae, certifications, and continuing professional development courses, which can be used to develop skills inventory of auditors.

- An auditor's performance is reviewed and evaluated after completing an audit engagement, combined with feedback from post-engagement surveys and interviews of audit clients.

- An internal audit plan showing resource requirements, such as time budget, staff budget, and travel budget.

- An assurance map showing qualifications of service providers on which the internal audit activity relies for assurance.

- A report from internal assessment of the internal audit activity.

Requiring a familiarity with the related Standards includes:

- Proficiency (*Standard* 1200)
- Due professional care (*Standard* 1220)
- Continuing professional development (*Standard* 1230)
- Resource management (*Standard* 2030)
- Coordination and reliance (*Standard* 2050)
- Engagement resource allocation (*Standard* 2230)
- Engagement supervision (*Standard* 2340)

1220—Due Professional Care

Internal auditors must apply the care and skill expected of a reasonably prudent and competent internal auditor. Due professional care does not imply infallibility.

1220.A1—Internal auditors must exercise due professional care by considering the:

- Extent of work needed to achieve the engagement's objectives.
- Relative complexity, materiality, or significance of matters to which assurance procedures are applied.
- Adequacy and effectiveness of governance, risk management, and control processes.
- Probability of significant errors, fraud, or noncompliance.
- Cost of assurance in relation to potential benefits.

1220.A2—In exercising due professional care, internal auditors must consider the use of technology-based audit and other data analysis techniques.

> **1220.A3**—Internal auditors must be alert to the significant risks that might affect objectives, operations, or resources. However, assurance procedures alone, even when performed with due professional care, do not guarantee that all significant risks will be identified.
>
> **1220.C1**—Internal auditors must exercise due professional care during a consulting engagement by considering the:
>
> - Needs and expectations of clients, including the nature, timing, and communication of engagement results.
>
> - Relative complexity and extent of work needed to achieve the engagement's objectives.
>
> - Cost of the consulting engagement in relation to potential benefits.

1220—Implementation Guide

Establishing a scope for implementation work includes the following requirements:

- Internal auditors acquiring the necessary education, experience, certifications, training, and continuing education to increase the level of skills and expertise so they can perform their work with due professional care

- Internal auditors understanding and applying the Mandatory Guidance of the IIA's IPPF and the IIA's Global Internal Audit Competency Framework

- Internal auditors understanding and conforming to the IIA's Code of Ethics and the organization's Code of Conduct and signing those documents for acknowledgment

Considerations for implementation require an understanding and exercising of due professional care at three different levels:

1. *Due professional care at the individual auditor level* (personal level) involves (a) considering the possibility of significant errors, fraud, and noncompliance; (b) conducting audit examinations and verifications to the same extent as would a reasonably prudent and competent auditor in the same or similar circumstances; and (c) providing a reasonable assurance, not an absolute assurance, that noncompliance or irregularities do not exist. Due professional care does not imply infallibility.

   Due Professional Care looks for Errors, Fraud, Irregularities, and Noncompliances

2. *Due professional care at the audit engagement level* (audit assignment level) involves (a) understanding the objectives and scope of the engagement, knowing the competencies required to conduct the audit work, and understanding any policies and procedures of the internal audit activity and the organization; (b) supervisory review of the engagement workpapers, audit results, and audit conclusions to be reported; (c) providing supervisory feedback to auditors who conducted the engagement; and (d) soliciting post-engagement surveys from audit clients.

   Due Professional Care Focuses on Objectives, Scope, Competencies, and Reviews

3. *Due professional care at the internal audit activity level* (audit department level) involves the CAE (a) assuming overall responsibility that due professional care is applied, developing measurement tools (e.g., conducting self-assessment exercises and analyzing metrics and key performance indicators [KPIs]); (b) assessing the performance of individual auditors as individuals and the internal audit activity as a whole through internal and external assessments; and (c) evaluating individual auditors through peer reviews, supervisory

feedbacks, audit client surveys, and other audit stakeholder feedbacks, representing a 360-degree review.

$$\text{Auditor Evaluation} = \text{Peer Reviews} + \text{Supervisor's Feedback} + \text{Audit Client Surveys}$$
$$+ \text{Stakeholder's Feedback} = \text{360-Degree Reviews}$$

Considerations for demonstrating conformance can be achieved through the following output documents:

- Audit engagement plan, work programs, and workpapers
- Auditor's performance review reports
- Supervisory reviews of engagement work as documented in workpapers
- Post-engagement feedback from supervisors to auditors
- Feedback from audit clients through surveys, interviews, and memos
- Auditor's signing the IIA's Code of Ethics and the organization's Code of Conduct documents
- Reports from internal and external assessments of the internal audit activity as part of the quality assurance and improvement program

Requiring a familiarity with the related Standards includes:

- Proficiency (*Standard* 1200)
- Proficiency (*Standard* 1210)
- Continuing professional development (*Standard* 1230)
- Engagement supervision (*Standard* 2340)
- Quality assurance and improvement program (*Standard* 1300)
- Requirements of the quality assurance and improvement program (*Standard* 1310)
- Internal assessments (*Standard* 1311)
- External assessments (*Standard* 1312)

1230—Continuing Professional Development

Internal auditors must enhance their knowledge, skills, and other competencies through continuing professional development.

1230—Implementation Guide

An internal auditor's long-term career goals and plans will shape the auditor's continuing professional development (CPD) plans. The CPD plan is a part of auditor's professional development plan (PDP). An auditor's CPD plan and PDP plan must be aligned with the CAE's career plans developed for that auditor.

Establishing a scope for implementation work needs the following input documents:

- Job descriptions stating job requirements for auditors
- Training policies and professional education requirements of a profession, organization, or industry

- Conformance with the Mandatory Guidance of the IIA's IPPF
- Self-assessments based on the IIA's Global Internal Audit Competency Framework or any other benchmarks
- A CPD plan that considers the internal audit's policies, auditors' training schedules, and the audit staff's surveys and feedbacks

Considerations for implementation include:

- An auditor's self-assessment tool becomes a basis for the auditor's PDP.
- The scope of an auditor's PDP plan can include on-the-job training, coaching, mentoring, job rotation, internal and external training programs (e.g., conferences and seminars), educational programs (e.g., online and offline courses, webinars, self-study programs, and research projects), professional certifications, and volunteering with professional associations and organizations.

  Job Rotation = Moving from Audit Function to Nonaudit Function

  Reverse Job Rotation = Moving from Nonaudit Function to Audit Function

- An auditor's PDP becomes the basis for the auditor's KPIs that could be incorporated into supervisory reviews, audit-client surveys, and annual performance reviews.
- An internal audit department's training and development policies support CPD in terms of number of hours of training (say 40 hours), which can be benchmarked with other internal audit departments.
- An auditor's PDP must be aligned or synchronized with that of the CAE's CPD plan.
- An auditor's business acumen can be measured or assessed through audit-client surveys and feedbacks, supervisor comments, and peer observations.
- An auditor can keep his or her knowledge, skills, and abilities (KSAs) current with guidance from the IIA's *Standards*, research publications, best practices, procedures, and techniques.
- An auditor can subscribe to newsfeeds or notification services related to the audit profession and industry-specific news.
- An auditor can acquire two types of proficiency: required proficiency and enhanced proficiency.

Required Proficiency = Continuing Education Credit Hours + Professional Certifications
+ Certificates of Completion
Enhanced Proficiency = On the Job Training Coaching + Job Rotation Mentoring
+ Internal and/or External Training

Considerations for demonstrating conformance require the following output documents:

- Self-assessment reports and benchmark studies
- Professional development and training plans
- Paying for membership dues and magazine subscriptions
- Evidence of completed training and educational programs with a proof of continuing education credits, certificates of completion, certificates of attendance, professional certifications, and college-level credits
- CPD plans for each auditor developed from the internal audit's policies, training schedules, and surveys and feedbacks from audit staff

Requiring a familiarity with the related Standards includes:

- Proficiency (*Standard* 1200)
- Proficiency (*Standard* 1210)
- Due professional care (*Standard* 1220)

1300—Quality Assurance and Improvement Program

The chief audit executive must develop and maintain a quality assurance and improvement program that covers all aspects of the internal audit activity.

Interpretation: *A quality assurance and improvement program is designed to enable an evaluation of the internal audit activity's conformance with the* Standards *and an evaluation of whether internal auditors apply the Code of Ethics. The program also assesses the efficiency and effectiveness of the internal audit activity and identifies opportunities for improvement. The CAE should encourage board oversight in the quality assurance and improvement program.*

1300—Implementation Guide

Establishing a scope for implementation work includes:

- Assurance engagements as stated in the Mandatory Guidance of the IIA's IPPF
- Consulting engagements as stated in the Mandatory Guidance of the IIA's IPPF
- Internal audit activity operations
- QAIP sources that include audit literature reviews, audit research studies, and best practices in the internal audit profession
- QAIP scope that includes both internal assessments and external assessments of the internal audit activity

Considerations for implementation include:

- Conforming to QAIP means conforming to the IIA's *Standards*, applying the Code of Ethics, and aligning with the definition of internal auditing and core principles.
- Each individual audit engagement is not required to conform to the IIA's *Standards*.
- Each individual audit engagement should conform to an established audit methodology primarily and by default with the *Standards*. Moreover, the audit methodology should be uniformly and consistently applied to all individual audit engagements.
- The audit methodology promotes continuous gradual improvement of the audit activity.

Considerations for demonstrating conformance can be found in the following output documents:

- The CAE's documents describing the QAIP itself
- The CAE's communication of QAIP results with the board and senior management about its findings, corrective actions plans, and corrective actions already taken
- Reports from external assessments provided by independent and qualified assessors
- Board's meeting minutes showing discussions and presentations made to the board and senior management

Requiring a familiarity with the related Standards includes:

- Requirements of the quality assurance and improvement program (*Standard* 1310)
- Internal assessments (*Standard* 1311)
- External assessments (*Standard* 1312)
- Reporting on the quality assurance and improvement program (*Standard* 1320)
- Use of "conforms with the international standards for the professional practice of internal auditing" (*Standard* 1321)
- Disclosure of nonconformance (*Standard* 1322)

1310—Requirements of the Quality Assurance and Improvement Program

The quality assurance and improvement program must include both internal and external assessments.

1310—Implementation Guide

Establishing a scope for implementation work includes:

- Audit QAIP coverage includes both internal assessments and external assessments where these assessments add value to the internal audit activity first and organization's stakeholders next.
- Internal assessments consist of rigorous and comprehensive processes; continuous supervision and testing of assurance and consulting work; and periodic validation of conformance with the IIA's *Standards* and the Code of Ethics. A report is issued to identify areas for improvement.
- External assessments are provided by an external and independent assessor or team of assessors to conclude whether the internal audit activity conforms to the IIA's *Standards* and the Code of Ethics. A report is issued to identify areas for improvement.
- The CAE conducts ongoing and continuous measurements and analyses using audit metrics and KPIs.
- The CAE monitors the outcomes of the internal and external assessments and develops and implements action plans related to any identified improvements through the QAIP.

Considerations for implementation include:

- Internal assessments consist of ongoing monitoring and periodic self-assessments in that order.
- Ongoing monitoring is achieved primarily through continuous activities such as engagement planning and supervision, standardized work programs and practices, standardized workpaper development procedures and sign-offs, and workpaper and report reviews. Continuous monitoring is related to delivering quality audits on an engagement-by-engagement basis.
- Periodic self-assessments are conducted internally to validate that ongoing monitoring is operating effectively and to assess whether the internal audit activity is in conformance with the IIA's *Standards* and the Code of Ethics. This conformance in turn also achieves alignment with the definition of internal auditing and the core principles.

Internal Assessments = Ongoing Monitoring + Periodic Self-Assessments

Ongoing monitoring is done first.

Periodic self-assessment is done next.

- External assessments are conducted at least once every five years by an independent and external assessor or a team from outside the audit function and outside the audit organization.

- A self-assessment may be performed in lieu of a full external assessment, provided it is validated by a qualified, independent, competent, and professional external assessor. Under these conditions, the scope of a self-assessment is the same as that of a full external assessment.

  An original self-assessment can be performed onsite by an internal assessor or by an external assessor.

  A self-assessment must be validated onsite by a separate independent external assessor regardless of who performed the original self-assessment.

- The goal of internal assessments and external assessments is the same: to determine whether an internal audit activity conforms to the IIA's *Standards* and the Code of Ethics.

Considerations for demonstrating conformance include the following output documents:

- Minutes of board meetings where internal external assessment plans and results were discussed.

- A request for services (RFSs) document that shows how the external assessors are vetted (screened), selected, and hired to do the external assessment work. This document combined with a benchmarking report demonstrates the exercise of due diligence on the part of the internal audit activity.

- Documents showing how internal assessments are conducted with review scope, approach plan, workpapers, and reports containing recommendations for improvement. These documents are accompanied by audit metrics and KPIs.

- Documents showing how external assessments are conducted with a report containing conclusions as to the degree of conformance (e.g., 85%); recommendations to improve internal audit quality, efficiency, and effectiveness; and corrective action plans required.

Requiring a familiarity with the related Standards includes:

- Quality assurance and improvement program (*Standard* 1300)

- Internal assessments (*Standard* 1311)

- External assessments (*Standard* 1312)

- Reporting on the quality assurance and improvement program (*Standard* 1320)

- Use of "conforms with the international standards for the professional practice of internal auditing" (*Standard* 1321)

- Disclosure of nonconformance (*Standard* 1322)

Audit Metrics and Key Performance Indicators—*Standard* 1310

Internal audit activity is a function requiring a measurement of its performance similar to other functions in an organization. Audit metrics and KPIs are self-checks for internal auditors to measure and manage progress of their own performance levels. Audit metrics and KPIs can be organized, structured, and monitored in terms of management KPIs, operational KPIs, strategic KPIs, professional KPIs, financial KPIs, and board-level KPIs.

Management KPIs

- Time to complete an audit engagement in hours or days (time to audit in hours or days)

- Average time to complete an audit engagement in hours or days (average time to audit in hours or days)

- Elapsed time between the audit fieldwork completion and audit report issuance (Longer time periods require improvements.)

- Average time to issue audit reports in days or weeks (This measures how much time was taken to issue an audit report after an audit engagement was completed.)

- Time since the last audit (in years) (This actual time should be compared with the planned audit cycle time, and proper actions should be taken.)

- Elapsed time between the audits (in years) (This actual time should be compared with the planned audit cycle time, and proper actions should be taken.)

- Time to take corrective actions by audit client management regarding audit recommendations (Longer time periods require audit monitoring and follow-up.)

- The longest time an auditor's job is open for months, quarters, and years

- The shortest time an auditor's job is open for months, quarters, and years

Operational KPIs

- Percentage of the annual audit plan completed (Higher percentage indicates successful audits while lower percentages indicate unsuccessful audits, where the latter results in residual risks.)

- Percentage of actual risks addressed, assured, or covered to the total number of risks discovered or uncovered (The difference results in an assurance gap.)

- Percentage of audit reports issued as scheduled or planned (This shows that the audit activity can deliver its reports on time and that it is disciplined in doing so.)

- Percentage of follow-up audits conducted as scheduled or planned (This indicates auditors' lack of seriousness and shows that auditors are there just to make recommendations and that they are not serious about whether they help the organization that they work for. It is a sign of disservice to the organization.)

- Percentage of recommendations implemented resulting from internal assessments and external assessments regarding internal audit activity's QAIP

Strategic KPIs

- Percentage of audit recommendations accepted by audit clients at a point in time (This indicates the usefulness [benefit] of audit recommendation to audit clients.)

- Percentage of audit recommendations rejected by audit clients at a point in time (This indicates the nonuse (no benefit) of audit recommendation to audit clients.)

- Percentage of audit recommendations implemented after they are accepted by audit clients at a point in time (This indicates that audit recommendations are practical and useful.)

- Percentage of unimplementable audit recommendations after they were accepted by audit clients at a point in time (This indicates that audit recommendations are theoretical in nature with no practical benefits.)

- Percentage of significant audit recommendations (vital few of 20/80 or 80/20 rule) to the total number of audit recommendations made in a year (This indicates that internal auditors are clearly adding and enhancing value to their organization.)

- Percentage of insignificant audit recommendations (trivial many of 20/80 rule) to the total number of audit recommendations made in a year (This indicates that internal auditors are not adding value to their organization.)

- Percentage of audit recommendations accepted and remaining open at a point in time (This indicates that audit clients have not decided to implement the recommendations for some reason.)

- Percentage of audit recommendations that were closed at a point in time (This indicates that audit clients have fully implemented the auditors' recommendations to the auditors' full satisfaction.)

- Overall audit client satisfaction rate (This is an aggregated measure of satisfaction-related information received from audit clients and other stakeholders through surveys, feedback, one-on-one meetings and interviews, memos, emails, and reports. This satisfaction rate is expressed in terms of a percentage.)

Professional KPIs

- Percentage of auditors certified in internal auditing with the CIA designation

- Percentage of auditors with audit-related multiple certifications

- Average number of professional certifications held by auditors

- Average number of continuing professional development (CPD) hours earned in a year by auditors

- Average number of years of auditor work experience in internal auditing

- Percentage of technology auditors to nontechnology auditors

- Average turnover of audit staff in a year

Financial KPIs

- Percentage of audits completed over budget

- Percentage of audits completed under budget

- Variance analysis between budgeted hours and actual hours

Board-Level KPIs

- Percentage of independent directors to total board members (The goal should be a higher percentage than in the industry.)

- Percentage of a company's executives on the board to total board members (The goal should be a smaller percentage than in the industry.)

- Percentage of shadow directors to total board members (The goal should be a zero percentage because shadow directors—for example, outsiders such as lobbyists, activists, friends, family members, consultants, and majority shareholders—can exercise greater pressure on and influence over the board.)

- Percentage of nonexecutive directors to risk management committee members (The goal should be a higher percentage because executive directors such as the CEO, CFO, and chief risk officer [CRO] can exercise greater influence on the risk committee, which is not good for the company.)

Audit Metrics and Key Performance Indicators— *Standard* 1310 *(Continued)*

- Percentage of independent directors to audit committee members (The goal should be a higher percentage because the audit committee oversees the entire financial reporting process and coordinates between internal auditors and external auditors, which is a major responsibility. The audit committee should not oversee the risk management and regulatory compliance functions as they are the responsibilities of senior management [executives].)

- Percentage of female directors to total board members (The goal should be a comparable percentage in the industry and nation's data.)

- Percentage of directors with little or no compensation or remuneration paid (The goal should be a zero percentage because it follows the simple principle of no money, no work. Two outcomes are possible here: say on pay and no pay, no say. Without comparable compensation and remuneration, directors are hired just for their name only to act as a rubber stamp for the CEO, directors simply become routine box checkers in their work, and they have no strong voice [or no teeth] in the board's work and decisions.)

- Percentage of board-level qualitative metrics to the total number of board-level metrics (Total metrics include both qualitative metrics and quantitative metrics, which should be given equal importance. Examples of quantitative metrics include (1) sales, revenues, profits, market share, and company stock prices year over year; and (2) earnings per share, return on investment, return on assets, return on equity, and return on capital. Examples of qualitative metrics include employee low morale, negative comments posted on social media by unhappy customers, cyberrisks, supply-chain risks, product recall risks, public relations risks, and customer dissatisfaction risks.)

1311—Internal Assessments

Internal assessments must include:

- Ongoing monitoring of the performance of the internal audit activity.

- Periodic self-assessments or assessments by other persons within the organization with sufficient knowledge of internal audit practices.

Interpretation: *Ongoing monitoring is an integral part of the day-to-day supervision, review, and measurement of the internal audit activity. Ongoing monitoring is incorporated into the routine policies and practices used to manage the internal audit activity and uses processes, tools, and information considered necessary to evaluate conformance with the Code of Ethics and the* Standards.

Periodic assessments are conducted to evaluate conformance with the Code of Ethics and the Standards.

Sufficient knowledge of internal audit practices requires at least an understanding of all elements of the International Professional Practices Framework.

1311—Implementation Guide
Establishing a scope for implementation work requires the following considerations:

- The scope of internal assessments includes both ongoing monitoring and periodic self-assessments with different focus. The difference in scope and focus is shown next:

  Ongoing monitoring takes a narrow scope and focuses on conformance with performance standards at the individual audit engagement level.

Periodic self-assessments take a broad scope and focus on conformance with all *Standards* (Attribute and Performance *Standards*) at the internal audit activity level.

- Both ongoing monitoring and periodic self-assessments require constant measuring, monitoring, and reporting of audit metrics and audit KPIs.

- All internal assessments must conform to the IIA's *Standards* and the Code of Ethics.

- Internal assessments focus on continuous improvement of the internal audit activity.

- The IIA's Quality Assessment Manual for the Internal Audit Activity or other guidelines and tools can help in conducting internal assessments.

- The relation between internal assessments and external assessments:

Internal assessments are done first.

External assessments are done last.

Internal assessments support external assessments.

Considerations for implementation include:

- Ongoing monitoring occurs routinely throughout the year with the implementation of standard work practices such as audit supervision, audit planning, audit program, work-paper reviews, and audit reports.

- During ongoing monitoring, checklists or automation tools can be used to ensure compliance with established practices and procedures and to ensure consistency in the application of performance standards.

- Ongoing monitoring requires feedback from audit clients immediately after an audit engagement, semiannually, or annually to determine how efficiently and effectively the internal audit work was performed during the engagement.

- Ongoing monitoring delivers quality audit results on an engagement-by-engagement basis.

- Periodic self-assessments are conducted by senior members of the internal audit activity, Certified Internal Auditors (CIAs), and competent internal audit professionals working in nonaudit departments of the same organization. These members can form a team with extensive experience and knowledge with IIA's IPPF, consisting of *Standards* and Code of Ethics. Conducting post-engagement reviews or analyzing metrics and KPIs can support the periodic self-assessment.

- A periodic self-assessment should be performed shortly before the external assessment to reduce the time and effort required to complete the external assessment.

- Audit metrics and KPIs should be measured during self-assessments and internal assessments.

- Results of ongoing monitoring and periodic self-assessments should be reported to the board at least annually.

Considerations for demonstrating conformance include the following output documents:

- Completed checklists that support workpapers reviews
- Submitted survey results from audit clients and other stakeholders
- Audit metrics and KPIs showing the efficiency and effectiveness of the internal audit activity

- Completed periodic self-assessments showing the scope and focus of work

- Internal assessment results presented to the board and senior management with corrective action plans and corrective actions taken

- Board meeting minutes

Requiring a familiarity with the related Standards includes:

- Quality assurance and improvement program (*Standard* 1300)

- Requirements of the quality assurance and improvement program (*Standard* 1310)

- External assessments (*Standard* 1312)

- Reporting on the quality assurance and improvement program (*Standard* 1320)

- Use of "conforms with the international standards for the professional practice of internal auditing" (*Standard* 1321)

- Disclosure of nonconformance (*Standard* 1322)

- Policies and procedures (*Standard* 2040)

- Engagement planning (*Standard* 2200)

- Performing the engagement (*Standard* 2300)

- Engagement supervision (*Standard* 2340)

- Communicating results (*Standard* 2400)

1312—External Assessments

External assessments must be conducted at least once every five years by a qualified, independent assessor or assessment team from outside the organization. The chief audit executive must discuss with the board:

- The form and frequency of external assessment.

- The qualifications and independence of the external assessor or assessment team, including any potential conflict of interest.

Interpretation: *External assessments may be accomplished through a full external assessment or a self-assessment with independent external validation. The external assessor must conclude as to conformance with the Code of Ethics and the* Standards; *the external assessment may also include operational or strategic comments.*

A qualified assessor or assessment team demonstrates competence in two areas: the professional practice of internal auditing and the external assessment process. Competence can be demonstrated through a mixture of experience and theoretical learning. Experience gained in organizations of similar size, complexity, sector, or industry, and technical issues is more valuable than less relevant experience. In the case of an assessment team, not all members of the team need to have all the competencies; it is the team as a whole that is qualified. The CAE uses professional judgment when assessing whether an assessor or assessment team demonstrates sufficient competence to be qualified.

An independent assessor or assessment team means not having either an actual or a perceived conflict of interest and not being a part of, or under the control of, the organization to which the internal audit activity belongs. The CAE should encourage board oversight in the external assessment to reduce perceived or potential conflicts of interest.

1312—Implementation Guide

Establishing a scope for implementation work includes:

- External assessments are required at least once every five years or more frequently by an independent and competent external assessor, either individually or a team, coming from outside the organization. Reasons for conducting assessments more frequently include changes in senior management, shorter business cycles, new CAE, changes in the audit policies and procedures, merger of two or more audit departments, and significant audit staff turnover.

- The goal of the external assessor is to validate that an internal audit activity conforms to the IIA's *Standards* and the Code of Ethics.

- The external assessor must be hired through an acquisition policy such as submitting an RFSs document followed by bidding and evaluation practices.

- The CAE must ensure that the external assessor will not impair independence, will maintain objectivity, and will be free of conflict-of-interest situations.

- The relation between internal assessments and external assessments is shown next:

Internal assessments are done first.

External assessments are done last.

Internal assessments support external assessments.

Considerations for implementation include:

- Two approaches to external assessments include (1) a full external assessment and (2) a self-assessment with independent external validation (SAIV). These two approaches will have the same comprehensiveness in terms of scope and size, as they evaluate the audit's conformance with the IIA's *Standards* and Code of Ethics.

- A full external assessment addresses: (1) the level of conformance with the IIA's *Standards* and Code of Ethics as evidenced from the audit charter, plans, policies, procedures, practices, and regulatory requirements; (2) the efficiency and effectiveness of the internal audit activity through a review of audit processes, QAIP requirements, and the audit staff's knowledge, experience, and expertise; and (3) the extent to which the audit activity adds value to the stakeholders and meets the expectations of senior management, operations management, and functional management.

- The work of SAIV is conducted by a qualified internal auditor first and later validated by a qualified external assessor. The work is conducted onsite.

SAIV = Qualified Internal Auditor for Onsite Self-Assessment
      + Qualified External Assessor for Onsite Validation

- External assessors must be competent in the professional practice of internal auditing (i.e., knowledge of IPPF's Mandatory Guidance and *Standards*) and must be knowledgeable in the external quality assessment process.

- External assessors must have work experience at the audit management level (i.e., CAE or similar), must have received the CIA designation, and must have received the IIA's quality assessment training course or similar training.

- The external assessment team may consist of specialists (e.g., risk analysts, IT auditors, statisticians, scientists, engineers, and actuaries) to provide assistance to the team members. Each team member does not need to possess all of the preferred competencies; rather, the team as a whole should possess the necessary competencies to deliver the best results.

- The external assessors, either individually or a team, must be objective. This means that they should be free from actual, potential, or perceived conflict-of-interest situations that could impair objectivity.

- The external assessors must be independent of the internal audit activity (audit department). They are not independent if they were: (1) recent previous employees of the internal audit department; (2) employees from another department of the organization (nonaudit department); (3) employees from a related organization, such as a parent company, an affiliate group, or a business division; or (4) reciprocal peer assessments between two audit departments. However, reciprocal peer assessments among three or more audit departments are considered independent.

Considerations for demonstrating conformance include the following output documents:

- A report from the external assessor describing observations and recommendations to management in order to improve the internal audit quality, efficiency, and effectiveness

- Minutes of a board meeting documenting the assessment results with action plans for improvement

- A benchmarking report showing how the external assessor was screened, selected, and hired (a vetting process) through an RFSs document that demonstrates the audit's commitment to a due diligence process (Note that the vetting process does not apply to guest auditors, who are borrowed auditors and employed in a nonaudit department of the same organization as that of the internal audit department.)

Requiring a familiarity with the related Standards includes:

- Quality assurance and improvement program (*Standard* 1300)
- Requirements of the quality assurance and improvement program (*Standard* 1310)
- Internal assessments (*Standard* 1311)
- Reporting on the quality assurance and improvement program (*Standard* 1320)
- Use of "conforms with the international standards for the professional practice of internal auditing" (*Standard* 1321)
- Disclosure of nonconformance (*Standard* 1322)

1320—Reporting on the Quality Assurance and Improvement Program

The chief audit executive must communicate the results of the quality assurance and improvement program to senior management and the board. Disclosure should include:

- The scope and frequency of both the internal and external assessments
- The qualifications and independence of the assessor(s) or assessment team, including potential conflicts of interest
- Conclusions of assessors
- Corrective action plans

Interpretation: *The form, content, and frequency of communicating the results of the quality assurance and improvement program is established through discussions with senior management and the board and considers the responsibilities of the internal audit activity and CAE as contained in the internal audit charter. To demonstrate conformance with the Code of Ethics and the* Standards, *the results of external and periodic internal assessments are communicated upon completion of such assessments, and the results of ongoing monitoring are communicated at least annually. The results include the assessor's or assessment team's evaluation with respect to the degree of conformance.*

1320—Implementation Guide

Establishing a scope for implementation work requires the following considerations:

- The CAE establishes the minimum criteria for conducting internal assessments and external assessments and communicates them to the board and senior management.

- The CAE is aware of previous internal and external assessments with their rating scales.

- The CAE is familiar with the IIA's *Standards* and Code of Ethics.

Considerations for implementation include four core elements:

1. Scope and frequency of both internal assessments and external assessments

    Internal assessments are done at least every year for large-size audit departments.

    Internal assessments are done at least every two years for small-size audit departments.

    External assessments are done at least every five years or more frequently.

    Ongoing monitoring, a part of internal assessments, requires a reporting of audit metrics and KPIs.

2. Qualifications and independence of the assessor(s) or assessment team

    Both internal assessors and external assessors must be qualified and competent to do their work.

    External assessors must be independent and objective from the audit activity in that they do not have actual, potential, or perceived conflicts of interests.

3. Conclusions of assessors

    External assessors express their opinions or conclusions on the results of their work.

    External assessors indicate the degree of conformance with the IIA's *Standards*, whether for each standard and/or a series or group of standards, with a rating scale.

    The conformance rating scale includes three types: (1) generally conforms (a top rating of conformance with the audit charter, polices, practices, processes, and *Standards*), (2) partially conforms (a middle rating of deviations from the *Standards* that do not preclude the audit activity from fulfilling its responsibilities), and (3) does not conform (a bottom rating of significant deficiencies that have a serious impact or that can preclude the audit activity from adequately fulfilling its responsibilities).

4. Corrective action plans that have been completed or yet to be completed

    The CAE reports the results of external assessments to the board and senior management at two different times: immediately after the assessment work was done and before the corrective actions were taken on recommendations and immediately after all the recommendations have been corrected.

The CAE adds the external assessor's recommendations to the ongoing monitoring processes on a proactive basis.

Considerations for demonstrating conformance include the following output documents:

- Board meeting minutes showing the CAE's discussions with the board and senior management about the scope, objectives, and frequency of both internal assessments and external assessments

- Procurement or acquisition documents showing how the external assessors are carefully screened, selected, and hired (i.e., vetted)

- Reports from internal assessments and external assessments with conclusions and recommendations

Requiring a familiarity with the related Standards includes:

- Quality assurance and improvement program (*Standard* 1300)
- Requirements of the quality assurance and improvement program (*Standard* 1310)
- Internal assessments (*Standard* 1311)
- External assessments (*Standard* 1312)
- Use of "conforms with the international standards for the professional practice of internal auditing" (*Standard* 1321)
- Disclosure of nonconformance (*Standard* 1322)
- Recognizing mandatory guidance in the internal audit charter (*Standard* 1010)
- Policies and procedures (*Standard* 2040)

1321—Use of "Conforms with the International *Standards* for the Professional Practice of Internal Auditing"

Indicating that the internal audit activity conforms with the *International Standards for the Professional Practice of Internal Auditing* is appropriate only if supported by the results of the quality assurance and improvement program.

Interpretation: *The internal audit activity conforms with the Code of Ethics and the* Standards *when it achieves the outcomes described therein. The results of the quality assurance and improvement program include the results of both internal and external assessments. All internal audit activities will have the results of internal assessments. Internal audit activities in existence for at least five years will also have the results of external assessments.*

1321—Implementation Guide

This *Standard* discusses the scenarios and situations under which a conformance statement can be used, whether it is a partial conformance with one or more *Standards* or a full conformance with all *Standards*. Here, conformance addresses both the IIA's *Standards* and the Code of Ethics. Note that external auditors are required to state that all of their attestation engagements and financial statement audits are conducted in conformance with the Generally Accepted Auditing Standards. On the other hand, internal auditors have specific conditions to meet prior to stating that their internal audit work conforms to the IIA's *Standards* and Code of Ethics.

Conformance = Internal Assessments and External Assessments

Nonconformance = No Internal Assessments and No External Assessments

Nonconformance = Internal Assessments without External Assessments

Establishing a scope for implementation work requires:

- The CAE is required to have a full and clear understanding of the QAIP requirements.

- The CAE reviews the results from recent internal assessments and external assessments.

- The CAE learns the expectations of the board about conformance to the IIA's *Standards*, educates board members about the scope and nature of such *Standards*, and explains to board members what it means to conform or not conform to those *Standards.*

Considerations for implementation include an understanding of the following scenarios:

- It is a nonconformance when the results of either the current internal assessment or the most recent external assessment do not conform to the IIA's *Standards* and Code of Ethics.

- It is a nonconformance when the age of the internal audit activity is five years or more and it did not complete an external assessment.

- It is a nonconformance when the internal audit activity did not conduct an internal assessment according to its published frequency and that a completed external assessment did not validate the internal assessment.

- It is a nonconformance when the external assessment was not done every five years and it requires that the internal audit activity must not use a statement that it is in conformance until the external assessment is completed and that it supports conformance with the IIA's *Standards* and Code of Ethics.

- It is a nonconformance when the external assessment concludes that the internal audit activity was not in compliance. Then the audit activity must immediately discontinue using a conformance statement until all the nonconformance items are corrected based on the next external assessment with full validation.

- Nonconformance becomes conformance after full validation by external assessors.

- It is a conformance when the age of the internal audit activity is less than five years and the recent self-assessment (a part of internal assessment) report stated that it was in compliance with the IIA's *Standards* and Code of Ethics.

Considerations for demonstrating conformance include the following output documents:

- Reports from internal assessments and external assessments with clear conclusions whether the internal audit activity has achieved conformance with the IIA's *Standards*

- Engagement plans, notifications, and schedules for internal and external assessments

- Internal audit charter

- Internal audit policies and procedures manual

- QAIP manual

- Board meeting minutes showing the CAE's communications with the board about the internal and external assessments and their results

Requiring a familiarity with the related Standards includes:

- Quality assurance and improvement program (*Standard* 1300)
- Requirements of the quality assurance and improvement program (*Standard* 1310)
- Internal assessments (*Standard* 1311)
- External assessments (*Standard* 1312)
- Reporting on the quality assurance and improvement program (*Standard* 1320)
- Disclosure of nonconformance (*Standard* 1322)

1322—Disclosure of Nonconformance

When nonconformance with the Code of Ethics or the *Standards* impacts the overall scope or operation of the internal audit activity, the chief audit executive must disclose the nonconformance and the impact to senior management and the board.

1322—Implementation Guide

This *Standard* discusses the disclosures required when an internal audit activity does not conform to the IIA's *Standards* and Code of Ethics and presents the impact of nonconformance on the overall scope or operation of the internal audit activity. This *Standard* presents examples of such nonconformances.

Establishing a scope for implementation work requires:

- The CAE is required to have a full and clear understanding of the QAIP requirements.
- The CAE reviews the results from recent internal assessments and external assessments.
- The CAE learns the expectations of the board about conformance to the IIA's *Standards* and Code of Ethics, educates board members about the scope and nature of such *Standards* and Ethics, and explains what it means to conform or not conform to those *Standards* and Ethics.

Considerations for implementation include:

- The CAE is required to communicate annually to the board and senior management about the results of internal and external assessments and the level of conformance with the IIA's *Standards* and Ethics. This communication is necessary to uncover impairments to independence or objectivity, audit scope restrictions or limitations, and resource limitations for auditors and audit clients.
- Examples of nonconformances include: (1) when the internal audit activity did not conduct external assessment at least once every five years; (2) when an internal auditor did not meet individual objectivity requirements during an audit engagement; (3) when an audit engagement did not have auditors possessing collective knowledge, skills, and experiences; and (4) when the CAE and managers and supervisors failed to consider risk when developing the audit plan.
- The CAE should be able to quantify (how much) the impact of nonconformance on the internal audit activity in fulfilling its responsibilities such as providing reliable assurance and consulting services, completing the audit plan, and addressing high-risk audit areas.

Considerations for demonstrating conformance require the following output documents:

- Board meeting minutes showing the impact of nonconformance with the *Standards* and ethics
- Private meetings with the audit committee
- One-on-one meeting with the board chair
- Memos or emails to senior management and the board

Requiring a familiarity with the related Standards includes:

- Quality assurance and improvement program (*Standard* 1300)
- Requirements of the quality assurance and improvement program (*Standard* 1310)
- Internal assessments (*Standard* 1311)
- External assessments (*Standard* 1312)
- Reporting on the quality assurance and improvement program (*Standard* 1320)
- Use of "conforms with the international standards for the professional practice of internal auditing" (*Standard* 1321)
- Individual objectivity (*Standard* 1120)
- Proficiency (*Standard* 1210)
- Planning (*Standard* 2010)

The IIA's Three Lines of Defense Model—*Standard* 1322

Similar to information systems security requiring multiple layers of defense (i.e., security controls using defense-in-depth and defense-in-breadth concepts) to protect technology assets (e.g., computers, networks, and mobile devices), organizations need three lines of defense (three layers of defense) to protect and preserve human assets (e.g., employees, customers, suppliers, vendors, visitors, and contractors), tangible assets (e.g., buildings, inventory, plant, and equipment), intangible assets (e.g., copyrights, trademarks, service marks, and patents), financial assets (e.g., cash, stocks, and bonds), and information assets (e.g., data, plans, policies, procedures, and practices). The scope of the three-lines-of-defense model applies to risk management and control activities and processes. The nature of this model includes vigilant employees observing people and things for unusual and strange behavior, manual control procedures, automated control procedures, and daily work rules and practices.

The idea behind the three-lines-of-defense model is that:

- If the first line of defense does not work for some reason, then the second line of defense comes into play to protect and preserve the assets.

- If the first line and second lines of defense do not work for some reason, the third line of defense (last line of defense) should work in protecting and preserving the assets.

The concept behind the three-lines-of-defense model is that two hands are stronger than one hand and that multiple lines of defense provide a much stronger support and protection than a single line of defense. This model can be installed at two levels: organization level and internal audit level.

THE IIA'S THREE LINES OF DEFENSE MODEL— *STANDARD* 1322 *(Continued)*

Organization Level: Three Lines of Defense

Examples of organization-level three-lines-of-defense follow. Although not officially and explicitly defined, outside auditors, such as external auditors, bank examiners, and regulatory auditors, can be treated and recognized as providing fourth-line-of-defense services.

First line of defense	Operational and functional management working in manufacturing, marketing, merchandising, procurement, IT, human resources, accounting, loss prevention, finance, and operations departments. This first defense is a form of initial exercise of controls through management controls and internal control measures. This defense is provided by risk owners and managers who own, manage, and oversee risks. These risk owners implement corrective actions to address process weaknesses and control deficiencies.
Second line of defense	Employees working in compliance function, health and safety department, customer service department, technical support group, environmental management, IT security analysts, physical security guards, legal staff, risk analysts, financial control analysts, product quality inspectors, internal quality assurance providers, and external quality assurance providers. This second defense is a form of intermediary exercise of controls and provides risk control and compliance.
Third line of defense	Internal auditors, physical security guards, fraud specialists, public relations officers, insurance claims adjusters, and corporate gatekeepers (e.g., accountants, auditors, and attorneys). This third defense is a form of final exercise of controls and provides risk assurance.
Fourth line of defense	Although not officially and explicitly defined, outside auditors, such as external auditors, bank examiners, and regulatory auditors, can be treated and recognized as providing fourth-line-of-defense services. These outside auditors can be asked to provide a separate and comprehensive review of an organization's risk management framework and practices (e.g., enterprise risk management), to assess the adequacy of the three lines of defense, and to report their review results to senior management, the board, and shareholders.

Both the second and third lines of defense provide oversight and/or assurance services over risk management. The key difference between the second and third lines is the concepts of independence and objectivity of internal auditors.[1]

Responsibilities may become blurred across internal audit function and second-line-of-defense functions when internal auditors are asked to assume second-line-of-defense activities due to their special skills and talents. Examples of these assumed activities include new regulatory requirements (e.g., assistance in training and implementation of Sarbanes-Oxley Act of 2002), change in business (e.g., entry into new markets, new products, and new lines of business), resource constraints (internal auditors are requested to fill the staffing and management gap), and efficiency in performing compliance and risk management functions better than the others.

---

[1] IIA, *Internal Audit and the Second Line of Defense*, IPPF's Supplemental Guidance, *Practice Guide* (January 2016), www.theiia.org.

Where safeguards to maintain internal audit's independence and objectivity are not possible, the responsibility for performing the second-line-of-defense activities should be reassigned to an internal nonaudit function or outsourced externally to a third-party provider. Moreover, the second-line-of-defense activities performed by internal audit should be referenced in the audit's charter document and/or included in the board update report issued at least annually by the internal audit department.

Internal auditors should avoid activities that compromise their independence and objectivity, including:

- Setting the risk appetite levels

- Owning, managing, and overseeing risks

- Assuming responsibilities for accounting, business development, and other first-line-of-defense functions

- Making risk-response decisions on the organization's management's behalf

- Implementing or assuming accountability for risk management or governance processes

- Providing assurance on second-line-of-defense activities performed by internal auditors

Audit Level: Three Lines of Defense

Similar to the three lines of defense found at an organization level, internal audit activity has three lines or layers of defense within its own department or function.

First line of defense	Staff auditor who is assigned to an audit engagement (engagement auditor), who developed the audit program, who prepared audit workpapers, and who drafted the initial audit reports can act as the first line of defense. Sign-off letters received from the engagement auditor after completing the audit work support and strengthen the audit work.
Second line of defense	In-charge auditor or lead auditor who reviewed the audit program, workpapers, and audit reports to confirm adherence to the audit plan, objectives, and scope can act as the second line of defense. Sign-offs received from the in-charge auditor or lead auditor support and strengthen the audit work completed.
Third line of defense	Audit supervisor or manager who reviewed the audit plan, audit program, workpapers, and audit reports to confirm adherence to the IIA's Standards, including the audit quality assurance standards, can act as the third line of defense. Sign-offs received from the audit supervisor or manager support and strengthen the audit work completed. Note that the audit supervisors and managers should act as the last line of defense (last resort) because there is no one after them to protect and defend the audit work.

2100—Nature of Work

The internal audit activity must evaluate and contribute to the improvement of the organization's governance, risk management, and control processes using a systematic, disciplined, and risk-based approach. Internal audit credibility and value are enhanced when auditors are proactive and their evaluations offer new insights and consider future impact.

2100—Implementation Guide

Establishing a scope for implementation work includes:

- The CAE should possess **business acumen** in understanding the concepts and principles of organizational governance, risk management, and control. Business acumen is a collective knowledge and understanding of business mission and vision; business objectives and goals; business strategies and plans; regulatory and legal requirements; and competitors' strategies and plans. This understanding can help the CAE in evaluating the effectiveness and efficiency of governance, risk management, and control (GRC) processes in the organization.

- The CAE and staff understand that the full scope and nature of internal audit work consists of improving the GRC processes.

Scope and Nature of Audit Work = Governance Processes + Risk Management Processes + Control Processes

- Internal auditors, supervisors, and managers need to apply their knowledge, experience, and best practices in the GRC processes to proactively highlight observed operational weaknesses and control breakdowns and make recommendations for improvement.

- The board is responsible for guiding the governance processes whereas senior management is accountable for leading risk management and control processes.

Board ⟶ Governance Processes

Senior Management ⟶ Risk Management and Control Processes

- The CAE will review and understand the board's charter and the audit committee's charter to understand the scope and nature of their duties, responsibilities, and accountabilities.

- The CAE will review and become familiar with the key organizational structures and roles of the chairman of the board, CEO, and other C-level executives such as CFO, chief information officer, and CRO.

Considerations for implementation include the following:

- Whereas the board is responsible for governance processes and senior management is accountable for risk management and control processes, the CAE is responsible for providing objective assurance and consulting services related to the GRC processes and to improve such processes.

Board ⟶ Governance

Senior Management ⟶ Risk Management and Control

Chief Audit Executive ⟶ Governance, Risk Management, and Control

- The CAE can assess the risks associated with the GRC processes only after assessing the maturity level of the GRC processes, maturity level of the organization's culture, and seniority of the individuals managing the GRC processes. Maturity levels can be either high (mature) or low (immature).

- A **fit-gap analysis** can be performed showing maturity or immaturity of GRC processes, as follows:

Mature GRC Processes + Mature Organization's Culture + Mature Senior Managers = Fit

Mature GRC Processes + Immature Organization's Culture + Mature Senior Managers = Gap

Mature GRC Processes + Mature Risk Management + Mature Controls = Fit

Mature GRC Processes + Mature Risk Management + Immature Controls = Gap

Mature GRC Processes + Immature Risk Management + Mature Controls = Gap

Immature GRC Processes + Mature Risk Management + Mature Controls = Gap

- The CAE can seek guidance from an established framework that senior management uses in guiding the risk assessment. Examples of these frameworks include the Committee of Sponsoring Organizations of the Treadway Commission's internal control (COSO's Internal Control) and COSO's enterprise risk management framework (COSO-ERM), the King Report on Corporate Governance, or International Standards Organization (ISO) 31000 for risk management. If the organization does not use any framework to guide the GRC processes, the CAE should recommend an appropriate framework for adaptation.

- The CAE assesses how her organization promotes business ethics and values, both internally within the organization and externally with its business partners. This assessment covers a review of mission, vision, and value statements; a code of conduct; hiring and training processes; an antifraud and whistleblowing policy; and a hotline and investigation process. Surveys and interviews can be used to measure whether the organization's efforts result in sufficient awareness of its ethical standards and values.

- The CAE ensures that his organization is effective in employee performance management and accountability matters. This scope covers a review of policies and processes related to employee compensation, objective setting (management by objective, MBO), performance evaluations, organization's KPIs, and incentive plans (bonuses and perks to management). This review can disclose unacceptable behavior of employees and management or excessive risk taking by management, which can be contrary to the organization's strategic objectives.

- The CAE appraises how her organization communicates risk and control information to employees and nonemployees. Internal reports, newsletters, memos and emails, staff meeting minutes, surveys, interviews, and audit assurance and consulting engagements all can be used to appraise the effectiveness of communicating risk and control information to all parties.

- The CAE assesses his organization's ability to coordinate governance activities and communicate governance information among various parties such as internal auditors, external auditors, audit committee, risk committee, and governance committee.

- The CAE can provide consulting services, as a preferred approach, when governance issues are known or the governance process is immature because consulting services provide recommendations for improvement of governance processes.

- The CAE can assign senior-level internal auditors to attend and observe meetings of governance-related bodies and advise them on an ongoing basis. This assignment is an example of continuous monitoring methods for the internal audit activity.

- The CAE understands that a review of his organization's governance processes must be based on a broad focus with a comprehensive scope due to its pervasive nature, not a narrow focus with a limited scope.

- The broad focus takes into account: (1) previous internal audit reports; (2) results of management assessments (e.g., compliance inspections, quality audits, and control self-assessments); (3) results of external assurance providers (e.g., legal investigators, government auditor general offices, called the Office of the Inspector General), public accounting firms, and reports from regulators; (4) results from the work of internal assurance providers or second-line-of-defense functions, such as health and safety, compliance, and quality; and (5) adverse incidents, such as natural disasters, manmade disasters, website hacking, data breaches, and computer glitches and crashes.

Considerations for demonstrating conformance require the following output documents:

- Internal audit charter describing the internal audit activity's roles and responsibilities related to the GRC processes
- Internal audit plans showing the audit schedules in performing the GRC processes
- Board meeting minutes discussing the GRC processes among the CAE, board, and senior management
- Audit engagement plans and reports showing a risk-based approach to audit the GRC processes

Requiring a familiarity with the related Standards includes:

- Governance (*Standard* 2110)
- Risk management (*Standard* 2120)
- Control (*Standard* 2130)

2110—Governance

The internal audit activity must assess and make appropriate recommendations to improve the organization's governance processes for:

- Making strategic and operational decisions.
- Overseeing risk management and control.
- Promoting appropriate ethics and values within the organization.
- Ensuring effective organizational performance management and accountability.
- Communicating risk and control information to appropriate areas of the organization.
- Coordinating the activities of, and communicating information among, the board, external and internal auditors, other assurance providers, and management.

2110.A1—The internal audit activity must evaluate the design, implementation, and effectiveness of the organization's ethics-related objectives, programs, and activities.

2110.A2—The internal audit activity must assess whether the information technology governance of the organization supports the organization's strategies and objectives.

2110—Implementation Guide

Establishing a scope for implementation work requires the following:

- The CAE must understand the definition of **governance** as the combination of processes and structures implemented by the board of directors to inform, direct, manage, and monitor the activities of the organization toward the achievement of its objectives.
- The CAE becomes familiar with the globally accepted governance frameworks and models (e.g., COSO, U.S. Business Roundtable, National Association of Corporate Directors

[NACD], and global governance models). The CAE understands that the effectiveness of these frameworks and models depends on the size, complexity, life cycle, maturity level, stakeholder structure, and legal and regulatory requirements in which the organization operates.

Larger organizations are found to have stronger governance mechanisms.

Smaller organizations are found to have weaker governance mechanisms.

- The CAE understands that GRC processes are highly interrelated:

  Effective governance activities consider risk.

  Risk management relies on effective governance.

  Effective governance relies on internal controls.

  Effective governance requires tone at the top, voice of the top, risk culture, risk appetite, risk tolerance, risk maturity, risk sensitivity, oversight of risk management, and organization's culture.

- The CAE recognizes that the two most important items in a board's risk management activities are risk appetite and risk tolerance.

- The CAE reviews the board's charter, audit committee's charter, and the board meeting agendas and minutes to understand the role of the board in establishing strategic and operational decision-making framework. Note that the board members are not guarantors of governance activity; instead, they are overseers, custodians, loyalists, stewards, protectors, fiduciaries, caretakers, shepherds, gatekeepers, defenders, and guardians.

- The CAE reviews and evaluates the amount and frequency of compensation and remuneration paid to board members using the "contract for services" document. The CAE determines if these compensations and remunerations are reasonable and comparable in the industry. The effectiveness of a board's function is directly related to members' compensation and remuneration amounts, meaning lower or no compensation and remuneration amounts can lead to ineffective boards. The same logic applies to a board's incentive programs, which include bonuses, stock options, termination and retirement packages, and perks.

- The CAE interviews with the C-level executives to gain a detailed understanding of specific governance processes and activities. These executives include chief governance officer, chief compliance officer, chief ethics officer, chief risk officer, and chief people officer (human resources). Consulting with the organization's independent external auditor is a good practice in this area.

- The CAE understands the key requirements of good governance include two parties, such as the board and the CEO. Both parties must be good for good governance to exist. The following relationships can apply based on specific conditions.

  Good Board + Good CEO = Good Governance
  Bad Board + Good CEO = Bad Governance
  Good Board + Bad CEO = Bad Governance
  Bad Board + Bad CEO = Worse Governance

Considerations for implementation need:

- The CAE identifies the organization's higher-risk governance processes, which are addressed through assurance and consulting engagements described in the final audit plan.

- The CAE is responsible for assessing and making recommendations to improve the organization's overall governance processes.

- The CAE reviews past audit reports and board meeting minutes and interviews the department-level heads, such as functional managers and senior managers, to find out what governance processes led to strategic and operational decisions.

- The CAE learns how the organization conducts its annual risk assessment exercise and how it provides oversight of its risk management processes and control activities. In this regard, the CAE can interview key risk management personnel in the C-level executive suite, such as chief compliance officer, chief risk officer, and CFO.

Considerations for demonstrating conformance require the following output documents:

- Board meeting minutes and materials showing that the board is actively monitoring the performance, compensation, and incentive packages offered to senior-level executives

- Signed ethics statements from senior-level executives and business partners to show their commitment to maintaining business ethics and values and to eliminating conflict-of-interest situations

- Internal audit reports issued related to governance from assurance-based engagements and consulting-based recommendations to improve the governance processes

Requiring a familiarity with the related Standards includes:

- Nature of work (*Standard* 2100)
- Risk management (*Standard* 2120)
- Control (*Standard* 2130)
- Governance frameworks and models (e.g., COSO, U.S. Business Roundtable, NACD, and global governance models)

2120—Risk Management

The internal audit activity must evaluate the effectiveness and contribute to the improvement of risk management processes.

Interpretation: *Determining whether risk management processes are effective is a judgment resulting from the internal auditor's assessment that:*

- *Organizational objectives support and align with the organization's mission.*

- *Significant risks are identified and assessed.*

- *Appropriate risk responses are selected that align risks with the organization's risk appetite.*

- *Relevant risk information is captured and communicated in a timely manner across the organization, enabling staff, management, and the board to carry out their responsibilities.*

The internal audit activity may gather the information to support this assessment during multiple engagements. The results of these engagements, when viewed together, provide an understanding of the organization's risk management processes and their effectiveness.

Risk management processes are monitored through ongoing management activities, separate evaluations, or both.

2120.A1—The internal audit activity must evaluate risk exposures relating to the organization's governance, operations, and information systems regarding the:

- Achievement of the organization's strategic objectives.

- Reliability and integrity of financial and operational information.

- Effectiveness and efficiency of operations and programs.

- Safeguarding of assets.

- Compliance with laws, regulations, policies, procedures, and contracts.

2120.A2—The internal audit activity must evaluate the potential for the occurrence of fraud and how the organization manages fraud risk.

2120.C1—During consulting engagements, internal auditors must address risk consistent with the engagement's objectives and be alert to the existence of other significant risks.

2120.C2—Internal auditors must incorporate knowledge of risks gained from consulting engagements into their evaluation of the organization's risk management processes.

2120.C3—When assisting management in establishing or improving risk management processes, internal auditors must refrain from assuming any management responsibility by actually managing risks.

2120 Implementation Guide

Establishing a scope for implementation work requires:

- The CAE and staff must understand the definitions of risk management, risk, risk culture, risk attitude, risk appetite, risk tolerance, risk sensitivity, risk maturity, and risk immunity.

- The following highlights the relationships among risk attitude, risk appetite, risk tolerance, and risk sensitivity.

    Risk Taker = High-Risk Appetite = High Tolerance to Risk = Risk Insensitive
    Risk Averter = Low-Risk Appetite = High Intolerance to Risk = Risk Sensitive

- There is a built-in conflict when the internal auditor who is making audit recommendations is a risk taker and the audit client who is receiving these audit recommendations is a risk averter. Under these conditions, the audit client's acceptance of recommendations will be low (i.e., low risk appetite).

- The CAE and staff must understand the various types of risks the organization can face, including strategic, financial, operational, pure, hazard, speculative, legal, regulatory, and reputation risks.

- Internal auditors, supervisors, and managers need to know how their organization's management identifies, assesses, and provides oversight for risks before they evaluate the management's risk assessment processes.

- Internal auditors' assessment of risk considers their organization's size, complexity, life cycle, maturity, stakeholder structure, and legal and competitive environment, including new risks resulting from recent changes in the organization's environment. Examples of these changes include new laws and regulations, new management staff, new organization structure, new processes (manual and automated), new computer systems, new markets and products, and new business entities through mergers and acquisitions.

- Total risks facing an organization are the summation of risks assessed by the organization's management and risks assessed by the internal auditors.

$$\text{Total Risks} = \text{Management-Assessed Risks} + \text{Auditor-Assessed Risks}$$

Management assesses risks first.

Auditors assess risks next.

The CAE integrates both management-assessed risks and auditor-assessed risks.

- Internal auditors must understand the relationships among risks, returns, and controls as follows:

    Risks and returns move in the same direction, meaning that higher risks yield higher returns and lower risks give lower returns.

    Risks and controls move in the same direction, meaning that higher risks need higher levels of controls and lower risks require lower levels of controls.

- Internal auditors evaluate risk management processes during assurance and consulting reviews related to a specific business area, function, system, or process. They identify significant risks arising from major threats or vulnerabilities. Both the board and senior management should treat vulnerabilities as a test of their leadership; a challenge to their traditions, customs, beliefs, and values; an opportunity for their company's growth, progress, and success; and a strategic move to beat their competitors.

- The CAE reviews and evaluates the senior management's incentive programs in place and their relation to risk management activities that management undertakes. Incentive programs can take several forms, such as promotions, bonuses, stock options, perks, and termination and retirement packages.

    There should be a match between a company management's risk-taking approaches, a company's stated risk appetite levels, and a company's incentive programs established for the management. In addition, there should be a match between a company's risk policy and risk appetite; otherwise, a risk policy gap can occur. This is because strong incentives encourage excessive risk taking at the expense of company's risk policy and its stakeholders, which is not good. Incentives need to be risk adjusted or risk corrected when the actual outcomes are less than the planned or expected outcomes.

$$\text{Risk Policy} = \text{Risk Appetite}$$

Aggressive risk appetite implies aggressive risk policy.

$$\text{Risk Policy Gap} = \text{Risk Policy} - \text{Risk Appetite}$$

- The CAE should ascertain whether the CRO or equivalent is computing value-at-risk (VAR). VAR is an estimate of the maximum amount of loss that can occur in a given time period (e.g., one year) and at a given confidence level (e.g., 95%). Risk appetite is directly related to the VAR amount, meaning that the higher the risk appetite, the larger the amount of VAR, implying more value is at risk. The VAR amount can be computed using the Monte Carlo simulation method.

- The CAE and staff recognizes and promotes that a company management with high regard for compliance with laws, rules, and regulations will have a high, positive reputation in the business community and society.

- Senior managers and functional managers must carefully consider the appropriate balance between controls and risks in their functions, programs, and operations. To emphasize, too many controls can result in an inefficient and ineffective organization; managers must ensure an appropriate balance between the strength of controls and the relative risk associated with particular functions, programs, and operations. **The benefits of controls should outweigh the costs of controls.** Managers should consider both qualitative and quantitative factors when analyzing costs against benefits.

Considerations for implementation include:

- Risk assessment is of two types: one done by the management of the organization (management's risk assessment) and the other one done by the internal audit activity of the same organization (auditor's risk assessment). Any gaps between the management's risk assessment and the auditor's risk assessment should be identified and reported to the board and senior management. A **fit-gap analysis** indicates what fits and what does not fit (gap).

  Risk Fit-Gap Analyses = Management's Risk Assessment − Auditor's Risk Assessment

  □ The CAE and staff can use an established risk management framework, such as COSO-ERM or the ISO 31000 Standard, to assist them in risk identification and risk reduction.

  □ The CAE understands management's risk environment, such as risk appetite, risk tolerance, and risk culture (risk profiles), through conversations with the board and senior management.

  □ The CAE evaluates management's risk responses after alerting managers to new emerging risks due to changes and old risks that were not adequately mitigated (not remedied or not fixed). Examples of these risk responses include accept, pursue, transfer, mitigate, avoid, reject, or reduce.

  □ A risk exists when management has accepted a level of risk that may be unacceptable to the organization. The CAE should discuss this matter with senior management first and with the board next only after senior management fails to offer a risk mitigation strategy. When senior management offers a risk mitigation plan, the internal audit activity can evaluate the adequacy and timeliness of remedial actions (establishing controls) taken through reviews of control designs, testing of controls, and monitoring of control procedures.

  A risk exists when controls do not mitigate or do not limit that risk.

  A risk does not exist when controls mitigate or limit that risk.

- An organization's management faces its own risks, such as failed business strategies; poor execution of strategic plans; unethical incentive programs at the expense of customers, suppliers, and employees' goodwill; questionable business practices; underestimating or miscalculating competitors' moves and actions; and ignoring compliance with government's laws, rules, and regulations.

- Just as an organization's management faces its own risks, internal auditors face their own risks arising from the nature of the audit work performed (audit-related risks). Examples of audit-related risks include audit failure risk, false assurance risks, and reputation risks. The CAE should ensure that corrective actions are taken for audit-related risks.

Considerations for demonstrating conformance include the following output documents:

- Internal audit charter documenting the auditor's roles and responsibilities related to risk management

- Internal audit plan showing the risk management audit schedules with timelines and staff resources assigned

- Board meeting minutes discussing risk management audit's conclusions and recommendations with the board and senior management

- Audit committee meeting notes discussing risk management audit's conclusions and recommendations with members of the audit committee

- A report showing fit-gap analysis of risk management

- Meeting notes from discussions with special task forces (e.g., employee wages and benefits) and special committees (e.g., finance committee)

Requiring a familiarity with the related Standards includes:

- Nature of work (*Standard* 2100)

- Governance (*Standard* 2110)

- Control (*Standard* 2130)

- Communicating the acceptance of risks (*Standard* 2600)

- Risk management frameworks such as COSO-ERM and ISO 31000

2130—Control

The internal audit activity must assist the organization in maintaining effective controls by evaluating their effectiveness and efficiency and by promoting continuous improvement.

> **2130.A1**—The internal audit activity must evaluate the adequacy and effectiveness of controls in responding to risks within the organization's governance, operations, and information systems regarding the:
>
> - Achievement of the organization's strategic objectives.
>
> - Reliability and integrity of financial and operational information.
>
> - Effectiveness and efficiency of operations and programs.
>
> - Safeguarding of assets.
>
> - Compliance with laws, regulations, policies, procedures, and contracts.
>
> **2130.C1**—Internal auditors must incorporate knowledge of controls gained from consulting engagements into evaluation of the organization's control processes.

2130—Implementation Guide

- The CAE and staff must understand the definitions of control, control concepts, control processes, and control environment.

- **Control** is any positive or negative action taken by management, the board, and other parties to manage risk and increase the likelihood that established objectives and goals will be achieved. Management plans, organizes, and directs the performance of sufficient actions to provide reasonable assurance that objectives and goals will be accomplished.

- Several **control concepts** exist, including controls by motivation dimension, controls by action dimension, controls by time dimension, and controls by function dimension.

Controls by motivation dimension include positive controls and negative controls. Positive controls will increase the motivation levels of employees, making them more sincere, honest, efficient (productive), and effective (achieving goals) in their work. Examples of positive controls include bonuses, incentives, promotions, praises, recognition, and wage increases. Negative controls will decrease the motivation levels of employees, making them less sincere, honest, efficient (productive), and effective (achieving goals) in their work. Examples of negative controls include punishments, demotions, disciplinary actions, threats, criticism, and wage decreases.

Controls by action dimension include feedforward controls, concurrent controls, and feedback controls. A feedforward control is a proactive control based on strategies, budgets, and plans. Examples include error prevention, inspection of incoming materials and products, employee training and development, operating budget, and capital budget. A concurrent control is a current control that is repeated daily and ongoing. Examples include supervision, monitoring, on-the-job training, employee or machine work scheduling, and completing assigned work activities and tasks. A feedback control is a reactive control used to evaluate past activity to improve future performance. It measures actual performance against a standard to ensure that a defined result is achieved. Examples include surveys from customers, employees, and suppliers and variance analysis from budgets.

Controls by time dimension include pre-controls (proactive controls), current controls (ongoing controls), and post-controls (reactive controls).

Controls by function dimension include preventive controls, detective controls, and corrective controls. Preventive controls are actions taken to deter undesirable events, such as errors, irregularities, and fraud, from occurring. Examples include policies, procedures, directives, standards, circulars, regulations, guidelines, and segregation of duties. Detective controls are actions taken to detect undesirable events that have occurred. The installation of detective controls is necessary to provide feedback on the effectiveness of preventive controls. Examples include reviews, comparisons, bank reconciliations, receivable and payable reconciliations, and physical counts. Corrective controls are actions taken to correct undesirable events that have occurred. They fix both detected and reported errors. Examples include correction procedures, documentation, control reports, and exception reports.

The following is a relationship among controls by action dimension, controls by time dimension, and controls by function dimension.

Feedforward Controls ⟶ Proactive Controls ⟶ Pre-Controls ⟶ Preventive Controls

Concurrent Controls ⟶ Ongoing Controls ⟶ Current Controls ⟶ Detective Controls

Feedback Controls ⟶ Reactive Controls ⟶ Post-Controls ⟶ Corrective Controls

- **Control processes** are the policies, procedures (both manual and automated), and activities that are part of a control framework, designed and operated to ensure that risks are contained within the level that an organization is willing to accept.

- The **control environment** is the attitude and actions of the board and management regarding the importance of control within the organization. The control environment provides the discipline and structure for the achievement of the primary objectives of the system of internal control. The control environment includes six essential elements:

1. Integrity and ethical values

2. Management's philosophy and operating style

3. Organizational culture

4. Assignment of authority and responsibility

5. Human resource policies and practices

6. Competence of personnel such as auditors and nonauditors

> The control environment is enhanced when a tone at the top or voice of the top promotes a high culture of ethical behavior and a low tolerance for noncompliance with laws, rules, and regulations.

> Proper Control Environment = High Culture of Ethical Behavior
> + Low Tolerance for Noncompliance with Laws,
> Rules, and Regulations

> An organization's control environment consists of developing and implementing business controls, which can be classified as hard controls and soft controls.

☐ *Hard controls* are formal, tangible, objective, and much easier to measure and evaluate than the soft controls. Examples of hard controls include budgets, dual controls, written approvals, reconciliations, authorization levels, verifications, and segregation of duties. Soft controls are informal, intangible, subjective, and difficult to measure and evaluate. Tools to evaluate hard controls include flowcharts, system narratives, testing, and counting. Higher-level managers and executives need more depth in soft skills and soft controls and less depth in hard skills and hard controls. Lower-level managers and executives need more depth in hard skills and hard controls and less depth in soft skills and soft controls.

☐ *Soft controls* are informal, intangible, subjective, and much harder to measure and evaluate than the hard controls. Examples of soft controls include an organization's ethical climate, integrity, values, culture, vision, people's behaviors and attitudes, commitment to competence, tone at the top, management philosophy, management's operating style, level of understanding and commitment, and communication. Tools to evaluate soft controls include self-assessments, questionnaires, interviews, workshops, and role playing. Higher-level managers and executives need more depth in soft skills and soft controls and less depth in hard skills and hard controls. Lower-level managers and executives need more depth in hard skills and hard controls and less depth in soft skills and soft controls.

Establishing a scope for implementation work includes:

■ The CAE and staff must understand the critical risks that could inhibit the organization's ability to achieve its objectives and the controls that have been implemented to mitigate such risks to an acceptable level. The following is a relationship between risks and controls.

Business strategies, plans, and policies are designed into controls.

Business controls are built into daily procedures and practices.

Business events and transactions create risks.

Controls mitigate risks to an acceptable level of risk tolerance.

■ The CAE and staff must be familiar with globally recognized, comprehensive control frameworks such as *Internal Control–Integrated Framework*, issued by the Committee of Sponsoring Organizations (COSO) of the Treadway Commission.

- A management control policy can state that: (1) senior management oversees the establishment, administration, and assessment of the organization's control system; (2) functional management is responsible for the design and assessment of controls within their operating areas; and (3) the internal audit management is responsible for evaluating the effectiveness of the control processes in place at a point in time.

- The CAE and staff must understand the five relationships between controls and risks:

  1. Standards, regardless of their source, and regulatory guidelines are developed based on best practices, which eventually become "controls" for auditors.

  2. Controls can manage current risks only and cannot predict future risks.

  3. Controls cannot always provide reasonable assurance that risks are being managed effectively due to built-in control weaknesses, control overrides, and control breakdowns.

  4. Controls must address root causes of problems and risks, not just symptoms.

  5. Internal auditors should focus on significant risks and provide reasonable assurance on the management of such risks using the Pareto principle and the rule of 80/20.

Considerations for implementation require:

- Controls are designed to mitigate risks at three levels of an organization: at the entity level (e.g., a retail company level), at an activity level (e.g., customer order processing at the retailer), and at the transaction level (e.g., a customer buying and paying for goods and services from a retailer).

- Internal auditors must assess the effectiveness of controls by using a **risk and control matrix**, which shows how controls are used to manage risks and whether controls are effective or ineffective. Prior to developing this matrix, auditors gather information through interviews of management; review of organizational plans, policies, and processes; and use of walk-throughs, surveys, internal control questionnaires, checklists, narratives, and flowcharts. After gathering such information, auditors evaluate the adequacy of control design and test the effectiveness of controls using inspections, confirmations, continuous auditing, data analytics (e.g., ratio analysis and trend analysis), and audit metrics.

- Internal auditors must evaluate the efficiency of controls through a **cost-benefit analysis**, meaning costs should not exceed benefits.

- Internal auditors must assess whether the level of a control is appropriate for the risk it mitigates. A **risk and control map** can help auditors to document the relationship between risks and controls. Possible outcomes from the risk and control mapping follow:

Some high risks are undercontrolled (open to fraud, threats, and vulnerabilities).

Some low risks are overcontrolled (waste of resources, delays in operations).

Some risks are not controlled at all (open to fraud, threats, and exposures).

Some controls are not needed (waste of resources, delays in operations).

Some controls do not address any risks (waste of resources, open to threats).

Some weak controls are overdesigned (waste of resources, delays in operations).

Some strong controls are underdesigned (open to fraud, threats, and vulnerabilities).

Some simple controls are overcomplicated (waste of resources, delays in operations).

Some complex controls are oversimplified (open to fraud, threats, and vulnerabilities).

Some controls and risks have no relationship (mismatch of design and function).

- The CAE promotes a **continuous improvement program** in maintaining effective controls with control evaluations using a control framework for uniformity and consistency. He may recommend the implementation of a control framework if one is not already in place. Specific actions include (1) training nonauditors in controls, control concepts, control processes, and a positive control environment; (2) encouraging nonauditors to self-monitor controls; (3) facilitating control and risk assessment sessions; and (4) educating management and nonauditors in the purposes and consequences of control efficiency, control effectiveness, control deficiencies, control breakdowns, control overrides, and control requirements.

Considerations for demonstrating conformance require the following output documents:

- Risk and control matrices
- Risk and control maps
- Narrative descriptions of walk-throughs
- Results of surveys, interviews, and meetings with management and nonmanagement
- Standard operating manual showing continuous improvements of controls
- Internal audit plans, work programs, workpapers, reports showing control evaluations, control testing, and control assessment exercises

Requiring a familiarity with the related Standards includes:

- Nature of work (*Standard* 2100)
- Governance (*Standard* 2110)
- Risk management (*Standard* 2120)
- Control framework
- COSO—Internal Control
- SOX 2002
- Cadbury Report

Foundations of Internal Auditing

This domain contains several major theoretical topics in internal auditing, such as mission, definition of internal auditing, core principles, internal audit charter, types of audit services, and Code of Ethics. It also presents the roles and responsibilities of management.

All these topics are tested at a combination of basic and proficient cognitive levels in Part 1 of the CIA Exam with a 15% weight given. Relevant International Professional Practices Framework (IPPF) *Standards* presented in the first section of this book (Professional *Standards*) include 1000 and 1010, and they should be studied together with this domain to answer the CIA Exam questions and Wiley's online test bank practice questions.

With respect to the CIA Exam, cognitive levels are labeled as proficient level and basic level. These cognitive levels suggest that more time and effort should be spent in studying and mastering the subject matter covered in the topics labeled as the proficient level. Comparatively less time and effort should be spent on the topics labeled as the basic level.

1.1 Mission of Internal Audit

The Mission of Internal Audit articulates what internal audit aspires to accomplish within an organization. Its place in the new International Professional Practices Framework-2017 (new IPPF of 2017) is deliberate, demonstrating how practitioners should leverage the entire framework to facilitate their ability to achieve the mission.

> The mission of internal audit is to enhance and protect organizational value by providing risk-based and objective assurance, advice, and insight.

1.2 Definition of Internal Auditing

The Definition of Internal Auditing states the fundamental purpose, nature, and scope of internal auditing:

> Internal auditing is an independent, objective assurance and consulting activity designed to add value and improve an organization's operations. It helps an organization accomplish its objectives by bringing a systematic, disciplined approach to evaluate and improve the effectiveness of risk management, control, and governance processes.

Internal audit activity is defined as a department, division, function, team of auditors, team of consultants, or other practitioner(s) that provides independent, objective assurance and consulting services designed to add value and improve an organization's operations. The internal audit activity helps an organization accomplish its objectives by bringing a systematic, disciplined approach to evaluate and improve the effectiveness of governance, risk management, and control (GRC) processes.

Internal audit function is a separate function in an organization similar to other functions, such as manufacturing, marketing, service, procurement, accounting, human resources, information technology (IT), and finance. The internal audit department employs several individuals with different job titles to conduct audits, including staff auditor, engagement auditor, in-charge auditor, lead auditor, senior auditor, supervisor, audit manager, and audit director.

Add value refers to asking what type of value and how much value an internal audit activity is adding to an organization. The internal audit activity adds value when:

- Its charter aligns with the audit committee's charter.

- Its charter is built around and derived from the audit committee's charter.

- Its charter's alignment with the audit committee's charter demonstrates integrity, objectivity, and independence of the internal audit activity.

- Its internal quality assurance assessments are combined with external quality assurance assessments.

- Its yearly, short-term audit plan (current and future) aligns with its long-term strategic plan for the internal audit activity.

- Its long-term strategic plan aligns and integrates with the organization's long-term strategic plan.

- It provides objective and relevant assurance services and consulting services to all of its stakeholders.

- It contributes to the effectiveness and efficiency of GRC processes.

- It hires, promotes, and retains highly skilled and competent auditors with continuing professional development.

Simply stated, internal audit adds value to the organization when it makes highly significant, high-impact, and high-quality audit recommendations to audit clients through audit work.

Significant recommendations are big in scope (nature and extent), size (magnitude), and strength (impact), which is in line with the Pareto principle of the vital few (20%) and the trivial many (80%), representing Pareto's rule of 20/80 or 80/20.

Moreover, value is added when audit-client's business operations are improved, policies are strengthened, procedures are simplified, processes are streamlined, practices match best practices, costs are decreased, revenues are increased, profits are increased, earnings per share are increased, market price per share is increased, employee morale is increased, customers are satisfied, actual risks are controlled, potential risks are avoided or minimized, supply-chains are strengthened, regulations are complied with, and competitors are made jealous. This value is seen either directly or indirectly from internal audits.

Value is not added or enhanced until the audit-client's management fully accepts and implements the internal auditors' recommendations. The audit-client's acceptance is not guaranteed because it depends on whether the auditors' recommendations will help or hurt the audit-client's business function. Value is not added when auditors make nitpicking findings and give token recommendations that waste resources, resulting from surface audits (superficial audits) using a checklist approach.

(a) Rules of Value and Return on Value

Value is defined and recognized when benefits exceed costs. Here, internal auditors are giving value and audit clients are receiving value through audits. Internal auditors are in a unique position to add and enhance value to audit clients because they can bring outside-in (new) perspectives and clear (fresh) insights to a business function, system, or operation.

As outsiders to an auditable area, internal auditors can visualize business areas needing improvement during their audit work, and internal auditors should take advantage of their unique position. Value is added to audit clients through audit recommendations. Value is enhanced and protected after it is added continuously.

Examples of **rules of value** are listed next.

- Value is added when internal auditors make recommendations to audit clients that reduce errors and delays and improve quality of daily operations.

- Value is enhanced when internal auditors make recommendations to audit clients that decrease operating costs and increase operating profits.

- Value is diminished or reduced when internal auditors make recommendations to audit clients that increase operating costs and decrease operating profits.

- When internal auditors make highly significant recommendations to audit clients with high-impact, high-quality, and positive outcomes, value is enhanced and auditors' reputation and respect is increased (i.e., audit's reputation risk is decreased). Significant recommendations are those that are big in scope (nature and extent), size (magnitude), and strength (impact) that can lead to positive outcomes.

- When internal auditors make highly insignificant (trivial and nitpicking) recommendations to audit clients with low-impact, low-quality, and negative outcomes, value is diminished and auditors' reputation and respect is decreased or damaged (i.e., audit's reputation risk is increased).

- When internal auditors make recommendations to audit clients, they should remember the **Pareto principle or 20/80 rule.** This means that auditors should recommend only the "vital few" recommendations that add real value (20%), not the "trivial many" that add no real value (80%). The "trivial many" implies making recommendations just for the sake of recommendations to increase the number of recommendations on record. Also, the "vital few" recommendations increase audit's reputation while the "trivial many" recommendations decrease audit's reputation.

Based on the rules of value, audit clients should attempt to compute a **return on value** (ROV) metric using the costs and investments required to implement internal auditors' recommendations and the associated and quantified benefits resulting from implementing such recommendations. Quantified benefits can be based on actual data, projected data, or estimated data. Note that, in order to keep their independence and objectivity goals in mind, internal auditors should not and must not be involved in computing, assisting, or reviewing the ROV metric.

ROV should be based on the Pareto principle of the "vital few" and the "trivial many."

ROV is increased when auditors' recommendations are based on the Pareto principle of the "vital few."

ROV is decreased when auditors' recommendations are based on the Pareto principle of the "trivial many."

Some auditors' recommendations can be significant in importance, requiring large amounts of investment (e.g., developing a new computer system). In such cases, senior management and the board may require investment justification from audit clients through a cost-benefit analysis before committing to the investment project. **Costs** include initial investment in equipment, computer systems, and employees and ongoing operating expenses. **Benefits** include operating cost reductions; productivity (efficiency) increases; product and service quality increases; employees' performance improvements; profit increases; and employee morale improvements.

Value in amount, ratio, or percentage can be computed as follows.

$$\text{Value in Amount} = \text{Benefits Amount} - \text{Costs Amount}$$
$$\text{Value Ratio} = \text{Benefits/Costs}$$
$$\text{Value Percentage} = (\text{Benefits/Costs}) \times 100$$

If the computed value ratio is equal to or greater than 1, the value is positive, accept the investment project; otherwise, reject the investment project.

If the computed value (ROV) percentage is equal to or greater than the expected or targeted ROV percentage, accept the investment project; otherwise, reject the investment project.

1.3 Core Principles

The **Core Principles** (CPs) of internal auditing, taken as a whole, articulate internal audit effectiveness. For an internal audit function to be considered effective, all Principles should be present and operating effectively. How an internal auditor, as well as an internal audit activity, demonstrates achievement of the Core Principles may be quite different from organization to organization, but failure to achieve any of the Principles would imply that an internal audit activity was not as effective as it could be in achieving internal audit's mission. The Core Principles are the foundation for internal audit's framework and support the internal audit's effectiveness.

A set of 10 Core Principles comprise the fundamentals essential to the effective practice of internal auditing. They are the foundational underpinnings of the Code of Ethics and the *Standards*, reflecting the primary requirements for the professional practice of internal auditing now and in the future. The Core Principles can be used as a benchmark against which to gauge the effectiveness of an internal audit activity. Thus, the Core Principles should be well expressed throughout the Code of Ethics and the *Standards*.

> CP1: Demonstrates integrity
>
> CP2: Demonstrates competence and due professional care
>
> CP3: Is objective and free from undue influence (independent)
>
> CP4: Aligns with the strategies, objectives, and risks of the organization
>
> CP5: Is appropriately positioned and adequately resourced
>
> CP6: Demonstrates quality and continuous improvement
>
> CP7: Communicates effectively
>
> CP8: Provides risk-based assurance
>
> CP9: Is insightful, proactive, and future-focused
>
> CP10: Promotes organizational improvement

The IIA's International Internal Audit Standards Board (IIASB) has conducted an assessment of how well the Core Principles are related to and evidenced in the Code of Ethics and the *Standards*. The following is the result of such assessment.

CP1: Demonstrates Integrity

Core principle 1 is embodied in Code of Ethics Principle and Rules of Conduct: Integrity as the common item. Several *Standards* reinforce the expectation of integrity. For example, integrity is required in maintaining objectivity (*Standard* 1120—Individual Objectivity) and in Communicating Errors or Omissions (*Standard* 2421—Errors and Omissions).

CP2: Demonstrates Competence and Due Professional Care

Core principle 2 is embodied in Code of Ethics Principle and Rules of Conduct: Competency as the common item. Competence and due care are required by several *Standards*: for example, 1200—Proficiency and Due Care, 1210—Proficiency, 1220—Due Professional Care, and 1300—Quality Assurance and Improvement Program.

CP3: Is Objective and Free from Undue Influence (Independent)

Core principle 3 is embodied in Code of Ethics Principle and Rules of Conduct: Objectivity as the common item. Several *Standards* require objectivity and independence. These include 1100—Independence and Objectivity, 1110—Organizational Independence, 1120—Individual

Objectivity, and 1130—Impairment to Independence or Objectivity. Furthermore, an internal audit charter codifies reporting relationships, organizational independence, authority, and access to information, as described in *Standard* 1000—Purpose, Authority, and Responsibility.

CP4: Aligns with the Strategies, Objectives, and Risks of the Organization

The consideration of organizational strategies, objectives, and risks when planning, executing, and reporting on engagements is evident in many current *Standards*. Examples include 2010— Planning, 2100—Nature of Work, 2110—Governance, 2120—Risk Management, 2130—Control, 2201—Planning Considerations, and 2000—Managing the Internal Audit Activity.

CP5: Is Appropriately Positioned and Adequately Resourced

The importance of internal audit's organizational placement and sufficient and appropriate resources is addressed in several *Standards*. Examples include 1000—Purpose, Authority, and Responsibility, 1110—Organizational Independence, 1111—Direct Interaction with the Board, and 2030—Resource Management.

CP6: Demonstrates Quality and Continuous Improvement

Core principle 6 is embodied in Code of Ethics Principle and Rules of Conduct: Competency as the common item. In addition, several *Standards* specify requirements associated with demonstrating quality and continuous improvement, including the 1330 series of *Standards* related to quality assurance and improvement programs and 1230—Continuing Professional Development. Other *Standards*, such as 2040—Policies and Procedures and 2340—Engagement Supervision, help create an internal audit environment to deliver quality services.

CP7: Communicates Effectively

Core principle 7 is evident in several *Standards* addressing chief audit executive communications with the board and management as well as communications from the internal audit activity. Examples include *Standards* 2020—Communication and Approval, 2060—Reporting to Senior Management and the Board, and the 2400 series related to communicating results of engagements.

CP8: Provides Risk-Based Assurance

Several existing *Standards* require internal audit work to be based on an assessment of risk, at both the overall program level and the individual engagement level. Also, the importance of this core principle, providing risk-based assurance to management and the board, is highlighted in several *Standards*, including 2010—Planning, 2201—Planning Considerations, 2060—Reporting to Senior Management and the Board, and 2600—Communicating the Acceptance of Risks.

CP9: Is Insightful, Proactive, and Future-Focused

Although this core principle is implied by several *Standards*, the existing Code of Ethics and *Standards* do not completely address it. Several Performance *Standards* reflect the result of insightful, proactive, and future-focused activities. Examples include *Standards* 2010—Planning, 2120—Risk Management, and 2060—Reporting to Senior Management and the Board. However, this core principle is not fully recognized in the Attribute *Standards*.

CP10: Promotes Organizational Improvement

The responsibility for internal audit to contribute to and promote organizational improvement is embedded in several *Standards*, including 2000—Managing the Internal Audit Activity, 2050—Coordination, 2100—Nature of Work, and 2500—Monitoring Progress. The 1300 series of *Standards* related to quality assurance and improvement programs also promotes organizational improvement within the internal audit activity.

1.4 Internal Audit Charter

Each internal audit function should have an internal audit charter (the charter) that describes the purpose, authority, and responsibility of the internal audit function. An audit charter should include the following critical components:

- The objectives and scope of the internal audit function

- The internal audit function's management reporting (i.e., functional and administrative reporting) position within the organization as well as its authority and responsibilities

- The responsibility and accountability of the chief audit executive (CAE)

- The internal audit function's responsibility to evaluate the effectiveness of the organization's GRC processes

The charter should be approved by the audit committee of the organization's board of directors. The charter should provide the internal audit function with the authorization to access the organization's records, personnel, and physical properties relevant to the performance of internal audit procedures, including the authority to examine any activities or entities. Periodically, the CAE should evaluate whether the charter continues to be adequate, requesting the approval of the audit committee for any revisions. The charter should define the criteria for when and how the internal audit function may outsource its work to external experts.

The charter is an internal company document and is not an external legal document. It is a formal and critical document, and it is a blueprint or roadmap for the internal audit activity because it contains the agreed-upon purpose, authority, and responsibility of an internal audit activity. In essence, the charter describes how the internal audit department performs and manages its work activities and how it operates in the short term and the long term. As such, the audit charter must be created with a clear understanding of the internal audit function.

Specifically, the charter document should define these elements:

- Objectives, purpose, scope, position (status), roles, and responsibilities of the internal audit activity, including its expectations by the board and senior management.

- Functional and administrative reporting lines within the management's hierarchy, including the level of authority and organizational placement. (See Exhibit 1.1.)

- Authority and budget are given to access records (physical and electronic), property (tangible and intangible), and personnel (internal and external) in order to perform audit engagements.

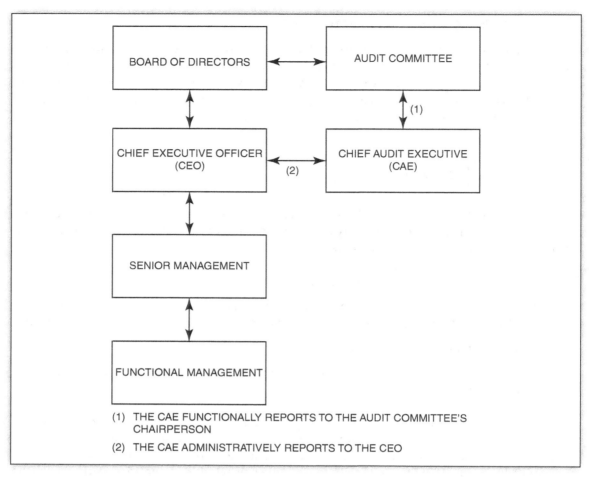

EXHIBIT 1.1 Chief Audit Executive Reporting Lines

Specifically, the charter document should require or describe these elements:

- The scope and nature of the CAE's nonaudit responsibilities, which can be either short term or long term (i.e., ongoing). Short-term nonaudit responsibilities require transition plans and require no changes to the charter. Long-term nonaudit responsibilities require no transition plans and require changes to the charter. In a way, all long-term changes to the CAE's roles and responsibilities are required to be documented in the charter (e.g., from audit work to nonaudit work and vice versa) with safeguards established to protect auditors' independence and objectivity. A **transition plan** states how an internal audit department moves its nonaudit responsibilities back to an organization's functional management.

  Short Term ⟶ Transition Plan Required ⟶ No Change to Audit Charter Required

  Long Term ⟶ No Transition Plan Required ⟶ Change to Audit Charter Required with Safeguards Established to Protect Independence and Objectivity

- The charter requires an internal audit plan that includes known audits (based on previous years) as well as unknown audits (unanticipated audits or special request projects), requiring contingency plans, such as enforce Plan B if Plan A does not work.

- The charter requires a financial budget that includes known costs and expenditures as well as unknown costs and expenditures, requiring contingency costs and expenditures.

- The charter requires a staff budget that includes internal staff (in-source) as well as external staff (co-source or outsource), requiring contingency staffing plans for handling emergencies and unexpected events.

- The charter requires a talent budget that includes the requirement and availability of internal staff's skill sets (e.g., education, knowledge, experience, and hard/soft skills) and external staff's skill sets (e.g., costs, risks, deliverables, expectations, education, knowledge, experience, and hard/soft skills). **Internal staff** includes internal auditors and noninternal auditors working within a company. **External staff** includes audit consultants, audit contractors, and external auditors.

- **Hard skills** are mostly quantitative in nature and include these:

  □ Analytical skills

  □ Technical skills

  □ Functional skills

  □ Problem identification and solving skills

  □ Decision-making skills

  □ Managing skills

  □ Application skills

  □ Integration skills

  Higher-level managers and executives need more depth in soft skills and soft controls and less depth in hard skills and hard controls. Lower-level managers and executives need more depth in hard skills and hard controls and less depth in soft skills and soft controls.

- **Soft skills** are mostly qualitative in nature and include these:

  □ People skills (interpersonal skills)

  □ Motivation skills

  □ Leadership skills

  □ Communications skills

  □ Presentation skills

  □ Coordination skills

  □ Project management skills

  □ Implementation skills

  □ Time-management skills

  □ Creative skills

  □ Critical-thinking skills

  Higher-level managers and executives need more depth in soft skills and soft controls and less depth in hard skills and hard controls. Lower-level managers and executives need more depth in hard skills and hard controls and less depth in soft skills and soft controls.

- The charter describes communication plans and protocols to be used when communicating audit work results (e.g., audit memos, letters, and reports) to the appropriate internal and external parties. These communication plans indicate the media, format, frequency, and recipients of various communications (e.g., what, how, when, and to whom to communicate).

■ The charter requires that the CAE discuss the IIA's Mission and adherence to Mandatory Guidance with the board and senior management.

1.5 Types of Audit Services

The IIA's Implementation *Standards* define two types of audit services: assurance services and consulting services. Each type of service is described next.

(a) Assurance Services

Assurance services involve the internal auditor's objective assessment of evidence to provide opinions or conclusions regarding an entity, operation, function, process, system, or other subject matters. The nature and scope of an assurance engagement are determined by the internal auditor. Generally, three parties are participants in assurance services:

1. The person or group directly involved with the entity, operation, function, process, system, or other subject matter—the process owner and/or the audit client

2. The person or group making the assessment—the internal auditor

3. The person or group using the assessment—the user (e.g., audit client, management, and outside parties)

In summary, assurance services are an objective examination of evidence for the purpose of providing an independent assessment on governance, risk management, and control processes for the organization. Examples of assurance services may include operational audits, financial audits, performance audits, compliance audits, and system security and privacy audits.

Examples of Assurance Services

Operational audits include a review of revenue, expenditure, production, treasury, and financial reporting cycles; and IT operational audits.

Financial audits include financial statement audits and financial statement analysis for identifying trends and patterns.

Performance audits include review of organization-wide performance measurement systems (e.g., productivity increase and cost reduction), employee incentive programs, and employee suggestion system. Performance audits also include a review of metrics and key performance indicators. Value-for-money audits are a part of performance audits in public sector and private sector organizations.

Compliance audits focus on adherence to plans, policies, procedures, laws, rules, regulations, and contracts, including risk and control assessment. The scope can also include lawsuits arising from contractual violations, employee discrimination, and product liabilities, hazards, and recalls. Examples include environmental audit; human resource policy audit; quality audit; third-party audit; review of related-party transactions; and contract compliance audits.

System security and privacy audits focus on reviewing security controls over computer systems, networks, mobile devices, data at the source, data in transit, and data in storage. The scope also covers privacy audits.

(b) Consulting Services

Consulting services are advisory in nature and are generally performed at the specific request of an engagement client. The nature and scope of the consulting engagement are subject to agreement with the engagement client. Consulting services generally involve two parties: the person or group offering the advice—the internal auditor, and the person or group seeking and receiving the advice—the engagement client. When performing consulting services, the internal auditor should maintain objectivity and not assume management responsibility.

In summary, consulting services are advisory in nature and provide great insights to clients. The nature and scope of these services are agreed with the client in advance and are intended to add value and improve an organization's governance, risk management, and control processes without the internal auditor assuming management responsibility. Examples of consulting services may include counsel, advice, facilitation, and training.

Examples of Consulting Services

Counsel may include data breaches and privacy breaches; cybersecurity issues such as ransomware and bitcoin fraud; and risks in cloud networks, social media platforms, and mobile technologies, including mobile apps.

Advice may include strategic planning; risk assessments; governance framework; control breakdowns; business process reviews, including process mapping; benchmarking studies; IT consulting in system design and development; design of performance measurement systems, big-data analytics, agile audits (targeted audits); and due diligence reviews.

Facilitation may include control self-assessments and internal control reviews.

Training may include internal control; audit-related quality assurance; regulatory compliance; big-data modeling; and data-mining applications.

1.6 IIA's Code of Ethics

The IIA's Code of Ethics comprises broad principles relevant to the profession and practice of internal auditing and more specific rules of conduct, which describe the behavior expected of both entities and individuals who perform internal audit services in accordance with the Definition of Internal Auditing (including IIA members, recipients of IIA certifications, and certification candidates). The purpose of the Code of Ethics is to promote an ethical culture in the global profession of internal auditing.

Code of Ethics is a statement of the principles and expectations governing the behavior of individuals and organizations in the conduct of internal auditing. It is a description of the minimum requirements for conduct. The Code describes behavioral expectations rather than specific activities.

(a) Introduction to the Code of Ethics

The purpose of the IIA's Code of Ethics is to promote an ethical culture in the profession of internal auditing. A code of ethics is necessary and appropriate for the profession of internal auditing, founded as it is on the trust placed in its objective assurance about governance, risk management, and control.

The Code of Ethics extends beyond the Definition of Internal Auditing to include two essential components:

1. Principles that are relevant to the profession and practice of internal auditing.

2. Rules of Conduct that describe behavior norms expected of internal auditors. These rules are an aid to interpreting the Principles into practical applications and are intended to guide the ethical conduct of internal auditors.

"Internal auditors" refers to IIA members, recipients of or candidates for IIA professional certifications, and those who perform internal audit services within the Definition of Internal Auditing.

(i) Applicability and Enforcement of the Code of Ethics

This Code of Ethics applies to both entities and individuals who perform internal audit services. For IIA members and recipients of or candidates for IIA professional certifications, breaches of the Code of Ethics will be evaluated and administered according to the IIA's Bylaws and Administrative Directives. The fact that a particular conduct is not mentioned in the Rules of Conduct does not prevent it from being unacceptable or discreditable, and therefore, the member, certification holder, or candidate can be liable for disciplinary action.

(b) Code of Ethics—Principles

The Code of Ethics—Principles discusses integrity, objectivity, confidentiality, and competency elements.

Internal auditors are expected to apply and uphold the following principles:

1. **Integrity**

   The integrity of internal auditors establishes trust and thus provides the basis for reliance on their judgment.

2. **Objectivity**

   Internal auditors exhibit the highest level of professional objectivity in gathering, evaluating, and communicating information about the activity or process being examined. Internal auditors make a balanced assessment of all the relevant circumstances and are not unduly influenced by their own interests or by others in forming judgments.

3. **Confidentiality**

   Internal auditors respect the value and ownership of information they receive and do not disclose information without appropriate authority unless there is a legal or professional obligation to do so.

4. **Competency**

   Internal auditors apply the knowledge, skills, and experience needed in the performance of internal audit services.

(c) Code of Ethics—Rules of Conduct

The Rules of Conduct also discuss integrity, objectivity, confidentiality, and competency elements, which are the same elements found in the Code of Ethics—Principles.

1. **Integrity**

   Internal auditors:

   1.1. Shall perform their work with honesty, diligence, and responsibility.

   1.2. Shall observe the law and make disclosures expected by the law and the profession.

   1.3. Shall not knowingly be a party to any illegal activity, or engage in acts that are discreditable to the profession of internal auditing or to the organization.

   1.4. Shall respect and contribute to the legitimate and ethical objectives of the organization.

2. **Objectivity**

   Internal auditors:

   2.1 Shall not participate in any activity or relationship that may impair or be presumed to impair their unbiased assessment. This participation includes those activities or relationships that may be in conflict with the interests of the organization.

   2.2 Shall not accept anything that may impair or be presumed to impair their professional judgment.

   2.3 Shall disclose all material facts known to them that, if not disclosed, may distort the reporting of activities under review.

3. **Confidentiality**

   Internal auditors:

   3.1 Shall be prudent in the use and protection of information acquired in the course of their duties.

   3.2 Shall not use information for any personal gain or in any manner that would be contrary to the law or detrimental to the legitimate and ethical objectives of the organization.

4. **Competency**

   Internal auditors:

   4.1 Shall engage only in those services for which they have the necessary knowledge, skills, and experience.

   4.2 Shall perform internal audit services in accordance with the *International Standards for the Professional Practice of Internal Auditing*.

   4.3 Shall continually improve their proficiency and the effectiveness and quality of their services.

1.7 Roles and Responsibilities of Management

Internal auditors, whether they are staff auditors, senior auditors, audit supervisors, audit managers, or audit directors, need to know the roles and responsibilities of their organization's management hierarchy in order to do their work properly during audit engagements, from audit planning to audit reporting.

When internal auditors conduct their audit work, they (1) deal directly with the functional managers as they are the primary, day-to-day, audit clients (audit customers) and (2) deal indirectly with the senior managers as they are the secondary audit clients. The board can be thought of as the final audit client. Here, management hierarchy is that functional managers report to senior managers (e.g., chief executive officer [CEO]) who in turn report to the board. The level of audit contact is shown next:

Functional managers = First level of audit contact

Senior managers = Second level of audit contact

Board members = Last level of audit contact

Next, we briefly describe the roles and responsibilities of the chief audit executive (CAE), the board of directors (board), the audit committee, senior management (senior managers), and functional management (functional managers) and the meaning of an organization's management.

The **chief audit executive** (e.g., director of internal audit or internal audit director) is a person in a senior position responsible for effectively managing the internal audit activity in accordance with the internal audit charter and the mandatory elements of the IPPF. In addition to communicating and reporting to the audit committee on audit-related matters, the CAE is responsible for developing and maintaining a quality assurance and improvement program (QAIP) that covers all aspects of internal audit activity and for continuously monitoring the effectiveness of the audit function. The CAE and/or senior audit staff should effectively manage and monitor all aspects of audit work on an ongoing basis, including any audit work that is outsourced. The CAE or others reporting to the CAE will have appropriate professional certifications and qualifications. The specific job title and/or responsibilities of the CAE may vary across organizations.

The **board** (e.g., a board of governors, a board of trustees, or a supervisory board) is the highest level of governing body in an organization charged with the responsibility to direct and/or oversee the organization's activities and hold senior management accountable. The board's responsibility of designing, maintaining, and operating an effective system of internal controls cannot be delegated to others within the organization or outside the organization (i.e., external parties).

The board is the top level (first layer) of the management hierarchy that governs and controls the entire organization. Although governance arrangements vary among legal jurisdictions and business sectors, typically the board includes senior management. If a board does not exist, the word "board" in the *Standards* may refer to a committee or another body to which the governing body has delegated certain functions (e.g., an audit committee). Individual members of the board join various board-level committees to address specific issues, problems, and concerns facing an organization. Examples of these committees include finance, governance, risk, ethics, nominating, audit, social responsibility, labor relations, wage and benefits, compensation, investigative, standing, grievance, human resources, and technology committee.

Audit committee members are board members who are responsible for establishing an appropriate internal audit function and ensuring that it operates adequately and effectively. The audit committee should be confident that the internal audit function addresses the risks and meets the demands posed by the organization's current and planned audit activities. Moreover, the audit committee is expected to retain oversight responsibility for any aspects of the internal audit function that are outsourced to a third party.

The audit committee should provide oversight to the internal audit function. Audit committee meetings should be on a frequency that facilitates this oversight and generally should be held four times a year at a minimum. Annually, the audit committee should review and approve internal audit's charter, budget and staffing levels, the audit plan, and overall risk assessment methodology. The committee approves the CAE's hiring, annual performance evaluations, and compensation.

The audit committee and its chair should have ongoing interaction with the CAE separate from formally scheduled annual meetings to remain current on any internal audit department, organizational, or industry concerns. In addition, the audit committee should have executive sessions with the CAE without members of senior management present as needed. The audit committee should receive appropriate levels of management information (e.g., audit plan, audit results, audit issues, audit staff changes and issues, high-risk audit areas, budgeted audit hours versus actual audit hours, and audit opinions) to fulfill its oversight responsibilities.

Senior management (e.g., C-level executives) represents the second layer of management hierarchy from the top down and often becomes members of the board. Senior management consists of C-level executives such as chief executive officer (CEO or the president), chief financial officer (CFO), chief information officer (CIO), chief people officer (human resources), chief governance officer, chief ethics officer, chief operating officer (COO), chief marketing officer, chief manufacturing officer, chief service officer, chief compliance officer, chief risk officer, chief legal counsel, and chief audit executive (CAE). The CEO reports to the board where the latter can hire and fire the former. The senior management group reports to the CEO, who in turn can hire and fire the senior managers except the CAE. The CAE has a dual reporting relationship to the board and the CEO. The senior management's responsibility of designing, maintaining, and operating an effective system of internal controls cannot be delegated to others within the organization or outside the organization (i.e., external parties).

Functional management (e.g., department managers, operations managers, regional managers, area managers, unit managers, branch managers, group managers, general managers, or divisional managers) is in charge of a single business function, department, operation, region, area, unit, branch, group, or division, such as marketing, manufacturing, service, operations, procurement, accounting, finance, treasury, human resources, and IT. Functional managers report to senior managers where the latter hire and fire the former. Functional managers are responsible for day-to-day operations of their departments and functions and implement the system of internal controls.

An **organization's management** refers to the board, audit committee, senior management, and functional management, not the internal audit management. This is because internal audit management is independent of other types of management due to the audit work performed on other departments or functions.

1.8 Sample Practice Questions

In the actual CIA Exam for Part 1, 125 multiple-choice (M/C) test questions appear. This book contains 125 M/C sample practice questions divided into syllabus-based domains using the approximate domain weight given in the exam. These questions are added at the end of each applicable domain of this book with the sole purpose of showing the flavor and structure of the exam questions and of creating a self-quiz experience. The answers and explanations for these questions are shown in a separate section at the end of this book. This separate section is titled "Sample Practice Questions, Answers, and Explanations." If CIA Exam candidates need to practice more sample questions to obtain a higher level of confidence, Wiley offers a separate online test bank software product with hundreds of similar sample practice questions.

1. What is the key word in the Institute of Internal Auditors (IIA) mission Statement of internal audit?

   a. Assurance

   b. Advice

   c. Value

   d. Insight

2. The new International Professional Practices Framework (IPPF) effective from 2017 contains which of the following that was **not** a part of the previous IPPF?

   a. Mission and Core Principles

   b. Definition of Internal Auditing and Practice Guides

   c. Code of Ethics and Glossary

   d. International Standards and local standards for internal auditing

3. Which of the following adds value to the others?

   a. Governance processes

   b. Risk management processes

   c. Internal audit activities

   d. Control processes

4. The IIA's definition of internal auditing emphasizes the effectiveness of which of the following?

   a. Value, cost, and benefit propositions

   b. Inherent risk, residual risk, and total risk

   c. Risk management, control, and governance processes

   d. Purpose, nature, and scope of work

5. The internal audit activity's Core Principles can be used as which of the following?

   a. Metrics

   b. Benchmarks

   c. Key performance indicators

   d. Dashboards

6. The internal audit activity's Core Principles describe which of the following?

   a. Efficiency

   b. Resources

   c. Plans

   d. Effectiveness

7. The internal audit activity's Core Principles underpin which of the following?

   a. Code of Ethics and Standards

   b. Efficiency and effectiveness

   c. Metrics and key performance indicators

   d. Resources and skills

8. The audit committee of an organization has charged the chief audit executive (CAE) with bringing the department into full compliance with the IIA *Standards*. The CAE's first task is to develop a charter. Identify the item that should be included in the statement of objectives.

   a. Report all audit findings to the audit committee every quarter.

   b. Notify governmental regulatory agencies of unethical business practices by organization management.

   c. Determine the adequacy and effectiveness of the organization's systems of internal controls.

   d. Submit departmental budget variance reports to management every month.

9. The internal audit charter normally requires the internal audit activity to focus on areas consisting of which of the following?

   a. High inherent risk and high residual risk

   b. High audit risk and high current risk

   c. Low inherent risk and low audit risk

   d. Low inherent risk and high outstanding risk

10. Consulting engagement objectives must be consistent with all of the following **except**:

   a. Organization's goals.

   b. Organization's values.

   c. Organization's strategies.

   d. Organization's objectives.

11. All of the following are examples of assurance services **except**:

   a. Financial engagement.

   b. Compliance engagement.

   c. Due diligence engagement.

   d. Training engagement.

12. All of the following are examples of consulting services **except**:

   a. Legal counsel engagement.

   b. System security engagement.

   c. Advice engagement.

   d. Facilitation engagement.

13. The IIA's Code of Ethics includes which of the following two essential components?

   a. Definition of internal auditing and administrative directives

   b. Principles and Rules of Conduct

   c. Integrity and objectivity

   d. Confidentiality and competency

14. A certified internal auditor (CIA) is working in a non–internal audit position as the director of purchasing. The CIA signs a contract to procure a large order from the supplier with the best price, quality, and performance. Shortly after signing the contract, the supplier presents the CIA with a gift of significant monetary value. Which of the following statements regarding the acceptance of the gift is correct?

   a. Acceptance of the gift would be prohibited only if it were noncustomary.

   b. Acceptance of the gift would violate the IIA Code of Ethics and would be prohibited for a CIA.

   c. Since the CIA is no longer acting as an internal auditor, acceptance of the gift would be governed only by the organization's code of conduct.

   d. Since the contract was signed before the gift was offered, acceptance of the gift would not violate either the IIA Code of Ethics or the organization's code of conduct.

15. An auditor, nearly finished with an audit, discovers that the director of marketing has a gambling habit. The gambling issue is not directly related to the existing audit, and there is pressure to complete the current audit. The auditor notes the problem and passes the information on to the chief audit executive (CAE) but does no further follow-up. The auditor's actions would:

   a. Be in violation of the IIA Code of Ethics for withholding meaningful information.

   b. Be in violation of the Standards because the auditor did not properly follow-up on a red flag that might indicate the existence of fraud.

   c. Not be in violation of either the IIA Code of Ethics or the Standards.

   d. Both a and b.

16. As used by the internal auditing profession, the IIA Standards refer to all of the following **except**:

   a. Criteria by which the operations of an internal audit department are evaluated and measured.

   b. Criteria that dictate the minimum level of ethical actions to be taken by internal auditors.

   c. Statements intended to represent the practice of internal auditing as it should be.

   d. Criteria that are applicable to all types of internal audit departments.

17. Which of the following situations would be a violation of the IIA Code of Ethics?

a. An auditor was subpoenaed in a court case in which a merger partner claimed to have been defrauded by the auditor's company. The auditor divulged confidential audit information to the court.

b. An auditor for a manufacturer of office products recently completed an audit of the corporate marketing function. Based on this experience, the auditor spent several hours one Saturday working as a paid consultant to a hospital in the local area, which intended to conduct an audit of its marketing function.

c. An auditor gave a speech at a local IIA chapter meeting outlining the contents of a program the auditor had developed for auditing electronic data interchange connections. Several auditors from major competitors were in the audience.

d. During an audit, an auditor learned that the company was about to introduce a new product that would revolutionize the industry. Because of the probable success of the new product, the product manager suggested that the auditor buy additional stock in the company, which the auditor did.

18. In applying the standards of conduct set forth in the Code of Ethics, internal auditors are expected to:

a. Exercise their individual judgment.

b. Compare them to standards in other professions.

c. Be guided by the desires of the auditee.

d. Use discretion in deciding whether to use them or not.

19. Reinforcing the Code of Conduct and ethical behavior standards for all internal auditors can protect which of the following?

a. Business risk

b. Audit failures

c. Audit false assurance

d. Audit reputation risk

Independence and Objectivity

This domain defines several major theoretical topics, such as independence and objectivity, including their impairments and threats. It presents the required elements of independence and relationships between independence and objectivity and between independence and ethics. The domain also summarizes various threatening and supporting factors in independence and objectivity and lists policies to promote objectivity.

All these topics are tested at a combination of basic and proficient cognitive levels in Part 1 of the CIA Exam with a 15% weight given. Relevant International Professional Practices Framework (IPPF) *Standards* presented in first section of this book (Professional Standards) include 1100, 1110, 1111, 1112, 1120, and 1130. They should be studied together with this domain to answer the CIA Exam questions and Wiley's online test bank practice questions.

With respect to the CIA Exam, cognitive levels are labeled as proficient level and basic level. These cognitive levels suggest that more time and effort should be spent in studying and mastering the subject matter covered in the topics labeled as the proficient level. Comparatively less time and effort should be spent on the topics labeled as the basic level.

2.1 Independence Defined

Independence is defined as the freedom from conditions that threaten the ability of the internal audit activity to carry out internal audit responsibilities in an unbiased manner. Independence allows internal auditors to carry out their work freely and objectively. This concept requires that internal auditors be independent of the activities they audit. Independence is achieved through organizational status and objectivity. It is the freedom from conditions that threaten the ability of the internal audit activity to carry out internal audit responsibilities in an unbiased manner. Simply stated, independence can come across as appearance that can be real or imaginary in the eyes of others.

Two professional attributes of internal auditors and internal audit activity are independence and objectivity, where organizational independence deals with the internal audit activity and individual objectivity deals with the internal auditors.

Independence ⟶ Internal Audit Activity

Objectivity ⟶ Internal Auditors

Internal audit activity is an independent function supporting an organization's business strategies and objectives and evaluating the effectiveness of governance, risk management, and control processes. The structure of an internal audit activity should be organized so that its board of directors (directors) has confidence that the internal audit activity can be impartial and not unduly influenced by senior managers and functional managers in day-to-day operations.

In this regard, the chief audit executive (CAE), internal audit director, or internal audit manager should not have any responsibility for operating the system of internal control and should report functionally to the audit committee.

The CAE is functionally accountable and reports directly to the audit committee on internal audit matters, such as the audit plan, audit findings and recommendations, hiring of the CAE, and the CAE's job performance and compensation.

The CAE reports administratively to the chief executive officer (CEO) who is not responsible for the day-to-day operational activities reviewed by internal audit.

Functional Reporting ⟶ Audit Committee

Administrative Reporting ⟶ Chief Executive Officer

(a) Elements of Independence

Independence comprises two elements:

1. **Independence of mind**—It is the state of mind that permits the conduct of an audit engagement without being affected by influences that compromise professional judgment, thereby allowing an individual auditor to act with integrity and exercise objectivity and professional skepticism.

2. **Independence in appearance**—It is the absence of circumstances that would cause a reasonable and informed third party, having knowledge of the relevant information, including any safeguards applied, to reasonably conclude that the integrity, objectivity, or professional skepticism of an audit organization or member of an audit engagement team had been compromised.

Therefore, it is important for internal auditors and internal audit organizations to maintain their independence so that their opinions, findings, conclusions, judgments, and recommendations will be impartial and reasonable and so that informed third parties will view them as impartial.

(b) Independence and Ethics

Ethical principles provide the foundation, discipline, structure, and the environment necessary to conduct an audit engagement independently. **These ethical principles include integrity, objectivity, resource utilization, and professional behavior.**

Internal audit management sets the tone for ethical behavior by maintaining an ethical culture, clearly communicating acceptable behavior and expectations to each employee, and creating an environment that reinforces and encourages ethical behavior. The ethical tone maintained and demonstrated by audit management and audit staff is an essential element of a positive ethical environment for the audit organization.

Performing audit work in accordance with ethical principles is a matter of personal and organizational responsibility. Ethical principles apply in preserving auditor independence, taking on only that work that the audit organization is competent to perform, performing high-quality work, and following the applicable standards cited in the audit report.

Here, **integrity** refers to auditors performing their work with an attitude that is objective, fact-based, non-partisan, and non-ideological with regard to audit clients and users of the audit reports.

Here, **objectivity** refers to auditors' objectivity in discharging their professional responsibilities in performing a credible audit work. Both integrity and objectivity are maintained when auditors perform their work and make decisions that are consistent with the broader interest of those relying on the audit report, including a company's senior management and its board of directors.

Here, **resource utilization** means proper handling of sensitive and confidential information or resources of the audit client organization, not for auditor's personal gain.

Here, **professional behavior** includes auditors putting forth an honest effort in performing their duties in accordance with the relevant technical and professional standards. In this regard, auditors should avoid any personal and professional conduct that could bring discredit to their work. Otherwise, an objective third party with knowledge of the relevant information can conclude that the auditors' work was professionally deficient.

2.2 Factors Threatening and Supporting Independence

This section contains two parts: factors threatening independence and factors supporting independence. Each part is presented separately.

(a) Factors Threatening Independence

Threats or impairments to organizational independence and individual objectivity may include organizational politics (OP); organizational conflict of interest; personal conflict of interest; audit engagement scope limitations; restrictions on access to records, personnel, and properties; and resource limitations in funding and budgeting.

Impairments to independence are the introduction of threats that may result in a substantial limitation, or the appearance of a substantial limitation, to the internal auditor's ability to perform an engagement without bias or interference.

- The CAE could report administratively to someone other than the CEO, such as the chief financial officer, general counsel, senior vice president of finance, chief accounting officer, or accounting controller. Under these conditions, the audit committee should document its rationale for this reporting structure, including mitigating controls available for situations that could adversely impact the objective of the CAE. In such instances, the audit committee should periodically (at least annually) evaluate whether the CAE is impaired and not unduly influenced by the administrative reporting line arrangement. Further, conflicts of interest for the CAE and all other audit staff should be monitored at least annually with appropriate restrictions placed on auditing areas where conflicts may occur.

- If the internal audit activity is not organizationally independent, it could impact the objectivity of the CAE.

- Conflict-of-interest situations for the CAE and staff could arise when auditing areas with known conflicts.

- OP is a major challenge to independence.

(i) More on Threats to Independence

Threats to independence can be identified at three levels: the internal audit organization (level 1), an internal audit engagement (level 2), and an individual internal auditor (level 3). The purpose of these levels is to (1) identify threats to independence; (2) evaluate the significance of the threats identified, both individually and in the aggregate; and (3) apply safeguards as necessary to eliminate the threats or reduce them to an acceptable level.

Internal auditors should reevaluate threats to independence, including any safeguards applied, whenever the audit organization becomes aware of new information or changes in facts and circumstances that could affect whether a threat has been eliminated or reduced to an acceptable level. Note that if the audit engagement team intends to use the work of specialists, it should assess the independence of the specialists. Internal auditors should conclude that independence is impaired if no safeguards have been effectively applied to eliminate an unacceptable threat or reduce it to an acceptable level. Safeguards are actions, individually or in combination, that auditors and audit organizations take that effectively eliminate threats to independence or reduce them to an acceptable level.

Because independence is an aspect of ethics, a threat to the auditor's independence that cannot be addressed through the application of safeguards is considered a form of **ethical conflict**.

Threats to independence may be created by a wide range of relationships and circumstances. Those circumstances that result in a threat to independence in one or more of the next seven broad categories may result in other threats as well, because threats are interlinked and intertwined.

1. **Self-interest threat**—The threat that a financial or other interest will inappropriately influence an auditor's judgment or behavior.

2. **Bias threat**—The threat that an auditor will, as a result of political, ideological, social, or other convictions, take a position that is not objective.

3. **Familiarity threat**—The threat that aspects of the relationship with management or personnel of an audit client's department or office, such as a close or long relationship or that of an immediate or close family member or close friend, will lead an auditor to take a position that is not objective. This means the auditor can show favors to these people.

4. **Undue influence threat**—The threat that influences or pressures from sources external to the internal audit organization will affect an auditor's ability to make objective judgments. (OP can also play a key role here.)

5. **Management participation threat**—The threat that results from an auditor taking on the role of management or otherwise performing management functions on behalf of the audit client, which will lead an auditor to take a position that is not objective.

6. **Structural threat**—The threat that an internal audit organization's placement within a company, in combination with the structure of the company being audited, will affect the audit organization's ability to perform work and report results objectively. (This means that an employee of a company is auditing his/her own employer.)

7. **Previous employment threat**—The threat that a current internal auditor previously worked in a nonaudit department, office, or division that is being audited today and will not appropriately evaluate the results of previous judgments made or services provided as part of the previous work when forming an audit judgment today. This is called a self-review threat, meaning the auditor is not able to criticize himself.

When evaluating threats to independence, an acceptable level is a level at which a reasonable and informed third party would likely conclude that an audit organization or auditor is independent. The concept of a reasonable and informed third party is a test that involves an evaluation by a hypothetical person. Such a person possesses skills, knowledge, and experience to objectively evaluate the appropriateness of the auditor's judgments and conclusions. This evaluation entails weighing all the relevant facts and circumstances that the auditor knows, or could reasonably be expected to know, at the time that the evaluation is made.

(ii) More on Organizational Politics

OP is a major challenge in maintaining independence due to its undue influence.

Extreme and unnecessary playing of OP can slowly lead to an organization's failure or decline. OP and impression management focuses on self-interest in response to opposition at the workplace. OP represents stubborn actions and nepotism shown at all levels of management, which conflicts with the goal congruence principle. Many employees feel that "freedom from office politics" is important to their job satisfaction.

EXAMPLE: A CASE OF ORGANIZATIONAL POLITICS

Some governmental agencies hire cronies (citizens who helped to elect a government official or a local politician). These cronies are fake employees. They are on the governmental payroll and receive regular paychecks, like normal employees, but they really do not work at the agency.

Two aspects of OP include positive OP and negative OP.

- Positive aspects of OP include exchanging favors (nepotism), forcing coalitions, and seeking sponsors at upper levels of the organization.

- Negative aspects of OP include whistleblowing, revolutionary coalitions, threats, and sabotage.

EXAMPLE: A POSITIVE ASPECT OF ORGANIZATIONAL POLITICS

A positive aspect of OP occurs when a senior manager intervenes in the hiring process and influences the human resource department to hire the manager's preferred, unqualified job candidate over another, qualified candidate.

In general, OP can show dysfunctional behavior (bad) when employees and managers feel that their internal workflow is either delayed or stagnant due to distractions from OP.

Why do employees and employers promote OP? Employees resort to OP when they are unwilling to trust career advancement solely to competence, hard work, or luck. An organizational climate or culture that places unreasonable barriers to individual or group success also promotes OP.

Another dimension to understanding the OP is by knowing its potential impact on the entire organization. OP can have positive impact and negative impact.

Organizational Politics = Positive Impacts + Negative Impacts

---

EXAMPLES

Positive impacts resulting from OP include gaining visibility for ideas, improving coordination and communication, developing teams and working groups, advancing one's career, and increasing esprit de corps.

Negative impacts resulting from OP include distraction from organizational goals, misuse of resources, and organizational conflict due to dysfunctional behavior of employees and managers alike.

Tactics that are common expressions of OP in the workplace include posturing (one-upmanship), empire building, making the superior look good (apple polishing), political favors (nepotism), creating power and loyalty cliques, reciprocating, engaging in destructive competition, and sabotaging (as a last resort).

Remedies to OP include creating openness and trust, measuring employee performance rather than personalities, integrating individual and organizational goals, implementing job rotation techniques, and practicing better work scheduling and timely career planning.

Rules for winning at OP include finding out what the supervisor expects, finding out how the grapevine works, finding a mentor, fighting over major issues only, and not hiring a family member or a close friend (nepotism).

Research on OP has indicated that

- The larger the organization and the higher the levels of management, the greater the perceived amount of political activity.
- People in staff positions are viewed as more political than those in line positions.
- Marketing people are viewed as more political than those in production.
- Organizational changes (i.e., employee movement due to changes in jobs) prompt more political activity than any other types of change.

Summary of Factors Threatening an Internal Audit Function's Independence Levels

- Restricted access to records, documents, information, facilities, properties, employees, and management
- Organizational misplacement of the CAE

- Reporting restrictions for the CAE with no autonomy

- Across-the-board budget cuts that can limit the scope of the audit work

- Less confidence in internal controls in the eyes of outside auditors due to compromised independence of the internal audit function

- Less reliance and low assurance on the work of internal auditors by outside auditors and third parties due to compromised independence of internal auditors

- OP played by senior internal management in hiring auditors; limiting the scope of audit work; controlling the timing of the audit work; limiting how much time to spend on the audit work; and deciding what employees to meet and what facilities to visit during the audit work

- Conflicts of interest between the audit staff and audit management

- Ethical conflict due to close relationships between the auditor and his or her family, friends, and colleagues working for the same company as the auditor

- Violating ethical principles, such as integrity, objectivity, resource utilization, and professional behavior by internal auditors

(b) Factors Supporting Independence

The next factors support an internal audit function's independence levels:

- Presence of a strong internal audit charter

- Requiring all audit committee members to be fully independent of the company

- Presence of strong governance processes and mechanisms

- Proper organizational placement of the internal audit function

- Strong reporting relationship of the CAE

- Segregation of duties between the audit function and other business functions

- Equitable salaries, bonuses, and profit sharing plans for auditors

- Signed conflict-of-interest statements by auditors

- Ethical training and conflict-of-interest training for internal auditors

- Unlimited access to records, documents, information, facilities, properties, employees, and management

- Effective human resource policies in demoting and terminating internal auditors for violating independence rules

- Auditor professionalism through education and certification

- Outsourcing the internal audit function

2.3 Objectivity Defined

Objectivity means independence of mind and appearance when conducting audit engagements, maintaining an attitude of impartiality, having intellectual honesty, and being free of conflicts of interest. Maintaining objectivity includes a continuing assessment of relationships with audit clients and other stakeholders. The concepts of objectivity and independence are closely related in that independence impairments affect auditors' objectivity. Simply stated, objectivity deals with the state of mind of an internal auditor, meaning whether she is objective or subjective when dealing with matters of interest.

An individual internal auditor's objectivity means performing job duties such as audit assignments and engagements free from bias and interference. A major characteristic of objectivity is to avoid any conflict-of-interest situations (situations in which a competing professional or personal interest exists, which can make it difficult for the individual to fulfill job duties impartially).

2.4 Factors Threatening and Supporting Objectivity

This section contains two parts: factors threatening objectivity and factors supporting objectivity.

(a) Factors Threatening Objectivity

Threats or impairments to individual objectivity may include personal conflicts of interest; auditor's cognitive biases and traps; organizational cultural traps; audit engagement scope limitations; restrictions on access to records, personnel, and properties; and resource limitations in funding.

For example, the objectivity of an auditor making audit recommendations to adopt internal control standards or reviewing management's new procedures prior to their implementation may be impaired when that same auditor participated in the design, installation, procedures development, implementation, or operation of the same internal control systems.

In a way, all the threats to independence also apply to objectivity because lack of independence leads to lack of objectivity. These threats include self-interest threat, bias threat, familiarity threat, undue influence threat, management participation threat, structural threat, and self-review threat.

(i) Personal Conflicts of Interest

Conflict of interest is a situation in which an internal auditor, who is in a position of trust, has a competing professional or personal interest. Such competing interests can make it difficult for the individual to fulfill job duties impartially.

(ii) Auditor's Cognitive Biases and Traps

Internal auditors should avoid the next six cognitive biases and traps rooted in their own personality zone (area) combined with an organization's culture traps that could affect auditors' objectivity.

1. **Mirror-imaging trap**—An auditor's false assumption that his or her thinking is the same as others thinking. With this trap, auditors are unwilling to examine or analyze other views, variations, or alternatives of the subject matter at hand. This is similar to saying "My way or the highway." Here, the real issue is that the auditor is blindly committing to a set of common assumptions and not challenging those assumptions. One way to avoid

the mirror-imaging trap is to have a peer review by people from different backgrounds, which provides a good safeguard of checks and balances.

2. **Target fixation trap**—Some individuals get fixated on one hypothesis, rely only on evidence that is consistent with their preconceptions, and ignore other relevant views. In a way, they lose sight of the big-picture perspectives and push for a quick closure.

3. **Analogy trap**—Arises when an auditor is unaware of differences between his or her own context and that of others. This is a case of inappropriate or incorrect use of analogies. The net result is that important knowledge and information is missing because the auditor fails to admit ignorance coming from:

   a. Insufficient study and data/information

   b. Inability to differentiate between old facts and new facts and not integrating those facts

   c. Inability to accept conflicting facts

4. **Projection trap** (halo and horn error)—Occurs when an auditor is conducting an employee's performance appraisals. The halo error occurs when an auditor projects one positive performance feature or incident onto the rest, resulting in an overall higher rating of that employee's performance. The horn error occurs when an auditor projects one negative performance feature or incident onto the rest, resulting in an overall lower rating of that employee's performance. Both halo and horn errors are based on a recent behavior bias.

5. **Stereotyping trap**—Results from maintaining the status quo (no changes) and discouraging creativity (requiring changes). This trap results from the auditor's personal bias.

6. **Stovepiping trap**—Acknowledging only one source of information or knowledge base as the official source and disregarding the other sources of information or knowledge base as unofficial sources. This trap is similar to a silo trap or legacy trap.

(iii) More on Human Behavior

Another aspect of understanding behavior is perception. **Perception** is the cognitive process people use to make sense out of the environment by selecting, organizing, and interpreting information. Perceptual distortions can occur in the workplace. These perceptual errors in judgment arise from inaccuracies in any part of the perceptual process. Examples include stereotyping, the halo effect, projection, and perceptual defense.

Stereotyping is placing an employee into a class category based on one or a few traits or characteristics. The **halo effect** is an overall impression of a person based on one characteristic, either favorable or unfavorable. **Projection** is the tendency to see one's own personal traits in other people. **Perceptual defense** is the tendency of perceivers to protect themselves by disregarding ideas, objects, or people that are threatening to them.

Examples of cognitive biases and traps include (1) an internal auditor in the audit engagement team having preconceptions about the operations of a function under audit that are strong enough to affect that auditor's objectivity and (2) an internal auditor on the audit engagement team having biases associated with political, ideological, or social convictions that result from membership or employment in or loyalty to a particular type of policy, group, entity, or level of organization that could affect his or her objectivity.

(iv) Organizational Culture Traps

Organizational culture traps can make someone unwilling to challenge the views and perspectives of subject matter experts and senior-level managers. Other examples include:

- Assuming that small things in one culture are small things in every culture, whereas the opposite can be true. For example, adhering to time schedules and waiting in lines or queues is well accepted in some cultures and is not followed at all in other cultures.

- Assuming that all cultures in all countries follow the same way as one culture in one country.

- American businesspeople may push for quicker decisions during negotiations, whereas Japanese businesspeople may push for building consensus and trust first, followed by faster decisions.

One way to avoid the organizational culture trap is to read as many books as possible covering organizational cultures and international cultures in order to gain a good working knowledge of various cultures.

Summary of Factors Threatening an Internal Auditor's Objectivity Levels

- Work pressures to produce major audit findings in volume and quickly

- Pressure from audit clients to ignore suspicious issues and major irregularities

- Groupthink behavior from the audit team (e.g., going along and not rocking the boat)

- Being a friend or relative of an audit client and therefore failing to report major negative audit findings

- Owning financial stock in the company where they are employed

- Bias in prejudging the client based on previous familiarity with the client (i.e., this time should be good because the last time was good)

- A former consulting auditor becoming an assurance auditor who must do a self-review of his/her own work and ignoring or overlooking errors, irregularities, or deficiencies in order to make him- or herself look good

- Personal and professional conflict-of-interest situations

- Cognitive biases and traps

- Organizational culture traps

(b) Factors Supporting Objectivity

These factors support an internal auditor's objectivity levels:

- Auditor's unbiased behavior

- Audit supervisory reviews of auditors' work

- Auditor's own self-control, self-discipline, and self-accountability mechanisms

- Equitable salaries, bonuses, and profit-sharing plans for auditors

- Auditor's sound judgment

- Ethical training and conflict-of-interest training for internal auditors
- Auditors working in a team environment
- Rotation of auditors between different audits and locations
- Internal and external quality assurance reviews of audit work to provide credibility, recognition, and validation
- Effective human resource policies in demoting and terminating internal auditors for violating objectivity rules
- Signed conflict-of-interest statements by auditors
- Auditor professionalism through education and certification
- Outsourcing the internal audit function

(c) Comparison between Independence and Objectivity

Independence and objectivity are two different concepts because someone can be independent but not objective and someone can be objective but not independent. In some cases, these two concepts are linked in that lack of independence leads to lack of objectivity. Hence, auditors should avoid situations that could lead reasonable and informed third parties to conclude that the auditors are not independent and thus are not capable of exercising objective and impartial judgment on all issues when conducting audit engagements and reporting on the audit work (i.e., audit results).

Independence originates from the organizational placement and assigned responsibilities as shown in an organization chart. This means the internal audit loses its independence if it is a part of another function (e.g., finance) or if it manages other functions (e.g., risk management, loss prevention, insurance, or regulatory compliance) because these functions are subject to internal audit. This situation could result in a compromise of independence. In summary, independence is achieved through reporting lines, professional and regulatory requirements, benchmarking, and an organization's cultural factors.

Objectivity deals with the mind-set of internal auditors, and it can be understood through organization's policies, such as employee performance evaluation policies, compensation policies, and conflict-of-interest policies, Here objectivity means the auditor being objective when conducting the audit work, documenting the work, evaluating the work results, developing audit findings, drawing audit conclusions, writing audit reports, and making audit recommendations, all based on facts gathered and evidence collected. The auditor is not subjective, working based on gut feel and insufficient evidence.

A clear comparison between independence and objectivity is shown next.

Independence = Unbiased Business Conditions = Internal Audit as an Activity

Objectivity = Unbiased Mental Attitudes or Mind-sets = Internal Auditor as a Person

Exhibit 2.1 summarizes factors threatening and supporting independence and objectivity concepts. This summary provides a big-picture perspective of these two complicated and confusing concepts.

EXHIBIT 2.1 A Summary of Independence and Objectivity Factors

	Independence	Objectivity
Factors that threaten	Internal auditors facing restricted access to records, documents, information, facilities, properties, employees, and management	Auditors facing work pressures to produce major audit findings in volume and quickly
	Organizational misplacement of CAE	Pressure from audit clients to ignore suspicious issues and major irregularities
	Reporting restrictions for CAE with no autonomy	Auditors facing groupthink behavior from audit team (e.g., going along and not rocking the boat)
	Across-the-board budget cuts that can limit scope of audit work	Auditor is friend or relative of audit client who fails to report major negative audit findings
	Outside auditors having less confidence in internal controls due to compromised independence of internal audit function	Auditors own financial stocks in company they are employed with
	Outside auditors and third parties having less reliance and low assurance on work of internal auditors due to compromised independence of internal auditors	Auditor bias in prejudging audit client based on previous familiarity with client (i.e., this time should be good because the last time was good)
	OP played by senior internal management in hiring auditors; limiting scope of audit work; controlling timing of audit work; limiting how much time to spend on audit work; and deciding which employees to meet and what facilities to visit during audit work	Former consulting auditor becoming assurance auditor who must do a self-review of own work and ignoring or overlooking errors, irregularities, or deficiencies in order to make self look good
	Conflict-of-interest between audit staff and audit management	Auditors' personal and professional conflict-of-interest situations
	Ethical conflict due to close relationships between auditors and family, friends, and colleagues working for same company as auditors	Auditors' cognitive biases and traps
		Organizational culture traps
	Internal auditors violating ethical principles, such as integrity, objectivity, resource utilization, and professional behavior	
Factors that support	Presence of strong internal audit charter	Auditors' unbiased behavior
		Audit supervisory reviews of auditors' work
	Requiring all audit committee members to be fully independent of company	Auditor's own self-control, self-discipline, and self-accountability mechanisms

Independence	Objectivity
Presence of strong governance processes and mechanisms	Equitable salaries, bonuses, and profit-sharing plans for auditors
Proper organizational placement of internal audit function	Auditors' sound judgment
Strong reporting relationship of CAE	Ethical training and conflict-of-interest training for internal auditors
Segregation of duties between audit function and other business functions	Auditors working in team environment
	Rotation of auditors between different audits and locations
Equitable salaries, bonuses, and profit-sharing plans for auditors	Internal and external quality assurance reviews of audit work to provide credibility, recognition, and validation
Signed conflict-of-interest statements by auditors	Effective human resource policies in demoting and terminating internal auditors for violating objectivity rules
Ethical training and conflict-of-interest training for internal auditors	
Unlimited access to records, documents, information, facilities, properties, employees, and management	Signed conflict-of-interest statements by auditors
	Auditor professionalism through education and certification
Effective human resource policies in demoting and terminating internal auditors for violating independence rules	Outsourced internal audit function
Auditor professionalism through education and certification	
Outsourcing the internal audit function	

2.5 Policies to Promote Objectivity

These policies can help promote an internal auditor's objectivity:

- Establishing a policy on salary, bonuses, profit sharing, and other compensation schemes for internal auditors that does not provide incentives to act contrary to the objectives of the internal audit function.

- Establishing a policy that internal auditors should not be responsible for the design, installation, procedures development, implementation, and operation of internal control systems. However, they are responsible for reviewing and evaluating the adequacy, efficiency, and effectiveness of such internal control systems. This means that consulting auditors and assurance auditors cannot be the same for the same type of consulting work and assurance work.

- Establishing a company's code of ethics that emphasizes the principles of objectivity, competence, confidentiality, and integrity, consistent with the IIA's professional internal audit guidance on codes of ethics.

- Establishing a policy on how to assess the independence of specialists used in audit engagements. Examples of specialists include risk management analysts, information technology auditors, statisticians, engineers, quality control analysts, big data analysts, actuarial scientists, control self-assessment analysts, and audit consultants.

- Establishing a policy on how to handle sensitive and confidential information, including privacy concerns.

- Establishing a policy that auditors should not use their auditing position for financial gain or professional gain.

- Establishing a policy that internally recruited internal auditors should not audit activities for which they were previously responsible until after one year of employment in the internal audit function.

- Establishing a policy on avoiding conflicts of interest of former employees of the organization performing external quality assessments in the audit department after a certain length of time in the previous employment. This is to avoid real or apparent threat to independence and objectivity.

- Establishing an external assessor policy stating that, either individually or as a team, they must have an objective mind. This means they should be free from actual, potential, or perceived conflicts of interest that could impair objectivity.

2.6 Sample Practice Questions

In the actual CIA Exam for Part 1, 125 multiple-choice (M/C) test questions appear. This book contains 125 M/C sample practice questions divided into syllabus-based domains using the approximate domain weight given in the exam. These questions are added at the end of each applicable domain of this book with the sole purpose of showing the flavor and structure of the exam questions and of creating a self-quiz experience. The answers and explanations for these questions are shown in a separate section at the end of this book. This separate section is titled "Sample Practice Questions, Answers, and Explanations." If CIA Exam candidates need to practice more sample questions to obtain a higher level of confidence, Wiley offers a separate online test bank software product with hundreds of similar sample practice questions.

1. Which of the following is **not** compromised when an internal auditor has compromised her independence of mind?

   a. Integrity

   b. Objectivity

   c. Continuing education

   d. Professional skepticism

2. When internal audit work is performed based on facts, it is referring to which of the following ethical principles?

   a. Integrity

   b. Objectivity

   c. Resource utilization

   d. Professional behavior

3. Organizational politics is a part of which of the following threats to independence of internal audit organization and to an individual internal auditor?

   a. Bias threat

   b. Familiarity threat

   c. Undue influence threat

   d. Management participation threat

4. A peer review can help in mitigating which of the following threats to an auditor's objectivity?

   a. Target fixation trap

   b. Mirror-imaging trap

   c. Analogy trap

   d. Projection trap

5. The silo trap, which is a threat to an auditor's objectivity, belongs to the:

   a. Stereotyping trap.

   b. Culture trap.

   c. Stovepiping trap.

   d. Conflicts-of-interest trap.

6. Which of the following will **not** help in identifying the overall risks to the internal audit function?

   a. Barrier analysis

   b. Root-cause analysis

   c. Assurance maps

   d. Risk maps

7. In which of the following situations does the auditor potentially lack objectivity?

   a. An auditor reviews the procedures for a new electronic data interchange connection to a major customer before it is implemented.

   b. A former purchasing assistant performs a review of internal controls over purchasing four months after being transferred to the internal auditing department.

   c. An auditor recommends standards of control and performance measures for a contract with a service organization for the processing of payroll and employee benefits.

   d. A payroll accounting employee assists an auditor in verifying the physical inventory of small motors.

8. Which of the following actions would be a violation of auditor independence?

a. Continuing on an audit assignment at a division for which the auditor will soon be responsible as the result of a promotion.

b. Reducing the scope of an audit due to budget restrictions.

c. Participating on a task force which recommends standards for control of a new distribution system.

d. Reviewing a purchasing agent's contract drafts prior to their execution.

9. According to the IIA *Standard* 1130—Impairment to Independence or Objectivity, which of the following is **not** a part of functional reporting to the board?

a. Audit charter

b. Audit risk assessment

c. Audit budgets

d. Audit plan

Proficiency and Due Professional Care

This domain defines several major theoretical topics, such as proficiency, competency, and due professional care. It discusses the need for internal auditors to improve their competency through continuing professional development and the relationship between professional judgment and competence. It presents competency levels for internal auditors in the form of hard skills and soft skills required to do a professional job.

All these topics are tested at a combination of proficient and basic cognitive levels in Part 1 of the CIA Exam with 18% weight given. Relevant International Professional Practices Framework (IPPF) *Standards*, such as 1200, 1210, 1220, and 1230, presented in the first section of this book (Professional *Standards*) should be studied together with this domain to answer the CIA Exam questions and Wiley's online test bank practice questions.

With respect to the CIA Exam, cognitive levels are labeled as proficient level and basic level. These cognitive levels suggest that more time and effort should be spent in studying and mastering the subject matter covered in the topics labeled as the proficient level. Comparatively less time and effort should be spent on the topics labeled as the basic level.

3.1 Proficiency and Competency Defined

(a) Proficiency Defined

Proficiency is defined as the ability to apply knowledge to situations likely to be faced and to deal with them without extensive recourse to technical research and assistance. There is a built-in and direct relationship between a person's proficiency and competency. A person needs to be fully proficient to become a fully competent person, as there are levels of proficiency and competency. This relationship is shown next.

$$\text{High-Level Proficiency} = \text{High-Level Competency}$$
$$\text{Low-Level Proficiency} = \text{Low-Level Competency}$$

(b) Competency Defined

Competency or **competence** is defined as the combination of knowledge, skills, and abilities (KSAs) obtained from education and experience necessary to conduct audit engagements. Competence enables auditors to make sound professional judgments as it includes possessing the technical knowledge and the hard/soft skills necessary for the assigned role and the type of audit work being done.

Competence is derived from a combination of education and experience (i.e., Competence = Education + Experience).

Education is a systemic and systematic process aimed at developing KSAs. It is a process that is typically, but not exclusively, conducted in traditional academic environments. Several ways of teacherless study methods, done outside of the academic environment, such as self-educating, self-teaching, and self-learning, can be considered education. The major difference is that these teacherless study methods do not go through rigorous testing and validation, as occurs in traditional academic environments. Therefore, what is really learned and retained through teacherless study methods is debatable.

Experience refers to workplace activities that are relevant to developing professional auditors. Experiences such as clerical work, administrative work, or assistant to the audit director positions do not qualify as relevant professional audit work. Competence is not necessarily measured by years of auditing experience because such a quantitative measurement may not accurately reflect the kinds of experience auditors gain in any given time period. Maintaining competence through a commitment to continuous learning and development throughout auditors' professional lives is important for auditors. This means that maintaining competence is not a one-time learning or a series of intermittent learnings.

(c) Core Competencies

Core competencies are the unique and collective capabilities (training and know-how) and specific competencies (skills, experience, and education) that a company has and its competitors do not have. Here the scope of competencies includes competencies of employees, products, and services. The idea is that if employees' competencies are at a higher level, a company's products and services will be at a higher level because it is employees who make products and deliver services. Note that a solid linkage can be established between competency and quality in that highly competent employees can deliver high-quality products and services, and vice versa.

$$\text{Highly Competent Employees} = \text{High-Quality Products and Services}$$
$$= \text{Great Competitive Advantage}$$

Competence is an individual's qualification necessary to carry out assigned job duties and responsibilities. The competence-rich situation creates a competency gap between the company and its competitors; the higher the competency-richness level, the larger the competency gap. Of course, a company's core competencies are a simple summation of all of its employees' competencies.

The goal of having all employees acquire the core competencies is to remove their talent gaps and skills gaps. **Talent management** means implementing and maintaining improvement programs to attract, acquire, develop, train, promote, and retain quality employees.

Competency Gaps = Talent Gaps + Skills Gaps

Core competencies are observable, measurable, and a critical set of key knowledge, skills, abilities, and behaviors employees need to have in order to successfully perform their job functions or work efficiently, effectively, and productively. Core competencies can help ensure that a person's performance, acting as an individual or as a member of a team, aligns with the organization's mission and strategy.

Audit managers can ask themselves two basic questions:

1. Does my department has competent employees that it needs?

2. Do my employees have multiple competencies (skills) so they can handle multiple job responsibilities, as needed?

Example

Online retailer Zappos follows the holacracy management model where its employees work in teams (called circles). Zappos employees have no job titles, no job descriptions, no managers, and only one partner (coordinator) for each circle. An employee can belong to more than one circle and can do more than one job, which is possible solely due to that employee's multiple skills and well-rounded competencies.

In general, four competency levels exist.

1. **Entry level**—Staff auditors, audit trainees, and audit interns (low competency level)

2. **Journeyman level**—Senior auditors, lead auditors, and in-charge auditors (medium competency level)

3. **Functional level**—Audit supervisors and audit managers knowledgeable in audit function and other business functions (high competency level)

4. **Expert level**—Subject matter experts (SMEs) well known in one industry or across industries for their in-depth knowledge and authoritative source in a subject (very high competency level). An SME is a general expert who is regarded as an authority with unusual competencies and skills by other people in the same profession. An SME has high visibility. For example, Michael E. Porter from the Harvard Business School is the well-known SME in the area of corporate strategy. Loosely stated, an external audit consultant, audit specialist, and outsourced audit staff can be called as an expert if he or she possesses certain unique skills and talent.

3.2 Due Professional Care Defined

Due professional care calls for the application of care and skill expected of a reasonably prudent and competent person in the same or similar circumstances. For example, due professional care is exercised when internal audits are performed in accordance with the IIA *Standards*. The exercise of due professional care requires that:

- Internal auditors be independent of the activities they audit.

- Internal audits be performed by those persons who collectively possess the necessary knowledge, skills, abilities, and disciplines to conduct the audit properly.

- Internal audit work be planned and supervised.

- Internal audit reports be objective, clear, concise, constructive, and timely.

- Internal auditors follow-up on reported audit findings to ascertain that appropriate action was taken.

A clear comparison between proficiency and due professional care is presented next.

- **Proficiency** refers to education, experience, professional development opportunities (e.g., seminars, training, and continuing education), and professional certifications (e.g., Institute of Internal Auditors' [IIA's] Certified Internal Auditor (CIA)).

- **Due professional care** refers to understanding the systematic and disciplined approach to internal auditing required by the IIA's International Professional Practices Framework (IPPF) and establishing an internal audit's policies and procedures manual for guidance to auditors.

3.3 Continuing Professional Development

Competence includes being knowledgeable about the specific audit requirements and having the skills and abilities to proficiently apply that knowledge on audit engagements. Continuing professional education (CPE) contributes to auditors' competence. The continuing competence of the audit organization's personnel depends in part on an appropriate level of CPE so that auditors maintain the KSAs necessary to conduct the audit engagement.

Determining what subjects are appropriate for individual auditors to satisfy the CPE requirements is a matter of professional judgment to be exercised by auditors and audit managers. When determining what specific subjects qualify for the CPE requirement, auditors may consider the types of KSAs and the level of proficiency necessary in order to be competent for their assigned roles in current audit engagements or future audit engagements. CPE programs are structured educational activities with learning objectives designed to maintain or enhance the auditors' competence to address audit engagement objectives and perform work in accordance with audit standards.

Examples of specific subjects that qualify for the CPE requirements may depend in part on the industry the auditors work for and on the audit profession as a whole. These subjects include audit standards; laws and regulations; analytical techniques such as statistics, data mining, and actuarial science; general ethics; time management, audit reporting and presentation; communications; project management; economics; information technology; and human resources management.

Examples of CPE's structured educational activities or programs can include internal training programs (e.g., courses, seminars, and workshops); external training programs (e.g., conferences, conventions, meetings, and seminars); web-based seminars; audio and video conferences; university and college courses; correspondence courses; developing CPE courses; and publishing articles and books.

Internal audit staff should have the requisite collective skill levels to audit all areas of the organization. Therefore, auditors should have a wide range of business knowledge, demonstrated through years of audit work and industry-specific experience, educational background, professional certifications, training programs, committee participation, joining professional associations, and job rotational assignments. Internal audit should assign staff to audit assignments based on areas of expertise and should, when feasible, rotate staff within the audit function.

Internal audit management should perform knowledge gap assessments at least annually to evaluate whether current staff members have KSAs commensurate with the organization's strategy and operations. Management feedback surveys, internal quality assurance program findings, and external quality assurance program findings are useful tools to identify and assess knowledge gaps. Any identified knowledge gaps should be filled and may be addressed through targeted staff hires, training, business line rotation programs, and outsourcing arrangements. The internal audit function should have an effective staff training program to advance professional development and a process to evaluate and monitor the quality and appropriateness of training provided to each auditor. Internal auditors generally receive a minimum of 40 hours of training in a given year.

3.4 Professional Judgment and Competence

Auditors must use professional judgment in planning and conducting the audit engagement and in reporting the audit results. Professional judgment includes exercising reasonable care and professional skepticism. **Reasonable care** includes acting diligently in accordance with applicable professional standards and ethical principles. Attributes of professional skepticism include a questioning mind, awareness of conditions that may indicate possible misstatement owing to error or fraud, and a critical assessment of evidence. **Professional skepticism** includes being alert to, for example, evidence that contradicts other evidence obtained or information that brings into question the reliability of documents or responses to inquiries to be used as evidence. Further, it includes a mind-set in which auditors assume that management is neither dishonest nor of unquestioned honesty. Auditors may accept records and documents as genuine unless they have reason to believe the contrary. Auditors may consider documenting procedures undertaken to support their application of professional skepticism in highly judgmental or subjective areas under audit.

A critical component of the audit engagement is that auditors use their professional knowledge, skills, and experiences, in good faith and with integrity, to diligently gather information and objectively evaluate the sufficiency and appropriateness of evidence. Professional judgment and competence are interrelated because judgments made depend on auditors' competence, as shown next.

Competent Auditors ⟶ Good Judgment

Incompetent Auditors ⟶ Poor Judgment

Issues or concerns regarding professional judgment are listed next.

- Professional judgment is a collection of experiences of all the audit team members, individual auditors, stakeholders, specialists, and audit management involved in an audit engagement.

- Professional judgment considers adhering to independence standards; maintaining objectivity and credibility; assigning competent audit staff; defining the scope of the audit work;

evaluating, documenting, and reporting the results of the audit work; and maintaining appropriate quality control over the audit engagement process.

■ Professional judgment considers any threats to the auditor's independence (real or apparent) and related safeguards that may mitigate the identified threats.

■ Professional judgment considers whether the audit team's collective experience, training, KSAs, and overall understanding of the engagement's subject matter are sufficient to assess the risks that the engagement's subject matter may contain a significant inaccuracy or could be misinterpreted. An example of collective experience is big data collection and data analytics.

■ Professional judgment deals with audit risk in arriving at improper audit conclusions. Determining the sufficiency and appropriateness of evidence to be used to support the audit findings and conclusions based on the engagement objectives and any recommendations reported is integral to the engagement process.

■ Professional judgment does not imply infallibility on the part of either the individual auditor or the audit organization. Absolute assurance is not attainable because of factors such as the nature of evidence (i.e., correct/incorrect evidence and complete/incomplete evidence) and characteristics of fraud (e.g., collusion and intentional acts and omissions).

■ Professional judgment does not mean eliminating all possible limitations or weaknesses associated with a specific audit engagement but rather identifying, assessing, mitigating, and concluding on them.

3.5 Competency Levels for Internal Auditors

Internal auditors must possess the business-related KSAs required to perform their audit work and to meet professional responsibilities of the internal audit activity. These KSAs, in addition to the core auditing principles and practices required, can be arranged by topic or subject matter. These KSAs can be acquired or developed over time and are classified as common skills, hard skills, and soft skills (the latter two are called general business skills).

(a) Common Skills

Common skills are a collection of skills from a variety of sources necessary to make an internal auditor more proficient and competent. These skills are in addition to the KSAs required from the core auditing principles and practices. Common skills include:

■ Business acumen (e.g., mission, vision, strategy, goals, objectives, and plans)

■ Critical thinking and logical reasoning (e.g., reasoning skills and problem-framing skills)

■ Communications (verbal and written)

■ Basic legal and ethical principles (e.g., due process, due care, due diligence, due professional care, duty of loyalty, duty of care, and duty of obedience)

■ Audit and legal evidence (e.g., direct evidence and documentary evidence)

■ Forensics and investigations (e.g., using computers to analyze crimes and fraud)

■ Analytical and functional knowledge (e.g., basic ratios, reasonableness analysis, audit metrics, and core business functions)

■ Assurance services and consulting services (financial, performance, compliance, and system security reviews and advice, facilitation, and training services)

- Risk management and insurance (e.g., governance, control, risk mitigation strategies, and risk recovery practices)

- Sampling and statistics (e.g., statistical sampling, nonstatistical sampling, and regression analysis)

- Information technology in systems development and systems security (e.g., control evaluation and testing and knowledge of system security principles and practices)

- Big data analytics and data mining (e.g., anomaly detection analysis, fraud analysis, predictive analytics, and descriptive analytics)

- Industry knowledge (e.g., retail and healthcare)

(b) Hard Skills

Hard skills are core KSAs learned and acquired by a person in his or her trade, vocation, and occupation through intensive and extensive education, training, testing, and validation to provide a lifetime career of choice and interest (i.e., job-related technical skills in a plumber, carpenter, electrician, teacher, accountant, engineer, lawyer, doctor, and auditor). Hard skills can be improved and enhanced through continued education, training, testing, and validation in a specific career. Most hard skills can be acquired through education, training, and development courses and work-related experiences. Simply stated, hard skills are career-building and career-enhancing KSAs.

> Hard Skills = Analytical and Technical Skills + Functional Skills
> + Problem-Solving and Decision-Making Skills
> + Managing and Management Skills + Application Skills + Integration Skills

Specifically, hard skills:

- Deal with knowing specific rules, methods, tools, techniques, procedures, and practices that are constant from job to job regardless of the work environment.

- Describe what a person knows and what a person can do certain things.

- Can be learned, acquired, and perfected over time. They are tangible and much easier to quantify.

- Are often listed as a job applicant's qualifications necessary for an open position (e.g., degrees and certificates).

- Help a person to get the job done on time with resources provided.

- Are considered as complements to soft skills.

Examples of hard skills are listed next.

- Quantitative, analytical, and technical skills (e.g., knowledge of basic mathematics, statistics, and probability theories to advanced regression/correlation analysis, and forecasting techniques)

- Qualitative, analytical, and technical skills (e.g., content analysis, factor analysis, cluster analysis, link analysis, canonical analysis, discriminant analysis, causal analysis, causality analysis, cost – benefit analysis, and neural research methods to analyze written words and conversation analysis to analyze spoken words)

- Functional skills (e.g., knowledge of accounting/finance, marketing, and operations)

- Problem-solving skills (e.g., identifying and differentiating between symptoms and real problems and equally solving structured and unstructured problems)

- Decision-making skills (e.g., making routine and nonroutine decisions with too little or too much information and differentiating between perfect and imperfect information)

- Managing skills (e.g., planning, organizing, directing, and controlling skills, which are the basic functions of managers and executives)

- Management skills (i.e., containing conceptual, human, and technical skills possessed by supervisors, managers, executives, and leaders, not in equal proportion but in proportion to their job)

- Application skills (e.g., the ability to put theory into practice; the ability to apply functional knowledge, say in marketing and operations)

- Integration skills (i.e., the ability to combine, e.g., marketing's functional knowledge with operations functional knowledge and vice versa)

(c) Soft Skills

Unlike hard skills, soft skills do not represent acquired KSAs. Instead, they represent natural skills (innate skills and born-with skills), such as common sense; the ability to deal with people and handle them in a proper manner; the ability to get along with people in difficult situations; and having a positive and flexible attitude. Soft skills are learned by trial-and-error effort in response to a changing environment.

Because some soft skills—such as interpersonal skills, people skills, leadership skills, creative skills, and entrepreneurial skills—are innate skills; they cannot be learned and acquired through education, training, or development programs. Other soft skills, such as communication skills, presentation skills, comprehension skills, time management skills, implementation skills, and coordination skills, can be learned and improved through education, training, and development programs because they are not fully innate skills.

> Soft Skills = People Skills + Social Skills + Critical Thinking Skills + Persuasion Skills + Collaboration Skills + Negotiation Skills + Communication Skills

Specifically:

- Soft skills deal with a person's character traits and interpersonal relationships with other people describing who they are and what their personality is.

- Most soft skills are natural, innate, and instinctive, which are difficult to acquire and change. They are intangible and much harder to quantify than hard skills.

- Soft skills are a major differentiator in people because they are a major requirement for employment and key criteria for success in a person's life.

- Soft skills are considered as complements to hard skills.

- Soft skills require teamwork, flexibility, patience, persuasion, time management, empathy, understanding, and listening to others.

- Major soft skills in business include communication skills, interpersonal skills (people skills), collaboration skills, persuasion skills, listening skills, coordination skills, time management skills, and project management skills.

Examples of soft skills are listed next.

- Interpersonal skills (i.e., dealing with an individual's attitudes about and behaviors toward others). Interpersonal skills can be considered the same as people skills.

- People skills (i.e., innate skills, meaning people are born with those skills). People skills can be considered the same as interpersonal skills.

- Communication skills (e.g., analyzing written and oral communications).

- Comprehension skills (e.g., understanding complex content in words, tables, charts, graphs, exhibits, and figures).

- Presentation skills (e.g., showing complex results in simple ways using tables, charts, graphs, exhibits, and figures).

- Coordination skills (e.g., working together in collaboration with employees in different departments to achieve common goals and objectives). These skills also are called collaboration skills.

- Implementation skills (i.e., bringing project and program new initiatives to a successful completion).

- Motivational skills (i.e., using hard-sell and/or soft-sell strategies).

- Negotiation skills (i.e., skills that yield a win-win, win-lose, lose-lose, and lose-win outcome between two parties).

- Time management skills (i.e., utilizing time more efficiently and effectively and doing more work with fewer resources).

- Diversity management skills (i.e., defining who is included or excluded from a group or subgroup and receiving sensitivity training [also called T-training]).

- Leadership skills (e.g., team-building skills; handling people; possessing interpersonal skills; managing motivation teamwork, conflicts, and crisis situations; and possessing contextual intelligence, emotional intelligence, and cognitive intelligence).

- Listening skills (e.g., asking relevant questions with an inquisitive mind and showing genuine curiosity and interest; requiring much more patience and carefulness than normal).

- Assertion skills (skills that enable people to get their needs met with minimal strife). By being assertive when the need arises, one can prevent the buildup of emotions that so often cause conflict.

- Creative skills (i.e., challenging common thinking and the status quo and coming up with groundbreaking and innovative thinking combined with game-changing ideas).

- Learning skills (i.e., the ability to understand what a person knows about his own learning styles and methods to acquire new knowledge in order to do his job now better than before and more efficiently and effectively). Learning skills include collaboration, communication, critical thinking, and creativity.

- Critical thinking skills (i.e., problem-framing skills requiring redefining a problem and reinventing a matched solution).

- Reasoning skills (skills based on logical thinking or logical reasoning and comprised of deductive, inductive, and abductive reasoning).

- Project management skills (i.e., managing resources to meet project goals and managing costs, schedules, deliverables, people, and quality).

- Social skills (e.g., interpersonal skills, people skills, coordination skills, mentoring, negotiation skills, and persuasion skills).

- Collaborative skills (i.e., a group effort requiring knowledge sharing and tool utilization to improve efficiency and increase output in production).

- Persuasion skills (i.e., ability to convince others to do something or to make others believe in something).

(d) Hard Skills versus Soft Skills

Hard skills represent what a person *knows*, and soft skills represent who a person *is*. It is important to note that employers need well-rounded employees with both hard and soft skills. Because hard skills are teachable, employers often look for job applicants with the required soft skills, which are not teachable that easily and quickly. This means that employers want new employees who are already equipped with soft skills to make their job effective and efficient. Note that business skills represent a Pareto principle in that 80% of achievements in a person's career are determined by soft skills and only 20% are determined by hard skills.

Specifically:

- People who possess both hard skills and soft skills can obtain and hold jobs very easily and quickly.

- People who possess only hard skills and no soft skills cannot obtain and hold a job.

- A person who has several soft skills and only few hard skills can obtain a job because hard skills can be taught and learned, whereas some soft skills cannot.

(e) Expanded Hard Skills and Soft Skills

The next table expands on some major hard skills and soft skills.

Communication skills	Oral communications, listening skills, written communications, presentation skills, report writing skills, memo writing skills; project status report writing skills, contract writing skills, weekly/monthly activity report writing skills, comprehension skills, negotiation skills, interviewing skills, and investigative skills. Communications can flow in four directions in an organization: up, down, horizontally, and diagonally. **Communication skills are ranked as a number 1 requirement for auditors.**
Assertion skills	Assertion (or assertive) skills enable people to get needs met with minimal strife. By asserting when needs arise, people can prevent the buildup of emotions that so often cause conflict. Both assertion skills and listening skills help to clear up two major sources of conflict: errors and lack of information. Internal auditors need more assertive skills than others because they deal with audit clients and other stakeholders in critical situations during their audit work. Auditors need to assert and summarize their understanding of audit client matters in a concise and succinct manner and should positively confirm with the audit client. In addition to auditors, managers and leaders must possess assertion skills.
Persuasion skills	Persuasion skills are the art of convincing someone to do something or to make someone believe in something. Persuasion deals with facts and actions. Factors such as persistence, perseverance, and determination are prerequisites to persuasion.

Leadership skills	Ability to inspire and lead others; explaining strategic mission and vision to others; possessing drive, integrity, and agility; motivating skills; listening skills; negotiation skills; coordination skills; diversity management skills; public servicing skills; organizational skills; ability to understand decision traps and decision biases; people skills (relationship-oriented issues and interpersonal dealings between and among individuals); assertion skills; time management skills; business acumen; creative skills; contextual intelligence; emotional intelligence, cognitive intelligence; problem-solving and decision-making skills; and reasoning skills. Essential skills for leaders include communication skills, listening skills, negotiation skills, and delegating skills. **Leadership skills are ranked as a number 4 requirement for auditors.**
Technical skills	Core business functional knowledge (functional skills); subject matter proficiency; quantitative skills; qualitative analysis; technology-oriented skills (e.g., robots, artificial intelligence, CAD, CAM, and lean Six Sigma skills); project management skills (Program Evaluation Review Technique [PERT]), and big data analytics. **Technical skills are ranked as a number 3 requirement for auditors.**
Social skills	Social skills operate in interactions between people and communication with other people, all within the established social rules, norms, relations, and expectations in a society. Social skills are learned through changes in people's attitude, thinking, and behavior over a period of time. Social skills build character traits like trustworthiness, respectfulness, rapport, responsibility, fairness, and above all an internal moral compass.
Reasoning skills	Reasoning skills are based on logical thinking or logical reasoning, which is comprised of deductive reasoning, inductive reasoning, and abductive (inference) reasoning. In deductive reasoning, conclusions are drawn when moving from general principles to specific cases. In inductive reasoning, conclusions are drawn when moving from specific cases to general principles. In abductive reasoning, conclusions lead to premises. Moreover, conclusions are drawn from hypothesis testing and heuristics (rules of thumb, intuition, and trial and error) where outcomes are likely to occur, but not with certainty. In abductive reasoning, one moves from outputs to inputs.
Problem-solving skills	Identifying and differentiating between symptoms and real problems and equally solving structured and unstructured problems. Problem-framing skills require reverse engineering a current problem (i.e., deconstructing a current problem) and forward engineering the same problem (i.e., reconstructing the same problem). It also includes redefining an old, unclear problem into a new, clear problem.
Decision-making skills	Making routine and nonroutine decisions with too little or too much information and differentiating between perfect and imperfect information. Note that problem-solving skills and decision-making skills go hand in hand because decisions are made in part to solve problems.
Twenty-first-century learning skills	The P21 Organization conducted a research study that identified four deep learning competencies and skills (called the four Cs) of twenty-first-century learning: collaboration, communication, critical thinking, and creativity.
Teamwork skills	Ability to follow or take direction from a leader, manager, supervisor, team leader, coach, or mentor; delegation skills; valuing and respecting opinions of others; handling cross-cultural diversity and sensitivity; and adaptability to changes and uncertainties. These skills require collaboration skills. **Teamwork skills are ranked as a number 2 requirement for auditors.**

(continued)

Managing skills	Managing human capital (people skills); listening skills; negotiation skills; motivating skills; coordination skills; managing a risk-based environment; assertion skills; and reasoning skills. In addition, managing skills require integration skills, application skills, creative skills, business acumen, managing decision-making and problem-solving processes; managing administrative activities; implementing strategy and innovation projects; handling conflict and change; managing diversity skills; organizational skills; and time management skills. Broadly speaking, managing skills are composed of conceptual, human, and technical skills. **Managing skills are ranked as a number 5 requirement for auditors.**
Critical thinking skills:	Ability to think objectively and analyze facts and evidence to form an opinion (judgment) with the ultimate goal of reaching an answer or conclusion. This ability is inwardly directed to maximize the thinker's rationality (rational thinking and logical thinking). It provides a self-regulated judgment and self-directed thinking, and it is not "hard" thinking, as the name suggests or implies. Critical thinking skills do not solve problems. Instead, they improve one's own process of thinking. They are used as a systematic approach to problem solving and decision making. Critical thinking skills include observation, interpretation, analysis, inference, evaluation, and explanation.
	Critical thinking skills provide the ability: to apply professional standards and industry standards; to differentiate between real problems and symptoms; to identify root causes of problems; to apply reasoning and logical skills such as inductive and deductive reasoning; and to apply professional judgment in collecting audit evidence and reporting audit results. Critical thinking skills also need reasoning skills and problem-framing skills.
Motivation skills	The ability to inspire others to do good things that are expected. These skills use hard-sell (stick approach with punishments) or soft-sell (carrot approach with incentives) techniques to get the expected results.
Negotiation skills	Skills that produce win-win, win-lose, lose-lose, and lose-win outcomes between two parties to a negotiation process who are trying to reach an agreement. These skills push for what one party wants while knowing what the other party wants.
	Negotiation skills are the ability to influence others to get what is wanted from them. It uses a hard approach (threats and insults) and a soft approach (calm and collected). Usually, if one party wins, the other party loses.
Career skills	Skills that help a person's career path with growth and versatility. Key elements include agility (e.g., flexibility and adaptability), accountability, productivity, self-direction, self-control, self-motivation, cross-cultural understanding and interaction, social skills, and self-initiatives.
Collaboration skills	Occurs when two or more employees or departments work together to achieve a common goal. Virtual teams, quality teams, audit teams, project teams, and distributed teams are examples of collaboration because team members work cooperatively and in a coordinated manner. In collaboration, face-to-face interaction is better than person-to-machine interaction.
	Technological collaboration tools include online calendars, spreadsheets, voicemails, electronic mails, chat systems, videoconferencing, workflow systems, messaging systems, virtual collaboration systems, and web-based software such as wiki.
	Nontechnical collaboration tools are less efficient and include manual systems such as paper and pencil, flipcharts, sticky notes, whiteboards, or chalkboards.
	For example, internal auditors in one division of a major company can work with auditors in other divisions of the same company when conducting similar audits or related audits to share common business knowledge and audit tools.

Interpersonal skills	Ways to improve interpersonal skills include touring facilities; managing by walking around; arranging brown-bag lunches, fireside chats, and face-to-face meetings; and communicating by phone, fax, text, email, voicemail, and intranet. Interpersonal skills are also called as people skills.
People skills	Innate skills (meaning people are born with those skills), although some parts can be learned, developed, and practiced. Research has proved that people who are successful possess more people skills, despite their lack of technical skills. People skills include conflict management, communication, listening, and interpersonal skills for better relationships and rapport building. People skills focus on getting along with coworkers and handling and treating coworkers with respect and dignity and to establish mutual trust and comfort levels. People skills can be thought of as interpersonal skills.
Business acumen skills	Knowledge of core business functions, such as operations, marketing, and finance (functional skills); commitment to mission and vision; ability to develop a grand strategy for the entire business and substrategies for each business line, to create and sustain value, to understand competitors and their business games, to come up with counterstrategies and counteractions to beat competitors, to treat shareholders and stakeholders equally and properly, to understand how business functions integrate and work with each other to create value; and implementing best practices or metapractices to create value and to improve business processes and functions in a sustainable manner.

(f) Required Skills for Internal Auditors

A summary of competency levels and business skills required of internal audit staff and management is presented next.

Role	Skills Needed
Staff auditors and senior auditors	Communication, assertion, persuasion, technical, social, reasoning, collaboration, people, teamwork, critical thinking, and business acumen
Audit supervisors and audit managers	Communication, technical, problem solving and decision making, managing, critical thinking, collaboration, people, and business acumen
Chief audit executive and internal audit director	Communication, leadership, problem solving and decision making, critical thinking, motivation, negotiation, creative, people, and business acumen

(i) Business Skills for Directors and Officers
All directors, officers, executives, and senior managers, including chief audit executives, need both hard skills and soft skills to perform their jobs more effectively and efficiently. However, the depth and the type of skills needed for an executive or manager depends on his or her level in the management hierarchy. This means that higher-level managers and senior executives need more depth in soft skills and less depth in hard skills. On the other hand, lower-level managers and junior executives need more depth in hard skills and less depth in soft skills. This is shown below:

Higher-Level Managers and Senior Executives Need More Depth in Soft Skills and Less Depth in Hard Skills

Lower-Level Managers and Junior Executives Need More Depth in Hard Skills and Less Depth in Soft Skills

3.6 Sample Practice Questions

In the actual CIA Exam for Part 1, 125 multiple-choice (M/C) test questions appear. This book contains 125 M/C sample practice questions divided into syllabus-based domains using the approximate domain weight given in the exam. These questions are added at the end of each applicable domain of this book with the sole purpose of showing the flavor and structure of the exam questions and of creating a self-quiz experience. The answers and explanations for these questions are shown in a separate section at the end of this book. This separate section is titled "Sample Practice Questions, Answers, and Explanations." If CIA Exam candidates need to practice more sample questions to obtain a higher level of confidence, Wiley offers a separate online test bank software product with hundreds of similar sample practice questions.

1. The relationship between proficiency and competency is:
   a. Direct
   b. Indirect
   c. Not tested
   d. Not observed

2. A person's competency can be derived from which of the following?
   a. Knowledge, skills, and abilities
   b. More theory and less practice
   c. Education and experience
   d. Less theory and more practice

3. Regarding competency levels, staff auditors belong to which of the following?
   a. Entry level
   b. Journeyman level
   c. Functional level
   d. Expert level

4. Regarding competency levels, audit consultants belong to which of the following?
   a. Entry level
   b. Journeyman level
   c. Functional level
   d. Expert level

5. Regarding competency levels, audit supervisors belong to which of the following?
   a. Entry level
   b. Journeyman level
   c. Functional level
   d. Expert level

6. Regarding competency levels, senior auditors belong to which of the following?
   a. Entry level
   b. Journeyman level
   c. Functional level
   d. Expert level

7. Due professional care for internal auditors is derived from which of the following?
   a. Internal audit manual
   b. Internal auditor education
   c. Internal auditor experience
   d. Internal auditor professional certification

8. Internal audit management should perform annually which of the following?
   a. Education gap assessment
   b. Competency gap assessment
   c. Talent gap assessment
   d. Skill gap assessment

9. Auditors' professional judgment does not mean:
   a. Eliminating all possible limitations.
   b. Identifying all possible limitations.
   c. Mitigating all possible limitations.
   d. Assessing all possible limitations.

10. Due professional care for internal auditors does not mean:
    a. Developing a systematic approach to audits.
    b. Attending audit-related professional seminars.
    c. Adhering to a disciplined approach to audits.
    d. Developing a structured approach to audits

11. Due professional care is not exercised when:
    a. The internal audit work is planned.
    b. The internal audit work is supervised.
    c. The internal audit reports are objective and clear.
    d. Internal auditors fail to follow up on repeated audit findings.

12. Professional judgment for internal auditors includes which of the following?
    a. Professional skills and professional work
    b. Strong evidence and documented procedures
    c. Reasonable care and professional skepticism
    d. Sufficient evidence and appropriate evidence

13. Regarding professional judgment, internal auditors cannot attain:
    a. Absolute assurance.
    b. Reasonable assurance.
    c. Possible assurance.
    d. Expected assurance.

14. Which of the following is the highest-ranked skill required at all levels of internal auditors?
    a. Assertion skills
    b. Career skills
    c. Persuasion skills
    d. Communication skills

15. Which of the following can help clear up major sources of conflict between internal auditors and their audit clients?
    a. Assertion skills and listening skills
    b. Leadership skills and managing skills
    c. Problem-solving skills and decision-making skills
    d. Social skills and teamwork skills

16. Audit teams need more of which of the following?
    a. Collaboration skills
    b. Communication skills
    c. Critical thinking skills
    d. Creativity skills

17. Internal auditors ranging from staff auditor to audit director need which of the listed skills?
    a. Technical skills
    b. Business acumen skills
    c. Social skills
    d. Motivation skills

18. Ensuring internal audit teams have the right competencies with right level of work experience and designing effective internal audit procedures can reduce the risk of which of the following?
    a. Business risk
    b. Audit failures
    c. Audit false assurance
    d. Audit reputation risk

19. Which of the following differs between assurance services and consulting services when exercising due professional care?
    a. Costs and benefits
    b. Complexity of work
    c. Extent of work
    d. Materiality

Quality Assurance and Improvement Program

This domain contains only a few key theoretical topics. It describes the required elements of the quality assurance and improvement program, including its reporting results. In addition, it discusses conformance or nonconformance with the IIA's *Standards*. It also shows how to apply total quality management (TQM) approaches to improve internal audit operations.

All these topics are tested at the basic cognitive levels in Part 1 of the CIA Exam with a 7% weight given. Relevant International Professional Practices Framework (IPPF) *Standards*, such as 1300, 1310, 1311, 1312, 1320, 1321, and 1322, presented in the first section (Professional *Standards*) of this book should be studied together with this domain to answer the CIA Exam questions and Wiley's online test bank practice questions.

With respect to the CIA Exam, cognitive levels are labeled as proficient level and basic level. These cognitive levels suggest that more time and effort should be spent in studying and mastering the subject matter covered in the topics labeled as the proficient level. Comparatively less time and effort should be spent on the topics labeled as the basic level.

4.1 Required Elements

A well-designed, comprehensive quality assurance (QA) program should ensure that internal audit activities conform to the Institute of Internal Auditors (IIA)'s professional *Standards* and the organization's internal audit policies and procedures. **The QA program contains two required elements, internal quality assessments and external quality assessments:**

$$\text{Audit QA} = \text{Internal Quality Assessment} + \text{External Quality Assessment}$$

The internal audit function should develop and document its internal assessment program to promote and assess the quality and consistency of audit work across all audit groups with respect to policies, procedures, audit performance, and workpapers. The QA review should be performed by someone independent of the audit work being reviewed. Conclusions reached and recommendations for appropriate improvement in internal audit process or staff training should be implemented by the chief audit executive (CAE) through the quality assurance and improvement program (QAIP). Action plan progress should be monitored and subsequently closed after a period of sustainability. Each organization should conduct an internal quality assessment exercise annually, and the CAE should report the results and status of internal assessments to senior management and the audit committee at least annually.

$$\text{Quality Assurance (QA) + Improvement Programs (IP)} = QA + IP = QAIP$$

The IIA recommends that an external quality assessment of internal audit be performed by a qualified independent party at least once every five years. The review should address compliance with the IIA's Definition of Internal Auditing, Code of Ethics, Core Principles, and Professional *Standards*. In addition, the review should address the internal audit function's charter, policies, and procedures, and any applicable legislative and regulatory requirements. The CAE should communicate the results, planned actions, and status of remediation efforts to senior management and the audit committee.

In addition, the internal audit function should contain five key characteristics that form the foundation on an effective QAIP:

1. Policy
2. Methodology and process
3. People
4. Systems and information
5. Communication and reporting

A list of highlights of internal assessment and external assessments follows.

- The goals of internal assessment and external assessment are the same regarding compliance and conformance with the IIA's *Standards* and the Code of Ethics and alignment with the Definition of Internal Auditing and the Core Principles.

- The scope of internal assessments consists of ongoing monitoring and periodic self-assessments, where the ongoing monitoring is conducted first and the periodic self-assessment is performed next. Internal assessments focus on continuous improvement of the audit activity.

- Ongoing monitoring, which takes a narrow scope, is an integral part of the day-to-day supervision and operation of the internal audit as they are blended into the audit policies, practices, tools, processes, and information. Ongoing monitoring focuses on individual audit engagements.

- Periodic self-assessments, which take a broad scope, focus on the entire internal audit activity as a whole.

- A self-assessment may be performed in lieu of a full external assessment, provided it is validated by a qualified external assessor and that the scope of a self-assessment is the same as that of a full external assessment.

- An external assessment can be done as a stand-alone and full external assessment or a self-assessment with independent external validation and assurance. The scope of external assessment can be expanded to provide comments on operations and strategy.

- Internal assessments are performed first, and external assessments are conducted second. Internal assessment supports external assessments.

- Internal assessments are conducted every year. External assessments are conducted every five years.

(a) Manufacturing Quality versus Audit Quality

Manufacturing-oriented companies have long been developing and maintaining comprehensive QA programs and quality control methods to continuously improve the quality of their products. Best practices in TQM are applied to manufacturing processes, primarily at three production stages, such as quality before, during, and after production. TQM is a management philosophy containing quality principles, practices, tools, and techniques to continuously improve the quality of products. Specifically, TQM focuses on QA plans, quality control practices, and continuous improvement programs. Later, TQM was introduced in service-oriented companies. Similarly, an internal audit activity, which is a part of service-oriented organizations, needs a comprehensive QAIP to conduct quality audit work and deliver quality results to its stakeholders. A comparison between manufacturing TQM and audit QAIP follows:

TQM in Manufacturing = QAIP in Internal Audit

Quality before Production = Audit Planning

Quality during Production = Audit Engagement

Quality after Production = Audit Reporting

(b) Potential Risks in Audit Quality Assessments

At least five types of risks exist when conducting internal assessments and external assessments: peer review risk, audit sampling risk, auditor cognitive risk, assessment rating risk, and assurance risk. Note that the last four risk types can be byproducts of the peer review or stand-alone risks in internal and external assessments. Each of these risks is briefly discussed next.

Peer review means that one colleague reviews and checks another colleague's work to ensure the work's accuracy, completeness, and quality. Peer reviews are done in a team environment during internal and external assessments to provide additional QA. **Peer review risk** is the risk that the review team:

- Fails to identify significant weaknesses in the reviewed audit organization's system of quality control for its auditing practice, its lack compliance with that system, or a combination thereof

- Issues an inappropriate opinion on the reviewed audit organization's system of quality control for its auditing practice, its compliance with that system, or a combination thereof

- Makes an inappropriate decision about the matters to be included in, or excluded from, the peer review report

In summary, peer review risk deals with not reporting significant weaknesses, issuing an inappropriate opinion, and making an inappropriate decision.

Audit sampling risk occurs when selecting specific audit engagements for review across many audit divisions of a large audit organization that completes many audit engagements in a year. As the peer review is based on selected tests, it is not designed to test every audit engagement, compliance with every professional standard, or every detailed component of the audit organization's system of quality control. This means that a peer review would not necessarily detect all weaknesses in the system of quality control or all instances of noncompliance with it. Specifically, audit sampling risk can arise based on whether (1) statistical or nonstatistical sampling methods are used when selecting audit tests for review; (2) auditors have sampling experience or not; and (3) auditors have considered sampling and nonsampling risks when selecting audit tests for review.

Auditor cognitive risk occurs from the auditor's own cognitive traps and biases, because these traps and biases are deeply embedded in people's own personality. Cognitive biases are human tendencies that can lead to human biases and that can act as judgment triggers (good or bad). Examples include stereotyping (i.e., maintaining the status quo and failing to invite creativity), target fixation (i.e., evidence is consistent with perceptions and no big-picture views), and projection traps (i.e., a recent behavior bias, resulting in halo errors and horn errors and seeing one's own traits in other people). Projection of current review results to future reviews is an example of a cognitive risk because future conditions can change, thus making the current review results invalid.

Assessment rating risk occurs when the rating system used in a peer review work is unfair and subjective. Possible rating types include pass, fail, or pass with deficiencies needing improvement, requiring ratings to be fair and objective. An auditor's cognitive traps and biases can influence the assessment rating risk.

Assurance risk means all the internal assessments and external assessments can result only in reasonable, not absolute, assurance. Usually, reasonable assurance is provided in performing and reporting in conformity with applicable professional standards. The real question is whether a reasonable assurance is good enough to accept.

4.2 Reporting Requirements

The CAE is required to report to the board and senior management at several critical points, as listed next.

- After internal assessments are completed, a report is issued identifying areas for improvement and showing corrective action plans.

- After external assessments are completed, a report is issued identifying areas for improvement and showing corrective action plans.

- After uncovering any impairments to independence or objectivity, audit scope restrictions or limitations, and resource limitations for auditors and audit clients, a report is issued with documented details and evidence.

- After completing internal assessments and external assessments, a report is issued showing the conformance rating scale, whether it generally conforms, partially conforms, or does not conform.

- After discovering a nonconformance outcome, a report is issued showing the impact of nonconformance by quantifying it as much as possible on specific areas, such as:
  - ☐ Providing reliable assurance services
  - ☐ Providing consulting services
  - ☐ Completing the audit plan

☐ Addressing high-risk audit areas

☐ Impact on the overall scope or operation of the internal audit activity

■ A report is issued by the external assessor describing observations and recommendations to management in order to improve internal audit quality, efficiency, and effectiveness.

■ A benchmarking report is issued showing how the external assessor went through a vetting process (i.e., how he or she was screened, selected, and hired) with a request for services document, all demonstrating internal audit's commitment to the due diligence process. Note that the vetting process does not apply to guest auditors.

4.3 Conformance versus Nonconformance

Whether it is an internal assessment or an external assessment, the QA review should eventually address compliance with the IIA's Definition of Internal Auditing, Code of Ethics, Core Principles, and *Standards*. Two outcomes are possible: conformance or nonconformance.

Conformance means compliance with the Definition of Internal Auditing, Code of Ethics, Core Principles, and *Standards*. Note that the Core Principles are a new requirement starting with the 2017 *Standards*. Conformance means both internal assessments and external assessments are carried out.

Examples of Conformance

■ There are no impairments or threats to independence and objectivity.

■ There are no audit scope restrictions or limitations.

■ There are no resource limitations for auditors and audit clients.

■ People performing internal and external assessments possess collective knowledge, skills, and experiences.

■ Risk was explicitly considered during the development of annual and individual audit plans.

■ There are no peer review risks and audit work sampling risks during internal and external assessments.

Nonconformance means noncompliance with the Definition of Internal Auditing, Code of Ethics, Core Principles, and *Standards*. Nonconformance means (1) there is no internal assessment and no external assessment and/or (2) internal assessments without external assessments. Nonconformance can become conformance after full validation by external assessors.

EXAMPLES OF NONCONFORMANCE

■ The internal audit activity did not conduct external assessment at least once every five years.

■ An internal auditor did not meet individual objectivity requirements during an audit engagement.

■ An audit engagement did not have auditors possessing collective knowledge, skills, and experiences.

■ The CAE and managers and supervisors failed to consider risk when developing the audit plan.

4.4 TQM in Internal Audit Operations

Many internal audit departments have installed TQM approaches to improve internal audit operations. One such approach is recommended by the U.S. Government Accountability Office, which outlined eight steps to apply and implement TQM approaches in audit operations.

1. **Initial quality assessment.** This step includes:

   a. Identifying the audit department's customers

   b. Establishing the needs of customers

   c. Setting priorities so as to best meet customers' needs

   d. Assessing the quality of audit products (audit reports) as perceived by audit customers as to timeliness, usefulness, responsiveness, and cost

   e. Interviewing customers so as to reveal pertinent information about the audits, audit staff performance, and the audit department as a whole

2. **CAE awareness.** Awareness training should stress the importance of TQM as a philosophy or an approach, not a program.

3. **Formation of a quality council.** Audit managers, audit supervisors, and audit staff members should be part of the quality council, and they should acquire the knowledge of TQM principles, practices, and tools. This council should report to the CAE. It should coordinate training and participate in prototypes.

4. **Fostering teamwork in audits.** The audit department should establish a participative environment that fosters teamwork and quality work. Audit plans, audit work programs, fieldwork, workpapers, and audit reports all require quality orientation and thinking.

5. **Development of prototypes.** To convince some auditors who are doubtful about the TQM philosophy, the quality council should demonstrate the practical value of new ways of organizing the audit work with highly visible prototypes and productivity initiatives. When tested and proven successful, these prototypes can convince the cautious of the audit staff.

6. **Celebration of success.** The audit department should publicize the achievements of the prototype to encourage the cautious and hesitant audit staff.

7. **Organizational implementation.** All units and all locations of the audit department should successfully implement audit quality methods, and appropriate recognition should be given for those units that are most successful. This provides motivation and promotes healthy competition.

8. **Annual audit quality review.** There should be an annual audit quality review for audit departments throughout the organization. The annual review, together with a rating system, will demonstrate the success of the implementation of quality in the audit department.

EXAMPLE: Internal Audit and TQM

An audit assignment can go wrong at any stage. It can be ill conceived, improperly directed, poorly planned, or badly implemented, and its results can be ineffectively communicated. For a variety of reasons, the audit can fail to meet its customers' needs.

An appropriate quality control system identifies or flags those factors that could jeopardize the quality of an audit and establishes processes or procedures that promptly identify and correct problems before they occur. For example, it is more effective to correct a planning-related problem in the planning phase than in a later phase (e.g., reporting phase).

An effective quality control system needs to do more than ensure the quality with which work was performed. It also needs to determine what the work accomplished and how customers and stakeholders viewed the result. This can be done by system approaches, such as surveys of customers and stakeholders, recommendation tracking and reporting systems, and auditor performance measurements and award/reward systems.

4.5 Sample Practice Questions

In the actual CIA Exam for Part 1, 125 multiple-choice (M/C) test questions appear. This book contains 125 M/C sample practice questions divided into syllabus-based domains using the approximate domain weight given in the exam. These questions are added at the end of each applicable domain of this book with the sole purpose of showing the flavor and structure of the exam questions and of creating a self-quiz experience. The answers and explanations for these questions are shown in a separate section at the end of this book. This separate section is titled "Sample Practice Questions, Answers, and Explanations." If CIA Exam candidates need to practice more sample questions to obtain a higher level of confidence, Wiley offers a separate online test bank software product with hundreds of similar sample practice questions.

1. When selecting people to work in the internal audit department, the vetting process does **not** apply to which of the following?
   a. External assessors
   b. Audit contractors
   c. Guest auditors
   d. External service providers

2. Which of the following is the key performance indicator for an internal audit activity?
   a. Number of audit clients satisfied
   b. Number of audit recommendations made
   c. Number of audit recommendations accepted
   d. Number of audit recommendations implemented

3. Which of the following provides assurance as the first line of defense over risks and exposures facing an organization?
   a. Internal auditors
   b. Senior managers
   c. Risk managers
   d. Operations managers

4. The scope of work in developing and maintaining a quality assurance and improvement program (QAIP) includes which of the following processes?
   I. Supervision
   II. Internal assessment
   III. Ongoing monitoring
   IV. External assessment

   a. I only
   b. I and II
   c. I, II, and III
   d. I, II, III, and IV

5. Which of the following is **not** included in the ongoing and periodic assessment dealing with measurements and analyses of performance metrics with respect to internal audit's quality assurance and improvement program (QAIP)?
   a. Money saved from the audit work
   b. Number of recommendations accepted
   c. Customer satisfaction
   d. Audit cycle time

6. If the results of the assessment of the internal audit's quality assurance and improvement program (QAIP) indicate areas for improvement, which of the following will implement such improvements?
   a. Audit committee of the board
   b. Chief audit executive
   c. Chief executive officer
   d. External auditor

7. All of the following stakeholders receive the results of internal and external quality program assessments of internal audit's activity from the chief audit executive (CAE) **except**:
   a. Functional managers
   b. Senior managers
   c. Board of directors
   d. External auditor

8. Which of the following is unique to the external assessment of an internal audit's activity when compared to internal assessment?
   a. Findings
   b. Conclusions
   c. Recommendations
   d. Overall opinion

9. Which of the following facilitates and reduces the cost of the external assessment of an internal audit's activity?

   a. A periodic internal assessment performed within a short time before an external assessment

   b. A periodic internal assessment performed in parallel with an external assessment

   c. A periodic internal assessment performed a long time before an external assessment

   d. A periodic internal assessment performed a short time after an external assessment

10. Which of the following is unique to external assessment of an internal audit's activity?

   a. Best practices

   b. Cost recoveries

   c. Benchmarking

   d. Expected deliverables

11. Which of the following is common between internal assessment and external assessment of an internal audit's activity?

   a. Audit standards

   b. Audit charter

   c. Code of ethics

   d. Definition of internal auditing

12. The scope of external assessment of an internal audit's activity should **not** be limited to which of the following?

   a. Assurance services

   b. Consulting services

   c. Leading practices

   d. Quality assurance and improvement program

Governance, Risk Management, and Control

This domain is very big in size as it contains 20 major theoretical topics. Its major focus is on an organization's governance, risk management, and control processes. It also presents the nature of compliance management as it relates to compliance with laws, rules, and regulations.

All these topics are tested at a combination of proficient and basic cognitive levels in Part 1 of the CIA Exam with a 35% weight given. Relevant International Professional Practices Framework (IPPF) Standards, such as 2100, 2110, 2120, and 2130, presented in the section entitled "Professional *Standards*" of this book should be studied together with this domain to answer the CIA Exam questions and Wiley's online test bank practice questions.

With respect to the CIA Exam, cognitive levels are labeled as proficient level and basic level. These cognitive levels suggest that more time and effort should be spent in studying and mastering the subject matter covered in the topics labeled as the proficient level. Comparatively less time and effort should be spent on the topics labeled as the basic level.

5.1 Governance Principles, Components, and Problems

In this section, topics such as an organization's governance principles, components, and problems are discussed. The section further details topics such as corporate governance definition, corporate governance principles, corporate governance components, and corporate governance problems. In addition, a summary of corporate governance problems is presented.

(a) Corporate Governance Defined

Corporate governance refers to the method by which a firm is being governed, directed, administered, or controlled and to the goals for which it is being governed. It is concerned with the relative roles, rights, and accountability of such stakeholder groups as owners, boards of directors, managers, executives, employees, labor unions, and others who assert to be stakeholders. Note that boards of governors or directors are not the guarantors of the governance process as long as they use good judgment.

(i) What Is Corporate Governance?

Corporate governance sets the right tone and proper stage for the entire corporation. While there is no standard definition of corporate governance, it can broadly be understood to refer to the system by which companies are directed and controlled, including the role of the board of directors, management, shareholders, and other stakeholders. Corporate governance provides the structure through which the objectives of the company are set and the means of attaining those objectives and monitoring performance are determined.

A weak form of corporate governance is one of the root causes of many problems that corporate management is facing today. A weak board means a weak governance and vice versa. Note that corporate governance and corporate ethics should support corporate management.

The issue of corporate governance is a direct outgrowth of the question of legitimacy. For business to be legitimate and to maintain its legitimacy in the eyes of the public, its governance must correspond to the will of the people and interests of stakeholders.

(ii) What Is a Corporation?

A **corporation** is a legal entity that is separate from its owners and shareholders, where it is responsible for paying debts it owes and receiving money it is owed, and where its owners and shareholders would not be responsible for the corporation's debts or liabilities.

An exception to this legal entity concept occurs in specific situations where courts are required to pierce (lift or remove) the corporate veil and where the corporation's owners and shareholders would be liable for the corporation's debts or wrongful conduct. Examples of these specific situations include misconduct, dishonest and improper actions, fraud, criminal acts, deceiving third parties, and setting up sham corporations based on "alter ego" theory by owners and shareholders. This means illegal and unethical acts cannot be hidden behind the name of a corporation and owners and shareholders cannot get away with bad acts.

Piercing the corporate veil applies to closely held corporations, single-person corporations, and shell corporations and does not apply to publicly traded corporations because the latter are assumed to have a better and proper corporate structure and organizational controls. Piercing the veil is based on the concept of equitable principle and deep rock doctrine.

Courts have decided to pierce the veil and found that a corporation's owners and shareholders are personally liable for the following:

- Failing to pay dividends to shareholders
- Installing ineffective or nonfunctioning board of directors and officers, who are simply box checkers, box tickers, and rubber-stamp approvers with no strong voice and no sharp teeth
- Controlling or majority shareholders mixing corporate assets with their assets and stealing corporate assets
- Using the corporation for their personal purposes
- Operating while undercapitalized or with inadequate capitalization amounts in the balance sheet
- Not maintaining accurate records and required documents

An old corporation can sue a new corporation when a former employee of the old corporation starts a new corporation to compete with the old one after signing a contract with the old corporation not to compete.

Courts have decided *not* to pierce the corporate veil when a corporation's management becomes creditors of a company and are subordinated to other creditors when the company becomes insolvent or goes bankrupt and the management becomes the new owners of the corporation (e.g., a management buyout plan). This is because a management buyout is a legal and ethical practice.

(iii) What Is a Corporate Constitution?
The essential elements of a corporate constitution include corporate charter (bylaws), director power and accountability (right to manage), and shareholder rights and duties (approve sale and purchase of company assets in a merger and acquisition). The purpose of a corporation may be anything that is lawful.

(b) Corporate Governance Principles

Business Roundtable supports eight guiding principles as part of good corporate governance practices.

   1. The board approves corporate strategies that are intended to build sustainable long-term value; selects a chief executive officer (CEO); oversees the CEO and senior management in operating the company's business, including allocating capital for long-term growth and assessing and managing risks; and sets the "tone at the top" for ethical conduct.

(Source: Business Roundtable, Principles of Corporate Governance, August 2016, Washington, DC. www.brt.org)

2. Management develops and implements corporate strategy and operates the company's business under the board's oversight, with the goal of producing sustainable long-term value creation.

3. Management, under the oversight of the board and its audit committee, produces financial statements that fairly present the company's financial condition and results of operations and makes the timely disclosures investors need to assess the financial and business soundness and risks of the company.

4. The audit committee of the board retains and manages the relationship with the outside auditor, oversees the company's annual financial statement audit and internal controls over financial reporting, and oversees the company's risk management and compliance programs.

5. The nominating/corporate governance committee of the board plays a leadership role in shaping the corporate governance of the company, strives to build an engaged and diverse board whose composition is appropriate in light of the company's needs and strategy, and actively conducts succession planning for the board.

6. The compensation committee of the board develops an executive compensation philosophy, adopts and oversees the implementation of compensation policies that fit within its philosophy, designs compensation packages for the CEO and senior management to incentivize the creation of long-term value, and develops meaningful goals for performance-based compensation that support the company's long-term value creation strategy.

7. The board and management should engage with long-term shareholders on issues and concerns that are of widespread interest to them and that affect the company's long-term value creation. Shareholders that engage with the board and management in a manner that may affect corporate decision-making or strategies are encouraged to disclose appropriate identifying information and to assume some accountability for the long-term interests of the company and its shareholders as a whole. As part of this responsibility, shareholders should recognize that the board must continually weigh both short-term and long-term uses of capital when determining how to allocate it in a way that is most beneficial to shareholders and to building long-term value.

8. In making decisions, the board may consider the interests of all of the company's constituencies, including stakeholders such as employees, customers, suppliers and the community in which the company does business, when doing so contributes in a direct and meaningful way to building long-term value creation.

LONG-TERM VALUE CREATION

A publicly held corporation's long-term value is created and sustained with three foundational and essential elements: corporate strategy, risk management, and management performance.

(c) Corporate Governance Components

To appreciate fully the legitimacy and corporate governance issues, it is important to understand the major groups that make up the corporate form of business organization. Only by so doing can one appreciate how the system has failed to work according to its intended design.

The four major groups needed in setting the stage are (1) shareholders (owners or stakeholders), (2) board of directors, (3) managers, and (4) employees. Overarching these groups is the charter issued by the state, giving the corporation the right to exist and stipulating the basic terms of its existence.

COMPONENTS OF CORPORATE GOVERNANCE

Four components of corporate governance include shareholders, board of directors, managers, and employees.

Under the U.S. corporate law, **shareholders** are the owners of a corporation. As owners, they should have ultimate control over the corporation. This control is manifested primarily in the right to select the company's board of directors. Generally, the number of shares of stock owned determines the degree of each shareholder's right.

Because large organizations may have hundreds of thousands of shareholders, they elect a smaller group, known as the **board of directors**, to govern and oversee the management of the business. The board is responsible for ascertaining that managers put the interests of the owners (i.e., shareholders) first. The third major group in the authority hierarchy is **management**—the group of individuals (managers) hired by the board to run the company and manage it on a daily basis. Along with the board, top management establishes overall policy. Middle- and lower-level managers carry out this policy and conduct the daily supervision of the operative employees. **Employees** are those hired by the company to perform the actual operational work. Managers are employees, too, but in this discussion, we use "employees" to refer to nonmanagerial employees.

(d) Corporate Governance Problems

Eleven types of governance problems exist:

1. Separation of ownership from control
2. Lack of board independence
3. Occurrence of insider trading scandals
4. Appearance of conflict-of-interest situations
5. Presence of interlocking boards
6. Presence of shadow directors
7. Presence of activist shareholders and directors
8. Experiencing ethical lapses and dilemmas
9. Failure to recognize cognitive traps and biases
10. Lack of reasoning skills in board members
11. Incomplete proxy materials

Each problem is explained further next.

(i) Separation of Ownership from Control

The separation of ownership from control is the major condition embedded in the structure of modern corporations that has contributed to the corporate governance problem. This means owners cannot control their own business or investment because management exercises control over the business. In the precorporate period, owners typically were themselves the managers. As public corporations grew and stock ownership became widely dispersed, a separation of ownership from control became common. Shareholders were owners in a technical sense, but most considered themselves to be investors rather than owners.

Other factors that added to management's power were the corporate laws and traditions that gave the management group control over the **proxy process**—the method by which the shareholders elected boards of directors. Over time, it was not difficult for management groups to create boards of directors of likeminded executives who simply collected their fees and deferred to management on whatever it wanted. The result of this process was that power, authority, and control began to flow upward from management rather than downward from the shareholders (owners). **Agency problems** developed when the interests of the shareholders were not aligned with the interests of the manager, and the manager (who is simply a hired **agent** with the responsibility of representing the owner's [principal's] best interest) began to pursue self-interest instead.

Market forces and agency costs aim to prevent or minimize agency problems. Examples of market forces include large shareholders and threat of takeover, where large institutional shareholders put pressure on company management to perform using their voting rights and where a constant threat of a takeover motivates company management to act in the best interest of the corporation owners. Examples of agency costs include cost of management compensation in terms of incentive plans (stock options), performance plans (performance shares), and cash bonuses; and costs imposed by lenders (creditors and bankers) in the form of constraints put on borrowers' actions to protect their investment (e.g., minimum liquidity levels, merger and acquisition activities, executive salaries, and dividend payments).

(ii) Lack of Board Independence

Board independence from company management is a crucial aspect of good corporate governance. It is here that the difference between inside directors and outside directors is most pronounced. Outside directors are independent from the firm and its top managers. In contrast, inside directors have some sort of ties to the firm. Sometimes they are top managers in the firm; other times they are family members or others with close ties to the CEO. To varying degrees, each of these parties is beholden to the CEO and, therefore, might be hesitant to speak out when necessary.

Another problem is managerial control of the board processes. CEOs often can control board perks, such as director compensation and committee assignments. Board members who rock the boat may find they are left out in the cold with little or no perks. Two issues surrounding compensation include CEO compensation, which is very controversial, and director compensation, which is very subjective or can be interpreted as self-dealing. A 100% independent director from outside of the company is ideal and preferred.

(iii) Occurrence of Insider Trading Scandals

According to the Fast Answers section of the U.S. Securities and Exchange Commission (SEC) website, insider trading has two faces: legal conduct and illegal conduct. **Legal insider trading,** in contrast to illegal insider trading, occurs when corporate insiders (e.g., directors, executives, officers, managers, and employees) buy and sell their own stock (security trading activity) in their own companies. The only requirement is that they must report their trading activity to the SEC.

Illegal insider trading refers generally to buying or selling a security, in breach of a fiduciary duty or other relationship of trust and confidence, while in possession of material, nonpublic information about the security. Insider trading violations may also include providing tips or clues about securities, securities trading by the person tipped, and securities trading by those who misappropriate such information. This type of trading leads to insider scandals.

Insider information can be positive information (good news about a company) and negative information (bad news about a company). Savvy individuals take advantage of today's good news and buy a company's stock today in hopes of increased price in the future. Individuals also take advantage of today's bad news and sell a company's stock today in fear of decreased price in the future.

Examples of Today's Positive or Negative Insider Information that Can Lead to Illegal Conduct Tomorrow

- Announcement of upcoming mergers, acquisitions, and divestitures between two or more companies (Mergers and acquisitions with a positive synergy could increase the stock price of the acquiring company and a negative synergy could decrease the stock price.)

- Announcement of new products and services into current and new markets that can increase sales, revenues, and profits

- Announcement of a new and lucrative sales contract that is signed or about to be signed that can increase sales, revenues, profits, and market stock price, including increase in employment

- Announcement of introduction of new and emerging technologies (e.g., robots, artificial intelligence, drones, and virtual reality) that can increase sales, revenues, and profits

- Announcement of new hires, promotions, demotions, transfers, terminations, resignations, and departures of officers, executives, and directors

- Announcement of new regulations and deregulations that can increase or decrease a company's sales, revenues, profits, and market share price

- Announcement of a company's data security breaches, ransomware attacks, and website crashes that can decrease a company's sales, revenues, profits, and market share price

- Announcement of lawsuits against a company from:
  1. Regulators in violation of laws, rules, and regulations
  2. Tax authorities in violation of tax laws
  3. Security agencies in violation of securities laws
  4. Stakeholders in violation of their individual rights
  5. Competitors in violation of free market economics regarding price violations
  6. Customers in violation of their privacy rights

- Announcement of wrongdoings and misdeeds by a company's directors, officers, and executives in terms of bribes, corruption, fraud, and sexual harassment

The SEC prosecutes individuals and organizations that violate insider trading laws because these laws protect investor confidence in the fairness and integrity of the securities markets.

Examples of Illegal Insider Trading Cases

- Corporate officers, directors, and employees who traded the corporation's securities after learning of significant, confidential corporate developments

- Friends, business associates, and family members, and other tippees of such officers, directors, and employees who traded the securities after receiving such information

- Employees of law, banking, brokerage, and printing firms who were given such information to provide services to the corporation whose securities they traded

- Government employees who learned of such information because of their employment by the government (e.g., employees at the regulatory agencies such as Federal Trade Commission, Federal Communications Commission, Department of Justice, and SEC)

- Other persons who misappropriated and took advantage of confidential information from their employers (e.g., consultants, contractors, suppliers, vendors, customers, and competitors)

In summary, illegal insider trading refers to breach of a fiduciary duty and a violation of trust and confidence and tipping others with material and nonpublic information about a company's stock security. All other forms of insider trading are legal.

(iv) Appearance of Conflict-of-Interest Situations

A **conflict of interest** means an individual's goals and objectives do not fit with the goals and objectives of that individual's organization. It is any relationship that is actual (or appears to be actual) and not in the best interest of the organization. Such a relationship would prejudice an individual's ability to perform his or her duties and responsibilities objectively. A conflict-free mind-set requires a full disclosure of financial interests or other conflicting matters, such as working for competing firms or owning stock of competing firms.

Examples of Conflict-of-Interest Situations

Favoring one:

- Executive over the other executives
- Contractor over the other contractors
- Company to merge with or acquire over other companies
- Supplier over other suppliers
- Employee over others in making hiring, promotion, demotion, transfer, and termination decisions

Conflict-of-interest situations are common in corporate settings due to different personalities and ambitions of people in higher-level positions where some people can get rich at the expense of others or benefit from illegal and/or unethical actions. Specific areas vulnerable to conflict-of-interest situations include:

- Contractual agreements between buyers and sellers of goods and services
- Developing compensation and incentive packages for directors and officers

- Sharing of investments and profits between two or more parties

- Taking advantage of insider or privileged information by selling or sharing it with others for personal or financial gain

- Returning favors to others through placing phonies and imposters on a company's payroll

Simply stated, when there is no conflict of interest, an individual cannot use a company's sensitive insider information for personal gain. Organizational politics can play a vital role in creating conflict-of-interest situations.

Poorly exercising or ignoring the **business judgment rule** can lead to a conflict-of-interest situation. The business judgment rule requires people to carefully exercise due care by acting on an informed basis, in good faith, and in the honest belief that their actions are in the best interests of the corporation. This rule can reduce the liability of directors and increase the legal immunity to directors and officers as long as the directors' and officers' actions fall within their authority. However, this rule can raise a doubt in the minds of directors and officers about whether their judgment is sound.

EXAMPLES

Sound Conflict-of-Interest Programs in the Banking Industry and Financial Institutions

- Bank examiners should not be scheduled to participate in assignments from which they must be disqualified because of an actual conflict or the appearance of a conflict of interest. Examples include (a) a borrowing relationship with a financial institution to be examined or an affiliate or (b) other relationships, such as employment of a spouse, household member, or close relative, at the institution to be examined.

- Bank examiners should not take out a loan or establish a line of credit at any state member bank, bank holding company, or its no-bank subsidiaries while employed at the main bank.

- All nonclerical employees should fill out, sign, and file all required financial disclosure forms so that potential conflicts are fully disclosed. Bank examiners must disclose all borrowing relationships with banking organizations, including credit card or credit lines even with zero balances.

- Appropriately trained staff should review the disclosure forms so that conflict-of-interest issues are identified and resolved in a timely manner. Legal staff should be consulted about any differences.

Controls to Implement Sound Conflict-of-Interest Programs

- Establish pre-employment screening policies to inform bank examiners about borrowing rules and investment prohibitions during the employee hiring interview process.

- Establish a financial disclosure program with forms and instructions to identify potential conflicts of interest.

- Establish a formal training and education program for all employees, reviewers of disclosure forms, and schedulers of bank examiners' work so that they are informed of their responsibilities.

(v) Presence of Interlocking Boards

Interlocking boards or interlocking directorates means some of the board of directors of a hiring company that hires its directors might (1) own shares in the hiring company, (2) become members of other company's boards, and (3) be working as executives in other companies. These activities are a concern to shareholders due to conflict-of-interest situations and time pressures on directors (i.e., spread their time too thin) to contribute fully and give complete attention to the hiring company. All these factors could affect a board member's judgment and decision-making qualities in a negative way. The chief audit executive (CAE) should evaluate board members' qualifications, education, and experience. The interlocking boards are also called overboarding.

(vi) Presence of Shadow Directors

Shadow directors are outsiders who do not sit on a company's board but can exert considerable influence over the board's strategies, plans, policies, programs, and practices. Examples of these shadow directors include lobbyists, activities, majority shareholders, friends, family members, and consultants. The presence of shadow directors is a major concern for shareholders and stakeholders.

(vii) Presence of Activist Shareholders and Directors

Some shareholders and directors are very aggressive in raising their concerns and in pushing their agenda to influence the board's decisions and actions in their favor. The difference between the shadow directors and activist directors is that shadow directors do not sit on a company's board, whereas the activist directors do sit on the board, like other board members. Proponents of activism say it keeps board members on their toes; opponents say it distracts the board's normal and regular activities.

Activist shareholders and investors are deeply dissatisfied with the insufficient disclosures of executive compensation (i.e., the CEO, executives, officers, and board chairperson and other members) due to excessive compensation packages in terms of their size, structure, and performance targets used in compensation contracts. Activists say these disclosures provided in proxy materials are not clear and complete to enable them to make an informed decision on executive compensation. "Say on pay" is the term used where proxy statements allow shareholders to make informed votes on executive compensation, and the term is somewhat effective in influencing or modifying the executive compensation practices.

Activist or special interest directors are raising hard questions about the board's assessment of environmental, social, economic, and governance issues. A board that is composed of one or more special-interest directors with potentially competing objectives would be more likely to become distracted by particular agenda. Consequently, such a board would be less able to focus on the large best interests of the corporation and its stakeholders.

A counterargument is that directors join a board only if they can appeal to a broad number of shareholders, not to a limited special-interest group. This means that shareholder-nominated directors would not be elected without a majority support from all other shareholders.

(viii) Experiencing Ethical Lapses and Dilemmas

Ethical lapses and dilemmas are one of the root causes of many problems that corporate management is facing today. Ethical lapses emerge from the gaps in applying the ethical principles and standards. Ethical dilemmas arise from the inability to identify and decide what is right or wrong. Most ethical dilemmas involve a conflict between the needs of the part and those of the whole—the individual versus the organization or the organization versus society as a whole. These issues are exceedingly difficult to resolve and often represent dilemmas.

Examples of Ethical Lapses and Dilemmas

- The supervisor of a travel agency was aware that her agents and she could receive large bonuses for booking 100 or more clients each month with an auto rental firm, although clients typically wanted the rental agency selected on the basis of lowest cost.

- The executive in charge of a parts distribution facility told employees to tell phone customers that inventory was in stock even if it was not. Replenishing the item only took one to two days, no one was hurt by the delay, and the business was kept from competitors.

- The project manager for a consulting project wondered whether some facts should be left out of a report because the marketing executives paying for the report would look bad if the facts were reported.

- A North American manufacturer operating abroad was asked to make cash payments (a bribe) to government officials and was told it was consistent with local customs, despite being illegal in North America.

(ix) Failure to Recognize Cognitive Traps and Biases

Cognitive traps can be deeply embedded in an individual's own personality or in the organization's culture (i.e., unwilling to challenge the experts and senior managers, respect for time, discipline, courtesy, and social mannerisms). An individual's personality influences a wide variety of work-related attitudes and behaviors. Cognitive biases are human tendencies that can lead to human biases and that can act as judgment triggers (good or bad).

These traps and biases can negatively impact the minds of any problem solver or decision maker who is solving big problems and who is making big decisions. Board members, executives, and officers of a corporation solve big problems and make big decisions that result in high-risk, high-impact, and big outcomes. Failure to recognize cognitive traps and biases can result in flawed decisions (poor actions and negative outcomes), judgment errors (misjudgments), and reasoning errors (illogical reasons).

$$\text{Judgment Errors} + \text{Reasoning Errors} = \text{Negative Outcomes}$$

EXAMPLES OF COGNITIVE TRAPS

- Stereotyping (i.e., maintaining the status quo and uninviting creativity)

- Mirror imaging (i.e., leaders and followers think alike)

- Target-fixation trap (i.e., evidence is consistent with perceptions and no big-picture views)

- Analogy trap (i.e., not using the factual data and information, the inability to blend new facts with old facts, and denying conflicting facts)

- Projection trap (i.e., a recent behavior bias, resulting in halo errors and horn errors and seeing one's own traits in other people)

- Stovepiping traps (i.e., accepting only one source of information as official and ignoring other sources as unofficial; this is similar to silo or legacy traps.)

- Perceptual defense traps (i.e., protecting themselves and disregarding ideas, objects, or people that are threatening to them)

Examples of Cognitive Biases

- Confirmation bias (i.e., accepting information that supports preconceptions and ignoring other information)

- Framing bias (i.e., how information is presented regardless of its factual content)

- Anchoring bias (i.e., making decisions based on subjective value and not on objective value and sticking with an initial value)

- Group bias (i.e., the effect of groupthink, resulting in a substitution of an individual's decision with a group's decision)

- Hindsight bias (i.e., crediting or discrediting previous decisions as if they were based on new and current information)

- Bandwagon bias (i.e., going along with others, doing the same thing as others do, blindly following others, and blindly believing others)

- Overconfidence bias (i.e., resulting in suboptimal decisions, such as poorly defining problems, poorly articulating objectives, and poorly identifying all alternatives)

- Availability bias (i.e., working with limited information that is gathered and ignoring other available information; this can result in information gaps.)

Cognitive traps and biases are summarized next:

Cognitive Traps and Biases → Flawed Decisions, Judgment Errors, and Reasoning Errors → Negative Outcomes → High Risk

(x) Lack of Reasoning Skills in Board Members

Learning and practicing reasoning skills can either minimize or eliminate reasoning errors and their associated judgment errors because reasons behind any action or decision must be valid and sensible. Logical reasoning consists of: (1) understanding the nature of argument construction, premises, consequences, conditions, and rules; and (2) understanding the several types of reasoning, such as deductive, inductive, inference, practical, and theoretical reasoning.

Deductive reasoning moves from general principles to specific cases and is used by mathematicians and philosophers.

Inductive reasoning moves from specific cases to general principles and is used by scientists.

Inference reasoning moves from outputs to inputs and is used by detectives. It specifically applies to hypothesis testing where conclusions lead to premises.

Practical reasoning is the ability to decide how to act in a specific situation. A cognitive bias can occur when ignoring unproductive possibilities in favor of productive possibilities. This means that all possibilities and all alternatives must be considered before taking a specific action.

Theoretical reasoning, also called speculative reasoning, is the ability to decide what to do next in a specific situation.

(xi) Incomplete Proxy Materials

Shareholders of publicly held corporations and companies registered with the SEC under the Securities Exchange Act of 1933 are required to receive a proxy statement from the corporation prior to a shareholder meeting (annual or special meeting) of a company. The information contained in the proxy statement must be filed with the SEC before soliciting shareholders to vote on the election of directors and the approval of other corporate actions and initiatives. Solicitations, whether by management or shareholders, must disclose all important facts about the issues on which shareholders are asked to vote.

In recent years, shareholder and director activism has greatly increased to influence corporate management through the shareholder-proposal process in the areas of social investing, economic welfare, and environment-related policy concerns and matters. These new matters are in addition to the traditional matters, such as a company's products, services, customers, suppliers, and competitors. For example, investors, especially institutional investors, are asking companies to report on the portfolio risk of their new initiatives and investments in social, economic, and environment areas.

Shareholders vote the proxy statements, and the proxy materials represent the voice of shareholders. Proxy voting is indirect and remote voting, instead of a direct and in-person voting, used because thousands and millions of shareholders cannot attend the scheduled shareholder meetings. Proxy voting is a convenient way of allowing shareholders to express their opinions and decisions on matters of interest to both shareholders and corporations.

A frequent complaint from investors, especially institutional investors, about proxy statements is that they do not disclose fully and fairly. These investors rely on disclosures to make investment decisions, performance metrics used in executive compensation, pay-for-performance alignment, governance profile of the company, shareholder rights, management's anti-takeover measures, and risk management oversight. Proxy materials that lack these disclosures are incomplete.

It is hoped that a corporation's future proxy statements communicate board strategies, board member skills and competencies, and noteworthy accomplishments to shareholders. This type of proactive information can help strengthen the board's oversight function and at the same time lead to a positive image of the board in the eyes of shareholders and create better relations between shareholders and board members. In addition, the board chairperson should use proxy statements to compare the company's governance structures and mechanisms with best practices in the industry. The chairperson should provide explanations for any deviations from the best practices along with reasons for such deviations.

(xii) Summary of Corporate Governance Problems

- Separation of ownership from control, meaning owners cannot control their business or investment because corporate management (hired talent) exercises control of the business

- Unclear roles of the board of directors

- Lack of board's full independence

- Issues surrounding very high compensation (Major issues include CEO compensation—e.g., salaries, bonuses, incentives, stock options, and perks—and outside director compensation.)

- Poor consequences of merger and acquisition projects due to bad decisions made, prevalent takeover waves and ugly anti-takeover options, and poorly advised divestiture of assets

- Insider trading scandals

- Board member liability, such as a board member's personal reputation risk

- Lack of strong voice or strong teeth for board of directors who are afraid to ask hard questions due to their submissive behaviors

- Shareholder and director activism that is spreading fast to all companies regardless of their size and structure

5.2 Governance Models and Frameworks

Globally, several organizations and legal and regulatory bodies have published a variety of governance models and frameworks. In most instances, governance appears to be a process or system and is not static. What distinguishes the approach in the Internal Audit Standards is the specific emphasis on the board and its governance activities.

This section discusses six governance models and frameworks:

1. Corporate Governance Guidelines of the U.S. National Association of Corporate Directors (NACD)

2. U.K. Cadbury Governance Framework

3. Australian Governance Framework

4. Germany's Corporate Governance Framework

5. South Africa's Corporate Governance Framework

6. Comparison of global governance models

(a) U.S. NACD's Corporate Governance Guidelines

(i) Overview

The U.S.-based NACD issues corporate governance guidelines for its own board of directors with an overview of the structure of the board and how it functions with respect to its most important responsibilities in serving the association's members and chapters.[1]

Although the NACD is a not-for-profit educational organization, its corporate governance guidelines contain all the essential elements of good corporate governance guidelines. Hence, they should be taken as a model framework for publicly held companies. However, before adopting or adapting these guidelines, publicly held companies should interpret them in the context of their own applicable laws, articles of incorporation, bylaws, committee charters, and other governing legal documents.

(ii) Board's Mission and Composition

NACD advances exemplary board leadership—for directors, by directors. The NACD team provides the information and insights that board members rely upon to confidently navigate business challenges and enhance long-term shareowner value. NACD amplifies the collective voice of directors and positions as the **Voice of the Director.** To this end, NACD focuses on

---

[1] NACD's Corporate Governance Guidelines (2015) and Key Agreed Principles (2011), Washington, DC, www.nacdonline.org.

meeting the needs of board members and supports the corporate directors to perform more effectively and efficiently.

The bylaws of NACD authorize between five and seventeen directors, but the governance committee can change the size of the board. The mix of directors consists of one insider, the CEO. The rest are outside independent directors. The CEO may not serve as the chairman of the board, as these two positions are separate. The board elects the individual directors who have been recommended by the governance committee. All directors are required to have a reputation for integrity, leadership, and the ability to exercise sound judgment. NACD requires that the board as a whole should have competency in four areas of corporate governance, accounting and finance, leadership, and management. The board seeks men and women who have diverse backgrounds and who are recognized as leaders in their respective fields. The governance committee in conjunction with the board and the CEO reviews the skills and characteristics required of new board members. The governance committee oversees the orientation of all new directors with the CEO and senior management.

(iii) Board's Duties and Responsibilities

The board of directors oversees the management of NACD through the CEO and senior management by providing guidance and strategic oversight. The board's duties and responsibilities are set out in the board's bylaws, committee charters, and governance guidelines, and include being responsible for:

- The size and composition of the board

- Selection, compensation, and evaluation of the CEO

- Planning management succession

- Reviewing and approving strategic and business plans, including financial objectives and budgets

- Election of board members

- Evaluation of the board's performance through metrics and key performance indicators

- Oversight of the financial reporting processes and accounting practices

- Assessment of the adequacy and effectiveness of systems of internal controls regarding finance, accounting, and legal and regulatory compliance

- Assessment and management of major risks

- Development of policies, procedures, and programs to ensure that the activities of the board and all employees are in compliance with legal and ethical conduct standards

- Review of governance policies and practices

(iv) Key Agreed Principles

The NACD's ten Key Agreed Principles are grounded in the common interest of shareholders, boards, and corporate management teams in the corporate objective of long-term value creation (through ethical and legal means), the accountability of management to the board, and ultimately the accountability of the board to shareholders for long-term value creation. These key principles provide a framework for board leadership and oversight in the critical areas of strategic planning, risk oversight, executive compensation, and transparency. Each principle is listed and briefly outlined.

I. Board Responsibility for Governance

Governance structures and practices should be designed by the board to position the board to fulfill its duties effectively and efficiently. Major focus includes (1) setting the tone at the top, (2) fulfilling the board's fiduciary obligations, and (3) requiring board members to act with integrity, objectivity, judgment, diplomacy, and courage in addition to possessing the knowledge and experience in business acumen and governance principles.

II. Corporate Governance Transparency

Governance structures and practices should be transparent—and transparency is more important than strictly following any particular set of best-practice recommendations. A major focus is communicating with shareholders using proxy statements to describe the company's governance practices, comparing them with best practices, disclosing deviations from the best practices, and explaining the reasons for such deviations.

III. Director Competency and Commitment

Governance structures and practices should be designed to ensure the competency and commitment of directors. Major focus includes (1) fulfilling the board's responsibilities of due care, duty of loyalty, and good faith; and (2) determining the right mix of skill sets and experiences for the directors to face ever-increasing challenges.

IV. Board Accountability and Objectivity

Governance structures and practices should be designed to ensure the accountability of the board to shareholders and the objectivity of board decisions. Major focus includes:

1. Accountability for oversight function

2. Objective in mind and in actions

3. Separation between the board's role and corporate management's role

4. No relationship with the company, such as family and friends

5. Conducting regular executive sessions

    a. Between and among the board members without the CEO

    b. Between the board and the CEO without senior management

    c. Between the board and senior management without the CEO

V. Independent Board Leadership

Governance structures and practices should be designed to promote some form of leadership for the board distinct from management. Major focus includes (1) assigning someone to lead the board and have a job title such as lead director, presiding director, or chairperson and (2) not allowing the CEO to serve as the board's chairperson.

VI. Integrity, Ethics, and Responsibility

Governance structures and practices should be designed to promote a corporate culture of integrity, ethics, and corporate social responsibility. Major focus includes: (1) understanding the meaning of "desired culture," "agreed culture," and "actual culture"; (2) establishing the tone of the corporate culture; and (3) conducting cultural audits and ethics audits.

VII. Attention to Information, Agenda, and Strategy

Governance structures and practices should be designed to support the board in determining its own priorities, resultant agenda, and information needs and to assist the board in focusing on strategy and its associated risks. Major focus includes: (1) establishing corporate priorities, board's priorities, and management's priorities and aligning them as one priority; (2) performing corporate strengths, weaknesses, opportunities, and threats (SWOT) analysis; and (3) establishing and measuring benchmarks for success.

VIII. Protection against Board Entrenchment

Governance structures and practices should encourage the board to refresh itself. Major focus includes: (1) establishing age limits and term limits for directors; (2) identifying underperforming and overperforming directors; and (3) establishing rules for renominating directors, especially for underperforming directors.

IX. Shareholder Input in Director Selection

Governance structures and practices should encourage meaningful shareholder involvement in the selection of directors. Major focus includes: (1) knowing the difference between contested elections and uncontested elections; and (2) adopting a majority voting process after considering the provisions in the articles of incorporation, bylaws, and state laws. In an uncontested election, a candidate who did not get a majority of the votes is required to resign. In contested elections, directors are elected by plurality voting.

X. Shareholder Communications

Governance structures and practices should be designed to encourage communication with shareholders. Major focus includes: (1) understanding various communication channels between shareholders and the company, including proxy statements, annual meetings, annual reports, special meetings, and virtual meetings; and (2) understanding various modes of meetings, such as in person, regular mail, electronic mail, and virtual mail. A major concern of shareholders is executive compensation. Minor concerns could include environmental, economic, social, and governance matters and political campaign donations.

(v) Board's Legal and Ethical Conduct

The board is responsible for establishing policies and programs to ensure that NACD activities are conducted in a legal and ethical manner. Topics such as committee roles, conflict of interest, code of ethics, whistleblower protection policy, and record retention and document destruction policy are discussed in this section.

(A) Committee Roles. The audit and finance committee and the governance committee have shared responsibility with regard to reviewing and monitoring compliance with laws, regulations, and NACD policies. For example, the audit and finance committee assist the board in fulfilling its oversight responsibility relating to finance, accounting, and legal and regulatory compliance matters.

Governance committee	Recommends for board approval a conflict-of-interest policy and a code of ethics
Audit and finance committee	Recommends for board approval a whistleblower protection policy and a record retention and document destruction policy

(B) Conflict of Interest. All directors must comply with the conflict-of-interest policy. It is the responsibility of each director to advise the chair of the board and the governance committee of any affiliation, relationship, or transaction that may create a conflict of interest with NACD. The board takes appropriate steps to identify any potential conflict-of-interest issues and to ensure that all directors voting on an issue are disinterested with respect to that issue.

(C) Code of Ethics. The board is responsible for overseeing corporate ethics. Each director and all employees are expected to adhere to the highest ethical standards. All directors are expected to comply with the NACD's Code of Ethics. The Code of Ethics is embodied in the following standards, requiring the commitment of directors, officers, employees, and chapter leaders to:

- Honesty, integrity, and transparency
- Acting responsibly
- Maintaining the public trust through full accountability
- Complying with the spirit and the letter of all applicable laws, regulations, and rules
- Avoiding conflict of interest, whether actual or apparent
- Responsible stewardship of resources
- Treating directors, officers, employees, and others with respect and fairness
- Reporting violations of this Code of Ethics to the designated third party and/or the chair of the audit and finance committee

(D) Whistleblower Protection Policy. All directors, officers, and employees are responsible for complying with the NACD's Whistleblower Protection Policy and to report violations and suspected violations in accordance with the policy. If anyone reports any activity believed to be illegal or improper, all the reporters will be protected against retaliatory actions and kept confidential during investigation. A company maintains a confidential hotline phone number for people to report.

(E) Record Retention and Document Destruction Policy. It is the policy of NACD to retain records, including paper records, electronic files, and voicemails, for the period of their immediate or current use, unless longer retention is necessary for historical reference or to comply with contractual or legal requirements. It is also the policy of NACD to not knowingly destroy a document if the destruction would result in a violation of the Sarbanes-Oxley Act of 2002. A formal, written record retention and document destruction policy will be distributed to all directors and employees.

(b) U.K. Cadbury Governance Framework

The Cadbury Report of the Committee on the Financial Aspects of Corporate Governance issued in December 1992 consists of internal controls, fraud, internal audit, external audit, financial reporting practices, audit committees, shareholders, corporate governance, the board of directors, and the code of best practice.

Regarding internal controls, the report says that directors should maintain a system of internal control over the financial management of the company, including procedures designed to minimize the risk of fraud. The directors should make a statement in the report and accounts on the effectiveness of their system of internal control, and the auditors should report thereon.

Regarding fraud, the report says that prime responsibility for the prevention and detection of fraud and other illegal acts is that of the board, as part of its fiduciary responsibility for protecting company assets. The auditor's responsibility is to properly plan, perform, and evaluate audit work so as to have a reasonable expectation of detecting material misstatements in the financial statements.

Regarding the internal audit, the report states that the function of the internal auditors is complementary to, but different from, that of the external (outside) auditors. The committee regards the internal audit as good practice for companies to establish internal audit function to undertake regular monitoring of key controls and procedures. Such regular monitoring is an integral part of a company's system of internal control and helps to ensure its effectiveness. An internal audit function is well placed to undertake investigations on behalf of the audit committee and to follow up any suspicion of fraud. It is essential that heads of internal audit should have unrestricted access to the chairman of the audit committee in order to ensure the independence of their position.

Regarding the external audit, the report says that an essential first step is to be clear about the respective responsibilities of directors and external auditors for preparing and reporting on the financial statements of companies, in order to begin to narrow the expectations gap. This gap is due to lack of understanding of the nature and extent of the external auditors' role. The gap is the difference between what audits do achieve and what it is thought they achieve or should achieve. The expectations gap is damaging not only because it reflects unrealistic expectations of audits but also because it has led various interested parties to be disenchanted with the value of audits.

The external auditors' role is to report whether the financial statements give a true and fair view, and the audit is designed to provide a reasonable assurance that the financial statements are free of material misstatements. The auditors' role is not (to cite a few of the misunderstandings) to prepare the financial statements, or to provide absolute assurance that the figures in the financial statements are correct, or to provide a guarantee that the company will continue to exist.

(c) Australian Governance Framework

The Australian Securities Exchange Corporate Governance Council defines governance as "the system by which companies are directed and managed. It influences how the objectives of the company are set and achieved, how risk is monitored and assessed, and how performance is optimized."

(d) Germany's Corporate Governance Framework

In 1998, the German government proposed changes for the reform of corporate governance. The KonTrag model in Germany affects control and transparency in business. Specifically, it impacts the board of directors, supervisory board, corporate capitalization principles, authorization of no-par-value shares, small nonlisted stock corporations, banks investing in industrial companies, and the acceptance of internationally recognized accounting standards, such as U.S. GAAP.

(e) South Africa's Corporate Governance Framework

The Institute of Directors in South Africa established the King Committee on Corporate Governance, which produced the King Report in 1994. The committee has developed a Code of Corporate Practices and Conduct, and compliance with the code is a requirement to be listed in the Johannesburg Securities Exchange in South Africa.

(f) Comparison of Global Governance Models

(i) Introduction to Global Governance

The corporate governance structure of joint stock corporations in a given country is determined by factors such as (1) the legal and regulatory framework outlining the rights and responsibilities of all parties involved in corporate governance, (2) the de facto realities of the corporate environment in the country, and (3) each corporation's articles of association or articles of incorporation. While corporate governance provisions may differ from corporation to corporation, many de facto and de jure factors affect corporations in a similar way. Therefore, it is possible to outline a model of corporate governance in a given country. De facto factors are real and factual things, which are based on practices, whereas de jure factors are official and right things, which are based on laws.[2]

Due to its dynamic process, the corporate governance structure in each country should be developed based on the response to country-specific factors and conditions. In each country, the corporate governance structure has seven characteristics or constituent elements, which distinguish it from structures in other countries:

1. Key players in the corporate environment

2. Share ownership pattern in the given country

3. Composition of the board of directors or boards in the German model

4. Regulatory framework

5. Disclosure requirements for publicly listed stock corporations

6. Corporate actions requiring shareholder approval

7. Interaction among key players

(h) Three Models of Corporate Governance

To date, researchers have identified three models of corporate governance in developed capital markets: the Anglo-U.S. model, the Japanese model, and the German model.

(i) Anglo-U.S. Model of Corporate Governance

The Anglo-U.S. model mostly governs corporations in the United Kingdom, the United States, Australia, Canada, and New Zealand. The Anglo-U.S. model is characterized by:

- Share ownership of individual, and increasingly institutional, investors not affiliated with the corporation (known as outside shareholders or outsiders)

- A well-developed legal framework defining the rights and responsibilities of three key players: management, directors, and shareholders

- A comparatively uncomplicated procedure for interaction between shareholders and corporations

Equity financing is a common method of raising capital for corporations in the United Kingdom and the United States. It is not surprising, therefore, that the United States is the largest capital market in the world and that the London Stock Exchange is the third largest stock exchange in

---

[2] EWMI/PFS Program, Lecturers on Corporate Governance, *Three Models of Corporate Governance* (December 2005), www.ewmi.org.

the world in terms of market capitalization after the New York Stock Exchange and Tokyo Stock Exchange.

There is a causal relationship between the importance of equity financing with stocks and bonds, the size of the capital market, and the development of a corporate governance system. The United States is both the world's largest capital market and the home of the world's most-developed governance system of proxy voting and shareholder activism by institutional investors. Note that institutional investors also play an important role in both the capital market and corporate governance in the United Kingdom.

In the United States, anti-monopoly legislation prohibits one bank from providing a multiplicity of services. Instead, commercial banks are used for loans, investment banks are used for equity, and consulting firms are used for proxy voting.

The composition of the board of directors includes both insiders (i.e., executive directors) and outsiders (nonexecutive directors or independent directors). An insider is a person who is either employed by the corporation (e.g., executive, manager, or employee) or has significant personal or business relationships with corporate management. An outsider is a person or institution that has no direct relationship with the corporation or corporate management.

(ii) Japanese Model of Corporate Governance

The Japanese model is characterized by:

- A high level of stock ownership by affiliated banks and companies

- A banking system characterized by strong, long-term links between bank and corporation

- A legal, public policy and industrial policy framework designed to support and promote *keiretsu* (industrial groups linked by trading relationships as well as cross-shareholdings of debt and equity)

- Boards of directors composed almost solely of insiders, and a comparatively low (in some corporations, nonexistent) level of input of outside shareholders, caused and exacerbated by complicated procedures for exercising shareholders' votes

Equity financing is important for Japanese corporations. However, insiders and their affiliates are the major shareholders in most Japanese corporations. Consequently, they play a major role in individual corporations and in the system as a whole. Conversely, the interests of outside shareholder are marginal.

(i) German Model of Corporate Governance

The German model governs German and Austrian corporations. Some elements of this model also apply in the Netherlands and Scandinavia. Furthermore, some corporations in Europe and Belgium have introduced some elements of the German model.

The German corporate governance model differs significantly from both the Anglo-U.S. model and the Japanese model, although some of its elements resemble the Japanese model.

Banks hold long-term stakes in German corporations, and, as in Japan, bank representatives are elected to German boards. However, this representation is constant, unlike the situation in Japan, where bank representatives are elected to a corporate board only in times of financial distress. Germany's three largest universal banks (i.e., banks that provide a multiplicity of services) play a major role, and public-sector banks are also key shareholders in some parts of the country.

Three unique elements of the German model distinguish it from the other models: board composition, shareholders' rights, and foreign ownership.

(i) Board Composition

Two different boards with separate members are in use. German corporations have a two-tiered board structure consisting of a management board (composed entirely of inside executives) and a supervisory board (composed of labor/employee representatives and shareholder representatives). The two boards are completely distinct; no one may serve simultaneously on a corporation's management board and supervisory board. The size of the supervisory board is set by law and cannot be changed by shareholders.

(ii) Shareholders' Rights

Voting rights restrictions are legal; these limit a shareholder to voting a certain percentage of the corporation's total share capital, regardless of share ownership position. Minority shareholders are especially subjected to voting rights restrictions.

Most German corporations have traditionally preferred bank financing (debt financing) over equity financing. As a result, German stock market capitalization is small in relation to the size of the German economy. Furthermore, the level of individual stock ownership in Germany is low, reflecting the citizen's conservative investment strategy. It is not surprising, therefore, that the corporate governance structure is geared toward preserving relationships between the key players: banks and corporations.

The percentage of foreign ownership of German equity is slowly becoming a significant factor due to increased number of foreign investors from inside and outside of the European Union and the globalization of capital markets. For example, when Daimler-Benz AG decided to list its shares on the New York Stock Exchange in 1993, it was forced to adopt U.S. GAAP. GAAP provides much greater financial transparency than the German accounting standards. Specifically, Daimler-Benz AG was forced to account for huge losses that it could have hidden under the German accounting rules.

Exhibit 5.1 highlights the nature and type of key players in the corporate environment in the Anglo-U.S. model, the Japanese model, and the German model of corporate governance.

EXHIBIT 5.1 Key Players in the Various Corporate Models

Anglo-U.S. Model	Japanese Model	German Model
Management, directors, shareholders (mostly institutional investors), government agencies, stock exchanges, self-regulatory organizations, and consulting firms, where the latter advises on proxy voting.	A main bank and an affiliated company with financial or industrial network, called *keiretsu*.	Banks have a major role; corporate shareholders have a minor role.

Anglo-U.S. Model	Japanese Model	German Model
Three key players: management, directors, and shareholders.	The main bank is a major shareholder in corporations and provides loans and issues bonds and equities.	Banks play multifaceted roles as shareholders, lenders, and issuers of both equity and debt.
Banks and corporations are not key institutional investors.		Banks also act as depository banks (custodian banks) and voting agents.
Boards of directors consist of both insiders and outsiders.	The main bank also provides settlement accounts and related consulting services.	The mandatory inclusion of labor and employee representatives on the supervisory board is unique.
Equity financing is a common method of raising capital.	Four key players: main bank, affiliated company, management, and government.	Two key players: banks and corporate shareholders.
	Boards of directors consist mostly of insiders.	Boards of directors consist of both insiders and outsiders.
	Equity financing is a common method of raising capital.	Debt financing is preferred over the equity financing to raise capital.

(j) Global Practices in Corporate Governance

Corporate governance practices differ considerably around the globe, although there are some common practices. Regardless, most of the problems are rooted in poor governance policies and practices; fraudulent accounting practices; and executives' excessive and abusive behavior. Specific issues deal with ownership, board composition, influence, power, and control, as described next.

- Ownership is heavily dispersed in the United States but is much more concentrated in Canada, Germany, Japan, and China. High levels of influence and control over corporate affairs are associated with high concentrations of ownership.

- National and state governments own major stakes of public companies in Germany, Italy, Japan, and China.

- French and German companies have different types of owners from those found in the United States and United Kingdom. In France, nonfinancial corporations and state governments are the largest shareholders. In Germany, both banks and nonfinancial corporations are owners. In addition, German banks own both debt and equity in the same corporation; they have direct voting power and proxy voting positions from bank depositors.

- Most public firm shares in China are controlled by state-owned or state-controlled shareholders; the remaining trading shares are owned by a combination of individual and institutional investors.

- In Brazil, China, France, and Russia, the government owns the largest companies in size.

- Owners and workers sit on boards in France, Germany, Japan, and China; outsiders and managers sit on boards in U.S., U.K., and Canadian companies.

- CEOs have considerable power over the selection of board members in many U.S. corporations as well as in Canada and the United Kingdom. In France and Germany, owners nominate and elect the board members.

- In Japan, both supplier and customer organizations acquire financial interests and ownership in Japanese corporations and are represented on the corporate board (*keiretsu*).

(k) Improving Corporate Governance

Efforts to improve corporate governance may be classified into two major categories:

1. Changes could be made in the composition, structure, and functioning of boards of directors.

2. Shareholders—on their own initiative or on the initiative of management or the board—could assume a more active role in governance.

Specifically, improving corporate governance requires increased:

- Change in the composition of the directors between inside directors (one is preferred) and outside directors (more are preferred)

- Role of shareholders with their initiatives to companies

- Role of company initiatives to shareholders

- Obligation of companies to fairly and fully disclose vital information to shareholders through proxy statements, management's discussion and analysis, compensation discussion and analysis, and other reporting avenues

In summary, improving corporate governance requires (1) changes in boards of directors to include more outside directors and (2) increased role of shareholders in the governance process.

5.3 Roles of the Board of Directors

The roles and responsibilities of board of directors of a company are varied and complex due to the board's unique position at the top of a company in guiding the company's direction. Some boards excel in their roles while most do not, due to the composition and qualifications of board members.

These complex roles can be subdivided into several roles:

- Understanding oversight function

- Understanding fiduciary duties

- Understanding legal and ethical obligations (e.g., legal entity, basic legal principles, such as due process, due care, duty of care, due diligence, duty of loyalty, duty of obedience; and basic ethical principles, such as the Golden Rule, means–ends cycle, might-equals-right principle, professional principle, goal congruence principle, and prudent person concept)

- Managing corporate affairs

- Managing access to information

- Handling legal liabilities and legal actions
- Acquiring knowledge about core functions of the businesses they represent

At the end of this section, we present guidelines from the Business Roundtable on the Key Responsibilities of the Board of Directors.

(a) Oversight Function

The shareholders of a corporation elect the board of directors to govern the company. The board, in turn, hires managers, executives, and officers to run the day-to-day business. The board represents the highest level in the management hierarchy of a company. The board governs the corporation to ensure that all employees perform their job duties in a legal, ethical, and controlled manner to achieve the organization's mission and vision.

(b) Fiduciary Duties

The board has three fiduciary duties: (1) duty of care (i.e., complying with the business judgment rule), (2) no self-dealing (i.e., fair to the company's business), and (3) corporate opportunities (i.e., exploring and identifying potential candidate companies for mergers, acquisitions, and divestitures).

(i) Duty of Care

The business judgment rule is a legal presumption that the directors and officers of a corporation have exercised duty of care by acting on an informed basis, in good faith, and in the honest belief that their actions are in the best interests of the corporation. Unless a plaintiff can give persuasive evidence against at least one of the criteria, corporate directors and officers are insulated from liability for breach of the duty of care.

(ii) No Self-Dealing

Regarding self-dealing, corporate directors and officers may pursue business transactions that benefit themselves as long as they can prove the transaction, although self-interested, was nevertheless intrinsically "fair" to the corporation (i.e., the transaction is initiated and completed at an arm's-length distance). A plaintiff must start by alleging the director or officer stood to gain a material economic benefit. The burden then shifts to the defendant to show the fairness of the transaction. The court considers both the terms and the process for the bargain (i.e., both a fair price and fair dealing). However, if the director shows that full disclosure was made to disinterested directors or disinterested shareholders, then the burden remains on the plaintiff.

(iii) Corporate Opportunities

As a part of fiduciary duties, it is acceptable for directors to inform one another of corporate opportunities that arise. Examples of these opportunities include identifying candidates for mergers, acquisitions, and divestitures; business expansions and contractions; introducing new products, new suppliers, new customers, new contractors, new technologies, and new business ventures; and bringing awareness of new laws and regulations. The scope and nature of divestitures include investment spin-offs, sell-offs, and close-offs and may involve write-offs.

(c) Legal and Ethical Obligations

The board of an organization is placed in a critical position with an oversight role for all of its shareholders and stakeholders. Hence, its members need to provide a delicate balance between basic legal principles and ethical principles. Any imbalance in these principles can lead to legal liabilities to the board and can damage reputation of the organization.

(i) Basic Legal Principles

Examples of basic legal principles applicable to the board include due process, due care, duty of care, due diligence, duty of loyalty, duty of obedience, and due regard, which are discussed next.

(A) Due Process.   Due process means following rules and principles so that an individual is treated fairly and uniformly at all times with basic rights protected. It also means fair and equitable treatment to all concerned parties so that no person is deprived of life, liberty, or property without due process of the law, which is the right to notice and a hearing. Due process mainly applies to governmental policy. Due process requires due care and due diligence.

(B) Due Care.   Due care means reasonable care that promotes the common good. It involves maintaining minimal and customary practices. Due care implies reasonable care and competence, not infallibility or extraordinary performance. Corporate directors and officers of a corporation must perform their duties in good faith and in a nonnegligent manner. Doing this requires due care and due diligence principles, which are part of due process. The concepts of due care and due diligence are similar to the prudent person or reasonable person concept.

> **Examples of Due Care**
>
> All employees must be trained in their jobs to show that a standard of due care has been taken in developing employees.
>
> Requiring acknowledgment of signed statements of conflict-of-interest and code of ethics documents from all employees ensures that employees have read and understood the documents.

(C) Duty of Care.   Duty of care is the legal obligation that each person has to others not to cause any unreasonable harm or risk of harm resulting from careless acts. A breach of the duty of care is gross negligence, which means reckless behavior with willful intent to harm people and damage property. An example of duty of care is that corporate directors and officers must use due care and due diligence when acting on behalf of a corporation.

(D) Due Diligence.   Due diligence requires organizations to develop and implement an effective system of controls, policies, and procedures to prevent and detect violation of policies and laws. In other words, due diligence is the care that a reasonable person exercises under the circumstances to avoid harm to other persons or to their property. Due diligence is another way of saying due care. Often a due diligence review is conducted when one company acquires or merges with another firm. Another concept related to due care is good faith, which means showing honesty in fact and honesty in intent. The concepts of due care and due diligence are similar to the prudent person concept.

> ### Examples of Due Care
>
> A business insurance policy is needed to protect physical assets against theft, loss, or damage.
>
> Good housekeeping in a computer data center is needed to prevent accidents, damages, and disasters in the center.

(E) Duty of Loyalty. Duty of loyalty is expected of board of directors and officers of a corporation; they have a duty not to act adversely to the interests of the corporation and to subordinate their personal interests to those of the corporation and its shareholders. These adverse actions include self-dealing, taking personal advantage of a corporate opportunity, and competing with the corporation, thus creating conflict-of-interest situations. Under the duty of loyalty, a corporation can sue a director or an officer to recover the secret profit made on a business transaction.

(F) Duty of Obedience. Duty of obedience is expected of officers and directors of a corporation to act within the authority conferred on them by state corporation statutes, articles of incorporation, corporate bylaws, and resolutions adopted by the board of directors.

(G) Due Regard. Due regard is a legal concept meaning treating all parties with equal interest and respect and with no bias. It requires an objective analysis based on facts and valid evidence. For example, due regard is required from a driver operating a moving machine and motor vehicles to protect people from accidents while keeping the safety and security of people around.

> ### SUMMARY OF LEGAL PRINCIPLES EXPECTED OF CORPORATE DIRECTOR AND OFFICERS
>
> - Due process (e.g., allowing a reasonable amount of time for one party to prepare and respond to another party's questions and requests. This also assumes that everyone will have a day in the court to represent oneself.)
> - Due care (e.g., reasonable care, good faith, be a prudent person, no harm, nor risk, and no breach of duty)
> - Duty of care (e.g., reckless behavior due to gross negligence)
> - Due diligence (e.g., honesty in fact and honesty in intent)
> - Duty of loyalty (e.g., no self-dealing, no stealing of company opportunities, no competition with the company, and no making of secret profits)
> - Duty of obedience (e.g., comply with state corporation statutes, articles of incorporation, and corporate bylaws)
> - Due regard (e.g., treating all parties with equal interest and respect and with no bias)

(ii) Basic Ethical Principles

The basic ethical principles applicable to the board of directors include the Golden Rule, the means–ends cycle, the might-equals-right principle, the professional principle, the goal congruence principle, and the prudent person concept, which are discussed next.

(A) Golden Rule. The Golden Rule means not knowingly doing harm to others and damaging others' property.

(B) Means–Ends Cycle. According to the means–end cycle, when ends are of overriding importance, unscrupulous means may be used to reach the ends.

(C) Might-Equals-Right Principle. According to the might-equals-right principle, justice is defined as the interest of the stronger, meaning that stronger people have an upper hand over weaker people.

(D) Professional Principle. According to the professional principle, a true professional will do things in such a way that he or she can explain them before a committee of peer professionals. Also, the law and the society expect higher levels of standards for professionals (e.g., doctors, teachers, nurses, engineers, actuaries, architects, accountants, and lawyers) than for nonprofessionals such as office clerks and administrative staff.

(E) Goal Congruence Principle. According to the goal congruence principle, actions, wills, and needs of employees should be subordinated to the greater good of the organization they work for. An employee should ask whether his or her goals are consistent with the organization's goals. This principle is similar to the utilitarian ethic (the greatest good should be done for the greatest number) and the organization ethic (employees do things for the good of the organization).

(F) Prudent Person Concept. The prudent person, who is not infallible or perfect, has the ability to govern and discipline him- or herself by the use of reason, does not neglect duty, and applies knowledge, skills, and sound judgment in the use of organization's resources. The prudent person concept is related to the goal congruence principle.

(G) Business Judgment Rule. This rule was created in a court of law when shareholders filed lawsuits against the directors and officers (D&Os) of a company challenging the board's actions/inactions and wrong/bad decisions.

The rule states that the board will not be liable for member actions or inactions as long as: they acted in a good faith and with good intent keeping the best interests of the company in mind; no self-dealing was involved; no insider information was misused; no fraud was committed; and no conflict-of-interest situation existed.

This judge-driven rule states that that courts will not second-guess a board's actions and inactions. The rule accepts that judgmental mistakes and errors are common and normal human conditions and concludes that the board should not be penalized in courts for members' honest and judgmental mistakes and errors. This rule allows a reasonable doubt to occur in the minds of managers or executives when taking a specific action or decision. The doubt is whether the judgment is sound or not.

The rule presumes that the D&Os of a corporation have exercised due care by acting on an informed basis, in good faith, and in the honest belief that their actions are in the best interests of the corporation. Unless a plaintiff can give persuasive evidence against at least one of the criteria, corporate D&Os are insulated from liability for breach of the duty of care.

(d) Corporate Affairs

The corporate affairs or public relations (PR) function of a company is the first point of contact or window to the outside world. By definition, the PR function handles major issues or problems facing the company, not day-to-day minor issues or problems. Usually, a PR spokesperson handles these topics:

- Crisis and issues management
- Social media platforms
- Negative press

- Natural disasters
- Cybersecurity

(i) Crisis and Issues Management

Crisis and issues management focuses on major issues, such as:

- When the CEO of a company gives testimonials at congressional hearings regarding corporate management's wrongdoings
- When company insiders share information with outsiders for personal gain, favor, or revenge
- When banks open illegal charge accounts and loan accounts without customers' approvals so bank management can receive unethical bonuses and promotions
- When senior management is involved in stock market trading scandals using insider information
- When a company pays less money to female employees compared to male employees doing the same work
- When employees at all levels and senior management at the high level are involved in workplace sexual harassment cases

(ii) Social Media Platform

Backlash from a social media platform (e.g., Facebook and Twitter) can be damaging to a company's reputation when customers post their negative comments about its products, services, employees, and management's policies and procedures and practices. A company needs to manage social media content and comments in a timely and proper manner and respond to customers' posts.

(iii) Negative Press

Negative press can be damaging to a company's reputation, which can decrease sales, revenue, profits, and stock market share price. Topics that can appear in the press include:

- Accidents and deaths resulting in product recalls
- Bad acquisitions and mergers that did not fit well
- Mishandling of customers
- Mistreatment of suppliers and vendors
- Illegal and unethical manipulation of software in motor vehicles to reduce the emission of pollution into air

(iv) Natural Disasters

Natural disasters, such as fires, floods, storms, hurricanes, and earthquakes, can displace employee workers and can damage or destroy a company's manufacturing plants, warehouses, and distribution center facilities, which can impede production, sales, and revenues. Another negative side effect of natural disasters is the inability of employees to go to work due to lack of transportation and housing.

(v) Cybersecurity

Cybersecurity issues include website crashes, computer system outages, customers' data breaches by hackers, and ransomware payments to hackers either through bitcoins or direct deposits into bank accounts. Company executives have been fired due to their inability to control cybercrime.

(vi) Internal and External Affairs Doctrine

It is hoped that the PR spokesperson understands the internal and external affairs doctrines to discharge duties properly and completely. Business affairs can be divided into internal affairs and external affairs of a business organization. Internal affairs doctrines and external affairs doctrines exist to handle different situations. In the United States, each state has the power to incorporate business organizations based on its laws, called lex incorporations. Each state's incorporation laws are different; some are flexible and some are not. Hence, states compete to attract business corporations to register in them. For example, the states of Delaware and Nevada became corporate havens or tax havens due to their flexibility in dealing with internal and external affairs of a corporation, and the court system fully approves these state laws and the lex incorporations. Some states extend the internal affairs doctrine internationally, which has permitted offshore (outside the U.S.) financial centers or other businesses.

(A) Internal Affairs Doctrine. The internal affairs doctrine states that the internal affairs of a corporation will be governed by the corporate statutes and case laws of the state in which the organization is incorporated (called lex incorporations). The scope of internal affairs addressing any issues and conflicting matters between shareholders and management (e.g., executives, officers, and directors) of a corporation includes:

- Voting rights of shareholders

- Distribution of dividends

- Distribution of company property

- Fiduciary obligations of management

(B) External Affairs Doctrine. The law views a corporation's external affairs differently from its internal affairs. External affairs are governed by the state in which the corporation is doing business. Examples of issues and matters include:

- Labor union matters

- Employment-related matters

- Tax-related issues and disputes

Within the external affairs doctrine, there are other matters governed by the state of incorporation and by the state in which the transaction takes place. On the top of this, federal laws may come into force when investment securities (e.g., SEC Commission and Department of Justice) and mergers, acquisitions, and divestitures (e.g., Federal Trade Commission or Federal Communications Commission) are involved. Examples of external affairs matters include:

- Contracts with third parties

- Mergers, acquisitions, and divestitures

- Sales of investment securities to third parties

(e) Access to Information

Similar to internal auditors, board members should have unlimited and unrestricted access to people, facilities, assets, and information to do their job. The type and nature of information needed is endless; major examples include:

- Financial performance results

- Nonfinancial performance results

- Regulatory and legal issues, such as lawsuits filed against a company

- Performance results on the key executives and senior management (e.g., the CEO, president, other C-level executives, vice presidents, and general managers).

In addition, information access types could be direct and formal or indirect and informal.

The best way to assess whether the board's access to information is proper is to understand how effective directors and ineffective directors go about getting that information.

- Effective board members invite direct, formal, and timely feedback from all interested parties, both inside and outside of the company.

- Ineffective board members invite indirect, informal, and untimely feedback from all interested parties, both inside and outside of the company.

- Effective board members receive the required information voluntarily and regularly.

- Ineffective board members seek out information they need on their own; it is not given to them voluntarily and regularly.

(f) Legal Liabilities and Legal Actions

Understanding legal liabilities and handling proper legal actions are some of the most important job duties and responsibilities of a board.

(i) Legal Liabilities

A company's executives or board members are primary and frequent targets for lawsuits initiated by company insiders and outsiders due to their deep pockets. When a new lawsuit is filed against a company and its directors and officers, the company's stock market price per share usually decreases, reflecting a negative opinion.

In addition to shareholders filing lawsuits against a company, many nonshareholders file lawsuits for various reasons; these non-shareholders include:

- Former and current employees

- Customers

- Suppliers

- Consultants

- Contractors

- Outsourced vendors

- Joint venture business partners
- Labor unions
- Competitors
- Tax authorities (federal and state)
- Regulators (e.g., SEC, Federal Trade Commission, Federal Communications Commission, and Department of Justice)
- Corporate lobbyists, activists, and watchdogs
- Third parties, such as insurance companies

Governmental agencies overseeing employee discrimination claims can also file lawsuits against a company.

During 1980s, not many individuals wanted board director positions. Concerned about increasing legal hassles emanating from stockholder, customer, and employee lawsuits, directors were quitting such positions or refusing to accept them in the first place. Although courts rarely hold directors personally liable in the hundreds of shareholder suits filed every year, there have been a few cases in which directors have been held personally and financially liable for their decisions.

The Private Securities Litigation Reform Act of 1995 made it more difficult for shareholders to bring class action lawsuits to federal courts. However, rather than stemming the tide of lawsuits, the act simply prompted shareholders to change their venue. Suits filed in federal courts decreased while suits filed in state courts increased. The Securities Litigation Uniform Standards Act of 1998 was designed to plug that loophole. The act says: "Any covered class action suit brought into any state courts shall be removable to the federal district courts for the district in which the action is pending."

(ii) Legal Actions

Sometimes, lower-level managers may take business-related actions with or without the explicit authority and power given to them by their upper-level managers. Examples of these actions could be dealing with outside contractors, suppliers, vendors, consultants, other businesses, and government authorities. A good example is actions between a purchasing manager and an employee in contracting with potential suppliers in purchasing materials, products, and services (i.e., a principal–agent relationship). The law views the validity of these actions differently, depending on whether these actions are *ultra vires* or *intra vires*.

- If the actions are taken without a proper authority, it is called *ultra vires* (i.e., beyond the power). These actions can be construed by law as invalid actions.

- If the actions are taken with a proper authority, it is called *intra vires* (i.e., within the power). These actions can be construed by law as valid actions.

(g) Core Business Knowledge

Manufacturing industry and service industry are the two major industries in any nation's economy, after excluding the agriculture industry. Three core functions in any business or industry are operations (i.e., manufacturing or service), marketing, and finance because they are the key functions that support a company's mission and vision and that generate revenues, incur costs, and make profits. Note that the nature and scope of core business functions within the manufacturing industry and service industry are different.

Core functions, especially operations, are defined differently based on the type of industry. For example, core business functions in the retail industry are defined as operations (i.e., procurement and merchandising), marketing, and finance. In the insurance industry, they are defined as operations (i.e., premiums [actuaries] and claims), marketing, and finance. In the manufacturing industry, core functions are defined as operations (i.e., production, supply chain, logistics, and inventory), marketing, and finance. In the service industry, core functions are defined as operations (i.e., planning and delivery), marketing, and finance.

The other two common functions of marketing and finance are the same regardless of the industry. Marketing includes product/brand management, marketing administration and communication, marketing research, advertising and promotion, service/brand marketing, marketing public relations, sales administration, and sales management. Finance includes accounting, such as financial, management, governmental accounting, and tax accounting; operating and capital budgets; debt and asset management; and periodic financial reporting.

Regardless of the industry, three common core business functions include: operations (i.e., manufacturing to produce goods or to provide services to customers); marketing to sell those goods and services; and (3) finance to invest money in those goods or services and to receive revenue and profits from making and selling those goods and services.

Support functions help the core functions to succeed and include human resources, information technology (IT), quality, legal, public relations, and other functions.

A primary difference between ineffective boards and effective boards is the amount and possession of core business knowledge among the board members about the company they represent in order to do their job properly and efficiently. This means that the higher the amount of core business knowledge members possess, the higher their contribution to the company, and the greater their effectiveness.

Knowledge Level → Contribution Level → Effectiveness Level

In other words, effective board members possess a complete and thorough knowledge (core competencies) about the company they represent; ineffective board members do not possess such knowledge. Board members possessing the right type of skills and competencies can become effective directors. Otherwise, skills and competency gaps can exist, resulting in an ineffective and inefficient board.

Board members can acquire the core business knowledge about their company or the industry they represent in these ways, among others:

- Enrolling in internal and external training and educational programs

- Attending core industry and cross-industry seminars, conferences, and forums

- Earning professional certificates in business topics from reputable organizations

- Attending executive training and developmental programs from reputable business schools

- Working for a series of companies in the same industry (Working for the same company for many years would not expand the member's core knowledge due to the limits of one-company-only experience.)

- Enrolling in continuing education programs, which can lead to a continuous board improvement path

- Starting a self-learning journey with peer networking, self-educating, self-teaching, or self-improving

According to an NACD report, only 7.5% of board time is spent on director education (i.e., 18.5 hours on director education out of a total of 245.1 hours spent on all board-related services in a year).[3] More time and attention is needed to improve core business knowledge of board members through continuing education programs.

Key Responsibilities of the Board of Directors

An effective system of corporate governance provides the framework within which the board and management address their key responsibilities.

(Source: Business Roundtable, Principles of Corporate Governance, August 2016, Washington, DC. www.brt.org)

A corporation's business is managed under the board's oversight. The board also has direct responsibility for certain key matters, including the relationship with the outside auditor and executive compensation. The board's oversight function encompasses a number of responsibilities, including:

1. **Selecting the CEO.** The board selects and oversees the performance of the company's CEO and oversees the CEO succession planning process.

2. **Setting the "tone at the top."** The board should set a "tone at the top" that demonstrates the company's commitment to integrity and legal compliance. This tone lays the groundwork for a corporate culture that is communicated to personnel at all levels of the organization.

3. **Approving corporate strategy and monitoring the implementation of strategic plans.** The board should have meaningful input into the company's long-term strategy from development through execution, should approve the company's strategic plans, and should regularly evaluate implementation of the plans that are designed to create long-term value. The board should understand the risks inherent in the company's strategic plans and how those risks are being managed.

4. **Setting the company's risk appetite, reviewing and understanding the major risks, and overseeing the risk management processes.** The board oversees the process for identifying and managing the significant risks facing the company. The board and senior management should agree on the company's risk appetite, and the board should be comfortable that the strategic plans are consistent with it. The board should establish a structure for overseeing risk, delegating responsibility to committees, and overseeing the designation of senior management responsible for risk management.

5. **Focusing on the integrity and clarity of the company's financial reporting and other disclosures about corporate performance.** The board should be satisfied that the company's financial statements accurately present its financial condition and results of operations, that other disclosures about the company's performance convey meaningful information about past results as well as future plans, and that the company's internal controls and procedures have been designed to detect and deter fraudulent activity.

---

[3] National Association of Corporate Directors report, October 2017 (www.nacdonline.org).

6. **Allocating capital.** The board should have meaningful input and decision-making authority over the company's capital allocation process and strategy to find the right balance between short-term and long-term economic returns for its shareholders.

7. **Reviewing, understanding, and overseeing annual operating plans and budgets.** The board oversees the annual operating plans and reviews annual budgets presented by management. The board monitors implementation of the annual plans and assesses whether they are responsive to changing conditions.

8. **Reviewing the company's plans for business resiliency.** As part of its risk oversight function, the board periodically reviews management's plans to address business resiliency, including such items as business continuity, physical security, cybersecurity, and crisis management.

9. **Nominating directors and committee members, and overseeing effective corporate governance.** The board, under the leadership of its nominating/corporate governance committee, nominates directors and committee members and oversees the structure, composition (including independence and diversity), succession planning, practices, and evaluation of the board and its committees.

10. **Overseeing the compliance program.** The board, under the leadership of appropriate committees, oversees the company's compliance program and remains informed about any significant compliance issues that may arise.

5.4 Characteristics of Effective and Ineffective Boards

McKinsey & Company, a premier management consulting firm, conducted surveys of global corporate governance and boards (i.e., boards of directors) practices in 2015 and 2016 to determine how the boards of private companies are creating or destroying value; how the scope and nature of a board's engagement work is changing; and how to build forward-looking, high-performing, and value-creating boards.

Major conclusions from the survey are listed next.[4]

- The biggest contributions can be made to strategy management followed by performance management, compliance management, investment management, risk management, and talent management, and the lowest contributions can be made to stakeholder management.

- Most directors said they would like to dedicate more time to strategy management followed by talent management, performance management, risk management, investment management, compliance management, and stakeholder management in that order.

The survey results are grouped into three profiles of boards—ineffective boards (low level), complacent boards (middle level), and striving boards (high level)—in the form of a hierarchy. Although striving boards are good, this book author imagined adding a fourth profile as effective boards (very high level) to represent the ultimate profile that every private company strives to reach.

---

[4] Conor Kehoe, Frithjof Lund, and Nina Spielmann, "Toward a Value-Creating Board," McKinsey & Company (February 2016), https://www.mckinsey.com/business-functions/strategy-and-corporate-finance/our-insights/toward-a-value-creating-board.

(a) Hierarchy of Boards

Forward-looking boards consist of individual board members whose business practices are high performing and value creating in nature and those individuals whose business practices can achieve their stated mission: vision, core values, goals, and objectives. At any point in time, a company's board can be placed in one of the four hierarchical levels, where level 1 is ineffective boards, level 2 is complacent boards, level 3 is striving boards, and level 4 is effective boards. This hierarchy of board practices is similar to Maslow's hierarchy of human needs (i.e., the lowest level is basic needs, such as food and shelter, and the highest level is self-actualization, such as reaching lifelong goals and aspirations), where people move on to the next levels after the basic needs are satisfied until they reach the self-actualization level. Similarly, company directors can be expected to move up the hierarchy from ineffective boards to effective boards as their board's practices get better and better over a period of time. One can think of ineffective boards and effective boards as the two extreme sides of a scale and complacent boards and striving boards falling in between. This four-level board hierarchy of practices is shown below with different impact levels on a company.

Levels	Impacts
4. Effective boards (top of the hierarchy)	Very high positive impact and very low negative impact
3. Striving boards	High positive impact and low negative impact
2. Complacent boards	Moderate positive impact and moderate negative impact
1. Ineffective boards (bottom of the hierarchy)	Low positive impact and high negative impact

(b) Ineffective Boards

Ineffective boards are at the lowest level of the practices hierarchy with low positive impact and high negative impact. A summary of practices that characterize ineffective boards follows. These practices are not listed in order of importance, and the list is not all inclusive.

- Ineffective boards are backward-looking, low-performing, and value-destroying boards because they do not understand the true mission, vision, and core values of the company they represent. In a way, ineffective boards are weakminded boards, where board members may not be fully independent of the company.

- Ineffective boards spend more time evaluating financial performance and little or no time evaluating nonfinancial performance. Examples of financial performance include sales and profits year over year; market share-price year over year; quarterly earnings per share; and returns on investment, sales, equity, assets, value, training, research, data, and capital.

- According to the NACD, nonfinancial performance is grouped into five categories:

  1. Products and services, such as percentage of revenue from new products and services

  2. Operations, such as percentage of total sales from digital operations and nondigital operations

  3. Talent and culture, such as percentage of employees in high-growth jobs

4. Market and reputational impact, such as market share ratios for new offerings, sales effectiveness ratios, and customer satisfaction rates

5. Resilience and sustainability, such as bond rating (A + or junk), stock market daily scores (low, average, or high), carbon use metrics, and sustainability indices

■ Board members take a very passive approach in regard to issues before the board (e.g., a box-checking or box-ticking approach and a rubber-stamped attitude).

■ The board has a low impact on the long-term value-creation process because there are no explicit strategies, plans, and actions. Company risks are not managed, hence they are ignored.

■ The board is low on completion rates on all of the required and assigned job duties and tasks.

■ The board members have a low culture of trust and respect in the boardroom and with other members of the board. There is no teamwork among the board members and with the senior management or key executives.

■ New board members do not receive onboarding, orientation, or induction training and educational programs.

■ The board spends too much time and effort looking backward (i.e., what happened?) and not enough time and effort looking forward (i.e., what is going to happen?).

■ The board deals with static-agenda issues in board meetings, such as reviewing routine and traditional quarterly financial, operating and capital budget, annual account, audit, compliance, regulatory, and performance reports. All these reviews fulfill the traditional fiduciary duty of directors.

■ Board members are known to be liabilities to a company due to their incomplete core business knowledge about the company they represent and their low or negative contribution to the company's growth.

■ The board has a low regard for laws, rules, regulations, and ethics.

■ Board members seek out information on their own; it is not given to them directly, voluntarily, and regularly.

■ Board members invite indirect, informal, and untimely feedback from all interested parties, both inside and outside of the company.

■ Board members do not have strong teeth or a loud voice; they do not ask uncomfortable and difficult questions about senior management and key executives, and they do not challenge them constructively. Ineffective boards are simply token boards.

In summary, ineffective board members are weakminded as they turn their heads the other way or close their eyes when the CEO and the management team is involved in illegal, unethical, or otherwise questionable business practices. Moreover, ineffective boards do not challenge the CEO's assumptions and approaches and operate in a suboptimal manner regarding:

■ Strategy formulation and implementation

■ Resource prioritization, allocation, and utilization

■ Problem-solving and decision-making processes

■ Risk-versus-return trade-offs

■ Performance-versus-incentives conflicts

Ineffective boards either consciously or subconsciously invite activist shareholders and directors due to their bad actions and poor image. These activists can create problems for the entire board with their selfish agenda.

(c) Complacent Boards

Complacent boards are little better than ineffective boards and are at level 2 of the practices hierarchy with moderate positive impact and moderate negative impact. The board's goal is to move up to the next level of striving board. A summary of practices that characterize complacent boards follows. These practices are not listed in order of importance, and the list is not all inclusive.

- Board members are passive in approaches and attitudes relating to board's matters.

- The board spends more time on strategy management and less time on talent management.

- Board members feel good about their contribution to the long-term value creation process.

- The board has a low completion rate on all the required job duties and tasks except for ensuring that management reviews the company's financial performance; setting the company's overall strategic framework; and approving the management strategy.

- The board is weak in the talent management area but is strong in ensuring a viable CEO succession-planning program.

- The board has a stronger sense of trust and teamwork and a stronger culture of trust and respect than normal.

- The board struggles to embrace formal and direct feedback from other directors; instead, it seeks informal and indirect evaluations about their peer directors.

(d) Striving Boards

Striving or trying boards are significantly better than complacent boards and are at level 3 of the practices hierarchy with high positive impact and low negative impact. These boards are trying very hard to reach the next highest level of effective boards. A summary of practices that characterize striving boards follows. These practices are not listed in order of importance, and the list is not all inclusive.

- Board members are aggressive in approaches and attitudes relating to board's matters.

- The board spends more time on strategy management and performance management and less time on stakeholder management.

- Board members feel very good about their contribution to the long-term value creation process.

- The board has a high completion rate on all required job duties and tasks as it spends more time than normal on all of them.

- The board seeks formal and direct feedback from other board members and conducts regular evaluations of them.

- The board exhibits a strong culture of trust and respect for the management team where they challenge each other constructively.

- The board is good at strategy management and performance management, including adjusting or adapting the strategy on a continuous basis.

(e) Effective Boards

Effective boards are at level 4 of the practices hierarchy with very high positive impact and very low negative impact. Effective boards can be thought of as exemplary, ideal, dream, or excellent boards that every public company director hopes to reach. In order to reach this level, effective boards need to strengthen owners' (investors') trust; gain the confidence of the general public; receive positive goodwill from shareholders and other stakeholders; and send positive signals to capital, financial, and stock markets to thrive. A summary of practices that characterize effective boards follows. These practices are not listed in order of importance, and the list is not all inclusive.

- Effective boards are forward-looking, high-performing, and value-creating boards because they understand the true mission, vision, and core values of the company they represent. In a way, effective boards are strongminded boards, where board members may be fully independent of the company.

- The board spends equal time evaluating financial and nonfinancial performance.

- The board spends equal time on strategy development; talent, risk, and performance management; mergers, acquisitions, and divestitures; and regulatory compliance matters.

- The board puts equal focus on internal risks (e.g., management's unethical practices; employee fraud; supply-chain risks; vendor collusion; production and service backlogs, bottlenecks, and inefficiencies; employee strikes and protests; website crashes; computer system outages; poor-quality products and services; and pressure to increase sales, profits, and stock market price) and external risks (e.g., cybercrime, such as ransomware; insider trading; shadow directors; corruption; competitor's aggressive moves; backlash from social media platforms; regulatory risks; product recalls and repairs; product and service warranty and guarantee claims; reputation risks; bad public relations; customer boycotts; labor union strikes and pickets; shareholder activists; industry lobbyists; computer data breaches; and negative press). Note that internal risks and external risks can contain a combination of known and unknown risks and anticipated and unanticipated risks.

- The board completes all the required job duties and tasks, including evaluating resource decisions, debating strategic alternatives, and assessing management's understanding of the value creation process.

- The board maintains a trust-based culture and respect toward the key executives and senior management.

- The board is fully engaged during strategy formulation and development, not after-the-fact review and rubber-stamp approval, so that the strategy can be stress-tested fully and repeatedly.

- The board is heavily involved in management succession planning and promotion matters by holding annual reviews of key executives and senior management. Members become active mentors for high-performing key executives and senior management.

- The board actively engages in operational areas of the company (e.g., visiting production plants, service facilities, sales offices, warehouse and distribution centers, research and development laboratories, and facilities of major suppliers and customers). This type of engagement is done in a collaborative effort, not in an intrusive manner.

- The board is not afraid to ask uncomfortable, tough, and sensitive questions of management to get to the root causes of problems and to clearly demonstrate strong teeth and loud voice.

- Board members should think like an active investor or a majority shareholder to fully understand how a company makes money with its products and services and to assess what business units or divisions create value or destroy value.

- The board deals with dynamic agenda issues in board meetings, such as:

  □ Reviewing strategic and competitive positions

  □ Reviewing key performance indicators

  □ Conducting 360-degree reviews and evaluations as a part of board reinvention efforts

  □ Performing annual risk reviews and risk-mitigation reviews

  □ Conducting talent management reviews

  □ Making investment decisions in mergers, acquisitions, divestitures, and capital budgets

  □ Fulfilling traditional fiduciary duties (e.g., reviewing routine and traditional quarterly financial reports, operating and capital budget reports, annual account reports, audit reports, compliance reports, regulatory reports, performance reports)

  □ Attending customer, supplier, and industry conferences and seminars as part of board member education

- Board members possess complete and thorough core business knowledge about their company's products, services, customers, suppliers, bankers, creditors, investors, regulators, and competitors. This knowledge in turn is considered as an asset of the company with consequent and associated positive contributions to the company's growth and prosperity.

- The board uses best practices or metapractices to improve its overall performance standards, to remove bias from decisions, and to avoid judgment traps. The business judgment rule applies here (the legal presumption that directors and officers of a corporation have exercised due care by acting on an informed basis, in good faith, and in the honest belief that their actions are in the best interests of the corporation; unless a plaintiff can give persuasive evidence against at least one of the criteria, corporate directors and officers are insulated from liability for breach of the duty of care).

- At least one board member should act as an integrator to bring disparate points made and varied discussions occurring in the boardroom together to keep the boardroom functional.

- The board has a high regard for laws, rules, regulations, and ethics.

- Board members receive information directly, voluntarily, and regularly.

- The board invites direct, formal, and timely feedback from all interested parties, both inside and outside of the company.

- The board pursues a continuous improvement strategy with a 360-degree review of key executives and senior management performance. It does not use a box-checking or box-ticking approach as a self-evaluation alternative to the 360-degree review.

In summary, effective board members are strongminded as they open their eyes and look straight into the eyes of the CEO and the management team when they are involved in illegal, unethical, or otherwise questionable business practices. Moreover, effective boards challenge the CEO's assumptions and approaches and operate in an optimal manner regarding strategy formulation and implementation; resource prioritization, allocation, and utilization; problem-solving and decision-making processes; risk-versus-return trade-offs, and performance-versus-incentives conflicts. Simply stated, an effective board is more than the sum of its parts due to greater synergy coming from board members with diverse skill sets, relevant work experience, and earned professional competencies.

5.5 Roles of Executives and Officers

The board of directors selects and hires the chief executive officer (CEO) or the president of a company. The CEO in turn selects and hires a management team consisting of several C-level (chief level) executives, such as chief marketing officer (CMO) and chief financial officer (CFO). For example, the CEO at the top and the CMO and CFO at the next level down form the management hierarchy or the chain of command. In reality, there could be several C-level executives reporting to the CEO and there could be several next-level-down employees reporting to each of the C-level executives.

Improperly defining and practicing employee reporting relationships is often deeply rooted in corporate governance, control, and ethical problems. Improper reporting relationships between and among the C-level executives creates control-related problems and poses ethical dilemmas due to conflict of interest, lack of separation of duties, and lack of independence and objectivity. Incompatible job functions and improper separation of duties can lead to fraud, collusion, and other irregularities. Corporate goal congruence is at risk when individual goals and interests dominate and conflict with the goals of the corporation. Proper organizational structure and reporting relationships can enforce clear lines of responsibility and accountability throughout the organization.

Most C-level executives are vice presidents or directors of a business division or group. The proper and improper reporting relationships between and among the C-level executives are described next.

- The CEO should report to the board of directors and can assume the role of the president but cannot assume the role of chair of the board or of CFO. A nonexecutive board member should assume the role of board chair.

- The CFO should report to the CEO or to the executive vice president (EVP) of finance. The CFO cannot assume the role of the CEO.

Having so many C-level executives directly reporting to the CEO is a challenging administrative task for the CEO to handle on a daily basis, especially when the CEO's time is a limited and critical resource. Some organizations have EVP or senior vice president (SVP) positions, and some C-level executives directly report to the EVP or SVP in order to reduce the CEO's workload. For example, the CFO, chief accounting officer (controller), chief treasurer, and chief administrative officer report directly to the EVP of finance.

Both the CEO and senior executive management must ensure that employee reporting relationships in the management hierarchy below that of the C-level executives (e.g., group/division heads, general managers, middle-level managers, and lower-level managers) are structured in such a way as to prevent conflict of interest, promote goal congruence, exercise control, and prevent ethical problems. Goal congruence, consistency, harmony, and a single and collective voice are the primary benefits accruing to private or public sector organizations resulting from this type of wide span of control (i.e., several lower-level employees report to one higher-level employee).

Next we discuss roles and responsibilities of 12 executives and officers:

1. Chief executive officer

2. Chief governance officer

3. Chief risk officer

4. Chief compliance officer

5. Chief ethics officer

6. Chief legal officer

7. Chief financial officer

8. Chief operations officer

9. Chief marketing officer

10. Chief people officer

11. Chief information officer

12. Gatekeepers

(a) Roles of the Chief Executive Officer

The CEO's management style, tone, and leadership skills set the stage for the entire corporation and determine the ultimate success or failure of the organization. The CEO is central to the strategic management process in setting the overall direction for the organization and mobilizing resources to accomplish the organization's mission, vision, goals, and objectives.

Along with the CFO, the CEO is the primary contact person for the stock markets, investment analysts, and the media in communicating financial and operational performance results. The CEO should possess more soft skills than hard skills and should have a thick skin to handle job-related pressures and criticisms. The management style and leadership skills of other senior executives and officers should be compatible with that of the CEO to ensure goal congruence. To ensure the CEO's independence and separation from the board, he or she cannot be the chair of the board of directors. However, the CEO is a part of the board, hired by the board's chair.

Business Roundtable defines the next specific roles and responsibilities for CEO and management.

The CEO and management, under the CEO's direction, are responsible for the development of the company's long-term strategic plans and the effective execution of the company's business in accordance with those strategic plans. As part of this responsibility, management is charged with the following duties.

(Source: Business Roundtable, Principles of Corporate Governance, August 2016, Washington, DC. www.brt.org)

1. **Business operations.** The CEO and management run the company's business under the board's oversight, with a view toward building long-term value.

2. **Strategic planning**. The CEO and senior management generally take the lead in articulating a vision for the company's future and in developing strategic plans designed to create long-term value for the company, with meaningful input from the board. Management implements the plans following board approval, regularly reviews progress against strategic plans with the board, and recommends and carries out changes to the plans as necessary.

3. **Capital allocation**. The CEO and senior management are responsible for providing recommendations to the board related to capital allocation of the company's resources, including but not limited to organic growth; mergers and acquisitions; divestitures; spin-offs; maintaining and growing its physical and nonphysical resources; and the appropriate return of capital to shareholders in the form of dividends, share repurchases, and other capital distribution means.

4. **Identifying, evaluating, and managing risks.** Management identifies, evaluates, and manages the risks that the company undertakes in implementing its strategic plans and conducting its business. Management also evaluates whether these risks, and related risk management efforts, are consistent with the company's risk appetite. Senior management keeps the board and relevant committees informed about the company's significant risks and its risk management processes.

5. **Accurate and transparent financial reporting and disclosures.** Management is responsible for the integrity of the company's financial reporting system and the accurate and timely preparation of the company's financial statements and related disclosures. It is management's responsibility—under the direction of the CEO and the company's principal financial officer—to establish, maintain, and periodically evaluate the company's internal controls over financial reporting and the company's disclosure controls and procedures, including the ability of such controls and procedures to detect and deter fraudulent activity.

6. **Annual operating plans and budgets**. Senior management develops annual operating plans and budgets for the company and presents them to the board. The management team implements and monitors the operating plans and budgets, making necessary adjustments in light of changing conditions, assumptions, and expectations, and keeps the board apprised of significant developments and changes.

7. **Selecting qualified management, establishing an effective organizational structure, and ensuring effective succession planning.** Senior management selects qualified management, implements an organizational structure, and develops and executes thoughtful career development and succession planning strategies that are appropriate for the company.

8. **Business resiliency.** Management develops, implements, and periodically reviews plans for business resiliency that provide the most critical protection in light of the company's operations. Two related topics follow.

   □ Risk identification. Management identifies the company's major business and operational risks, including those relating to natural disasters, leadership gaps, physical security, cybersecurity, regulatory changes, and other matters.

   □ Crisis preparedness. Management develops and implements crisis preparedness and response plans and works with the board to identify situations (such as a crisis involving senior management) in which the board may need to assume a more active response role.

(b) Roles of the Chief Governance Officer

The overall role of the chief governance officer (CGO) is to promote good corporate governance practices. The CGO position must be a permanent one, not a one-time job created to handle a corporate crisis situation. Stakeholders will invite the permanent establishment of a CGO position since it sends a positive signal to the capital markets. This good news in turn increases the market price of a company's stock and lowers the cost of capital for the company. The corporation's internal environment consisting of directors and management must be supportive of good governance principles and in hiring and proper functioning of a CGO job. In order to fulfill the roles and responsibilities, the CGO should have free and full access to all board members and the chair of the board. The CGO should report to the board, not to the CEO, to preserve independence and objectivity. Note that corporate governance practices vary greatly around the world, just as legal and ethical practices do.

Specifically, these are the roles and responsibilities of a CGO:

- Establish the goals of good corporate governance, addressing board oversight, exacting ethical behavior, creating trust, and hiring competent management.
- Make corporate board members and management accountable for their actions.
- Develop governance principles, policies, and practices, covering the composition of the board; qualities of nonmanagement (nonexecutive) directors; the composition and responsibilities of various committees; and the allocation and balance of power among the owners, management, and the board.
- Communicate freely and fully about governance principles and policies, both inside and outside of the organization.
- Notify government regulators and authorities through periodic filings to them about the governance accomplishments. Do the same thing with the general public through news media.
- Provide training to management and nonmanagement employees of the organization about good governance principles, policies, and practices.
- Seek to employ best practices in corporate governance that other organizations have implemented successfully through benchmarking.
- Reexamine and reevaluate governance principles, policies, and practices, and update them as needed on an ongoing basis.
- Conduct governance audits, management reviews, and self-assessment reviews periodically and proactively to ensure continuous improvement in corporate governance practices.
- Analyze outside-in views (i.e., stakeholders' views about company management) and inside-out views (i.e., company management views about stakeholders) to identify disconnections between these views and to integrate them in a coherent manner.

(c) Roles of the Chief Risk Officer

The chief risk officer (CRO) should report functionally to the board of directors or risk committee of the board and administratively to the CEO. The CRO should not report administratively to the chief financial officer (CFO), chief administrative officer (CAO), chief operating officer (COO), or chief audit executive (CAE) for independence reasons because the CRO will be conducting risk management reviews in finance and operations functions.

Specifically, the roles and responsibilities of the CRO are to:

- Monitor the entire organization's risk profile.
- Develop an enterprise-wide risk architecture or risk framework that is linked down to each business unit or division.

- Develop an inventory of risks, both current and potential, with associated trigger points or events as guidance to employees.

- Develop an inventory of controls or risk mitigation action steps to address each of current and potential risks in order to bring risks to an acceptable level.

- Acquire property insurance and business insurance to protect business assets (tangible and intangible) from damage, destruction, accidents, fire, floods, theft, or loss.

- Seek alternative risk transfer tools as an option to traditional insurance (e.g., multiline or multiyear insurance, multiple trigger policies, securitization, captives insurance, and finite risk insurance policies).

- Coach business unit line managers and staff managers how to develop risk-versus-reward trade-offs, especially when pursuing new business opportunities.

- Anticipate potential new risks facing the organization after analyzing internal changes (e.g., new business, products, services, processes, customers, and suppliers) as well as external changes (e.g., economic, political, technical, regulatory, and international).

- Develop organization-wide business continuity and contingency plans for addressing business disasters as well as IT disasters.

- Manage enterprise-wide risks so that there are no unpleasant surprises to the firm's senior management, audit committee, and board of directors.

- Work with the internal audit department in developing audit plans to identify high-risk areas for audit.

- Work with the legal department in understanding risks arising from lawsuits filed either internally or externally.

- Estimate the value-at-risk (VaR) amount for each risk type or risk category using the Monte Carlo method or other estimation methods. Then the CRO can back-test the actual VaR amount with the estimated or forecasted VaR amount and determine the reasons for the differences. The CRO should recheck and revisit assumptions and parameters that went into the VaR estimation for accuracy and validity.

- Determine periodically whether the organization's risk model provides real value to the organization in the short or the long term.

- Conduct risk management audits, special management reviews, and risk self-assessment reviews periodically and proactively to manage risks facing an organization.

(d) Roles of the Chief Compliance Officer

Organizations have a legal and ethical obligation to comply with the various federal, state, and local laws, rules, regulations, circulars and bulletins, directives and executive orders, government orders, and ordinances pertinent to a specific business area. Noncompliance with these laws and regulations can lead to fines, civil and/or criminal penalties, probation, and jail punishments (prison time), thus creating reputation (image) risk. Compliance with industry and/or organization standards, including professional standards, can increase the quality of products and services, which in turn can enhance an organization's reputation and image in the marketplace. Adherence to generally accepted business principles and concepts could have similar effect as complying with standards.

The reader is advised to obtain the original laws, regulations, and standards from the official sources for a better understanding of the provisions, requirements, and conditions of the laws, regulations, and standards.[5]

Regulatory risk arises from noncompliance with laws and regulations, executive orders, directives, circulars, bulletins, and ordinances that could result in adverse publicity in the news media. Regulatory risk is related to reputation (image) risk in that noncompliance with laws and regulations will tarnish the reputation of an organization.

Specifically, the roles and responsibilities of a chief compliance officer (CCO) include:

- Hiring the needed staff to enforce and monitor laws and regulations.
- Understanding the applicable laws and regulations.
- Establishing communication systems with regulators and government authorities.
- Conducting training classes in laws and regulations to all employees at all levels.
- Requiring all employees to be mindful of laws and regulations as a part of their day-to-day job duties and job descriptions.
- Educating all employees about the cost of compliance and of noncompliance as a part of cost-benefit analysis conducted for major laws, rules, and regulations.
- Conducting compliance audits, special management reviews, and self-assessment reviews periodically and proactively to reduce regulatory risks.

(i) Compliance Costs and Benefits

Corporate management says it costs a significant amount of resources to comply with the often-confusing and duplicating laws, rules, and regulations in terms of record-keeping and monitoring activities. Management does not readily see a direct and positive benefit from compliance. Regulators, however, say these laws, rules, and regulations are developed for the benefit of the entire society and that the cost of compliance should be treated as a cost of doing business. This is a never-ending debate, but in the end, government wins due to its constitutional power. A tradeoff analysis should be performed between the cost of compliance versus the cost of noncompliance.

(ii) Decision Criteria for Compliance

Business organizations might be implicitly or explicitly using the next decision criteria when deciding to fully comply with the government's specific rule, regulation, or acts:

- Compliance is favored when the cost of noncompliance is higher than the cost of compliance.
- Compliance is not favored when the cost of noncompliance is lower than the cost of compliance.

(e) Roles of the Chief Ethics Officer

The board of directors in cooperation with the CEO can install a chief ethics officer position. This person is assigned responsibility and authority to promote a positive ethical climate in the organization through his or her leadership skills.

---

[5] www.regulations.gov.

The specific roles and responsibilities of a chief ethics officer are listed next.

- Work with the internal audit department in developing audit plans and to identify areas of audit addressing ethical violations.

- Work with the legal department in pursuing cases that violated ethical principles either inside the company (e.g., employees and management) or outside (e.g., customers, suppliers, vendors, and contractors).

- Conduct ethics audits, special management reviews, and self-assessment reviews periodically and proactively to ensure continuous improvement in ethical matters.

- Encourage employees and others to report ethical violations through whistleblower telephone hotlines, email, or other means that will be kept confidential.

- Conduct training classes for managers and nonmanagers about ethical principles that include actions and consequences and referencing to all the applicable laws and regulations.

- Analyze outside-in views (i.e., stakeholders' views about company management) and inside-out views (i.e., company management views about stakeholders) to identify disconnections between these views and to integrate them in a coherent manner.

(f) Roles of the Chief Legal Officer

The corporate chief legal officer (CLO), corporate legal counsel, or corporate general counsel:

- Establishes policies and procedures relating to prosecution of identified instances of fraud, waste, and abuse cases, and employee criminal acts.

- Oversees the implementation of ethics program throughout the organization.

- Handles patent, trademark, and copyright violations by individuals or organizations.

- Reviews discrimination suits filed by employees, contractors, and consultants against the corporation.

- Is involved in labor union negotiations.

The specific roles and responsibilities of the CLO are listed next.

- Participate in the due diligence process during proposed mergers or acquisitions as part of SMEs from operations, finance, IT, and marketing.

- Develop business contracts and provide technical support to management to enforce contractual terms and conditions.

- Work with investment bankers and brokers in developing prospectus documents and filing securities regulation applications during stock and bond offerings to potential investors.

- Participate in labor union negotiations for a win-win outcome.

- Conduct in-house training classes for functional managers and executives regarding interpretation of laws, regulations, the Uniform Commercial Code, and court cases.

- Establish a solid and sustainable chain of knowledge linked through the entire legal management hierarchy to ensure core knowledge competencies.

- Conduct legal audits, management reviews, and self-assessment reviews periodically and proactively to ensure continuous improvement in legal matters.

- Comply with professional standards and code of ethics established by the American Bar Association for the legal profession (www.abanet.org).

- Analyze outside-in views (i.e., stakeholders' views about company management) and inside-out views (i.e., company management views about stakeholders) to identify disconnections between these views and to integrate them in a coherent manner.

(g) Roles of the Chief Financial Officer

The chief financial officer (CFO), as a member of senior management, is usually responsible for both accounting and treasury functions and more. Both the controller and the treasurer report to the CFO, and the CFO in turn reports to the firm's CEO. The CFO plays an important role in strategic planning, capital budgeting and the investment decision-making process, stockholder relations, safeguarding of assets, financial statement analysis, and financial reporting for the firm.

The **controller or chief accounting officer** is usually responsible for financial accounting (e.g., billing, accounts payable, and payroll), general accounting (e.g., general ledger), cost accounting (e.g., inventory accounting and product/service costing), operating and capital budgeting, financial statement preparation, taxes, and coordination with internal auditors and external auditors. The controller reports to the CFO.

The **treasurer** is usually responsible for working capital management (e.g., credit management, collecting accounts receivable, cash disbursements, and short-term borrowing and investing), external financing with banks and other financial institutions (e.g., long-term borrowing, leasing, and investor relations), risk management (e.g., interest rate risk and foreign exchange rate risk), insurance, pension funds, and dividend disbursement to investors. The treasurer reports to the CFO.

The specific the roles and responsibilities of the CFO are listed next.

- Change from police role to team player role. (However, the custodial role of protecting the organization's assets is here to stay.)

- Maximize shareholder value by increasing revenues, decreasing costs, and increasing profits in a legitimate and ethical manner.

- Integrate accounting, treasury, and finance activities for maximum efficiency and effectiveness.

- Lower total manufacturing costs, marketing costs, administrative and selling costs, and service costs in order to lower selling prices, increase sales volume, and increase profits.

- Link finance service costs to cash flows and gross profits.

- Increase faster finance service deliveries to internal customers to achieve their total satisfaction.

- Innovate new finance service techniques and processes by leveraging technology to improve quality and to reduce costs.

- Eliminate non-value-added activities in finance services to trim waste and lower costs.

- Focus more on value-added activities in finance services to provide a solid value to customers and the organization.

- Identify key drivers of cost, quality, risks, expenses, revenues, profits, business growth, competition, and performance. Focus on the root causes of these drivers and understand why these drivers go up and down.

- Seamlessly integrate back-end systems with front-end systems for (1) maximum data consistency, completeness, and accuracy; (2) better customer service and satisfaction; and (3) stronger connection of disparate and disconnected business processes.

- Build standardized, transparent, and repeatable finance service processes to provide stable, consistent, and quality services that internal customers expect.

- Understand that increases in sales velocity increase inventory velocity, which in turn increases the velocity of production or service, finance, human capital, and systems. The goal is to synchronize these velocities in a cohesive manner.

- Implement the goal congruence concept by linking individual employee goals with those of the department/division and the organization. Remove or reduce the competing or conflicting goals.

- Implement cross-cutting best practices across business units, divisions, departments, and functions through breaking silos and building bridges.

- Link employee rewards, bonuses, and promotions to employees' true performance and tangible results, and empower employees.

- Build solid working relationships with C-level executives in marketing, manufacturing, IT, human resources, and other functions through formal and informal approaches at the workplace.

- Foster ethical values and cultural sensitivity in light of workforce diversity.

- Encourage employees to acquire and improve their knowledge, skills, and abilities (KSAs) continuously through targeted training courses, management development programs, and professional certifications.

- Establish a solid and sustainable chain of knowledge linked through the entire management hierarchy to ensure adequate core knowledge competencies for all levels of employees in the organization.

- Invite finance audits, self-audits, special management reviews, and self-assessments periodically and proactively to ensure continuous improvement in finance quality, cost, and delivery.

- Encourage employees at all levels of the organization to think differently and radically (i.e., out-of-the-box thinking) at all times, which can lead to new perspectives providing best-of-breed solutions.

- Participate in the succession planning process for key positions.

- Adhere to accounting, auditing, treasury, and finance professional and ethical standards established by the respective professional bodies.

- Analyze outside-in views (i.e., stakeholders' views about company management) and inside-out views (i.e., company management views about stakeholders) to identify disconnections between these views and to integrate them in a coherent manner.

(h) Roles of the Chief Operations Officer

The chief operations officer or chief operating officer (COO) is a key person in the C-level executive suite in charge of either manufacturing operations or service operations.

The specific roles and responsibilities of a COO are listed next.

- Integrate production, inventory, logistics, and transportation activities for maximum efficiency and effectiveness.

- Lower total manufacturing and service costs in order to lower selling prices, increase sales volume, and increase profits.

- Link production and service costs to cash flows and gross profits.

- Increase faster product and service deliveries to customers to achieve their total satisfaction (i.e., shorter order-to-delivery cycle).

- Innovate new production and service techniques and processes by leveraging technology to improve quality and to reduce costs.

- Eliminate non-value-added activities in production and service to trim waste and to lower costs.

- Focus more on value-added activities in production and services to provide a solid value to customers and the organization.

- Identify key drivers of cost, quality, risks, expenses, revenues, profits, business growth, competition, and performance. Focus on the root causes of these drivers and understand why the drivers go up and down.

- Seamlessly integrate back-end systems with front-end systems for (1) maximum data consistency, completeness, and accuracy; (2) better customer service and satisfaction; and (3) stronger connection of disparate and disconnected business processes.

- Build standardized, transparent, and repeatable production and service processes to provide stable, consistent, and quality products and services that both internal and external customers expect.

- Understand that increases in sales velocity increase inventory velocity, which in turn increases the velocity of production or service, finance, human capital, and systems. The goal is to synchronize these velocities in a cohesive manner.

- Implement the goal congruence concept by linking individual employee goals with those of the department/division and the organization. Remove or reduce the competing or conflicting goals.

- Implement cross-cutting best practices across business units, divisions, departments, and functions through breaking silos and building bridges.

- Link employee rewards, bonuses, and promotions to employees' true performance and tangible results, and empower employees.

- Build solid working relationships with C-level executives in marketing, finance, human resources, and other functions through formal and informal approaches at the workplace.

- Foster ethical values and cultural sensitivity in light of workforce diversity.

- Encourage employees to acquire and improve their knowledge, skills, and abilities continuously through targeted training courses, management development programs, and professional certifications.

- Establish a solid and sustainable chain of knowledge linked through the entire management hierarchy to ensure core knowledge competencies for all levels of employees in the organization.

- Invite production and service audits, management reviews, and self-assessments periodically and proactively to ensure continuous improvement in quality, cost, and delivery.

- Encourage employees at all levels of the organization to think differently and radically (i.e., out-of-the-box thinking) at all times, which can lead to new perspectives providing best-of-breed solutions.

- Participate in the succession planning process for key positions.

- Adhere to professional and ethical standards established by the respective professional bodies.

- Analyze outside-in views (i.e., stakeholders' views about company management) and inside-out views (i.e., company management views about stakeholders) to identify disconnections between these views and integrate them in a coherent manner.

(i) Roles of the Chief Marketing Officer

The chief marketing officer (CMO) is a key person in the C-level executive suite and is in charge of both sales and marketing functions. The heads of the sales function and the marketing function report to the CMO.

The specific roles and responsibilities of the CMO are listed next.

- Integrate marketing and sales activities for maximum synergy, efficiency, and effectiveness.

- Lower marketing and sales costs in order to lower selling prices, increase sales volume, and increase profits.

- Link marketing and sales costs to cash flows and net profits since marketing and sales costs are part of administrative costs, which are subtracted from operating profits to result in net profits.

- Increase faster product and service deliveries to customers to achieve their total satisfaction (i.e., faster time to market of products and services).

- Innovate new marketing and sales techniques and processes by leveraging technology to improve quality and to reduce costs.

- Eliminate non-value-added activities in marketing and sales to trim waste and lower costs.

- Focus more on value-added activities in marketing and sales to provide a solid value to customers and the organization.

- Identify key drivers of cost, quality, risks, expenses, revenues, profits, business growth, market segments, customer loyalty, competition, and performance. Focus on the root causes of these drivers and understand why these drivers go up and down.

- Seamlessly integrate back-end systems with front-end systems for (1) maximum data consistency, completeness, and accuracy; (2) better service and satisfaction of internal and external customers; and (3) stronger connection of disparate and disconnected business processes

- Build standardized, transparent, and repeatable marketing and sales processes to provide stable, consistent, and quality products and services that customers expect.

- Understand that increases in sales velocity increase inventory velocity, which in turn increases the velocity of production or service, finance, human capital, and systems. The goal is to synchronize these velocities in a cohesive manner.

- Implement the goal congruence concept by linking individual employee goals with those of the department/division and the organization. Remove or reduce competing or conflicting goals.

- Implement cross-cutting best practices across business units, divisions, departments, and functions through breaking silos and building bridges.

- Link employee rewards, bonuses, and promotions to employees' true performance record and tangible results.

- Build solid working relationships with C-level executives in operations, finance, human resources, and other functions through formal and informal approaches at the workplace.

- Foster ethical values and cultural sensitivity in light of workforce diversity.

- Encourage employees to acquire and improve their knowledge, skills, and abilities continuously through targeted training courses, management development programs, and professional certifications.

- Establish a solid and sustainable chain of knowledge linked through the entire management hierarchy to ensure core knowledge competencies for all levels of employees in the organization.

- Invite marketing, sales, distributor, and competitor audits; customer perception audits; special management reviews; and self-assessments periodically and proactively to ensure continuous improvement in the marketing and sales of products and services.

- Encourage employees at all levels of the organization to think differently and radically (i.e., out-of-the-box thinking) at all times, which can lead to new perspectives providing best-of-breed solutions.

- Participate in the succession planning process for key positions.

- Adhere to the American Marketing Association's Code of Ethics and Professional Standards established for marketers and salespeople (www.ama.org).

- Analyze outside-in views (i.e., stakeholders' views about company management) and inside-out views (i.e., company management views about stakeholders) to identify disconnections between these views and integrate them in a coherent manner.

(j) Roles of the Chief People Officer

The chief people officer (CPO) or chief human resources officer or its equivalent is a key person in the C-level executive suite. The CPO treats talented and competent employees as the company's most valuable assets because they provide the company with a competitive advantage.

The specific roles and responsibilities of the CPO are listed next.

- Link human resource (HR) strategy to business strategy.

- Support all employees of the organization from hiring to firing.

- Develop human talent acquisition and retention strategies that are sustainable over longer periods of time.

- Develop an HR manual describing policies, procedures, and standards expected of employees.

- Establish and encourage self-service systems so employees can:

  □ Select healthcare benefits and life insurance coverage.

  □ Schedule paid-time off and vacations.

  □ Participate in attitude and satisfaction surveys.

  □ Enroll in training and development courses.

- Conduct employee exit interviews to understand the reasons for leaving the organization. Incorporate the lessons learned from these exit interviews into the employee hiring-to-rehiring cycle.

- Integrate HR administrative tasks with the HR strategic tasks for maximum efficiency and effectiveness.

- Develop a "one system of record" to capture employee information in one place by integrating back-end systems with front-end systems through automation, such as business application systems (e.g., payroll and personnel systems) and web-based systems (e.g., resume requests, interview requests, job offers made, and job offers accepted). Some benefits of integrated systems include:

  □ Maximum data consistency, completeness, and accuracy

  □ Better internal customer service and satisfaction

  □ Stronger connection of disparate and disconnected business processes

- Link HR costs to cash flows and gross profits, and lower total HR costs to increase profits.

- Increase faster HR service deliveries to internal customers to achieve their total satisfaction.

- Innovate new HR service techniques and processes by leveraging technology to improve quality and reduce costs.

- Eliminate non-value-added activities such as HR administrative and clerical tasks to reduce inefficiencies and lower costs.

- Focus more on value-added activities such as HR strategic tasks to provide a solid value to internal customers and the organization.

- Identify key drivers of cost, quality, risks, expenses, revenues, profits, business growth, competition, and performance. Focus on the root causes of these drivers and understand why these drivers go up and down.

- Build standardized, transparent, and repeatable HR service processes to provide stable, consistent, and quality services that internal customers expect.

- Understand that increases in sales velocity increase inventory velocity, which in turn increases the velocity of production or service, finance, human capital, and systems. The goal is to synchronize these velocities in a cohesive manner.

- Implement the goal congruence concept by linking individual employee goals with those of the department/division and organization. Remove or reduce the competing or conflicting goals.

- Implement cross-cutting best practices across business units, divisions, departments, and functions by breaking silos and building bridges.

- Link employee rewards, bonuses, and promotions to employees' true performance and tangible results, and empower employees.

- Build solid working relationships with C-level executives in marketing, finance, operations, IT, and other functions through formal and informal approaches at the workplace.

- Foster ethical values and cultural sensitivity in light of workforce diversity, and provide cross-cultural orientation and preparation.

- Encourage employees to acquire and improve their KSAs continuously through targeted training courses, management development programs, and professional certifications.

- Establish a solid and sustainable chain of knowledge linked through the entire management hierarchy to ensure adequate core knowledge competencies for all levels of employees in the organization.

- Invite HR audits, special management reviews such as benefits auditing, and self-assessments periodically and proactively to ensure continuous improvement in the HR function.

- Encourage employees at all levels of the organization to think differently and radically (i.e., out-of-the-box thinking) at all times, which can lead to new perspectives providing best-of-breed solutions.

- Participate in the succession planning process for key positions.

- Adhere to professional and ethical standards established by the respective professional bodies.

- Analyze outside-in views (i.e., stakeholders' views about company management) and inside-out views (i.e., company management views about stakeholders) to identify disconnections between these views and integrate them in a coherent manner.

(k) Roles of the Chief Information Officer

The chief information officer (CIO) or chief technology officer (CTO) or its equivalent is a key person in the C-level executive suite. Forward-looking companies are treating an organization's information resource as a valuable asset and as a strategic weapon against competition.

The specific roles and responsibilities of the CIO are listed next.

- Link IT strategy with business strategy.

- Integrate IT administration, planning, system development and maintenance, telecommunications and networks, and computer operations functions for maximum efficiency and effectiveness.

- Deliver value-based information to functional and senior management to facilitate quality decision making and to gain a competitive advantage.

- Reduce investment in stovepipe (legacy) systems and slowly retire them by developing new systems that integrate seamlessly with other systems.

- Align system processes with business processes to increase employee performance and productivity by reducing paper-driven manual systems and end-user ad hoc systems.

- Ensure that business application systems (e.g., accounts payable and inventory) are flexible and that they do not limit internal and external customer service offerings.

- Improve data quality, data usability, data integration, data communications, and data sharing to authorized individuals.

- Implement a business continuity plan for stable business functions and operations with resilient computer systems.

- Implement data dictionaries and metadata repositories to facilitate data management and control.

- Link IT service costs to cash flows and gross profits.

- Increase faster IT service deliveries to internal customers to achieve their total satisfaction.

- Implement new IT technologies and processes by leveraging technology to improve quality and to reduce costs.

- Eliminate non-value-added activities in IT service to trim waste and lower costs.

- Focus more on value-added activities in IT services to provide a solid value to internal customers and the organization.

- Identify key drivers of cost, quality, risks, expenses, revenues, profits, business growth, competition, and performance. Focus on the root causes of these drivers and understand why these drivers go up and down.

- Seamlessly integrate back-end systems with front-end systems for (1) maximum data consistency, completeness, and accuracy; (2) better customer service and satisfaction; and (3) stronger connection of disparate and disconnected business processes.

- Build standardized, transparent, and repeatable IT service processes to provide stable, consistent, and quality products and services that customers expect.

- Understand that increases in sales velocity increase inventory velocity, which in turn increases the velocity of production or service, finance, human capital, and systems. The goal is to synchronize these velocities in a cohesive manner.

- Implement the goal congruence concept by linking individual employee goals with those of the department/division and organization. Remove or reduce competing or conflicting goals.

- Implement cross-cutting best practices across business units, divisions, departments, and functions by breaking silos and building bridges.

- Link employee rewards, bonuses, and promotions to employees' true performance and tangible results, and empower employees.

- Build solid working relationships with C-level executives in marketing, manufacturing, finance, HR, and other functions through formal and informal approaches at the workplace.

- Foster ethical values and cultural sensitivity in light of workforce diversity.

- Encourage employees to acquire and improve their KSAs continuously through targeted training courses, management development programs, and professional certifications.

- Establish a solid and sustainable chain of knowledge linked through the entire management hierarchy to ensure adequate core knowledge competencies for all levels of employees in the organization.

- Invite IT audits, special management reviews, and self-assessments periodically and proactively to ensure continuous improvement in IT service quality, cost, and delivery.

- Encourage employees at all levels of the organization to think differently and radically (i.e., out-of-the-box thinking) at all times, which can lead to new perspectives providing best-of-breed solutions.

- Participate in the succession planning process for key positions.

- Adhere to IT professional and ethical standards established by the respective professional bodies.

- Analyze outside-in views (i.e., stakeholders' views about company management) and inside-out views (i.e., company management views about stakeholders) to identify disconnections between these views and integrate them in a coherent manner.

(l) Roles of Gatekeepers

Gatekeepers include external auditors, attorneys, securities analysts, credit rating agencies, and investment bankers, who inform and advise the board of directors and the shareholders. It has been reported that these gatekeepers are not fulfilling their gatekeeper or agent role to its fullest extent. These gatekeepers should be serving investors, creditors, and stockholders by assuming the role of independent monitor or watchdog and by avoiding conflict-of-interest situations that can compromise their independence and objectivity.[6]

Gatekeepers are in a way policemen to prevent corporate management wrongdoing, such as manipulating earnings (earnings management), financial restatements and misstatements, capitalizing expenses, deferring or misclassifying expenses, hiding liabilities, engaging in off-balance-sheet transactions, and other types of financial fraud to increase stock market price and receive big bonuses.

Gatekeepers such as external auditors provide financial certification and verification services to investors externally and to corporate directors and senior managers internally. These services lower the cost of capital for a corporation and thereby increase its stock price. Both shareholders and the board depend on gatekeepers for an unbiased flow of information that is not edited, filtered, or modified in favor of corporate management. Effective corporate governance requires a chain-of-actors including directors, managers, and gatekeepers, where the latter cannot become the weakest link. Taking this chain-of-actors to its extreme, the board of directors, internal auditors, and the SEC can also be viewed as gatekeepers. For example, the SEC monitors and takes severe actions against misleading or fraudulent securities registration and offering of stocks and bonds; stock market trading scandals; deceptive computer trading practices; insider trading scandals; self-dealing allegations; and misleading financial misstatements to defraud investors.

---

[6] John C. Coffee, Jr., *Gatekeepers: The Professions and Corporate Governance* (Cambridge, UK: Oxford University Press, 2006).

Based on corporate scandals, gatekeepers are not fulfilling their watchdog role in preventing and/or detecting fraud or other irregularities. Gatekeepers should not wear blinders and cannot ignore red flags, be indifferent to sins of omission, or do perfunctory audits or investigations.

Gatekeepers should increase their positive reputational capital and decrease their negative reputational capital by exhibiting unbiased and professional behavior in preventing unethical and illegal business practices. Gatekeepers can act as a first line of defense (LOD) at the entrance of a gate or a last line of defense at the exit of a gate.

Organizations should do the following to preserve good governance principles:

- The board should be active and independent of corporate management to discharge board's fiduciary responsibilities. The board should not approve loans to the CEO or other executives.

- The gatekeepers in cooperation with the board should protect the rights of whistleblowers who report corporate management wrongdoing.

- A principal–agent relationship between the gatekeepers and the corporation must be reconsidered and restructured. This relationship is similar to a purchasing manager (principal) and an employee (buyer and agent) in a procurement or purchasing department.

Organizations should **not** do the following to preserve good governance principles:

- Organizations should not do opinion shopping for accounting, auditing, financial and investment consulting, and legal services.

- A hiring organization's management should not have conflict-of-interest situations with management of a hired organization that provides accounting, auditing, financial and investment consulting, and legal services.

5.6 Roles of the Audit Committee

Audit committee is the most important board-level committee as it deals with development of financial statements (e.g., income statement and balance sheet) and coordination between internal audits and external audits. A board member with formal education in accounting and finance with professional certification in accounting and who previously worked on an audit committee for another company is a qualified candidate to be assigned to the audit committee (i.e., financial expert on the board). A board's standards require that fully independent directors serve on the audit, compensation, nominating, and governance committees. The highest standards of independence apply to the audit committee due to its work with financial statements and internal controls. The audit committee is discussed separately due to its financial importance to stockholders, investors, and owners and as audit champion to internal auditors.

(a) Overview

Vibrant and stable capital markets depend on, among other things, reliable, transparent, and objective financial information to support an efficient and effective capital allocation process. The vital oversight role audit committees play in the process of producing financial information has never been more important. As capital markets continue to digest various corporate governance reforms, audit committees have been forced to refine—some would say redefine—their mission. And with these changes, the natural tension between the board's dual roles as an advisor to management and a fiduciary to shareholders is heightened, with audit committee often at the center of the tension. Quite fundamentally, the capital market system today expects more from an audit committee than it ever has. How audit committees react to these changing expectations is a key factor in restoring credibility in financial information.[7]

The audit committee's key responsibility—overseeing the process that produces reliable and credible financial statements while ensuring the company has effective internal controls—requires it to conduct activities that earlier had been executed mostly by management. Today, audit committees are also expected to retain and compensate the external auditors, grasp all of the key information included in a company's financial reporting, and oversee risk management and compliance with laws and regulations affecting the company. This change is occurring in an environment that demands transparency.

(b) Charter and Evaluation

Charters—the clearest articulation of the audit committee's purpose, composition, roles and responsibilities, and authority—are public documents. That makes it even more important for committees to evaluate regularly whether their charters are appropriate and whether the committees are discharging all their responsibilities. Committee evaluations, useful in identifying areas for improvement and training needs, raise new concerns over putting results in writing.

(c) Financial Statements

In today's world, financial statements are extremely dense and, too often, difficult to understand. Indeed, they are so complicated that many audit committees struggle to grasp them or to feel completely confident they portray business results in the most effective way, particularly in areas where the accounting is highly technical and complex. Although many individual investors do not read the full financial statements, that does not diminish the importance of the audit committee's role in ensuring they are understandable and transparent for those companies and individuals who do. Audit committees can bring the discipline to ensure companies provide information to the investor world that is digestible and reliable.

(d) Risk Management and Internal Control

When people talk about risk, they often mean different things—such as insurance or hedging, or regulatory, product, or technology risk. While audit committees long have overseen how companies respond to financial reporting risks, some now are overseeing the effectiveness of management's responses to additional types of risk, the kinds just mentioned as well as other risks that might prevent a company from achieving its strategic objectives. It is vital that the board agrees on the scope of the audit committee's oversight, so the board can ensure all key risks are monitored somewhere at the board level. Then the audit committee needs to understand those risks within its purview and be confident that management's responses—the internal controls it has established and operate—are satisfactory and that management's process for identifying and assessing risk is sound. And in the same way that audit committee should ensure proper transparency of financial statements, it also should ensure that management's reporting on the effectiveness of internal control over financial reporting is complete and understandable.

---

[7] *Audit Committee Effectiveness: What Works Best,* 3rd ed. (Altamonte Springs, FL: Institute of Internal Auditors Research Foundation, 2005).

(e) Oversight of Management and Internal Audit

Audit committees always have needed to balance their fiduciary role with their role as advisors to management. However, as audit committee responsibilities have increased and the external pressure to emphasize their fiduciary role mounts —questioning and pressing management more, trusting less—tensions naturally increase.

RESPONSIBILITIES OF AUDIT COMMITTEE AND ITS RELATIONSHIP WITH CORPORATE MANAGEMENT

Regarding relationships with corporate management, audit committees should press more and trust less of corporate management. The principal responsibilities of an audit committee are to:

- Ensure that published financial statements are fair and proper and are not misleading.
- Ensure that internal controls are adequate.
- Follow up on allegations of material, financial, ethical, and legal irregularities in response to whistleblower reports.
- Ratify the selection of the external auditor.
- Hire, retain, and terminate the CAE of the internal audit function.
- Coordinate between the external auditors and internal auditors.
- Ensure the integrity of financial reporting and nonfinancial reporting to shareholders and stakeholders.
- Ensure that related-party transactions are fair and proper.
- Ensure that a record retention policy and a document destruction policy are in place and are effective.
- Press more and trust less with corporate management.

Of course, audit committees must evaluate whether what management is telling them is supportable. Many audit committees look to the internal audit function for that insight and rely on internal audit's objective assessment of risk and control in operational, compliance, and reporting areas. Audit committees should consider whether the internal audit function has the proper stature in the company. The audit committee will benefit from this proper audit stature, and it is in the committee's self-interest to be internal audit function's champion.

(f) Relationship with External Auditors

External auditors play one of the key gatekeeper roles in capital markets. Audit committees should own the relationship with external auditors—and if they do not and it is evident that management still does, the committees need to take immediate steps to own the relationship. When audit committees own the relationship, there is direct reporting by external auditors, ongoing communication, frequent meetings, and robust discussions about audit scope and audit results. External auditors pay more attention to greater levels of detail, evaluating potential services to determine whether the committee will grant its preapproval, taking steps to ensure the auditors' independence, and considering how well the auditors perform.

(g) Compliance and Ethics

Witnessing how quickly corporate and personal reputations can be destroyed has provided a wake-up call for many directors. They recognize that often the greatest harm is caused by an individual's unethical actions. Therefore, ethics, codes of conduct, and tone at the top are vital in protecting a company against reputation risk. While failing to comply with legal and regulatory requirements may be caused by carelessness or process problems—more neglect than outright malfeasance—to the outside world, such lack of compliance simply looks as if the company does not care enough about compliance to focus on it, all leading to reputation problems. Many audit committees are playing a central role in addressing the evolving regulatory expectations for board-level involvement in compliance and ethics.

(h) Committee Composition

It has become more challenging to recruit qualified members to an audit committee due to requirements for independence and financial literacy, limitations on the number of audit committees on which a director can serve, and concerns around liability. The significant workload and time commitment required of audit committee members may be responsible for shifting committee composition, with active board chairs, CEOs, and presidents constituting a smaller portion of audit committee members than they did in the past.

(i) Meetings Agenda

Audit committees have to steer their agenda and must not abdicate their responsibility to management. Audit committee chairs often provide the foundation for effective audit committee meetings, driving the agenda, facilitating the discussion, holding pre-meetings to explore issues, and ensuring the right people are present. Audit committee members also must prepare thoroughly for meetings. And the meetings need to have active meaningful participation, not just presentations, which sometimes require that presenters be coached in advance of meetings.

(j) Training

With the intricate nature of companies' business activities, the complexity of accounting transactions and policies, and frequent changes to financial accounting standards, even the most experienced audit committee members can benefit from training. New audit committee members also need robust orientation, allowing them to understand their role and the company's financial reporting process, so they can add value sooner.

(k) Resources and Special Investigations

Audit committees' right and willingness to access needed resources further supports their shift to being self-sufficient and autonomous. This shift requires that the audit committee is ready to direct special investigations. Crises may develop suddenly and arise in unexpected places. Committees directing a special investigation must be able to act quickly, ensure the investigating firm is independent, be comfortable with the level of communication, cooperate with regulators, and ensure appropriate remedial actions.

5.7 Roles of Board-Level Committees

Board-level committees are an effective way to focus on key issues and problems facing an organization because each issue or problem requires a dedicated approach, resources, and attention to solve it. For example, committees are extensively used in the public sector. In this section, we present several specific board-level committees, not including the audit committee, which is presented in a separate topic due to its importance to internal auditors.

Individual members of the board of directors of an organization join various board-level committees to address specific tasks, issues, problems, and concerns facing that organization. The rationale behind establishing committees is divide and conquer: It is better and easier to handle several small-size issues separately than to handle one big-size issue. Committee members can spend more time on and pay more attention to a small committee than to a large one.

Committees have high visibility and high impact on organizations due to their strategic-level representation of executive management and board members as their decisions affect the entire company. The outcome of a committee's work is a new or revised policy, plan, or procedure to make current things better or future things even better. Committees are employed in both private and public organizations, managed by committee chairpersons, and they take big-picture perspectives.

The committee should contain nonexecutive and independent directors with no potential for conflict of interest and who exercise due diligence. Committee members' formal education, skills, and work experience are important factors in assigning them to committees. In addition, each committee should have its own "committee charter" describing primary objectives to be achieved, tasks to be accomplished, and roles and responsibilities to be fulfilled, all approved by the chair of the board.

The following presents some variations in establishing committees.

- Some companies may consolidate many of these 25 committees into a few committees.
- Global corporations may have more committees than a major domestic U.S. corporation.
- Banks, healthcare, transportation, and financial industries will establish a regulatory and compliance committee in contrast to others because they are heavily regulated.
- Banks will establish an asset and liability committee in contrast to nonbanks because assets and liabilities are their core business.
- A software development company will establish an intellectual property (IP) committee to address and protect its IP assets.
- A manufacturing or retail company will establish a supply-chain committee due to its core business in contrast to other companies.

Every publicly held corporation has a nominating committee, and all companies have an HR committee.

The next 25 committees are discussed in this section.

1. Governance committee
2. Strategic management committee
3. Finance committee
4. Risk committee
5. Ethics committee
6. Nominating committee
7. Social responsibility committee
8. Labor relations committee

9. Wage and benefits committee

10. Compensation committee

11. Investigative committee

12. Standing committee

13. Grievance committee

14. Human resources committee

15. Technology committee

16. Public relations committee

17. Legal committee

18. Supply-chain committee

19. Intellectual property committee

20. Policy committee

21. Regulatory and compliance committee

22. Steering committee

23. Special committee

24. Ad hoc committee

25. Asset and liability committee

(a) Governance Committee

The governance committee maximizes the effectiveness of the board through an annual review and evaluation of the structure, size, composition, development, and selection of board members and board committees. Major responsibilities of this committee are governance, risk, and control matters. In some companies or countries, the governance committee is part of a nominating committee. Specifically, the governance committee:

- Recommends for board approval a conflict-of-interest policy and a code of ethics document.
- Oversees the succession planning process for the CEO and other key executives.
- Promotes orientation (onboarding) training and educational programs for directors.
- Evaluates the performance of members of the other board-level committees as well as the governance committees themselves.

In addition, the board may delegate the investigation of a potential conflict of interest to the governance committee.

(b) Strategic Management Committee

The strategic management committee ensures that the mission and vision of an organization is current and up-to-date and that it reflects the organization's current strategy and strategic plans. The major responsibility of this committee is to make sure that the strategic plan is properly understood and fully implemented across the business divisions and functions of the entire organization.

(c) Finance Committee

The finance committee controls major commitments of funds and ensures that capital expenditure budgets and operating budgets are consistent with strategic and operational plans. It also focuses on long-term investments planning; raising new capital; declaring dividends; and handling mergers, acquisitions, and divestitures (i.e., disinvestments such as spin-offs and sell-offs).

(d) Risk Committee

The risk committee ensures that its organization fully adopts a time-tested and well-proven enterprise risk management (ERM) framework and model to accomplish its overall objectives and to realize full and real value from the use of such a framework and model. The risk committee:

- Focuses on how to approve, measure, and monitor risk appetite and risk tolerance of an organization with strategies, plans, policies, and procedures.

- Identifies and evaluates the pros and cons of all current, future, known, and unknown risks.

- Ensures that risk-mitigation strategies and efforts are in place to handle each of these risks.

- Requests an operating budget and a capital budget for managing risks in its organization. A specific line item in the budget can be called risk capital (i.e., capital-at-risk), risk reserves, or loss reserves to pay for all actual losses, damages, disasters, accidents, fines, penalties, and legal costs incurred to handle all undesirable risk outcomes.

- Ensures that risk management estimates the total amount of value at risk (VaR) for each risk type and for all risk types. The VaR provides a big-picture perspective of total exposure (i.e., value at loss) facing the organization, which can be computed with Monte Carlo method.

The scope of the risk committee's work includes both financial areas (e.g., stocks, bonds, mutual funds, money market securities, pensions, options, swaps, off-balance-sheet items, and hedges) and nonfinancial areas (e.g., operational, credit, market, technology, political, contractual obligations, and lawsuits filed against and by the company). A typical composition of the risk committee, installed by the CEO, can include senior managers, functional managers, and C-level executives such as the chief risk officer, CFO, CIO, CTO, CAE, chief legal officer, CPO, and others.

(e) Ethics Committee

The ethics committee reviews complaints received from insiders and outsiders of an organization about unethical behavior by its managers, nonmanagers, and executives. It coordinates with the organization's legal counsel in determining a plan of action in handling these unethical behaviors, such as bribery, corruption, fraud, manipulation of financial and operational outcomes, and misreporting of truth in performance. It also looks into any violation of the U.S. Foreign Corrupt Practices Act of 1998, which is applicable to inside and outside of the United States. Bribery and corruption risks are a major concern here.

(f) Nominating Committee

The nominating committee provides input and control over the selection of candidates for the board of directors and key executive positions, such as the CEO. In some companies or countries, the nominating committee is a part of governance committee. Nominating committee members are responsible not only for selecting candidates with the best individual credentials for board membership but also for ensuring the strength of a board as a whole. A major concern is whether underperforming board members are renominated for another term.

(g) Social Responsibility Committee

The corporate social responsibility (CSR) committee focuses on social matters, such as exploiting child labor by employing them in unsafe offshore manufacturing plants; dumping industrial pollution into lakes and rivers; and encouraging philanthropic activities, such as giving donations to charitable organizations. The scope of CSR committee can also include a review of product safety, employee safety, environmental issues (e.g., pollution and climate change), public policy, community outreach, and community giving.

(h) Labor Relations Committee

The labor relations committee handles labor union matters, contracts, and bargaining rights of unions. It also deals with problems and issues between a company's management and its union leaders.

(i) Wage and Benefits Committee

The wage and benefits committee oversees employee wages and benefits programs and ensures that they are consistent with the organization's objectives and that committee's fiduciary responsibilities are properly discharged. The committee conducts benchmarking studies and surveys on employee wages and benefits with other companies in the same industry and other industries in general.

(j) Compensation Committee

The compensation or remuneration committee focuses on compensation arrangements for the board of directors and key executives that help achieve the organization's objectives and do not emphasize short-term results at the expense of long-term performance. The scope of work includes executive compensation, board compensation, and incentive packages (bonuses, stocks, and perks) for executives and the board members. The committee should ensure that the incentive packages do not contain language that rewards unnecessary and unwanted risk taking by board members and executives. That is, undue risk taking must be discouraged.

An increasing number of countries consider it good practice for compensation (remuneration) policy and employment contracts for board members and key executives to be handled by a special committee of the board comprised either wholly or by a majority of independent directors. There are also calls for a remuneration committee that excludes executives that serve on each other's remuneration committees (i.e., the same executive working on cross-committees), which could lead to conflicts of interest.

(k) Investigative Committee

The investigative committee handles financial restatements to answer questions from securities regulators. This committee also reviews insider trading scandals and unethical behavior in raising new capital in financial markets. The investigative committee is also called a special committee because it handles rare issues.

(l) Standing Committee

The standing committee focuses on periodically and independently reviewing and evaluating directors' compensation and remuneration packages, including those of executives. The goal is to make sure that these compensation packages are in line with those of other companies in the same industry and to adjust polices accordingly. An important task of the standing committee is to review stakeholder and shareholder relations.

(m) Grievance Committee

The grievance committee deals with several types of grievances, such as nonunion employee, union-employee, customer, supplier, and contractor grievances alleging unfair practices and discrimination matters.

(n) Human Resources Committee

The HR committee deals with setting policies and procedure in hiring, training, developing, and terminating employees in coordination with functional management. It also deals with employment or hiring contracts for employees and independent contractors. A special focus is placed on handling complaints such as whistleblowing issues and consequent retaliations.

(o) Technology Committee

The technology committee focuses on investments in technology, automation projects, cyber-risks, cyberattacks, malware attacks, ransomware attacks, data breaches, website crashes, and other computer-related risks. The technology committee is also called a steering committee to approve and monitor investments into technology projects.

(p) Public Relations Committee

The PR committee deals with crisis situations facing a company. Specifically, the PR committee:

- Deals with product recalls for manufactured products and poor-quality problems (e.g., *E. coli*) in processed and prepared products.

- Looks into how management responds to crisis situations and resolves them in a timely or proper manner. (Lack of timely and proper response or simply no response can destroy goodwill and reputation of a company.)

- Addresses negative comments posted by its customers on social media networks based on experiences with the company's products and services. (Failure to address these comments can lead to reputation risk.)

Examples of crisis situations that raise serious public relations issues include:

- Defective airbags in automobiles, resulting in deaths and accidents
- Car makers manipulating software that decreases pollution emitting from automobiles
- Airline employees' unacceptable behavior toward customers
- Oil companies dumping polluted materials into rivers and lakes, killing sea life and polluting drinking water

A corporation's reputation risk is a major concern here.

(q) Legal Committee

The legal committee handles legal matters, such as lawsuits, fines, punishments, and imprisonments. The source of lawsuits can include competitors, customers, employees, suppliers, vendors, contractors, and regulatory agencies. Not handling these lawsuits in a timely and proper manner can increase reputation risk.

(r) Supply-Chain Committee

The supply-chain committee focuses on risks such as product tampering by suppliers in the supply chain, counterfeit products, or embedding malware and ransomware programming code in assembling or delivering computer software and equipment. Product recalls and product contaminations are a major risk here.

(s) Intellectual Property Committee

The intellectual property (IP) committee works on protecting the ownership of copyrights, trademarks, service marks, trade secrets, and patents owned by a company. It also deals with violation or infringement of IP rights. The risk of ransomware attack is possible with IP rights where hackers copy, steal, and sell a company's IP assets.

(t) Policy Committee

The policy committee establishes or reviews organization-wide policies on major topics or issues, including:

- Workforce diversity
- Sexual harassment
- Executive succession planning
- Management development training programs
- Employee hiring, training, promotion, and termination programs
- Equal wages and benefits for all employees
- Access to and use of social media networks
- Use of company email server per personal use or use of personal email server for business use
- Disclosure of confidential, personal, and medical information, and insider trading

(u) Regulatory and Compliance Committee

The regulatory and compliance committee focuses on compliance with existing laws, rules, and regulations (LRR) affecting a company or industry. It also looks into how new regulations will affect a company's revenue and profit structure. Management conducts cost-benefit analyses for both current and new regulations. It estimates the negative consequences (negative impacts) in terms of fines and penalties due to noncompliance with LRR. Reputation risks increase in direct proportion to the increase in noncompliance with LRR due to fines, penalties, and negative publicity. It requires that all employees and management should have a high regard for compliance with LRR and that the committee compares the cost of compliance with LRR with the cost of noncompliance with LRR. Legal risk in terms of severe fines and penalties are a major concern here.

(v) Steering Committee

The steering committee, also called a technology committee, approves and monitors investments into technology projects. Other reasons for establishing a steering committee are to manage a major real estate development program or to plan to build a public park in a city.

(w) Special Committee

A special committee can be installed to handle one-of-a-kind or rare issues or topics, such as investigating fraud and unethical behaviors of senior management and discussing compensation or remuneration matters for directors, key executives, and senior management team that appeared in recent news media. Other reasons for establishing a special committee is to conduct a survey about information security practices, data breaches, cybercrimes, and website crashes in a company.

(x) Ad Hoc Committee

An ad hoc committee (also known as last-minute committee, as-needed committee, or on-the-spot committee) is installed to address temporary and emergency problems (e.g., employee protests on the streets for minimum wages). It brings a problem-specific team consisting of board members and others who possesses the relevant knowledge and skills to address a particular emergency. The committee is disbanded after its work is complete.

(y) Asset and Liability Committee

An asset and liability committee (ALC) is normally installed in financial service companies to establish policies and strategies, make and implement liquidity risk decisions, and actively monitor the organization's liquidity risk profile. The liquidity risk profile consists of high-quality liquid asset amounts, unencumbered asset amounts, contingency funding amounts, and stress-test ratio results. Liquidity risk results when a company is unable to fund increases in assets and unable to meet financial obligations as they come due without incurring unacceptable losses.

The ALC operates in the first line-of-defense (LOD) model and second LOD model, not in the third LOD model. In the first LOD model, the ALC proposes risk appetite levels, risk targets, and risk limits, including managing liquidity risks, market risks, and capital risks. The company's independent risk management function ensures that these proposals are appropriate and consistent with its stated risk profile. In the second LOD model, the ALC performs oversight responsibilities, such as reviewing liquidity risk profiles, monitoring conformance to the company's stated risk appetite, overseeing decision making related to managing assets and liabilities, reacting to changing market conditions, and ensuring the adequacy of the liquidity and capital resources. The liquidity risk is a major concern here.

5.8 Roles and Rights of Shareholders and Stakeholders

Both shareholders and stakeholders have basic roles to perform and rights to achieve in any size and type of organization. In addition to discussing these roles and rights, we present initiatives of shareholders and corporations and laws governing shareholder lawsuits.

(a) Roles of Shareholders Defined

Shareholders are owners of and investors in a corporation. The purpose of the corporation is to enhance shareholder value through effective and efficient management practices. Three types of shareholders exist: majority shareholders, minority shareholders, and activist shareholders. Each has different roles and rights.

Basically, **majority shareholders** are controlling shareholders who own less than 50% of the equity. **Minority shareholders** are noncontrolling shareholders who own less than 10% of the equity due to the number of shares they own in a company.

Activist shareholders, who can be considered minority shareholders, own less than 10% of outstanding shares and put public pressure on a company's management to:

- Change its major policies, investment and disinvestment practices, or financing structure (debt and equity proportions).
- Increase revenues and profits.
- Decrease fixed costs in its cost structure.
- Increase the dividend payout ratio.
- Distribute dividends as stock dividends, not as cash dividends, in order to increase their ownership percentage.

Activist shareholders (once called corporate raiders) use several forms of activism to express their displeasure with a company's management, including proxy fights, adverse publicity campaigns, and lawsuits. Many corporate boards have developed best practices and trained and educated the board members to increase their knowledge and skills to combat activist shareholders' efforts. In other words, the competency of board members is on the rise to fight activist shareholders and other challengers.

(b) Rights of Shareholders Defined

Shareholders have a right to vote and a right to file lawsuits. They have voting rights, cumulative voting rights, proxy voting rights, preemptive rights, and take-along rights, as described next. They can also file class action and derivative lawsuits.

(i) Voting Rights

Every active shareholder has a basic right to vote due to stock ownership and can elect a company's board members; vote on stock splits, spin-offs, mergers, acquisitions, and divestiture plans; and vote in regard to compensation for executives and board members. Shareholders exercise their voting rights with in-person or mail-in ballots.

(ii) Cumulative Voting Rights

Shareholders can assign their votes to one or more candidates for board member instead of voting separately for each member. Each shareholder requires a number of votes proportionate to his or her shareholdings (i.e., number of shares [say 50] multiplied by the number of open board positions [say 2] equals 100 votes). Ten to 15% of votes is required to select one board member. This approach allows minority shareholders to select some members of the board.

(iii) Proxy Voting Rights

Shareholders are authorized to vote on behalf of other shareholders who cannot attend the scheduled general board meeting. Some counties allow mail-in ballots for proxy voting.

(iv) Preemptive Rights

Preemptive rights are the first right given to existing shareholders to participate in any new capital increase (i.e., can purchase new shares issued by a company). They prevent a company from selling new shares on favorable terms to only some shareholders or to non-shareholders.

(v) Take-Along Rights

When a controlling or majority shareholder sells enough equity shares to a new shareholder, the new shareholder will inherit all the rights of the controlling shareholders. This means that the original owner's rights can be transferred to subsequent owners or new owners can take along all the rights of the old owners.

(c) Ownership Pyramid

Some companies have complex legal structures with straight shareholdings in one company or cross-shareholdings in two or more companies so a parent company can exercise control over its subsidiary companies in a pyramid organizational structure.

$$\text{Company A} \rightarrow \text{Company B} \rightarrow \text{Company C} \rightarrow \text{Company D}$$

Here, straight shareholdings means that Company A is an owner of some shares of Companies B, C, and D. Cross-shareholdings means that Company A is a parent company that owns 10% of Company B (Subsidiary 1), Company B owns 15% of Company C (Subsidiary 2), and Company C owns 5% of Company D (Subsidiary 3).

(d) Class-Action Lawsuits

Class-action lawsuits are filed by one or more shareholders of a company on behalf of other shareholders of the same company, all having the same problems, complaints, and grievances with the company's management. These lawsuits can save significant amounts of total legal expenses when each shareholder needs to file a lawsuit. An example is a lawsuit filed against the board for not addressing cyberattacks and data breaches in a timely and proper manner.

(e) Derivative Lawsuits

Derivative lawsuits are filed by shareholders on behalf of a corporation against an offending party for damages caused to the corporation when the corporation itself fails to bring a lawsuit against the offending party. Here the shareholders' goal is to recover damages due the corporation in which the recovered money is deposited into the company's treasury account after paying for the legal expenses. The recovered money does not go into the pockets of any shareholders.

(c) Roles and Rights of Stakeholders Defined

Stakeholders, other than shareholders, have a right to file lawsuits and grievances, but they have no right to vote. The purpose of a corporation is to serve a wider range of interests of its stakeholders and to solve various issues facing its stakeholders.

Stakeholders is a broad term that includes shareholders (stockholders) and nonshareholders. Stakeholders have a built-in stake in a corporation, meaning whatever a company's management does or does not do can directly or indirectly affect them both economically and socially. The types of stakeholders include shareholders (owners and investors), employees, management, creditors, labor unions, customers, suppliers and vendors, consultants and contractors, regulators, business partners, and citizens and society, each with different and conflicting roles, objectives, and expectations. Note that some stakeholders, such as employees and customers, can also become shareholders if they own their company's stocks.

Shareholders are the first stakeholders of a corporation and expect dividends, capital gains, and investment growth.

Employees are the internal prime stakeholders. They expect stable employment and decent wages and benefits to them and to their family.

Management is responsible for running a company and meeting the demands of various stakeholders.

Creditors are not the owners and are protected by contracts, covenants, and collaterals for lending their money to a corporation. They are concerned about the solvency of the corporation in terms of receiving interest payments and the principal amount of loans.

Labor unions protect the rights and obligations of their member employees. At times, they are in conflict with corporate management regarding wages, working conditions, and discrimination lawsuits.

Customers are the external prime stakeholders who purchase a company's good and services to meet their needs and wants.

Suppliers and vendors provide products and materials to operate a company. They expect to be paid after completing their work.

Consultants and contractors provide various services and expect to be paid after completing their work.

Regulators issue laws, rules, and regulations to protect the interests of businesses and their customers and expect compliance with such laws.

Business partners (e.g., joint ventures, insurance companies, and outsourcing firms) are external companies that collaborate and coordinate with a company to provide goods and services and expect the company to operate ethically and legally with trust and good reputation.

Citizens and society expect charitable contributions; sponsor educational, environmental, and health training programs; and develop and improve local community relations. They expect companies to become good corporate citizens.

An effective corporate governance model requires that all shareholders and stakeholders will have a common purpose and principles of transparency, accountability, fairness, and responsibility, as described next.

- Transparency—Full disclosure of financial and nonfinancial information

- Accountability—An independent and competent governing body that admits their own actions and inactions

- Fairness—Treating investors and noninvestors equally

- Responsibility—Fulfilling its defined roles with duty of care and duty of loyalty combined with exercising due process and due diligence

(d) Initiatives of Shareholders and Corporations

Initiatives are new programs and projects to make current and future things better as they are done on a proactive basis to address current problems and issues. Both shareholders and corporations have their own initiative agendas to improve each other and as a response to each other.

Examples of **shareholder initiatives** include increases in:

- Filing of shareholder lawsuits against directors especially with respect to buyout offer prices.

- Shareholder activist groups through organizing and exercising power over company management.

- Filing of shareholder resolutions at annual meetings through booklets of shareholder questions.

A rationale behind the shareholder initiatives is to protect the shareholders from courts, applying the legal concept of piercing the corporate veil.

Examples of **corporation initiatives** include:

- Increasing amounts of full disclosure of information to investors that affects their investment decisions.

- Showing full accountability and transparency to shareholders about business activities, financial condition, and tender offers made during mergers and acquisitions.

- Avoiding conflict-of-interest situations by board members and executives.

- Avoiding the use of insider information for personal gain by board members and executives.

- Avoiding personal use of company assets and taking personal loans by directors, officers, and executives.

- Maintaining arm's-length relationships with related entities and third parties during business transactions.

(e) Laws Governing Shareholder Lawsuits

Shareholder activist groups are increasingly suing companies for major or minor reasons, and most of these suits are settled out of court. Examples of major reasons for these lawsuits include paying a high price for the acquisition of new assets and receiving a low price for the divestiture of existing assets. The U.S. Private Securities Litigation Reform Act of 1995 was issued to curb the filing of frequent and frivolous class action lawsuits in federal courts. A loophole in the act diverted the cases from federal courts, which increased the filings of such lawsuits in state courts. The U.S. Securities Litigation Uniform Standards Act of 1998 was issued to plug that loophole;

according to this act, state court filings will be referred to federal district courts for the district in which the action is pending. This means that all lawsuits must be filed in federal courts, which come under the provisions of the 1995 act.

5.9 Scope of Board-Level Audits

The chief audit executive or an outside consultant can conduct a board-level audit for publicly held companies periodically to ensure that all board-level activities and programs are functioning effectively and efficiently. This audit work also looks at the effectiveness of the board's oversight responsibilities by reviewing corporate governance, risk management, and control policies, procedures, and activities. The following are the required levels of audit clients when conducting board-level audits and when using 360-degree performance reviews with all of the audit stakeholders together to obtain a well-rounded feedback and big-picture assessment.

First-level audit clients → Board members and board chairperson

Second-level audit clients → Executives and officers

Third-level audit clients → Vice presidents and division heads

Fourth-level audit clients → General managers and functional managers

(a) Audit Scope

The audit scope depends on the type and size of an organization, meaning that a large organization may need a bigger scope than a small organization, which may need a smaller scope. Eighteen specific audit areas are listed next; they can be combined into a few major audit groups or teams for convenience and relevancy purposes.

1. Onboarding programs
2. Skills and competency levels
3. Compensation audit
4. Interlocking and shadow directors
5. Reputation management
6. Strategic audit
7. Stakeholder audit
8. Due diligence audit
9. Performance metrics audit
10. Legal and insurance audit
11. Board-level committee audit
12. Risk management audit
13. Social responsibility audit
14. Ethics audit
15. Compliance audit

16. Corporate sustainability audit

17. Cybersecurity awareness audit

18. Governance audit

(i) Inputs to the Board Audit

A company's board is composed of several members from inside and outside of the company where one member is elected as the chair of the board. Several input documents exist or are required either prior to or during the board audit; these include:

- Board's charter and bylaws
- Board's organization chart
- Board members' resumes and job descriptions
- Company's strategic plans
- CEO's status reports to the board's chair
- Board's financial budget
- Board's minutes of meetings with meeting agenda
- Directors' contract for services
- Board's special studies and reports
- Company survey results
- Outside consultant reports
- Quarterly and annual financial reports
- Stakeholder complaints and reports
- Company annual reports
- Board-level committee charter and reports
- Board's and CEO's press briefings

(b) Specific Audits

Details of each specific audit or review are presented next.

(i) Onboarding Programs

An onboarding program for first-time directors and new directors is an educational and training program with the essential information needed to understand a company and start contributing value to the company. It is also called a job orientation program, job induction program, or job preview program (most suitable to regular and low-level employees) providing practical advice as to what to do and what not to do during board meetings and other interactions with senior management and outsiders (e.g., the press). The program provides a job description and checklists on various topics to familiarize people with the company's strategy, operations, products, services, markets, customers, and suppliers. The National Association of Corporate Directors (NACD) provides an onboarding guide for new directors (www.nacdonline.org).

(ii) Skills and Competency Levels

As more and more publicly held companies are engaged in a globally complex business environment, the skills and competency levels of the board of directors must be current with the business environment so they can make informed and intelligent decisions. Therefore, directors must possess the right skills and competencies. Otherwise, skills and competency gaps can exist, resulting in an ineffective and inefficient board. All directors must have a thorough understanding and ability to apply both hard skills and soft skills to the company they represent. Many directors do not possess the right type and mix of skills needed to do their jobs because they acquired those jobs based on personal contacts and informal selection criteria. NACD provides certificate and training programs for directors to increase their skills and competency levels (www.nacdonline.org).

For example, a high-tech company might require the directors to possess technology and business skills; a bank or financial institution might require directors to possess accounting, finance, and business skills; a marketing-oriented company might require directors to possess marketing, sales, and business skills; and a durable-goods manufacturing company might require directors to possess engineering, manufacturing, and business skills.

(iii) Compensation Audit

The compensation, remuneration, incentive, and bonus package for executives and directors has been a hotly debated topic for many years. The right compensation package for a specific organization is not easy to determine except by conducting benchmarking studies with other similar and competing organizations. Ideally, a compensation package is linked to performance levels, which is not easy to do because of uncertainty of future outcomes. For example, a CEO who is hired to turn around a troubled company will demand much higher compensation package than otherwise due to the uncertain outcomes he or she may face.

Usually compensation packages contain two elements: a fixed element and a variable element. Fixed items include a yearly base salary with defined increments, termination and retirement amounts, some perks, and severance pay. Bonuses, promotions, stock options, and some perks can be variable elements.

Major concerns when reviewing the effectiveness of the compensation committee are listed next.

- Are committee members fully independent directors from outside the company?

- Is the clawback provision invoked against the CEO and CFO to reduce their compensation and bonuses when financial statements are restated due to their wrongdoing, either knowing or unknowing?

- Are compensation-related disclosures written in plain English with clear and complete content that is full and fair in presenting all material information to investors? These disclosure topics can include:

  □ Related-party transactions exceeding certain dollar amounts

  □ Valuation of perquisites (perks)

  □ Performance targets and thresholds with a balance between the needs of investors for full disclosure and this potentially sensitive information ending up in the hands of competitors

□ Postemployment compensation disclosures, including potential payments from retirement plans, nonqualified deferred compensation, and healthcare benefit payments

□ Summary compensation tables showing total compensation package listing the annual increase in accrued value of pension benefits and the fair value basis for reporting option grants

□ Performance graphs providing a quick performance comparison in close proximity to compensation disclosures that are valuable to investors. These graphs are a readily accessible and noncontroversial source for performance comparisons that shareholders often use in their proposals and decisions.

Note that the SEC allows a company to apply the **safe harbor principle,** where it can exclude key information regarding performance targets and thresholds if that information may be competitively damaging or harmful to the company if disclosed. The SEC also requires companies to include a compensation discussion and analysis section in their annual reports that integrates the strengths of a principle-based approach with a broad focus and a rule-based approach with a narrow focus.

(iv) Interlocking and Shadow Directors

Having interlocking directors and shadow directors is a major concern because it defies good corporate governance principles and dilutes the effectiveness of a board's function. **Interlocking directors** or interlocking directorates mean some company board members also are working on other company boards, thus presenting a conflict-of-interest situation. In addition, these directors may spread themselves too thin, which means they do not have enough time to pay full attention to one company's issues.

Shadow directors are outsiders who do not sit on a company's board but can exert considerable influence over the board's strategies, plans, policies, programs, and practices. Examples of shadow directors include lobbyists, activists, majority shareholders, friends, family members, and consultants. The presence of shadow directors is a major concern to shareholders and stakeholders.

(v) Reputation Management

Reputation is what outsiders think about a company, its products and services, and its management, board, employees, suppliers, bankers, and investors. It represents an image of a company, which is an outside-in view. Boards are increasingly taking responsibility for overseeing reputational risk as a part of managing a company's reputation. It is much easier to destroy a company's or a person's reputation than to create it. There are two types of reputation: an organization's reputation and a director's personal reputation. An organization's reputation can include product, service, customer, supplier, management, brand, and compliance reputation.

Factors that can create a positive or negative reputation include:

■ Handling of cybersecurity risks (e.g., ransomware)

■ Product safety issues, including product recalls

■ Customer and employee safety issues

■ Regulatory compliance or noncompliance

- Mishandling of supply chain matters

- Mishandling of public relations (PR) matters

- Mismanaging of social media matters

- Handling of stakeholder relations

- Management's ethical or unethical behavior

For example, cybersecurity liabilities can occur with higher frequency with bigger severity amounts. Positive reputation can be differentiated from negative reputation, as shown next.

Positive Reputation	New customer acquisitions
	Competitive advantage
	Increased brand value
	Higher shareholder value with increased stock market price
	Increased revenues and profits
	Good public relations
	High regard for compliance with laws, rules, regulations, and ethics
	Higher customer goodwill
	Innovative management
	Overall higher corporate value
Negative Reputation	Current customer defections
	Competitive disadvantages
	Decreased brand value due to tarnished brand perceptions
	Lower shareholder value due to drop in stock market price
	Decreased revenues and profits
	Bad public relations
	Low regard for compliance with laws, rules, regulations, and ethics
	Lower customer goodwill
	Higher turnover in management
	Inability to hire talented employees
	Status quo management
	Lower corporate value

EXAMPLES

Some situations that can create negative reputations are listed next.

- An airline company's website crashed and computer systems malfunctioned without backup systems, resulting in hundreds of flights canceled and thousands of passengers stranded at airports.

- Airline companies mishandled customers due to overbooking of flight tickets.

- Automobile companies recalled millions of cars and trucks due to defective manufacturing.

- An automobile company's senior management was involved in illegal manipulation of software to show low levels of pollution.

- An automobile air bag manufacturer made defective air bags that killed many people inside vehicles.

- Many organizations experienced severe cyberattacks and massive data breaches due to weak security controls.

These negative reputation cases have cost the companies involved millions of dollars in fines and repairs, declines in sales, profits, and market stock price, loss of jobs, bankruptcies, low asking price in mergers and acquisitions, negative goodwill, and bad image.

(vi) More on a Director's Personal Reputation

With the increased presence of activist shareholders and directors on a company's board, individual directors are often targeted and challenged with lawsuits, demands, damaging insinuations, humiliations, and insults, resulting in a destruction of personal reputation of directors (i.e., personal reputation risk). A risk mitigation strategy for these risk-prone directors is to purchase a reputational insurance policy covering indemnification instruments, which are like performance or warranty bonds. These insurance policies aim to absolve board members of damaging insinuations made by activists and other stakeholders. Risk insurance is a part of clawback strategy, and it is a very clear way to repair personal damage done through corporate wrongdoings. There are two components to the cost of reputation: cost of damage (i.e., current costs) and cost of lost opportunity (i.e., future costs), as shown:

$$\text{Cost of Reputation} = \text{Cost of Damage} + \text{Cost of Lost Opportunity}$$
$$\text{Reputation Costs} = \text{Current Costs} + \text{Future Costs}$$

Major reasons for a director's personal reputation risk caused by activists and nonactivists are listed next.

- Activists are unhappy with the board's actions and inaction.

- Activists have overexpectations of board members.

- Activists place unreasonable demands on board members.

- Activists want more than what board members can deliver.

- Ineffective directors cannot meet even reasonable demands from activists.

- Incompetent directors have outdated skills and experiences and do not understand their roles.

(vii) Strategic Audit

The strategic audit is a systematic and structured review of identifying issues and problems in the understanding and execution of the approved corporate strategy in various business functions and activities and making recommendations to resolve such issues and problems. Strategic audits should focus on deciding whether a corporation is creating a value-based organization, not a profit-maximization, wealth-maximization, or stock-price maximization organization. Ensure that the board members and senior managers have stress-tested the corporate strategy document before approving and releasing it to the entire corporation.

(viii) Stakeholder Audit

The stakeholder audit is a systematic and structured review of issues and problems related to stakeholders (e.g., rights and privileges) and making recommendations to resolve such issues and problems. Stakeholders include shareholders, employees, customers, suppliers, vendors, unions, contractors, consultants, and regulatory authorities.

(ix) Due Diligence Audit

Due diligence audits are performed in several areas of business. They provide a safety valve to management that is: planning to acquire, manage, or consolidate with other businesses; starting joint ventures; and performing environmental impact studies. These due diligence audits are the minimum managerial requirements to ensure that all applicable laws and regulations are met and that risks and exposures are minimized. For example, due diligence audits are risk management tools for banks, land buyers, and lending agencies when a buyer is purchasing land or accepting it as a gift. Here the buyer wants to minimize potential legal liability resulting from the land acquisition.

Due diligence audits are team-based efforts with internal and external auditors, lawyers, engineers, IT staff, and other specialists. Three phases in this audit include: information gathering, information analysis, and information reporting. Information gathering involves collecting information through document reviews, interviews, and meetings. Information analysis may include analytical reviews, including ratio analysis, regression analysis, and other quantitative techniques. Information reporting includes writing a balanced report based on facts with an executive summary. In addition to writing reports, oral reports can be used for immediate response and clarification of issues and findings.

(x) Performance Metrics Audit

The CAE should ensure that the board measures, monitors, and manages board-level metrics and key performance indicators with a focus on quantitative (financial) and qualitative (nonfinancial) measures. Here, it can be assumed that what is not measured is not managed. Performance metrics can be financial and nonfinancial in nature, as described next.

Financial Metrics	Sales and profits year over year
	Market share price year over year
	Earnings per share
	Return on investment, sales, equity, assets, value, training, research, data, and capital
Nonfinancial Metrics	Cybersecurity risk
	Customer satisfaction
	Product quality and safety
	Workplace safety and security
	Eployee morale
	Key employee turnover
	Workplace diversity
	Supplier/vendor relationship
	Regulatory compliance
	Negative comments posted on social media about a company's products and services (require a careful monitoring as they can increase the company's reputation risk)

(xi) Legal and Insurance Audit

Legal obligations are what the directors and officers (D&Os) of a company are legally required to adhere to in discharging their job duties and responsibilities. Examples of legal obligations include due process, due care, due diligence, due professional care, duty of loyalty, duty of care, and duty of obedience. Legal liabilities arise when these legal obligations are not properly met. Here the audit concern is to ensure that all lawsuits filed against board members and against the organization (i.e., all legal liabilities) are resolved properly and timely with case-aging analysis done. The case-aging analysis is similar to account-aging analysis, showing how long a case was open.

One way to address the legal obligations and liabilities is to acquire a D&O insurance policy with an adequate amount of coverage at an appropriate cost to protect the D&Os' personal assets. Due to recent corporate scandals, public companies and their D&Os face a greater scrutiny by U.S. federal regulators regarding corporate conduct and wrongdoing than ever before.[8]

Examples: Laws and Regulations Affecting the D&Os' Insurance

Several laws and regulations affecting D&Os' insurance include:

- Sarbanes-Oxley Act of 2002 dealing with internal control, fraud, and ethics.

- U.S. Department of Justice's renewed focus on individual accountability issued in 2015. These increased accountability guidelines give a "cooperation credit" in the context of corporate wrongdoing with forthcoming facts with open mind for reduced fines and punishments.

- U.S. Securities and Exchange Commission's increased efforts on corporate wrongdoing in securities fraud, stock market trading scandals, and financial misstatements.

- Foreign Corrupt Practices Act of 1998 for bribery and fraud.

- U.S. Department of Labor and the National Labor Relations Board for joint employer liability regarding the right to control a single employee in 2015.

- U.S. Securities Litigation Uniform Standards Act of 1998 to curb the filing of frequent and frivolous class action lawsuits against a company.

Scope and Nature of D&Os' Issues

- Shareholder derivative lawsuits

- Shareholder class-action lawsuits

- Merger and acquisition issues

- Spin-offs (divestitures)

- Bankruptcy

- Employment-related liability cases

- Cyberrisk cases

- Corporate investigations of fraud and wrongdoings

At a minimum, companies should acquire these types of insurance policies:

- D&O liability insurance

- Transactional risk insurance

- Data loss insurance

---

[8] National Association of Corporate Directors, *Evolving Directors & Officers Liability Environment, Emerging Issues & Considerations* (Washington, DC: Author, 2017), www.nacdonline.org/.

Examples: Laws and Regulations Affecting the D&Os' Insurance *(Continued)*

- Regulatory investigations insurance
- Cyberinsurance
- Business interruption insurance

The legal and insurance audit should:

- Ascertain whether a corporation's bylaws contain specific language requiring the company to indemnify current and former D&Os to the fullest extent permitted by law.

- Regarding corporate investigations, ensure that a company has purchased a "look-back" insurance coverage to address payment for previously incurred defense costs or investigation costs. Some "look-back" coverage will pay for costs incurred after a securities claim is resolved.

- Regarding spin-off transactions, ensure that the existing company retains all of the prior acts liability and the new company does not purchase any prior acts protection or coverage. There should be uniform D&O coverage at least in the first year after the spin-off transaction for both companies to avoid "finger-pointing" behavior.

- Ensure that the D&O insurance policy adequately covers actions during and after a potential bankruptcy. Ensure that a runoff insurance policy is purchased prior to entering bankruptcy, not after. Note that insurance recoveries should not be subject to bankruptcy stays.

- Ensure that a company has purchased runoff coverage or tail insurance for claims that might arise after closing of mergers and acquisition, bankruptcy, or spin-off transactions based on decisions that were made prior to the transaction.

- Ensure that D&Os have sufficient limits of liability coverage through regression loss analysis of claims filed, industry trends, fit-gap analysis, and benchmarks against peer companies. Multiple layers of insurance coverage are better than a single layer of insurance for D&Os who are on the move to higher levels of responsibility.

- Conduct a case-aging analysis to determine the elapsed time between the case-filed date and the analysis-date or case-resolved date. Determine whether the elapsed time is excessive or not after comparing it to a policy or standard.

(xii) Board-Level Committee Audit

Committees have high visibility and high impact on organizations due to their strategic representation of executive management. The decisions of board members affect the entire company. The outcome of a committee's work is a new or revised policy, plan, or procedure to make current things better or future things even better. Several types of committees are established in both private and public sector organizations, managed by committee chairs, and they take big-picture perspectives.

The basic audit concerns are to ensure that all board-level committees have a specific charter document, that they have solved the known problems, and that they have found resolutions to the reported issues.

Major audit concerns include lack of financial experts sitting on the audit committee and lack of independent directors on the audit committee. The highest standards of independence rule applies to the audit committee due to its responsibility in overseeing financial statements and internal control systems.

(xiii) Risk Management Audit

Through his or her leadership skills, the chief risk officer (CRO) (or equivalent position) must assign proper responsibility and authority and exact clear accountability to promote a risk acceptable mind-set in the organization. It is important to recognize that not all risks can be eliminated, be known, or be ignored. The only thing that matters is that all risks must be controlled and managed. However, even after installing safeguards (controls), a residual risk always exists. That risk is either accepted or self-insured. The risk management audit primarily focuses on the risk management framework since it is the highest level of the risk hierarchy and because it encompasses all risk components. The major audit objective is to ensure that the risk management framework is current and appropriate for the needs of the company.

At a minimum, the CRO or designee must conduct a risk management self-audit in these areas:

- Various types of business risks, such as financial risk (e.g., off-balance-sheet items, swaps, options, hedge funds, and derivatives; foreign exchange risk), and trade risks, such as increased international trade barriers and increased tariffs

- Political risk (possibility of asset expropriation by foreign governments and political instability)

- Technical risk (resulting from the use of leading-edge and bleeding-edge technologies)

- Product risk (unmet customer needs, poor design quality, and poor production quality)

- Project risk (time delays and cost overruns)

- Reputation risk (resulting from product defects, recalls, and service mishaps; and rumors and bad publicity, which are reflected in lower stock prices)

- Legal risk (resulting from current and anticipated lawsuits)

Major audit concerns are determining whether the CRO is managing key risk indicators, derisking efforts, and value-at-risk amounts. In addition, the CRO or designee must issue an audit report listing the deficiency findings and recommendations for improvement.

(xiv) Social Responsibility Audit

The social responsibility audit is a systematic and structured review of identifying issues and problems in the understanding and fulfilling of economic, legal, ethical, and philanthropic responsibilities and making recommendations to resolve such issues and problems. A full scope of social responsibility of a corporation can include four major areas: economic, legal, ethical, and philanthropic responsibility.

Special audit areas include (1) whether the company's products are made by child labor in offshore manufacturing plants, (2) whether employees are receiving less than minimum wages and working in dangerous conditions; (3) whether the company is polluting or removing pollution from the environment; and (4) whether the company's products contain any animal skin or parts, which is against the beliefs of animal activists.

(xv) Ethics Audit

The chief ethics officer and staff should develop an ethics manual describing expected behavior of employees and other stakeholders. The contents of this manual may include these items:

- Written policies and procedures on conflicts of interest and code of conduct
- Restrictions regarding accepting or giving gifts and travel by procurement, contracting, marketing, and sales personnel
- Requirement for written disclosures on executives' financial condition and outside earned income activities
- Rules regarding employing relatives (nepotism)
- Rules regarding putting ghost, imposter, or shadow employees on the payroll
- Ways to protect the organization's property and information
- Descriptions of allowed political contributions and activities
- Treatment of sales of stock acquired pursuant to exercise of stock options to comply with conflict-of-interest requirements
- Restrictions on sharing or using insider information for financial gain
- Protections for whistleblowing employees

Other aspects of ethics audits can include how the company's management and employees handle various groups or activities, such as:

- Shareholders, creditors, and investors
- Stock markets and investment analysts
- Employees and labor unions
- Regulators and government authorities
- Suppliers, vendors, contractors, consultants, and customers
- Purchasing agents, buyers, and salespeople
- Related parties and third parties
- Mergers, acquisitions, and divestitures activities

Here the audit concern is whether these activities are handled ethically or unethically.

Because culture affects ethics, they should be audited together. Whether an act is ethical or unethical depends on whether a culture is good or bad. A good culture encourages ethical behavior (e.g., honesty, integrity, and equity). A bad culture encourages unethical behavior (e.g., bribes, corruption, and collusion). It has been reported that the number of workplace ethical misconduct (i.e., rule-breaking incidents) increases and the compliance rate with laws decreases the higher up in the management hierarchy you go.

(xvi) Compliance Audit

When conducting a compliance audit, there are three major audit concerns:

1. Management's attitude toward compliance with the laws, rules, and regulations (LRRs). Company management with a high regard for compliance with LRRs will have a high, positive reputation in the business community and society, and vice versa.

2. Cost of noncompliance with LRRs.

3. Cost of compliance with LRRs.

The chief audit executive and staff should study the costs of compliance and of noncompliance with LRRs over a specific period (e.g., last five years) and identify trends and patterns. If the trend shows that costs are increasing, the audit staff should determine reasons and root causes for such increases.

A key concern when conducting a compliance audit is the cost of noncompliance and not so much of cost of compliance. This is because a company's reputation depends on noncompliance with the LRRs and the cost of noncompliance. The higher the noncompliance rate is, the higher the noncompliance costs, and the greater the reputation costs (or the greater the loss of reputation). Compliance with the LRRs and incurring costs for compliance are expected of all organizations as part of doing business, regardless of their size.

For example, a bank's policy on compliance with LRRs in the area of lending practices and programs can include the following:

- Commissions, gifts, bribes, and kickbacks of anything of value should not be received for procuring loans.

- Loans made in connection with any political election to any political party should comply with all applicable laws and regulations, such as the U.S. Foreign Corrupt Practices Act and the U.S. Federal Election Campaign Act.

- Loans to executives, officers, and principal shareholders should not be based on any special treatment, and there should be no appearance of conflicts of interest, as per the Financial Institutions Regulatory and Interest Rate Control Act.

- Independent appraisals and evaluations should be received for all real estate loans prior to making the final credit decision in conformance with the Financial Institutions Reform, Recovery, and Enforcement Act.

- All loan applicants should be fully informed of the annual interest rate, finance charges, amount financed, total monthly payments, and repayment schedule as mandated by the Federal Reserve's Truth in Lending Act (Regulation Z).

- Mortgage life insurance coverage for real estate loans should comply with the sales practices, sales commission limits, and disclosure requirements as defined in the Federal Reserve's policy statements.

(xvii) Corporate Sustainability Audit

A corporate sustainability audit focuses on (1) whether a corporation can survive or die (e.g., Enron and Toys R Us Corporations) in the long term and (2) determining what and how the board of directors and senior management are prepared to continue corporate growth and prosperity and to prevent corporate decline.

The scope of the audit includes a review of environmental, social, and governance (ESG) matters and a review of non-ESG matters such as products, services, sales, revenues, costs, profits, market share, and market price of a company's stock. Note that the ESG matters are related to outside of a corporation's boundaries and the non-ESG matters are related to inside of a corporation's boundaries. An audit objective is to determine how much attention is given to the ESG matters and non-ESG matters and in what proportion and whether these two matters are integrated. An example of a company that did not pay proper and timely attention to the ESG matters was British Petroleum's (BP's) oil spill disaster case.

An audit report is issued to the chairperson of the board and senior managers with details of findings (problems) and recommendations (solutions).

(xviii) Cybersecurity Awareness Audit

The scope of cybersecurity awareness audit is to review whether the board members and senior manager of a corporation are aware of the cybersecurity threats and attacks (e.g., data breaches and ransomware attacks). The audit objective is to determine what policy and security control mechanisms the board is overseeing and their effective implementation.

Cybersecurity is no longer a technical issue left to IT management, Instead, it has become a major corporate issue due to its severe negative consequences, leading to financial risks and reputational risks (e.g., Target and Sony Corporation's data breaches).

(xix) Governance Audit

The corporate governance audit is a systematic and structured review of issues and problems related to disclosure and transparency in the areas of financial condition shown in the balance sheet, performance reporting, ownership, and board responsibilities and recommendations to resolve such issues and problems. The governance audit is the final audit of corporate governance practices. It determines whether a corporation is using the right governance framework for its business (i.e., the framework is current and appropriate).

To this end, the board chair must manage and monitor governance risk indicators (GRIs), which are warning signs of impairments or threats to governance principles and mechanisms. Corrective actions are needed to fix these GRIs. A list of GRIs is presented next.

- No policy on age limits, term limits, service-year limits, and tenure limits for directors. This means directors can work for the same company for 10 years or longer, which prevents the influx of new blood, new thinking, new insights, new experiences, and diverse perspectives. Board members are a close-knit society similar to a country club or social club of elites. They have long experience, but it is the one-year experience that is repeated many times.

- No policy on director nominations or renominations, especially in regard to underperforming directors.

- No clear criteria on a director's required skill sets, relevant work experience, and professionalism with education and certificates of proficiency and competency, all leading to ineffective boards.

■ No percentage limit on a director's equity ownership in the company.

■ No dollar limits on a director's commercial relationship (e.g., contracts on selling, buying, trading, brokering, and supplying some products or services) with the company.

■ No clear picture on how the size and nature of executive compensation, incentives, and perquisites are designed and how it is linked to executives' targeted and actual performance.

■ No time limits on a director's previous management job in the company until after a reasonable time has elapsed. (Such limits ensure a director's independence and objectivity.)

■ No new director hired in the last 5 or 10 years (shows stagnation at the board level).

■ Board composed of a few independent directors and many nonindependent directors. (A percentage must be decided on, such as two-thirds or three-fourths of independent directors.)

■ Same board chair and CEO (no separation exists between the chair's role and the CEO's role). The goal is to keep these roles separate to avoid conflicts of interest and to place a cross-check on each person's work. Also, when the CEO retires, he or she should not be appointed as a board member or board chair (because he or she could influence the board's function).

■ No executive sessions between independent directors and outside directors for a long time without the CEO. (Excluding the CEO would allow board members to measure the CEO's performance.)

■ No executive sessions between the board and the CEO for a long time without the presence of other senior managers, officers, and executives. (Excluding them would enable the board to measure the performance of other senior managers, officers, and executives.)

■ Leaderless board. There is no full-time and permanent position as board chair. Instead, board members take on the chair's job on a part-time and rotating basis (such as monthly, quarterly, yearly, per meeting, as needed or ad hoc, crisis, or per request). In the absence of a full-time board chair, individual responsibilities cannot be assigned fully and individual accountabilities cannot be exacted correctly, thus leading to a chaotic and finger-pointing environment. This means the chair is not in the same job long enough to be held accountable and to determine his or her real contribution because the board member is working on a borrowed time.

■ Incomplete and noncurrent succession planning for key management positions. The board stops the succession planning at the CEO level and does not extend it down three or four levels below the CEO level. This means that no backup management is available to continue the business after the CEO level.

■ Minimal participation of women and minorities on the board. Boards should conduct benchmark studies with best-in-class companies to find out the optimal level of participation (a 50–50 rate is ideal) after considering diversity goals in gender, minority, and ethnicity.

■ Use of immature and outdated frameworks for governance, risk management, and control processes, resulting in a greater exposure to new threats and vulnerabilities and missed opportunities, all resulting in unpreparedness.

■ Failure of board members to put hard questions to the CEO and senior management in order to maintain good rapport with them. Instead, board members are using box-ticking, box-checking, rubber-stamp approaches and not exercising strong teeth, thus becoming a weak board. Under these conditions, it is hard to make the CEO and senior management accountable for their actions and inactions.

- Table testing documents (i.e., simply reading at a table), instead of stress testing or deep testing to prove that the strategy works in real life.

- Shortage of directors due to a personal reputation risk, resulting from legal liabilities and propaganda in the media. Hence, many good executives are avoiding sitting on company boards, thinking that becoming a director is not worth the risk.

- Recycled directors (the same director serves on multiple company boards). Because of this, directors are stretched too thin to attend board meetings and have no time to prepare in advance of the meetings in order to ask hard questions. As a result, some directors are merely token directors who appear just to collect fees, perks, and bonuses.

- Inadequate company-sponsored D&O insurance, so directors and officers are not fully protected against lawsuits by shareholders, stakeholders, competitors, and the government and from personal reputation risk. High deductible amounts and large monthly premium payments for these insurance policies make them cost prohibitive for many directors and officers working in small and mid-cap companies. (A mid-cap company is a company listed on the over-the-counter stock market exchange.)

- Board chair who fails to identify underperforming directors and continues to renominate or reappoint them, thus perpetuating incompetent and ineffective boards.

5.10 Organizational Culture

Organizational culture is a set of shared values and norms guiding both employees' and managers' behavior. **Organizational culture** refers to a system of shared meaning held by employees that distinguishes their organization from other organizations. Organizational culture provides direction to employees and helps them understand how things are done in the organization. In other words, organizational culture defines the rules of the game, which are very difficult to understand.

A strong culture provides stability (asset) to an organization; at the same time, it can become a major barrier to change (liability). Every organization has a culture, and that culture can have a significant influence on employees' attitudes and behaviors. *The outcome of an organization's culture can be good or bad.*

Organizational Culture = Good (Asset) or Bad (Liability)

Researchers have identified seven characteristics that capture the essence of an organization's culture: innovation and risk taking, attention to detail, outcome (results), task orientation, people orientation, team orientation (team versus individual), aggressiveness (competitive versus easygoing), and stability (status quo versus growth).

Culture has two sides: functional culture (good) and dysfunctional culture (bad). The functional aspects of culture include a boundary-defining role, a sense of identity and commitment, stability of the social system through standards, and a control mechanism to guide and shape the attitudes and behaviors of employees. The dysfunctional aspects of a strong culture include barriers to change, to diversity, and to acquisitions and mergers.

Organizational Culture = Functional Culture + Dysfunctional Culture

Culture is first formed from the founder's philosophy, which is reflected in hiring employees at all levels. Later, the current top management sets the general climate of what is acceptable behavior and what is not. Culture is transmitted to employees through stories, rituals, material symbols, and language.

Culture is shared among employees through widened span of control, flattened organization structures, introduction of teams, reduced formalization, and empowerment to ensure that every employee is pointed in the same direction to achieve organization's common goals and objectives (i.e., goal-congruence principle).

Culture is made more customer-responsive through employee selection, training and socialization, organization structures, empowerment, leadership, performance evaluation, and reward systems.

(a) Organizational Culture and Ethics

Culture affects ethics. Whether an act is ethical or unethical depends on whether a culture is good or bad. A good culture encourages ethical behavior (e.g., honesty, integrity, and equity). A bad culture encourages unethical behavior (e.g., bribes, corruption, and collusion). A combination of the next five practices can create a more ethical and strong culture:

1. Be a visible role model by taking the ethical high road.
2. Communicate ethical expectations through a code of ethics.
3. Provide ethical training to address ethical dilemmas.
4. Reward work-related ethical acts visibly and publicly; punish unethical ones invisibly and privately.
5. Provide protective mechanisms to employees through ethical counselors, whistleblower protection, ombudsmen, or ethical officers.

The number of acts of workplace ethical misconduct (i.e., rule-breaking incidents) increases and the compliance rate with laws decreases as the management level increases up in the management hierarchy.

(b) Organizational Culture and Behavior

Organizational culture drives organizational behavior, which is concerned with the study of what employees do in an organization and how their behavior affects the organization's performance. It emphasizes behavior as related to concerns such as jobs/positions; work assignments and tasks; employee absenteeism, turnover, productivity, and performance; and management—all connected with employment-related situations. These concerns in turn are translated into core topics, such as motivation, leadership, communication (written and oral), groups/teams, learning and listening, attitudes, perceptions, change and conflict management, work design, and work-related stress. *The outcome of an organization's behavior can be good or bad.*

Organizational Culture → Organizational Behavior
Organizational Behavior = Good (Asset) or Bad (Liability)

Organizational behavior studies three determinants of behavior in organizations: individuals, groups, and structures. In addition, it applies the knowledge gained about individuals, groups, and the effect of structures on behavior in order to make organizations work more effectively and efficiently.

$$\text{Organizational Behavior} = \text{Individuals} + \text{Groups} + \text{Structures}$$
$$\text{Organizational Behavior} = \text{Organizational Effectiveness} + \text{Organizational Efficiency}$$

An organizational behavior model is developed by identifying dependent and independent variables to understand employee behavior, where independent variables impact dependent ones.

A dependent variable, which is the focus of organizational behavior, is the key factor to explain or predict and is affected by some other factor(s). Examples of dependent variables include productivity, absenteeism, turnover, deviant workplace behavior, organizational citizenship behavior, and job satisfaction.

An independent variable is the presumed cause of some change in the dependent variable. The independent variable is further divided into three levels: individual level (lowest level), group level (middle level), and organization level (highest level).

$$\text{Independent Variable} = \text{Individual Level} + \text{Group Level} + \text{Organization Level}$$

The **individual level** deals with issues such as personality and emotions, values and attitudes, ability, perception, motivation, individual learning and decision making, and biographical characteristics (e.g., age and gender).

The **group level** deals with issues such as group decision making, leadership and trust, group structure, communication, work teams, conflict, group power, and group or organizational politics.

The **organization level** deals with issues such as organizational culture, human resource policies and practices (e.g., employee selection processes, training and development programs, and performance evaluation methods), and organization structure and design.

Note that organizational behavior can be functional and dysfunctional, because behavior has two sides. **Functional behavior** means everyone is pulling in the same direction, which is good. **Dysfunctional behavior** means someone is pulling in different directions, which is bad.

$$\text{Organizational Behavior} = \text{Functional Behavior} + \text{Dysfunctional Behavior}$$

Three related concepts in organizational behavior include the law of effect, the goal-congruence principle, and the level of interest and commitment. The level of interest and commitment is a requirement of the goal-congruence principle.

- The **law of effect** states that behavior that is positively rewarded tends to be repeated and behavior that is negatively reinforced tends to be inhibited.

- According to the **goal-congruence principle,** an employee's goals and objectives should be aligned with that of the organization where the employee works, which is not an easy thing to achieve. One way to achieve goal congruence is to link results of employees' job performance appraisals to the organization's goals and objectives.

- An employee's **level of interest and commitment** to the organization should equal management's interest and commitment, which also is not easy to achieve. One way to ensure employees' level of interest and commitment is to link results of employees' job performance appraisals to the organization's goals and objectives.

(c) Organizational Culture and Change

Organizational change means organizational renewal that requires greater flexibility, capability, and adaptability. Organizational change is the first and foremost requirement for an organization to develop, perform, succeed, transform, or innovate. Organizational change in turn depends on organizational culture and organizational behavior. Organizations must change to survive in a competitive environment, because the status quo does not work anymore. This thinking requires that everyone in the organization believes in and accepts the change. Ideally, managers are architects or agents of change rather than victims of change.

When introducing changes, managers often are surprised that things do not turn out as planned. This is because the change process is not carried out properly. The change itself is not the problem. When managers are acting as agents of change, their company will be much more responsive, flexible, and competitive. *The outcome of an organization's change process can be good or bad.*

$$Organizational\ Change = Organizational\ Culture + Organizational\ Behavior$$
$$Organizational\ Change = Good\ (Asset)\ or\ Bad\ (Liability)$$

An organization can change by:

- Reengineering business policies, processes, jobs, and procedures to eliminate waste and duplication.

- Outsourcing nonstrategic or noncore business functions or activities to outsourced companies.

- Partnering with major suppliers and customers for synergies.

- Implementing total quality management programs for improving quality.

- Redesigning the organizational structure to fit the organizational strategy.

- Renovating physical plants and facilities to keep them efficient and modern.

- Installing computer-based systems and technologies to realize cost savings and productivity gains.

- Understanding its own products, services, markets, and customers and those of competitors through business intelligence–gathering methods.

- Installing performance measurement methods (metrics and scorecards) and reward systems (monetary and nonmonetary methods).

(i) Resistance to Organizational Change

Organizational change comes in all forms, sizes, shapes, and with various degrees of impacts and consequences for employees. Some of the most common reasons for resistance to change are listed next.

- Surprise

- Inertia

- Misunderstanding
- Emotional side effects
- Lack of trust
- Fear of failure
- Personality conflicts
- Lack of tact
- Threats to job status or security
- Breakup of work groups

Management faces the challenge of foreseeing and neutralizing resistance to change, as the resistance is both rational and irrational.

Management theorists have offered at least six options to overcome resistance to change, including:

1. Education and communication
2. Participation and involvement
3. Facilitation and support
4. Negotiation and agreement
5. Manipulation and co-optation
6. Explicit and implicit coercion

Situational appropriateness is the key to success.

Manipulation occurs when managers selectively withhold or dispense information and consciously arrange events to increase the chance that a change will be successful. Co-optation normally involves token participation, and the impact of participants input is negligible.

Explicit and implicit coercion is involved when managers who cannot or will not invest the time required for other strategies force employees to go along with a change by threatening them with termination, loss of pay raises or promotions, transfer, and so forth.

(d) Organizational Culture and Development

Organizational development focuses on employees' behavior and the interactions and interrelationships between employees. Organizational development takes organizational strategy into account and becomes an input to organizational change. It is a systematic approach to planned change programs intended to help employees and organizations function more effectively. Organizational development combines knowledge from various disciplines, such as behavioral science, psychology, sociology, education, and management.

Organizational development is a process of fundamental change in an organization's culture. For organizational development programs to be effective, not only must they be tailored to unique situations, but they also must meet common objectives in order to develop trust. Problem-solving skills, communication, and cooperation are required for success.

The outcome of an organization's development process can be good or bad.

Organizational Strategy → Organizational Development → Organizational Change

Organizational Development = Organizational Culture + Organizational Behavior
+ Organizational Change

Organizational Development = Good (Asset) or Bad (Liability)

(i) Organizational Culture Traps

Organizational culture traps can make someone unwilling to challenge the views and perspectives of subject matter experts and senior-level managers. Other examples include:

- Assuming that small things in one culture are small things in every culture, whereas the opposite can be true. For example, adhering to time schedules and waiting in lines is well accepted in some cultures and is not followed at all in other cultures.

- Assuming that all cultures in all countries follow the same manner as one culture in one country.

- American businesspeople pushing for quicker decisions during negotiations in contrast to Japanese businesspeople pushing for building consensus and trust first followed by faster decisions.

One way to avoid the organizational culture trap is by having an open mind and by reading many articles and books on organizational and international cultures in order to gain a good working knowledge of various cultures.

(e) Summary of Organizational Culture

Corporate management is the major culprit behind corporate failures and management's misdeeds, misconduct, and misbehaviors—all of which point to an organization's culture and its personality. A list of important topics, issues, concerns, and dimensions about organizational culture is presented next.

- Organizational culture can be good or bad, an asset or a liability, soft or hard, fixed or variable, healthy or unhealthy, low risk or high risk, strong or weak, positive or negative, toxic or nontoxic, right actions or wrong actions, and effective or ineffective.

- Culture is doing the right things at the right times and in the right manner.

- Engaged and empowered employees will always have good things to say and positive comments to make about their organization's cultural accomplishments and improvements, which reflects their job satisfaction and work performance. The reverse is also true.

- Individual audit engagements are positively affected by a positive organizational culture and negatively affected by a negative organizational culture. This means that a negative culture creates mistrust toward internal auditors and their work, leading to roadblocks and impairments due to organizational culture traps.

- Organizational culture is conveyed from top-level managers to lower-level managers to frontline employees through reports, memorandums, meetings, letters, face-to-face communications, policies, the intranet, procedures, and dealings with outsiders such as customers, suppliers, and regulators.

- Culture is like oxygen holding the entire organization together to operate, survive, and endure. It is invisible, powerful, and silent.

- Culture is like a strong glue that holds an organization's employees and management together.

- Culture can be compared to an onion. Its layers can be peeled away to understand the real culture at the top-level management, middle-level management, lower-level management, and frontline employees (entry-level employees) in that order (i.e., from top to bottom). The culture from the top to bottom management may be consistent or inconsistent from one layer of the onion to another.

- Culture is reflected and embedded in an organization's mission/vision, strategy, policies, procedures, programs, plans, and business practices.

- Culture is either directly or indirectly related to **ethics and compliance** in that a healthy culture can lead to ethical practices and compliance with laws and regulations; unhealthy culture can lead to unethical practices and noncompliance with laws and regulations. Usually, toxic managers and leaders practice toxic cultures such as unethical and illegal behaviors and actions. They practice such behaviors because they are known as rule-breakers.

- Culture is related to **risk** in that risk culture reflects and represents the risk appetite and mind-set of a person facing a risk, which leads to a question of whether that person is risk-aware or risk-unaware. Risk culture means whether an organization's culture is risk resistant or risk prone (i.e., risk immunity). For example, in a risk-prone culture, innovation is invited; in a risk-resistant culture, innovation is not invited (i.e., the culture expresses the not-invented-here syndrome). Risk culture is rooted in people's beliefs, values, customs, and traditions, which are hard to change. In a risk-aware culture, risk thinking is integrated into the job descriptions of all employees and managers so that it becomes a part of their daily routine work instead of a separate way of working.

Risk culture also asks whether a person is proactive or reactive in risk situations. Proactive persons invite innovation, change, risk, and improvements; reactive ones disinvite innovation, change, risk, and improvements. Reactive persons believe in the not-invented-here syndrome; proactive persons welcome or attempt innovations. Other reactive examples include "We have been doing things the same way all along" or "It is the way we do things around here."

According to the Financial Stability Board, four major areas that can influence in assessing an organization's risk culture include tone at the top, accountability, effective communication and challenge, and incentives. Culture begins with the tone at the top.

- Culture is related to **workplace behavior,** whether it is exhibiting dysfunctional or disorderly behavior. Toxic leaders can exert their office (position) power over subordinate employees by doing certain unwanted things to employees (e.g., sexual harassment) and by making discriminatory comments to employees (e.g., racial slurs).

- Culture is related to **discrimination** in the workplace. Management's attitudes toward employee hiring and firing policies, promotion and travel policies, and work assignments based on certain criteria (e.g., age, sexual orientation, race, and ethnicity) can lead to allegations of discrimination, which poses potential legal liabilities to an employer.

- Culture is related to **strategy,** whether it is a mild strategy or an aggressive one. A mild strategy reflects and supports status quo thinking with little or no innovation in introducing new products and services into current and new markets. An aggressive strategy is the opposite of a mild strategy.

■ Culture is related to the **control environment,** where design, implementation, and operation of business controls depend on management's attitudes toward those controls. Managers with an indifferent or careless culture would not pay proper attention to implementation of controls. They may even bypass or circumvent operational controls to conduct misdeeds. In an indifferent culture, managers can sabotage or override controls or be involved in collusion with insiders and/or outsiders.

■ Culture does not provide a simple view with homogeneous entity. Instead, it is a complex view with heterogeneous entity in terms of micro-culture and macro-culture. For example, someone can look at culture from two views, such as micro-culture and macro-culture. A micro-culture is small, contained behavior of individuals or teams and has an internal focus. A macro-culture is large in size, exhibits uncontrolled behavior, and has an external focus.

■ A strong culture tends to rely on two-way conversations between parties, including:

   □ A collaborative approach in decision making between management and employees.

   □ A team-based effort to get things done.

   □ Employees' positive or negative attitude toward the organization's governance.

   □ Management's relationships with customers, employees, public community, and other stakeholders.

   □ How management handles crisis situations and negative events.

   □ How management behaves toward competitors.

   Communications from top management (tone at the top) is one-way conversation, which represents a weak culture.

■ Simple and clear communications within an organization can include using newsletters, fireside chats, group meetings, one-on-one meetings, interviews, and the intranet to bring cultural awareness regarding policies on workplace violence, business conduct, harassment, and discrimination.

(f) Auditing Organizational Culture

World-class internal audit functions incorporate the review of their corporate culture into every audit engagement, not as a stand-alone or an ad hoc audit when needed or requested. Some special issues arise in reviewing corporate culture due to its sensitive nature and because no concrete evidence is available, unlike traditional assurance reviews.[9]

The next audit procedures can help in reviewing or assessing the corporate culture.

■ Determine whether an organization's culture maturity model is stone-age culture or modern-age culture or in between.

   Characteristics of **stone-age culture** are described next.

   □ A closed shop for limited members only

   □ Mistrust

---

[9] Adapted from Institute of Internal Auditors, "Auditing Culture—A Hard Look at the Soft Stuff," *Global Perspectives and Insights*, no. 3, 2016; https://global.theiia.org/knowledge/Public%20Documents/2016-Feb-GPI-English.pdf.

□ Insensitivity to cultural norms and deviations (e.g., corruption, bribes, and fraud are accepted)

□ Rigid organizational structure (i.e., tall structures with several management hierarchical levels and formal and strict job titles with threats, insults, and punishments)

□ Class discrimination (i.e., rich or poor, educated or uneducated)

□ All exclusiveness (i.e., no outsiders)

□ Low expectations from employees

□ Innovation is discouraged

□ Intuition-based risk taking discouraged

□ Weak leadership

Characteristics of **modern-age culture** are described next.

□ Open shop for all members

□ Trust

□ Sensitivity to cultural norms and deviations (e.g., ethical actions and good behavior)

□ Flexible organizational structure (i.e., flat structure with few management hierarchical levels and loose job titles with no threats, insults, and punishments)

□ No class discrimination (i.e., rich or poor, educated or uneducated)

□ All inclusiveness (both insiders and outsiders)

□ High expectations from employees by raising the bar

□ Innovation is encouraged

□ Calculated risk taking encouraged

□ Strong leadership

Leaders in the modern-age culture set a strong tone at the top, practice management by example, seek best practices through benchmarking, and provide a forward-looking direction.

■ The CAE first should inform the CEO about the assessment of culture (culture audit) in all audit engagements prior to talking to the board and audit committee to gain initial support from the CEO and later from the senior management. Ideally, the CEO, board, and audit committee are champions of the continuous assessment of culture. Next, the CAE should seek the support of senior management and operational management because they are the key managers that make the culture audit happen. Senior management in turn must inform the functional managers in their chain of command. Any resistance to the culture audit at any management level is a red flag indicating cultural problems.

■ The CAE should ensure that soft culture audit findings, which are based on subjective matters, are treated delicately and differently from the hard findings based on hard evidence found in traditional compliance audits. All assumptions and timelines must be verified so as not to reach false conclusions and wrong allegations quickly that can create ill will between the audit function and audit clients.

- Because there is no hard proof and there is no concrete evidence (solid evidence) available in culture-related audit findings, internal auditors can use surveys (employees and customers), interviews (employee exit interviews and management interviews), customer complaints (wrong prices, poor quality, shipping delays and problems, and product returns), and metrics (culture indicators and scorecards) to increase the concreteness of evidence. In some cases, seeing is *not* believing.

- The CAE should ensure that internal auditors assigned to culture-related audit projects have business acumen and receive sensitivity training.

A relationship between the three lines of defense and auditing culture is presented next.

First line of defense	Business line management (business unit or division management, functional or departmental management, and frontline supervisors and managers) is responsible for establishing and communicating expected outcomes, value in adhering to code-of-conduct, and promote good cultural behaviors.
Second line of defense	Oversight function provides advice and support to the first line of defense. These oversight functions include the ethics, compliance, legal, and regulatory offices. The oversight function develops policies, procedures, and programs for adherence in order to minimize culture-related risks and for compliance purposes.
Third line of defense	Internal audit function: Evaluates adherence to the organization's culture-related standards. Evaluates whether the corporate culture supports the organization's mission, vision, and strategy. Assesses the overall organization's culture personality. Identifies areas with weak culture and turns them into areas with strong culture.

5.11 Organizational Ethics

Organizational or corporate ethics play an important role in ensuring good corporate governance and better corporate management. Corporate ethics and corporate governance support corporate management. Ethical lapses and dilemmas are root causes of many problems that corporate management faces today.

Ethics can be defined broadly as the study of what is right or good for human beings. It attempts to determine what people ought to do or what goals they should pursue. Business ethics, as a branch of applied ethics, is the study and determination of what is right and good in business settings. Unlike legal analyses, analyses of ethics have no central authority, such as courts or legislatures, upon which to rely; nor do they follow clear-cut, universal standards. Nonetheless, despite these inherent limitations, it is still possible to make meaningful ethical judgments.

SCOPE OF ETHICS MANAGEMENT

The scope of ethics management is too broad as it includes several categories, such as societal ethics, public ethics, personal ethics, business ethics, management ethics, professional ethics, a nation's ethics, government ethics, family ethics, environmental ethics, and individual versus group ethics.

(a) Personal Ethics and Business Ethics

Broadly speaking, ethics can be divided into personal ethics and business ethics. Personal ethics deal with how an individual conducts his or her own life on a day-to-day basis. Business ethics deal with how a business organization conducts its own business, whether it is a proprietorship, partnership, or corporation. Personal ethics affect business ethics because it is the same individual working for the same business organization. This individual brings his or her own beliefs, attitudes, behaviors, and values (moral compass) to the workplace. Hence, personal ethics are integrated with business ethics.

(b) Law, Ethics, and Economics

(i) Law

Law reflects society's codified ethics and is generally regarded as a minimum standard of behavior for individuals and organizations. It is good to respond to the spirit as well as the letter of law, assuming law is the floor and ethics are the ceiling on behavior and operating above minimum required between the floor and the ceiling. Illegal acts are by definition violations of laws, rules, or regulations. They are failures to follow requirements of laws or implementing regulations, including intentional acts (e.g., fraud, irregularities, and not fully disclosing in financial statements), unintentional noncompliance acts (e.g., errors), and criminal acts. Abuse occurs when the conduct of an activity or function falls short of expectations for prudent behavior. Abuse is distinguished from noncompliance in that abusive conditions may not directly violate laws or regulations. Abusive activities may be within the letter of the laws and regulations but violate their spirit or the more general standards of impartial behavior and, more specifically, the ethical behavior. This means that abusive acts can be legal but unethical.

Some corporate executives are under the false impression that their actions are above the legal and ethical principles and that they will not get caught for their bad behavior. Instead, they should realize that nobody is above the law. Honesty and integrity should be the hallmark of the management profession for business managers and executives.

It is illegal for corporate management to create complicated and convoluted business divisions and ventures to simply divert the law, thus creating illusory profits and deceiving stakeholders. The underlying, implicit intent could be to increase the company's stock price and to receive higher compensation for executives because compensation levels are tied to performance levels (i.e., profits, stock prices, and earnings per share). If caught, these executives can be fined, punished, and imprisoned for conducting illegal activities and for their bad behavior. Human greed is at play here.

(ii) Ethics

Ethics deal with deciding and acting on what is right or wrong in a particular situation. Basically, ethics is concerned with knowing what is good and bad and separating them. The next guidelines can help business managers and executives to be ethical in business settings.

Most ethical dilemmas involve a conflict between the needs of the part and those of the whole—the individual versus the organization or the organization versus society as a whole. Managers faced with tough ethical choices often benefit from a normative approach—one based on norms and values—to guide their decision making.

Four normative approaches are the utilitarian approach, the individualism approach, the moral-rights approach, and the justice approach. The utilitarian approach is based on the ethical concept that moral behaviors produce the greatest good for the greatest number. The individualism approach is based on the ethical concept that acts are moral when they promote the individual's best long-term interests, which ultimately leads to the greater good. The moral-rights approach is based on the ethical concept that moral decisions are those that best maintain the rights of those people affected by them. The justice approach is based on the ethical concept that moral decisions must be based on standards of equity, fairness, and impartiality.

Three types of justice are of concern to business managers: distributive, procedural, and compensatory justice. Distributive justice requires that people not be treated differently based on arbitrary characteristics. Procedural justice emerges from the concept that rules should be clearly stated and consistently and impartially enforced. Compensatory justice requires that individuals should be compensated for the cost of their injuries by the party responsible and that individuals should not be held responsible for matters over which they have no control.

It is unethical for corporate management to create illusory profits and manipulate profits to increase their company's stock price using creative accounting practices, thus deceiving stakeholders. The underlying, implicit intent could be to increase the company's stock price and to receive higher compensation for executives because compensation levels are tied to performance levels (i.e., profits, stock prices, and earnings per share). If caught, these executives can be fined, punished, and imprisoned for conducting unethical activities. Note that illegal activities and unethical activities go hand in hand sometimes but not always.

(iii) Economics
Economics deals with effective and efficient allocation and utilization of scarce resources to produce goods and to provide services to citizens of a country or a nation. These scarce resources are money, men, machinery, and materials, often called the 4Ms.

(iv) Law and Ethics
The generally accepted view of ethics is that ethical behavior is above behavior required by the law. In many respects, the law and ethics overlap because the law embodies notions of ethics. That is, the law may be seen as a reflection of what society thinks are minimal standards of conduct and behavior. Both law and ethics have to do with what is deemed appropriate or acceptable, but law reflects society's codified ethics. Therefore, if a person breaks a law or violates a regulation, that person is also behaving unethically.

It is important to understand that the law does not address all realms in which ethical questions might be raised. Thus, both law and ethics have clear roles to play in society. In other words, not all unethical actions are illegal (e.g., Dumpster diving is unethical but is legal in some states) and not all illegal actions are unethical (e.g., trespassing is illegal but is ethical). Note that trespassing is involved in conducting Dumpster diving, meaning that illegal acts are done unethically. Similarly, pirated software, movies, music, sports, and other entertainment acts are illegal and unethical in the United States but not in most other countries.

Laws and ethics relating to bribery, corruption, and violation of intellectual property rights vary greatly between the United States and other countries. Bribery, corruption, and violation of intellectual property rights are illegal and unethical in the United States but not in most other countries.

(v) Interactions among Law, Ethics, and Economics

Business managers and executives can use Venn diagrams to understand the interactions (i.e., connections and disconnections) among law, ethics, and economics (profits). A firm's legal, ethical, and economic goals can be depicted in a Venn diagram showing how certain decisions address these goals. Four overlapping areas and their associated scenarios are possible when these three goals interact, as shown in Exhibit 5.2.

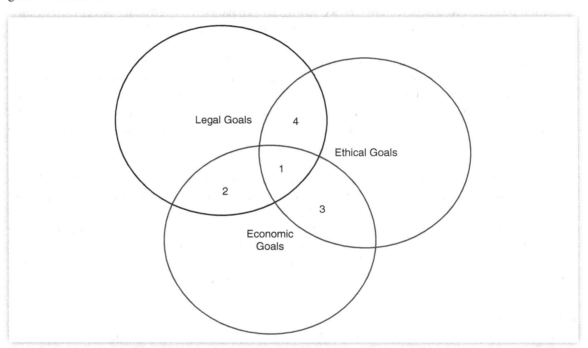

EXHIBIT 5.2 Venn Diagram

Scenario 1 in the exhibit addresses all three goals, meaning that management's decisions are profitable, legal, and ethical. This is an ideal solution and the best situation because the diagram meets the legal, ethical, and economic goals. Here, there is a connection with the law, ethics, and economics, which is a rare situation in practice.

Scenario 2 addresses only legal and economic goals, not ethical ones. It means that management's decisions are legal and profitable but not ethical. The ethical aspect of the decision needs to be carefully considered before proceeding with this scenario. Here, there is a disconnect with ethics.

HOW CAN THE VENN DIAGRAM HELP MANAGERS?

Business managers can use Venn diagrams to understand the interactions (i.e., connections and disconnections) among law, ethics, and economics (profits). A firm's legal, ethical, and economic goals can be depicted in a Venn diagram to show how certain decisions address these goals.

Scenario 3 addresses only ethical and economic goals, not legal ones. It means that management's decisions are ethical and profitable but not legal. It could be that the law may be vague or does not address the current issue. A general belief is that if something is ethical, there is a good chance it is also legal, but management cannot assume that this is true and needs to proceed carefully with this scenario. Here, there is a disconnect with the law.

Scenario 4 addresses only legal and ethical goals, not economic ones. It means that management's decisions are legal and ethical but not profitable. Here, management has a choice of avoiding this decision altogether or finding ways to make it profitable, because this decision contradicts the profit maximization goal. However, there may be a compelling reason (e.g., government mandate to clean up pollution) to make this decision. Here, there is a disconnect with economics.

(c) Basic Ethical and Legal Principles and Ethical Dilemmas

Basic ethical and legal principles guide managers and executives to handle ethical and legal problems and issues on a day-to-day basis. When these principles are understood and implemented, they can reduce ethical dilemmas and embarrassments and legal risks and protect reputations in the eyes of the public.

Private and public sector managers and executives often face ethical dilemmas during their job duties. Some examples of these ethical dilemmas may help to clarify the definition of business or government ethics.

- In an interaction between a pharmaceutical company and a medical researcher, the company management threatens the researcher if she releases negative test results (bad news) to the public about its drugs.

- In an interaction between government attorneys and a government executive, attorneys are fired improperly for whistleblowing on the government and not following the executive's unethical instructions, despite the Ethics in Government Act and the Whistleblower Protection Act.

- In an interaction between a local oil company and local government officials, the oil company was allowed to dump toxic waste into a nearby lake, which is used for drinking water, in exchange for creating more local jobs when the oil company expands its plant processing capacity. The toxic waste kills fish and causes seaweed to grow in the lake.

- In the interaction between federal environmental regulators and management of a coal-fired power plant, regulators relaxed rules to allow the very old plant to be reopened after it was closed earlier due to excessive air pollution. The plant required modernization work to reduce air pollution, and the work was not completed when the plant reopened.

- In relationships between employees and employers, many issues arise regarding worker safety and compensation, civil rights (such as equal treatment, privacy, and freedom from sexual harassment), and the legitimacy of whistleblowing. Previous employees working as contractors can raise tax and legal issues.

- In relationships between businesses and their customers, ethical issues permeate marketing techniques, product safety, price discrimination, and consumer protection.

- In relationships between businesses and their owners, ethical questions involving corporate governance, shareholder voting, and management's duties to shareholders can pose problems.

- Relationships among competing businesses involve numerous ethical matters, including fair competition and the effects of collusion in price fixing and other matters.

- In relationships between buyers and vendors, suppliers, contractors, and consultants, showing favors and receiving bribes and expensive gifts are common.

- In interactions between gatekeepers (e.g., external auditors, attorneys, securities analysts, and investment bankers) and their owners and investors of a company, gatekeepers do not always discharge professional responsibilities in the financial securities and capital markets due to conflicts of interest, job security, groupthink, and greed.

- Interactions between business and society at large present additional ethical dimensions, such as pollution of the physical environment, commitment to the community's economic and social infrastructure, and depletion of natural resources.

- On the international level, issues such as bribery of foreign officials, exploitation of less-developed countries, and conflicts among differing cultures and value systems are difficult to control and monitor.

- In interactions among company management and investors and the stock market, company management can manipulate earnings and profits (earnings management) to boost its stock prices and to receive big bonuses when the actual financial results are less than expected.

- In interactions among company management and the bond market and the stock market, company management can hide its debt through off-balance-sheet accounting practice to realize higher bond and stock prices. This practice is unethical although not illegal because generally accepted accounting principles allow it.

- In interactions between company management and the board of directors, company management can pull off financial shenanigans (a form of financial fraud) against the company. The board of directors may not be able to prevent and detect such acts, but it is legally liable for such unethical conduct on part of company management.

- In interactions between a company's buyers and sellers, both parties may be subject to unethical and illegal tactics (e.g., poison pills) to win or lose the business transactions of mergers and acquisitions.

(d) Types of Ethics

Basically, ethics can be of two types: the normative approach and the descriptive approach. Managers faced with tough ethical choices often benefit from taking a **normative approach**—one based on norms and values—to guide their decision making. Normative ethics are concerned with supplying and justifying a coherent moral system of thinking and judgment. They ask: "What ought to be?" The normative approach includes utilitarian, individualism, moral rights, and justice approaches. An application of the normative approach can occur when a decision is made to recruit, hire, train, and promote both men and women equally.

The **descriptive ethics** approach is concerned with describing, characterizing, and studying the morality of a people, culture, or society. It also compares and contrasts different moral codes, systems, practices, beliefs, and values. This approach asks a basic question: "What is?" The business judgment rule is a legal presumption that directors and officers of a corporation have exercised due care by acting on an informed basis, in good faith, and in the honest belief that their actions are in the best interests of the corporation. Unless a plaintiff can give persuasive evidence against at least one of the criteria, corporate directors and officers are insulated from liability for breach of the duty of care. A downside is that some people may adopt the view that "if everyone is doing it, it must be acceptable," which is not right. Examples include discrimination, speeding while driving a car, padding expense accounts, and deceptive advertising.

NORMATIVE APPROACH VERSUS DESCRIPTIVE APPROACH

- The normative approach deals with "what ought to be" or "what ought not to be" in the prevailing set of ethical standards.

- The descriptive approach focuses on "what is" in the prevailing set of ethical standards.

- "What ought to be" should be compared with "what is" to see what is going on in the real world.

Three major approaches to thinking about business ethics include the conventional, principles, and ethical tests approaches.

The **conventional approach** to business ethics is essentially an approach whereby a decision or practice is compared with prevailing norms of acceptability. It is called the conventional approach because it is believed that this is the way that general society thinks.

The **principles approach** includes utilitarian ethics, virtue ethics, and the Golden Rule and augments the conventional approach to business ethics. Utilitarian ethics focus on providing the greatest good for the greatest number. The Golden Rule includes not knowingly doing harm to others.

The **ethical tests approach** is based on practice while the principles approach is based on philosophy (e.g., servant leadership). Showing common sense, presenting one's best self, making something public, and airing out are examples of ethical tests approaches.

(e) Models of Management Ethics

The three models of management ethics include immoral management, moral management, and amoral management.

The **immoral management** model holds that management's motives are selfish and greedy and that management cares only about its own or its company's gains. For example, if Company A knowingly commits a wrongful act that is detrimental to Company B, Company A has exhibited an immoral type of management ethics. Immoral management decisions, behaviors, actions, and practices are discordant with ethical principles. This model represents unethical behavior and follows an exploitative strategy.

Moral management, as expected, exhibits ethical behavior and follows an integrity strategy. It conforms to the highest standards of ethical behavior or professional standards of conduct.

Amoral management can be intentionally or unintentionally amoral. Intentionally amoral managers do not factor ethical considerations into their decisions, actions, and behaviors because they believe business activity resides outside the sphere to which moral judgments apply. They think that different rules apply in business than in other areas of life. Unintentionally amoral managers do not think about business activity in ethical terms. These managers are simply casual about the negative effects of their decisions on others. They lack ethical perception and moral awareness and do not stop to consider that their actions have ethical dimensions or consequences. Amoral management contains both intentional behavior and unintentional behavior, and follows compliance strategy.

(f) Elements of Making Moral Judgments

The six major elements or capacities that are essential to making moral judgments include:

1. Moral imagination
2. Moral identification and ordering
3. Moral evaluation
4. Tolerance of moral disagreement and ambiguity
5. Integration of managerial and moral competence
6. A sense of moral obligation and integrity

Moral imagination refers to the ability to perceive that a web of competing economic relationships is, at the same time, a web of moral or ethical relationships. Developing moral imagination means not only becoming sensitive to ethical issues in business decision making but also developing the perspective of searching out subtle places where people are likely to be detrimentally affected by managers' decision making or behaviors.

Moral identification and ordering refers to the ability to discern the relevance or nonrelevance of moral factors that are introduced into a decision-making situation. The goal of **moral evaluation** is to integrate the concern for others into organizational goals, purposes, and legitimacy. In the final analysis, though, managers may not know the "right" answer or solution, although moral sensitivity has been introduced into the decision-making process. The important point is that amorality has not prevailed or driven the decision process.

Tolerance of moral disagreement and ambiguity is an extension of a managerial talent or facility that is present in all decision-making situations managers face. **Integration of management and moral competence** combines management's knowledge, skills, and abilities with moral values that provide a future-looking perspective. **A sense of moral obligation and integrity** requires the intuitive or learned understanding that moral fibers—a concern for fairness, justice, and due process to people, groups, and communities—are woven into the fabric of managerial decision making and are integral components that hold systems together.

(g) Role of Corporate Code of Ethics

Ethics involve knowing what is right or wrong, proper or improper. Ethics form basic ground rules for individuals to follow. They reside within a person and are personal matters. Since people run businesses, personal ethics are business ethics and vice versa. Also, ethics are indivisible or inseparable (i.e., they are the whole thing or nothing).

CORPORATE CULTURE AND CORPORATE ETHICS

Corporate culture is identified formally in written statements of corporate vision or mission statements or as a set of basic qualities, values, beliefs, or commitments.

Corporate culture raises the overall sense of ethical behavior in a way that is easy to understand and accept. Corporate culture needs to include the ethical element.

A good corporate culture should incorporate a substantial part of corporate ethics, explicitly or implicitly.

A person's competence, integrity, and objectivity are the roots of ethical behavior. Professionals have stricter rules and higher expectations about their ethical behavior than others do. According to Stephen Landekich, professionalism means that a person acts and is expected to act as an expert at a reliable level of conduct.[10] A professional not only acts in a manner beyond reproach but also is careful about any related conditions and circumstances that might appear improper or be so perceived by others. Consequently, a code of ethics is a distinct mark of an established profession.

(h) Conflicts of Interest

The conflict-of-interest policy often is considered a part of overall ethics policies. Conflict-of-interest concerns sometimes constitute the main part of ethics standards. According to Stephen Landekich's research, all major companies believe that conflicts between an employee's activities or personal interests and company interests are one of the most significant causes of concern with regard to proper business conduct. The guiding principle is that the best interests of the company must motivate the employee's acts. Anything that might be inconsistent with this principle constitutes an actual or potential conflict of interest or the appearance of a conflict of interest. For example, if a fund manager puts more time and energy into managing his own personal funds at the expense of company funds, it is a conflict-of-interest situation.

Companies uniformly prohibit conflicts of interest, unless employees have obtained written company approval. Such a basic clause may appear within a code of ethics or in a separately issued policy. In either case, typical conflict-of-interest situations are described in considerable detail.

Landekich gathered a concise set of standards on conflicts of interest taken from a company's corporate code of conduct. For example:

- Employees are forbidden to have direct or indirect ownership interests (excluding publicly traded securities of large companies listed on a stock exchange) or profit participation in organizations selling or buying goods or services to or from the company where such relationship may reasonably lead to a conflict of interest.

- Employees or members of their families may not receive compensation, services, gifts, or entertainment from such organizations which receipt could reasonably be construed to have influenced the employee in dealing with them on behalf of the company.

---

[10] Stephen Landekich, *Corporate Codes of Conduct* (Montvale, NJ: Institute of Management Accountants, 1989).

ETHICS POLICY

The ethics policy is contained in the corporate policies, internal auditing policies, or conflict-of-interest policies.

Only 5% of ethics are written. Ethics and quality attributes of a person are interrelated; one needs the other to work more effectively.

- In accordance with the personnel policy concerning "Outside Employment," the company prohibits its employees from engaging in outside employment with a supplier, customer, competitor, or a firm that may become employer in the foreseeable future where such a relationship may reasonably lead to a conflict of interest.

- Certain employees will be required to sign conflict of interest statements annually.

- Employees who have questions regarding what constitutes a conflict of interest should discuss the matter with their division management.

- Mortimer Dittenhofer and Rebecca Klemm undertook a research project for the Institute of Internal Auditors (IIA) to determine attitudes of internal auditors relative to 20 ethics issues.[11] These 20 situations (issues) were grouped into eight ethics classifications. General comments on the eight classifications follow.

    1. **Confidentiality**—There is a definite agreement between employees' attitudes and the perceived positions of their employers. No substantial differences were noted regarding staff level, location, or industry.

    2. **Honesty and Objectivity**—Employees seem stricter about violating these areas of ethics than their employers. All were consistent about action to take.

    3. **Loyalty**—The answers were not clear-cut. There was little agreement between auditors' and employers' positions. Whistleblowing appears to cause differing attitudes about loyalty.

    4. **Conflict of Interest**—Auditors and their employers agree as to the action to take. Auditors outside the United States seem to be more hardline. There were no major differences in the other categories. However, the percentages in the industrial groups varied significantly.

    5. **Gifts**—Internal auditors are stricter than their organizations. Generally, there is congruity in all classifications.

    6. **Professional Competence**—This area dealt with evidence and disclosure. Auditors' opinions and the perceived positions of their employers did not display a high degree of concern over this topic.

    7. **Striving for Proficiency and Effectiveness**—There is less concern, and the perceived organizations' opinions are somewhat less concerned.

    8. **High Standards of Morality and Dignity**—There was general disagreement about an internal auditor going to a city from an employer-paid training session to apply

---

[11] Mortimer Dittenhofer and Rebecca Klemm, *Ethics and the Internal Auditor, IIA Monograph Series IIA* (Altamonte Springs, FL: IIA, 1983).

for a new job. It appears that there are less firm positions and that attitudes are less comparable. This is an unethical practice.

In conclusion, audit practitioners apparently are aware of unethical positions. They recognize unethical behavior and, on an organizational basis, are prepared to take action and impose sanctions on those who act improperly.

(i) Factors Influencing Ethical Standards

In a study, Steven Brenner and Earl Molander asked a group of managers to list factors that they believed influenced ethical standards.[12] Factors causing *higher* ethical standards included:

1. Public disclosure, publicity, media coverage, and better communication

2. Increased public concern, public awareness, consciousness and security, better-informed public, and societal pressures

3. Government regulation, legislation and intervention, and federal courts

4. Education of business managers, increase in manager professionalism, and education

5. New social expectation of the role that business is to play in society, and the attitudes of young adults

6. Greater sense of social responsibility on the part of organizations, and greater awareness of the implications of their actions

7. Business responsiveness, corporate policy changes, and top management's emphasis on ethical action

Factors causing *lower* ethical standards included:

1. Society's lower standards, social decay, more permissive society, growth of materialism and hedonism, loss of church and home influence, and less quality, more quantity desires

2. Competition, pace of life, the stress of trying to succeed, current economic conditions, and the cost of doing business

3. Political corruption, loss of confidence in government, politics, political ethics, and climate

4. People being more aware of unethical acts, constant media coverage, and communications that create an atmosphere for crime

5. Greed, desire for gain, worship of the dollar as a measure of success, selfishness, and a lack of personal integrity and moral fiber

6. Pressure for profit from within the organization from superiors or stockholders, corporate influences on managers, and corporate policies

It is easy to rationalize unethical conduct in business because of the prevailing theory that executives must provide stockholders with the greatest possible return on their investments (i.e., profit). This leads us to believe that ethical practices are rarely rewarded when compared to profits.

---

[12] Steven N. Brenner and Earl A. Molander, *Is the Ethics of Business Changing?* (Boston: Havard Business School Press, 1989).

KEY CONCEPTS TO REMEMBER: Corporate Code of Ethics

The best reason for establishing a code of conduct within an organization is that such codes express standards of individual behavior for members of the organization.

■ An example of unacceptable behavior that should be included in a conflict-of-interest policy is providing a mailing list of company employees to a relative who is offering training that might benefit the organization. A conflict-of-interest policy should prohibit any activity contrary to the best interests and well-being of the organization.

■ A conflict-of-interest policy should include, among other things, that an employee shall not: accept money, gifts, or services from a customer; borrow from or lend money to vendors; and use company information for private purposes. The conflict-of-interest policy for a private firm (e.g., manufacturing company) should not include that the employee not participate in the management of a public agency.

■ A firm's code of ethics contains the statement "Employees shall not accept gifts or gratuities over $50 in value from persons or firms with whom our organization does business." This provision is designed to prevent employees from granting excessive sales allowances.

■ Several years ago a large financial institution developed and distributed a code of conduct to all its officers and employees. The best audit approach to provide the audit committee with the highest level of comfort about the code of conduct would be to fully evaluate the comprehensiveness of the code and compliance therewith and to report the results to the audit committee.

■ A review of an organization's code of conduct revealed that it contained comprehensive guidelines designed to inspire high levels of ethical behavior. The review also revealed that employees were knowledgeable of its provisions. However, some employees still did not comply with the code. To enhance its effectiveness, the code of conduct should contain provisions for disciplinary action in the event of violations.

(j) Options for Facilitating Ethical Behavior

An organization has several options to facilitate ethical behavior. The options require careful planning and proper implementation with sincere interest and commitment. According to Wayne Moore and Mortimer Dittenhofer, the presentation of the code of conduct plays an important role in how important employees view the code.[13] If the code of conduct is presented casually to new employees along with other material related to the employment entrance process, such as insurance forms, tax deduction forms, pension information, and others, it will be considered a perfunctory document of minimal importance or significance. However, if the code is covered in a training program, and top management attends and participates, employees will view the code as a major element of organizational governance and a positive guide to attitude and behavior.

An alternative to distributing the code in a training program is for the CEO to transmit it with a personal letter. This tone-from-the-top message should explain that the code governs conduct at all levels of the organization. The letter may include a statement that says infractions will be dealt with seriously. It should be made clear that the excuse "I did what was best for the organization" will not be acceptable.

---

[13] Wayne G. Moore and Mortimer A. Dittenhofer, *How to Develop a Code of Conduct*, IIA Monograph Series IIA (Altamonte Springs, FL: IIA, 1992).

CONFLICT-OF-INTEREST POLICY

A conflict-of-interest policy should state that employees should not do business with family members as customers or suppliers even though no fraud appears to have been committed.

Another successful method for introducing new employees to the code of conduct is in a workshop where they see examples of ethics in practice. This is a good way to expose them to role-playing exercises relating to the most common types of infractions and to the potential disciplinary action that could be taken as a result. In addition to this initial exposure to the code of conduct, ongoing training is also needed. This training may be most effective when done by individual supervisors, usually in conjunction with employee training, orientation, or professional development courses. An effective way to impress the concept of ethics on each new employee is for supervisors to explain that ethical conduct is a core value of the organization that employees are expected to comply with throughout their careers. This subject should be discussed each time the supervisor focuses on performance issues with an individual.

In some cases, code of conduct training can be done more broadly through a seminar or meeting. If properly designed, such sessions can be effective. In other cases, ethics videos are used, either separately or as part of additional training. This type of presentation is most effective if the CEO or a member of top management participates in the videotape and provides supporting comments. Also, the presentation is enhanced if a knowledgeable individual is available to answer questions.

To keep the ethics momentum going, the code of conduct document needs to be updated periodically. The updating team should consider such elements as infractions not originally or specifically covered in the original code, changes in the organization's policies, environmental and organizational changes with material impact on the organization and its employees, and definitions and descriptions that are not clear.

(k) Monitoring Compliance with the Code of Conduct

Corporate governance objectives are also formulated in voluntary codes and standards (i.e., codes of conduct) that do not have the status of law or regulation. While such codes play an important role in improving corporate governance arrangements, they might leave shareholders and other stakeholders with uncertainty about the status of codes and their implementation. When codes and principles are used as a national standard or as an explicit substitute for legal or regulatory provisions, market credibility requires that their status in terms of coverage, implementation, compliance, and sanctions is clearly specified.

The codes of conduct document should be distributed to all employees annually. Employees must acknowledge receipt of the document, and they must read, understand, and sign it, agreeing that they will abide by the contents of the document.

World-class organizations have developed codes of conduct for their firms. These codes should comply with the definition of a "code of ethics" set out in Section 406 of the Sarbanes-Oxley Act of 2002. In addition, the code must provide for an enforcement mechanism and protection for persons reporting questionable behavior (i.e., whistleblowing). The board of directors must approve any waivers of the code for directors, executives, or officers of the organization.

Compliance with the code of conduct is an ongoing responsibility of each employee and is primarily based on the honor system. Employees should be asked to certify or sign a form asserting that they have complied with the code or to list exceptions to such compliance. These surveys may be administered by operating management or a staff group, such as legal, employee relations (human resources), or internal auditing.

(I) Ethics and Fraud in Financial Reporting

In 1987, the Report of the National Commission on Fraudulent Financial Reporting (Treadway Commission) made recommendations for public companies to improve their financial reporting process.[14] The commission made specific recommendations on the Code of Corporate Conduct.

The public company should develop and enforce written codes of corporate conduct. Codes of conduct should foster a strong ethical climate and open channels of communication to help protect against fraudulent financial reporting. As a part of its ongoing oversight of the effectiveness of internal controls, a company's audit committee should review annually the program that management establishes to monitor compliance with the code.

A strong corporate ethical climate at all levels is vital to the well-being of the corporation, all its constituencies, and the public at large. Such a climate contributes importantly to the effectiveness of company policies and control systems and helps influence behavior that is not subject to even the most elaborate system of controls. Consequently, a strong corporate ethical climate emphasizing accountability helps to protect a company against fraudulent financial reporting.

A written code of corporate conduct strengthens the corporate ethical climate by signaling to all employees standards for conducting the company's affairs. Well-defined ethical standards and guidelines for acceptable behavior promote ethical decision making at all levels of the organization and help resolve ethical dilemmas that arise.

To succeed, a code of corporate conduct must have the full support of management and the board of directors. The most influential factors in determining the code's effectiveness are the attitude and the behavior of the top officers and directors, who set the example for the entire company. The CEO, in particular, has a special role; the CEO's attitude, behavior, and expectations of others strongly influence the actions of other upper-level managers.

ACTIVITIES TO ENSURE A STANDARD LEVEL OF CONDUCT

Proper hiring practices

Competitive levels of compensation

Performance incentives

Company tradition and reputation

Control mechanisms

Proper organization structure

---

[14] *Report of the National Commission on Fraudulent Financial Reporting,* October 1987.

The development of a corporate code of conduct is not an overnight task. A company must invest the necessary time, energy, and resources to ensure that the code is tailored to its circumstances. Since those circumstances will evolve to meet changing demands, the company must update the code periodically.

Finally, the full support of management and the board is needed to ensure that the code receives widespread understanding and support. Employees representing all levels of the corporation should be encouraged to participate in the code's development and evolution in an appropriate fashion. Such collaboration can minimize cases of noncompliance due to lack of understanding and can promote acceptance and adherence. In addition, the code and any amendments must be publicized throughout the corporation.

A code of corporate conduct can also help establish an environment where open communication is expected, accepted, and protected. Management needs a free flow of information to assist it in directing the company's operations, especially in a large, decentralized business. This need is critical in assessing the risk of fraudulent financial reporting. An atmosphere of open communication allows an employee, when confronted with suspected fraud, to bring the problem to the attention of someone high enough in the corporation to solve it without fear of reprisal.

The code must also provide an accessible internal complaint and appeal mechanism. This mechanism should be designed to facilitate internal disclosure, particularly those involving allegations of fraudulent financial reporting or other misconduct. The mechanism could take a variety of forms, such as the use of an ombudsman.

Such internal procedures offer a number of advantages. They allow management to correct inadvertent mistakes and mistakes that may result from bad judgment or failure to recognize a problem. They also encourage employees to act in good faith and tend to ensure the validity of any complaint. In addition, effective internal action may make external disclosures to government authorities or other third parties unnecessary.

BUSINESS PRACTICES THAT CONSTITUTE AREAS OF ETHICAL DILEMMA

Hidden defects in products

Unfair credit practices

Deceptive advertising

Overselling

Overcharging

Unreal delivery dates

Products that are unhealthy

The code of corporate conduct should protect employees who use these internal procedures against reprisal. Failure to adopt guarantees against reprisal and to provide an effective internal complaint procedure could undermine the vitality of codes of conduct and encourage a call for antiretaliatory legislation. Retaliation is still occurring despite legislation.

The Treadway Commission observed a great deal of diversity in written codes of corporate conduct. Some are general; others are specific in their content and direction. Corporate management should develop a code that fits the particular circumstances of its business. Nearly all codes of conduct, however, should include a conflict-of-interest policy, to prevent actual or apparent improprieties in connection with business transactions; a corporate policy of compliance with domestic and foreign laws affecting its business, including those laws relating to financial disclosures; and a policy of confidentiality relating to the company's proprietary information.

TOOLS TO MONITOR ETHICAL COMPLIANCE

Annual survey

Periodic query

Ethics review board

Policy guidance

Employee indoctrination

Periodic review by internal audit

Adequate monitoring and enforcement mechanisms are indispensable to the success of a code of conduct. Management is responsible for determining how best to establish adequate monitoring and enforcement mechanisms and for implementing them. This responsibility is typically carried out through the legal department, internal audit department, or a separate ombudsman function.

The board of directors should be responsible through the audit committee for reviewing the program that management establishes to monitor compliance with the code of conduct. Employees at all levels should understand that violating the law or compromising the company's code of conduct can result in serious disciplinary actions (including dismissal and criminal or civil proceedings where appropriate) and that no employee is exempt from the code.

Written codes of corporate conduct have further advantages. Such codes foster a strong ethical climate, helping to create a work environment that appeals to company personnel at all levels. With an effective code, a company's employees may be more highly motivated, and the company may be able to attract and retain better employees.

ETHICS IMPLEMENTATION PROCEDURES

Ethics committee

Hotline phone

Counsel for guidance

Compliance review board

Internal complaint and appeal mechanism

Ombudsman

(m) Integrating Ethical Standards in Complex Situations

It is good to integrate ethical standards with company policies and procedures, conflict-of-interest statements, job/position descriptions, employee performance evaluations, vision/mission statements, posters and marketing/advertising materials, product packing materials, management employment contracts, legal contracts with outsiders, purchase orders and invoices, employment/job applications, and company annual reports.

Ethics-related statements should be included in so many places for reinforcement purposes and because not everyone will have access to the same ethics-related materials. For example, a consultant may not have access to job descriptions and employee performance evaluations that an employee would have. Similarly, outsiders such as investors and creditors would have more access to a company's annual report than to a company policy manual or job application or description.

Another way to integrate ethical standards in complex situations is to measure a manager's performance based on both quantitative and qualitative factors. Usually managers' bonuses or other rewards are based on how well they meet their quantitative goals, such as increase in revenues or decrease in costs. While these goals are good, managers should also be measured on qualitative factors, such as quality; working relations with customers, suppliers, and employees; and productivity levels.

DOUBLE STANDARD FOR ETHICS

Most businesspeople hold to ethical behavior in their private lives but cease to be private persons in their organizational lives. This indicates that people have double standards (i.e., two different roles) as far as ethics are concerned: one standard for private lives and one standard for their organizational lives.

An organization's goals are interrelated. This fact should be considered during the establishment and evaluation of individual manager's goals and actual performance.

By placing emphasis on only one or a few goals, the other related goals may be in jeopardy. For example, focusing on increasing revenues or decreasing costs alone is not enough because these goals might have been achieved by jeopardizing or manipulating other related goals, such as too much or too little inventory; or too much or too little maintenance expense; or expensing fixed asset acquisitions instead of capitalizing.

(n) Code of Ethics and the Internal Auditor

After the board and senior management approves the written code of ethics or code of conduct document, it should encourage the timely and confidential communication of suspected fraud, misconduct, or abuse to a higher-level person, for example, within a bank. Such a code is intended to foster a culture of integrity and accountability. An ethics officer or chief legal counsel can provide advice to all employees regarding ethics-related questions. The ethics officer performs annual reviews of the ethics policy and discusses ethics at all levels of the bank. Internal auditors monitor the effectiveness of the ethics program and whistleblower policy. Internal auditors should assess the corporate culture and ethics processes to identify any governance-related weaknesses. Internal auditors should assure the board that suspected fraud and misconduct are promptly reported, investigated, and addressed.

A comprehensive policy on code of ethics for a bank follows; it can be applied to any organization because it represents a model policy document consisting of nine essential elements.[15]

---

[15] *The U.S. Comptroller's Handbook*, www.occ.gov.

■ A bank's code of ethics should address the following nine essential elements:

1. **Conflicts of interest.** A conflict of interest occurs when an individual's private interests conflict with the bank's interests.

2. **Insider activities.** Directors, executives, and officers should refrain from financial relationships that are or could be viewed as abusive, imprudent, or preferential. In addition, laws and regulations (e.g., The SEC Rules and the bank's Regulation O) prohibit certain insider activities.

3. **Self-dealing and corporate opportunity.** Employees, officers, executives, and directors are prohibited from using corporate property, information, or their positions for personal gain. Usurpation of a corporate opportunity is a breach of fiduciary duty.

4. **Confidentiality.** All bank employees and directors must maintain the confidentiality of bank, customer, and personnel information.

5. **Fair dealing.** Employees, officers, and directors should not conceal information, abuse privileged information, misrepresent material facts, or engage in any other unfair dealing practice.

6. **Protection and use of bank assets.** Company assets should be used for legitimate business purposes.

7. **Compliance.** All bank employees, officers, and directors must comply with applicable laws and regulations.

8. **Whistleblower policy.** The board and senior management of an organization should ensure that there is a process for employees to report legitimate concerns about suspected illegal, unethical, or questionable practices taking place within the organization with protection from reprisal. This process includes the ability to escalate operational problems, inappropriate conduct, policy violations, or other risks to the organization for investigation. The suspected individuals can be internal to the organizations (e.g., employees, supervisors, managers, executives, and the board members) and external to the organization (e.g., contractors, consultants, suppliers, and vendors).

9. **Consequences.** Employees, officers, and directors should have a clear understanding of the consequences of unethical, illegal, or other behaviors that do not align with the bank's Code of Ethics. Consequences can include fines, penalties, imprisonment, demotions, terminations.

In summary, an ethics officer develops, reviews, updates, and communicates the code of ethics to all employees. Internal auditors monitor the effectiveness of the ethics program and whistleblower policy.

(o) Ethics Audit

Specifically, the chief ethics officer or designee should perform an ethics audit by:

■ Working with the internal audit department in developing audit plans and identifying areas of audit addressing ethical violations.

■ Working with the legal department in pursuing cases that violated ethical principles either inside the company (e.g., employees and management) or outside (e.g., customers, suppliers, vendors, and contractors).

- Conducting ethics audits, special management reviews, and self-assessment reviews periodically and proactively to ensure continuous improvement in ethical matters.

- Encouraging employees and others to report ethical violations through a whistleblower telephone hotline, email, or other means that will be kept confidential.

- Conducting training classes for managers and nonmanagers about ethical principles that include actions and consequences and referencing all applicable laws and regulations.

- Analyzing outside-in views (i.e., views of stakeholders about company management) and inside-out views (i.e., views of company management about stakeholders) to identify disconnections between these views and to integrate them in a coherent manner

- Issuing an audit report describing significant findings and recommendations to management for corrective actions to take

5.12 Corporate Social Responsibility

Corporations have obligations to be good citizens of the local, national, and international communities in which they do business. Failure to meet these obligations can result in damage to the corporation, both in immediate economic terms and in longer-term reputational value. Sustainability of a corporation is a major part of its social responsibility.

(a) What Is Corporate Social Responsibility?

A corporation should be a good citizen and contribute to the communities in which it operates by making charitable contributions and encouraging its directors, managers, and employees to form relationships with those communities. A corporation also should be active in promoting awareness of health, safety, and environmental issues, including any issues that relate to the specific types of business in which the corporation is engaged. Organizations must comply with the ISO 26000 Standard regarding social responsibility.

WHAT IS ISO 26000?

The International Organization for Standardization (ISO) has developed an international standard providing guidelines for social responsibility, known as ISO Standard 26000. The goal is to encourage voluntary commitment by business organizations to social responsibility with common guidance on concepts, definitions, and methods of evaluation. The core issues addressed in this standard include (1) environment, (2) human rights and labor practices, (3) organizational governance and fair operating practices, and (4) consumer issues and community involvement and society development (www.iso.org).

The social responsibility of business encompasses the economic, legal, ethical, and discretionary (philanthropic) expectations that society has of organizations at a given point in time.[16] Archie Carroll's four-part definition attempts to place economic and legal expectations of business in context by relating them to more socially oriented concerns. These social concerns include ethical responsibilities and philanthropic (voluntary/discretionary) responsibilities. This definition, which includes four kinds of responsibilities, elaborates and builds on the definition proposed by McGuire.

---

[16] Archie B. Carroll, "The Four Faces of Corporate Citizenship," *Business and Society Review* 100, no. 1 (1998): 1–7.

(i) Economic Responsibilities

First, there are business's economic responsibilities. It may seem odd to call an economic responsibility a social responsibility, but, in effect, this is what it is. First and foremost, the American social system calls for business to be an economic institution. That is, it should be an institution whose orientation is to produce goods and services that society wants and to sell them at fair prices—prices that society thinks represent the true values of the goods and services delivered and that provide business with profits adequate to ensure its perpetuation and growth and to reward its investors. While thinking about its economic responsibilities, business employs many management concepts that are directed toward financial effectiveness—attention to revenues, costs, strategic decision making, and the host of business concepts focused on maximizing the long-term financial performance of the organization.

SUMMARY OF ECONOMIC RESPONSIBILITIES

The economic responsibility required of business by the U.S. society includes things such as (1) be profitable, (2) maximize sales, (3) minimize costs, (4) make sound strategic decisions, and (5) be attentive to dividend policy.

(ii) Legal Responsibilities

Second, there are business's legal responsibilities. Just as society has sanctioned our economic system by permitting business to assume the productive role mentioned earlier, as a partial fulfillment of the social contract, it has also laid down the ground rules—the laws—under which business is expected to operate. Legal responsibilities reflect society's view of "codified ethics" in the sense that they embody basic notions of fair practices as established by our lawmakers. It is business's responsibility to society to comply with these laws. If business does not agree with laws that have been passed or are about to be passed, our society has provided a mechanism by which dissenters can be heard through the political process. In the past decades, our society has witnessed a proliferation of laws and regulations striving to control business behavior.

As important as legal responsibilities are, legal responsibilities do not cover the full range of behaviors expected of business by society. The law is inadequate for at least three reasons.

1. The law cannot possibly address all the topics, areas, or issues that business may face. New topics continually emerge, such as Internet-based business (e-commerce) and genetically engineered foods.

2. The law often lags behind more recent concepts of what is considered appropriate behavior. For example, as technology permits more exact measurements of environmental contamination, laws based on measures made by obsolete equipment become outdated but are not frequently changed.

3. Laws are made by lawmakers and may reflect the personal interests and political motivations of legislators rather than appropriate ethical justifications. A wise sage once said: "Never go to see how sausages or laws are made." It may not be a pretty picture.

SUMMARY OF LEGAL RESPONSIBILITIES

The legal responsibility required of business by the U.S. society includes things such as (1) obey all laws and adhere to all regulations, (2) obey Foreign Corrupt Practices Act, (3) fulfill all contractual obligations, and (4) honor warranties and guarantees.

(iii) Ethical Responsibilities
Because laws are important but not adequate, ethical responsibilities embrace those activities and practices that are expected or prohibited by societal members even though they are not codified into law. Ethical responsibilities embody the full scope of norms, standards, and expectations that reflect a belief of what consumers, employees, shareholders, and the community regard as fair, just, and in keeping with the respect for or protection of stakeholders' moral rights.

In one sense, changes in ethics or values precede the establishment of laws because the changes become the driving forces behind the initial creation of laws and regulations. For example, the civil rights, environmental, and consumer movements reflected basic alterations in societal values and thus may be seen as ethical bellwethers foreshadowing and leading to later legislation. In another sense, ethical responsibilities may be seen as embracing and reflecting newly emerging values and norms that society expects business to meet, even though they may reflect a higher standard of performance than that currently required by law. Ethical responsibilities in this sense are often ill defined or continually under public scrutiny and debate as to their legitimacy and thus often are difficult for business to agree on. Regardless, business is expected to be responsive to newly emerging concepts of what constitutes ethical practices.

Superimposed on these ethical expectations emanating from societal and stakeholder groups are the implied levels of ethical performance suggested by a consideration of the great ethical principles of moral philosophy, such as justice, rights, and utilitarianism.

For the moment, let us think of ethical responsibilities as encompassing those areas in which society expects certain levels of moral or principled performance but which it has not yet articulated or codified into law.

> **SUMMARY OF ETHICAL RESPONSIBILITIES**
>
> The ethical responsibility expected of business by the U.S. society includes things such as (1) avoid questionable practices; (2) respond to spirit as well as letter of law; (3) assume law is a floor on behavior; (4) operate above minimum required; (5) do what is right, fair, and just; and (6) assert ethical leadership.

(iv) Philanthropic Responsibilities
Fourth, there are business's voluntary/discretionary or philanthropic responsibilities. These are viewed as responsibilities because they reflect current expectations of business by the public. These activities are voluntary, guided only by business's desire to engage in social activities that are not mandated, not required by law, and not generally expected of business in an ethical sense. Nevertheless, the public has an expectation that business will engage in philanthropy. Thus, this category has become a part of the social contract between business and society. Such activities might include corporate giving, product and service donations, volunteerism, partnerships with local government and other organizations, and any other kind of voluntary involvement of the organization and its employees with the community or other stakeholders.

> **WHAT IS A SOCIAL AUDIT?**
>
> Social audit is a systematic analysis and testing of an organization's success in achieving its social responsibility. It is a systematic attempt to identify, measure, monitor, and evaluate an organization's performance with respect to its social efforts, goals, and programs. The social audit is a systematic and structured study of identifying issues and problems in the understanding and fulfilling of economic, legal, ethical, and philanthropic responsibilities, and making recommendations to resolve such issues and problems.

The distinction between ethical responsibilities and philanthropic responsibilities is that the latter typically are not expected in a moral or an ethical sense. Communities desire and expect business to contribute its money, facilities, and employee time to humanitarian programs or purposes, but they do not regard firms as unethical if they do not provide these services at the desired levels. Therefore, these responsibilities are more discretionary, or voluntary, on business's part, although the societal expectation that they be provided is always present. This category of responsibilities is often referred to as good corporate citizenship.

In essence, then, our definition forms a four-part conceptualization of corporate social responsibility (CSR) that encompasses the economic, legal, ethical, and philanthropic expectations placed on organizations by society at a given point in time. The implication is that business has accountability for these areas of responsibility and performance. This four-part definition provides us with categories within which to place the various expectations that society has of business. Because each of these categories is considered an indispensable facet of the total social responsibility of business, the conceptual model more completely describes the kinds of expectations that society has of business. One advantage of this model is that it can accommodate those who have argued against CSR by characterizing an economic emphasis as separate from a social emphasis. This model offers these two facets along with others that collectively make up CSR.

SUMMARY OF PHILANTHROPIC RESPONSIBILITIES

The philanthropic responsibility desired of business by the U.S. society includes things such as (1) be a good corporate citizen, (2) make corporate contributions, (3) provide programs supporting community (e.g., education, health and human services, culture, arts, and civic duties), and (4) provide for community development and betterment on a voluntary basis.

(b) The Pyramid of Corporate Social Responsibility

A helpful way of graphically depicting the four-part definition is envisioning a pyramid composed of four layers. The pyramid portrays the four components of CSR, beginning with the basic building block of economic performance (making a profit) at the base. At the same time, business is expected to obey the law, because the law is society's codification of acceptable and unacceptable behavior. Next is business's responsibility to be ethical. At its most basic level, this is the obligation to do what is right, just, and fair and to avoid or minimize harm to stakeholders (employees, consumers, the environment, and others). Finally, business is expected to be a good corporate citizen—to fulfill its voluntary or discretionary or philanthropic responsibility to contribute financial and human resources to the community and to improve the quality of life.

PYRAMID LAYERS OF CORPORATE SOCIAL RESPONSIBILITY

A socially responsible firm should strive to:

- Be a good corporate citizen (top).
- Be ethical.
- Obey the law.
- Make a profit (base).

The most critical tensions, of course, are those between economic and legal, economic and ethical, and economic and philanthropic responsibilities. The traditionalist might see this as a conflict between a firm's "concern for profits" and its "concern for society," but it is suggested here that this is an oversimplification. A CSR or stakeholder perspective would recognize these tensions as organizational realities but would focus on the total pyramid as a unified whole and on how the firm might engage in decisions, actions, policies, and practices that simultaneously fulfill all its component parts. This pyramid should not be interpreted to mean that business is expected to fulfill its social responsibilities in some sequential fashion, starting at the base. Rather, business is expected to fulfill all its responsibilities simultaneously.

(c) Social Audit

Social audit is a systematic analysis and testing of an organization's success in achieving its social responsibility. It is a systematic attempt to identify, measure, monitor, and evaluate an organization's performance with respect to its social efforts, goals, and programs. The social audit is a systematic and structured review of identifying issues and problems in the understanding and fulfilling of economic, legal, ethical, and philanthropic responsibilities, and making recommendations to resolve such issues and problems.

(d) Sustainability Responsibilities

A corporate sustainability responsibility focuses on (1) whether a corporation will survive or die (e.g., Enron and Toys R Us Corporations) in the long term and (2) determining how the board of directors and senior management are prepared to continue corporate growth and prosperity and to prevent corporate decline.

A corporation's sustainability policy addresses developing strategies to enhance environmental management, to reduce negative social outcomes from discrimination and injustice, and to improve corporate governance. This policy deals with environmental, social, and governance (ESG) issues, as shown in the following table.

Environmental issues	Greenhouse gas emissions
	Pollution from factories and automobiles
	Climate change matters (e.g., cyclones, tornadoes, hurricanes, mud slides, and wildfires)
	Water, air, and food quality problems
	Disposing and recycling of factory and household waste
Social issues	Racial and gender diversity problems at the level of the board and executive and frontline employees
	Community relations and services
	Community event sponsorships
Governance issues	Corporate tax strategies
	Tax havens to hide profits and evade taxes in offshore banks
	Off-balance-sheet activities to misreport assets and liabilities
	Supply-chain management issues (e.g., transporting toxic chemicals, inserting fake and dangerous parts and components into finished goods during product assembly and transportation; and experiencing unexpected supplier-labor strikes and supplier-plant shutdowns)
	Political and lobbying spending data

Recently, more and more shareholders and investors are demanding that boards of directors of public companies provide them with sustainable investment strategies and associated disclosures on the ESG matters. Shareholders and investors use this information during proxy voting decisions. Therefore, corporations should provide a Management's Discussion and Analysis (MD&A) of how their ESG strategy and performance relates to its overall business strategy and performance.

ESG Matters versus Non-ESG Matters. As mentioned, ESG matters focus on environmental, social, and governance issues. Non-ESG matters focus on making and selling products and services and taking care of employees, customers, suppliers, and other stakeholders, all to increase sales revenues, profits, market share, and the market price of a company's stock. However, corporate management found out very quickly that a focus only on non-ESG matters is not enough to survive and grow in business. Instead, management found out that it needs to focus on ESG matters as much as non-ESG matters because these two matters are interconnected. Note that the ESG matters are related to outside of a corporation's boundaries and the non-ESG matters are related to inside of a corporation's boundaries. An example of a company that did not pay proper and timely attention to the ESG matters was the British Petroleum's (BP's) oil spill disaster case. Hence, corporate sustainability goal is achieved when the board and senior management deal with issues coming from inside the corporate boundaries as well as the issues coming from outside the corporate boundaries.

$$\text{Sustainability Matters} = \text{ESG Matters} + \text{Non-ESG Matters}$$

Shareholders and investors strongly believe that a company can face sustainability risks when it does not invest in ESG initiatives, integrate the ESG strategy into the company's strategy, blend the ESG sustainability analysis and investment impact analysis into the traditional financial analysis, and integrate the ESG reporting into the traditional financial reporting.

$$\text{Sustainability Risk} = \text{Environmental Risk} + \text{Social Risk} + \text{Governance Risk}$$

Global research as proven the positive and negative impacts of ESG issues on a company's market share price across multiple industries. Shareholders and investors are asking company management to develop responsible, sensible, and sustainable investment strategies addressing ESG matters.

$$\text{Investment in ESG} \rightarrow \text{Increase in Share Price}$$
$$\text{No Investment in ESG} \rightarrow \text{Decrease in Share Price}$$

For example, companies have become inoperable and their work facilities destroyed during severe tornadoes, hurricanes, and cyclones. Some companies went out of business because they had no backup facilities and disaster recovery plans, and some companies became operational after incurring significant costs to recover from the damage. Consequently, companies lost sales and profits because they could not produce goods, and employees lost their wages because they could not go to work due to damage to their homes.

In summary, the total social responsibility of business entails the concurrent fulfillment of the firm's economic, legal, ethical, philanthropic, and sustainability responsibilities. In equation form, this might be expressed as follows.

$$\text{Total Corporate Social Responsibility} = \text{Economic Responsibilities} + \text{Legal Responsibilities} + \text{Ethical Responsibilities} + \text{Philanthropic Responsibilities} + \text{Sustainability Responsibilities}$$

5.13 Risk Concepts, Risk Types, and Risk Management Processes

In this section, we present four important and related topics—risk concepts; risk types; risk vocabulary; and risk management tools and managing corporate risks. It is important to understand the risk concepts and the types of risks prior to learning the terms presented in the risk vocabulary and risk management tools.

(a) Risk Concepts

Risk concepts include three major terms: vulnerabilities, threats, and risks. Risks are precursors to vulnerabilities and threats. Threats are further divided into threat sources and threat events.

A vulnerability is a flaw, loophole, or weakness in a business function, operation, system, plan, policy, procedure, or practice, and design and implementation of internal controls that could be exploited or triggered by a threat source. Vulnerabilities are susceptible to risk sources that can lead to undesirable events with negative consequences. For example,

- A computer system may be flawed due to its poor design of functions and features and insufficient security controls.

- A plan, policy, procedure, or practice may have loopholes that employees and others can use to circumvent a company's intentions and controls.

- Employees may exhibit their weaknesses such as incompetency, dishonesty, bad attitude, and unethical and illegal behavior.

Threat is any circumstance or event with a potential to negatively impact an organization's operations (e.g., mission, function, image, or reputation), assets, information, or individuals on a daily basis. This event is carried out with a computer system or a manual system via unauthorized access, destruction, disclosure, modification of information, and customer service denial. Threats exploit vulnerabilities, resulting in risks.

Threat sources or risk sources are the places where potential risks can originate. These places consist of people, systems, facilities, equipment, machines and devices, processes, operations, functions, tasks and activities, plans, policies, procedures, and practices. Each business initiative or project is a candidate for introducing or creating risks. Threat sources can be found when new products are developed and when new markets are entered with current and new products. Note that a threat source can exploit a particular system's or operation's vulnerability.

Threat events or risk events are tasks and activities taking place every day in an organization. Examples of threat events include when:

- A customer places an order to purchase goods and services.
- Customers are paying for goods and services that they purchased.
- A retailer is shipping a product that a customer ordered and paid for.
- A marketing department introduces a new advertising campaign.
- A new computer system is just put into operation.
- A new employee is hired.

The presence of a threat event does not mean that it will necessarily cause actual harm or loss. To become a risk, a threat must take advantage of vulnerabilities in systems, functions, and operations.

Risk is defined as the probability or possibility of an undesirable event occurring that will have a negative impact on the achievement of objectives, including damage to property and/or loss of: revenues and profits, market share, competitive advantage, goodwill, rights to intellectual property, talented employees, strategic suppliers, loyal customers, life, and property. Risk is measured in terms of consequence (impact) and likelihood (probability).

$$Risk = Impact \times Likelihood$$

Controls reduce or eliminate risks. A relationship exists between vulnerabilities, threats, risks, and controls, as follows:

$$Vulnerabilities \rightarrow Threats \rightarrow Risks \rightarrow Controls$$

Lack of adequate and/or inappropriate controls often increase the vulnerabilities in a system. One needs to focus on vulnerabilities first, threats next, before managing the risks with appropriate controls later. Moreover, when vulnerabilities are eliminated, risks are eliminated, too.

(b) Risk Types

The chief risk officer (CRO) must identify as many risk types as possible—both current and future (potential) risks as well as known and unknown risks. Each risk alternative for satisfying the business requirements must be evaluated for the 26 risk types discussed in this section. A risk evaluator reviews each of these risks to determine the overall impact of significant variations from the original assumptions on which the expected success of the alternative is based.

This section discusses 26 types of risks and suggests best practices to reduce them. Most of these risks are interrelated and interconnected with a magnifying effect. For example, legal risk and regulatory risk would magnify the reputation (image) risk of an organization. Some risks have a cascading effect; for example, noncompliance with contractual terms and conditions can lead to financial risk (i.e., loss of money due to payment of penalties) and legal risk (lawsuits resulting from violation of contractual rights). Therefore, these 26 risk types should be viewed from a total business context, instead of on a piecemeal basis.

Four common **best practices** are applicable to each type of risk:

1. Acquire traditional and nontraditional insurance coverage to protect tangible and intangible assets.
2. Conduct surveys of employees, customers, suppliers, and the industry.
3. Perform benchmarking studies to understand existing and new risks better.
4. Keep the chain of knowledge strong and current through continuously acquiring of knowledge, skills, and abilities (KSAs) for all employees.

(i) Human Capital Risk

Human capital (people) risk is very significant and the most risky one to watch for. Some causes for people risk involve employee carelessness; fatigue; memory lapses; inattention; destructive (sabotage) mind; collusion; unacceptable and uncontrolled behavior with negative attitudes; and disgruntled, unmotivated, and unhappy employees. A subtle cause includes cultural risk resulting from workforce diversity. Human resources management can play an important role in managing and controlling people risks.

A major risk item in the people risk category results from using ineffective pre-employment screening practices and improper employee reference-checking practices. If these practices are not conducted safely (i.e., legally and ethically), they can lead to potential legal risks in the form of discrimination, retaliation, and defamation lawsuits.

The goal is to conduct these practices without jeopardizing employees' privacy and legal rights. The scope of these practices includes hiring new employees (i.e., checking for education, work experience, work habits, and reasons for leaving) and talking to former employers about prospective employees. Furthermore, if these practices are not conducted at all or are conducted negligently, they can lead to hiring incompetent employees with poor performance records, misconduct (e.g., sexual harassment), and workplace violence, theft, and fraud.

There are 14 **best practices** to reduce people risks:

1. Install a chief human resource officer.

2. Perform employee background checks.

3. Establish policies, controls, and procedures approved by the legal department to ensure consistency and fairness in handling employee reference requests (i.e., giving and getting references).

4. Balance between getting too much information and too little information when obtaining references about prospective employees.

5. Balance between giving too much information and too little information when responding to a reference request about former employees.

6. Provide training, development, and educational programs or courses to employees taught by training consultants or corporate university staff.

7. Install coaching and mentoring programs.

8. Establish individual and/or group incentives.

9. Provide fair and equitable pay and salaries.

10. Respect individuals while keeping diversity in mind.

11. Empower employees.

12. Achieve a ranking as one of the best places to work.

13. Install a chief learning officer to improve employees' performance and productivity.

14. Conduct human capital audits, special management reviews, and self-assessment reviews periodically and proactively to reduce people risks.

(ii) Managing Risk

If people are the major root cause of most problems in an organization, managing is next in line because managing is done by and through people. Managing risk stems from the inability and incompetence of managers and executives in controlling risks and in managing and implementing new programs, projects, business acquisitions, products, policies, procedures, processes, and technology. Managing risk also comes from not exhibiting leadership skills.

Five best practices to reduce managing risks are listed next.

1. Install a general manager for a business unit or division.

2. Perform basic management functions, such as plan, direct, organize, and control tasks.

3. Learn and apply hard and soft skills.

4. Learn time management and leadership skills.

5. Conduct management audits, special management reviews, and self-assessment reviews periodically and proactively to reduce managing risks.

(iii) Strategic and Business Risks

Strategic and business risks come from not executing the business strategic plan properly and timely, and when the goals of managers and nonmanagers are incongruent with those of the organization. These risks also arise from changes in the internal and external environment. Strategic and business risks are big risks facing an organization due to their great impact on its mission.

Five best practices to reduce strategic and business risks are listed next.

1. Install a chief strategist.

2. Develop a strategic management process.

3. Perform basic management functions, such as plan, organize, direct, and control tasks.

4. Learn and apply hard and soft skills.

5. Conduct strategic management process audits, special management reviews, and self-assessment reviews periodically and proactively to reduce strategic risks.

(iv) Financial and Economic Risks

Financial and economic risks arise from many sources since most corporate risks are eventually translated into money so senior management can understand the risks better. One financial risk is that cash inflows and outflows will not be synchronized.

Sixteen sources of financial and economic risks are listed next.

1. Interest rate risk resulting from changes in interest rates

2. Credit risk resulting from changes in credit ratings for bonds

3. Exchange rate risk resulting from changes in foreign currency exchange rates

4. Investment risk resulting from off-balance-sheet accounting practices (a hidden financial risk)

5. Financial reporting risk resulting from financial restatements or misstated financial results

6. Fraud risk resulting from misconduct of managers, nonmanagers, and outsiders

7. Merger and acquisition risks resulting from not executing the merger or acquisition properly or ethically, leading to penalties and punishments

8. Tax risk resulting from misinterpretation of the tax code, paying less taxes than required, or taking deductions that are not allowed by the tax code, resulting in a tax liability

9. Revenue risk resulting from overstated reporting of sales, management misdirected sales, and errors in sales reporting due to improper sales cut-offs

10. Cost risk from project cost overruns due to low estimates at the start and unexpected additional costs later

11. Speculative risk, such as hedging techniques and use of derivatives

12. Audit risk resulting from the inability of the auditor to detect fraud, not considering the risks the audited organization is facing, issuing an incorrect opinion on the financial statements, and conducting the audit work negligently and unprofessionally

13. Liquidity risk resulting from the organization's inability to pay bills and meet other financial obligations when due

14. Market risk, which is the part of an investment security's risk that cannot be eliminated by diversification

15. Portfolio risk, which is connected with an investment when it is held in combination with other assets

16. Leverage risk resulting from excessive debt

Seven **best practices** to reduce financial and economic risks are listed next.

1. Install a chief financial officer.

2. Develop financial policies, procedures, and standards.

3. Provide honest financial reporting with integrity attached.

4. Conduct training classes on tax laws and code.

5. Use forensic accounting and auditing techniques to detect and investigate fraud.

6. Develop a culture of controls.

7. Conduct financial audits, management reviews, and control self-assessment reviews periodically and proactively to reduce financial risks.

(v) Product and Service Quality Risks

Quality risk results from producing inferior quality products, which in turn increases warranty costs and product recall costs. Risk also results from delivering poor-quality services to customers.

Five **best practices** to reduce product quality risks are listed next.

1. Install a chief quality officer.

2. Implement ISO 9000 and 14000 Series Standards and Six-Sigma approaches.

3. Install statistical process control techniques.

4. Implement quality management tools.

5. Conduct product and service quality audits, management reviews, and quality self-assessment reviews periodically and proactively to improve product and service quality.

(vi) Production and Process Risks

Production risk results from not adhering to product design specifications and not following the generally accepted world-class manufacturing best practices. There could be a mismatch between changes to engineering drawings (blueprints) and final product design specifications. Production risk also includes manufacturability risk, purchasing or procurement errors, ignoring product safety requirements, manufacturing errors, delays due to unavailability of materials, and disruption in the supply chain. Purchasing risk results from purchasing the wrong materials and parts, buying materials and parts that are of inferior quality, or buying a greater quantity than what is needed. Processes are used to manufacture a product in that process design will affect the product design and vice versa.

Eight **best practices** to reduce production and process risks are listed next.

1. Install a chief manufacturing officer.

2. Design for manufacturability.

3. Design for quality.

4. Design for environment to control pollution.

5. Design for safety.

6. Establish long-term contracts with suppliers.

7. Conduct training classes for production staff and product engineers.

8. Conduct operations audits, management reviews, and self-assessment reviews periodically and proactively to reduce production and process risks.

(vii) Service and Process Risks

Service risk results from providing poor or delayed service to customers, leading to dissatisfied and eventually lost customers. The net result is increased warranty costs and service cost refunds. Processes are used to deliver a service in that process design will affect the service design and vice versa.

There are four **best practices** to reduce service risks:

1. Install a chief service officer.

2. Implement service industry standards.

3. Conduct benchmarking studies.

4. Conduct service audits, management reviews, and self-assessment reviews periodically and proactively to reduce and process risks.

(viii) Organizational Risk

Organizational risk is the mismatch between organizational structure and business strategy. It also deals with whether management is forward-looking or not or whether organizational culture meets the competitive environment. Organizational risk can also result from goal-incongruent behavior of employees, improper reporting relationships, and unclear lines of responsibility and accountability.

Six **best practices** to reduce organizational risks are listed next.

1. Install a chief organizational development officer.
2. Cultivate a corporate culture.
3. Design a proper organizational structure and reporting relationships.
4. Encourage innovation and creativity.
5. Link the business unit/division mission and strategy to the corporate mission and strategy through active employee participation and direct involvement.
6. Conduct organizational and culture audits, management reviews, self-assessment reviews, and employee surveys periodically and proactively to reduce organizational risks.

(ix) Contract Risk

Contract risk results from not complying with the contractual terms and conditions, leading to default, penalties, and late deliveries. Contract risk leads to financial and legal risks.

Five **best practices** to reduce contract risks are listed next.

1. Install a contract officer.
2. Involve the chief legal officer and his/her staff in developing and reviewing the contracts for language, terms, and conditions.
3. Install project management controls.
4. Monitor the contractor's performance.
5. Conduct contract audits, project management reviews, and self-assessment reviews periodically and proactively to reduce contract risks.

(x) Information Risk

Information risk stems from lack of quality, objectivity, utility, and integrity in information and IT systems, whether manual or automated. One example is that old technology will cease to meet the system requirements at some point during the system life. Another example is using inappropriate hardware and software technologies and architectures. Information risk also includes general and application risks resulting from inadequate controls in IT and user functions. Intelligence-based company information can be stolen to blackmail the company for money or sold to competitors for financial gain.

Seven **best practices** to reduce information risks are listed next.

1. Install a chief information officer.
2. Develop an IT corporate governance framework.

3. Conduct IT risk assessments and evaluations.

4. Establish general controls and application controls.

5. Comply with the Information Quality Act.

6. Install strict controls over taking company data home even for business purposes.

7. Conduct technical IT audits, reviewing IT general and application controls, conducting industry surveys, benchmarking studies, special management reviews, and technical self-assessment reviews periodically and proactively to reduce information risks.

(xi) Trade Risk

Trade risk results from violating transborder data flow rules and not complying with a specific country's and international trade laws and regulations. Trade risks can increase tariff and nontariff costs to the importing country. Trade wars and retaliatory measures are possible.

Four **best practices** to reduce trade risks are listed next.

1. Involve the chief globalization officer in trade dealings.

2. Comply with international trade laws and regulations for both importing and exporting countries.

3. Understand the global economic, political, and cultural environments.

4. Conduct trade audits, management reviews, and self-assessment reviews periodically and proactively to reduce trade risks.

WHAT ARE TRANSBORDER DATA FLOWS AND PRIVACY?

The term "transborder data flows" refers to the movement and storage of data by automatic means across national or federal boundaries. These data flows deal with global privacy concerns. International data networks, connecting thousands of terminals, make it possible to exchange all kinds of data in a minimum of time and without respecting national frontiers.

In general, such transborder activity is composed of three elements:

1. Database of origin—the initial system from where the data is communicated
2. Transmission mechanism—a through-flow station
3. Database of destination—the final destination and storage of the transmitted data, ready for use

Often the flow of information passes through several stations or countries. For instance, the land of destination sometimes has no facilities to process the information, so the data is first sent to another country.

For example, data should not be encrypted when it is flowing over some borders. One approach taken is to transmit a copy of such data unencrypted along with the encrypted data.

(xii) Control Risk

When controls are lax and not followed, fraudulent activities can take place, and employees may take advantage of system weaknesses. Proper design and implementation of effective controls can reduce risks.

Five **best practices** to reduce control risks are listed next.

1. Install a chief audit executive to conduct internal audits within the company to evaluate and monitor the effectiveness of control systems.

2. Install a controller position in business units or divisions to establish and monitor the effectiveness of accounting controls.

3. Implement controls, such as directive, preventive, detective, corrective, and compensating controls.

4. Motivate and educate employees to reduce the temptation to perpetuate fraud and to cultivate a culture of controls.

5. Conduct control audits, management reviews, and control self-assessment reviews periodically and proactively to reduce control risks.

(xiii) Research and Development Risks

Research and development (R&D) risks result when R&D staff and product engineers design and develop new products without a real understanding of the marketplace and of customers' real needs. Lack of innovation or lack of encouragement to innovate also increases R&D risk.

Five **best practices** to reduce R&D risks are listed next.

1. Install a chief R&D officer.

2. Gather information about customer requirements through the use of voice of the customer (VOC) and quality function deployment (QFD) techniques.

3. Inform the product development team about the results of VOC and QFD.

4. Provide marketing training to R&D staff and product engineers.

5. Conduct R&D audits, management reviews, and technical self-assessment reviews periodically and proactively to reduce R&D risks.

(xiv) Technology Risks

Technology risks deal with whether the organization is using leading-edge technology or not. Technology risk can affect security risk because the technology could be new and unproven, and security may be difficult to implement in such technology. Leading-edge, bleeding-edge, cutting-edge, and whiz-bang technologies should be implemented with caution as they may not have real use, may not yield fair return on investment, and may cause implementation risks.

Six **best practices** to reduce technology risks are listed next.

1. Install a chief technology officer.

2. Separate hype from help.

3. Separate fact from opinion.

4. Deploy proven technologies.

5. Perform cost-benefit analysis, SWOT (strengths, weaknesses, opportunities, and threats) analysis, gap analysis, option analysis, and return on investment analysis as part of initial justification.

6. Conduct technology audits, management reviews, and technology self-assessment reviews periodically and proactively to reduce technology risks.

(xv) Digital and Security Risks

Digital risk results from Internet activities, such as cyberincidents and violation of intellectual property rights, copyrights, trademarks, and patents. Security risks arise when computer systems, networks, users, and outsiders are not complying with established security policies, procedures, rules, and standards or when security policies, procedures, rules, and standards are not adequate or not communicated properly to all employees. Digital risks and security risks are related to each other, and they can lead to loss of revenues and reputation.

Thirteen **best practices** to reduce digital and security risks are listed next.

1. Install an information security officer.

2. Develop an IT security governance framework.

3. Involve the chief risk officer in the development and communication of digital policy.

4. Deploy proven security technologies on the Internet.

5. Conduct threat, vulnerability, and risk assessments periodically.

6. Integrate physical, network, personnel, and information security across the entire organization by creating a culture of security.

7. Develop consistent security procedures across business partners, suppliers, vendors, franchisees, and customers.

8. Issue acceptable use policies, mobile device use policies, software restriction policies, business use of Internet policies, cloud storage use policies, and social media use policies to control employees' behavior at work using computers and using their own mobile devices for business use at work and home.

9. Install preventive, detective, and corrective security controls over facilities, employees, outsiders (external service providers), systems, data, and processes.

10. Communicate security policies to all employees in an easily understandable manner.

11. Penetrate computer systems by using "red team," "blue team," or "white team" security testing concepts.

12. Implement national and international security standards (e.g., NIST, COBIT, ITIL, EU, OECD, and ISO).

13. Conduct digital and security audits, special management reviews and investigations, and self-assessment reviews periodically and proactively to reduce digital and security risks.

(xvi) Project and Program Risks

Project/program risks are viewed from schedule and technical aspects. Schedule risk is evaluated for the extent to which a project is subject to unexpected delays in meeting the technical objectives of the system, regardless of cost. Items of concern include lack of technical skills, lack of enough user/IT staff, and lack of physical facilities. Further, delays in budgeting and acquisition cycles must be considered.

Technical risk is evaluated for the probability that all or part of the technical objectives of a project will prove difficult to achieve due to unforeseen problems, regardless of cost or schedule. This includes management and user acceptance risks as well as those of a purely technical nature. Generally, the alternative that is closest to the status quo and presents the least extension of the state of the art presents the least exposure to such risks.

Six **best practices** to reduce project and program risks are listed next.

1. Install a project/program manager.
2. Develop work breakdown structure techniques.
3. Use program evaluation and review technique/critical path method (PERT/CPM) project planning methods.
4. Issue regular project status reports.
5. Monitor project team member and contractor performance.
6. Conduct project audits, project management reviews, and project self-assessment reviews periodically and proactively to reduce project and program risks.

(xvii) Communication Risks
Communication risks are the inability of employees or management to communicate or listen effectively, which leads to wrong interpretation of information and inappropriate actions.

Five **best practices** to reduce communication risks are listed next.

1. Install a chief communication officer or its equivalent.
2. Develop multidimensional communication formats (e.g., top-down, bottom-up, diagonal, and horizontal directions).
3. Provide training courses in effective listening and communication techniques.
4. Issue newsletters to employees to share company performance matters such as sales, revenues, and profits.
5. Conduct communication audits, management reviews, self-assessment reviews, and employee surveys periodically and proactively to reduce communication risks.

(xviii) Regulatory and Reputation Risks
Regulatory risk arises from noncompliance with laws and regulations, executive orders, directives, circulars, bulletins, and ordinances that could result in adverse publicity in the news media. Regulatory risk is related to reputation risk (image problem) in that noncompliance with laws and regulations will tarnish the reputation of an organization.

Five **best practices** to reduce regulatory risks are listed next.

1. Install a chief compliance officer or its equivalent.

2. Thoroughly understand applicable laws and regulations.

3. Establish communication systems with regulators and government authorities.

4. Conduct training classes in laws and regulations.

5. Conduct compliance audits, special management reviews, and self-assessment reviews periodically and proactively to reduce regulatory risks.

(xix) Environmental Risks

Environmental risks come from not complying with laws and regulations regarding water contamination and air pollution and their associated health-related problems.

Four **best practices** to reduce environmental risks are listed next.

1. Install an environmental officer or its equivalent.

2. Understand environmental laws and regulations.

3. Implement ISO 14000 Standards and industry standards.

4. Conduct environmental audits, special management reviews, and self-assessment reviews periodically and proactively to reduce environmental risks.

(xx) Outsourcing Risks

Outsourcing risks result when outsourced vendors deliver poor-quality products and services, deliver completed projects that do not meet requirements and specifications, and incur cost overruns and time delays.

Five **best practices** to reduce outsourcing risks are listed next.

1. Establish a contract officer for outsourcing projects.

2. Develop fully executed contracts in conjunction with the corporate legal department.

3. Insert a "right to audit" clause in the contract.

4. Monitor the outsourced vendor with periodic progress reports and on-site visits.

5. Conduct outsourcing vendor audits, performance reviews, and vendor self-assessment reviews periodically and proactively to reduce outsourcing risks.

(xxi) Privacy Risks

Privacy risks originate from divulging or releasing personal financial information, personal medical information, trade secret formulas, and other sensitive information (e.g., salaries) about an individual to unauthorized parties.

Six **best practices** to reduce privacy risks are listed next.

1. Install a privacy officer or its equivalent.

2. Develop and communicate privacy policies that contain consequences for not complying with the policies.

3. Understand privacy laws and regulations.

4. Implement policies and procedures for controlling and releasing personal information to third parties.

5. Provide employee orientation classes by the human resources department at the time of hiring.

6. Conduct privacy audits, special management reviews, and privacy self-assessment reviews periodically and proactively to reduce privacy risks.

Some examples of U.S. privacy laws and regulations include the Fair Credit Reporting Act, which protects consumer report information; the Gramm-Leach-Bliley Financial Modernization Act of 1999, which protects nonpublic personal information collected and used by financial institutions; and the Health Insurance Portability and Accountability Act (HIPAA) of 1996, which protects health information collected by health plans, healthcare clearinghouses, and healthcare providers. In the United States, the Federal Trade Commission is responsible for ensuring consumer protection and market competition.

An example of an international privacy law is European Union's directive concerning the transfer of data over countries. The directive mandates that companies engaging in transborder data flow maintain an "adequate level" of protection for such data.

(xxii) Implementation and Operational Risks
Implementation risk results from poor practices in installing a new business strategy, a new computer system, program, or project; establishing a new policy, procedure, or service; or assimilating a new business into an existing one. These risks also arise when a change is not properly and timely implemented or executed. Also, when implementation efforts are inadequate, inefficient, and incomplete, operational risks will increase in that people may not use a new computer system or use it in a wrong way. Operational risks come after implementation risks.

Seven **best practices** to reduce implementation and operational risks are listed next.

1. Install an implementation or operational officer.

2. Develop standard operating procedures and instructions for employees to follow.

3. Develop computer system design and operation manuals.

4. Perform testing, validation, and verification methods for new computer systems.

5. Provide training on how to use a new system, policy, or procedure.

6. Provide due diligence guidelines for acquiring new businesses.

7. Conduct implementation and operational audits, management reviews, and self-assessment reviews periodically and proactively to reduce implementation and operational risks.

(xxiii) Marketing and Sales Risks
Marketing and sales risks stem from the inability to promote, advertise, and sell products to customers that scientists, researchers, and engineers have created, designed, and developed. These risks also include risks resulting from price fixing or disruption in the supply chain or using illegal telemarketing practices.

Seven **best practices** to reduce marketing and sales risks are listed next.

1. Install a chief marketing officer.

2. Gather information about customer requirements for products (i.e., use VOC and QFD techniques).

3. Inform the product development and R&D teams about the results of VOC and QFD.

4. Provide product training to marketing and sales staff.

5. Integrate marketing and sales functions.

6. Establish a chief telemarketing officer.

7. Conduct routine marketing and sales audits, customer perception audits, special management reviews, and self-assessment reviews periodically and proactively to reduce marketing and sales risks.

(xxiv) Nature and Catastrophic Risks

Nature and catastrophic risks result from tornadoes, hurricanes, earthquakes, fire, floods, storms, rain, water leakages, power outages (e.g., blackouts and brownouts), wind-related accidents, and other emergencies.

Six **best practices** to reduce nature and catastrophic risks are listed next.

1. Install a contingency officer or its equivalent.

2. Develop crisis management plans.

3. Install emergency preparedness programs.

4. Develop business continuity, contingency, and communication plans for the entire organization (i.e., Plan A, Plan B, and Plan C).

5. Acquire traditional insurance coverage.

6. Conduct catastrophic audits, crisis management reviews, emergency preparedness drills, and emergency readiness self-assessment reviews periodically and proactively to reduce nature and catastrophic risks.

(xxv) Legal and Reputation Risks

Similar to financial risks, many sources for legal risks exist. There are 12 risks:

1. Not complying with health and safety regulations (e.g., Occupational Safety and Health Act regulations in the United States)

2. Employee and contractor sexual harassment complaints

3. Employee age discrimination suits

4. Inability to prevent employees from using illegal software

5. Patent violations

6. Contract-related lawsuits

7. Product liability suits

8. Product recalls

9. Product tampering

10. Employee criminal acts

11. Conflict-of-interest situations

12. Other illegal activities

Legal risk is related to reputation risk (image problem), similar to the regulatory risk, which could result in adverse publicity in the news media subjecting the organization to special investigations and government inquiries.

Seven **best practices** to reduce legal and reputation risks are listed next.

1. Install a chief legal officer or its equivalent.

2. Provide in-house training classes to employees by legal and human resource departments to comply with applicable laws and regulations.

3. Provide guidelines on acquiring and installing software from reputable vendors.

4. Provide guidelines regarding downloading of official software.

5. Restrict employees bringing software, mobile devices, or personal computers to work from their home.

6. Restrict employees from taking company data and software home.

7. Conduct legal audits, illegal software audits, legal management reviews, and legal self-assessment reviews periodically and proactively to reduce legal risks.

(xxvi) International Risks

International risks are the combination of political, economic, and cultural risks associated with conducting business in a foreign country. Political risk addresses unstable governments and asset expropriation while economic risk deals with currency fluctuations, interest rate changes, and the like. For example, in some countries, culture may prevent implementation of security controls because people believe in mutual trust in each other.

Four **best practices** to reduce international risks are listed next.

1. Install a chief globalization officer.

2. Work with government authorities in streamlining international trade laws and regulations.

3. Provide training to employees in understanding international laws, regulations, and culture.

4. Conduct global audits, global management reviews, and global self-assessment reviews periodically and proactively to reduce international risks.

(xxvii) Summary of Various Types of Risks

Many organizations face various types of risks and exposures. Hence, the chief risk officer must identify as many risk types as possible, including both current and potential risks. Each risk alternative for satisfying the business requirements must be evaluated for the selected risk types. The evaluator reviews each risk to determine the overall impact of significant variations from the original assumptions and expectations.

Most of these risks are interrelated and interconnected with a magnifying effect. For example, legal risk and regulatory risk would magnify the reputation (image) risk of an organization. Some risks have a cascading effect; for example, noncompliance with contractual terms and conditions can lead to financial risk (i.e., loss of money due to payment of penalties) and legal risk (lawsuits resulting from violation of contractual rights). Therefore, all risk types should be viewed from a total business context, instead of on a piecemeal basis.

(c) Risk Vocabulary

This section presents from a conceptual viewpoint risk vocabulary as it relates to a general risk management program and enterprise risk management (ERM) framework. A number of risk-related terms are discussed.

Risk

Risk is the possibility of an event occurring that will have an impact on the achievement of objectives. Risk is measured in terms of impact and likelihood. Risks can be classified or categorized into three types: static versus dynamic, subjective versus objective, and pure versus speculative. Risk is uncertainty about loss. Risks should be avoided where possible; if not, they should be managed well. There are at least six types of risks, including pure, strategic, operational, financial, hazard, and speculative.

Risk Management

Risk management is the total process of identifying, assessing, controlling, and mitigating risks as the risk deals with uncertainty. Risk management includes risk assessment (risk analysis); cost-benefit analysis; the selection, implementation, test, and evaluation of safeguards (risk mitigation); risk financing (risk funding); and risk monitoring (reporting, feedback, and evaluation). It is expressed as:

$$\text{Risk Management} = \text{Risk Assessment} + \text{Risk Mitigation} + \text{Risk Financing} + \text{Risk Monitoring}$$

The ultimate goal of risk management is to minimize the adverse effects of losses and uncertainty connected with pure risks. Risk management is broken down into two major categories: risk control and risk financing.

Audit Risk

Audit risk is the risk that an auditor may unknowingly fail to appropriately modify his or her opinion on financial statements that are materially misstated. It is also defined as the risk that an auditor may fail to detect a significant error or weakness during an examination. Audit risk is defined below.

$$\text{Audit Risk} = \text{Inherent Risk} \times \text{Control Risk} \times \text{Detection Risk}$$

Inherent risk is the susceptibility of a management assertion to a material misstatement, assuming that there are no related internal control structure policies or procedures. Control risk is the risk that a material misstatement in a management assertion will not be prevented or detected on a timely basis by the entity's internal control structure policies or procedures. Detection risk is the risk that the auditor will not detect a material misstatement present in a management assertion.

Heat Maps

A heat map is a visual map highlighting a major activity of interest, using a data visualization technology. It can be applied to several situations, such as (1) a risk heat map, (2) an attacker's heat map, (3) a website's heat map, and (4) an organization's governance, risk, and compliance (GRC) heat map showing data outliers and problem areas. A *risk heat map* can show the impact (consequences) and probability (likelihoods) on a matrix. The impact can be labeled as very low, low, medium, high, and very high impact on a scale of 1 to 5. Similarly, the likelihood (riskiness) can be labeled as very less, less, medium, high, and very high probability between 0% and 100%. Color-coded heat maps highlight a major risk element or component to draw attention.

An *attacker's heat map* shows an attacker's activity as an output from threat intelligence efforts. This map can help victim organizations build a profile of past and current attacker's activity, helping the organizations better understand when, where, and how they will be attacked again in the future.

A *website's heat map* tracks website visitors' click behavior and browsing habits. These maps help a web administrator visualize how visitors are interacting with the website.

An *organization's GRC heat map* can show a quick comprehension of data when its reports are blended into its dashboards. These maps improve the efficiency and effectiveness of risk and compliance staff because they can highlight outliers or other problem areas quickly for their attention.

Probability of Ruin

The probability of ruin is the likelihood of liabilities exceeding assets for a given time period. As the probability of ruin increases, an asset's value decreases and the value-at-risk (VaR) increases.

Residual Risk

Residual risk is the risk remaining after management takes action to reduce the impact and likelihood of an adverse event, including control activities in responding to a risk. Residual risk is current risk; it is also called unmanaged risk, leftover risk, or net risk after existing controls are applied. Residual risk is the portion of inherent risk that remains open after management executes its risk responses.

Several equations are available to express the difficult concept of residual risks:

$$Residual \ risks = Total \ risks - Mitigated \ risks = Unmitigated \ risks$$

$$Residual \ risks = Unmitigated \ risks = Unmanaged \ risks$$

$$Residual \ risks = Accepted \ risks = Retained \ risks$$

$$Residual \ risks = Potential \ risks - Covered \ risks = Uncovered \ risks$$

$$Residual \ risks = Total \ risks - Control \ measures \ (controls \ applied$$

$$Residual \ risks = Total \ risks - Transferred \ risks \ or \ Shared \ risks$$

$$Residual \ risks = Potential \ risks - Countermeasures \ (controls \ applied$$

$$Residual \ risks = Uncovered \ risks = Unaddressed \ risks = Unresolved \ risks$$

$$Residual \ risks = Uncommitted \ risks$$

Risk Acceptance

Risk acceptance means accepting a potential risk and continuing with operating a process or system. It is like accepting risks as part of doing business (a kind of self-insurance). Risk acceptance is also called risk tolerance and risk appetite in order to achieve a desired result.

Risk Retention

Risk retention means some low-level risks are retained on a temporary basis until further study and analysis. Risk retention is most appropriate for situations in which there is a low probability of occurrence (frequency) with a low potential severity. Such risks seldom occur, and, when they do happen, the financial impact is small or negligible. Severity dictates whether a risk should be retained. If the potential severity is more than the organization can afford, retention is not recommended. Frequency determines whether the risk is economically insurable. The higher the probabilities of loss, the higher the expected value of loss and the higher the cost of transfer.

Risk Culture

Risk culture, which is a part of an organization's culture, primarily deals with tone at the top and voice of the top. Risk culture is often the root cause of an organization's scandals, rumors, and downfall, all leading to reputation risk and corporate failures such as tarnished image and financial damage such as bankruptcy.

Risk culture deals with risk-taking and reward-getting approaches, as described next.

- Strong incentives for management encourage risk-taking approaches.
- Weak incentives for management encourage risk-inhibiting approaches.
- There should be a strong link and a calculated balance between risk-taking and reward-getting approaches.
- There should be a balance between excessive downside risks (e.g., loss of revenues and profits) and upside rewards (e.g., larger amounts of bonuses).

In general, strong incentives for management encourage a greater chance of manipulation of business transactions, such as increases in revenues and decreases in costs. Strong incentives also encourage misreporting of business results (e.g., earnings per share and returns on investment, equity, capital, and assets) to earn greater rewards and returns, such as bonuses and promotions.

Risk culture has two basic components: risk behaviors and risk attitudes. Risk behaviors indicate why and how individuals behave or act on things the way they do and how that behavior or those actions affect the overall risk of their organizations. In other words, risk behaviors reflect risk-taking and risk-inhibiting approaches. Risk attitudes reflect a person's risk perceptions and predispositions about risk that can be labeled as risk taker, risk neutral, and risk averter.

Risk Appetite

Risk appetite is the level of risk that an organization is willing to accept. It documents the overall principles that an organization follows with respect to risk taking, given its business strategy, financial objectives, and capital resources. Often stated in qualitative terms, a risk appetite defines how an organization weighs strategic decisions and communicates its strategy to key stakeholders with respect to risk taking. It is designed to enhance management's ability to make informed and effective business decisions while keeping risk exposures within acceptable boundaries.

An organization's risk appetite statement must be matched with its risk policy; otherwise, a risk policy gap can exist. A risk policy gap is the difference between the risk policy and risk appetite. Note that risk policy is derived from risk strategy.

Specific points regarding risk appetite are listed next.

- Risk appetite must balance risk-based decisions and risk-based rewards or returns.

- Risk appetite changes with changes in a nation's economy, business conditions, and competitive forces.

- Risk appetite should be developed and implemented based on the risk capacity (i.e., the maximum amount of risk to handle) and risk maturity (i.e., mature versus immature) of an organization, meaning that mature organizations have already utilized all of their risk capacity or risk-handling capabilities at their disposal with their resources.

- Risk appetite is directly related to value at risk (VAR), meaning that the higher the risk appetite, the larger the amount of VAR. The implication is that more value is at risk the higher the risk appetite.

- Risk appetite is closely linked with risk tolerance in terms of an organization's performance levels.

- Risk appetite must remain within the outer boundaries and inner boundaries of risk tolerance

Risk tolerance has a range of minimum and maximum amounts and levels of risk, and risk appetite falls within this defined range. An example of risk tolerance is when a retailer states that customer merchandise returns should fall between 1% and 2% of gross merchandise sales revenue.

The relationship between risk appetite, risk tolerance, and risk universe is shown next:

Risk Appetite < Risk Tolerance < Risk Universe

Risk Pursuance
Risk pursuance means acknowledging the increased risks and analyzing or exploring different approaches and methods to fully understand the size, scope, and severity of those risks for increased performance. The organization adopts aggressive growth strategies such as introducing new products and services and expanding facilities and operations. It sends a positive signal to further study and exploit risks that can result in either risk acceptance or risk rejection, not to exceed the target residual risk. This increased performance can result from a greater change in organizational strategies, policies, procedures, practices, and programs.

Risk Assessment
Risk assessment includes identification, analysis, measurement, and prioritization of risks. Risk assessment (risk analysis) is the process of identifying the risks and determining the probability of occurrence, the resulting impact, and additional safeguards that would mitigate this impact. It includes risk measurement and prioritization.

Risk Assignment
Risk assignment consists of transferring or assigning risk to a third party by using other options to compensate for the loss, such as an insurance company or outsourcing firm.

Risk Avoidance

Risk avoidance eliminates the risk causes and/or consequences (e.g., add controls that prevent the risk from occurring, remove certain functions of the system, or shut down the system when risks are identified). It is like reducing, avoiding, or eliminating risks by implementing cost-effective safeguards and controls. Risk situations that have high severity and high frequency of loss should be either avoided or reduced. Risk reduction is appropriate when it is possible to reduce either the severity or the frequency. Otherwise, the risk should be avoided or transferred. Examples of risk avoidance controls include separating threats from assets or assets from threats to minimize risks and separating resource allocation from resource use to prevent resource misuse.

Risk Control

Risk control identifies the presence or lack of effective controls in the form of prevention, detection, and correction of risks. Risk control focuses on minimizing the risk of loss to which an organization is exposed. The situation of high frequency and low severity should be managed with additional controls (loss control). Risk control includes risk avoidance and risk reduction.

Risk Financing

Risk financing concentrates on arranging the availability of internal funds to meet occurring financial losses. It also involves external transfer of risk. Risk financing includes risk retention and risk transfer, a tool used by captive insurers. Risk retention applies to risks that have a low expected frequency and a low potential severity. Risk transfer (e.g., buying insurance) applies to risks that have a low expected frequency and a high potential severity. Insurance should be purchased for losses in excess of a firm's risk retention level.

When losses have both high expected frequency and high potential severity, it is likely that risk retention, risk transfer, and loss control all will need to be used in varying degrees. Common methods of loss control include reducing the probability of losses (i.e., frequency and severity reduction) and decreasing the cost of losses that do occur (i.e., cost reduction). Note that "high" and "low" loss frequency and severity rates are defined differently for different firms.

Risk financing includes internal funding for risks (self-insurance and residual risk) and external transfer of risks, such as insurance and hedging. Funding retention can be unfunded or funded. Unfunded retention is treated as part of the overall cost of doing business. A firm may decide to practice funded retention by making various preloss arrangements to ensure that money is readily available to pay for losses that occur. Examples of funded retention include use of credit, reserve funds, self-insurance, and captive insurers.

Risk Limitation

Risk limitation means limiting or containing risks by implementing controls (e.g., supporting, preventive, and detective controls) that minimize the adverse impact of a threat's exercising a vulnerability or by authorizing business operation to continue for a limited time during which additional risk mitigation efforts by other means is installed.

Risk Mapping

Risk mapping involves profiling risk events to their sources (i.e., threats and vulnerabilities), determining their impact levels (i.e., low, medium, or high), and evaluating the presence or lack of effective controls to mitigate risks.

Risk Mitigation

Risk mitigation involves implementation of preventive, detective, and corrective controls along with management, operational, and technical controls to reduce the effects of risks. Risk mitigation includes designing and implementing controls and control-related procedures to minimize risks.

Risk mitigation is a systematic methodology used by senior management to reduce organization risks. Risk mitigation can be achieved through any one or combination of the following risk mitigation options.

Risk Rejection. Risk rejection or risk ignorance is not a wise choice, as all major risks must be managed.

Risk Assumption (Acceptance). Risk acceptance is recognizing a risk and its potential consequences and accepting that risk. This usually occurs when there is no alternate risk mitigation strategy that is more cost effective or feasible. Risk acceptance is associated with risk tolerance and risk appetite.

Risk assumption involves accepting the potential risks and continuing operating the system or process. At some point, management needs to decide if the operation, function, or system is acceptable, given the kind and severity of remaining risks. Risk acceptance is linked to the selection of safeguards since, in some cases, risk may have to be accepted because safeguards (countermeasures) are too expensive (in either monetary or nonmonetary factors).

Merely selecting safeguards does not reduce risk; those safeguards need to be implemented effectively. Moreover, to continue to be effective, risk management needs to be an ongoing process. This requires a periodic assessment and improvement of safeguards and reanalysis of risks.

Risk Avoidance. Risk avoidance involves avoiding risk by eliminating the cause and/or consequence of the risk by, for example, adding controls that prevent the risk from occurring, removing certain functions from the system, or shutting down the system when risks are identified. Risk avoidance is appropriate when it is possible to reduce either the severity or the frequency of a risk.

Risk Reduction (Limitation). This means limiting the risk by implementing controls (supporting, preventive, and detective controls) that minimize the adverse impact of a threat or vulnerability.

Risk Transfer. This means transferring the risk by using other options to compensate for the loss, such as purchasing insurance, coinsurance, or outsourcing. It involves finding another person or organization that can manage project risk(s) better. Risk transfer is appropriate for a risk with a low expected frequency and a high potential severity. Risk protection can be thought of as insurance against certain events. Risk protection involves doing something to allow the project to fall back on additional or alternate resources should the scheduled resource(s) fail.

Risk Contingency. Proper planning is done to define the necessary steps needed if an identified risk event should occur.

Risk Compliance. This means complying with all the applicable laws and regulations in a timely and proper manner in order to reduce compliance risk.

Residual Risk. This refers to the risk remaining after the implementation of new or enhanced controls. Organizations can analyze the extent of the risk reduction generated by the new or enhanced controls in terms of the reduced threat likelihood or impact. Practically no system or process is risk free, and not all implemented controls can eliminate the risk they are intended to address or reduce the risk level to zero.

Implementation of new or enhanced controls can mitigate risks by:

- Eliminating some of the system's vulnerabilities (flaws and weaknesses), thereby reducing the number of possible threat source/vulnerability pairs.

- Adding a targeted control to reduce the capacity and motivation of a threat source (e.g., if technical controls are expensive, then consider administrative and physical controls).

- Reducing the magnitude of the adverse impact (e.g., limiting the extent of a vulnerability or modifying the nature of the relationship between the IT system and the organization's mission).

If the residual risk has not been reduced to an acceptable level, the risk management cycle must be repeated to identify a way of lowering the residual risk to an acceptable level.

Risk Monitoring

Risk monitoring addresses internal and external reporting and provides feedback into the risk assessment process, continuing the loop.

Risk monitoring or risk evaluation, the third and final process of risk management, is a continual evaluation process since change is constant in most organizations. Eight changes are possible:

1. New businesses are acquired.
2. New products are introduced.
3. New services are provided.
4. Networks are updated and expanded.
5. Network components are added or removed.
6. Application software is replaced or updated with newer versions.
7. Personnel changes are made.
8. Security policies are updated.

These changes mean that new risks will surface and risks previously mitigated may again become a concern. Thus, the risk monitoring process is ongoing and evolving.

Risk Transfer

Risk transfer involves payment by one party (the transferor) to another party (the transferee, or risk bearer). Ten forms of risk transfer are available:

1. Hold-harmless agreements.
2. Incorporation.

3. Diversification.

4. Hedging.

5. Insurance and re-insurance.

6. New contract.

7. Re-contracting.

8. Risk sharing.

9. Risk spreading.

10. Business partnerships.

Risk transfer is most likely ideal for a risk with a low expected frequency and a high potential severity.

Alternative Risk-Transfer Tools

Five alternative risk-transfer tools, other than traditional insurance, are described next. Of the five, multiple-trigger policies and risk securitization tools are more commonly used.

1. **Captive insurance methods**, where a noninsurance firm is created for the purpose of accepting the risk of the parent firm that owns an insurer. Captives combine risk transfer and risk retention.

2. **Financial insurance contracts**, which are based on spreading risk over time, as opposed to across a pool of similar exposures. These contracts usually involve a sharing of the investment returns between the insurer and the insured.

3. **Multiline/multiyear insurance contracts**, which combine a broad array of risks (multiline) into a contract with a policy period that extends over multiple years (multiyear). For example, a pure risk may be combined with a financial risk.

4. **Multiple-trigger policies**, which reflect the source of the risk, are not as important as the impact of the risk on the earnings of the firm. A pure risk is combined with a financial risk. The policy is "triggered," and payment is made, only upon the occurrence of an adverse event.

5. **Risk securitization**, which involves the creation of securities such as bonds, or derivatives contracts, options, swaps, or futures that have a payout or price movement linked to an insurance risk. Examples include catastrophe options, earthquake bonds, catastrophe bonds, and catastrophe equity puts.

Risk Registers. Risk registers document the accepted risks below the strategic level and include current risks and unchanged residual risks, lack of effective key internal controls, and lack of mitigating factors (e.g., contingency plans and monitoring activities). Risk registers provide direct links among risk categories, risk aspects, audit universe, and internal controls.

Risk Spreading or Sharing. Risk spreading and sharing involves spreading and sharing risks with other divisions or business units of the same organization. Risk sharing is viewed as a special case of risk transfer in which the risk is transferred from an individual to a group, from one division to another, or from one business unit to another. Risk sharing is a form of risk retention, depending on the success of the risk sharing arrangement.

Financial Risks. Financial risks are risks arising from volatility in foreign currencies, interest rates, and commodities. They include credit risk, liquidity risk (bankruptcy risk), interest rate risk, and market risk.

Hazard Risk. Hazard risks are risks that are insurable, such as natural disasters, various insurable liabilities, impairment of physical assets and property, and terrorism.

Strategic Risk. Strategic risk is a high-level and corporate-wide risk, which includes strategy risk, political risk, economic risk, regulatory risk, reputation risk, global risk, leadership risk, customer risk, and market brand management risk. It is also related to failure of strategy and changing customer needs and business conditions.

Operational Risk. Operational risk is a risk related to the organization's internal systems, products, services, processes, technology, and people.

Hazard. Hazard is a condition that creates or increases the probability of a loss. Three types of hazards exist: (1) physical hazard, (2) moral hazard, and (3) morale hazard. Physical hazard is a condition of the subject of insurance that creates or increases the chance of loss, such as structural defects, occupancy, or similar conditions. Moral hazard is a dishonest predisposition on the part of an insured that increases the chance of loss. Morale hazard is a careless attitude on the part of an insured that increases the chance of loss or causes losses to be greater than would otherwise be the case.

Hedging. Hedging is taking a position opposite to the exposure or risk. This can be done with financial derivatives, such as futures contracts, forward contracts, options, and swaps. A perfect hedge is not possible because financial derivatives used to hedge do not move together, leaving some risk. The idea behind hedging is to minimize risk. A value is created for shareholders if corporate hedging does not duplicate the shareholders' "homemade" hedging.

Natural Hedges. Natural hedges are created from the relationship between revenues and costs of a business unit or a subsidiary. The more revenues over the cost, the better protection is. The key is the extent to which cash flows adjust naturally to currency changes due to exchange-rate fluctuations. One way to explore the likelihood of a natural hedge is to determine whether a subsidiary's revenue and cost functions are sensitive to domestic or global business conditions.

Many types of risks may be relatively correlated with each other. Consequently, combining these risks produces a form of natural hedging. The traditional silo approach could actually reduce the overall efficiency of the firm's risk management activities by destroying the natural hedging that exists at the enterprise-wide level.

Insurance. Insurance is an economic device whereby an individual or a corporation substitutes a small certain cost (the premium) for a large uncertain financial loss (the claim, or contingency insured against) that would exist if it were not for the insurance policy (contract). Insurance is most appropriate for situations in where there is a low frequency and a high severity of occurrence. Insurance is a risk transfer mechanism.

Insurable Interest. Insurable interest is an interest that might be damaged if the peril insured against occurs; the possibility of a financial loss to an individual or a corporation that can be protected against through insurance.

Self-Insurance. Self-insurance is a risk-retention program that incorporates elements of the insurance mechanism where the self-insured organization pays the claims rather than an insurance company.

Peril. Peril is the cause of possible loss, the event insured against. "Open peril" is a term used to describe a broad form of property insurance in which coverage applies to loss arising from any fortuitous cause other than those perils or causes specifically excluded.

Portfolio Risk. Portfolio risk considers risk and return of a firm when it is investing in acquisition or expansion projects. Management needs to find the relationship between the net present values (NPVs) for new projects and the NPVs for existing projects. In a portfolio framework, the trade-off between risk and expected NPV for different combinations of investments can be analyzed.

Pure Risk. Risk is a possibility or chance of loss. Many types of risks exist, including pure risk, speculative risk, static risk, dynamic risk, subjective risk, and objective risk. Pure risk is a condition in which there is a probability of loss (e.g., default of a debtor or disability). Risk management is a scientific approach to the problem of dealing with the pure risks facing an individual or an organization in which insurance is viewed as simply one of several approaches for dealing with such risks. The techniques of insurance and self-insurance are commonly limited to the treatment of pure risks, such as fire, product liability, and worker's compensation. Traditionally, the risk management tools—avoidance, loss control, and transfer—have been applied primarily to the pure or hazard risks facing a firm. Several types of pure risks exist, including personal, property, liability, and performance risks.

Speculative Risk. Speculative risk exists when there is uncertainty about an event that could produce either a profit or a loss. It involves the chance of loss or gain (e.g., hedging, options, and derivatives).

Static Risk. Static risk, which can be either pure or speculative, stems from an unchanging society that is in stable equilibrium. Examples of pure static risk include the uncertainties due to such random events as lightning, windstorms, and death. Business undertakings in a stable economy illustrate the concept of speculative static risk.

Dynamic Risk. Dynamic risk, in contrast to static risk, is produced because of changes in society. Dynamic risks also can be either pure or speculative. Examples of sources of dynamic risk include urban unrest, increasingly complex technology, and changing attitude of legislatures and courts about a variety of issues.

Subjective Risk. Subjective risk refers to the mental state of an individual who experiences doubt or worry as to the outcome of a given event. In addition to being subjective, a particular risk may be either pure or speculative and either static or dynamic.

Objective Risk. Objective risk differs from subjective risk primarily in the sense that it is more precisely observable and therefore measurable. In general, objective risk is the probable variation of actual from expected experience.

Derisking. If risking means risk taking, derisking means risk-lessening, risk-downsizing, or risk modifying. It can also include reducing a current risk or a future risk with various methods of risk transferring, risk sharing, risk-shifting (surety bonds, performance bonds, and blanket bonds), or risk spreading with third parties. Examples of these methods include self-insurance; reinsurance; coinsurance; captive insurance; financial engineering; joint ventures; risk securitization through using financial securities (e.g., financial bonds, financial options, and puts) as collateral for security; and incorporation methods (e.g., a public corporation is less risky than a private corporation; a regular corporation is less risky than a proprietorship or partnership; and a limited liability corporation is less risky than a regular corporation).

Value at Risk. Value at risk (VaR) is the maximum amount of loss that can occur in a given time period (e.g., one year) and at a given confidence level (e.g., 95%). The VaR needs to be established for each risk type or risk category that is documented in risk descriptions and risk discussions. The amount of VaR is the amount of risk capital (i.e., capital at risk) needed to withstand a particular loss. Risk appetite is directly related to the VaR, meaning that the higher the risk appetite, the larger the amount of VaR, implying more value is at risk. An example of VaR is that we are 95% confident that our organization will have to incur $500,000 loss in the next year due to cyberattacks, resulting from cyberrisks of data breaches. A **back-testing** of the VaR amount should be performed by comparing the actual VaR with the estimated VaR. The root causes for major variances should be found.

(d) Risk Management Tools and Measuring Corporate Risks

This section discusses two topics related to risk management, including a presentation of risk management tools, and how to manage corporate risks with best practices.

(i) Risk Management Tools

Measuring risk can be difficult. A variety of approaches are used ranging from simply adjusting costs up or benefits down, adjusting risk levels, dollar amounts, and probabilities of events occurring, including quantitative methods and qualitative methods. Thirteen of the more commonly used tools and techniques are listed and discussed next.

1. Business impact analysis
2. Cost-benefit analysis
3. SWOT analysis (situation analysis)
4. Sensitivity analysis
5. Fit-gap analysis
6. Option analysis
7. Outcomes analysis
8. Economic analysis
9. Root-cause analysis
10. Expected value analysis
11. Subjective scoring methods
12. Quantitative methods
13. Qualitative methods

It is good business practice to combine some of the above tools and methods to obtain broad perspectives and comprehensive picture of risks.

(A) Business Impact Analysis. A business impact analysis is a critical step to understanding the impact of various threats, exposures, and risks facing an organization. This analysis can be applied to any business function, operation, or mission. The results of the business impact analysis are then integrated into business strategies, plans, policies, and procedures.

(B) Cost-Benefit Analysis. In order to allocate resources and implement cost-effective security identifying all possible controls and evaluating their feasibility and effectiveness, should conduct a cost-benefit analysis for each proposed control to determine which controls are required and appropriate for their circumstances.

The cost-benefit analysis can be qualitative and quantitative. Its purpose is to demonstrate that the costs of implementing controls can be justified by a reduction in the level of risk. A cost-benefit analysis for proposed new controls or enhanced control encompasses:

- Determining the impact of implementing the new or enhanced controls.

- Determining the impact of *not* implementing the new or enhanced controls.

- Estimating the costs of the implementation. These may include hardware and software purchases; reduced operational effectiveness if system performance or functionality is reduced for increased security; cost of implementing additional policies and procedures; cost of hiring additional personnel to implement proposed policies, procedures, or services; and training and maintenance costs.

- Assessing the implementation costs and benefits against system and data criticality to determine the importance of implementing the new controls, given their costs and relative impact.

The organization will need to assess the benefits of the controls in terms of maintaining an acceptable mission posture for the organization to achieve. Just as there is a cost for implementing a needed control, there is a cost of *not* implementing it. By relating the result of not implementing the control to the mission, organizations can determine whether it is feasible to forgo its control implementation.

(C) SWOT Analysis. The scope of situation analysis or SWOT analysis includes an assessment of an organization's key strengths (S), weaknesses (W), opportunities (O), and threats (T). It considers several factors, such as the firm itself, the organization's industry, its competitive position, functional areas of the firm, and firm management.

(D) Sensitivity Analysis. Sensitivity analysis includes scenario (what-if) planning and simulation studies. It indicates how much change in outputs will occur in response to a given change in inputs. As applied to investments, sensitivity analysis indicates how much an investment's return (or net present value) will change in response to a given change in an independent input variable, with all other factors held constant. This technique can be used on one variable at a time or on a group of variables (sometimes referred to as scenario analysis). Typically, investment returns are more sensitive to changes in some variables than to changes in others.

(E) Fit-Gap Analysis Fit-gap analysis determines the difference between the actual outcome and the expected outcome. It asks two basic questions:

1. How much fit is there?

2. How much gap is there?

After the root causes of the gap are identified, the gap can be reduced, though not eliminated, through strategies, contingency plans, and specific action steps.

(F) Option Analysis. Option analysis is more a framework for critical thinking than a model. It requires analysts to ask if all choices for managing uncertainty have been considered. Option analysis may be subdivided into sequential decision analysis and irreversible investment theory. For example, a complex risk decision may require developing multiple choices, such as Option A, Option B, Option C, and Option D.

(G) Outcomes Analysis

Outcomes analysis is a comparison of a model's inputs to corresponding actual outputs. These comparisons can assess the accuracy of estimates or forecasts or provide evidence of poor performance. Statistical tests or expert judgment can be used in outcomes analysis. It is better to use a range of forecasts of tests instead of a single test, because a single test can have a built-in weakness. Back-testing is a form of outcomes analysis.

(H) Economic Analysis. The scope of economic analysis includes breakeven analysis, capital budgeting analysis (e.g., payback period, net present value, internal rate of return, and profitability index), and financial ratio analysis (e.g., return on investment, on value, on quality, on assets, on training, on equity, on data, and on sales). The analysis mainly deals with quantitative data in terms of dollars and ratios.

(I) Root-Cause Analysis. Root causes are fundamental deficiencies or problems that result in a nonconformance. These deficiencies or problems must be corrected to prevent their recurrence. Root causes link undesirable events to their sources. Measuring a problem's root causes involves determining the sources of identified risks (known risks) and understanding the positive and negative impacts of those known risks on other areas of an organization. Corrective controls must address and reduce the root causes of problems at their source, not just the symptoms. Root-cause analysis is a technique used to identify conditions that initiate the occurrence of an undesirable activity, state, or an event. It is a part of risk management techniques.

(J) Expected Value Analysis. Expected value analysis involves the assignment of probability estimates to alternative outcomes and summing the products of the various outcomes. For example, the price of crude oil per barrel today is $10.80 and there is a 25% probability of the price rising to $11.50 in the next year, a 25% chance it will fall to $10.50, and a 50% chance of a slight increase to $11.00. The expected value (EV) of the future price of one barrel of crude oil would be:

$$EV = 0.25 \times \$11.50 + 0.25 \times \$10.50 + 0.50 \times \$11.00 = \$11.00$$

(K) Subjective Scoring Methods. Subjective scoring methods involve assigning weights to responses to questions addressing areas that may introduce elements of risk. The resulting "risk" score may be just one component of an overall subjective project or investment evaluation. Evaluation criteria are individually weighted to reflect the concept of inherent risk. Identified risk factors should be limited to a few points for manageability and understandability and for meaningful interpretation of the results.

(L) Quantitative Methods Exposure Factor. This risk metric provides a percentage measure of potential loss—up to 100% of the value of the asset.

Single Loss Exposure Value. This value is computed by multiplying the asset value with the exposure factor. This risk metric presents the expected monetary cost of a threat event. For example, an earthquake may destroy critical IT and communications resources, thereby preventing an organization from billing its clients for perhaps a week—until replacement resources can be established—even though the necessary information may remain intact.

Financial losses from a single event could be devastating. Alternatively, the threat of operational errors costing individually from hundreds to a few thousands of dollars—none devastating or even individually significant—may occur many times a year with a significant total annual cost and loss of operational efficiency.

Annualized Rate of Occurrence. Threats may occur with great frequency, rarely, or anywhere in between. Seemingly minor operational threats may occur many times every year, adding up to substantial loss, while potentially devastating threats, such as a 100-year flood, fire, or hack that destroys critical files, may occur only rarely. Annualizing threat frequency allows the economic consequences of threat events to be addressed in a sound fiscal manner, much as actuarial data for insurance enables insurance companies to provide valuable services to their clients.

Probability of Loss. Probability of loss is the chance or likelihood of expected monetary loss attributable to a threat event. For example, loss due to operational error may extend from a 1/10 chance of losing $10 million annually to a 1/100 chance of losing $1 billion annually, provided the right combinations of conditions are met. Note that there is little utility in developing the probability of threat events for anything but relatively rare occurrences. The annualized probable monetary loss can be useful in budgeting.

Annualized Loss Expectancy. The simplest expression of annualized loss expectancy is derived by multiplying the annualized rate of occurrence (i.e., threat frequency) with the single loss exposure value. For example, given an annual rate of occurrence of 1/10 and a single loss exposure of $10 million, the expected loss annually is $1/10 \times \$10$ million = $1 million. This value is central in the cost-benefit analysis of risk mitigation and in ensuring proportionality in resources allocated to protection of assets.

(M) Qualitative Methods

Qualitative methods include judgment and intuitive (gut feel) approach, checklists, self-assessments, focus groups, interviews, surveys, and the Delphi technique. In the Delphi technique, subject matter experts present their own views of risks independently and anonymously, and their views are centrally compiled. The process is repeated until consensus is obtained. The Delphi technique is a method used to avoid groupthink, as subject matter experts do not meet face-to-face to make decisions.

(ii) Managing Corporate Risks

Five **best practices** should be implemented to manage corporate risks on an ongoing basis.

1. **Manage existing safeguards and controls.** The day-to-day management of existing safeguards and controls ranges from the robust access control for information assets, to enforcement of systems development standards, to awareness and management of the physical environment and associated risks. Many other essential areas of safeguard and control must be administered and practiced daily. These include, but are not limited to, personnel procedures, change control, information valuation and classification, and contingency planning.

2. **Periodically assess risks.** In order to determine whether all necessary and prudent safeguards and controls are in place and efficiently administered, associated risks must be assessed periodically, preferably with quantitative risk assessment. An insecure IT environment may appear on the surface to be securely administered, but quantitative risk assessment can reveal safeguard or control inadequacies. Effective application of the results of that assessment, through risk mitigation and associated cost/benefit analysis, can lead to the assurance of efficient safeguards or control of the organization assets and improved bottom-line performance.

3. **Mitigate risks by implementing and efficiently administering safeguards and controls.** It is important to remedy situations where risk assessment shows that safeguards or controls are not in place or are not effectively administered.

4. **Risk assessment and strategic planning.** Quantitative risk assessment, applied in the consideration of alternative strategic plans, can reveal unacceptable risks in an otherwise sound business case. Failure to assess the risks associated with alternative strategic plans can result in the implementation of plans at significant monetary loss. That loss is a consequence of being unaware of, or inadequately considering, risks.

5. **Implement an enterprise risk management program.**

5.14 Globally Accepted Risk Management Frameworks

Several globally accepted risk management frameworks are available to provide a variety of perspectives with different and useful purposes in risk management. We define enterprise risk management in general followed by eight specific risk management frameworks.

(a) Enterprise Risk Management

In this section we define risk from two perspectives: pure risk and organization risk. From a pure risk viewpoint, risk is defined as the possibility of a loss (financial and/or nonfinancial). From an organization viewpoint, risk is defined as a risk of failure (upside risk) and a risk of success (downside risk).

There are several types of **pure risks**, including personal, property, liability, and performance risks. Risk management is a scientific approach to the problem of dealing with the pure risks facing an individual or an organization. Insurance is viewed as simply one of several approaches for dealing with pure risks. The techniques of insurance and self-insurance are commonly limited to the treatment of pure risks, such as fire, product liability, and worker's compensation claims. Traditionally, risk management tools—avoidance, loss control, and transfer—have been applied primarily to the pure or hazard risks facing an organization.

Organizational risks are discussed from two contrasting viewpoints—a risk of failure (upside risk) and a risk of success (downside risk)— where the former is managed well due to fear and the latter is not managed well due to overconfidence. This is shown in the next equation.

$$\text{Organizational Risks} = \text{Risk of Failure} + \text{Risk of Success}$$

Risk of failure can result from increased threats and vulnerabilities facing an organization; low-performing senior management and the board; increased competition; poor-quality products and services; inappropriate revenue, cost, and profit structure; bad customer service; mediocre employees, increased legal liabilities; and, above all, a decrease in the customer base. Management should recognize the risk of failure early and develop strategies to reduce or eliminate the chances of failure with new thinking and radical approaches to turn a risk of failure into a risk of success.

Risk of success can result from decreased threats and vulnerabilities facing an organization; high-performing senior management and the board; managed competition; high-quality products and services; appropriate revenue, cost, and profit structure; good customer service; talented employees, decreased legal liabilities; and, above all, an increase in the customer base. An example of downside risk is the inability to fulfill unexpected increases in demand for products and services and the inability to sustain expected business growth. The risk of success must be recognized, protected, and sustained and not taken it for granted due to complicit management and overconfidence because a risk of success can eventually turn into a risk of failure when the former is ignored.

(i) Yesterday's Risk Management

Traditionally, an organization's risk management was focused on pure risks and handled on a piecemeal basis and in an ad hoc manner. Risk was recognized only when a disaster occurred and only when huge amounts of losses occurred (i.e., financial and/or nonfinancial losses). Some organizations have taken insurance coverage to protect against losses or some have operated with self-insurance. Each department, operation, function, or division handled risk in its own way, and senior management and the board did not know how much total risk the entire organization was facing at any point in time. Risk was not explicitly considered in the organization's governance processes and oversight mechanisms. There was no chief risk officer position at the senior management level to handle organization-wide risks.

Risks were not a part of business strategy and management performance, resulting in a mismatch between:

- Risk identification and risk containment.
- Risk-resource allocation and risk-resource usage.
- Risk planning and risk execution.
- Risk-based costs and risk-based benefits.
- Risk-based decisions and risk-based results.
- Responsibility for risks and accountability of risks.

Some organizations establish a limited budget to cover financial losses; others did not. In summary, a silo approach was taken to handle risk management, and risk was not integrated within the entire organization.

(ii) Today's Risk Management

Today, many forward-looking organizations have established an enterprise risk management (ERM) business philosophy to manage risks in a comprehensive and integrated manner in one place. Senior management and the board know how much total risk the entire organization is facing at any point in time due to ERM's holistic and big-picture views of all major risks. These organizations have established a chief risk officer position with a budget and staff at the senior management level to handle organization-wide risks. Risks are a part of business strategy and management performance. Some organizations establish a limited budget to cover financial losses; others do not. In summary, an integrated approach is taken to handle risk management.

The correct sequence of elements of a business strategy and management performance is shown next.

Mission/Vision/Core Values → Goals/Objectives → Strategies → Decisions → Results (Performance)

Strategies → Known and Unknown Risks (ERM) → Decisions → Results (Performance)

(iii) Risk Management before and after ERM
A summary of an organization's risk management status from two timelines—before ERM and after ERM—is presented next.

(A) Risk Management before ERM
- More emphasis was placed on pure risks dealing with insurance coverage and losses or self-insurance and little or no emphasis was placed on organizational risk.

- Risks had low visibility because they were discretely managed and monitored at lower levels of management.

- Risk was not an explicit part of an organization's strategy and management's performance. Only the chief executive officer or president was responsible and accountable for risk management.

- The risk assessment process was considered a scientific approach, left to mathematicians, technicians, and actuaries who develop risk models and come up with risk scenarios, which may not be useful to management due to misleading and confusing interpretations.

- Employees had little or no risk awareness due to lack of training and because risk awareness was not built into their job descriptions.

- Management considered only risk drivers arising inside of an organization (e.g., sales, revenue, costs, profits, technology, and employees). It ignored risk drivers coming from outside of the organization (e.g., competitive, supply-chain, production, reputation, social media, regulatory, and political risk; union strikes).

- More focus was placed on risk containment and less focus was placed on risk identification.

- More focus was placed on risk of failure and less focus was placed on risk of success.

- More focus was placed on known risks and less focus was placed on unknown risks (i.e., whitespace).

- More focus was placed on risk detection and correction and less focus was placed on risk anticipation and prevention.

- More focus was placed on reaction and less focus was placed on proactive responses.

- More focus was placed on a narrow view of risks and less focus was placed on a broad view of risks.

- The risk management process is less structured, organized, disciplined, managed, and integrated than it should be.

(B) Risk Management after ERM

- Equal emphasis is placed on both pure risks and organization risks.

- Risks take on high visibility because they are continuously managed and monitored at higher levels of management.

- Risk is explicitly part of an organization's s strategy and management's performance. All senior management, board members, and all employees are responsible and accountable for risk management.

- The risk assessment process is considered a combination of art (judgment and strategy) and science (risk models and model outcomes).

- Greater levels of risk awareness are found in employees due to constant and continuous training and because risk awareness is built into their job descriptions.

- Management considers risk drivers arising inside and outside of an organization.

- There is an equal focus on:

  □ Risk containment and risk identification.

  □ Risk of failure and risk of success.

  □ Known and unknown risks.

  □ Risk anticipation, prevention, detection, and correction.

  □ A broad view and a narrow view of risks.

- There is more focus on proactive responses and less focus on reaction.

- The risk management process is structured, organized, disciplined, managed, and integrated.

(b) Risk Management Frameworks

Eight specific risk management frameworks are discussed here:

1. U.S. COSO's Framework for Enterprise Risk Management

2. IIA's Enterprise Risk Management

3. U.S. OMB's Framework for ERM and Internal Control

4. Switzerland ISO Risk Management—ISO Standard 31000

5. Switzerland ISO/IEC Risk Assessment—ISO Standard 31010

6. RIMS ERM Risk Maturity Model

7. U.K. Federation of European Risk Management Association

8. U.K. BS 31100 Standard—Code of Practice for Risk Management

(i) U.S. COSO's Framework for Enterprise Risk Management

The U.S. Committee of Sponsoring Organizations of the Treadway Commission (COSO) has issued its new and updated version in June 2017 titled Enterprise Risk Management (ERM): Integrating with Strategy and Performance.[17]

(A) COSO's Definition of Risk and Uncertainty.   The U.S. COSO-ERM defines **risk** as the possibility that events will occur and affect the achievement of strategy and business objectives. Here, risks are related to the potential for events, often considered in terms of severity. In some instances, risks may relate to the anticipation of an event that does not occur (i.e., unknown risks).

An **event** is defined as a single occurrence or a set of occurrences. An u**ncertainty** is defined as the state of not knowing how potential events may or may not manifest. A s**everity** is defined as a measurement of considerations, such as the likelihood and impacts of events or the time it takes to recover from events (i.e., recovery time and efforts).

$$Risk = Severity = Likelihood \times Impact$$

$$Risk = Severity = Recovery\ Time\ and\ Effort$$

(B) COSO's Risk Framework.   The Framework highlights the importance of ERM in strategic planning and embedding it throughout an organization because risk influences and integrates strategy and performance across all departments and functions. The Framework is a set of 20 principles organized into five interrelated components:

Component 1: Governance and Culture. Governance sets the organization's tone, rein-forcing the importance of and establishing oversight responsibilities for ERM. Culture pertains to ethical values, desired behaviors, and understanding of risk in the entity. This component is supported by the principles of (1) exercises board risk oversight, (2) establishes operating structures, (3) defines desired culture, (4) demonstrates commit-ment to core values, and (5) attracts, develops, and retains capable individuals.

Component 2: Strategy and Objective-Setting. The ERM strategy and objective-set-ting work together in the strategic planning process. A risk appetite is established and aligned with strategy; business objectives put strategy into practice while serving as a basis for identifying, assessing, and responding to risk. This component is supported by the following principles of (1) analyzes business context, (2) defines risk appetite, (3) evaluates alternatives strategies, and (4) formulates business objectives.

Component 3: Performance. Risks that may impact the achievement of strategy and busi-ness objectives need to be identified and assessed. Risks are prioritized by severity in the context of risk appetite. The organization then selects risk responses and takes a portfolio view of the amount of risk it has assumed. The results of this process are reported to key risk stakeholders. This component is supported by the following principles of (1) identi-fies risk, (2) assesses severity of risk, (3) prioritizes risks, (4) implements risk responses, and (5) develops portfolio view.

Component 4: Review and Revision. By reviewing entity performance, an organization can consider how well the ERM components are functioning over time and in light of substantial changes, and what revisions are needed. This component is supported by the

---

following principles of (1) assesses substantial change, (2) reviews risk and performance, and (3) pursues improvement in ERM.

Component 5: Information, Communication, and Reporting. ERM requires a continual process of obtaining and sharing necessary information, from both internal and external sources, which flows up, down, and across the organization. This component is supported by the following principles of (1) leverages information and technology, (2) communicates risk information, and (3) reports on risk, culture, and performance.

Examples of communicating methods include electronic messages; third-party materials; informal discussions and meetings; training and seminars; public events; internal documents; employee performance evaluations; annual management reviews; social media; newswires; whistleblower hotlines; and escalation protocols and procedures to report inappropriate behavior and exceptions in standards of conduct. High-quality information is accessible, accurate, appropriate, current, reliable, and above all has integrity.

(C) COSO's Risk Responses.
For all risks identified, management selects and deploys a **risk response strategy** from five categories: accept, avoid, pursue, reduce, and share.

1. **Accept.** No action is taken to affect the severity of the risk. This response is appropriate when the risk is already within risk appetite. A risk that is outside the entity's risk appetite and that management seeks to accept will generally require approval from the board or other oversight bodies.

2. **Avoid.** Action is taken to remove the risk, which may mean ceasing a product line, declining to expand to a new geographical market, or selling a division. Choosing avoidance suggests that the organization was not able to identify a response that would reduce the impact of the risk to an acceptable amount of severity. The decision to "avoid" is considered as a part of the alternative strategy-setting process that could introduce new risks to the organization.

3. **Pursue.** Action is taken that accepts increased risk to achieve increased performance. This may involve adopting more aggressive growth strategies, expanding operations, or developing new products and services. When choosing to exploit risk, management understands the nature and extent of any changes required to achieve desired performance while not exceeding the target residual risk.

4. **Reduce.** Action is taken to reduce the severity of the risk. This involves any of myriad everyday business decisions that reduce residual risk to an amount of severity aligned with the target residual risk profile and risk appetite.

5. **Share.** Action is taken to reduce the severity of the risk by transferring or otherwise sharing a portion of the risk. Common techniques include outsourcing to specialist service providers, purchasing insurance products, and engaging in hedging transactions. As with the reduce responses, sharing risk lowers residual risk in alignment with risk appetite.

These five categories of risk responses assume that the risk can be managed within the organization's risk appetite and within an acceptable variation in actual performance. In some instances, management may need to consider another (alternative) course of action when the stated five categories do not represent the desired course of action.

Examples of alternative actions include: (1) review and revise the business objectives; (2) review and revise the business strategy; and (3) review, recalibrate, and exceed (increase) the risk appetite when the organization repeatedly accepts risks that approach or exceed appetite as part of its usual operations and when the benefit from exceeding the appetite is greater than the cost of exceeding the risk appetite.

Management selects and deploys risk responses while considering factors such as business context; costs and benefits; obligations and expectations; regulatory requirements; new business opportunities that were not previously considered; risk priority; risk severity; and risk appetite. The last three factors are given further attention below.

Risk priority. The priority assigned to the risk informs the allocation of resources. Risk reduction responses that have large implementation costs (e.g., system upgrades and increases in personnel) for lower-priority risks need to be carefully considered and may not be appropriate given the assessed severity.

Risk severity. It is a measurement of risk in terms of impact and likelihood of events and the time it takes to recover from such events. Risk response should reflect the size, scope, and nature of the risk and its impact on the organization. For example, in a transaction or production environment, where risks are driven by changes in volume, the proposed response is scaled to accommodate increased activity.

Risk appetite. Risk response either brings risk within the risk appetite of the organization or maintains the current status. Management identifies the response that brings residual risk to within the appetite. For example, a combination of purchasing insurance and implementing internal responses (e.g., developing new strategies and installing new controls) can reduce the risk to an acceptable variation in actual performance. The relationships between risk appetite, tolerable risk, and residual risk are shown next.

Residual risk = Acceptable variation in actual performance = Tolerable risk = Risk appetite

Single risk response = Optimum residual risk

Multiple risk responses = Optimum residual risk

Residual risk can be less than or equal to the risk appetite, but it cannot be greater than that.

Residual risk can be less than or equal to the tolerable risk, but it cannot be greater than that.

Note that a risk response may change the risk profile. For example, fruit farmers may purchase weather-related insurance for floods or storms that would result in production levels dropping below a certain minimum volume. The risk profile for production levels would account for the potential performance outcomes covered by insurance.

Once management selects a risk response, control activities are necessary to ensure that those risk responses are executed as intended. Management must recognize that risk is managed but not eliminated. Some residual risk will always exist, not only because resources are limited but because of future uncertainty and limitations inherent in all tasks, activities, functions, or operations.

(D) COSO's Lines of Accountability Model. All levels of an organization's management must be responsible and accountable for the ERM, regardless of their job title and their management hierarchy. Here, higher-level management comprises the chief executive officer (CEO), president, other C-level executives, vice presidents, general managers, and other senior managers leading the key operating units or business functions.

In addition to the higher-level managers, there will be some middle-level managers and many lower-level managers and supervisors who are directly involved in implementing (executing) the ERM strategies, where strategies are translated into policies and procedures at a detailed level. The roles of various management levels are shown next.

Higher-Level Management → Develops ERM Strategy

Middle-Level and Lower-level Management → Implements ERM Strategy

As management accountability follows management responsibility, the lines of accountability model is shown next.

- The board of directors is accountable to the external stakeholders (i.e., shareholders, owners, and investors) for the entire ERM program along with other responsibilities.

- The CEO is accountable to the board of directors for the entire ERM program.

- Each C-level executive and other senior managers are accountable for the CEO for his or her portion of the ERM program.

- Each middle-level manager and lower-level manager and supervisor is accountable to the next higher-level manager for his or her portion of the ERM program.

- In other words, each person at the lower-level of management hierarchy is accountable to another person at the highest-level of management hierarchy for his or her portion of the ERM program.

The three lines of the accountability model include the core business function, support functions, and assurance functions.

First Line of Accountability: Core Business Functions. Operational management at all levels of the hierarchy is responsible for identifying and managing the performance outcomes and risks resulting from practices and systems to which they are accountable. The first line is also responsible for the risks inherent to the strategy and business objectives. As the principal owners of risk, they set business objectives, establish acceptable variation in performance outcomes, train personnel, and reinforce risk responses. In short, the first line implements and executes the day-to-day tasks to manage performance outcomes and risks taken to achieve strategy and business objectives. If a separate risk management function or team is established in the first line, it must exercise an unbiased oversight in risk-related matters.

Core business functions are defined differently based on the type of industry. For example, core business functions in the (1) retail industry are defined as operations (i.e., procurement and merchandising), marketing, and finance; (2) insurance industry are defined as operations (i.e., premiums [actuaries] and claims), marketing, and finance; (3) manufacturing industry are defined as operations (i.e., production and supply chain), marketing, and finance; and (4) service industry are defined as operations (i.e., planning and delivery), marketing, and finance.

Regardless of the industry, three common core business functions include (1) operations (i.e., manufacturing to produce goods or providing services to customers), (2) marketing to sell those goods and services, and (3) finance to invest money in those goods or services and to receive revenue and profits from making and selling those goods and services.

Management roles within different organizations may change. For example, a chief technology officer (CTO) may play a second-line role in a financial services company due to its support function, but in a technology company the same position would play a first-line role due to its core function.

Second Line of Accountability: Support Functions. Support functions assist and advise core functions to succeed. Support functions (business-enabling functions) in operating units include its management and personnel responsible for managing and monitoring day-to-day performance outcomes and ERM. They provide guidance and establish standards and evaluate adherence to defined standards. The second line is independent of the first line and can challenge the first line to manage performance outcomes and take prudent risks. In some companies, independent teams (e.g., outside consultants and subject matter experts) without separate and distinct reporting lines may provide some degree of challenge.

The management and personnel working in the support functions possess specialized skills, such as technical risk management expertise (e.g., risk analysts), finance, (e.g., financial analysts), product/service quality management (e.g., quality control analysts), information technology (e.g., IT security analysts), accounting (e.g., internal control analysts), compliance (e.g., compliance analysts), legal (e.g., legal analysts), human resources (e.g., HR analysts), procurement (e.g., purchase analysts), manufacturing (e.g., production control analysts), public relations (e.g., a company spokesperson), and others. If a separate risk management function or team is established in the second line, it must exercise an unbiased oversight in risk-related matters.

Specifically, the second-line management responsibilities include:

- Intervening directly in modifying and supporting the first-line in appropriate risk responses.

- Supporting management policies, defining roles and responsibilities, and setting targets for implementation.

- Providing ERM guidance, supporting management to identify trends and emerging risks, and providing training on ERM processes.

- Assisting management in developing processes and risk responses to manage risks and issues.

- Monitoring the adequacy and effectiveness of risk responses, accuracy, and completeness of reporting, and timely remediation of deficiencies.

- Escalating identified or emerging risks exposures to management and the board for risk awareness and potential action.

Third Line of Accountability: Assurance Functions. Assurance functions, most commonly internal audit, often provide the last line of accountability by performing audits or reviews of ERM practices, identifying issues and improvement opportunities, making recommendations, and keeping the board and executive management up-to-date on matters requiring resolution.

The two factors that distinguish the third line of accountability from the first and second lines of accountability are:

- The high level of independence and objectivity of internal auditors (enabled by direct reporting to the board).

- The authority of internal auditors to evaluate and make recommendations to senior management on the design and operating effectiveness of the entity overall.

External auditors expressing an opinion on the fairness of the financial statements, by itself, does not include a significant focus on the ERM. Nor does it result in the external auditor forming an opinion on the entity's ERM. Where, however, law or regulation requires the external auditor to evaluate a company's assertions related to internal control over financial reporting and the supporting basis for these assertions, the scope of the external audit work directed at those areas will be extensive and sufficient information and assurance will be gained. Under these circumstances, external auditors also become a part of the third line of accountability, similar to internal auditors. Imagining further, external auditors or regulatory auditors can be thought of as a fourth line of accountability if they are asked to conduct a separate and comprehensive review of an ERM and the three lines of accountability where such review results are reported to senior management, the board, and shareholders.

(E) COSO's Benefits of Enterprise Risk Management. With an ERM framework for optimizing strategy and performance, organizations that integrate ERM throughout the entity can realize many benefits, including, though not limited to:
- Increasing the range of opportunities, after considering both positive and negative aspects of risk.

- Identifying and managing risk entity-wide, after knowing that a risk that originated in one part of the entity can impact a different part of the same entity.

- Increasing positive outcomes while reducing negative surprises. ERM allows entities to improve their ability to identify risks and establish appropriate responses, reducing surprises and related costs or losses, while profiting from advantageous developments.

- Reducing performance variability. For some, the challenge is less with surprises and losses and more with variability in performance. Performing ahead of schedule or beyond expectations may cause as much concern as performing short of scheduling and expectations. Enterprise risk management allows organizations to anticipate the risks that would affect performance and enable them to put in place the actions needed to minimize disruption and maximize opportunity.

- Improving resource deployment in the face of finite resources, to assess overall resource needs, to prioritize resource deployment, and to enhance resource allocation.

- Enhancing enterprise resilience or agility, which is the ability to anticipate and respond to change, not only to survive but also to evolve and thrive. A simple a way to define resilience or agility is the ability to get up and run after falling down.

These benefits highlight the fact that risk should not be viewed solely as a potential constraint or challenge to setting and carrying out a strategy. Rather, the change that underlies risk and the organizational responses to risk give rise to strategic opportunities and key differentiating capabilities.

Risk is not a strategic constraint. Rather, risk is a strategic opportunity.

(F) COSO's Guidance to Management and the Board. Organizations need to be more adaptive to change. They need to think strategically about how to manage the increasing volatility, complexity, and ambiguity of the world, particularly at the senior levels in the organization and in the boardroom where the stakes are highest.

Guidance to Management. Management will gain a better understanding of how the explicit consideration of risk may impact the choice of strategy. ERM enriches management dialogue by adding perspective to the strengths and weaknesses of a strategy as conditions change, and to how well a strategy fits with the organization's mission and vision. It allows management to feel more confident that they've examined alternative strategies and considered the input of those in their organization who will implement the strategy selected.

Once strategy is set, ERM provides an effective way for management to fulfill its role, knowing that the organization is attuned to risks that can impact strategy and is managing them well. Applying ERM helps to create trust and instill confidence in stakeholders in the current environment, which demands greater scrutiny than ever before about how a company is actively addressing and managing these risks.

Guidance to the Board. Every board has an oversight role, helping to support the creation of value in an entity and prevent its decline. Traditionally, ERM has played a strong supporting role at the board level. Now boards are increasingly expected to provide oversight of enterprise risk management.

The board's risk oversight role may include, but is not limited to:

- Reviewing, challenging, and concurring with management on (1) proposed strategy and risk appetite, (2) alignment of strategy and business objectives with the entity's stated mission, vision, and core values, (3) significant business decisions, including mergers acquisitions, capital allocations, funding, and dividend-related decisions, (4) response to significant fluctuations in entity performance or the portfolio view of risk, and (5) responses to instances of deviation from core values.
- Approving management incentives and remuneration.
- Participating in investor and stakeholder relations.

Over the longer term, ERM can also enhance enterprise resilience or agility, which is the ability to anticipate and respond to change. It helps organizations identify factors that represent not just risk, but change, and how that change could impact performance and necessitate a shift in strategy. By seeing change more clearly, an organization can design its own plan; for example, should it defensively pull back (e.g., disinvest) or offensively push forward (e.g., invest) in a new business? ERM provides the right framework for boards to assess risk and embrace a mindset of resilience or agility.

(G) COSO's ERM Misconceptions and Outlooks. The following is a list of misconceptions about COSO's ERM practices and a summary of future directions of ERM (outlooks). These outlooks consist of several emerging trends that will have either a positive or negative effect on the future ERM.

ERM's Misconceptions

Misconception 1:	ERM is a separate function or department, similar to marketing and finance functions or departments.
Truth 1:	ERM is not a separate function or department as it is fully integrated into all functions or departments with the same strategy and objectives for all functions or departments.
Misconception 2:	ERM is simply a passive list of inventory of all risks.
Truth 2:	ERM has a broader view of risk-related active practices to manage all risks.
Misconception 3:	ERM is just an internal control mechanism found only in accounting, finance, and auditing functions.
Truth 3:	ERM focuses on many things, such as internal control, governance, risk management, strategy, objectives, and performance. ERM's principles apply at all levels and across all functions of an organization.
Misconception 4:	ERM is just a checklist of yes or no.
Truth 4:	ERM is not a checklist as it is a set of principles, processes, and systems. It is a learning and monitoring mechanism with the goal of improving an organization's performance.
Misconception 5:	ERM is only good for large Fortune 500 for-profit companies.
Truth 5:	ERM can be useful to all sizes (i.e., small, medium, or large) and for all types of organizations (i.e., for-profit firms, not-for-profit organizations, social enterprises, governmental agencies, and government corporations).

ERM's Outlooks

Trend 1:	Use of big data, collected either from inside or outside of an organization, is rapidly growing to explore new business opportunities that can increase revenue and profits. New ways of analyzing the big data (data analytics) and new ways of presenting the big-data results (data visualization tools) can help the ERM strategies and practices to view in a new light.
Trend 2:	New areas of technology are being researched and deployed. Examples include artificial intelligence software, robots, drones, proximity sensors, and other automation initiatives to make employees more productive and customers more satisfied than before.
Trend 3:	As value from risk management exceeds the cost of risk management, greater levels of implementation of ERM strategies and practices result.
Trend 4:	As an organization's resilience mechanisms get stronger and stronger, ERM's strategies and practices can handle new and high-impact risks.
Trend 5:	As an organization's risk appetite levels increase and its subsequent risk-taking practices increase, management will explore new business opportunities to improve the organization's overall performance. When these new opportunities are successful, they put more pressure on management to increase the risk appetite and risk-taking levels and vice versa. Note that an organization's risk culture can either help or hinder the risk-taking practices. A change in the risk culture is required to improve an organization's performance.

(ii) IIA's Enterprise Risk Management

Enterprise risk management (ERM) is prescribed as an organizational use of a risk framework. This section defines ERM and discusses Institute of Internal Auditors (IIA) survey results, approaches to ERM, and implementation of ERM.

(A) ERM Defined. Traditionally, corporate risk management focused on partial portfolios of risks (silo approach), specifically on financial and hazard risks. The scope was narrow, ignoring all the other risks impacting the organization. It did not exploit the "natural hedges" and "portfolio effects" in the organization and tended to treat risk as a downside phenomenon. Enterprise risk management (ERM), however, focuses on total portfolio of risks, including financial, hazard, strategic, and operational risks. The scope of ERM is much broader than the traditional view with the objective of creating, protecting, and enhancing shareholder value. ERM treats risk as both upside and downside phenomena since ERM integrates all risks.

When creating shareholder value, management needs to understand that risks and opportunities go together. The key is to determine if the potential benefits of a given opportunity exceed the risks. During this exercise, management needs to consider derisking opportunities, meaning becoming a market leader by reducing the risks. This will lead to earnings growth, revenue growth, and expense control/reduction followed by earnings consistency from year to year.

ERM is defined as a rigorous and coordinated approach to assessing and responding to all risks that affect the achievement of an organization's strategic and financial objectives. This includes both upside and downside risks. ERM risks are classified as financial, hazard, strategic, and operational risks.

> **Financial risks**—Risks arising from volatility in foreign currencies, interest rates, and commodities. They include credit risk, liquidity risk (bankruptcy risk), and market risk.
>
> **Hazard risks**—Risks that are insurable, such as natural disasters, various insurable liabilities, impairment of physical assets, and terrorism.
>
> **Strategic risks**—High-level and corporate-wide risk, which includes political risk, regulatory risk, reputation risk, leadership risk, and market brand risk. It is also related to failure of strategy and changing customer needs and business conditions.
>
> **Operational risks**—Risks related to the organization's systems, processes, technology, and people.

(B) IIA Survey Results. The IIA Research Foundation conducted a multi-industry global survey of chief financial officers, chief audit executives, chief corporate counsels, and chief risk officers to understand trends and emerging practices in ERM.

A summary of major survey results follows.

- Key drivers of ERM are a desire for a unifying framework and corporate governance regimes.

- The top five motivating factors that were identified as driving ERM activity were: (1) desire for a unifying framework (more than 50% of respondents); (2) corporate governance guidelines (38%); (3) mandates from the board of directors; (4) competitive pressures; and (5) desire for stability in earnings.

- Organizations view ERM as a tool to help manage their most important business issues, such as corporate governance, value management, change management, capital management, and contingency planning.

- The chief financial officer is the most likely senior executive to coordinate and oversee risk management or compliance activities (90%).

- The executive who will be responsible for overseeing ERM activities: chief audit executive (30%), chief financial officer (24%), and chief risk officer (21%).

- Organizational barriers need to be overcome to implement ERM. The top five barriers include: (1) organizational culture; (2) unclear benefits; (3) lack of formalized process, language, and definitions (4) organizational "turf"; and (5) lack of tools.

- More than 60% of organizations identify implementing risk management programs through a change management model (high-level key lever). Low-level use of key levers, such as personnel management or compensation, may make ERM implementation very difficult.

- Most organizations include financial or operational risks in their internal auditing plan, but less than half consider strategic risks. For example, 63% of respondents reported that the finance function had a formal risk assessment process. In contrast, only 21% of respondents reported activity related to the human resource function.

- ERM may initially be more of a management information tool than a driver of corporate performance. ERM is seen as an analytical tool rather than as a performance management system.

- A variety of tools and metrics are used, such as risk mapping or optimization software. Risk metrics includes value at risk and earnings at risk.

(C) Approaches to ERM.   An ERM approach can be viewed in three dimensions. The first dimension represents the range of organization operations. This includes business units or locations, starting small as pilot projects and eventually rolling out to the entire enterprise (i.e., institutionalization). The second dimension represents the sources of risk (hazard, financial, operational, and strategic). This may include property catastrophe risk and currency risk. The third dimension represents the types of risk management activities or processes (risk identification, risk measurement, risk mitigation, and risk monitoring).

Within this ERM universe, two general models of ERM have emerged that are not mutually exclusive. These models are a measurement-driven approach and a process-control approach. A measurement-driven approach focuses on identifying the key risk factors facing an organization and understanding their materiality and probability of occurrence. Risk mitigation activities are focused on the most material risks with appropriate mitigation strategies. Specific steps in the measurement-driven model include assess risk (risk factors and profiles), shape risk (impacts, mitigate, and finance), exploit risk (plans and opportunities), and keep ahead (monitor change and loop). A process-control approach focuses on key business processes and accompanying uncertainties in the execution of the business plan. The emphasis is on linking the process steps, reporting relationships, methodologies, and data collection and reporting to ensure informed decision making. The goal is to manage risk events by achieving consistency of application across the business process spectrum, thereby limiting the possibility of surprise occurrence. The process-control model assumes that good processes can control risks.

Some organizations are approaching ERM in two ways: the push approach and the pull approach. In the push approach, corporate or division management tries to implement ERM throughout the organization. In the pull approach, individual business units will adopt ERM at their own pace.

Scorecards, action plans, and monitoring are part of the ERM approach. Scorecards include metrics, a time frame for managing the risk, and a link to shareholder value. Action plans include identifying a risk champion and determining milestones. Monitoring includes progress reviews and review for validity of metrics.

(D) Implementation of ERM. First, senior management support and commitment is needed to properly implement the ERM program in the organization. A dedicated group of cross-functional staff is needed to push it through the organization. Employees should see the ERM program as an enhancement to existing processes, rather than as a new, stand-alone process. The implementation should proceed incrementally and leverage early wins.

Most organizations implement the ERM program incrementally. Some begin by layering additional sources of risk, one at a time, into their exiting processes for risk assessment and risk mitigation. Some embrace all sources of risk at the outset but tackle the processes one at a time, with most starting with risk assessment. Others take on all risk sources and all processes but on a small, manageable subset of their operations as a pilot project. Most all seek early wins that will help build momentum and confidence and promote further development toward their ideal ERM process.

(iii) U.S. OMB's Framework for ERM and Internal Control

This section presents two topics: the Framework for Enterprise Risk Management and the Framework for Internal Control. Although these two topics are discrete in nature, they must be connected for maximum benefit.

(A) OMB's Framework for Enterprise Risk Management. The U.S. Office of Management and Budget (OMB) defines risk as the effect of uncertainty on objectives.

The OMB defines "extended enterprise" as consisting of interdependent relationships, parent–child relationships, and relationships external to an organization. This means that no organization is self-contained, and risk drivers can arise outside of organizations that extend beyond the internal enterprise.

Examples of outside risk drivers are listed next.

- A major disruption in a supply-chain (i.e., supply-chain risk)
- A major fire in a supplier's manufacturing plant (i.e., production risk)
- A long employee-union strike in a supplier's manufacturing plant (i.e., production risk)
- Continued pressure from government regulators for compliance with laws and regulations (i.e., noncompliance risk when laws are not followed)
- Customers' boycotting a company's products from purchase (i.e., reputation risk)
- Customers' backlash and negative comments posted on social media platforms (i.e., reputation risk)

Because of these relationships, risk must be managed between the parties in an appropriate and timely fashion. Although a normal enterprise cannot control the risks generated from the extended enterprise, it can constrain the risk-taking or risk-addressing plans undertaken by the internal enterprise. In other words, the internal enterprise needs to accommodate the risks from extended enterprise, and must not ignore or disregard such risks.[18]

$$\text{Total risks} = \text{Risks from internal enterprise} + \text{Risks from extended enterprise}$$

According to the OMB, risk management is a series of coordinated activities to direct and control challenges or threats to achieving an organization's goals and objectives. Enterprise risk management is an effective organization-wide approach to addressing the full spectrum of the organization's external and internal risks by understanding the combined impact of risks as an interrelated portfolio rather than addressing risks only within silos.

ERM provides an enterprise-wide, strategically aligned portfolio view of organizational challenges that provides better insight about how to most effectively prioritize resource allocations to ensure successful mission delivery. While organizations cannot respond to all risks related to achieving strategic objectives and delivering performance goals, they must identify, measure, and assess risks related to mission delivery. ERM objectives are expressed in equation form below.

$$\text{ERM objectives} = \text{Achievement of business objectives} + \text{Delivery of performance goals}$$

Effective risk management:

- Creates and protects value.
- Is an integral part of all organizational processes.
- Is part of decision making.
- Explicitly addresses uncertainty.
- Is systematic, structured, and timely.
- Is based on the best available information.
- Is tailored and responsive to evolving risk profiles.
- Takes human and cultural factors into account.
- Is transparent and inclusive.
- Is dynamic, iterative, and responsive to change.
- Facilitates continual improvements of the organization.

(B) Benefits from Enterprise Risk Management. ERM is beneficial since it addresses a fundamental organizational issue: the need for information about major risks to flow both up and down the organization and across its organizational structures to improve the quality of decision making. ERM seeks to open channels of communication so that managers have access to the information they need to make sound decisions.

ERM reflects forward-looking management decisions and balances risks and returns so an organization can enhance its value to its stakeholders. To this end, these risk-based concepts must be understood: risk appetite, risk tolerance, risk portfolio, risk profiles, and risk awareness.

> **Risk appetite**—Risk appetite is the broad-based amount of risk an organization is willing to accept in pursuit of its mission and vision. It is established by the organization's

---

[18] U.S. Office of Management and Budget, *Management's Responsibility for Enterprise Risk Management and Internal Control* (OMB Circular No. A-123), July 2016, www.omb.gov.

senior managers and serves as the guidepost to set strategies and select objectives. An organization's governance process should include a process for considering risk appetite and risk tolerance levels. The concept of risk appetite is a key to achieving effective ERM and is essential to consider in determining risk responses. Although not required to be documented, risk appetite should be documented to minimize confusion and must be considered both quantitatively and qualitatively.

Risk tolerance—Risk tolerance is the acceptable level of variance in performance relative to the achievement of objectives. It is generally established at the functional level by operational managers. In setting risk tolerance levels, management considers the relative importance of the related objectives and aligns risk tolerance with risk appetite.

Risk portfolio—A portfolio view of risk provides insight into all areas of an organization's exposure to risk (e.g., finance, operations, marketing, IT, human resources, performance, and reputation). A comprehensive and complete risk portfolio can result in fewer unanticipated outcomes and can lead to a better assessment of current risks and future risks.

Risk profiles—Risk profiles provide a thoughtful analysis of significant risks an organization is facing toward achieving its strategic objectives and identifying options for addressing such risks. These risk profiles indicate the aggregate level and types of risk that management is willing to assume. Risk profiles show a prioritized inventory of the most significant risks that were identified and assessed through the risk assessment process. They must consider risks from a risk portfolio perspective and must identify the sources of uncertainty, both positive (opportunities) and negative (threats). In addition, risk profiles show risk responses and act as an input to develop risk appetite and risk tolerance. Risk profiles are expressed in equation form below.

Risk profiles = Positive sources (opportunities) + Negative sources (threats)

Risk profile = Risk appetite + Risk tolerance

Risk awareness— Risk awareness requires organizations to incorporate the importance of risk into employee job descriptions and policy and procedure manuals, as a way of doing business. Specifically, risk awareness can be increased through company newsletters, training and educational programs for employees, case studies showing real-life risky situations of how risks are created and managed, and checklists of do's and don'ts.

Risk responses—Risk responses take many forms, such as risk acceptance, risk avoidance, risk reduction, and risk sharing. Formulation of risk responses should consider the organization's risk appetite and risk tolerance levels. As part of developing the risk profile, management must determine those risks for which the appropriate response includes implementation of formal internal control activities. Each type of risk response is briefly described next.

Risk acceptance—No action is taken to respond to the risk based on the insignificance of the risk; or the risk is knowingly assumed in order to seize an opportunity.

Risk avoidance—Action is taken to stop the operational process or the part of the operational process causing the risk.

Risk reduction—Action is taken to reduce the likelihood or impact of the risk.

Risk sharing—Action is taken to transfer or share risks across the organization or with external parties, such as insuring against losses. Risk sharing is also called risk spreading or risk transferring.

(C) Role of Auditors in Enterprise Risk Management. An organization's management is responsible for ERM systems. Internal auditors or external auditors conduct independent and objective audits, evaluations, and investigations of an organization's operations and programs, which includes aspects of internal control and risk management systems. Management uses the results of such evaluations, including accompanying findings and recommendations, to monitor the design or operating effectiveness of these systems at a specific time or of a specific function or process. Auditors are also responsible for keeping management informed about risks that they detect, including fraud risks, and thereby provide information to management for use in the identification and assessment of risks.

OMB's Framework for Internal Control. Internal control is a process effected by an organization's oversight body (the board), management, and other personnel (employees) that provides reasonable assurance that the objectives of the organization are achieved. These objectives can be broadly classified into one or more of these categories:

- Operations—Effectiveness and efficiency of operations
- Reporting—Reliability of reporting for internal and external use
- Compliance—Compliance with applicable laws, rules, and regulations

A subset of the categories of objectives is the safeguarding of all assets. Management designs an internal control system to provide reasonable assurance regarding the prevention or prompt detection and correction of unauthorized acquisition, use, or disposition of an organization's assets.

Internal control is an integral part of the entire cycle of strategic planning, goal, objective setting, budgeting, operations, accounting, and auditing. It must support the effectiveness and the integrity of every step of the process and provide continual feedback to management.

Managers must carefully consider the appropriate balance between risks, controls, costs, and benefits in their operations. For example, too many controls can result in inefficiencies, while too few controls might increase risks to an unacceptable level. The benefits of controls should outweigh the costs after considering both qualitative and quantitative factors.

Management's responsibility is to develop and maintain effective internal control that is consistent with its established risk appetite and risk tolerance levels. In addition, management is responsible for establishing and integrating internal control into its operations in a risk-based and cost-beneficial manner, in order to provide reasonable assurance that the organization's internal control over operations, reporting, and compliance is operating effectively.

Achieving the objectives of external reporting and compliance to it are largely based on laws, rules, regulations, and standards. These objectives depend on how activities within the organization's internal controls are performed and reported. Generally, management and directors have greater discretion in setting internal reporting objectives that are not driven by external parties or bodies. However, organizations may choose to align internal reporting and external reporting objectives to all internal reporting to better support the external reporting. This alignment is shown below.

Laws, Rules, Regulations, and Standards → External Reporting

Management and Directors → Internal Reporting

Total Reporting = External Reporting + Internal Reporting

Internal controls have built-in weaknesses. This means that no matter how well an internal control system is designed, implemented, or operated, it cannot provide absolute assurance that *all* of an organization's objectives are met. This is because factors outside the control or influence of management can affect an organization's ability to achieve its objectives. For example, natural disasters (e.g., fire, flood, tornados, or cyclones) or man-made disasters (e.g., violence, terrorism, strikes, and protests) can affect an organization's ability to achieve all of its objectives. Therefore, effective internal controls that are currently operating can provide reasonable assurance, not absolute assurance, that an organization achieves its objectives.

(D) Relationships between Risk Management and Internal Controls. ERM seeks to encompass the range of major risks that threatens organizations' ability to implement their mission and strategy. Organizations should build their capabilities, first to conduct more effective risk management, then to implement ERM, rating those risks in terms of impact (high, medium, or low), and finally building internal controls to monitor and assess the risk development at various time-points. This relationship is shown next.

Conduct Risk Management → Implement ERM → Build Internal Controls → Monitor and Assess Risks
(First)   (Next)   (Next)   (Last)

(iv) Switzerland ISO Risk Management—ISO Standard 31000

The International Organization for Standardization (ISO) in Geneva, Switzerland, develops and issues standards in several areas of business and industry. Two ISO standards related to risk management include Risk Management—Principles and Guidelines (ISO Standard 31000:2011) and Risk Management—Risk Assessment Techniques (ISO/IEC Standard 31010:2011).

ISO Standard 31000:2011 focuses on risk management. It sets out principles, a framework, and a process for the management of risk that is applicable to any type of organization in the public or private sector. It does not mandate a one-size-fits-all approach, but rather emphasizes the fact that the management of risk must be tailored to the specific needs and structure of the particular organization. Risks affecting organizations may have consequences in terms of societal, environmental, technological, safety, and security outcomes; commercial, financial, and economic disciplines; as well as social, cultural, and political reputation impacts. It also addresses crisis management, earthquakes, floods, storms, and hurricanes.

Using ISO 31000 can help organizations increase the likelihood of achieving objectives, improve the identification of opportunities and threats, and effectively allocate and use resources for risk treatment. The Standard can be applied to any organization, regardless of size, activity, or sector. However, the standard cannot be used for certification purposes although it does provide guidance for internal or external audit programs. Organizations using it can compare their risk management practices with an internationally recognized benchmark, providing sound principles for effective management and corporate governance.

Major highlights of the ISO 31000 Standard are listed next.

- It was written from a technical point of view for risk management analysts and managers and for subject matter experts, not for business managers and analysts.

- It defines risk as "effect of uncertainty on objectives."

- It is globally applicable to all types of industries due to its flexibility, adaptability, and simplicity. It is most helpful to rapidly changing organizations.

- It moves risk management from a reactive posture to a proactive posture in creating, capturing, and sustaining value, all in alignment with the organization's objectives.

- It contains three major components: core principles, framework, and processes in managing risks.

- It provides a solid foundation and practical and specific recommendations on how to implement the core principles of effective risk management.

(v) Switzerland ISO/IEC Risk Assessment—ISO Standard 31010

The ISO/IEC Standard 31010:2011 focuses on risk assessment, which helps decision makers understand the risks that could affect the achievement of objectives as well as the adequacy of controls already in place. The Standard focuses on risk assessment concepts and processes and the selection of risk assessment techniques. The Standard can be applied to any type of risk, whatever its nature, whether having positive or negative consequences, and is not intended for the purpose of certification.

(vi) RIMS ERM Risk Maturity Model

The Risk and Insurance Management Society (RIMS) has developed a very popular risk maturity model (RMM) and published it in 2008 as an umbrella framework for the risk management field. The RMM framework covers several risk management frameworks, such as the ISO 31000, British Standard (BS) 31100, COSO, the Institute of Risk Management's Federation of European Risk Management Associations (FERMA), and others.[19]

The RMM's methodology is divided into seven attributes, 25 competency drivers, and 68 key readiness indicators. Organizations can benchmark their own ERM programs against the RMM methodology to assess their own strengths and weaknesses in risk management.

The risk maturity model consists of five stages from 1 to 5 where "1" is Ad hoc (the lowest, immature level), "2" is Initial, "3" is Repeatable, "4" is Managed, and "5" is Leadership (the highest, mature level). The goal of many organizations is to reach stage 3 in the short term and to reach stage 5 in the long term. For example, the repeatable stage (3) gives consistent and predictable results.

Two important questions that any organization should ask itself are (1) whether its risk management processes are formal/mature or informal/immature and (2) whether its risk framework is fully adopted or partially adopted. Several benefits and value can accrue to organizations when their risk management framework and processes are formal, mature, and fully adopted.

The seven attributes cover the planning and governance of an ERM program, execution of assessments, and aggregation of risk information. These seven attributes represent the best practices of an ERM program and are listed next.

1. **Adoption of ERM-based processes**—This attribute measures an organization's risk culture and considers the degree of management support for the ERM program.

2. **ERM process management**—This attribute measures the extent to which an organization has adopted an ERM methodology throughout its culture and decision making. It indicates how well the ERM program follows the best practices from identification to monitoring of risks.

---

[19] RIMS Risk Maturity Model, www.riskmaturitymodel.com.

3. **Risk appetite management**—This attribute evaluates the level of awareness around risk–reward trade-offs, accountability for risks, defining risk tolerances, and whether the organization is effective in closing the gap between potential risks and actual risks.

4. **Root-cause discipline**—This attribute assesses the extent to which an organization identifies risk by source or root cause and distinguishes between real risks and symptoms of risks. Identification of root causes can strengthen management responses and risk mitigation efforts.

5. **Uncovering risks**—This attribute measures the quality of and coverage of risk assessment efforts. It examines the methods of collecting risk information and the risk assessment process; identifies trends and correlations that can be uncovered from risk information; and focuses on risk areas that may be uncovered in the "whitespace" that do not have a readily identifiable owner or associated control function. Risk coverage rates rest solely on risk discovery rates.

6. **Performance management**—This attribute determines the degree to which an organization executes its mission, vision, and strategy. It evaluates the strength of planning, communicating, and measuring the core enterprise goals and analyzes how actual progress deviates from expectations.

7. **Business resiliency and sustainability**—This attribute evaluates the extent to which business continuity planning and operational planning activities are carried out to ensure a long-term sustainability. It requires that the business continuity plans are agile and resilient.

Each attribute includes a set of competency drivers that outline the key readiness indicators or activities involved in achieving each driver. These driver/indicator pairs cover the entire risk management process, including administration, outreach, data collection, data aggregation, and analysis or risk information. Each competency driver is scored on three assessment dimensions: effectiveness (measures the frequency of key risk assessment activities [quarterly or annually]), proactivity (measures whether risk management is proactive or reactive in nature), and coverage (measures the breadth and depth of risk management efforts spread through all horizontal and vertical departments).

Benefits of the RIMS-RMM framework for risk-mature organizations include (1) a positive correlation between the high risk scores and high credit ratings that can help in raising new capital in the capital markets and (2) an increase in the market value (capitalization value) through increased stock prices. These benefits accrue to organizations because their risks are properly controlled and well managed.

(vii) RIMS-IIA Collaboration
In 2012, the RIMS and the Institute of Internal Auditors jointly issued an executive report titled "Risk Management and Internal Audit: Forging a Collaborative Alliance." Basically, this report addresses two topics of importance to internal auditors: the evolution of risk management and the role of internal audit in ERM.

According to this joint report, RIMS and the IIA define the ERM in different ways.

RIMS—"ERM is a strategic business discipline that supports the achievement of an organization's objectives by addressing the full spectrum of its risks and managing the combined impact of those risks as an interrelated risk portfolio."

IIA—"ERM is a structured, consistent, and continuous process across the whole organization for identifying, assessing, deciding on response to and reporting on opportunities and threats that affect the achievement of its objectives."

The RMM's definition of ERM focuses on best practices and disciplined approaches. The IIA's definition of ERM focuses on processes.

Both risk practitioners and internal auditors have a common focus on the same standards.

Note that both risk practitioners and internal auditors use the same specific risk management standards in their work, such as the ISO 31000, the IIA's International Professional Practices Framework, and COSO's ERM framework. They both face the same challenges regarding blending siloed risk strategies, handling of interrelated and interconnected risks, and uncovering unknown risks in the whitespace.

(viii) U.K.'s Federation of European Risk Management Association

In 2002, the Federation of European Risk Management Association (FERMA) adopted the Risk Management Standard originally published by the Institute of Risk Management, the Association of Insurance and Risk Managers, and the Public Risk Management Association in the United Kingdom.[20]

A summary of the technical highlights of the FERMA guide follows.

Risk management is a process that increases the chance (probability) of success and reduces the chance (probability) of failure toward achieving an organization's objectives. It consists of four components: risk assessment, risk reporting, risk treatment, and risk monitoring.

Risk management = Risk assessment + Risk reporting + Risk treatment + Risk monitoring

Risk assessment is an overall process of risk analysis and risk evaluation. **Risk analysis** is further divided into risk identification, risk description, risk estimation, risk techniques, and risk profiles.

Risk identification reveals how much an activity is exposed to uncertainty and volatility. Tools and techniques to identify risks include brainstorming, questionnaires, business process studies, industry benchmarking, scenario analysis, risk assessment training and workshops, audits and inspections, and risk discovery with intense analysis.

Risk description presents or displays the identified risks in a structured format, such as a table, spreadsheet, matrix, graph, or a simple narrative.

Risk estimation quantifies the possible amounts of consequence (impact) and the probability of occurrence (likelihood) that are useful in calculating the amount of risk (i.e., Risk = Impact × Likelihood). Consequences are divided into three parts: upside risk (opportunities), downside risk (threats), and hybrid risk (contains both upside risk and downside risk).

Risk techniques are used in risk analysis and include upside risks, downside risks, and hybrid risks. Examples of **upside risks** include research and development efforts, business impact analysis, test marketing, sales prospecting, and market survey. Examples of **downside risks** include vulnerability analysis; threat analysis; fault tree analysis; and failure mode and effect analysis. Examples of **hybrid risks** include SWOT analysis; business continuity planning methods; statistical analysis; event tree analysis; modeling and simulation techniques; decision making under conditions of risk and uncertainty; and business analysis focusing on economic, political, social, legal, technical, and environmental factors.

---

[20] "A Risk Management Standard" @IRM 2002, www.theirm.org.

Risk profiles are the output of risk analysis and indicate the significant rating given to each risk and provide a tool for prioritizing risk treatment efforts. The relationship between risk assessment and risk profiles is shown below.

Risk assessment = Risk analysis + Risk evaluation

Risk analysis = Risk identification + Risk description + Risk estimation + Risk profiles

Risk evaluation is composed of two parts: risk criteria and risk treatment. In **risk criteria**, estimated risks are compared against the established risk criteria (risk standards). In **risk treatment**, risks are modified or mitigated to an acceptable level of risk in several ways, such as accept, avoid, or transfer.

Risk evaluation = Risk criteria + Risk treatment

Risk reporting includes both internal reporting (e.g., board, business units, and individuals) and external reporting (e.g., stakeholders wanting both financial and nonfinancial performance information).

Risk monitoring is a continuous process to identify, assess, and control all risks to management's satisfaction. This monitoring can be achieved through regular audits and compliance reviews.

Risk monitoring = Regular audits + Compliance reviews

A brief presentation of the management highlights of the FERMA guide follows.

- The FERMA guide defines risk as the "combination of the probability of an event and its consequences."

- It is a simple guide that outlines a practical and systematic approach to the management of risk for business managers.

- It does not discuss the root causes of risks as a key component to effective risk management. Root causes link undesirable events to their sources.

- It believes that there are upside risks (opportunities to benefit), downside risks (threats to success), and/or hybrid risks (both upside risks and downside risks) in any risk-related situations.

- It believes that job descriptions of all employees (managers and nonmanagers) must reflect their responsibility regarding managing risks and promoting operational efficiencies. A risk-awareness culture must be encouraged in all employees, meaning that all employees must be on the lookout for risks all the time.

- It states that risk treatment practices should include effective internal controls and should comply with all applicable laws, rules, and regulations.

- It stresses the importance of the risk monitoring process as a tool for continuous improvement.

- The FERMA's risk management process is very similar to the ISO 31000 Standard.

(ix) U.K. BS 31100 Standard: Code of Practice for Risk Management
The British Standards Institution (BSI) issued Standard BS ISO 31100:2011: "Code of Practice for Risk Management." For all practical purposes, the BS 31100 Standard is similar to the ISO 31000 Standard. What is different is that the BS 31100 Standard uses a risk maturity model to improve an organization's risk management capability.

5.15 Effectiveness of Risk Management

The effectiveness of risk management is determined in part by how much an organization is using a risk management framework, its sources for discovery of risks, the maturity level of the framework, and its outcomes. Topics such as risk maturity, risk discovery, risk sources, and risk outcomes are presented in this section, as an approach to knowing how to use a risk management framework.

(a) Risk Maturity

Use of an enterprise risk management program is suggested as an organizational use of a risk framework. Organizations use this framework in different ways depending on whether they are risk mature or risk immature. Risk maturity deals with whether an organization is using a proper risk management framework to manage all of its risks. It asks two basic questions: (1) Has an organization established and does it use a proper risk management framework to assess all of its risks? and (2) Is that risk framework sufficient, current, and complete? Two possible outcomes are:

- **Mature** and sophisticated organizations use a formal risk management framework. A suggestion is to continue to improve.
- **Immature** and unsophisticated organizations use an informal risk management framework. A suggestion is to make more improvements.

(b) Risk Discovery

Risk discovery means determining how much of the risk universe is identified, unearthed, or uncovered during a risk assessment exercise. Risk discovery or discovery rate depends on the risk coverage or risk penetration rate (i.e., digging deeper and deeper into the risk universe to discover major and unknown risks). The higher the coverage rate, the greater the discovery rate and vice versa. Note that there is an inverse relationship between residual risks and discovered risks, meaning that the lower the residual risks, the higher the discovered risks and vice versa. Risk discovery also depends on whether the risk assessment exercises are based on surface or intense analysis. Surface analysis reveals superficial, insignificant, and minor risks (i.e., it is like picking low-hanging fruit); intense analysis reveals significant and major risks. Significant risks are big in scope (nature and extent), size (magnitude), and strength (impact). Auditors need to identify significant risks only.

Risk sources are the places where potential risks can originate. These places consist of people, systems, facilities, equipment, machines and devices, processes, operations, functions, tasks and activities, policies, procedures, and practices. Each business initiative or project is a candidate for introducing or creating risks. Examples of these sources are when new products are developed and when new markets are entered with current and new products.

Before proceeding with managing risks, auditor or manager needs to understand how risks arise in an organization in the first place, including their sources. An organization's management takes on new initiatives or projects from their strategic plans or business plans in order: to reduce costs; to increase revenues, profits, and market share; to improve employee morale, performance, and productivity; and for other purposes. *These new initiatives are new sources for new risks.* Examples of risk sources from business plans are listed next.

- New product development
- Modification of health benefit programs for employees

- New mergers, acquisitions, and divestitures
- New market entry with current and new products
- New manufacturing plants and processes
- New computer system for sales order management
- New retail stores, warehouses, and distribution centers
- New logistics and suppliers systems
- Modification of procurement and inventory systems

(c) Risk Outcomes

Risk outcomes are an integral part of business outcomes because they go hand in hand. The implementation or execution of business plans and policies can result in positive outcomes (positive effects lead to successes), negative outcomes (negative effects leading to failures), and hybrid outcomes (a mix of positive and negative effects). A source of these negative outcomes can be inherent risks and uncertainties built into those plans and policies. Note that these three outcomes are possible with any business activity, project, or process. Positive outcomes can be thought of as opportunities that should be seized or pursued; negative outcomes, as threats that should be reduced or avoided. The goal of risk managers is to turn negative outcomes into positive outcomes through risk mitigation efforts and control mechanisms. These outcomes are expressed in equation form below.

$$\text{Positive Outcomes} = \text{Opportunities}$$
$$\text{Negative Outcomes} = \text{Threats or Vulnerabilities}$$
$$\text{Negative Outcomes} \rightarrow \text{Positive Outcomes}$$
$$\text{Vulnerabilities} \rightarrow \text{Threats} \rightarrow \text{Risks} \rightarrow \text{Controls}$$

Exhibit 5.3 shows risk sources with their opportunities and threats.

EXHIBIT 5.3 Risk Sources, Opportunities, and Threats

Risk Sources	Opportunities	Threats
New product development	New revenues and profits Greater return on investment (ROI)	Product failures Loss of investment and reputation Giving away new ideas to competitors
Modify health benefit programs for employees	Improved employee morale Better workplace environment	Higher premium rates and some unhappy employees due to inadequate health coverage
New mergers, acquisitions, and divestitures	Increased revenues and profits Decreased costs Increased market share	Lower market share and stock price than expected Receiving less money than expected Paying more money than expected Actual performance is less than planned performance

Risk Sources	Opportunities	Threats
New market entry with current and new products	Increased revenues and profits	Loss of revenues and profits Heavy competition
New manufacturing plants and processes	Increased costs savings Efficient operations Increased machine and labor productivity levels	Increased costs Lack of skilled employees Lower productivity levels due to learning curve effects
New computer system for sales order management	Increased cost savings Increased revenues and profits Systems as a competitive tool	Incomplete and inaccurate design of system functions Lack of built-in security features and business controls Vulnerability to system crashes and hacking on websites and data files Loss of privacy and confidentiality for employees, customers, and suppliers
New retail stores, warehouses, and distribution centers	Increased revenues and profits Increased cost savings due to deployment of new technologies Greater ROI	Large capital investment required Unavailability of store associates due to unwilling to work in retail Poor customer service Actual sales less than planned sales Lower ROI
New logistics and supplier systems	Increased delivery efficiencies Increased cost savings Increased employee productivity levels Increased efficiency in internal operations	Suppliers' failure due to lack of serious commitment Suppliers' poor performance in quality, cost, and delivery Lack of backup suppliers
Modify procurement and inventory systems	Can realize economies of scale in purchasing materials to reduce procurement costs Can exercise bargaining power with manufacturers and suppliers to drive material's prices lower	Excess inventory buildup and investment tied up due to excessive procurement of materials Inventory obsolescence Increased inventory costs Loss of sales due to heavy competition, resulting in excess inventory levels

(d) Using a Risk Management Framework

A five-step suggested approach to using a risk management framework in an organization follows.

1. Identify the risk universe in full containing current risks, future risks, known risks, and unknown risks.

2. Select a specific risk area from the risk universe and identify all the vulnerabilities associated with this risk area. A meaningful question is "What are we vulnerable for today and tomorrow and how?"

3. Identify all the threat types, threat events, and threat sources associated with these vulnerabilities. A relevant question is "What threats are we facing now and in the future?"

4. Derive risks from the identified vulnerabilities and threats. Ask "What can go wrong?"

5. Inventory all the controls in place today and identify what controls are needed in the future to reduce or eliminate risks. Match the risks to the controls with a risk and control matrix and risk maps. Make sure that each vulnerability, threat, and risk has a corresponding and effective control in place or planned to be in place. A specific question is "What controls do we need now and in the future?"

Risk management tools, such as risk and control matrices and risk maps, can be used during the analysis of vulnerabilities, threats, risks, and controls. Exhibit 5.4 presents examples of such vulnerabilities, threats, risks, and controls.

EXHIBIT 5.4 Analysis of Vulnerabilities, Threats, Risks, and Controls

Vulnerabilities	Threats	Risks	Controls
Unqualified employees	Participating in collusion and stealing of property	Work-related errors Incorrect application of policies and plans Loss of money Loss of property	Establish better hiring and training programs with ethical values
High employee turnover	Unstable workforce and difficulty in manpower planning	Lack of completed work assignments Loss of skilled employees Low employee morale	Install employee incentive and motivation programs to make work interesting and satisfying
Unethical and illegal business practices	Manipulating research and survey results Suppressing major problems	Loss of sales revenues and profits Loss of customer goodwill	Instill a risk-awareness culture and require a signed code of conduct document
Poor governance oversight practices	Weak board of directors Weak tone at the top Lack of direction from the board	Ineffective governance results with major negative consequences Lack of stewardship High reputation risk Increased shareholder activism to gain control	Develop job descriptions Implement training and educational programs (e.g., onboarding) Require board members to become certified in board governance
Questionable marketing practices	Misleading marketing programs Deceptive advertising campaigns	Loss of customers Loss of reputation Government fines and penalties	Implement training and educational programs in truth-in-marketing and truth-in-advertising laws and regulations

Vulnerabilities	Threats	Risks	Controls
Unethical procurement practices	Incomplete and inaccurate purchasing bids and contracts Taking bribes from suppliers	Loss of quality in materials purchased Lower return on inventory investment	Instill a risk-aware culture Require a signed code of conduct document for buyers and purchasing agents
Poorly designed and secured computer systems	Computer hacking and hardware malfunctions Software glitches Website crashes and shutdowns Data breaches	Loss of customers Loss of sales and revenues Loss of reputation Loss of competitive advantage Loss of data	Implement an agile system development methodology with sufficient business functions and security controls

5.16 Internal Audit's Role in the Risk Management Process

Risk management is a systematic and disciplined process in managing and controlling organization-wide risks, which is often referred to as enterprise risk management. The scope and nature of this process is to identify, assess, manage, and control potential undesirable events or situations to provide reasonable assurance regarding the achievement of the organization's objectives because risks can impede the achievement of those objectives. Risks can be current and future risks as well as known and unknown risks.

(a) Evolution of Risk Management

It is interesting to note how the risk management field has evolved from a defensive strategy to an offensive strategy. The evolution occurred in three stages: the traditional stage, integrated stage, and contemporary stage.

Traditional (basic) risk management used a defensive approach. It is cost-benefit driven with a focus on risk transfer mechanisms such as insurance policies and hedging operations. It treated risks as an expense item in the budget through buying an insurance policy or participating in hedging operations. It primarily focused on handling insurable, contractual, hazard-based, and transactional risks. Moreover, it treated risks as siloed, treating each risk separately and discretely.

Integrated (advanced) risk management is an improvement over traditional risk management but is not as comprehensive as it can be. It combined individual risk functions, such as premiums and claims, to minimize insurable losses through prevention methods and severity reductions. It identified, analyzed, and coordinated risks from other risk activities and functions within an organization. For example, its goal was to prevent automobile accidents, worker injuries, property damages, and human life losses.

Contemporary (modern) risk management is a comprehensive risk management effort due to its focus on the entire organization's risk management issues, called ERM. ERM handles uncertainty and threats facing an organization and encourages a framework for board oversight of risk management. It is driven by a risk–reward trade-off and takes an offensive role to assess interconnected or interrelated portfolios of risks that were ignored before. Here, the goal is to add value to organizations.

Specifically,

- ERM's scope is much broader, deeper, and more responsive than prior risk management efforts due to its consideration of strategic, operational, and financial risks and due to its accommodation of business continuity plans.
- Risk-based decisions are guided by risk appetite statements.
- ERM's processes and methods are used to manage unwanted deviations from expectations, which are linked to corporate strategy.
- ERM's span of focus includes crossing siloed departments, building internal alliances, exhibiting flexibility and agility, addressing emerging risks, and enhancing strategic decision-making capabilities.

The three stages of evolution of risk management are shown next.

Traditional →   Integrated → Contemporary
(Defensive strategy)   (Offensive strategy)

(b) Role of Internal Audit in ERM

The role of internal audit in ERM is divided into three discrete sections: assurance activities, consulting services, and forbidden services. Five core assurance activities should be undertaken, seven risk-based consulting services can be performed with appropriate safeguards and proper disclosures and disclaimers, and six forbidden activities should *not* be undertaken except in emergency situations or in a very small business environment. The activities are forbidden because they may lead internal auditors to take on management roles and responsibilities in risk management that could impair their independence and objectivity.

Specific activities in the ERM program are shown next.

Assurance activities:	Reviewing the management of key risks
	Evaluating the reporting of key risks
	Evaluating risk management processes
	Giving assurance that risks are correctly evaluated
	Giving assurance on the risk management processes
Consulting services:	Developing ERM strategy for board approval
	Championing the establishment of ERM
	Maintaining and developing the ERM framework
	Consolidated reporting on risks
	Coordinating ERM activities
	Coaching management in responding to risks
	Facilitating identification and evaluation of risks

Forbidden activities: Setting the risk appetite

Imposing risk management processes

Management assurance on risks

Taking decisions on risks responses

Implementing risk responses on management's behalf

Accountability for risk management program

If an organization has established a formal risk management function staffed with risk managers and risk specialists, internal auditors should focus more on providing assurance services and focus less on providing consulting services in order to provide more value to the organization with assurance services.

(c) Collaboration between Risk Professionals and Internal Auditors

This joint report states that risk management and internal audit functions will be more effective when they work together rather than separately, especially when there is a common understanding of each other's roles. The next four collaborative practices can result in recognizable value.

1. Link the audit plan and the enterprise risk assessment and share other work products. Doing so provides assurance that significant risks are being identified effectively.

2. Share available resources wherever and whenever possible. Doing so allows for efficient use of scarce resources (e.g., financial, staff, and time).

3. Cross-leverage each function's respective competencies, roles, and responsibilities. Doing so provides communication depth and consistency, especially at the board and senior management levels.

4. Assess and monitor strategic risks. Doing so allows for deeper understanding and focused action on the most significant risks.

(d) Audit Roles

The chief audit executive is an ERM champion and should use risk-based audit plans that are consistent with the organization's goals. Internal auditing is the implementation arm of an ERM program. Internal auditors act as facilitators in cross-functional risk assessment workshops conducted in the business units. **Best practices** in running workshops include length of the workshop, preparation for the workshop, risk agreement, capturing the discussion, software selection, anonymous voting, instantaneous reporting and feedback, and selection and training of the facilitator.

Internal auditors must be process owners and subject matter experts. Both internal auditors and other employees of the organization should view ERM as a value-added activity since it is both inward looking and forward thinking.

Internal auditors should think like managers and focus on business objectives rather than an audit universe. Doing this requires new skill levels for internal auditors, including facilitation skills, skills in risk scorecards, and developing risk frameworks and metrics.

(e) Audit Tools

Traditional audit tools, such as checklist approaches and internal control questionnaires, may not work in implementing an ERM program. Internal auditors should move away from the perception of being policemen. ERM can improve the efficiency of internal auditing function since they accomplish more with less.

Some organizations have set up ERM committees, consisting of representatives from strategic planning, human resource, internal auditing, risk management, and loss prevention.

When companies fail to manage risk, opportunities are missed and shareholder value can be lost. Consequently, both internal pressures and external pressures develop to improve corporate governance. With respect to corporate governance, internal auditors can play an important role in ensuring that senior management, the audit committee, and the board of directors are fully informed of the organization's risk profiles and exposures.

5.17 Internal Control Concepts and Types of Controls

Due to its large scope and size, this section is broadly divided into three major topics: business control systems, management control systems, and corporate control systems.

(a) Business Control Systems

Topics covered in business control systems are listed next.

- Control characteristics
- Control requirements
- Combination, complementary, compensating, and contradictory controls
- Control assessment
- Cost-benefit analysis
- Cost versus controls versus convenience
- Controls by dimension
- Specific types of controls by function and by objectives
- Controls in business application systems
- Inventory of controls in business application systems
- Summary of controls

(i) Control Characteristics

Control is any positive and negative action taken by management that would result in accomplishment of the organization's goals, objectives, and mission. Controls should not lead to compulsion or become a constraint on employees. Controls should be natural and should be embedded in the organizational functions and operations. Moreover, controls should be accepted by the employees using or affected by them. Use and implementation of controls should be inviting, not inhibiting. Controls should be seen as beneficial from the employee's personal and professional viewpoints. Ideally, controls should facilitate the achievement of employees' and organizational goals and objectives. In other words, any control that does not help or promote in achieving the goals and objectives should not be implemented. Controls should be effective and efficient. Controls should not cost more than the benefits derived.

(ii) Control Requirements

The auditor needs to understand the control requirements of an application system or a business operation before assessing control strengths and weaknesses. In other words, there should be a basis or baseline in place (i.e., standards, guidelines, and benchmarks) prior to control measurement and assessment. In the absence of a baseline of standards, auditor's findings, conclusions, and recommendations will be questioned and will not be accepted by the auditee. Usually the basis is

- Internal control principles.
- Operating standards for manual and automated operations both in system-user areas and information systems (IS) areas.
- Application system development or maintenance methodology standards.
- Technical standards.
- Operations standards.
- Administrative standards.
- Industry standards.
- Auditee's operating standards.
- Generally accepted accounting principles.
- Generally accepted IT standards.
- Generally accepted auditing standards.
- Generally accepted government auditing standards.
- Generally accepted IS control objectives and techniques.
- Generally accepted system security principles.
- Organization's policies and procedures.
- Control philosophy of management.
- Risk and exposure levels of the system or operation under consideration.
- Management's tolerance to risk levels.
- The nature and type of industry (i.e., financial, regulated).
- Government, tax, legal, accounting, regulatory requirements.
- Management's directives and circulars.
- Good business and management practices.

(iii) Combination, Complementary, and Compensating Controls

Controls or control measures should prevent, reduce, or even eliminate potential risks and exposures. Controls should also prevent and detect errors, omissions, and irregularities. Controls are needed within and around a computer-based application system as well as in computer operations. Controls are additive.

(A) Combination Controls.   Rarely would a single control suffice to meet control objectives. Rather, a combination of controls or complementary controls is needed to make up a whole and to provide a synergistic effect.

Some examples of combination controls are listed next.

- Supervisory reviews and approvals combined with organization's policies, procedures, and standards
- A combination of controls from the five types of controls (i.e., directive, preventive, detective, corrective, and recovery)
- A specific general control (e.g., full-volume backups) combined with another specific general control (e.g., incremental backups)
- A specific general control combined with one or more application system controls
- A specific application system control combined with one or more general controls
- System-user controls in one user department combined with controls in other system-user departments
- IS controls in one IS section or department combined with controls in other IS sections or departments
- System-user controls combined with IS controls
- Manual controls combined with automated controls
- One-application system controls combined with other and related application system controls
- Application system controls combined with operating systems software controls
- Application system controls combined with database system controls
- Application system controls combined with automated program library management system controls
- Application system controls combined with automated access-control security system controls
- Application system controls combined with automated data file management system (e.g., tape, cartridges, and disk) controls
- Application system controls combined with automated documentation system controls
- Application system controls combined with automated report balancing system controls
- Application system controls combined with data communication system controls
- Application system controls combined with data dictionary system controls
- Application system controls combined with telecommunication system controls
- Application system controls combined with general data processing controls
- Physical-access security controls combined with logical-access security controls
- A user identification code combined with a password code to make user authentication more assured

An example of a combination of controls is a situation where fire-resistant materials are used in the computer center (a preventive control) to prevent a fire while smoke and fire detectors are used to detect smoke and fire (a detective control) and fire extinguishers are used to put out the fire (a corrective control). Here a single preventive control would not be sufficient. All three controls are needed to be effective.

(B) Complementary Controls.

Complementary controls (hand-in-hand controls) have an important place in both the manual and the automated control environment. Complementary controls are different from compensating controls in that, in the latter, category weak controls in one area or function are balanced by strong controls in other areas or functions, and vice versa. A function or an area need not be weak to use complementary controls. Complementary controls can enhance the effectiveness of two or more controls when applied to a function, program, or operation. These individual, complementary controls are effective as stand-alones and are maximized when combined or integrated with each other. In other words, complementary controls have a synergistic effect.

Some examples of complementary controls include:

- External security software functions can complement the security features available in applications software and vice versa.

- Security features within a database management system can complement the security functions available in the applications software.

- External security software functions can complement the security features available in the following systems software products: tape/disk management system, report distribution system, operator console automation system, job-control validation system, job-scheduling system, problem/change management system, online program development facilities, online teleprocessing monitors, database management systems, and job rerun software.

- External security software functions can complement the security features available in hardware devices (access keys, smart cards, access cards) and biometrics devices.

- Data editing and validation routines operating during data entry into the computer system can complement the same routines operating during data updating into the master files.

- Manual controls can complement automated controls and vice versa.

- The following areas can complement each other: administrative controls, physical security controls, personnel security controls, technical security controls, emanations security controls, operations controls, applications controls, procedural controls, environmental controls (heat, humidity, air-conditioning), and telecommunications security controls.

(C) Compensating Controls.

Normally the auditor will find more control-related problems if it is a first-time audit of an area. Generally the more frequently an area is audited, the less the probability of many control weaknesses. Therefore, determining the nature of efficient and effective operations needs both audit instinct and business judgment. During the control evaluation process, the auditor should consider the possibility of availability of compensating controls as a way to mitigate or minimize the impact of inadequate or incomplete controls. In essence, the concept of compensating controls deals with balancing of weak internal controls in one area with strong internal controls in other areas of the organization. Here the word "area" can include a section within a user or IS department.

An example of a weak control is a situation where data control employees in the IS department are not reconciling data-input control totals to data-output control totals in an application system.

This control weakness in the IS department can be compensated for by strong controls in the user department where end users reconcile their own control totals with those produced by the application system. Sometimes automated compensating controls and procedures are needed to shorten the lengthy manual controls and procedures (e.g., replacing a manual report balancing system with an automated report balancing system).

Compensating controls are needed whenever

- Manual controls are weak.

  □ **Solution:** Look for strong computer controls or other.

- Computer controls are weak.

  □ **Solution:** Look for strong manual controls or other.

- Interface controls between manual and automated systems are weak.

  □ **Solution:** Look for strong controls in either the receiving or the sending system,

- Functional (system) user controls are weak.

  □ **Solution:** Look for strong IS controls or other.

- IS controls are weak.

  □ **Solution:** Look for strong controls in system-user departments or other IS departments.

- Third-party manual controls are weak.

  □ **Solution:** Look for strong controls in the in-house system in either the manual or the automated part.

- Third-party computer controls are weak.

  □ **Solution:** Look for strong controls in the in-house system in either the manual or the automated part.

- Physical-access security controls are weak.

  □ **Solution:** Look for strong logical-access security controls.

- Logical-access security controls are weak.

  □ **Solution:** Look for strong physical-access security controls, supervisory reviews, or more substantive testing.

- A specific general control is weak.

  □ **Solution:** Look for a strong and related application control(s).

- An application system control is weak.

  □ **Solution:** Look for a strong and related general control(s).

- Employee performance is weak.

  □ **Solution:** Look for strong supervisory reviews and more substantive testing.

(D) Contradictory Controls. Two or more controls are in conflict with each other. Installation of one control does not fit well with the other controls due to incompatibility. This means, implementation of one control can affect another, related control(s) negatively. Examples include: (1) Installation of a new software patch can undo or break another related, existing software patch either in the

same system or other related systems. This incompatibility can be due to errors in the current patch(s) or previous patch(s) or that the new patches and the previous patches were not fully tested either by the software vendor or by the user organization. (2) Telecommuting work and organization's software piracy policies could be in conflict with each other if a noncompliant telecommuter implements such policies improperly and in an unauthorized manner when he purchases and loads unauthorized software on the home/work personal computer.

(iv) Control Assessment

During an assessment of control strengths and weaknesses, the auditor might run into situations where a business function, system, or manual/automated procedure is overcontrolled or under-controlled. This means that there may be too many controls in one area and not enough controls in other areas. Also, there may be duplication or overlapping of controls between two or more areas. Under these conditions, the auditor should recommend to eliminate either some user controls, some IS controls, some manual controls, some automated controls, or a combination of them. The same may be true of situations where a system or operation is oversecured or undersecured, and where an application system is overdesigned or underdesigned. This assessment requires differentiating between relevant and irrelevant information; considering compensating controls, which is discussed later; considering interrelationships of controls, which is also discussed later; and judging materiality and significance of audit findings taken separately and as a whole.

CONTROL ASSESSMENT CHALLENGE

The key issues are to know how much control is needed, how to measure it, how to evaluate whether a control is deficient or sufficient, and how to balance it.

Rarely can a single finding lead to the conclusion of an unacceptable audit or uncontrolled area. Usually a combination of control weaknesses is required to call an area unacceptable. For example, a finding such as "housekeeping is poor in the data center" alone or in combination with "there are 'No Smoking or Eating' signs in the data center" will not qualify for giving an unacceptable or uncontrolled audit rating. The audit findings must be significant. The nature of the operation (e.g., automated or manual and sensitive or routine), criticality of the system (high risk versus low risk), costs to develop and maintain controls, and the materiality (significance) of the finding are more important criteria to consider than simple observation of control weaknesses. Note that materiality is relative, not absolute. What is material to one organization may not mean the same to another. Audit judgment plays an important role in deciding what is material, what is a significant control weakness, what is an efficient operation, what is an effective system, and which should be considered separately and as a whole. In other words, the auditor needs to focus on the entire environment of the audited operation or system and take a big-picture approach instead of taking a finding-by-finding approach. A cost-benefit analysis might help the auditor in the process of evaluating controls.

(v) Cost-Benefit Analysis

A cost-benefit analysis is advised during the process of designing each type of control into an application system during its development and maintenance as well as during its operation. Ideally, costs should never exceed the benefits to be derived from installing controls. However, costs should not always be the sole determining factor because it may be difficult or impractical to quantify benefits such as timeliness, improved quality and relevance of data and information, and improved customer service and system response time. When controls are properly planned, designed, developed, tested, implemented, and followed, they should meet one or more of the following 12 attributes: (1) practical, (2) reliable, (3) simple, (4) complete, (5) operational, (6) usable, (7) appropriate, (8) cost-effective, (9) timely, (10) meaningful, (11) reasonable, and (12) consistent.

(vi) Costs versus Controls versus Convenience

Costs of controls vary with their implementation time and the complexity of the system or operation. Control implementation time is important to realize benefits from installing appropriate controls. For example, it costs significantly more to correct a design problem in the implementation phase of an application system under development than it does to address in the early planning and design phases.

There are **trade-offs** among costs, controls, and convenience factors. The same is true between system usability, maintainability, auditability, controllability, and securability attributes of systems. For example:

- High-risk systems and complex systems and operations require more controls.

- Excessive use of tight-security features and control functions can be costly and may complicate procedures, degrade system performance, and impair system functionality, which could ultimately inhibit the system's usability.

- System users prefer as few integrity and security controls as possible, only those needed to make the system really usable.

- The greater the maintainability of the system, the easier it is for a programmer to modify it. Similarly, the greater the maintainability of the system, the less expensive it is to operate in the long run.

(vii) Controls by Dimension

Control can be viewed through three different dimensions of timing: precontrol, concurrent control, and postcontrol (see Exhibit 5.5).

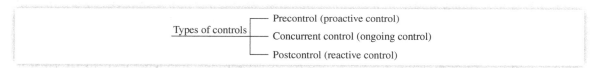

EXHIBIT 5.5 Types of Controls

Precontrol (e.g., policy) anticipates problems and is proactive in nature. Concurrent control is exercised through supervision and monitoring. Postcontrol identifies deviations from standards or budgets and calls for corrective action, and is similar to feedback control. Precontrol and feedforward control are interrelated since they deal with future-directed actions. Forecasting, budgeting, and real-time computer systems are examples of feedforward controls. Precontrol is the most preferred action; the least preferred action is postcontrol. The difference is when a corrective action is taken—the sooner the better.

A feedback control is used to evaluate past activity in order to improve future performance. It measures actual performance against a standard to ensure that a desired result is achieved. Feedback control has been criticized because corrective action takes place after the fact (reactive).

Feedback control can allow costs to build up due to their back-end position. An example is human resource managers holding exit interviews with employees who have resigned to go to work for competitors. Management tabulates the interviewee's responses and uses the information to identify problems with training, compensation, working conditions, or other factors that have caused increased turnover. Other examples include customer surveys, increased finished goods inspections, increased work-in-process (WIP) inspections, variance analysis, postaction controls, monitoring product returns, and evaluating customer complaints.

A feedforward control attempts to anticipate problems and effect timely solutions (proactive), and hence is important to management. An example is when a key auditee employee will not be available for a few weeks for audit work due to illness, and the audit supervisor reschedules the audit work to be done in this auditable area. Other examples include: defect prevention by quality control inspection of raw materials and WIP, quality control training programs, budgeting, forecasting inventory needs, and advance notice of a purchase.

(viii) Specific Types of Controls

Controls prevent the adverse effects of risks. Many different types of control activities have been described, including directive controls, preventive controls, detective controls, corrective controls, manual controls, computer controls, and management controls (see Exhibit 5.6).

The complexity of an entity and the nature and scope of activities affect its control activities. Complex organizations with diverse activities may face more difficult control issues than simple organizations with less varied activities. An entity with decentralized operations and an emphasis on local autonomy and innovation presents different control circumstances than a highly centralized one. Other factors that influence an entity's complexity and, therefore, the nature of its controls include location and geographical dispersion, the extensiveness and sophistication of operations, and information processing methods. All these factors affect an entity's control activities, which need to be designed accordingly to contribute to the achievement of the entity's objectives.

Control activities can also be classified by specified control objectives, such as ensuring completeness, timeliness, accuracy, and authorization of transactions, which are applicable to both manual and computer processing environments (see Exhibit 5.6).

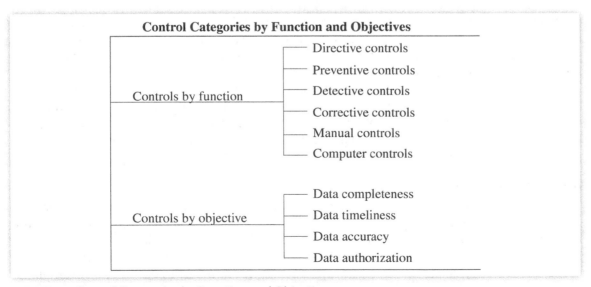

EXHIBIT 5.6 Control Categories by Function and Objective

(b) Controls by Function

Controls can be classified according to the function they are intended to perform.

Directive controls ensure the occurrence of a desirable event. Specific examples of directive controls include: requiring all members of the internal auditing department to be Certified Internal Auditors and providing management with assurance of the realization of specified minimum gross margins on sales. Other examples include policies, directives, guidance, and circulars.

Preventive controls are needed to avoid the occurrence of an unwanted event. Examples include segregation of duties, use of checklists, use of systems development methodology, competent staff, use of passwords, authorization procedures, and documentation. Segregation of duties means duties are divided among different people to reduce the risk of error or inappropriate actions. For example, it includes dividing the responsibilities for authorizing transactions, recording them, and handling the related asset. A manager authorizing credit sales would not be responsible for maintaining accounts receivable records or handling cash receipts. Similarly, salespersons would not have the ability to modify product price files or commission rates. It calls for a separation of the functional responsibilities of custodianship, record keeping, operations, and authorization. Other examples include (1) separating threats from assets to minimize risks and (2) separating resource allocation from resource use to prevent resource misuse.

Detective controls are needed to discover the occurrence of an unwanted event. The installation of detective controls is necessary to provide feedback on the effectiveness of the preventive controls. Examples include reviews and comparisons, bank reconciliations, account reconciliations, and physical counts.

Corrective controls are needed to correct after an unwanted event has occurred. They fix both detected and reported errors. Examples include correction procedures, documentation, and control and exception reports.

Manual controls include budgets, forecasts, policies and procedures; reporting; physical controls over equipment, inventories, securities, cash, and other assets, periodically counted and compared with amounts shown on control records.

Computer controls include general controls and application controls. General controls include data center operations controls, system software controls, access security controls, and application system development and maintenance controls. Application controls are designed to control application processing, helping to ensure the completeness and accuracy of transaction processing, authorization, and validity. Many application controls depend on computerized edit checks. These edit checks consist of format, existence, reasonableness, and other checks on the data, which are built into each application during its development. When these checks are designed properly, they can help provide control over the data being entered into the computer system. Computer controls are performed to check accuracy, completeness, and authorization of transactions.

(i) Controls by Objectives

Examples of data completeness controls include use of prenumbered forms, obtaining transaction authorization, and system logging of transactions. Examples of data timeliness controls include use of electronic mail to send urgent messages instead of phone and use of facsimile to send urgent letters instead of regular mail. Examples of data accuracy controls include use of batch and hash totals, check digits, balance controls, and system-assigned numbers to documents. Examples of data authorization controls include management approvals, two-person controls, and overrides.

KEY CONCEPTS TO REMEMBER: How Many Controls Are There?

- Accounting controls are well defined with a body of professional standards published. They help ensure there is full accountability for physical assets and that all financial transactions are recorded and reported timely and accurately.

- Administrative controls help ensure resources are safeguarded against waste, loss or fraud, and misappropriation, and support the accomplishment of organization's goals and objectives. These controls include accurate and timely management information, and effective and efficient processes for planning, productivity improvement, quality control, legal and regulatory compliance, and improving economy and efficiency.

- Auditing controls are the system of checks and balances in effect throughout the organization.

- Operating controls include segregation of duties, dual controls, joint custody, rotation of duties, adherence to prescribed policies and procedures, and employees taking vacations.

- Operational controls include controls that are not clearly defined and completely communicated due to constant changes and several functional departments involved in the operating chain. They are not supported by clear standards and are subject to greater misinterpretation.

- Input controls prevent or detect the entry of inaccurate or incomplete data into a computer system.

- Output controls ensure that computer outputs (reports, files, and listings) are distributed only to authorized people.

- Hardware controls must have existing rigid and clear standards in order to operate in different operating environments.

- Physical security controls are rigid, well defined, and subject to less misinterpretation.

- An organizational control system's components include objectives, standards, and an evaluation-reward system.

- A financial control system's components include budgeting, financial ratio analysis, and cash management.

- A managerial control is the result of proper planning, organizing, and directing. Its ultimate objective is to promote organizational effectiveness, which is the degree to which the organization achieves its short-term and long-term objectives. Components of managerial controls include forestalling management fraud and protecting assets. Components do not include implementing plans.

(ii) Controls in Business Application Systems

The scope of business application system controls includes controls over data origination, preparation, and data input; data processing; system-related file maintenance; data output; application system documentation; spreadsheet work; data integrity; and user satisfaction assessment. Each area is discussed next.

(iii) Data Origination, Preparation, and Data Input Controls

There are several approaches to data preparation and data entry into the application system. In some cases, the data are captured on a paper (source) document like a sales or purchase order.

The source documents are batched into small groups and entered into the system either by functional users or central data-entry operators through the use of terminals. In other cases, there is no externally generated source document since the customer calls in and places an order with the organization.

Other approaches include use of factory data collection devices for factories; automated teller machine recorders for banks; point-of-sale (POS) recorders for the retail business with or without bar codes; magnetic ink character recognition devices for the banking industry for customer checks and deposit tickets; optical character recognition devices to read credit card statements, insurance premium notices, and utility company billings; optical mark reading devices to read pencil marks made in specific locations on preprinted forms to be used in grading structured examination questions; scanners for document image processing; and voice recognition input devices used to recognize human voice in airline and parcel industries to route packages.

Regardless of the method used to capture the data, the entered data are edited and validated for preventing or detecting errors and omissions. Therefore, access controls and data editing and validation controls are important to ensure that quality data are entering into the application system.

WHAT CAN GO WRONG IN DATA PREPARATION AND ENTRY?

- Adequate separation of duties may not be maintained over data origination, data preparation, data input, data update, and data output activities between and among system users and data processors.

- Design of forms and documents used for data input preparation and the design of input terminal screens may not match or may be too complex for the skill level of the system user. Consequently, data are entered incorrectly and improperly.

- Source transactions may be inaccurate, unauthorized, or lost during movement from department to department, during data entry, and/or during data processing.

- Transaction errors may not be properly prevented, detected, or corrected and resubmitted in a timely manner.

- Data input errors, irregularities, omissions, and data alterations are the most common computer-related problems leading to fraud, crime, and abuse.

The following are red flags that suggest vulnerability to data errors: old application system with high program maintenance, large volume of data for processing, frequent processing and updating activity, numerous transaction types and sources, large number of coded data elements, high employee turnover (e.g., data entry clerks, operators, programmers, system analysts), inadequate training, complex data structures, and lack of standards related to security, access, and program-change control.

Data Processing Controls
Although there are some common controls, controls will be different between batch and online processing. Similar to data input, data editing and validation controls are important during

computer processing. Therefore, more use of program-based processing controls is needed to ensure data integrity and security. These controls include limit check, range test, validity check, table lookup, reasonableness test, sequence check, comparison test, check digit test, ratio test, and relationship test.

What Can Go Wrong in Process Validation and Editing?

- Transactions may be processed in the wrong fiscal period.

- Transactions may be improperly classified, valued, summarized, or reported.

- Adequate data editing and validation controls may not be available in application program processing logic to prevent or detect errors, omissions, or irregularities.

- Application program processing jobs may take longer due to inefficient data file structures, poor choice of design techniques, poor selection of data file access methods, poorly structured program logic, and/or ineffective program statements.

- Backout or fallback procedures may not be available for programs, causing abnormal termination, or due to other operational problems during computer-job processing.

System-related File Maintenance Controls. The auditor will encounter many system-related files during an audit of the application system. These files contain valuable data for audit analysis and reporting purposes. Major concerns for the auditor should be who can access and update these files. Some examples of these files are:

- **Master files.** Examples of master files are customer files, vendor files, employee files, account files.

- **Transaction files.** Transaction files are detail files used with the master files. Routine and repeat transactions are collected into transaction files and then used to update the master data files.

- **Backup files.** Backup files contain program or data files.

- **Program files.** Program files contain source, object, or executable code.

- **Table files.** Table files contain data such as office codes, state codes, postal Zip codes, department codes, tax codes, and plant codes. These tables are used during program execution for data editing, validation, and referencing purposes.

- **Summary/history files.** Summary files contain a history of transactions such as month-to-date, quarter-end, year-end, or last five years' data. These transactions are maintained in a summary form.

- **Archive files.** Archive files contain data or programs that are infrequently used and yet important to store for many useful reasons.

- **Control files.** Control files contain parameter-related information such as dates, cycles, and reports. These parameters are used in processing computer jobs.

- **Print files.** Print files contain data and program files waiting to be printed. These files are stored in a spool area and wait until the current print job is completed. When their turn comes up, these files are printed.

- **Report files.** Report files contain report records for each application system–generated output.

■ **Command files.** Command files contain certain key commands (e.g., execute, copy, delete, write) required by an application program, operating system, or other support systems software. Commands are supplied to various programs during their execution.

■ **Work files.** Work files are any files that are created, used, and then deleted at the end of one job step. Work files are also called scratch files. Normally work files are used to sort data files. Application programs create these files as needed. Work files are temporary in nature.

■ **Temporary files.** A temporary file is one that lasts for the duration of the job regardless of the successful completion or termination of the job. The operating system automatically deletes all such files when the job terminates. Sometimes programmers have the application program create a temporary cross-reference file from an input file and then use it in the downstream (subsequent job) processing.

■ **Log files.** A log file is a data file or command file that contains data and commands that are logged during computer job and program processing. Log files can be created by an operating system, application system, database system, telecommunication system, or security system. For example, a database system may create before-and-after images of records during an update process in a database log file. Log files are also temporary in nature.

■ **Document image files.** An image file is created out of a document such as a loan, credit, or employment application; payment invoice; and purchase order. These documents are then stored and retrieved as needed. An image file can be downloaded or uploaded to and from the host computer and the microcomputer.

■ **User files.** User files are created by each user of the system for the user's personal library and use.

■ **Transmission files.** Transmission files are the ones waiting to be transmitted from one location to the other, from one computer system to the other, from one entity to the other, or from one time zone to the other.

What Can Go Wrong in File Maintenance?

■ A computer file may be lost or damaged due to bad write/read head error or disk failure on an input/output device.

■ Both the original and backup file may be stored on the same magnetic media (e.g., disk, tape, cartridge) or physical area, thus losing both.

■ System files may be erased, destroyed, or unlogged intentionally or accidentally.

■ Before (from) and after (to) image record reporting may not be available when database or data files are updated, thus losing accountability.

■ Identification of production data files could be difficult because file names may not consistently indicate whether files are related to production application systems.

Data Output Controls. There are many output devices in use today. Traditionally, system outputs are in the form of hard-copy reports. Online viewing of reports on a terminal, computer, or mobile device is common today.

What Can Go Wrong in System Output Activities?

- Exception reporting may not be available to focus on deviations.

- Report balancing rules may not be documented or may be changed without authorization.

- Unneeded reports may be sent to system users.

- System output reports may be delivered to wrong users.

- System outputs (i.e., reports, lists, screens) may be lost, delayed, or truncated due to incorrect sizes between receiving and sending data fields.

- System users may not clearly understand the system outputs.

- System outputs may not be accurate or complete.

Balancing, distribution, and retention of system outputs are of major concern to the auditor since they affect the quality and timeliness of data and usefulness of the system.

Application System Documentation Controls. System documentation is a key element of audit evidence. Without correct and complete documentation, new users cannot be trained properly, programmers cannot maintain the system correctly, users of the system cannot make any meaningful references to the system functions and features, management or others cannot understand the system functions and features, and reviewers of the systems (e.g., auditors) cannot make an objective evaluation of the system functions and controls.

Six types of documentation manuals (systems, user, program, computer operations, help-desk, and network control) can be expected in a well-run IT organization. Each type of documentation is targeted for a specific individual or department, sometimes more than one department. For example, help-desk and network control manuals are very much needed by both end users and help-desk staff for an online system or one that is connected to outside third-party data-processing services for access during in-house processing. See Exhibit 5.7 for details of these six types of documentation manuals, which would be developed during system development work.

EXHIBIT 5.7 Application System Documentation Types and Contents

Documentation Type	Documentation Contents
Systems manual	System flowchart; systems requirements; system functions; design specifications; screen layouts; sample reports
Program manual	Program flowcharts; program functions; file layouts; program specifications
Computer operations manual	Job setup procedures; job narratives; job rerun and restart procedures; file backup procedures; report distribution procedures
User manual	System functions; sample screen and report layouts; report balancing procedures; file maintenance procedures; error correction procedures
Help-desk manual	Contact names and phone numbers of users and IT staff; problem diagnostic and reporting procedures; problem escalation procedures; problem logging, tracking, and closing procedures
Network control manual	Information about circuits, nodes, line, modems; problem diagnostic procedures; problem reporting and resolution procedures; network backup and contingency procedures

What Can Go Wrong in Application Documentation?

- User manuals/guides or documentation may not be available to understand how the system works, or it may not be current.

- System/program documentation may not be available to facilitate system/program maintenance, or it may not be current.

- Help-desk/network documentation may not be available to facilitate system/network diagnosis and troubleshooting, and it may not be current.

- Operations documentation may not be available to operators to facilitate operations and troubleshooting of operational problems, and it may not be current.

Spreadsheet Controls. Spreadsheet software is getting more powerful and simpler to use. Some applications include financial budgeting, project/product costing, payroll, word processing, analytical comparison, and others. Problems can arise: (1) through improper usage of spreadsheet software; (2) due to inadequate planning, design, and documentation of spreadsheet application; and (3) due to human errors. The consequences of these problems and errors are significant as the outputs of spreadsheets are used in decision making.

What Can Go Wrong in Spreadsheet Software and Its Use?

- Applicable quality control techniques such as author verification (desk checking) and supervisory review may not be available over spreadsheets to ensure that they are error-free.

- Spreadsheet work may not be documented clearly and completely.

- Formulas and key data may not be protected from writing over.

- The most frequent errors in spreadsheets occur during data entry and formulation.

- Errors or mistakes during data entry may not have been noticed or corrected in a timely manner.

- Assumptions and instructions related to the planning, operation, and interpretation of the spreadsheet application may not be documented clearly and adequately.

Data Integrity Controls. Data integrity is the heart of any application. Data integrity controls ensure the reliability and usability of data and information in making management decisions. The higher the integrity of controls, the greater the credibility and reliability of the application system. Here the term "data integrity" refers to five control attributes: completeness, accuracy, authorization, consistency, and timeliness. The interrelationships of the five control attributes are shown in Exhibit 5.8.

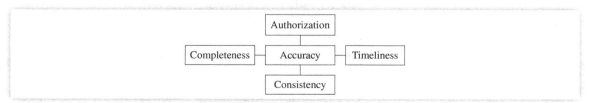

EXHIBIT 5.8 Interrelationships of Control Attributes

The objectives of a data integrity review are to ensure that basic internal controls such as documented procedures, access controls, management reviews, audit trails, and automated program-processing controls are established and to verify that they are functioning properly and effectively. Directive, preventive, detective, corrective, and recovery controls should be established in each application system during system development, system maintenance, and system operations activities to achieve the five control attributes of data integrity.

DATA INTEGRITY RULES AND CONTROLS

- A directive control will ensure that people follow data integrity rules consistently.
- A preventive control will stop a data integrity violation from happening.
- A detective control will recognize a data integrity violation.
- A corrective control will fix or repair the damage done by a data integrity violation.
- A recovery control will help in recovering or restoring from a disaster caused by a data integrity violation.

Specifically:

Data completeness refers to the presence or absence of information. All required data elements must be present for a transaction or record to be complete. Examples include all numeric places should be filled and a check cannot be issued unless all fields have a valid value.

Data accuracy asks whether data values have been entered into the system correctly and whether data values have been distorted during processing. The sources of the data in terms of where they came from and incorruptibility of data are also important here. This means that the received data are unchanged (no additions, changes, and deletions from the original order, without repetition and omission) with positive assurance and an acceptable degree of confidence. Examples include checking for numeric ranges, spelling errors, data duplication, and data omission.

Data authorization looks at whether transactions are authorized by appropriate personnel for proper accountability. The person who is approving the transactions is also important here. Moreover, authorization function should be tailored or responsive to the requirements of the application system.

Data consistency asks whether policies, procedures, and standards have been uniformly applied. This refers to the relation between intra-data elements and intra- and inter-records and files. Examples include a Requestor's name cannot equal an Approver's name, and an Approver's name cannot equal a Signatory's name in a check-approval scenario. The causes of data inconsistencies can be due to invalid, untimely, incomplete, and inaccurate data.

Data timeliness means that data are not stale for intended use and that they are current. Management needs to understand the need for establishing controls to ensure data integrity. This understanding makes the system more effective and useful.

User Satisfaction Assessment.   Assessment of system user satisfaction is a very important part of the audit of an application system. This is because it is the system user who paid for the system, who owns the system, and who uses the system.

In fact, the system is not successful and useful if the system user is not satisfied with system functions and results. One way to assess user satisfaction is to conduct user surveys periodically. System usability should be a major concern for the user and the auditor.

ISSUES IN USER SATISFACTION

- The application system may not be user-friendly, that is, may not be easy to use.

- System users may not be satisfied with the performance of the system, that is, online system response time may be too slow or batch job turnaround time may be too long.

- The application system may not be available to system users for use when it is needed and where it is needed.

- The application system may not be providing the right kind of information needed to run business operations.

- The application system may not be giving users control reports, exception reports, summary reports, aging reports, error reports, productivity reports, and audit trail reports.

- Functional users may not have documented and tested plans and procedures for operating their application systems during a power outage, natural disaster, or system failure.

- Access to an application system may take a longer time due to too many screens, menus, submenus, or steps to get into programs. Usually the greater the number of screens, the longer it takes to move from one screen to the other.

(c) Inventory of Controls in Business Application Systems

Application controls are designed to control computerized application systems, helping to ensure the completeness and accuracy of transaction processing, authorization, and validity. The following list provides the nature of each control (preventive, detective, and corrective); the type of control (completeness, accuracy, continuity, authorization, consistency, and security) is indicated where necessary.

Preventive Controls

- **Brevity codes.** A shortened form of standardized messages that reduces the amount of input required by valid users while often hiding the message type, or other information obtained from the user interface, from unauthorized users. This control increases data accuracy.

- **Data attribute checks.** Verification that data have particular attributes (e.g., length, type, content).

- **Validity checks.** These are tests for the validity of codes such as state, tax rates, Social Security number, customer number, vendor number, or employee number. Usually table lookups are performed for data comparison. This accuracy control is a preventive and a detective control.

- **Compatibility tests.** Compatibility tests are used to determine whether an acceptable user is allowed to proceed in the system. This test focuses on passwords, access rules, and system privileges. This is a security control.

- **Processing parameters.** The flexible use of parameters facilitates operation and customized reporting features can be used to specify dates (beginning and ending), processing frequency and cycles (daily, weekly, monthly), report numbers, computer-job numbers, and locations (plant numbers, office numbers, or store numbers). This is a continuity control.

- **Prenumbered forms.** Sequential numbers on individual source documents or input forms (i.e., purchase orders or invoices) are preprinted to allow subsequent detection of loss or misplacement of documents and forms. This is a completeness control.

- **System-assigned numbers.** These are the same as prenumbered forms except that the system automatically assigns the sequential numbers. This is an accuracy control.

- **Precoded forms/screens.** Fixed data elements or fields are entered or printed on input forms, source documents, terminal screen menus, or report listings to prevent errors in data coding and data entry, for example, on turnaround documents such as utility bills. A variation of this is called **preformatting,** the display of a document with blanks for data items to be entered by the system user or the data entry operator. This is an accuracy control.

- **Turnaround documents.** Source documents and input forms can be designed in such a way that they achieve two purposes: (1) to serve as a bill, invoice, or notice to a customer or a user and (2) to use the same document when returned as an input document for entering the necessary data into the computer system. This is an accuracy control.

- **Reference values or codes kept outside the program.** For ease of system or program maintenance, it is better to keep frequently used or changing values or codes (i.e., Social Security numbers, tax rates, pay classes) outside the program as an external table or other means (LEVEL 88 values in COBOL programs), and not embedded in the programming statements. Table lookups are provided. This is a continuity control.

- **Transaction cancellation.** The system can be designed in such a way as to cancel each transaction record after it is used in order to prevent its repeated use. Examples are purchase orders, receiving reports, invoices, sales returns, and the like. The system flags repeated use of the same document number; this is analogous to manual stamping of "paid" or "processed." Cancellation also can be used to reverse or back-out previous transactions for any reason. This is a completeness control.

- **Management approvals.** Supervisors or managers should be required to approve sensitive and important transactions that others entered into the system or calculated using the system. This is achieved by entering a secret keyword or number as a means of authorization. This is an authorization control.

- **Concurrent access controls.** For database systems, concurrent access (updates) to the same record or file by multiple users is a concern as it affects data integrity. Usually automatic file/record locking facilities are used to prevent concurrent accesses. These controls are required to minimize the possibility of destroying data records. This is a security control.

- **Two-person controls.** Two individuals review or approve the work of each other. Examples are: one person initiates a transaction and the other person approves it, one person counts inventory or cash while the other person observes it. The purpose is to provide accountability or accuracy in dealing with sensitive or high-risk transactions or activities to minimize fraud or other irregularities. This is an accuracy control.

- **Overrides.** Overrides can include manual and system-based overrides. The system should prevent unauthorized individuals overriding exceptions or errors. A report should be produced showing who did what. This is a security and authorization control.

Detective Controls

- **Summary integrity check.** This is a method for checking the correctness of data by comparing data with a "summary" of the data. It is similar to a batch-control technique.

- **Batch totals.** To ensure accuracy in data entry and processing, control totals can be compared by the system with manually calculated and entered control totals using the data fields such as quantities, line items, documents, or dollars. This is a completeness control.

- **Hash totals.** This is a technique for improving data accuracy, whereby totals are obtained on identifier (meaningless) data fields such as account number, Social Security number, part number, or employee number. These totals have no significance other than for internal system control purposes. This is an accuracy control.

- **Limit check.** The program tests specified data fields against defined high- or low-value limits (e.g., quantities or dollars) for acceptability before further processing. This is an accuracy control. Examples of error messages: transaction is over $30,000, purchase order is over $50,000, or multiple price change number cannot be higher than 9999. The limits can be based on transaction values and times.

- **Reasonableness test.** This test can be used to determine whether input data, updated data, calculated data, or output data are reasonable. Ascending/descending checks for numeric and alphabetic data can be performed. Tolerance tests measuring dollar or percentage deviation of vendor invoice from purchase-order amount can be designed. This test is specific to an application-system function. This is an accuracy control. Examples of error messages: Airline passenger departure flight time is not reasonable with arrival flight time for the same day or customer order quantity is not reasonable with historical order.

- **Check digit.** This is a digit, derived by a mathematical formula, that is a function of the other digits within a word or number. It is a checksum calculated on each digit of a numeric string. It is used for testing accuracy of transcription, transposition, data entry, and data processing, and detects such errors. Part numbers, stock-keeping numbers, credit card numbers, employee numbers, and account numbers can be check-digited. This is an accuracy control. Examples of error messages: Invalid check-digit must be zero through six. Invalid check digit on transfer number. Check digits can be operated on any part of the number as long as they are applied consistently.

- **Overflow check.** This is a limit check based on the capacity of a computer memory or data file area to accept data. This programming technique can be used to detect the truncation of a financial or quantity data-field value after computation (e.g., addition, multiplication, and division). Usually the first digit is lost. This is an accuracy control.

- **Format checks.** These are used to determine that data are entered in the proper mode, as numeric or alphabetical characters, within designated fields of information. The proper mode in each case depends on the data record definition. These are accuracy controls. Examples of error messages: Invalid transaction format. Invalid date format, date must be mm-dd-yy.

- **Date checks.** These can be used to record transactions in the proper accounting (fiscal) month; they relate to logical consistencies between transaction dates and events. These are continuity controls. Examples of error messages: Merchandise date received should be after the date shipped. Budget transaction date out of range. Control card "to" date is less than "from" date the job canceled.

- **Label check.** This is a processing control whereby a computer application program verifies internal file labels for tapes to ensure that the correct data file is used in the processing. This is a continuity control. Example of error message: Wrong file is mounted.

- **Completeness test.** This is a programming test to determine whether data entries have been made in data fields that should be left blank. It can be used to detect missing data fields or records. This is a completeness control.

- **Range test.** This is the same as "limit check," but this term is used when both high and low values are used for testing. It can also define include and exclude values. This is an accuracy control. Examples of error messages: Percentage must be between 10 and 75 inclusive or price change number must be in range 1000 through 1999.

- **Range check.** This is a verification that data are within a certain range of values.

- **Discrete value check.** This is verification that data either have certain permissible values or do not have other restricted values, out of a wider set of possible values.

- **Record count.** This is a processing control whereby information such as maximum, active, inactive, and available record counts will ensure proper size of the file and avoid loss of records. This is a continuity control. Example of error message: Transaction counts and actual record counts do not agree.

- **Sign test.** This is a test for a numeric data field containing a designation of an algebraic sign such as + or −, which can be used to denote, for example, debits or credits for financial data fields. This is an accuracy control. Example of error message: Sign is inconsistent with transaction type.

- **Size test.** This test can be used to test the full size of the data field. For example, a Social Security number in the United States should have nine digits. This is a completeness control. Examples of error messages: Line quantity or total may not be more than five digits long, or numeric postal Zip code must be either five or nine digits.

- **Sequence check.** This is a way of testing for a certain sequence of record types or transaction numbers during computer processing. It can also be used to test the sequence of purchase orders, receiving reports, invoices, and the like. It is also called "anticipation control" and depends on the system and its design logic. This is a completeness control. Examples of error messages: Missing transaction No. 06 or missing record type 09.

- **Duplicate checks.** These are the same as sequence checks but look for duplication. These are completeness controls. Examples of error messages: multiple tax records or multiple account records.

- **Cross-field editing.** Cross-field editing tests for the validity of multiple data fields simultaneously with a logical and predefined relationship to each other in the same record. This is a consistency control. Examples of error messages: No tax on taxable department. Tax amount received or paid on a nontaxable item or department. Incorrect telephone area code compared to postal Zip code.

- **Cross-record editing.** This is the same as cross-field editing, but the tests are performed among multiple records. This is a consistency control. Examples of error messages: Account number in a transaction record does not match with the master file. Department number not on file for the store/plant/office.

- **System matching.** The system matches certain transactions, such as purchase order numbers to receiving report numbers to vendor invoices or shipping advices to billing numbers, and lists unmatched transactions for review and follow-up. This is a completeness control. Examples of error messages: Account number does not match with the recording code. Tax percentage calculated does not match with tax tables.

- **Field combination tests.** One or more data fields are tested for the right combination. These are accuracy controls. Examples of error messages: invalid plant number for the business division; city and/or state cannot have city code; no price found for the given item/style; if the style number is entered, then the house number must also be entered; invalid employee number for the location; or invalid payclass for the given subclass.

■ **Run-to-run totals.** These are processing controls whereby output control totals resulting from one process (cycle, program, or module) are used as input control totals over subsequent processing. The control totals are used as a verification mechanism (automatically or manually) and link one process or cycle to another in a sequence. The control totals can be grouped by dollars, records, or in some other way. This control ensures program-processing accuracy. These are continuity controls. Examples of error messages: Database-beginning records total plus transaction activity records total is not equal to ending-records total, or net amount is not equal to total cost plus transportation cost – discount.

■ **Suspense file.** In this technique, computer files are designed to contain unprocessed or partially processed transactions awaiting further action. All pending or rejected transactions (errors) can be maintained in a suspense file for later review and correction. This will ensure that all errors are corrected. This is a completeness control. Examples of error messages: Transaction is rejected or transaction is incomplete or suspended.

■ **Header and trailer record verification.** This is a processing-control technique used to verify the accuracy of header information in a first record of a file and to verify the accuracy of a control total in the trailer or last record for comparison with accumulated counts or values of records processed. This is an accuracy control. Examples of error messages: Wrong file entered for processing or trailer record counts do not equal accumulated counts.

■ **Balance controls.** The system can be designed to balance transactions using a system- or function-dependent technique whereby an out-of-balance condition is automatically detected and reported. This is an accuracy control. Examples of error messages: The total sum of units or dollars must equal the sum of units or dollars for each location.

■ **System logging of transactions.** This is a processing control whereby the system maintains a log to record user ID, password, transaction number, department number, terminal ID, date, and time to provide an electronic audit trail. This is a security control.

■ **Comparison controls.** The program is designed to compare certain values in the same or different records to determine accuracy and reasonableness. These are consistency controls. Examples are: listing of differences between prices on purchase orders and purchase invoices, listing of differences between stock-status dollar values and general-ledger amounts, listing of shipment values and billed amounts, comparison of merchandise total plus freight plus tax amount with purchase-invoice total, comparison of quantities of product sold in the last quarter with quantities in inventory and reports of slow-moving inventory based on criteria built into the program, and comparison of debit-dollar totals with credit-dollar totals for financial accounting journal entry transactions. This technique is dependent on the application system's function.

■ **Computation controls.** The program logic includes columnar footing and cross-footing, extensions, and postings to ensure mathematical and processing accuracy. Most techniques described here are dependent on the application system's functions. These are accuracy controls. Examples of error messages: Total quantity must be the sum of all line quantities.

■ **Ratio test.** This is a mathematical calculation whereby one data element is divided into another to yield a ratio value. This is a consistency control. An example is: Return on investment/assets (ROI/ROA) is calculated as dividing the data element "operating or net income" in the numerator by the data element "investment or assets" in the denominator.

- **Rounding technique.** For financial and accounting calculations such as multiplication and division, the system analyst or programmer should decide how to handle rounding calculations and decimal point rounding rules consistently across and within all programs and systems. This is an accuracy control.

- **Relationship test.** This is a comparison of values to validate a logical or defined correlation; it is also referred to as a conditional test. For example, an invoice date must be the same as or earlier than the related payment date. This is a consistency control.

- **Descriptive read-back.** This is a design technique whereby a code or number is converted to its description and appears on the computer terminal screen for human inspection to determine its accuracy and completeness. This is an accuracy control. An example is when a customer number is entered, his or her name and address will appear on the screen to ensure that the right customer record is accessed.

- **Data checks.** The system analyst or programmer should test for the presence of blank spaces when numeric data are expected to be received in a numeric data field or should test for division by zero when a division is expected with a nonzero value. This prevents program failure during processing as a result of missing or improper data. These are accuracy controls.

- **Key verification.** Important data elements or fields need to be key verified by rekeying to verify data entry accuracy. This is an accuracy control. Example of error message: Incorrect account number, check it.

- **One-for-one checking.** Critical reports or input documents should be compared one-for-one with subsequent outputs to ensure accuracy and completeness of data entry and computer processing.

- **Cross footing.** Cross footing compares horizontal (rows) and vertical (columns) totals in a table or report to be equal. This is an accuracy control.

Corrective Controls

- **Program comments.** The consistent inclusion of English comments in the program will help programmers understand the program's functions and features during its maintenance. This is a consistency control.

- **Job control comments.** The consistent inclusion of English comments in the job control language will help the maintenance programmer and the data control analyst understand the purpose of job control language. This is a consistency control.

- **Automatic error correction.** The system is designed to correct errors automatically on the basis of predefined criteria and in cases where human intervention is not immediately needed. This is a continuity control.

- **Overrides by supervisors.** The system should be designed so that the ability to override certain critical and sensitive errors is limited to supervisors and managers using a password control. This is both a continuity control and an authorization control.

- **Audit trail report.** The system should provide a clear and complete listing of audit trail reports for tracing and verification purposes. This is an accuracy control.

- **Control report.** The system should provide a clear and complete listing of batch control and system logging reports for user balancing and verification purposes. This is an accuracy control.

- **Exception report.** This is a report produced on request or in response to certain specified conditions and highlights exceptions or deviations from the anticipated situation. The type of report and its details depend on the application system's function. This is an accuracy control.

- **Error report.** A report showing all rejected transactions in error, indicating the severity level of the error and the required action to correct the error. This is an accuracy control.

- **Before/after image record reporting for file maintenance.** To ensure data integrity, the system must report the data field values both before and after the changes so functional users can detect data-entry and update errors. This is an accuracy control.

- **Clear and complete error messages.** To facilitate error correction, all error messages should be easy to understand and meaningful. They should neither be cryptic or negative, nor use code numbers. This is a continuity control.

- **Error total.** To facilitate error correction and increase employee productivity, error totals should be provided by error type, department, position, transaction, plant, store, or company. Errors can be totaled as dollars, quantities, or records. This is an accuracy control.

- **Documentation.** Correct, up-to-date system, programming, computer operations, network control, help desk, and user manuals (documented procedures) will help system analysts, programmers, computer operators, network control analysts, and functional users correct errors, answer questions, and resolve problems during maintenance, operation, and use of the system. This is a continuity control.

- **Automatic backup and recovery.** The system is designed to provide automated periodic backup of all required disk files, as opposed to needing human intervention to ensure timely recovery from a disaster. In some systems, file restoration and recovery are automatic. This is a continuity control.

- **Journaling.** All application system transactions should be captured on a journal file so that recovery can be made should a system failure occur. This is a continuity control.

- **Checkpoint control.** All application system batch jobs requiring more than one hour of CPU processing time need to be designed with a checkpoint control so that automatic backup of files is made every 15 or 30 minutes to facilitate a recovery should a disaster occur. This is a continuity control.

- **Transaction back-out.** All application systems (database or not) should have the ability to back out or reverse invalid or improper transaction data should a processing problem or error occur. This is a continuity control.

- **Recovery logging.** For database systems, a recovery log can be used to record system status information as well as information describing the changes made to the database. Both before images and after images of the database pages affected by an update can be stored in the recovery log, which can be accessed by means of rollback and roll-forward techniques. This is a continuity control.

- **Fallback procedure.** In the event of a failure of transactions or the system, the program has the ability to fall back to the original or alternative method for continuation of processing. This is a continuity control.

(i) Summary of Controls

(A) Operational Application System Controls.   Exhibit 5.9 provides a summary of preventive, detective, and corrective controls as they relate to IT in operation. Implementation of these controls would help IT management in strengthening overall controls.

EXHIBIT 5.9 Operational Application System Preventive, Detective, and Corrective Controls Summary

Preventive Controls	Detective Controls	Corrective Controls
Data dictionary	Batch control totals	Program comments
Structured techniques	Hash totals	Job control comments
Programming and documentation standards	Limit checks	Automatic error correction
	Reasonableness checks	Overrides by supervisors
Processing parameters	Check digits	Audit trail reports
Online prompting	Overflow checks	Control reports
Self-help features	Format checks	Exception reports
Default options	Date checks	Productivity reports
Good screen design	Label checks	Aging reports
Field highlighting	Completeness tests	Error reports
Screen diagnostic messages	Range tests	Before/after image reporting
Prenumbered forms	Record counts	Clear and complete error messages
System-assigned numbers	Sign test	
Precoded forms and screens	Size test	Error totals
Turnaround documents	Sequence checks	Documentation
Data ownership	Duplicate checks	Automated backup and recovery mechanisms
Data classification	Cross-field checking	
Table lookups	Cross-record checking	Journaling
Passwords	System matching	Data retention
Transaction cancellation	Field combination tests	Checkpoint controls
Data encryption	Validity checks	Transaction backout
Management approvals	Run-to-run totals	Recovery logging
Concurrent access controls	Suspense files	Fallback procedures
Two-person controls	Header/trailer record verifications	
Fault-tolerant controls	Balance controls	
System or manual overrides	System logs	
	Comparison controls	
	Computation controls	
	Ratio tests	
	Rounding techniques	
	Descriptive readback	
	System walk-throughs	
	Data checks	
	Key verification	
	One-for-one checking	
	Crossfooting	

(B) Information Technology Management.   Operating management has the ultimate responsibility for the implementation of cost-effective controls in manual or automated systems. Management activities range from strategic planning to operational control. Strategic planning requires external,

very broad, future-oriented data, whereas operational control requires information that is largely internal, narrow, and current.

Feedforward controls help management in anticipating problems. Exhibit 5.10 presents a summary of preventive, detective, and corrective controls as they relate to information systems environment. Implementation of these controls would help IT management in strengthening overall controls.

EXHIBIT 5.10 Information Systems Environment Preventive, Detective, and Corrective Controls Summary

Preventive Controls	Detective Controls	Corrective Controls
Policies, procedures, standards	Project management tools	Exception reports
Separation of duties	Control parameters	Progress reports
Job (position) descriptions	Operating/capital budgets	Control reports
Short-range plans	Tolerance limits	Error reports
Long-range plans		Special reports
System access rules		

(C) Information Technology Operations. Exhibit 5.11 presents a summary of preventive, detective, and corrective controls as they relate to functional areas of IT operations. Implementation of these controls would help IT management in strengthening overall controls.

EXHIBIT 5.11 Functional Areas of IT Operations Preventive, Detective, and Corrective Controls Summary

Preventive Controls	Detective Controls	Corrective Controls
Establish IT steering committee	Install smoke and fire detectors and fire alarms	Automate the report balancing procedures
Establish service-level agreements	Require system logging of transactions	Use comments in job execution language
Establish and enforce computer center policies, procedures, and standards	Reduce computer operator intervention by installing console management system	Provide periodic backup of data and programs, and rotate them through off-site storage
Establish a problem, change, and configuration management function	Review system activity logs, journals, and exception reports	Facilitate system recovery and restart procedures
Install help-desk function to support system users	Rotate key employees in the computer center	Install automated job recovery software
Establish a separate and centralized network control function	Require employees to take vacations	Develop fallback systems and procedures
	Acquire or develop an automated job accounting information system	Install fault-tolerant devices and software to recover from a system failure
Require periodic audits of the computer center		
Establish a chargeback system	Ensure running of correct version of production programs	
Eliminate manual job scheduling practices	Compare production resource usage	
Discourage printing of hardcopy reports	Install water detection measures and environmental control devices	
Install automated tape and disk management systems		
Install computer capacity management function		

(D) Data and Network Communications. Exhibit 5.12 presents a summary of preventive, detective, and corrective controls as they relate to data and network communications. Implementation of these controls would help IT management in strengthening overall controls.

EXHIBIT 5.12 Network Communications Preventive, Detective, and Corrective Controls Summary

Preventive Controls	Detective Controls	Corrective Controls
Policies, procedures, and standards	Contingency plan testing	Contingency plan maintenance and update
Encryption techniques	Network line utilization statistics	Network diagnostic data collection tools with automatic corrective action
Transborder data transmission laws	Network diagnostic tools	
Training and education plans	Network testing capabilities	Network routing capabilities
Problem and change management system	Test cables and connectors prior to power-up for each node	Networking monitoring tools
Fault-tolerance network design practices	Periodic inventory of network equipment	Recovery mechanisms such as checkpoints, rollback and roll-forward features in the database
Resilient network design principles such as redundant equipment and components; alternate paths, routes, nodes, and circuits and lines; and parallel links	Install physical security devices	
	Implement logical security mechanisms	Recovery techniques from computer viruses
Contingency plan development	Message sequence numbers	
Network management tools	Checksum techniques	
Install quality cables for LAN network	Computer viruses detection tools	

System Security and Information Protection. Privacy of information is important and is protected by logging and analyzing system usage, implementing program change controls, and separating personal/personnel data from operating or statistical data. Both management and auditors can be equally liable for security breaches occurring in the organization. Situational pressures (e.g., gambling, drugs), opportunities to commit fraud (e.g., weak system of controls), and personal characteristics (e.g., lack of integrity, honesty) are major causes of fraud, whether computer-related or not. There is nothing new about the act of committing fraud. There is no new way to commit fraud because someone somewhere has already tried it.

Exhibit 5.13 presents a summary of preventive, detective, and corrective controls as they relate to security function. Implementation of these controls would help IT management in strengthening overall controls.

EXHIBIT 5.13 Security Function Preventive, Detective, and Corrective Controls Summary

Preventive Controls	Detective Controls	Corrective Controls
Establish a computer security management (steering) committee	Require all employees to wear badges	Provide application system–generated error reports to users for review
Establish a computer security function	Provide last activity/sign-on data on computer terminals	

(continued)

EXHIBIT 5.13 Security Function Preventive, Detective, and Corrective Controls Summary *(Continued)*

Preventive Controls	Detective Controls	Corrective Controls
Assign asset responsibility to employees and exact accountability Distribute job descriptions with security responsibility Generate a security awareness among employees Encourage legal ownership of software and protection of copyrighted (intellectual) property Provide guidelines to protect confidentiality of data and information Establish a quality control technique for computer security function Require audits of data processing systems and operations by auditors Issue guidelines for software development and maintenance methodology focusing on computer security design	Inform the user of any unauthorized attempts to guess his password Install continuous area surveillance mechanisms Review system activity logs, journals, and exception reports to detect security violations Conduct periodic security audits Require that employees take vacations Insert dummy names and known addresses as decoys into financially related mailing lists to detect their unauthorized use Provide dummy data files for intruders to trap while reviewing the data Control program changes to ensure that only authorized changes are made	Provide periodic backup of data and programs, and rotate through offsite storage Establish system recovery/restart guidelines in applications and systems software Implement vital records retention programs

(E) Contingency planning. Exhibit 5.14 presents a summary of preventive, detective, and corrective controls as they relate to contingency planning. Implementation of these controls would help IT management in strengthening overall controls.

EXHIBIT 5.14 Contingency Planning Preventive, Detective, and Corrective Controls Summary

Preventive Controls	Detective Controls	Corrective Controls
Conduct risk analysis Establish the planning committee Prioritize application systems Revisit the data storage and retention practices Install electronic vaulting Purge data and program files periodically Issue guidelines on how to discard/dispose of used paper records, mechanical records, and electronic records Develop disaster awareness among employees Establish system recovery/restart guidelines in applications and systems software	Establish recovery organization with clearly defined responsibilities Establish recovery logging procedures Conduct disaster recovery training Conduct recovery testing Conduct periodic fire drills Maintain a problem log during plan testing	Provide periodic backup of data and programs, and rotate through offsite storage Test the disaster recovery plan Install automated job recovery software Test the emergency procedures Obtain sufficient insurance coverage Implement vital records retention programs Develop fallback systems and procedures Update the planning document Issue a report of lessons learned from testing

(F) Application Development. Exhibit 5.15 presents a summary of preventive, detective, and corrective controls as they relate to information systems acquisition, development, and maintenance. Implementation of these controls would help IT management in strengthening overall controls.

EXHIBIT 5.15 Information Systems Acquisition, Development, and Maintenance Preventive, Detective, and Corrective Controls Summary

Preventive Controls	Detective Controls	Corrective Controls
Establish a software development management (steering) committee Establish a software quality assurance function Issue software development methodology guidelines Establish a data administration and database administration function Encourage auditor and management participation and reviews Require active user participation and receiver user sign-off letters Issue guidelines for software usability, maintainability, securability, auditability, and controllability criteria Implement good project management techniques Use structured techniques for analysis, design, programming, and testing Inspect and test software independently	Practice peer reviews Use program tracing tools and techniques Practice structure walk-throughs Use automated documentation aids Practice software verification and validation techniques Use software debugging tools during testing Design data-editing and validation control routines into the software Inspect and test software independently	Design automated error correction features into applications software Produce before-and-after image (from and to) reports for correction errors during data file maintenance activities Design audit trail reports, control reports, aging reports, and exception reports for user and auditor review Use preprocessors to make programs more readable Use interactive program debugging tools Use comments in computer programs and job execution language Design checkpoint, recovery/restart procedures into the software

(G) End User Computing. Lack of adequate separation of duties is a potential control weakness in a microcomputer or minicomputer environment. Direct supervision and frequent work reviews should be conducted to balance the control weaknesses.

When uploading data to a host computer, the data conversion programs residing on the host computer should reject inaccurate or incomplete data before updating any host-resident data files. Control totals should be developed between the micro- and the host computer and reconciled automatically by the program. Uploading is one source of computer viruses, and its effects on other programs and data files are unknown.

Exhibit 5.16 presents a summary of preventive, detective, and recovery controls as they relate to small computers and end-user computing. Implementation of these controls would help IT management in strengthening overall controls.

EXHIBIT 5.16 Small Computer and End User Computing Preventive, Detective, and Corrective Controls Summary

Preventive Controls	Detective Controls	Corrective Controls
Establish a PC or microcomputer support function Issue policies, procedures, and standards Establish controls in application programs used for mini- and midrange computers (e.g., label checking, recovery procedures, batch and file balancing, audit trails) Require a user ID and a password prior to accessing the PC system Initiate a preventive maintenance program for the PCs Install program change controls for end user–developed systems Require documentation for end user–developed and maintained systems	Install physical security devices Implement logical security mechanisms Test end user–developed software	Develop control reports Develop audit trail reports Develop exception reports Develop error reports Develop activity aging reports

(H) Third-Party Services. Almost every IT department uses third-party service providers such as outsourcing. Management should be cautious about knowing what to outsource and when.

Exhibit 5.17 presents a summary of preventive, detective, and corrective controls as they relate to third-party services. Implementation of these controls would help IT management in strengthening overall controls.

EXHIBIT 5.17 Summary of Controls Related to Third-Party Services

Preventive Controls	Detective Controls	Corrective Controls
Legal contracts with right to audit clauses Nondisclosure agreements Noncompeting agreements Work proposals with clear and measurable deliverables Copyright protection awareness	Periodic review and modification of contracts Logical access and physical access security controls Time reporting Review of work products and deliverables	Periodic progress reporting Exit interviews Ad hoc or regular reports to monitor third-party vendor's work

(d) Management Control Systems

Topics such as control systems, closed control systems, open control systems, and specific management controls are discussed in this section.

(i) Control Systems Defined

All control systems contain two variables, input variable (reference value) and output variable (controlled value). Control systems are of two types, closed control systems and open control systems. The main difference is that closed systems have a feedback mechanism while open systems do not have a feedback mechanism. Hence, closed systems are much stronger, more effective, and fully complete than the open systems. In a feedback mechanism, actual output of a system is fed back to the input end (reference value) for comparison with the desired output (controlled value).

Most business control systems (e.g., paying bills to vendors by checks where a check is cleared a bank is the feedback mechanism) and engineering control systems (e.g., a thermostat to control a room temperature where the thermostat is the feedback mechanism) are examples of closed control systems due to their feedback mechanisms. Here, closed control systems provide feedback to indicate (1) whether a control has worked or not worked operationally, (2) whether a control is effective or ineffective in achieving objectives, (3) whether an error or a deviation has occurred or not occurred, and (4) whether errors and deviations were corrected or not corrected. There is no improvement in management's plans and actions without timely feedback.

(ii) Closed Control Systems

Closed control systems contain six elements to operate, including a process element, measurement element, comparison element, error element, control element, and correction element. Each element with its purpose is described below.

- **Process element** transforms inputs to outputs and sets performance standards.

- **Measurement element** observes output and sends error signals to comparison element to decide if there are errors or deviations (feedback).

- **Comparison element** is a person or device comparing inputs to measured output and sending error signals.

- **Error element** sends error or deviation signals from input to the control element.

- **Control element** decides what actions to take when it receives error or deviation signals.

- **Correction element** makes changes in the process to remove errors and deviations.

Note that the measurement element, comparison element, and error element are the basic functions of a feedback mechanism.

(iii) Open Control Systems

Open control systems contain three elements to operate, including a process element, control element, and correction element. What is missing in an open control system is the measurement element, comparison element, and error element, which are the basic functions of a feedback mechanism. An example of an open control system is an electric fireplace to heat a room where the room temperature cannot be regulated due to lack of a thermostat, which acts as a feedback mechanism.

(A) Management Controls. Management controls, in the broadest sense, include the plan of organization, methods, and procedures adopted by management to ensure that its goals and objectives are met. Management controls, also known as internal controls, include accounting and administrative controls.

Management control systems must be integrated with ongoing management practices and, where appropriate and effective, with other management initiatives, such as productivity improvement, quality improvement, business process improvement, reengineering, and performance measures and standards. Examples of management practices include periodic staff meetings, quarterly management reviews, budget planning and execution, and variance analysis.

Management control systems must be effective and efficient—balancing the costs of control mechanisms and processes with the benefits the systems are intended to provide or control. They should identify who is accountable and provide accountability for all activities.

(B) Traditional Management Controls.   Management controls include the process for planning, organizing, directing, and controlling the entity's operations. They include the management control systems for measuring, reporting, and monitoring operations. Specifically, they include automated and manual systems, policies and procedures, and other ongoing management activities that help ensure risks are managed and controlled. Internal auditing is an important part of management control.

Managerial control can be divided into feedforward and feedback controls. A feedforward control is a proactive control such as defect prevention, inspection, training, and budgeting. A feedback control is used to evaluate past activity to improve future performance. It measures actual performance against a standard to ensure that a defined result is achieved. Examples of feedback controls include surveys and variance analysis.

(C) Contemporary Management Controls.   Many new management controls have evolved over the years, including economic-value-added (EVA), market-value-added (MVA), activity-based costing (ABC), open-book management, and the balanced scorecard system.

EVA is a financial control technique that is defined as a company's net (after-tax) operating profit – the cost of capital invested in the company's tangible assets. It captures all the things a company can do to add value from its activities, such as running the business more efficiently, satisfying customers, and rewarding shareholders. Each job, department, or process in the organization is measured by the value added.

MVA measures the stock market's estimate of the value of a company's past and projected capital investment projects. For example, when a company's market value (the value of all outstanding stock plus the company's debt) is greater than all the capital invested in it from shareholders, bondholders, and retained earnings, the company has a positive MVA, an indication that it has created wealth. A positive MVA usually goes hand-in-hand with a high EVA measurement.

ABC attempts to identify all the various activities needed to provide a product or service and allocate costs accordingly. Because ABC allocates costs across business processes, it provides a more accurate picture of the cost of various products and services. In addition, it enables managers to evaluate whether more costs go to activities that add value or to activities that do not add value. They can then focus on reducing costs associated with non-value-added activities.

Open-book management first allows employees to see for themselves—through charts, computer printouts, meetings, and reports—the financial condition of the company. Second, it shows individual employees how their job fits into the big picture and affects the financial future of the organization. Finally, it ties employee rewards to the company's overall success. The goal of open-book management is to get every employee thinking like a business owner rather than like a hired hand—what money is coming in and where it is going. Open-book management helps employees appreciate why efficiency is important to the organization's success. It turns the traditional control on its head.

The **balanced scorecard system** is a comprehensive management control system that balances traditional financial measures with measures of customer service, internal business processes, and the organization's capacity for learning and growth. The financial perspective reflects a concern that the organization's activities contribute to improving short- and long-term financial performance (e.g., net income and return on investment). Customer service indicators measure such things as how customers view the organization, as well as customer retention and satisfaction. Internal business process indicators focus on production and operating statistics, such as order fulfillment or cost per order. The learning and growth indicator focuses on how well resources and human capital are being managed for the company's future. Metrics may include employee retention and the introduction of new products.

(D) Specific Management Controls.   Management controls are a part of closed control systems because management always wants feedback on their plans and actions. Management controls can be divided into several ways, such as positive controls, negative controls, feedforward controls, concurrent controls, feedback controls, proactive controls, ongoing controls, reactive controls, pre-controls, current controls, and post-controls.

Positive controls will increase the motivation levels of employees in making them sincere, honest, efficient (productive), and effective (achieving goals) in their work (e.g., bonuses, promotions, and wage increases).

Negative controls will decrease the motivation levels of employees in making them sincere, honest, efficient (productive), and effective (achieving goals) in their work (e.g., punishments, demotions, and wage decreases).

Feedforward and feedback controls are based on actions. A feedforward control is a proactive control, such as error prevention, inspection of incoming materials and products, employee training and development, and operating and capital budgeting. A feedback control is a reactive control used to detect errors and to evaluate past activity to improve future performance. It measures actual performance against a standard to ensure that a defined result is achieved. Examples of feedback controls include surveys from customers, employees, and suppliers and variance analysis from budgets.

Management controls can also be viewed through three different dimensions of timing: pre-control (proactive control), concurrent control (ongoing control), and post-control (reactive control).

> Feedforward Controls → Proactive Controls → Pre-Controls
>
> Concurrent Controls → Ongoing Controls → Current Controls
>
> Feedback Controls → Reactive Controls → Post-Controls

(e) Corporate Control Systems

Control strategies should be linked to business strategies in that controls and the control environment in an organization should facilitate the achievement of business goals and objectives. This section defines controls and classifies the controls into several ways.

(i) Definition of Controls

Control is any positive and negative action taken by management that would result in accomplishment of the organization's goals, objectives, and mission. Controls should not lead to compulsion or become a constraint on employees. Controls should be natural and should be embedded in the organizational functions and operations. More so, controls should be accepted by the employees using or affected by them. Use and implementation of controls should be inviting, not inhibiting.

Controls should be seen as beneficial from the employee's personal and professional viewpoints. Ideally, controls should facilitate the achievement of employee's and organizational goals and objectives. In other words, any control that does not help or promote in achieving the goals and objectives should not be implemented.

Controls should be effective and efficient. Controls should not cost more than the benefits derived. Controls reduce risks, but they cannot completely eliminate all risks due to their high-cost nature. Note that current controls address current risks only, as new risks always emerge, new controls are needed in a timely manner to address new risks; otherwise, new control-related problems can occur.

Examples of Controls

Examples of controls include directive controls, preventive controls, detective controls, corrective controls, recovery controls, manual controls, and computer controls. The reason so many types of controls exist is that different controls work at different times for different purposes. Note that some controls can have a combined and synergistic effect.

Business control A is effective 90% of the time and business control B is effective 90% of the time. What is the combined effect of controls A and B?

The combined effect is 99%. In combination, both controls are ineffective only 1% of the time (i.e., $0.1 \times 0.1 \times 100 = 1\%$). This means the combined controls are effective 99% of the time (i.e., $100\% - 1\%$).

(A) Classification of Controls. Controls can be classified into four major categories: management controls, accounting and administrative controls, operational controls, and internal controls. The reason for classifying controls into different categories is that different controls work best in different departments or functions.

Management controls, in the broadest sense, include the plan of organization, methods, and procedures adopted by management to ensure that its goals and objectives are met (i.e., these controls ensure goal congruence principle). Management control systems must be effective and efficient—balancing the costs of control mechanisms and processes with the benefits the systems are intended to provide or control. They should identify who is accountable and provide accountability for all activities.

Management control systems must be integrated with ongoing management practices and, where appropriate and effective, with other management initiatives, such as productivity, quality, and business process improvement; reengineering; and performance measures and standards.

Examples of Management Control Practices

Management control practices include periodic staff meetings, quarterly management reviews, budget planning and execution, and variance analysis.

Management controls include the process for planning, organizing, directing, and controlling the entity's operations. These include the management control systems for measuring, reporting, and monitoring operations—specifically, automated and manual systems, policies and procedures, rules of behavior, individual roles and responsibilities, and other ongoing management activities that help ensure risks are managed and controlled.

Accounting controls are defined in professional standards published by accounting authorities. They help ensure there is full accountability for physical assets and that all financial transactions are recorded and reported in a timely and accurate fashion.

Examples of Accounting Controls

Accounting controls include transaction accuracy and authorization controls that address checks and balances.

Administrative controls help ensure resources are safeguarded against waste, loss, fraud, abuse, and misappropriation and support the accomplishment of organization's goals and objectives.

Examples of Administrative Controls

These controls include accurate and timely management information and effective and efficient processes for planning, productivity improvement, quality control, legal and regulatory compliance, and improving economy and efficiency of operations.

Operational controls are the day-to-day procedures and mechanisms used to control operational activities. The goal is to ensure that they are carried out effectively and efficiently. They also address computer security methods focusing on mechanisms primarily implemented and executed by people and computer systems. These controls are put in place to improve the security of a particular computer system or group of systems. They often require technical or specialized expertise and often rely on management and technical controls.

Examples of Operational Controls

These controls include controls over job/machine scheduling, shipping, and billing activities; technical controls over computer systems, software, and data; and routines to maintain machinery and equipment in working order.

Internal control is a process within an organization designed to provide reasonable assurance regarding the achievement of five primary objectives:

1. The reliability and integrity of information
2. Compliance with policies, plans, procedures, laws, regulations, and contracts
3. The safeguarding of assets
4. The economical and efficient use of resources
5. The accomplishment of established objectives and goals for operations and programs

Examples of Internal Controls

Internal controls include procedural checks and balances that safeguard assets and ensure data integrity and separation of duties.

The internal control system is intertwined with an entity's operating activities and exists for fundamental business reasons. Internal controls are most effective when they are built into the entity's infrastructure and are part of the essence of the enterprise. They should be "built in" rather than "built on." "Building in" controls can directly affect an entity's ability to reach its goals and supports quality initiatives of the entity. The quest for quality is directly linked to how businesses are run.

5.18 Globally Accepted Internal Control Frameworks

Seven globally accepted internal control frameworks or models are discussed in this section:

1. The Committee of Sponsoring Organizations (COSO) of the Treadway Commission's Integrated Framework for Internal Control, which has been adopted in the United States

2. Criteria of Control (CoCo) in Canada

3. Control Self-Assessment (CSA) in the United States

4. Cadbury Report of the Committee on the Financial Aspects of Corporate Governance in the United Kingdom

5. Turnbull Model in the United Kingdom

6. King Model in South Africa

7. KonTraG Model in Germany

(a) COSO's Integrated Framework for Internal Control in the United States

The U.S. Committee of Sponsoring Organizations of the Treadway Commission (COSO) released its 2013 updated version of *Internal Control—Integrated Framework*. COSO is recognized as a leading framework for designing, implementing, and conducting internal control and assessing the effectiveness of internal control. The Framework continues to emphasize the importance of management judgment in a system of internal control, with the 2013 update enhancing and clarifying items to ease use and application. Enhanced items include (1) formalizing the old concepts as new principles, (2) expanding the reporting of nonfinancial reporting and internal reporting, and (3) reflecting changes in the business and operating environments. It provides clarity for the user in designing and implementing systems of internal control and for understanding requirements for effective internal control.[21]

The new Framework summarizes changes taking place in the business and operating environments over the past several decades, including:

- Expectations for governance oversight.

- Globalization of markets and operations.

- Changes and greater complexities of business.

- Demands and complexities in laws, rules, regulations, and standards.

- Expectations for competencies and accountabilities.

---

[21] COSO, *Internal Control–Integrated Framework*, Executive Summary, May 2013. https://na.theiia.org/standards-guidance/topics/documents/executive_summary.pdf.

- Use of and reliance on evolving technologies.

- Expectations relating to preventing and detecting fraud.

(i) Definition of Internal Control

Internal control is not a static, serial, and independent process but a dynamic and integrated process. The Framework applies to all types of entities: large-size, mid-size, small, for-profit, not-for-profit entities and government bodies. Note that a smaller entity's system of internal control may be less formal and less structured than that of a larger entity, yet it still may have effective internal control.

Internal control is defined in this way: "Internal control is a process effected by an entity's board of directors, management, and other personnel, designed to provide reasonable assurance regarding the achievement of objectives relating to operations, reporting, and compliance."

(ii) Concepts of Internal Control

This broad definition reflects five fundamental concepts.

1. Internal control is geared to the achievement of objectives in one or more categories of operations, reporting, and compliance. Every entity sets out on a mission, establishing objectives it wants to achieve and strategies for achieving them. Objectives may be set for an entity as a whole or be targeted to specific activities within the entity. Although many objectives are specific to a particular entity, some are widely shared. For example, objectives common to virtually all entities are achieving and maintaining a positive reputation within the business and consumer communities, providing reliable financial statements to stakeholders, and operating in compliance with laws and regulations.

   An internal control system can be expected to provide reasonable assurance of achieving objectives relating to the reliability of financial reporting and compliance with laws and regulations. Achievement of those objectives, which are based largely on standards imposed by external parties, depends on how activities within the entity's control are performed.

   However, achievement of operations objectives—such as a particular return on investment, market share, or entry into new product lines—is not always within the entity's control. Internal control cannot prevent bad judgment or decisions or external events that can cause a business to fail to achieve operations goals. For these objectives, the internal control system can provide reasonable assurance only that management and, in its oversight role, the board are made aware, in a timely manner, of the extent to which the entity is moving toward those objectives.

2. Internal control is a process consisting of ongoing tasks and activities, which is a means to an end, not an end in itself. Internal control is not one event or circumstance but a series of actions that permeate an entity's activities. These actions are pervasive and are inherent in the way management runs the business.

   Business processes, which are conducted within, or across, organization units or functions, are managed through the basic management processes of planning, executing, and monitoring. Internal control is a part of these processes and is integrated with them. It enables them to function and monitors their conduct and continued relevancy. Internal control is a tool used by management, not a substitute for management.

This conceptualization of internal control is very different from the perspective of some observers who view internal control as something added on to an entity's activities, or as a necessary burden, imposed by regulators or by the dictates of overzealous bureaucrats, or unnecessarily dependent on a person's attitude.

The internal control system is intertwined with an entity's operating activities and exists for fundamental business reasons. Internal controls are most effective when they are built into the entity's infrastructure and are part of the essence of the enterprise. They should be "built in" rather than "built on."

"Building in" controls can directly affect an entity's ability to reach its goals and supports quality initiatives of the entity. The quest for quality is directly linked to how businesses are run and how they are controlled.

Quality initiatives become part of the operating fabric of an enterprise, as evidenced by

□ Senior executive leadership ensuring that quality values are built into the way a company does business.

□ Establishing quality objectives linked to the entity's information collection and analysis and other processes.

□ Using the knowledge of competitive practices and customer expectations to drive continuous quality improvement.

These quality factors parallel those in effective internal control systems. In fact, not only is internal control integrated with quality programs; usually it is critical to their success.

Building in controls also has important implications in regard to cost containment and response time.

□ Most enterprises face highly competitive marketplaces and need to contain costs. Adding new procedures separate from existing ones adds costs. By focusing on existing operations and their contribution to effective internal control, and by building controls into basic operating activities, an enterprise often can avoid unnecessary procedures and costs.

□ Building controls into the fabric of operations helps trigger development of new controls necessary to new business activities. Such automatic reactions makes entities more nimble and competitive.

3. Internal control is effected by people, which means it is not merely about policy and procedure manuals, systems, and forms but about people and the actions they take at every level of an organization to effect internal control. The board of directors, management, and other personnel in an entity effect internal control. The people of an organization accomplish it by what they do and say. People establish the entity's objectives and put control mechanisms in place.

Similarly, internal control affects people's actions. Internal control recognizes that people do not always understand, communicate, or perform consistently. Each individual brings to the workplace a unique background and technical ability and has different personal needs and priorities.

The realities affect, and are affected by, internal control. People must know their responsibilities and limits of authority. Accordingly, a clear and close linkage needs to exist between people's duties and the way in which they are carried out. Such a link also must exist with the entity's objectives.

The organization's people include the board of directors, management, and other personnel. Although directors might be viewed as primarily providing oversight, they also provide direction and approve certain transactions or policies. As such, the board of directors is an important element of internal control.

4. Internal control is able to provide reasonable, but not absolute, assurance to an entity's senior management and board of directors. No matter how well designed and operated, internal control can provide only reasonable assurance to management and the board of directors regarding achievement of an entity's objectives. Limitations are inherent in all internal control systems.

These limitations include the realities that human judgment in decision making can be faulty, persons responsible for establishing controls need to consider relative costs and benefits, and breakdowns can occur because of human failures, such as simple errors or mistakes. Additionally, controls can be circumvented by collusion of two or more people. Finally, management has the ability to override the internal control system.

5. Internal control is adaptable to the entity structure. It is flexible in application for the entire entity or for a particular subsidiary, division, operating unit, or business process. It is a choice between flexible structure and rigid structure.

(iii) Objectives of Internal Control

The COSO Framework provides for three categories of objectives, which allow organizations to focus on differing aspects of internal control.

1. **Operations objectives**—Pertain to effectiveness and efficiency of the entity's operations, including operational and financial performance goals and safeguarding of assets against loss.

2. **Reporting objectives**—Pertain to internal and external financial and nonfinancial reporting and may encompass reliability, timeliness, transparency, or other terms as set forth by regulations, recognized standard setters, or the entity's policies.

3. **Compliance objectives**—Pertain to adherence to laws and regulations to which the entity is subject.

(iv) Components of Internal Control

Internal control consists of five interrelated and integrated components: control environment, risk assessment, control activities, information and communication, and monitoring activities. These components are derived from the way management runs a business and are integrated with the management processes. Each component is detailed in Exhibit 5.18.

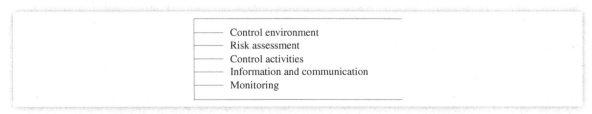

- Control environment
- Risk assessment
- Control activities
- Information and communication
- Monitoring

EXHIBIT 5.18 Five Components of Internal Control

(A) Control Environment. The control environment is the set of standards, process, and structures that provide the basis for carrying out internal control across the organization. The board of

directors and senior management establish the tone at the top regarding the importance of internal control, including expected standards of conduct. Management reinforces expectations at various levels of the organization. The control environment comprises:

- The integrity and ethical values of the organization.

- The parameters enabling the board of directors to carry out governance oversight responsibilities.

- The organizational structure and assignment of authority and responsibility.

- The process for attracting, developing, and retaining competent individuals.

- The rigor around performance measures, incentives, and rewards to drive accountability for performance.

The resulting control environment has a pervasive impact on the overall system of internal control.

(B) Risk Assessment. Every entity faces a variety of risks from external and internal sources. Risk is defined as the possibility that an event will occur and adversely affect the achievement of objectives. Risk assessment involves a dynamic and iterative process for identifying and assessing risks to the achievement of objectives. Risks to the achievements of these objectives from across the entity are considered relative to established risk tolerances. Thus, risk assessment forms the basis for determining how risks will be managed.

A precondition to risk assessment is the establishment of objectives, linked at different levels of the entity. Management specifies objectives within categories relating to operations, reporting, and compliance with sufficient clarity to be able to identify and analyze risks to those objectives. Management also considers the suitability of the objectives for the entity. Risk assessment also requires management to consider the impact of possible changes in the external environment and within its own business model that may render internal control ineffective.

Precondition   → Condition   → Postcondition
(Actions & Changes)   (Objectives)   (Risks)

(C) Control Activities. Control activities are the actions established through policies and procedures that help ensure that management's directives to mitigate risks to the achievement of objectives are carried out. Control activities are performed at all levels of the entity, at various stages within business processes, and over the technology environment. They may be preventive or detective in nature and may encompass a range of manual and automated activities, such as authorizations and approvals, verifications, reconciliations, and business performance reviews. Segregation of duties is typically built into the election and development of control activities. Where segregation of duties is not practical, management selects and develops alternative control activities.

(D) Information and Communication. Information is necessary for the entity to carry out internal control responsibilities to support the achievement of its objectives. Management obtains or generates and uses relevant and quality information from both internal and external sources to support the functioning of other components of internal control. Communication is the continual, iterative process of providing, sharing, and obtaining necessary information.

Internal communication is the means by which information is disseminated throughout the organization, flowing up, down, and across the entity. It enables personnel to receive the clear message from senior management that control responsibilities must be taken seriously. The full scope of internal communication can be upward, downward, horizontal, and diagonal.

External communication is twofold: It enables inbound communication of relevant external information, and it provides information to external parties in response to requirements and expectations. External parties include regulators, external auditors, business partners, and government authorities.

(E) Monitoring Activities. Ongoing evaluations, separate evaluations, or some combination of the two are used to ascertain whether each of the five components of internal control, including controls to effect the principles within each component, is present and functioning. Ongoing evaluations built into business processes at different levels of the entity provide timely information. Separate evaluations, conducted periodically, will vary in scope and frequency depending on assessment of risks, effectiveness of ongoing evaluations, and other management considerations. Findings are evaluated against criteria established by regulators, recognized standard-setting bodies, management, and the board of directors. Industry criteria and best practices should also be considered during the evaluation of findings. Deficiencies are communicated to management and the board of directors as appropriate.

(F) Internal Control Components and Principles. As shown next, the five components of internal control include control environment, risk assessment, control activities, information and communication, and monitoring. Each component is presented along with its major principles or concepts, resulting in a total of five components and 17 principles. All 17 principles apply to operations, reporting, and compliance objectives.

Component 1: Control Environment

1.1	Demonstrate commitment to integrity and ethical values
1.2	Exercise oversight responsibility
1.3	Establish structure, responsibility, and authority
1.4	Demonstrate commitment to competence
1.5	Enforce accountability

Component 2: Risk Assessment

2.1	Define objectives and risk tolerance
2.2	Identify, analyze, and respond to risk
2.3	Assess fraud risk
2.4	Analyze and respond to change

Component 3: Control Activities

3.1	Design control activities
3.2	Design activities for information systems
3.3	Implement control activities

Component 4: Information and Communication

4.1	Use quality information
4.2	Communicate internally
4.3	Communicate externally

Component 5: Monitoring

5.1	Perform monitoring activities
5.2	Remediate deficiency

(G) Effective Internal Control. An effective system of internal control provides reasonable assurance regarding achievement of an entity's three categories of objectives: operations, reporting, and compliance. To this end, two requirements are that each of the five components and relevant principles must be present and functioning and that all five components must operate together in an integrated manner due to their interdependence. When these requirements are met, it can be said that an effective system of internal control reduces, to an acceptable level, the risk of not achieving an entity's objectives, whether it is one, two, or three objectives. Here, only two outcomes are possible, as discussed next.

(H) Benefits from Achieving Objectives or Risk of Not Achieving Objectives. When a major deficiency exists with respect to the presence and functioning of a control component or related control principle, or with respect to the components operating together in an integrated manner, the organization cannot conclude that it has met the requirements for an effective system of internal control.

The COSO Framework requires judgment in designing, implementing, and conducting internal control and assessing its effectiveness. The use of judgment, within the boundaries established by laws, rules, regulations, and standards, enhances management's ability to make better and informed decisions about internal control but cannot guarantee perfect outcomes.

(I) Relationship of Internal Control Objectives and Components. There is a direct relationship between objectives, which are what an entity strives to achieve, and the components, which represent what is needed to achieve the objectives. Information is needed for all three objective categories—to effectively manage business operations, to prepare financial statements reliably, and to determine compliance. All five components are applicable and important to the achievement of operations objectives. Each component cuts across and applies to all three objectives categories. Examples are listed next.

- Financial and nonfinancial data generated from internal and external sources, which is part of the information and communication component, is needed to effectively manage business operations, develop reliable financial statements, and determine that the entity is complying with applicable laws.

- Also relevant to all three objectives categories is the establishment and execution of control policies and procedures to ensure that management plans, programs, and other directives are carried out—representing the control activities component.

WHAT INTERNAL CONTROLS CAN AND CANNOT DO

What Internal Controls Do

Internal control can help an entity achieve its performance and profitability targets and can prevent loss of resources. It can help ensure reliable financial reporting. And it can help ensure that the enterprise complies with laws and regulations, avoiding damage to its reputation and other consequences. In sum, it can help an entity get to where it wants to go and avoid pitfalls and surprises along the way.

What Internal Controls Cannot Do

Unfortunately, some people have unrealistic expectations. They look for absolutes, believing that internal control can ensure an entity's success—that is, it will ensure achievement of basic objectives or will, at the least, ensure survival.

Even effective internal control can only help an entity achieve these objectives. It can provide management information about the entity's progress, or lack of it, toward their achievement. But internal control cannot change an inherently poor manager into a good one. And shifts in government policy or programs, competitors' actions, or economic conditions can be beyond management's control. Internal control cannot ensure success, or even survival.

Some people also think internal control can ensure the reliability of financial reporting and compliance with laws and regulations. This belief is also unwarranted. An internal control system, no matter how well conceived and operated, can provide only reasonable—not absolute—assurance to management and the board regarding achievement of an entity's objectives. The likelihood of achievement is affected by limitations inherent in all internal control systems. These limitations include the realities that judgments in decision making can be faulty and control breakdowns can occur because of simple errors or mistakes.

Additionally, controls can be circumvented by the collusion of two or more people, and management can override the system. Another limiting factor is that the design of an internal control system must reflect the fact that there are resource constraints, and the benefits of controls must be considered relative to their costs.

Thus, while internal control can help an entity achieve its objectives, it is not a panacea.

(J) Responsibility for Internal Control. Who is responsible for establishing and ensuring an adequate and effective internal control environment within the organization? It is management, the audit committee, and the board of directors—not the auditors. Auditors are responsible for ensuring an adequate and effective system of internal control in the organization. Here the term "management" refers to senior management, operating management, and department/section management. The term "auditors" refers to both internal and external (independent) auditors. For example, company management is responsible for ensuring the adequacy of disclosures in the financial statements of a publicly held company.

According to the COSO study, everyone in an organization has responsibility for internal control: management, board of directors, internal auditors, and other personnel.

Management. The chief executive officer is ultimately responsible and should assume ownership of the system. More than any other individual, the CEO sets the tone at the top that affects integrity and ethics and other factors of a positive control environment.

In a large company, the CEO fulfills this duty by providing leadership and direction to senior managers and reviewing the way they are controlling the business. Senior managers in turn assign responsibility for establishment of more specific internal control policies and procedures to personnel responsible for the unit's functions.

In a smaller entity, the influence of the CEO, often an owner-manager, is usually more direct. In any event, in a cascading responsibility, a manager is effectively a chief executive of his or her sphere of responsibility. Of particular significance are financial officers and their staffs, whose control activities cut across, as well as up and down, the operating and other units of an enterprise.

Board of Directors. Management is accountable to the board of directors, which provides governance, guidance, and oversight. Effective board members are objective, capable, and inquisitive. They also have knowledge of the entity's activities and environment and commit the time necessary to fulfill their board responsibilities. Management may be in a position to override controls and ignore or stifle communications from subordinates, enabling a dishonest management that intentionally misrepresents results to cover its tracks.

A strong, active board, particularly when coupled with effective upward communications channels and capable financial, legal, and internal audit functions, is often best able to identify and correct such a problem.

Internal Auditors. Internal auditors play an important role in evaluating the effectiveness of a control system and contribute to its ongoing effectiveness. Because of the internal audit function's organizational position and authority in an entity, it often plays a significant monitoring role.

Other Personnel. Internal control is, to some degree, the responsibility of everyone in an organization and therefore should be an explicit or implicit part of everyone's job descriptions. Virtually all employees produce information used in the internal control system or take other actions needed to effect control. Also, all personnel should be responsible for communicating upward problems in operation, noncompliance with the code of conduct, or other policy violations or illegal actions.

A number of external parties often contribute to the achievement of an entity's objectives. External auditors, bringing an independent and objective view, contribute directly through the financial statement audit and indirectly by providing information useful to management and the board in carrying out their responsibilities. Others who provide information to the entity useful in effecting internal control are legislators and regulators, customers and others transacting business with the enterprise, financial analysts, bond raters, and the news media. External parties, however, are not responsible for, nor are they a part of, the entity's internal control system.

(K) Limitations of Internal Controls. Internal controls have limitations because they cannot prevent bad judgment, cannot prevent bad decisions, and cannot prevent external adverse events or incidents (e.g., customers boycotting a company's products due to that company's management's negative views on some social issues; increases in inflation and interest rates) that can cause an organization to fail to achieve its operational goals. In other words, even an effective system of internal control can experience a failure. In addition, people (employees) can be a weak link in the chain-of-controls due to their mistakes, carelessness, and fatigue. Management needs to understand the next limitations when selecting, designing, developing, and implementing internal control systems:

- Suitability of objectives established as a precondition to internal control

- Reality that human judgment in decision making can be faulty and subject to bias

- Breakdowns that can occur because of human failures, such as simple errors

- Ability of management to override internal control

- Ability of management, other personnel, and/or third parties (e.g., vendors and suppliers) to circumvent controls through collusion

- External adverse events beyond the organization's control (e.g., a foreign country's government seizing domestic U.S. company's assets for political reasons)

These limitations preclude the board and senior management from having absolute assurance of the achievements of the entity's objectives; in other words, internal control provides reasonable assurance but not absolute assurance.

Reasonable Assurance → Yes

Absolute Assurance → No

Factors to Be Considered When Understanding Limitations of Internal Controls. The six factors listed next need to be considered when understanding limitations of internal controls (see Exhibit 5.19).

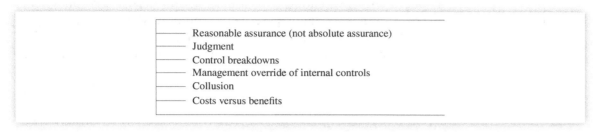

Reasonable assurance (not absolute assurance)
Judgment
Control breakdowns
Management override of internal controls
Collusion
Costs versus benefits

EXHIBIT 5.19 Factors to Be Considered When Understanding Limitations of Internal Controls

1. **Reasonable assurance.** Reasonable assurance certainly does not imply that an internal control system will fail frequently. Many factors, individually and collectively, serve to provide strength to the concept of reasonable assurance. The cumulative effect of controls that satisfy multiple objectives and the multipurpose nature of controls reduce the risk that an entity may not achieve its objectives. However, because of the inherent limitations discussed earlier, there is no guarantee that, for example, an uncontrollable event, a mistake, or an improper reporting incident could never occur. In other words, even an effective internal control system can experience a failure. *Reasonable assurance is not absolute assurance.*

2. **Judgment.** The effectiveness of controls will be limited by the realities of human frailty in the making of business decisions. Such decisions must be made with human judgment in the time available, based on information at hand, and under the pressures of the conduct of business. Some decisions based on human judgment may later, with the clairvoyance of hindsight, be found to produce less than desirable results, and may need to be changed.

    The fact that decisions related to internal control must be made based on human judgment is described further in the discussion of control breakdowns, management override, and costs versus benefits.

3. **Control breakdowns.** Even if internal controls are well designed, they can break down. Personnel may misunderstand instructions. They may make judgment mistakes. Or they may commit errors due to carelessness, distraction, or fatigue. Temporary personnel executing control duties for vacationing or sick employees might not perform correctly. System changes may be implemented before personnel have been trained to react appropriately to signs of incorrect functioning.

4. **Management override.** An internal control system can only be as effective as the people who are responsible for its functioning. Even in effectively controlled entities—those with generally high levels of integrity and control consciousness—a manager might be able to override internal control.

The term "management override" is used here to mean overruling prescribed policies or procedures for illegitimate purposes with the intent of personal gain or an enhanced presentation of an entity's financial condition or compliance status. Override practices include deliberate misrepresentations to bankers, lawyers, accountants, and vendors and intentionally issuing false documents, such as purchase orders and sales invoices.

Management override should not be confused with management intervention, which represents management's action to depart from prescribed policies or procedures for legitimate purposes. Management intervention is necessary to deal with nonrecurring and nonstandard transactions or events that otherwise might be handled inappropriately by the control system.

Provision for management intervention is necessary in all internal control systems because no system can be designed to anticipate every condition. Management's actions to intervene are generally overt and commonly documented or otherwise disclosed to appropriate personnel, whereas actions to override usually are not documented or disclosed, with an intent to cover up the actions.

Management Override versus Management Intervention

- *Management override* is departing from prescribed policies or procedures for illegitimate purposes and is not documented or disclosed.

- *Management intervention* is departing from prescribed policies or procedures for legitimate purposes and is documented or disclosed.

5. **Collusion.** The collusive activities of two or more individuals can result in control failures. Individuals acting collectively to perpetrate and conceal an action from detection often can alter financial data or other management information in a manner that cannot be identified by the control system. For example, there may be collusion between an employee performing an important control function and a customer, supplier, or another employee. On a different level, several layers of sales or divisional management might collude in circumventing controls so that reported results meet budgets or incentive targets.

6. **Costs versus benefits.** Resources always have constraints, and entities must consider the relative costs and benefits of establishing controls. In determining whether a particular control should be established, the risk of failure and the potential effect on the entity are considered along with the related costs of establishing a new control.

Cost and benefit measurements for implementing controls are done with different levels of precision. Generally, it is easier to deal with the cost side of the equation, which in many cases can be quantified in a fairly precise manner. The benefit side often requires an even more subjective valuation. Nevertheless, certain factors can be considered in assessing potential benefits: the likelihood of the undesired condition occurring, the nature of the activities, and the potential financial or operating effect the event might have on the entity.

The complexity of cost-benefit determination is compounded by the interrelationship of controls with business operations. Where controls are integrated with, or "built into," management and business processes, it is difficult to isolate either their costs or benefits.

Similarly, many times a variety of controls may serve, individually or together, to mitigate a particular risk. Cost-benefit determinations also vary considerably depending on the nature of the business. High-risk activities definitely require cost-benefit analysis while low-risk activities might not.

The challenge is to find the right balance. Excessive control is costly and counterproductive. For example, customers making telephone orders will not tolerate order acceptance procedures that are too cumbersome or time-consuming. Too little control, however, presents undue risk of bad debts. An appropriate balance is needed in a highly competitive environment. And, despite the difficulties, cost-benefit decisions will continue to be made.

Three Lines of Defense Model. Authors Douglas Anderson and Gina Eubanks make a strong case for using the Three Lines of Defense (LOD) model, which addresses how specific duties related to risk and control should be assigned and coordinated.[22]

The benefits of clearly defining responsibilities related to governance, risks, and control are that gaps in controls and duplication of duties related to risk and control are minimized. Succinctly, the Three LOD model advocates for clearly defined responsibilities for three aspects of risk: risk ownership, risk monitoring, and risk assurance.

Risk ownership is the first line of defense and deals with functions that own and manage risks.

Risk monitoring is the second line of defense and deals with various risk control and compliance functions that monitor risks.

Risk assurance is the third line of defense and deals with internal audit, which provides independent assurance on the effectiveness of control and compliance functions.

Exhibit 5.20 provides a summary of COSO's Three LOD model.

EXHIBIT 5.20

Risk Category	First LOD	Second LOD	Third LOD
Risk ownership—Creates and manages the risks and takes the right risks	Focuses on management controls and internal control measures. Involves front-line managers, midlevel managers, process owners, and business owners.		*(continued)*

[22] Douglas J. Anderson and Gina Eubanks, "Leveraging COSO Across the Three Lines of Defense," Institute of Internal Auditors and COSO, July 2015, www.theiia.org.

EXHIBIT 5.20 *(Continued)*

Risk Category	First LOD	Second LOD	Third LOD
Risk monitoring—Provides management and/or oversight functions		Involves support functions, such as financial control; physical and information security; risk management; quality; health and safety; inspection; compliance; legal; environmental; and supply chain.	
Risk assurance—Provides assurance to senior management and the board over the first and second LOD efforts			Involves internal auditors who do not perform management functions to protect their objectivity and independence. Internal auditors have a primary reporting line to the board. Regulatory auditors, external auditors, quality auditors, tax auditors, environmental auditors, and other outside auditors or entities are not involved.

(b) CoCo Model in Canada

The Canadian Institute of Chartered Accountants has issued 20 "criteria of control" (CoCo) as a framework for making judgments about control. The term "control" has a broader meaning than internal control over financial reporting. CoCo defines control as "those elements of an organization (including its resources, systems, processes, culture, structure, and tasks) that, taken together, support people in the achievement of the organization's objectives." It defines three categories of objectives:

1. Effectiveness and efficiency of operations
2. Reliability of internal external reporting
3. Compliance with applicable laws, regulations, and internal policies

CoCo is the basis for understanding control in an organization and for making judgments about the effectiveness of control. The criteria are formulated to be broadly applicable. The effectiveness of control in any organization, regardless of the objective it serves, can be assessed using these criteria. The criteria are phrased as goals to be worked toward over time; they are not minimum requirements to be passed or failed.

CoCo defines four types of criteria: purpose, commitment, capability, and monitoring and learning. The **purpose** type groups criteria that provide a sense of the organization's direction and address objectives (including mission, vision, and strategy); risks (and opportunities); policies; planning; and performance targets and indicators. The **commitment** type groups criteria that provide a sense of the organization's identity and values and address ethical values, including integrity, human resource policies, authority, responsibility, accountability, and mutual trust. The **capability** type groups criteria that provide a sense of the organization's competence and address knowledge, skills, and tools; communication processes; information; coordination; and control activities. The **monitoring and learning** type groups criteria that provide a sense of the organization's evolution and address monitoring the internal and external environment, monitoring performance, challenging assumptions, reassessing information needs and information systems, follow-up procedures, and assessing the effectiveness of control.

(c) Control Self-Assessment Model in the United States

Control self-assessment (CSA) deals with evaluating the system of internal control in any organization. CSA is a shared responsibility among all employees in the organization, not just internal auditing or senior management. The examination of the internal control environment is conducted within a structured, documented, and repetitive process. The formal assessment approach takes place in workshop sessions with business users as participants (process owners) and internal auditors as facilitators (subject matter experts) and as nonfacilitators (note takers). The purpose of the sessions is conversation, mutual discovery, and information sharing.

(i) Audit-Facilitated Approach to CSA

Two types of people conduct internal audit engagements: internal auditors and non-internal auditors. Auditors conducting audit engagements are based on an audit plan and include assurance audits, consulting audits, and compliance audits.

Nonauditors performing audit-related work include self-assessments of risks and controls, which are proactive in nature, meaning nonauditors are reviewing, assessing, and evaluating their own work. These self-assessments, although not traditional audits, are conducted by audit clients (a business unit's functional employees and managers), consultants, and process owners where the latter are a part of audit clients.

Self-assessments mean self-reviews, self-examinations, self-tests, self-evaluations, self-rating, self-ranking, self-grading, self-certifications, and self-reporting of a business function, department, operation, process, or system, which are conducted by nonauditors after they are trained and are facilitated by internal auditors, using questionnaires, templates, and checklists. Note that internal auditors do not prepare or develop the questionnaires; do not conduct the self-assessments; and do not write the self-assessment reports. Instead, nonauditors perform these tasks. Here, internal auditors act as facilitators of self-assessments; they do not act as regular auditors.

There are obvious **benefits** to audit clients and internal auditors from these self-assessments. Benefits to audit clients include (1) identifying strengths and weaknesses in their business functions, (2) establishing controls to minimize significant risks, and (3) promoting as an exercise of risk awareness and control consciousness. Benefits to internal auditors are that the self-assessments can reduce the overall scope of an audit to some extent and can increase audit efficiency to some extent due to time and effort saved from prior work done by the audit clients during the self-assessments.

Four **participants** in the self-assessments exercise have specific roles:

1. Audit client employees, supervisors, and consultants conduct self-assessments.

2. Process owners perform self-evaluations.

3. Audit client managers issue self-certifications, similar to the CEO and CFO, certifying their company's financial statements.

4. Internal auditors act as trainers, facilitators, and subject matter experts on risk and control matters, including as note takers (nonfacilitators) during training classes and workshops given to audit clients. Note that the original audit clients who were trained by internal auditors can later train other employees (i.e., train the trainer) either in the same department or in other departments. These specific roles are briefly presented next.

   Audit clients conduct self-assessments (i.e., client-facilitated).

   Process owners perform self-evaluations (i.e., client-facilitated).

   Audit client managers issue self-certifications (i.e., client-facilitated).

   Auditors act as trainers, facilitators, subject matter experts, and note takers during training classes and workshops. Later they review and use the self-assessment results only after independent validations and verifications (audit-facilitated).

Auditors should use professional skepticism and professional judgment when reviewing, understanding, and using the results of self-assessments prepared by audit clients due to audit clients' built-in bias of reviewing and evaluating their own work (i.e., a strong motive to look good). When audit clients conduct risk and control self-assessments, two outcomes are possible because they have little or no experience in conducting such assessments: false positive results and false negative results. A **false positive result** can occur when a business activity or control is rated as effective when it is ineffective. A **false negative result** can occur when a business activity or control is rated as ineffective when it is effective. Internal auditors need to understand the reasons for these ratings of effective or ineffective and proceed with caution.

(ii) Elements of CSA
CSA has five elements:

1. Up-front planning and preliminary audit work

2. Process owners gathering with a meeting facilitator

3. A structured agenda to examine risks and controls of the process

4. A note taker and electronic voting technology to input comments and opinions

5. Reporting the results and the development of corrective action plans

(iii) Scope of CSA
CSA can be done either as a stand-alone project or as a supplement to traditional audit work. CSA is not suitable to finding fraud or in compliance reviews (e.g., regulatory audits, or when participants have conflicting objectives, as in third-party contracts. However, CSA can be utilized in numerous situations, business issues, and industries, regardless of size. It is a management

tool that has equal application to horizontal (organization-wide), vertical (single department), and diagonal (process inquiries) issues.

(iv) Effect on Auditors

CSA can be used to assess business and financial statement risks, control activities, ethical values, and control effectiveness; the controls that mitigate those risks; and overall compliance with policies and procedures.

During the assessment process, there is a constant interactive dialogue between auditor and auditee as well as between auditees. This interaction increases communication and builds trust and confidence between each party. At the same time, it is educational to both parties because there is a knowledge transfer between auditor and auditee. Auditors gain a greater knowledge of business functions while auditees gain a better understanding of and appreciation for controls and the business process of which they are a part.

The increased communication and the knowledge transfer adds value to the organization in the following ways:

- Auditors accomplish control assessment.
- Auditees understand the purpose of controls.
- Management takes responsibility for the development and maintenance of the control environment.
- Process improvement issues are identified and resolved (i.e., implemented or deferred).

(v) Interrelationships between CSA, CoCo, and COSO

CSA can be an effective tool for accomplishing the objectives of both CoCo and COSO. CSA acts as a link to the CoCo and COSO.

The CSA audit can address the four elements of the CoCo framework: purpose, commitment, capability, and monitoring and learning. Both commitment and capability are examples of soft controls (e.g, risk assessment, the achievement of business objectives and goals, and the attitude of people toward controls).

(vi) Conclusion

CSA is a dynamic business process improvement and control-enhancing technique. In relation to internal auditing, CSA is like total quality management and continuous process improvement techniques in relation to other parts of the organization. The only difference is how the CSA program is implemented in each organization, but the benefits are real and long lasting.

(d) Cadbury Report in the United Kingdom

The Cadbury Report of the Committee on the Financial Aspects of Corporate Governance issued in December 1992 consists of internal controls, fraud, audit (internal and external), financial reporting practices, audit committees, shareholders, corporate governance, the board of directors, and the code of best practice.

Regarding internal controls, the report says that directors maintain a system of internal control over the financial management of the company, including procedures designed to minimize the risk of fraud. The directors should make a statement in the report and accounts on the effectiveness of their system of internal control and the auditors should report thereon.

Regarding fraud, the report says that prime responsibility for the prevention and detection of fraud and other illegal acts is that of the board, as part of its fiduciary responsibility for protecting the assets of the company. The auditor's responsibility is to properly plan, perform, and evaluate his or her audit work so as to have a reasonable expectation of detecting material misstatements in the financial statements.

Regarding the internal audit, the report states that the function of the internal auditors is complementary to, but different from, that of the external (outside) auditors. The committee regards the internal audit as good practice for companies to establish internal audit function to undertake regular monitoring of key controls and procedures. Such regular monitoring is an integral part of a company's system of internal control and helps to ensure its effectiveness. An internal audit function is well placed to undertake investigations on behalf of the audit committee and to follow up any suspicion of fraud. It is essential that heads of internal audit should have unrestricted access to the chairman of the audit committee in order to ensure the independence of their position.

Regarding the external audit, the report says that an essential first step is to be clear about the respective responsibilities of directors and external auditors for preparing and reporting on the financial statements of companies, in order to begin to narrow the "expectation gap." This gap is due to lack of understanding of the nature and extent of the external auditors' role. The gap is the difference between what audits do achieve and what it is thought they achieve or should achieve. The expectations gap is damaging not only because it reflects unrealistic expectations of audits but also because it has led to disenchantment with the value of audits to the various interested parties.

The external auditors' role is to report whether the financial statements give a true and fair view, and the audit is designed to provide a reasonable assurance that the financial statements are free of material misstatements. The auditors' role is not (to cite a few of the misunderstandings) to prepare the financial statements, or to provide absolute assurance that the figures in the financial statements are correct, or to provide a guarantee that the company will continue to exist.

(e) Turnbull Model in the United Kingdom

In 1998, the London Stock Exchange developed a Combined Code for Corporate Governance. The code requires that company directors should, at least annually, conduct a review of the effectiveness of the system of internal control and report to shareholders that they have reviewed the effectiveness of all three types of controls: financial, operational, and compliance control.

(f) King Model in South Africa

The Institute of Directors in South Africa has established the King Committee on Corporate Governance that produced the King Report in 1994. The committee has developed a Code of Corporate Practices and Conduct, and compliance with the code is a requirement to be listed in the Johannesburg stock exchange (JSE) Securities Exchange in South Africa.

(g) KonTraG Model in Germany

In 1998, the German government proposed changes for the reform of corporate governance. The model affects control and transparency in business. Specifically, it impacts the board of directors, supervisory board, corporate capitalization principles, authorization of no-par-value shares, small non-listed stock corporations, banks investing in industrial companies, and the acceptance of internationally recognized accounting standards.

5.19 Effectiveness and Efficiency of Internal Controls

This section focuses on examining the adequacy, effectiveness, and efficiency of internal controls after defining various terms.

(a) Control Defined

Control is any action, either positive or negative, taken by management, the board, and other parties to manage risks and the increase the likelihood that established objectives and goals will be achieved. Management plans, organizes, and directs the performance of sufficient actions to provide reasonable assurance that objectives and goals will be achieved. Thus, control is the result of proper planning, organizing, and directing by management. The control environment includes six elements:

1. Integrity and ethics values
2. Management's philosophy and operating style
3. Organizational structure
4. Assignment of authority and responsibility
5. Human resource policies and practices
6. Competence of personnel

(b) Internal Control Defined

Internal control is defined as a process used by an organization's management to help achieve its business objectives, such as: (1) run its operations effectively and efficiently (i.e., operations); (2) report reliable information about its operations for internal and external use (i.e., reporting); and (3) comply with all applicable laws, rules, and regulations (i.e., compliance). Organizations design, implement, and operate internal controls to achieve their objectives related to operations, reporting, and compliance, as shown:

Objectives Identified → Controls Designed → Controls Established → Objectives Achieved

Internal controls represent management's specific plans, programs, projects, and activities, which are then embedded and built into an organization's policies, operating procedures, business practices, manual systems, and automated systems operating in core business functions, such as operations, marketing, and finance. Internal controls are also built into activities of business partners, outsourced partners, and third-party entities through written contracts. Internal controls safeguard assets (physical and nonphysical), protect people (employees and nonemployees), and secure vital data and information. In simple terms, internal controls can come across as lists of do's and don'ts and very complicated language in contracts.

(c) Internal Control System

An **internal control system** is a continuous built-in component of operations, effected by people, that provides reasonable,, not absolute, assurance that an organization's objectives will be achieved. Here, "people" means:

1. Board of directors with oversight responsibilities regarding overseeing management's design, implementation, and operation of an internal control system.

2. Management with its strategic, tactical, and operational responsibilities, specifically in the design, implementation, and operating effectiveness of an internal control system.

3. Employees with their day-to-day work activities and job responsibilities, specifically helping management in the design, implementation, and operating an internal control system and in reporting issues related to internal controls.

4. Auditors and compliance officers with their responsibilities in reviewing and evaluating the effectiveness and efficiency of internal controls.

The systems of control exist to ensure the achievement of intended results, to promote operating efficiency, and to encourage compliance with policies and other established constraints. Although internal auditors have a definite interest in verifying the results of business activity, their primary concern must be the continuing effectiveness of the systems of control that influence business results.

The important qualities that must be evaluated are adequacy, effectiveness, and efficiency. It is not intended that the auditor should evaluate adequacy or effectiveness in absolute terms, nor is it intended that the auditor judge efficiency in absolute terms.

(d) Adequate Internal Controls

In evaluating adequacy, the auditor analyzes systems to determine whether they include design features proper to the circumstances and reasonably sufficient to effect control. The evaluation of adequacy begins by the comparison of "what should be" to "what is." Initial audits and audits of proposed procedures or organization structures focus primarily on the adequacy of control.

The systems of control must detect and correct errors and irregularities when preventive controls fail. Sound systems of control contain safeguards that counteract failures in other controls.

The features of the control system that encourage compliance with these requirements include the separation of duties, the employment of persons likely to comply, the establishment of authority limits, and the communication of expected conduct.

(e) Effective Internal Controls

In general, **effectiveness** is the degree to which an organization achieves a stated goal or objective. Effective control is present when management directs systems and people in such a manner as to provide a reasonable assurance that the organization's objectives and goals are achieved.

In evaluating effectiveness, the auditor measures the degree of compliance with control features and the extent to which compliance serves the intended purposes. The question that must be answered is: "Do the controls work?"

Internal controls are **effective** when:

- People (employees) are effective because it is people who plan, design, develop, and implement internal controls.

- Standards for internal control are established to provide criteria for assessing the design, implementation, and operational effectiveness of internal controls and internal control systems.

- There is an audit plan that is flexible to accommodate the changes in management strategies, external conditions, and risks. Gaps in audit coverage can be determined as shown:

  Audit Plan = Planned Audit Coverage

  Audit Coverage Gap = Planned Audit Coverage − Actual Audit Coverage

- The CAE forms an overall opinion about the adequacy and effectiveness of the control processes. The expression of such an opinion is based on sufficient audit evidence obtained through the completion of internal audits and, where appropriate, reliance on the work of other assurance providers (e.g., bank examiners, compliance auditors, and external auditors) as well as on management's self-assessments.

- Specific roles in an internal control system are well defined, meaning that everyone in the organization has a responsibility for internal control. These roles include the board of directors, management at all levels, and employees at all levels. However, internal auditors, external auditors, regulatory auditors, and compliance officers are not considered part of an organization's internal control system because management has the responsibility for internal control systems.

- An internal audit function maintains an effective system of internal controls on its outsourced audit function because internal controls cannot be delegated to a third party. Under these circumstances, the audit committee and CAE should provide active and effective oversight of outsourced auditors, including staffing levels and their talent levels.

- A risk and control matrix shows how controls are used to manage risks and whether controls are effective or ineffective. Control-related information is gathered and controls are designed and tested as shown:

  Gather Information → Interviews, Reviews, Walkthroughs, and Flowcharts

  Control Design and Test → Inspections, Confirmations, Continuous Auditing, and Data Analytics

The existence of significant control discrepancies or control weaknesses does not necessarily mean all the entire control processes are weak and bad. In fact, the nature and extent of risk exposure and the level of potential consequences determine whether the effectiveness of the control processes are jeopardized and unacceptable risks exist.

(f) Efficient Internal Controls

In general, **efficiency** is the use of minimal resources, such as raw materials, machinery, energy, money, and people, to provide a desired volume of output or outcome. Efficiency is related to performance and productivity in that efficient performance accomplishes objectives and goals in an accurate and timely fashion with minimal use of resources. In contrast, economical performance accomplishes objectives and goals at a cost commensurate with the risk.

The systems of control should promote operational efficiency. The features of control systems that promote operational efficiency include the processes used to select and train personnel, establish procedures, set performance requirements, measure results, and provide incentives. Managerial policies, laws, and regulations and sound fiduciary principles establish bounds within which the organization can conduct its business.

In evaluating efficiency, the auditor judges the practicality of controls in terms of their costs relative to their intended benefits. An internal auditor's evaluation of efficiency is restricted to the controls themselves; it does not extend to measures of operating performance associated with the functioning of such controls. In judging efficiency, the internal auditor must decide whether the benefits provided by the controls exceed their cost.

Internal controls are **efficient** when:

- Costs related to controls do not exceed their corresponding benefits.
- A risk and control map is used to document the relationship between risks and controls and to determine their efficiency. Possible outcomes could be:
  - Some high risks are undercontrolled.
  - Some low risks are overcontrolled.
  - Some risks are not controlled at all.
  - Some controls do not address any risks.
  - Some controls are not needed.
- Controls are designed in such a manner that they do not prevent threats and vulnerabilities and that they do not protect business features and functions, resulting in a waste of resources. Possible outcomes between control design and control operations could be that some weak controls are overdesigned and some strong controls are underdesigned.
- Controls are established with control simplicity and control strength in mind, which may result in some simple controls being overcomplicated and some complex controls being oversimplified.
- Employees are doing more work with less resources, meaning their productivity rate increases.

(g) Issues in Internal Controls

Three major issues in internal controls are presented next.

1. People are the major limiting factor or roadblock in ensuring the adequacy, effectiveness, and efficiency of internal controls because:
   a. The behavior of people is unexpected or unpredictable.
   b. People design and develop products and services.
   c. People establish processes, policies, and procedures.

   d. People evaluate the adequacy, effectiveness, and efficiency of internal controls.

   e. People have built-in strengths and weaknesses.

2. Internal controls can be overridden or manipulated, thus hurting an organization financially, operationally, and strategically.

3. Retrofitting a weak internal control system costs excessive amounts of money due to replanning, redesigning, redeveloping, retesting, and reimplementing the retrofitted controls.

5.20 Compliance Management

This section discusses roles and responsibilities of regulators and compliance managers. A compliance management audit program is presented along with compliance and noncompliance costs, and the effects of regulation and deregulation are highlighted.

(a) Roles of Regulators and Compliance Managers

The roles of government regulators and the compliance managers at the organizations affected by regulations are different and opposite; regulators issue laws, rules, and regulations (LRRs) while compliance managers implement those LRRs. Various governmental authorities (regulators) at local, state, and federal levels pass LRRs to control the conduct of business organizations for the good of the society and to collect tax revenues for proper functioning of government. The government needs these tax revenues to provide services to citizens and businesses. Corporate management can get a reasonable assurance about compliance with LRRs through compliance audits. The government has the constitutional power and the legal right to fine and punish business organizations for failing to comply with required LRRs.

To fulfill their roles, government regulators can perform retrospective analysis and flexibility analysis while compliance managers can conduct barrier analysis and cost-benefit analysis.

$$\text{Regulatory Analysis} = \text{Retrospective Analysis} + \text{Flexibility Analysis}$$
$$+ \text{Barrier Analysis} + \text{Cost-Benefit Analysis}$$

$$\text{Regulators} = \text{Retrospective Analysis} + \text{Flexibility Analysis}$$

$$\text{Compliance Managers} = \text{Barrier Analysis} + \text{Cost-Benefit Analysis}$$

(b) Retrospective Analysis

Retrospective analysis requires government regulators to modify, streamline, reduce, or repeal existing and significant LRRs periodically. The purpose is to reduce the existing regulatory burden (excessive costs and unreasonable times) on affected organizations and to promote economic growth and job creation in a country. Regulators are required to quantify burden costs and cost reductions resulting from the retrospective analysis.

The need for retrospective analysis makes sense when regulators consider the number of LRRs already issued, how sometimes new LRRs were released, or how old LRRs were amended in a rush due to difficult political environments and lobbyist pressures.

(c) Flexibility Analysis

Regulators at all levels of government can perform a **flexibility analysis** prior to releasing a new rule, regulation, act, circular, executive order, directive, ordinance, or guidelines to determine whether the proposed guideline is flexible or rigid for businesses to implement and the public to obey. To do so, regulators must do an in-depth, systematic, and thorough analysis to avoid unintended, negative consequences. Possible questions that regulators can ask themselves include:

- Does this new rule, regulation, or act look like a one-size-fits-all effort? Are there different sizes to fit different people? Providing choices, options, and alternatives, combined with doing sensitivity analysis (what-if analysis) can answer these questions. An example of what-if analysis is: If condition A1 occurs, then implement the X1 to X5 guidelines.

- Is this new rule, regulation, or act complex, confusing, fragmented, contradictory, duplicative, or overlapping with existing rules, regulations, or acts?

- Does this new rule, regulation, or act fall under one jurisdiction (i.e., one court) or under multiple jurisdictions (i.e., more than one court)? Handling in one jurisdiction is much simpler and easier than handling in multiple jurisdictions because multiple jurisdictions add complexity to the judicial system.

- Is this new rule, regulation, or act cost-effective and time-consuming?

- Is this new rule, regulation, or act safe and secure to citizens?

- Is this new rule, regulation, or act providing a real or imaginary benefit? Are the benefits achieved at the end the same as at the beginning?

(d) Barrier Analysis

Barrier analysis identifies the roadblocks that were placed or will be placed when planning, implementing, and changing some important activity in an organization. Specifically, this analysis can ask questions, such as what is standing in the way of implementing and complying with a new law, rule, or regulation.

Barrier analysis can be divided into major or minor factors and external or internal sources of data used in the analysis. Major factors that can impede the implementation of a new LRR include huge amounts of capital investment required, hiring a new support staff, developing new computer systems for implementing and monitoring the system's performance, and training the workforce. Minor factors can include day-to-day coordination of work activities and reporting to regulatory authorities on a scheduled basis. Examples of external sources include:

- Availability and quality of suppliers/vendors in procuring required ingredients, raw materials, parts, and components.

- Economic conditions in a country, such as interest rates, inflation rates, and wage rates.

- The nature and scope of competitors' actions or inactions.

Examples of internal sources include old policies, old procedures, old standards, old cultures, and old mind-sets.

(e) Cost-Benefit Analysis

The **cost-benefit analysis** (CBA) or benefit-cost analysis is used for many purposes, such as a planning tool, a decision-making criterion, and a means to evaluate investments. The CBA has four major elements that should be factored in for consideration:

1. Total business and system costs with the IT investment in a new system

2. Total business costs without the IT investment in a new system

3. Tangible benefits (e.g., decrease in labor cost, production materials cost, overhead costs, inventory cost, development cost, and implementation cost)

4. Intangible benefits (e.g., increased employee morale, increased management supervision and control, and increased goodwill, reputation, and value)

Note that costs and benefits could be one-time or recurring.

Many advantages to performing a CBA reach far beyond its ability to facilitate ultimate decision-making processes. A comprehensive CBA will include a documented path that clearly reveals the rationale behind a decision. When a CBA is performed correctly, all assumptions, theories, methods, and procedures are labeled and can be easily extracted from the decision or traced to the decision itself. This allows for the modification or clarification of any individual elements throughout the life of the project.

The CBA itself is structured as a systematic and organized collection of facts underlying a decision being made about a particular set of alternatives. It ensures that there is a standardization and objectivity in the decision-making process. The CBA is a particularly accommodating tool when evaluating seemingly noncomparable alternatives or solutions.

(f) Compliance Management Audit Program

The key concern when conducting a compliance management audit is the cost of noncompliance (e.g., fines, penalties, imprisonment, and fees) and not so much of cost of compliance (e.g., cost of implementation, cost of training, and cost of reporting). This is because reputation of a company depends on noncompliance with the laws, rules, and regulations and the cost of noncompliance. The higher the noncompliance rate is, the higher the noncompliance costs, and the greater the reputation costs (or the greater the loss of reputation).

The compliance audit management program requires a three-step process:

1. Understand relevant laws, rules, and regulations.

2. Test compliance with laws, rules, and regulations.

3. Develop action plans to comply with laws, rules, and regulations.

The compliance audit can be performed by functional business analysts, independent consultants, contractors, or internal/external auditors. Based on the audit report, management should develop action plans showing the timetables and resources required to conform to the missed laws, rules, and regulations. A checklist describing who should do what and when would help management in implementing action plans.

An example of using an internal control questionnaire to determine compliance with the Foreign Corrupt Practices Act of 1977 is presented next.

1. Has the organization adopted written policies that prohibit the offering or payment of improper or illegal payments, bribes, kickbacks, or loans to or from foreign government officials? The same question holds true for officials of a foreign government instrumentality; a foreign political party; a foreign party official; a candidate for foreign political office; or a person whom the organization's employee believes will give such money to those foreign officials.

2. Has the policy been communicated to all employees of the organization?

3. If an allowable payment is made, did the organization properly record the transaction without trying to conceal the activity?

4. Does the allowable payment consist only of a payment made to expedite or secure the performance of a routine governmental action by a foreign official, foreign political party, or foreign party official?

(g) Compliance Costs and Benefits

Corporate management says it costs a significant amount of resources to comply with the often confusing and duplicating laws, rules, and regulations in terms of record-keeping and monitoring activities. Management does not readily see a direct and positive benefit from compliance. Yet regulators say these laws, rules, and regulations are developed with a purpose for the benefit of the entire society. Regulators say that the cost of compliance should be treated as a cost of doing business. This is a never-ending debate, but in the end, the government wins due to its constitutional power. A trade-off analysis should be performed between the cost of compliance and noncompliance.

(i) Total Cost of Compliance
The **total cost of compliance** is both compliance costs and noncompliance costs.

Compliance costs are a combination of these costs:

- Planning costs

- New equipment, installation, software, and hardware costs

- Hiring costs

- Training costs

- Subject matter expert consulting costs

- Collecting and compiling compliance data

- Implementation costs

- Reporting costs

- Continuous monitoring costs

- Overall administrative and management costs for supervision and follow-up efforts

Noncompliance costs are a combination of these costs:

- Government fines and penalties
- Legal fees
- Court costs
- Case preparation costs
- Legal expert consulting fees
- Nonquantified loss of image and reputation costs resulting from negative publicity in news media and public's rejection of purchase and use of the affected company's products and services
- In a way, noncompliance costs are data evidence costs, meaning data was shown to regulatory authorities as a proof-of-evidence when regulators allege organizations for noncompliance with laws and regulations.

(ii) Decision Criteria for Compliance

Business organizations might be implicitly or explicitly using the following decision criteria when deciding to fully comply with the government-specific LRRs:

- Compliance is favored when the cost of noncompliance is higher than the cost of compliance.
- Compliance is not favored when the cost of noncompliance is lower than the cost of compliance.

(iii) Regulation versus Deregulation

In general, government regulations affect at least two parties, such as businesses and consumers (society), in terms of costs and benefits of different amounts. Businesses can incur additional expenses for compliance with new regulations. If the same, new regulation is removed, repealed, or canceled (i.e., deregulation), the same businesses would not incur the additional expenses. For example, when a government deregulates certain environmental laws, businesses benefit financially from not having to comply and costs to consumers increase in terms of polluted air and water and damaged health. Generally speaking, this relationship holds true for regulation and deregulation:

Regulation = More costs to businesses and more benefits to consumers

Deregulation = Fewer costs to businesses and fewer benefits to consumers

(iv) Assessment Rating for Compliance Process

It is always good to comply 100% with a specific rule, regulation, or act to realize its intended benefits. Both regulators and compliance managers at affected organizations can develop a rating system to assess the degree of compliance with a specific rule, regulation, or act. This is because there may be a very few companies with a rating system of "not met" (0% compliance) or "fully met" (100% compliance); and most companies could fall in between 0% and 100%. This systematic rating can help the court system to decide the amounts of fines and penalties to charge and the affected organizations to estimate the amount of work to complete. The systematic rating system is briefly discussed next.

> **Not met**—The affected organization did not provide any evidence to regulatory auditors to satisfy them that any portion of the new rule, regulation, or act is implemented and in operation. The compliance rating is 0% compliance.

Minimally met—The affected organization provided some evidence to regulatory auditors to satisfy them that a small portion of the new rule, regulation, or act was implemented and in operation. The compliance rating is approximated to 25% compliance.

Partially met—The affected organization provided a large amount of some evidence to regulatory auditors to satisfy them that about half of the new rule, regulation, or act was implemented and in operation. The compliance rating is approximated to 50% compliance.

Substantially met—The affected organization provided some evidence to regulatory auditors to satisfy them that a large portion of the new rule, regulation, or act was implemented and in operation. The compliance rating is approximated to 75% compliance.

Fully met—The affected organization provided full and complete evidence to regulatory auditors to satisfy them that the entire new rule, regulation, or act was fully implemented and in operation. The compliance rating is 100%.

5.21 Sample Practice Questions

In the actual CIA Exam for Part 1, 125 multiple-choice (M/C) test questions appear. This book contain 125 M/C sample practice questions divided into syllabus-based domains using the approximate domain weight given in the exam. These questions are added at the end of each applicable domain of this book with the sole purpose of showing the flavor and structure of the exam questions and of creating a self-quiz experience. The answers and explanations for these questions are shown in a separate section at the end of this book. This separate section is titled "Sample Practice Questions, Answers, and Explanations." If CIA Exam candidates need to practice more sample questions to obtain a higher level of confidence, Wiley offers a separate online test bank software product with hundreds of similar sample practice questions.

1. Internal controls are:
   a. Open systems.
   b. Closed systems.
   c. Standalone systems.
   d. Ad hoc systems.

2. Regarding compliance management, compliance costs are **not**:
   a. Data collection costs.
   b. Data analysis costs.
   c. Data reporting costs.
   d. Data evidence costs.

3. Regarding corporate social responsibility, which of the following should be the ultimate goal of corporations?
   a. Social goal
   b. Environmental goal
   c. Sustainability goal
   d. Philanthropic goal

4. Regarding risk management, derisking does **not** mean:
   a. Risk elimination.
   b. Risk mitigation.
   c. Risk management.
   d. Risk-return balancing.

5. Control self-assessments are done better when they are:
   a. Auditor controlled.
   b. Auditor facilitated.
   c. Auditor planned.
   d. Auditor designed.

6. Which of the following establishes a corporation's governance mechanism?
   a. Stockholders
   b. Corporate bylaws
   c. Board of directors
   d. Corporate officers

7. A corporation must be managed on which of the following principles?
   a. Corporate governance
   b. Corporate control
   c. Corporate law
   d. Corporate ethics

8. The major issue embedded in the structure of modern corporations that has contributed to the corporate governance problem has been:
   a. Separation of purchase from lease.
   b. Separation of suppliers from producers.
   c. Separation of ownership from control.
   d. Separation of employees from independent contractors.

9. Which of the following is the major reason for agency problems to exist?
   a. Owner interest
   b. Self-interest
   c. Community interest
   d. Corporate interest

10. The practice of obtaining critical information from a company in good faith and then using that information for one's own personal financial gain is called:

a. Financial trading.

b. Insider trading.

c. Shareholder trading.

d. Investor trading.

11. Which of the following is **not** an example of ethical dilemma facing a business manager involving a conflict between the:

a. Part versus whole.

b. Individual versus organization.

c. Organization versus society.

d. Individual versus family.

12. Abusive acts can be:

a. Legal but unethical.

b. Ethical but illegal.

c. Legal and ethical.

d. Illegal and unethical.

13. Which of the following statement is **not** true about ethics and law?

a. Ethical behavior resides above legal behavior.

b. Law embodies notions of ethics.

c. Law addresses all ethical questions.

d. Law and ethics have clear roles to play in the society.

14. Which type of social responsibility embraces those activities and practices that are expected or prohibited by societal members even though they are **not** codified into law?

a. Ethical responsibilities

b. Legal responsibilities

c. Philanthropic responsibilities

d. Economic responsibilities

15. Which of the following refers to the corporate behavior in response to market forces or legal constraints?

a. Social obligation

b. Social responsibility

c. Social responsiveness

d. Social attitude

16. All of the following provide effective relationships in the organization's governance framework **except**:

a. Organizational processes.

b. Governance.

c. Risk management.

d. Internal controls.

17. Which of the following internal audit assessments belong to specific governance processes?

a. Whistleblower processes

b. Risk management audit process

c. Internal control over financial reporting

d. Fraud risks

18. Risk registers describe direct links between which of the following?

a. Risk acceptance and risk avoidance

b. Risk categories and risk aspects

c. Risk assignment and risk sharing

d. Risk limitation and risk spreading

19. Risk can be categorized as:

a. Objective-subjective and perils-hazards.

b. Objective-subjective, physical-moral-morale, and pure-speculative.

c. Static-dynamic, subjective-objective, and pure-speculative.

d. Objective-subjective, physical-moral-morale, pure-speculative, and perils-hazards.

20. The three most commonly used methods of loss control are:

a. Risk retention, risk avoidance, and risk transfer.

b. Self-insurance, diversification, and risk transfer.

c. Frequency reduction, severity reduction, and cost reduction.

d. Insurance transfers, frequency reduction, and severity reduction.

21. Self-insurance differs from the establishment of a reserve fund in that:

   a. Establishing a reserve fund is a form of risk retention.

   b. Self-insurance involves prefunding of expected losses through a fund specifically designed for that purpose.

   c. Self-insurance requires the existence of a group of exposure units large enough to allow accurate loss prediction.

   d. Self-insurance requires the formation of a subsidiary company.

22. The purchase of insurance is a common form of:

   a. Risk retention.

   b. Risk transfer.

   c. Risk avoidance.

   d. Loss control.

23. Which of the following **best** represents the fit-gap analysis as a risk management tool?

   a. This analysis determines the difference between the actual outcome and the expected outcome.

   b. This analysis is used for managing uncertainty as it may be subdivided into sequential decision analysis and irreversible investment theory.

   c. This analysis deals with quantitative data in terms of dollars and ratios.

   d. This analysis involves assigning weights to responses to questions addressing areas that may introduce elements of risk.

24. Which of the following financial and accounting practices is **not** a risk for public corporations?

   a. Financial engineering

   b. Earnings management

   c. Creative accounting

   d. Off-the-books accounts

25. Which of the following has been determined to be a reasonable level of risk?

   a. Minimum risk

   b. Acceptable risk

   c. Residual risk

   d. Total risk

26. Which of the following enterprise risk management (ERM) frameworks addresses market risk?

   a. Strategic risks

   b. Operational risks

   c. Financial risks

   d. Hazard risks

27. The scope of enterprise risk management (ERM) should encompass which of the following?

   I. Hazards

   II. Opportunities

   III. Strengths

   IV. Weaknesses

   a. I only

   b. II only

   c. I and II

   d. III and IV

28. Which of the following is **best qualified** to manage the enterprise-wide risk management program?

   a. Chief risk officer

   b. Board of directors

   c. Chief financial officer

   d. Chief governance officer

29. An exception report for management is an example of which type of control?

   a. Preventive control

   b. Detective control

   c. Corrective control

   d. Directive control

30. Organizational procedures allow employees to anticipate problems. This type of control is known as:

   a. Feedback control.

   b. Strategic control.

   c. Feed-forward control.

   d. Performance appraisal.

31. As part of a total quality control program, a firm not only inspects finished goods but also monitors product returns and customer complaints. Which type of control **best** describes these efforts?

a. Feedback control

b. Feedforward control

c. Production control

d. Inventory control

32. To be successful, large companies must develop means to keep the organization focused in the proper direction. Organization control systems help keep companies focused. These control systems consist of which of the following components?

a. Budgeting, financial ratio analysis, and cash management

b. Objectives, standards, and an evaluation-reward system

c. Role analysis, team building, and survey feedback

d. Coaching, protection, and challenging assignments

33. Closed control systems consist of six elements. Identify one of the six elements.

a. Transforming inputs to outputs and setting performance standards

b. Adequately securing data files

c. Approval of audit charter

d. Establishment of independent audit function

34. The three **basic** components of all organizational control systems are:

a. Objectives, standards, and an evaluation-reward system.

b. Plans, budgets, and organizational policies and procedures.

c. Statistical reports, audits, and financial controls.

d. Inputs, objectives, and an appraisal system.

35. Which of the following management control systems measures performance in terms of operating profits minus the cost of capital invested in tangible assets?

a. Open-book management system

b. Economic value-added system

c. Activity-based costing system

d. Market value-added system

36. A comprehensive management control system that considers both financial and nonfinancial measures relating to a company's critical success factors is called a(n):

a. Balanced scorecard system.

b. Economic value-added system.

c. Activity-based costing system.

d. Market value-added system.

37. The term "risk appetite" means which of the following?

a. Risk avoidance

b. Risk limitation

c. Risk acceptance

d. Risk spreading

38. Residual risk is also known as which of the following?

a. Audit risk

b. Pure risk

c. Current risk

d. Inherent risk

39. Residual risk is calculated as which of the following?

a. Known risks minus unknown risks

b. Actual risks minus probable risks

c. Probable risks minus possible risks

d. Potential risks minus covered risks

40. Which of the following is closely linked to risk acceptance?

a. Risk detection

b. Risk prevention

c. Risk tolerance

d. Risk correction

41. Which of the following risk concepts can be assumed to have no mitigating controls?

a. Business risk

b. Residual risk

c. Inherent risk

d. Current risk

42. When dealing with employees, which of the following is **not** an example of possible management's negative actions if whistleblowing employees report misconduct of management?
   a. Reduced duties
   b. Coercion of political activity
   c. Reassignment of work location
   d. Reshuffling of work schedules

43. Which of the following was **not** a major shareholder initiative?
   a. Rise of shareholder activist groups
   b. Shareholder-initiated golden parachutes
   c. Shareholder resolutions and annual meetings
   d. Shareholder lawsuits

44. When dealing with stakeholders, which of the following ethical and legal principles is **not** applicable?
   a. Due process
   b. Due diligence
   c. Due care
   d. Duty of loyalty

45. Which of the following is the ultimate goal of shareholder and investor communications?
   a. Honesty
   b. Consistency
   c. Clarity
   d. Effectiveness

DOMAIN 6

Fraud Risks

This domain contains several major theoretical topics as they relate to fraud. It describes how to interpret fraud risks, fraud types, fraud indicators, and awareness of fraud and controls required to prevent and detect fraud risks. It presents audit tests required to detect fraud and integrates analytical relationships to detect fraud. It discusses interrogation and investigation techniques used in fraud discovery, including forensic auditing. This domain shows how to use a framework for managing fraud risks and uses big data to perform fraud analytics to detect fraud. The role of internal auditor in preventing and detecting fraud is briefly discussed.

All these topics are tested at a combination of proficient and basic cognitive levels in Part 1 of the CIA Exam with a 10% weight given. The only relevant International Professional Practices Framework (IPPF) *Standard* directly addressing fraud is *Standard 1220*—Due Professional Care, and the Sarbanes-Oxley Act of 2002 presented in the appendix also discusses fraud. Other *Standards* also touch on the fraud. This *Standard 1220* and the appendix of this book should be studied together with this domain to answer the CIA Exam questions and Wiley's online test software practice questions.

With respect to the CIA Exam, cognitive levels are labeled as proficient level and basic level. These cognitive levels suggest that more time and effort should be spent in studying and mastering the subject matter covered in the topics labeled as the proficient level. Comparatively less time and effort should be spent on the topics labeled as the basic level.

6.1 Interpretation of Fraud Risks

(a) Fraud Defined

Fraud is a generic term that embraces all the multifarious means that human ingenuity can devise, which are resorted to by one individual, to get an advantage over another by false representations. It includes all surprise, trick, cunning, and unfair ways by which another is cheated. *Fraud* is a term of law, applied to certain facts as a conclusion from them, but it is not in itself a fact. It has been defined as any cunning deception or artifice used to cheat or deceive another.

Cheat and defraud means every kind of trick and deception, from false representation and intimidation to suppression and concealment of any fact and information by which a party is induced to part with property for less than its value or to give more than it is worth for the property of another. The terms *fraud* and *bad faith* are synonymous when applied to the conduct of public offenders.

(b) Characteristics of Fraud

An organization's management should consider the potential for fraud when identifying, analyzing, and responding to risks. Three risk factors contribute to the design, implementation, and operating effectiveness of assessing fraud risks: the types of fraud, fraud risk factors, and response to fraud risks. The three risk factors include incentive/pressure, opportunity, and attitude/rationalization. Note that these three fraud risk factors do not necessarily indicate that fraud exists but are often present when fraud occurs.[1]

1. **Incentive/pressure**—Management, other employees, or external parties (e.g., for some improper payments) have an incentive or are under pressure, which provides a motive to commit fraud.

2. **Opportunity**—Circumstances exist, such as the absence of controls, ineffective controls, or the ability of management to override controls, that provide an opportunity to commit fraud.

3. **Attitude/rationalization**—Individuals involved are able to rationalize committing fraud. Some individuals possess an attitude, character, or ethical values that allow them to knowingly and intentionally commit dishonest acts. Generally, the greater the incentive or pressure, the more likely an individual will be able to rationalize the acceptability of committing fraud.

Management uses the fraud risk factors to identify fraud risks. While fraud risk may be greatest when all three risk factors are present, one or more of these factors may indicate a fraud risk. Other information provided by internal and external parties can also be used to identify fraud risks. This information may include allegations of fraud or suspected fraud reported by the office of the inspector general or internal auditors, personnel, or external parties who interact with the entity.

[1] *Federal Internal Control Standards* (*Green Book*) (Washington, DC: Government Accountability Office, September 2014), www.gao.gov.

Management can perpetrate fraud by directly or indirectly manipulating accounting records; overriding controls, sometimes in unpredictable ways; or committing other fraudulent or improper acts.

(c) Response to Fraud Risks

Management analyzes and responds to identified fraud risks so that they are effectively mitigated. Fraud risks are analyzed through the same risk analysis process performed for all identified risks. Management analyzes the identified fraud risks by estimating their significance, both individually and in the aggregate, to assess their effect on achieving the defined objectives. As part of analyzing fraud risk, management also assesses the risk of management override of controls. The oversight body oversees management's assessments of fraud risk and the risk of management override of controls so that they are appropriate.

Management responds to fraud risks through the same risk response process performed for all analyzed risks. Management designs an overall risk response and specific actions for responding to fraud risks. It may be possible to reduce or eliminate certain fraud risks by making changes to the entity's activities and processes. These changes may include stopping or reorganizing certain operations and reallocating roles among personnel to enhance segregation of duties. In addition to responding to fraud risks, management may need to develop further responses to address the risk of management override of controls. Further, when fraud has been detected, the risk assessment process may need to be revised.

(d) Fraud Risks from Misstatements

Fraud risk is a part of audit risk, making up a portion of inherent and control risk. Fraud risk consists of the risk of fraudulent financial reporting and the risk of misappropriation of assets that cause a material misstatement of the financial statements. The auditor should specifically assess and document the risks of material misstatements of the financial statements due to fraud and should consider fraud risk in designing audit procedures. The auditor may determine the risks of material fraud concurrently with the consideration of inherent and control risk but should form a separate conclusion on fraud risk. The auditor should evaluate the risk of fraud throughout the audit.

The auditor must plan and perform the audit to obtain reasonable assurance about whether the financial statements are free of material misstatement, whether caused by error or fraud. Accordingly, the auditor should evaluate the **risks of material misstatement due to fraud (fraud risk)**. The primary factor that distinguishes fraud from error is that the action causing the misstatement in fraud is *intentional*.

Two types of misstatements are relevant to the auditor's consideration of fraud in an audit of financial statements—misstatements arising from fraudulent financial reporting and misstatements arising from misappropriation of assets.

1. **Misstatements arising from fraudulent financial reporting**—Intentional misstatements or omissions of amounts or disclosures in financial statements to deceive financial statement users. They could involve intentional alteration of accounting records, misrepresentation of transactions, intentional misapplication of accounting principles, or other means.

2. **Misstatements arising from misappropriation of assets**—Involve thefts of an entity's assets that result in misstatements in the financial statements. The misappropriation

could involve theft of property, embezzlement of receipts, fraudulent payments, or other means. Safeguarding controls relate to protecting assets against loss from unauthorized acquisition, use, or disposition.

In considering misstatements arising from misappropriation of assets, the auditor should consider fraud risks associated with improper payments. Some improper payments made by federal government entities could involve fraud.

An **improper payment** is any payment that should not have been made or that was made in an incorrect amount (including overpayments and underpayments) under statutory, contractual, administrative, or other legally applicable requirements.

The auditor is responsible for obtaining reasonable, but not absolute, assurance about whether the financial statements are free of material misstatement. Reasonable assurance is a high level of assurance. Absolute assurance cannot be attained because of the nature of audit evidence and the characteristics of fraud, and the auditor's report does not provide absolute assurance. A properly planned and performed audit might not detect a material misstatement, and the subsequent discovery of a material misstatement does not, in and of itself, provide evidence that the auditor did not conform with auditing standards.

In addition, the auditor should evaluate situations or transactions that could be indicative of abuse, which is distinct from fraud and illegal acts. Abuse involves behavior that is deficient or improper (but not necessarily fraudulent or illegal) when compared with behavior that a prudent person would consider reasonable and necessary business practice, given the facts and circumstances. Abuse also includes misuse of authority or position for personal financial interests or those of an immediate or close family member or business associate. Abuse does not necessarily involve fraud or violations of laws, regulations, or provisions of a contract or grant agreement.

The auditor is not required to detect abuse as the determination of abuse is subjective. Accordingly, the auditor does not provide reasonable assurance of detecting abuse. However, if indications of abuse that could result in material misstatement of the financial statements or other financial data come to the auditor's attention, the auditor should apply audit procedures specifically directed to determine whether abuse has occurred and the effect, if any, on the financial statements. The auditor should consider both quantitative and qualitative factors in making judgments about the materiality of possible abuse and about related audit procedures. After performing these additional procedures, the auditor may discover that the abuse represents potential fraud or illegal.

(i) Other Types of Misstatements

Because fraud risk takes many forms, it is difficult to list or interpret fraud risks correctly due to problems in identifying and detecting various fraudulent activities. However, fraud risks can be broadly interpreted as falling into these major categories:

- Over- or underreporting of:
    - Production unit count in a manufacturing factory or plant
    - Unit count of sales or dollar count of sales
    - On-hand inventory count in a factory, plant, warehouse, and retail store
    - Product and service invoices and shipping dates

  □ Customer merchandise returns to a retailer or manufacturer

  □ Operating, marketing, and administrative expenses

  □ Gross income and net income

- Credit or debit card chargeback fraud

- Payroll fraud with ghost employees

- Advertising fraud due to intentional false billing errors

- Investment fraud (bitcoin fraud, affinity fraud, and microcap fraud)

(e) Profiles of Fraud Perpetrators

Understanding what the fraudulent acts are and what the profiles (traits) of fraud perpetrators are can help in interpretation of fraud risks. In addition, classification of fraudulent crimes into white-collar crime and organizational crime can better facilitate the interpretation of fraud risks.

(i) Acts and Profiles of Fraud Perpetrators

(A) Acts of Fraudulent Behavior. A list of fraudulent behavior acts about which an internal auditor must be concerned is presented next.

- Significant changes in the behavior of the defrauder (e.g., easygoing attitude, irregular work habits, and expensive social life)

- Knowledge that the defrauder is undergoing emotional trauma at home or in the workplace

- Knowledge that the defrauder is betting heavily

- Knowledge that the defrauder is drinking heavily

- Knowledge that the defrauder is heavily in debt

- Audit findings of errors or irregularities that are considered immaterial when discovered

- The defrauder works quietly, works hard, works long hours, often works alone.

- The defrauder appears to be living beyond his/her means.

- The defrauder has an expensive car or clothes.

(B) Profiles of Fraud Perpetrators

Traits of Managers. According to Joseph Wells, personality traits of managers associated with frauds include wheeler-dealers, management that is feared, impulsive, too number-oriented, and insensitive to people (especially to employees).[2] Obviously, the contrast is management that is friendly, calm, generous with time, self-confident, and goal oriented.

Many frauds occur where an autocratic management arbitrarily sets budgets for lower-level managers to meet. When these budgets are unattainable, the managers have a choice to either cheat or fail. When their jobs, reputations, and careers are at stake, cheating is sometimes easier than failing.

---

[2] Joseph Wells, *Fraud Examination: Investigative and Audit Procedures* (New York: Quorum Books, 1992).

Traits of Employees. The next traits are suggested as indicating fraudulent behavior.

- Managers and executives seem to be the major sources of ethical attitudes within organization. That is, there is pressure from superiors to commit unethical behavior. Superiors pressure subordinates to support incorrect viewpoints, sign false documents, overlook superiors' wrongdoing, and do business with superiors' friends. The chief executive officer sets the ethical tone of the organization.

- Be wary of employees who never take vacations, live beyond their means, or suffer from mood swings.

- About two males are arrested for embezzlement to every one female.

- About one-third of male and female embezzlers are 22 to 29 years of age; they constitute the largest groupings of all.

White-Collar Crime. **White-collar crime** is a breach of trust, confidence, or fiduciary duty. Someone relies on and trusts another, to his or her economic detriment. White-collar crime is classified as that directed against consumers and that directed against employers. It is caused by greed and by weak internal control mechanisms. Jack Bologna defines white-collar crime as occupational, corporate, economic, or financial.[3]

The common characteristics of each of the so-called white-collar crimes are intentional deception (fraud theft, embezzlement, and corruption), destruction of property (industrial sabotage), gross negligence (product liability), and failure to comply with government regulations on environmental pollution, unfair pricing practices, untrue advertising, unsafe and unhealthy products, stock fraud, tax fraud, and others. *High-level employee crimes are perceived to be based on economic greed while low-level employee crimes are perceived as based on economic need.*

In his book *White Collar Crime*, Edwin Sutherland gave examples of white collar violations by larger American corporations.[4] These violations involved, among others:

- Restraints of trade

- Misrepresentation in advertising

- Patent, trademark, and copyright infringements

- Unfair labor practices

- Illegal rebates

Sutherland found that many of the corporations were serial and serious repeaters.

Irwin Ross, writing for *Fortune* magazine, compiled statistics on fraud committed by the largest industrial and nonindustrial corporations.[5] He included five kinds of offenses, all of which were committed for the benefit of the organization rather than for personal profit:

1. Bribe taking or bribe giving by high-level corporate officials (including kickbacks and illegal rebates)

---

[3] Jack Bologna, *Handbook on Corporate Fraud* (Stoneham, MA: Butterworth-Heinemann, 1993).
[4] Quoted in Gary S. Green, *Occupational Crime* (Chicago: Nelson-Hall, 1990). Originally from Edwin O. Sutherland, *White Collar Crime* (New York: CBS, 1961).
[5] Quoted in Green, *Occupational Crime*. Originally from Irwin Ross, "How Lawless Are Big Companies?" *Fortune*, December 1, 1980.

2. Criminal fraud

3. Illegal campaign contributions

4. Tax evasion

5. Criminal antitrust violations

Profile of a Corporate Fraudster

- Extravagant purchases or lavish lifestyle

- Unexplained mood swings or compulsive behavior (e.g., workaholics, alcohol or drug abusers, overeaters, gamblers)

- Unable to deal with pressure

- Able to rationalize their thefts

- Able to exploit internal control weaknesses to cover up their fraud

- Reluctance to take vacations or be away from the office

- Chronic job frustration, low morale

- Unusually close ties to vendors or a sudden switch in a long-term vendor

- Suggestions of heavy personal debt

Source: Association of Certified Fraud Examiners, *White Paper Journal* 7, no. 5 (October/November 1993). Original source was from *The Fraud Prevention Primer*, KPMG Canada.

Profiles of Organizational Crime. Research by Edwin Sutherland, Marshall B. Clinard, and Peter Yeager found these profiles for organizations committing crime:

- The oil, pharmaceutical, and motor vehicle industries and their management were the most likely to violate the law.

- Firms that were relatively more prosperous tended to pollute illegally more often.

- Larger corporations in general commit no more violations per unit size than do smaller corporations.In some cases, larger corporations had more infractions generally, but smaller corporations had more violations per unit size.

- More diversified firms will violate more often. (This is because they are exposed to a greater number of regulations. More diversified firms seem more likely to violate labor and manufacturing laws than those less diversified.)

- Firms with more market power had slightly fewer violations per unit size than less dominant firms, which suggests that market power may diminish pressures to violate the law.

- Firms and industries with greater labor concentration tend to have more official censures for labor violations.[6]

---

[6] Quoted in Green, *Occupational Crime*, based on research studies conducted by Sutherland, Clinard, and Yeager in 1949, 1980, and 1983.

6.2 Types of Fraud

Various types of fraud exist, depending on the purpose, place, and people who are perpetrating the fraudulent activities. Because fraud has so many dimensions, it can be classified in eight ways:

1. Management fraud
2. Employee fraud
3. Identity fraud
4. Investment fraud
5. Internet fraud
6. Stock promotion fraud
7. Chargeback fraud
8. Miscellaneous fraud

Each type of fraud is discussed next.

(a) Management Fraud, Materiality, and Misstatements

Management considers the types of fraud that can occur within the entity to provide a basis for identifying fraud risks. Fraud involves obtaining something of value through willful misrepresentation. The court system (judicial or adjudicative) will determine whether an act qualifies as fraud.

The three types of management fraud are listed next.

1. **Fraudulent financial reporting**—Intentional misstatements or omissions of amounts or disclosures in financial statements to deceive financial statement users. This could include intentional alteration of accounting records, misrepresentation of transactions, or intentional misapplication of accounting principles.
2. **Misappropriation of assets**—Theft of an entity's assets. This could include theft of property, embezzlement of receipts, or fraudulent payments.
3. **Corruption**—Bribery and other illegal acts.

Fraud risk factors represent inherent or control risk factors. The auditor should evaluate fraud risk factors in assessing inherent and control risk. Although fraud is usually concealed, the presence of fraud risk factors that indicate incentive/pressure, opportunity, or attitude/rationalization might alert the auditor to a significant risk of fraud. However, fraud risk factors do not necessarily indicate that fraud exists.

Examples of fraud risk factors are classified by the two types: fraudulent financial reporting and fraudulent misstatements related to misappropriation of assets. These two risk factors are organized by the three conditions: incentive/pressure, opportunity, and attitude/rationalization. Examples follow.

Examples of Fraud Related to Misstatements Arising from Fraudulent Financial Reporting

Incentive/pressure—Incentive exists for management to report reduced program costs or costs that are consistent with budgeted amounts, or excessive pressure exists to meet unrealistic deadlines, goals, or other requirements.

Opportunity—Key financial statement amounts are based on significant estimates that involve subjective judgments or uncertainties that are difficult to corroborate, or management is in a position to override controls for processing adjustments or unusual transactions.

Attitude/rationalization— Employees perceive that penalties exist for reporting honest results, or employees consider requirements, such as performance targets, unrealistic.

Examples of Fraud Related to Misstatements Arising from Misappropriation of Assets

Incentive/pressure—Employees who are disgruntled because of impending layoffs have an incentive to misappropriate assets; pressure to meet programmatic objectives, such as for rapid benefit payments, increases the risk of fraudulent improper payments.

Opportunity—Employees have access to assets that are small in size and value or the authority to disburse funds; a program has weaknesses in internal control related to fraudulent improper payments.

Attitude/rationalization—Employees believe that management is unethical; individuals believe they are entitled to the entity's assets.

In addition to fraud, management considers other forms of misconduct that can occur, such as waste and abuse. Waste is the act of using or expending resources carelessly, extravagantly, or to no purpose. Abuse involves behavior that is deficient or improper when compared with behavior that a prudent person would consider reasonable and necessary operational practice given the facts and circumstances. This includes the misuse of authority or position for personal gain or for the benefit of another. Waste and abuse do not necessarily involve fraud or illegal acts. However, they may be an indication of potential fraud or illegal acts and may still impact the achievement of defined objectives.

Management fraud tends to involve a number of people with conspiracy in mind. It occurs because senior managers, due to their position of power, circumvent internal controls. According to Bologna, the major symptoms of management fraud are the intentional understatement of losses and liabilities and overstatement of assets or profits.

Examples of Symptoms of Management Fraud

- Profits can be manipulated by overstating revenues or understating costs.

- Revenues can be overstated by recording fictitious sales, recording unfinalized sales, recording consignments as sales, or recording shipments to storage facilities as sales.

- Costs can be manipulated by deferring them to the next accounting period or understating them in the current period. This is accomplished by such ploys as overstating ending inventories of raw materials, work-in-process, and finished goods or understating purchases of raw materials.

In almost every case of management fraud, signs (**red flags**) of the fraud exist for some time before the fraud itself is detected or disclosed by a third party. These signs include:

- Knowledge that the company is having financial difficulties, such as frequent cash flow shortages, declining sales and profits, and loss of market share.

- Signs of management incompetence, such as poor planning, organization, communication, and controls; poor motivation and delegation; management indecision and confusion about corporate mission, goals, and strategies; management ignorance of conditions in the industry and in the general economy.

- Autocratic management, low trust of employees, poor promotion opportunities, high turnover of employees, poorly defined business ethics.

Some of accounting-related transaction-based red flags include:

- Cash flow is diminishing.
- Sales and income are diminishing.
- Payables and receivables are increasing.
- Unusual or second endorsements on checks.
- Inventory and cost of sales are increasing.
- Income and expense items are continually reclassified.
- Suspense items are not reconciled at all or reconciled in an untimely manner.
- Suspense items are written off without explanation.
- Accounts receivable write-offs are increasing.
- Journal entries are adjusted heavily at year-end.
- Old outstanding checks.
- Heavy customer complaints.

Accounting Fraud by High-Level Managers

- Early booking of sales
- Expense deferrals
- Inventory overstatement
- Expense account padding

In planning and performing inventory procedures, auditors should be aware that reported methods of fraudulently misstating inventory have involved:

- Nonexistent items recorded as inventory.
- Goods that have been sold (and recorded as sales) included in inventory.
- Goods shipped between two sites and recorded as inventory at both locations.
- Scrap materials substituted for genuine inventory for the physical inventory observation.
- False invoices or journal entries.
- Inflated inventory costs.
- Inventory that has been excluded from the physical count because management states it has been sold when, under the terms of the bill-and-hold arrangement, title has not yet passed to the customer.
- Inadequate reserves for slow-moving and obsolete inventory.[7]

---

[7] American Institute of Certified Public Accountants, *Audit of Inventories, Auditing Procedure Study* (New York: Author, 1993).

Materiality represents the magnitude of an omission or misstatement of an item in a financial report that, in light of surrounding circumstances, makes it probable that the judgment of a reasonable person relying on the information would have been changed or influenced by the inclusion or correction of the item.

Materiality is based on the concept that items of little importance, which do not affect the judgment or conduct of a reasonable user, do not require auditor investigation. Materiality has both quantitative and qualitative aspects. Even though quantitatively immaterial, certain misstatements could have an important impact on or could warrant disclosure in the financial statements for qualitative reasons.

For example, intentional misstatements or omissions (fraud) usually are more critical to financial statement users than are unintentional errors of equal amounts. This is because users generally consider an intentional misstatement more serious than clerical errors of the same amount.

Regarding management fraud, materiality is closely related to misstatements, meaning that financial statement accounts (e.g., assets, liabilities, and equity) and operational results (e.g., production, sales, inventory, revenues, expenses, and income) could be misstated or misreported for management's personal gain to receive increased bonuses and promotions. Here, significant and intentional irregularities and omissions, which are an indication of fraud, are a major concern. However, significant and unintentional errors and clerical errors of the same amounts are not a major concern.

Here, the terms "intentional misstatements" and "unintentional misstatements" have very different meanings; the former is more damaging to the company than the latter in terms of changing the outcomes in reporting a financial loss as a gain and vice versa. These misstatements are the result of management's explicit and devious plans and goals for personal gain.

Materiality judgments are made after analyzing quantitative and qualitative considerations where, for example, quantitative considerations may include management manipulating sales and income levels and qualitative considerations may include management manipulating emission control software in automobiles to reduce air pollution. Both of these manipulations are illegal.

Materiality

The term "materiality" has several meanings:

Planning materiality—A preliminary estimate of materiality in relation to the financial statements taken as a whole, primarily based on quantitative measures. It is used to determine design materiality and tolerable misstatement, which in turn are used to determine the nature, extent, and timing of substantive audit procedures. It is also used to identify significant laws and regulations for compliance testing.

Design materiality—The portion of planning materiality that the auditor allocates to line items, accounts, or classes of transactions (such as disbursements). The auditor usually sets this amount the same for all line items or accounts as this amount is usually sufficient for testing.

Disclosure materiality—The threshold for determining whether to report items separately in the financial statements or in the related notes. This may differ from planning materiality.

Reporting materiality—The threshold for determining whether an unqualified opinion can be issued. In the reporting phase, the auditor assesses audit results to determine whether uncorrected misstatements (known and likely) are either quantitatively or qualitatively material. This decision is a matter of auditor judgment. There need not be a direct relationship between reporting and planning materiality when making these judgments. If uncorrected misstatements are determined to be material, the auditor would be precluded from issuing an unqualified opinion on the financial statements.

Misstatements

The term "misstatements" has several interpretations, and the auditor should quantify the effects of the misstatements and classify them as either known misstatement, which is the amount of misstatement actually found, or likely misstatement, which is the auditor's best estimate of the amount of the misstatement in the population. (Likely misstatement includes known misstatement.) For sampling applications, this amount is the projected misstatement. Another related misstatement is tolerable misstatement, which is explained next.

Tolerable misstatement (formerly "test materiality") is the materiality the auditor uses to test a specific line item, account, or class of transactions. Tolerable misstatement is defined as the maximum error in a population of transactions or account balance that the auditor is willing to accept. Based on judgment, the auditor may set tolerable misstatement equal to or less than design materiality and may set different amounts of tolerable misstatement for different line items or accounts or assertions.

If computer software is used to calculate sample size when conducting substantive tests, the auditor should understand how the software handles expected or projected misstatements. The auditor may detect misstatements during substantive tests or other procedures. The auditor should evaluate misstatements individually and in the aggregate in both quantitative and qualitative terms. Based on the evaluation of all misstatements, the auditor should determine the type of audit report (i.e., qualified opinion or unqualified opinion) to issue on the financial statements. External auditors focus on the fair and full presentation of financial statements, and internal auditors focus on the internal reporting of operational results.

(b) Employee Fraud

Embezzlement and corruption are two major types of employee fraud. The crime of embezzlement consists of the fraudulent misappropriation of the property of an employer by an employee to whom the possession of that property has been entrusted. Here is the difference between embezzlement and larceny: Embezzlement occurs when the embezzler gains initial possession of property lawfully but subsequently misappropriates it. Larceny is committed when property is taken without the owner's consent.

Common embezzlement techniques include these schemes:

- **Cash disbursement embezzlement** involves the creation of fake documents or false expense entries using phony invoices, time cards, and receipts.

- **Cash receipts fraud** involving the lapping of cash or accounts receivable. Here the embezzler "borrows" from today's receipts and replaces them with tomorrow's receipts. Other examples are skimming, where the proceeds of cash sales are intercepted before any entry is made of their receipts, and granting fake credits for discounts, refunds, rebates, returns, and allowances, possibly through collusion with a customer.

- **Theft of property** involves assets such as tools, supplies, equipment, finished goods, raw materials, and intellectual property, such as software, data, and proprietary information.

Accounting Fraud by Lower-Level Employees

- Check kiting
- Lapping of receivables
- Phony vendor invoices
- Phony benefit payment claims
- Expense account padding

Corruption is another common type of employee fraud. Vendors, suppliers, service providers, and contractors often corrupt the employees of an organization on both a small-scale level (e.g., gifts and free tickets of nominal value) and a large-scale level (e.g., commissions, payoffs, free trips, free airline tickets and hotel accommodations).

KEY CONCEPTS TO REMEMBER: Symptoms of Employee Fraud

- Adjusting journal entries that lack management authorization and supporting details
- Expenditures that lack supporting documents
- False and improper entries in books of accounts
- Destruction, counterfeiting, and forgery of documents that support payments
- Short shipments received
- Overpricing of goods purchased
- Double billing
- Substitution of inferior goods

(c) Identity Fraud

Identity theft means a fraud committed or attempted by one person using the identifying information of another person without the explicit authority of the second person. **Identifying information** means any name or number that may be used, alone or in conjunction with any other information, to identify a specific person, including any:

- Name, Social Security number, date of birth, official state or government issued driver's license or identification number, alien registration number, government passport number, employer or taxpayer identification number

- Unique biometric data, such as fingerprint, voice print, retina or iris image, or other unique physical representation

- Unique electronic identification number, address or routing code (e.g., a bank's routing number and account number); and credit/debit card number with personal identification number (PIN)

- Telecommunication identifying information or access device, such as cell/mobile phone number and a personal device's serial number.

Identity theft can occur in several ways:

- Data breaches by hackers in a retail environment where hackers steal customers' personal and financial information.

- Data leakages by company insiders, such as employees and contractors.

- **Pretext calling** by a fraudster in a banking environment. Pretext callers use pieces of a customer's personal information to impersonate an account holder to gain access to that individual's account information. Armed with personal information, such as an individual's name, address, and Social Security number, a pretext caller may try to convince a bank's employee to provide confidential account information. While pretext calling may be difficult to spot, there are measures banks can take to reduce the incidence of pretext calling, such as limiting the circumstances under which customer information may be disclosed by telephone. A bank's policy could be that customer information is disclosed only through email, text message, a letter, or in-person meeting.

(d) Investment Fraud

Three types of investment fraud include affinity fraud, bitcoin Ponzi schemes, and microcap fraud.

Affinity fraud involves either a fake investment or a normal investment where the fraudster lies about important details, such as the risk of loss, the track record of the investment, or the background of the promoter of the investment scheme. It is called affinity fraud because the fraud victims are members of identifiable groups of people, such as friends, family, relatives, and colleagues; religious groups; ethnic communities; or elderly persons.

Many affinity frauds are Ponzi or pyramid schemes, where money given to the promoter by new investors is paid to earlier investors to create the illusion that the so-called investment is successful. This tricks new investors into investing in the scheme and lulls existing investors into believing their investments are safe. In reality, even if there is an actual investment, the investment typically makes little or no profit. The fraudster simply takes new investors' money for his or her own personal use, often using some of it to pay off existing investors who may be growing suspicious. Eventually, when the supply of investor money dries up and current investors demand to be paid, the scheme collapses, and investors discover that most of or all of their money is gone.

Here are five tips to avoid affinity fraud:

1. Before investing, make sure to research the promoter's background and the investment itself before investing to determine its legitimacy.

2. Never make an investment based solely on the recommendation of a member of an organization or group to which you belong.

3. Do not fall for investments that promise spectacular profits or guaranteed returns.

4. Be skeptical of any investment opportunity that you cannot get put in writing.

5. Do not be pressured or rushed into buying an investment before you have a chance to research the opportunity.

Bitcoin Ponzi schemes involve using virtual currency or digital currency where fraudsters lure investors into Ponzi and other schemes and use these currencies to facilitate fraudulent, or simply fabricated, investments or transactions. The fraud may also involve an unregistered offering or trading platform. These schemes often promise high returns for getting in on the ground floor of a growing Internet phenomenon. A major attraction to using virtual currencies in transactions is their greater privacy benefits and less regulatory oversight than transactions in conventional (flat) currencies, such as the U.S. dollar. Virtual currencies are traded on online exchanges for conventional currencies or used to purchase goods or services online such as clothes and shoes.

Common red flags of fraud for bitcoin Ponzi schemes are listed next.

- High investment returns with little or no risk
- Overly consistent returns
- Unregistered investments
- Unlicensed sellers
- No minimum investor qualifications required
- Investments not in writing
- Difficulty in receiving payments
- Investments enlisted by national, ethnic, or religious affiliation groups or sponsored by respected leaders, prominent members, or celebrities

Microcap fraud is involved in the over-the-counter (OTC) market for securities where the market is designed for and comprised of companies with small amounts of assets and low stock prices. Microcap stocks are low-priced stocks issued by the smallest of companies, including penny stocks, which are the very lowest-priced stocks. As such, they are more susceptible to stock manipulation. Publicly available information about microcap companies often is scarce, making it easier for fraudsters to spread false information. In addition, it is often easier for fraudsters to manipulate the price of microcap stocks because microcap stocks historically have been less liquid than stocks of larger companies. Liquid investments are those stocks that can be sold easily.

Companies quoted on small exchanges, such as the OTC markets and bulletin boards, do not have to apply for listing or meet any minimum financial standards. Companies that trade their stocks on major exchanges undergo a formal application process and must meet minimum listing standards. For this reason, there is a greater tendency to perpetrate fraud on small exchanges, such as the OTC markets and OTC bulletin boards.

Some Red Flags to Watch for when Investing in a Microcap Stock

- Little or no assets, false press releases, and minimal revenues
- Insiders own large amounts of stock
- Unusual external auditing issues
- Odd items appear in the footnotes of financial statements
- Stock trading was suspended due to spam and for other reasons
- Frequent changes in company name or type of business
- Company issues a lot of shares without a corresponding increase in the company's assets
- Increase in stock price or trading volume linked to promotional activities

(e) Internet Fraud

Internet-based frauds are occurring at an alarming rate because the Internet is where most people (mass audience) are going to search, learn, study, research, share, listen, entertain, and do other things. In addition, the Internet is a useful way to reach a mass audience without spending a lot of time or money. A website, online messages, or spam emails can reach large numbers of people with minimum effort. It is easy for fraudsters to make their messages look real and credible, and sometimes it is hard for investors to tell the difference between fact and fiction.

Four ways how fraudsters can trick investors using the online channels are listed next.

1. **Online investment newsletters**—Although most online newsletters are good, some operate as tools for fraud. Some companies pay online newsletters to tout, or recommend, their stocks to the public. Touting is not illegal as long as newsletters disclose who paid them, how much they are getting paid, and the form of the payment (usually cash or stock). But fraudsters often lie about the payments they receive and their track records in recommending stocks.

2. **Online bulletin boards**—Begun as information sharing tools, online bulletin boards can be used as hiding places for one fraudster using multiple aliases. Although some messages may be true, many turn out to be bogus or even scams. Fraudsters may use online discussions (online chats) to pump up a company or pretend to reveal "inside" information about upcoming announcements, new products, or lucrative contracts. For example, one person can easily create the illusion of widespread interest in a small, thinly traded stock by posting numerous messages under various aliases. Here the problem is not knowing what is real or fake.

3. **Pump-and-dump schemes**—Schemes having two parts. In the first part, promoters try to boost the price of a stock with false or misleading statements about the company. Once the stock price has been pumped up, fraudsters move on to the second part, where they seek to make a profit by dumping their own stock holdings into the market. After

these fraudsters dump their shares and stop hyping the stock, the price of the stock typically falls, and investors lose their money. Usually these schemes involve unknown and small-size microcap companies that are traded on OTC stock market exchanges. Here the problem is not knowing what is hype or real.

4. **Spam emails or junk emails**—Often are used to promote bogus investment schemes or to spread false information about a company. With a bulk email program, spammers can send personalized messages to millions of people at once for much less than the cost of cold calling or traditional mail. Many scams, including advance fee frauds, use spam to reach potential victims. Here the problem is not knowing what is real or unreal.

Stock Promotion Fraud

Fraudsters who conduct stock promotions are often paid promoters or company insiders who stand to gain by selling their shares after creating a buying frenzy and pumping up the stock price. The promoters or insiders make profits for themselves by creating losses for unsuspecting investors.

Fraudsters may promote a stock in seemingly independent and unbiased sources, including social media, investment newsletters, online advertisements, emails, Internet chat rooms, and direct mail.

The four red flags of investment fraud are listed next.

1. Aggressive stock promotion

2. Guaranteed high investment returns

3. Pressure to buy immediately

4. Unsolicited stock recommendations

Even if a promoter makes specific disclosures about being compensated for promoting a stock, be aware that fraudsters may make such disclosures to create the false appearance that the promotion is legitimate. Additionally, the disclosures may not reveal that the underlying source of the compensation is a company insider or affiliate.

Before investing in a company based on a stock promotion, carefully research the investment and keep in mind that the promoter may be trying to get you to buy into the hype in order to sell his or her own shares at your expense.

Chargeback Fraud

A **chargeback** occurs when a customer who purchased merchandise from a retailer or a product from a company (e.g., a manufacturer, reseller, distributor, wholesaler) was not happy either with the product or with non-product-related matters and files a claim with a bank to get his or her money back. The customer paid the retailer or other seller with a charge card (debit or credit card). When the customer files a chargeback claim, the bank contacts the seller and gives a temporary credit to the customer and charges the seller for the amount of the purchase until the final investigation among the customer, bank, and seller is completed. Most chargeback claims by customers are genuine, but some are fraudulent claims. In summary, a chargeback claim, which is a financial claim, involves a customer (buyer), intermediary (customer's bank that issued the charge card and paid the seller), and a retailer (seller). In a way, a chargeback fraud is a financial fraud.

According to the Chargeback Gurus (www.chargebackgurus.com), two types of chargeback fraud can occur:

1. **Friendly fraud** occurs when cardholders report to their bank that a charge was fraudulently made on their card, even though the customers knowingly made the purchase themselves. Typically, customers may file a claim if they are unsatisfied with the purchase (e.g., price, design, or performance), the customer service experience, the shipping times, or the merchandise return policy. To prevent this problem, sellers should reassess their back-office policies and procedures.

2. **Family fraud** occurs when someone in a family uses another family member's card for a purchase and the cardholder reports the charge as fraudulent to the bank. Many times this type of fraud is unintentional and nonmalicious. In these situations, sellers need to establish chargeback recovery procedures.

Miscellaneous Fraud

Miscellaneous fraud addresses topics such as theft of assets, fraud by frequency, fraud involving conspiracy, and varieties of fraud. There are many varieties of frauds, limited only by the ingenuity of the perpetrators. From a discovery point of view, fraud can be classified in a number of ways. The reason for this classification is that different approaches and procedures are required to discover each type of fraud and to control the occurrence of each type.

Howard Davia and coauthors present four types of fraud (see Exhibit 6.1):[8]

1. Theft of assets

2. Fraud by frequency

3. Fraud by conspiracy

4. Varieties of fraud

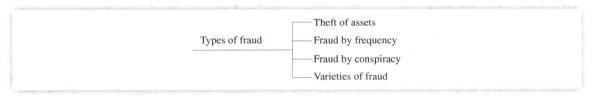

EXHIBIT 6.1 Types of Fraud

Theft of Assets. Theft of assets is classified into three categories:

1. Theft of assets that appears openly on the books as distinct accounting entries. (Fraud open on the books is the least difficult to discover.)

2. Theft of assets that appears on the books but is hidden as a part of other larger, otherwise legitimate accounting entries. This type of theft is very difficult to discover due to complexity. (Fraud hidden on the books)

3. Theft of assets that is not on the books and could never be detected by an examination of "booked" accounting transactions. (Fraud off the books is the most difficult to discover.)

[8] Howard R. Davia, Patrick C. Coggins, John C. Wideman, and Joseph T. Kastantin, *Management Accountant's Guide to Fraud Discovery and Control* (New York: John Wiley & Sons, 1992).

Fraud open on the books includes criminal acts that involve discrete entries in the accounting records. Here the term *discrete entry* means that the fraud involves the entire transaction; if that transaction is selected by an auditor for examination, this type of fraud offers the best chance for discovery (e.g., a fraudulent duplicate payment that stands by itself).

Fraud hidden on the books involves acts of fraud that are included in accounting entries that appear on the books but are not discrete entries. That is, the amount of the fraud is always buried in a larger, legitimate accounting entry, never appearing as a discrete amount (e.g., kickbacks).

In **fraud off the books**, the amount of the fraud is neither a discrete accounting entry nor a hidden part of an accounting entry. It is the loss of a valuable asset for the victim. Examples include diverting vending machine sales money and conversion of payments on accounts receivable that have been written off.

Fraud by Frequency.   Another way of classifying fraud is by its frequency of occurrence: nonrepeating or repeating. In **nonrepeating fraud**, a fraudulent act, even though repeated many times, is singular in nature in that it must be triggered by the perpetrator each time (e.g., a weekly payroll check requires a time card every week in order to generate the fraudulent paycheck).

In **repeating fraud**, a defrauding act may occur many times; however, it needs to be initiated only once. It then keeps running until it is stopped. It could possibly recur in perpetuity (e.g., a salaried payroll check that does not require input each time in order to generate the paycheck; it continues until a stop order is issued).

Three Elements of Fraud

1. Intent to defraud
2. Commission of a fraudulent act
3. Accomplishment of the fraud

For the auditor, the significance of whether a fraud is nonrepeating or repeating lies in where to look for the evidence. For example, the auditor would have to review a computer application program to obtain evidence of a repeating fraud involving skimming of a few cents off every bank customers' account service charge.

Fraud Involving Conspiracy.   Fraud can be classified as that involving conspiracy, that which does not involve conspiracy, and that involving partial (pseudo-) conspiracy. Here the word *conspiracy* is synonymous with *collusion*. It has been proven that most frauds involve conspiracy, either bona fide or pseudo. In the bona fide conspiracy, all parties involved are fully aware of the fraudulent intent; in the pseudoconspiracy, one or more of the parties to the fraud is innocent of fraudulent intent.

Varieties of Fraud.   Fraud can be grouped into two varieties: (1) "specialized" fraud, which is unique to people working in certain kinds of business operations, and (2) "garden-variety" frauds, which all people are likely to encounter in general business operations.

Examples of specialized fraud include embezzlement of assets entrusted by depositors to financial institutions (e.g., banks, savings and loans, credit unions, pension funds) (called custodial fraud) and false claims for life, health, auto, and property insurance coverage.

Eight types of garden-variety frauds are common today:

1. Kickbacks
2. Defective pricing
3. Unbalanced contracts or purchase orders
4. Reopening completed contracts
5. Duplicate payments
6. Double payments
7. Shell payments
8. Defective delivery

According to Jack Bologna, corporate fraud can be generated internally (perpetrated by directors, officers, employees, or agents of a corporation for or against it or against others) and externally (perpetrated by others—suppliers, vendors, customers, hackers) against the corporation.[9] Bologna includes management fraud, where there is intentional overstatement of corporate or division profits, as a part of corporate fraud. Management fraud is inspired, perpetrated, or induced by managers who seek to benefit in terms of promotions, job stability, larger bonuses, and status symbols.

6.3 Indicators of Fraud

(a) Identification and Assessment of Fraud Risks

To identify fraud risks (including any related to fraudulent improper payments), the auditor should perform the following procedures:

- Evaluate the information obtained in the procedures described in the context of the three conditions that generally are present when fraud occurs—incentive/pressure, opportunity, and attitude/rationalization. While fraud risk might be greatest when all three of these conditions are evident, observation of one or more of these conditions might indicate a fraud risk.

- Where revenue is (or is expected to be) material, evaluate whether there are fraud risks related to revenue recognition (e.g., through premature recognition or fictitious revenue). If the auditor concludes that improper revenue recognition does not represent a fraud risk, the auditor should document the reasons supporting that conclusion.

- Evaluate the possibility that management could override controls, even if specific fraud risks have not been identified.

- For each identified fraud risk, determine whether it relates to (1) specific financial statement account balances or classes of transactions and related assertions or, (2) more pervasively, to the financial statements as a whole. Generally, relating fraud risks to the individual accounts, classes of transactions, and assertions helps in designing audit procedures in response to these risks.

- As part of understanding internal control sufficient to plan the audit, (1) evaluate whether programs and controls that address identified fraud risks have been suitably designed and

---

[9] Bologna, *Handbook on Corporate Fraud.*

implemented, and (2) determine whether these programs and controls mitigate these risks, or whether specific control deficiencies increase these risks.

■ Assess the identified fraud risks. Evaluate the significant aspects of each of these risks, including the type of misstatement, the significance and pervasiveness of the risk, and the likelihood that a material misstatement could result.

(b) Response to Assessed Fraud Risks

The auditor must respond to the assessed risks of material misstatement due to fraud. The nature and significance of these fraud risks, as well as programs and controls that address identified fraud risks, influence the auditor's response. The auditor should use professional judgment in determining the appropriate response for the circumstances and exercise professional skepticism in gathering and evaluating audit evidence.

The response should

1. Affect the overall conduct of the audit.
2. Address fraud risks that relate to management override of controls.
3. Involve the nature, extent, and timing of audit procedures for any risks that relate to specific financial statement account balances or classes of transactions and related assertions.

In some instances, the audit strategy and audit plan could, for reasons other than responding to fraud risk, include procedures and personnel and supervisory assignments that are sufficient to respond to a fraud risk. In those instances, the auditor may conclude that no further response is required. For example, with respect to timing, audit procedures could be planned as of the date that the reporting period ends, both as a response to a fraud risk and for other reasons.

The auditor should respond to the fraud risks in ways that have an overall effect on the conduct of the audit:

1. **Assignment of personnel and supervision**—The auditor should assign audit team staffing and/or supervision so that the knowledge, skill, and ability of personnel assigned significant responsibilities are commensurate with the auditor's assessment of the fraud risks. For example, the auditor may assign a fraud specialist or more experienced staff member or may increase supervision in response to identified fraud risk specialists.

2. **Review of accounting principles**—The auditor should review management's selection and collective application of significant accounting principles, particularly those related to subjective measurements and complex transactions.

3. **Unpredictability of audit procedures**—The auditor should incorporate an element of unpredictability in the selection of audit procedures from reporting period to reporting period. For example, the auditor may perform substantive procedures on selected account balances and assertions not otherwise tested due to their materiality and risk, adjust the timing of audit tests, use a different method to select items for testing, or perform procedures at different locations or at locations on an unannounced basis. Statistical sampling selection usually provides an element of unpredictability as to the specific items tested. Generally, the auditor should not inform entity personnel of specific audit procedures prior to performing them, as personnel may take actions to further conceal any fraudulent activity. However, the auditor usually will make arrangements to conduct

audit work at specific sites in advance and will instruct entity personnel to locate certain documentation so the auditor may test it upon arrival.

The auditor should perform procedures to specifically address the risk that management can perpetrate fraud by overriding controls as follows:

1. **Examine journal entries and other adjustments**—The auditor should examine journal entries and other adjustments for evidence of possible material misstatement due to fraud. These include reclassifications, consolidating entries, and other routine and non-routine journal entries and adjustments. The auditor should

   ■ **Obtain an understanding of the financial reporting process and the controls over journal entries and other adjustments:**

      □ Identify and select journal entries and other adjustments for testing;

      □ Determine the nature, extent, and timing of the testing (ordinarily including tests of journal entries and other adjustments at the end of the reporting period); and

      □ Inquire of individuals involved in the financial reporting process about inappropriate or unusual activity related to the processing of journal entries and other adjustments.

2. **Review of accounting estimates**—The auditor should review accounting estimates for biases that could result in material misstatement due to fraud. In preparing financial statements, management is responsible for making judgments or assumptions that affect significant accounting estimates and for monitoring the reasonableness of these estimates on an ongoing basis. The auditor should evaluate whether differences between estimates best supported by the evidence and estimates included in the financial statements indicate possible bias by management, even if the estimates are individually reasonable. If so, the auditor should reconsider the estimates taken as a whole.

   The auditor also should perform a retrospective review of significant accounting estimates used in the prior year's financial statements, focusing on sensitive or subjective aspects, to determine whether they indicate possible bias by management. The auditor should be alert for aggressive or inconsistently applied estimates (e.g., significant changes in allowances for uncollectible accounts that may be tied to performance measures in an effort to improve collections).

3. **Evaluate business rationale for significant unusual transactions**—The auditor should evaluate the business rationale for any significant unusual transactions, considering whether

   ■ The form of these transactions is overly complex;

   ■ Management has discussed the nature of and accounting for these transactions with those charged with governance;

   ■ Management is placing more emphasis on particular accounting treatments than on the underlying economics of the transactions;

   ■ Transactions that involve related parties require review and approval by those charged with governance; and

   ■ Transactions involve previously unidentified related parties or related parties that do not have the substance or financial strength to support them without assistance from the entity.

For fraud risks related to specific financial statement account balances or classes of transactions and related assertions, the specific response will depend on the types of risks and the specific balances or classes and assertions, but it generally should involve both substantive procedures and control tests. The response should involve examining one or more of the following:

- **Nature** of audit procedures—for example, obtaining related evidence from independent external sources rather than internal sources

- **Extent** of audit procedures—for example, increasing sample sizes

- **Timing** of audit procedures—for example, performing substantive procedures at or near the end of the reporting period rather than at an interim date

(i) Risk Factors, Red Flags, and Symptoms of Fraud

(A) Risk Factors in Fraud. Internal auditors should be aware of risk factors related to general fraud as well as computer fraud.

Risk Factors Related to General Fraud (Red Flags of Corporate Fraud)

- Infighting among top management
- Low morale and motivation among employees
- Understaffed accounting departments
- High level of complaints against the organization from customers, suppliers, or regulatory authorities
- Inconsistent and surprising cash flow deficiencies
- Decreasing sales or income while accounts payable and receivable are rising
- Company line of credit is used to its limit for long periods of time
- Significant excess inventory
- Increasing number of year-end adjusting journal entries

Source: Association of Certified Fraud Examiners, "The White Paper" 7, no. 5 (October/November 1993). Original source was from: KPMG Canada, *The Fraud Prevention Primer.*

The degree of fraud can be linked to an organization's environment.

- **High fraud environment**—Low management integrity, poor control environment, loose accountability, and high pressure for results

- **Low fraud environment**—A culture of honesty, management openness, and employee assistance programs, and total quality management

The user-friendliness of computer systems and the increase in user computer literacy combined with a lack of or inadequate system controls could have a significant effect on computer crime and fraud. The rewards of computer crime can be greater than other crimes, and there is less chance of being discovered and convicted. Weak laws, embarrassment, expense, and time are the reasons given for not prosecuting computer criminals. For example, under the current laws, it is difficult to prosecute employees (insiders) of a company for perpetrating computer fraud. This is compounded by the fact that it is difficult to prove malicious intent. A computer is used as a tool but is also the means to perpetrate fraud. The motivations for, or causes of, computer abuse or fraud include

- Situational pressures
- Opportunities
- Personal or financial gain
- Revenge

Situational pressures can include when an honest employee becomes addicted to alcohol or drugs, or incurs large debts because of gambling. Opportunities are provided by weak policies and procedures and/or a poor system of controls or a lack of audit trails. Given the opportunity, employees will find shortcuts around certain controls. Some employees will steal given any opportunity. System users can reveal system vulnerabilities due to their close working knowledge of the system, both manual and automated. Other causes of computer abuse and fraud include personal or financial gain and revenge against employers and coworkers.

Creating a team environment can help employees feel that they are a part of the decision-making process and be content with their jobs. This in turn motivates employees to behave in a normal manner and be less tempted to commit computer crime and fraud. Empowering employees is a positive thing to do here.

Control/Audit Risks: Computer Fraud and Crime

- Good internal controls do not deter some employees, who will always steal. However, good internal controls do detect fraud at an early date and therefore lessen the loss. Internal controls are there for honest employees.
- Most computer crimes and frauds are committed internally, by employees of the organization.
- More damaging and more serious frauds are being committed by individuals outside the organization, such as consultants, contractors, and hackers.
- Some people will take advantage of any weakness in the computer system and company policies and procedures as well as their employment position.
- Application program development and maintenance work are equal targets for computer crime and fraud activities.
- Additions, deletions, and changes to computer data files are major sources of computer crime and fraud, including data breaches, data stealing, and data loss.
- Employees may sell computer-based client/customer lists, vendor names and addresses, bid information, or other sensitive and confidential information to competitors and others for money, to take revenge, or for other reasons.
- Employees may walk out the door with the organization's data and programs on disks and tapes.
- Third-shift service bureau employees may conduct computer work for their own clients without the knowledge of service bureau management.
- For each irregularity or fraud discovered, there might be hundreds of dead ends.
- Applications software reliability is one of the weakest links in the security and fraud chain.
- Programmers, systems analysts, tape librarians, database analysts and administrators, and functional users all are capable of committing computer crime and fraud.
- Passwords and other identification codes can be cracked via brute-force approaches.
- Spool area print files can be the targets of fraud where files can be copied before they are printed.

(B) Red Flags for Fraud. **Red flags** do not signal that a fraud has occurred but rather that the opportunity for a fraud exists. Some examples of red flags are listed next.

- Concealed assets
- Missing or destroyed records and documents
- Split purchases
- Excessive voids or refunds
- Rapid turnover of financial managers and executives

According to Belden Menkus, all types of frauds, including computer frauds, are characterized by certain contributing factors related to the values and motivations of the fraud perpetrator and the management of the defrauded organization.[10] Understanding how computer fraud can occur will not eliminate the menace; however, auditors have no alternative but to ferret out weaknesses and develop counterstrategies. The eight factors that contribute to computer fraud are listed next.

1. **Inadequate design of the information system**—Inadequate design deals with the flaws and errors in the system. The system's performance does not rest on a reliable foundation and its results are not predictable in any reasonable or consistent fashion. This provides opportunity for fraud.

2. **Aggregation of the information system's transaction processing steps prevents reviews of what is taking place**—The separation of duties within the system may be reduced or eliminated as a result of information system design techniques that are inherently interlinked and integrated. Verification of transaction operations becomes difficult if not impossible.

3. **Insufficient discrimination as to the legitimacy of transactions processed by the information system**—Data editing and validation routines at data entry and update activities may not be available or may too primitive to be of any use.

4. **Error toleration by the information system—either in data content or processing results**—Users may establish some arbitrary upper limit on individual errors that would disguise fraudulent activity as apparent error. This means that fraud perpetrators who are not greedy or careless are almost impossible for the auditor to detect, except by accident.

5. **Detachment of the information system's ongoing operation from the physical or functional reality that it is supposed to reflect**—For example, an inventory database does not reflect the actual items. In this situation, although a set of numbers looks right, they may be essentially worthless.

6. **Unrestrained, unmediated remote access to an information system that is subject to possible compromise or manipulation**—Sometimes it is difficult to isolate the actual identity or even the location of the individual perpetrating the fraud.

7. **Restricted ability to collect sufficient knowledge about the fraud itself, especially its scope and the extent of the loss that has occurred**—Fraud perpetrators may not

---

[10] Belden Menjus, "Eight Factors Contributing to Computer Fraud," *Internal Auditor* (October 1990).

leave sufficient evidence of their actions, or they may destroy the evidence (as when the system permits files to be modified without leaving any trace of what was added, changed, or deleted).

8. **Limits in the investigative tools for analyzing the knowledge that auditors may gain about the fraud**—The volume, volatility, and complexity of data that must be considered in detecting and investigating computer frauds may exceed the auditor's ability to deal with the size and scope of audit work in a timely manner.

Business Risks: Fraud

- Employee hiring efforts could be ineffective since computer criminals usually have the same characteristics as people whom organizations are seeking to employ.

- Employees will not take seriously a code of conduct if it is not consistently enforced.

- Not prosecuting employees caught in committing a computer crime could send a wrong signal to other employees that illegal acts are acceptable.

- If organizations quietly suspend without prosecuting employees who committed computer crime and fraud, the problem is never solved, and the suspended employee will find another job where he or she is more than likely to resume such behavior.

- If the employee's rights are violated either by improper search or by lack of evidence when suspected of computer crime, the organization may be legally liable for damages.

- Computer crime will never be completely eliminated because the elements of controls are themselves subject to human error and manipulation.

(ii) Professional Skepticism in Fraud

The planning and performance of an audit are to be carried out by an auditor with an attitude of professional skepticism. This means that the auditor neither assumes that management is dishonest nor assumes unquestioned honesty. An objective evaluation of the situation and of management integrity are important considerations for the auditor. *The auditor needs to balance between excessive audit costs due to suspicion and time constraints.*

The auditor should use professional skepticism in establishing the audit scope and in gathering audit evidence. The auditor needs to be aware of the inherent limitations of the auditing process, which include flaws in the audit procedures, auditor errors, risks created by management override of controls, collusion, forgeries, and unrecorded transactions.

The audit engagement needs to be planned so as to provide reasonable assurance of determining material errors or irregularities. *Errors are unintentional mistakes. Irregularities are intentional distortions, misrepresentations, and fraud.*

The auditor's understanding of the internal control structure influences the degree of professional skepticism applied in the course of the audit. The auditor gains an understanding of the internal control structure through previous experiences in the auditable area and by reviewing evidence obtained through preliminary audit survey work, which includes inquiry, inspection, and observation. *The more comfortable the auditor is with the internal control structure, the less skeptical he or she would be.*

KEY CONCEPTS TO REMEMBER: Sequence of Audit Activities Related to Professional Skepticism

- Review the internal control structure.
- Perform audit planning work.
- Determine the audit scope.
- Collect audit evidence.
- Review accounting estimates.
- Issue an audit opinion.

It is good to remain skeptical throughout the course of an audit even if the preliminary survey results indicate no existence of irregularities. If internal auditors discover errors and irregularities during the audit, they are required to inform the audit committee by quantifying their effects after obtaining sufficient evidence of their existence. In essence, it is good for internal auditors to maintain a posture of professional skepticism at all times.

(iii) Management Representations versus Risk

The auditor needs to assess the risk of management misrepresentations and to consider the effects of such risks in establishing an overall audit strategy and the scope of the audit.

Examples of Situations (Red Flags) that Could Lead to Risk of Management Misrepresentations

- Frequent disputes about aggressive application of generally accepted accounting principles
- Excessive emphasis on meeting targets upon which management compensation program is based
- Evasive responses to audit inquiries
- Employees lack necessary knowledge and experience yet develop various estimates including accounting
- Supervisors of employees generating estimates appear careless or inexperienced in reviewing and approving the estimates
- A history of unreliable or unreasonable estimates
- Constant crisis conditions in operating and accounting areas of the organization
- Frequent and excessive back orders, shortages of materials and products, delays, or lack of documentation of major transactions exist
- No restrictions on access to computer-based application systems initiating or controlling the movement of assets
- High levels of transaction processing errors
- Unusual delays in providing operating results and accounting reports

Value of Audit Client Representations

Audit client representations are not good substitutes for effective auditing procedures.

(iv) Review of Accounting Estimates

Many assumptions go into accounting estimates. The internal auditor should understand these assumptions and should determine whether the assumptions are subjective and are susceptible to misstatements and bias.

The auditor should show professional skepticism during the review and evaluation of the reasonableness of accounting estimates. These estimates contain both subjective and objective factors. Professional skepticism is important with regard to subjective factors where personal bias could be significant.

Examples of Accounting Estimates

- Uncollectible receivables
- Allowance for loan losses
- Revenues to be earned on contracts
- Subscription income
- Losses on sales contracts
- Professional membership or union dues income
- Valuation of financial securities
- Trading versus investment security classifications
- Compensation in stock option plans and deferred plans
- Probability of loss
- Obsolete inventory
- Net realizable value of inventories
- Losses in purchase commitments
- Property and casualty insurance accruals
- Loss reserves
- Warranty claims
- Taxes on real estate and personal property

In addition to review, the auditor should test management's process of developing accounting estimates or develop an independent estimation. The auditor can compare prior estimates with subsequent results to assess the reliability of the process used to develop estimates. The auditor should also review whether the accounting estimates are consistent with the entity's operational plans and programs.

6.4 Awareness of Fraud

Fraud-awareness initiatives include fraud training and education for managers, supervisors, employees, and stakeholders (e.g., customers and suppliers) with responsibility for implementing antifraud programs and efforts. Benefits of these initiatives are to (1) prevent potential fraud, (2) create a culture of integrity and compliance within an organization, and (3) better detect potential fraud.

Examples of Leading Practices in Antifraud Efforts

- Provide training and educational programs when employees are hired and retrain periodically. Maintain records of training to show compliance with requirements. Usually, the human resources department is responsible for coordinating these training programs.

- Provide more frequent and more targeted training to employees working in high-risk positions or functional areas. Maintain records of training to show compliance with requirements.

- Blend antifraud training programs with existing ethics training, code of conduct training, and compliance training programs.

- Provide information on how and where to report fraud incidents, including information on reporting mechanisms and what to report.

- Send a positive message with benefits of fraud risk management programs (e.g., increased revenues and profits and good morale), the cost of fraud, and consequences of engaging in fraud, such as sanctions, disciplinary actions, and other punishments.

Examples of Educational Activities Related to Fraud Control

- Newsletters highlighting the results of cases or information on fraud schemes
- Fraud risk indicators that communicate red flags to employees
- Computer-based trainings that are available on demand, such as audios or videos about fraud issues

6.5 Controls to Prevent or Detect Fraud Risks

Fraud prevention results in big savings because when fraud is prevented, there are no detection or investigation costs. This means a dollar spent in preventing fraud saves many more dollars later on. Therefore, greater attention should be paid to preventive controls rather than detective controls and recovery controls.

(a) Preventive Controls in General

Some examples of preventive controls are listed next.

- Sharing the company vision with all employees
- Distributing fraud policies and programs
- Conducting proactive audits using discovery sampling techniques
- Database query facilities and data mining tools
- Providing a hotline for fraud reporting by employees and others
- Monitoring employee performance
- Enforcing employee vacation privileges

- Discouraging collusion between employees, customers, or vendors with policies clearly explained to them
- Establishing a sound system of internal controls (both formal and informal)
- Providing fraud awareness training programs
- Providing employee assistance programs to deal with personal and work-related pressures
- Establishing physical security and information systems security controls
- Enforcing existing internal controls and fraud policies with the understanding that dishonesty will be punished
- Establishing separation of duties, dual custody, and dual controls
- Establishing total quality management programs
- Creating a positive work environment with open-door policy to facilitate open communications
- Creating teamwork with self-directed teams or quality circles
- Assigning responsibility for fraud prevention programs
- Hiring honest employees
- Publishing a code of ethics
- Establishing a system of authorizations and independent checks and balances
- Encouraging employee empowerment

(b) Detective Controls in General

Some examples of detective controls are listed next.

- Building audit trails in business transactions (whether automated or not)
- Testing controls
- Conducting regular internal audits
- Conducting surprise internal audits
- Conducting employee performance evaluations
- Watching employee lifestyle changes
- Observing employee behavior toward work, the organization, and other employees
- Periodically taking physical inventory of assets, financial securities, and other valuable items

(c) Computer Fraud–Related Controls

Good business practices include management (directive) controls, such as performing pre-employment screening procedures, requiring employees to sign a code of conduct, and conducting periodic training programs in computer security and privacy policies and procedures.

System-based preventive, detective, and recovery controls are also needed to combat computer crime and fraud in the electronic age.

(d) Preventive Controls

Preventive controls can help in restricting the access of potential perpetrators to the computer facility, computer terminals, data files, programs, and system libraries. Separation of duties, rotation of duties, backup personnel, and a good system of internal controls are some examples of preventive controls.

(e) Detective Controls

Detective controls can help in discovering fraud in the event a perpetrator slips past established prevention mechanisms. Some tips and procedures for fraud detection are listed next.

- Auditors should take a fresh approach to looking at the data (middle-of-the-month review instead of month-end).
- They should break the normal pattern of reporting (obtain early or late reports, ad hoc reports instead of scheduled), change review timing to throw things off their track (random times, not month-end, quarter-end, or year-end), and run normal reports at unusual times.

Audit hooks can help in monitoring the computer fraud. Audit hooks are embedded in application programs and are flagged when incoming and processed transactions meet prescribed criteria. If auditors requested and designed the audit hooks, they should provide the test data and assist in testing the computer system.

(f) Recovery Controls

Recovery controls can help to limit losses (financial or other) resulting from a well-planned and well-executed computer fraud and crime.

Prior to auditing for fraud, the organization must answer these questions:

- What does it have that someone would want to steal?
- How would someone go about stealing from it?
- How vulnerable is it?
- How can it detect fraud and crime?

6.6 Audit Tests to Detect Fraud, Including Discovery Sampling

It has been said that most frauds are detected by accident, not by planned effort. This should not stop auditors from planning to detect fraud. Some known approaches to detect fraud include testing; statistical sampling, especially discovery sampling methods; computer-assisted audit techniques; data query; and data mining tools.

(a) Tools and Techniques

Some examples of fraud-related audit tools include analytical techniques, charting techniques, recalculations, confirmations, observations, physical examinations, inquiries, and document reviews.

Examples of statistical techniques include **discovery sampling**, a type of sampling procedure that has a specified probability of including at least one item that occurs very rarely in the population. Multiple regression analysis can be used to find relationships between two or more variables of interest.

Examples of computer-assisted audit techniques include finding exceptions in data through analysis of computer files. These files are searched for invoice or payment duplication or other anomalies.

Data query tools are used to search the database for known conditions of data sequencing and data dependencies. Auditors can query many points within a database. Data mining tools can be used to detect abnormal patterns in data.

(b) Steps to Take when Fraud Is Suspected

Handling suspected fraud is a difficult thing to do. It must be dealt with properly and with care. Amateurs in the personnel or audit department playing at being investigators can cause many unforeseen problems and unpleasant surprises. If cases of suspected fraud are not handled properly, employee morale and trust can be shattered. Unsubstantiated charges can bring on lawsuits for defamation, illegal firing, false arrest, invasion of privacy, and stress. Confrontations with suspected employees can be staged before allegations are even documented or verified. Evidence that may support the charges often can go uncollected or be mishandled.

Jack Bologna provides these tips that could help in investigating internal corruption charges:

- Qualify the source of the allegation (i.e., check on the source's identity, credibility, knowledgeability, and reliability).

- Determine whether the source knows the information firsthand (personal knowledge) or whether it has been passed on by another (hearsay).

- Determine the motives of the source (revenge, spite, jealousy, pique, and money).

- If the source demands money before disclosing details, beware. Do not front money until verifiable information has been given and has been confirmed through independent means (other credible witnesses or documents).

- Qualify all further information about the alleged corruption (i.e., verify and corroborate the charges through other independent sources and documents).

- Never take disciplinary action without a complete record of the corruption allegation, including the identity of the source of the allegations and his or her written account of the allegations. (An oral account is not enough.)

- Confirm the allegations through documents and the testimony (written and subscribed to) of other knowledgeable witnesses.

- Approach the vendors, suppliers, or others alleged to be involved; elicit their responses and enlist their cooperation.

- Interview the suspected employee to seek his or her version of the situation (e.g., Did the vendor make the offer or did the employee solicit the vendor?).[11]

Another related question that should be asked is: Should the investigation and audit proceed with inside resources (i.e., security department staff, legal department staff, or audit department staff, or a combination)? If the insiders are trained properly, work can proceed in-house. If they are not properly trained, it is advisable to go outside to a reputable and experienced private detective, legal firm, consultant, public accounting firm, or other.

(i) Document Examination

Document examination is a part of gathering evidence for fraud. This technique uncovers perpetrators' efforts to conceal fraud by cover-up schemes involving documents. Documents can be altered, forged, created, changed, duplicated, or misplaced. According to Joseph Wells, most internal frauds are concealed by manipulating source documents, such as purchase orders, sales invoices, credit memorandums, and warehouse removal slips.[12] Investigators should be aware that missing documents, destroyed records, modified records, errors, or omissions can be attributed to human error, carelessness, or accident as well as deliberate action on the part of a suspect.

Guidelines for Document Examination

- Always search for the strongest possible evidence.
- Investigate without delay.
- Do not ignore small clues or leads.
- Look for facts you can confirm or refute.
- Be persistent and creative.
- Concentrate on the weakest link in the fraud chain.

Source: Joseph Wells, Association of Certified Fraud Examiners, Austin, Texas, 1992.

(ii) Examining Accounting Records

According to Wells, one of the easiest ways to detect fraud in accounting records is by looking for weaknesses in the various steps of the accounting transaction cycle. Legitimate transactions leave a trail that can be followed. Most transactions start with a source document, such as an invoice, a check, or a receiving report.

[11]Bologna, *Handbook on Corporate Fraud.*
[12]Wells, *Fraud Examination.*

These source documents become the basis for journal entries, which are chronological listings of transactions with their debit and credit amounts. Journal entries are made in various accounting journals. The entries in the journals are then posted or entered into the accounts. The amounts in the accounts are summarized to become the financial statements for a period.

When fictitious entries are made to the accounting records, source documents are normally absent, fabricated, or altered. These documents, together with the journal entries, accounts, and financial statements, leave a trail that can reveal many frauds. The next guidelines help in searching for overstatement or understatement of amounts in financial statements:

■ When searching for an understatement in the financial statements, one usually begins with the source documents and works forward to the financial statements. If the financial statements are understated, sometimes the information from the invoice will be deleted or altered.

■ When searching for an overstatement in the financial statements, one starts with the financial statement and works backward to the source documents. Normally true overstatements will not have legitimate supporting documentation.

Analyzing past records can reveal some insights that can be used to establish the operating standards. These records should include the:

■ Normal rate of loss per a specific time period

■ Number and nature of transactions processed per day

■ Number and nature of exceptional transactions handled

■ Number and nature of people movement in and out per day

(iii) Documenting Fraud

Documenting fraud is as important, if not more, as conducting the fraud investigation. Documenting fraud is a continuous effort from inception to completion of the fraud investigation. During the documentation period, a great deal of evidence is in the form of documents. Wells states that many examiners (auditors) pay too much attention to documents. It is easy to get bogged down in details when examining records and lose sight of a simple fact: Documents do not make cases; witnesses do. The documents make or break the witness. So-called paper cases often confuse and bore juries. Only relevant documents should be collected. In order to guarantee document acceptance by the courts, one should provide

■ Proof that the evidence is relevant and material

■ Proper identification of the item

■ Proof of the chain of custody of the document

Early in the case, the relevance of documents cannot be easily determined. For that reason, it is recommended that all documents possible be obtained; if they are not needed, they can always be returned or destroyed. General rules regarding the collection of documents include

■ Obtain original documents where feasible. Make working copies for review, and keep the original segregated.

■ Do not touch originals any more than necessary; they may later be needed for forensic analysis.

- Maintain a good filing system for the documents. This is especially critical where large volumes of documents are obtained. Voluminous documents can be sequentially stamped for easy reference.[13]

(iv) Obtaining Documentary Evidence

Three principal methods exist for obtaining documentary evidence: subpoenas, search warrants, and voluntary consent[14] (see Exhibit 6.2).

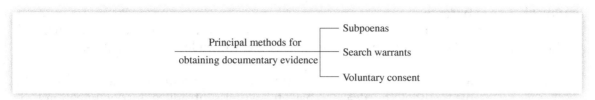

Principal methods for obtaining documentary evidence
- Subpoenas
- Search warrants
- Voluntary consent

EXHIBIT 6.2 Principle Methods for Obtaining Documentary Evidence

Subpoenas are ordinarily issued by the court or grand jury and can take three forms. A subpoena *duces tecum* calls for the production of documents and records, whereas a regular subpoena is used for witnesses. If the examiner is not an agent of the grand jury or the court, obtaining documents by subpoena is not possible. Subpoenas can call for the production of documents at a grand jury or deposition at a specified time. A forthwith subpoena is usually served by surprise and reserved for those instances where it is thought the records will be secreted, altered, or destroyed.

Search warrants are issued by a judge upon presentation of probable cause to believe the records are being used or have been used in the commission of a crime. An affidavit is usually used to support the request for the search warrant. The affidavit must describe the reason(s) the warrant is requested, along with the place the evidence is thought to be kept.

Courts do not issue search warrants lightly, as the Constitution protects individuals against unreasonable searches and seizures. Search warrants are almost never used in civil cases. Although there are provisions in the law for warrantless search, examiners should avoid such searches at all costs. Searches can be conducted by voluntary consent.

Documents can be obtained by **voluntary consent**, and this is the preferred method. The consent can be oral or written. In the case of obtaining information from possible adverse witnesses or from the target of the examination, it is recommended that the consent be in writing.

(v) Types of Evidence

The examiner or auditor needs to be familiar with the types of evidence in order to obtain the right kind of evidence. Basically, evidence falls into one of two categories, either direct or circumstantial (see Exhibit 6.3).

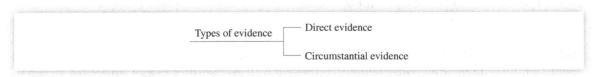

Types of evidence
- Direct evidence
- Circumstantial evidence

EXHIBIT 6.3 Types of Evidence

---

[13] Ibid.
[14] Ibid.

Direct evidence is that which shows *prima facie* the facts at issue. What constitutes direct evidence depends on the factors involved. For example, in the case of kickbacks, direct evidence might be a check from the person making the kickback directly to the target.

Circumstantial evidence is that which would indirectly show culpability. For example, in the case of a kickback allegation, cash deposits of unknown origin deposited to the account of the target around the time of the suspect transaction could be circumstantial evidence.

(vi) Organization of Evidence

One of the biggest problems in fraud cases is keeping track of the amount of paper generated. Good organization of documents in complex cases usually includes these guidelines.

- Segregate documents by either witness or transaction. Chronological organization is the least preferable method. The idea is to have the witness introduce the document, not the examiner or auditor.

- Make a "key document" file for easy access to the most relevant documents. Purge this file periodically of less important documents.

- Establish a database early on when volumes of information exist. The database should include, at a minimum, date of the document, individual from whom the document was obtained, date the document was obtained, brief description of the document, and subject to whom the document pertains.

Legal Rules of Evidence

There are strict legal rules regarding the handling of evidence and the chain of custody thereof. If the examiner is operating under a lawful order of the courts that compels a custodian of records to furnish original documents, the documents should be copied, preferably in the presence of the custodian, before being removed from the premises. The custodian keeps the copies. If not operating under a court directive and the records are being provided voluntarily by the custodian, the examiner may retain copies instead of originals.

- Maintain a control log of events and documents in the case of voluminous evidence and complex cases. The purpose of maintaining a brief chronology of events is to establish the chain of events leading to the proof. The chronology may or may not be made a part of the formal report. At a minimum, it can be used for analysis of the case and kept in a working paper binder.

(c) Charting Techniques

Three types of charting techniques for documenting fraud are link network diagrams, time flow diagrams, and matrices (see Exhibit 6.4).[15]

Link network diagrams show the relationships among persons, organizations, and events. Different symbols can be used consistently to represent different entities (e.g., a square for an organization, a circle for a person, and a triangle for an event). A solid line can represent connection

---

[15] Ibid.

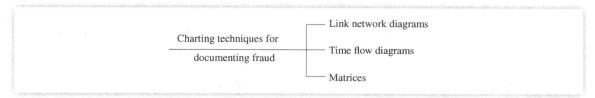

EXHIBIT 6.4 Charting Techniques for Documentary Fraud

between entities, and broken lines can show presumed relationships. The diagram should be clear and simple to understand.

Time flow diagrams show the relationships of significant events, in the order in which they occurred. A **matrix** is a grid that shows the relationship or points of contact between a number of entities. Known contact can be differentiated from presumed contact by use of different marks, such as a solid dot or an open dot. In complex cases, a matrix is a useful preliminary step to identify the relative status of the parties by showing the number of contacts of each. Later the matrix can be converted into a table or a chart. For example, a matrix can be used to identify the direction and frequency of telephone traffic between suspect parties.

(i) Business and Individual Records

Original documents are preferred and should be obtained wherever possible. If necessary, the examiner should furnish the record custodian a receipt for the property. If the originals cannot be obtained, the examiner can settle for copies. The exact records obtained will vary from case to case, but where applicable, basic business records often include these:

- Organization of the business such as article of incorporation
- Financial statements and tax returns
- Customer lists
- Business diaries, address, telephone, text messages, facsimile, and email records
- Personnel records, including employment application
- Bank account records, deposit slips, and canceled checks
- Relevant contracts or agreements
- Computer programs and data file disks

Originals of individual records are usually easier to obtain than originals of business records. Some of the more relevant individual records include these:

- Bank account records, deposit slips, and canceled checks
- Financial statements and tax returns
- Credit card statements and payment records
- Telephone, facsimile, text messages, and email records

(ii) Memorandum of Interview

It is a good practice to write a memorandum addressed to the case file any time evidence comes into or leaves the hands of the fraud examiner or auditor. Whether it is included in the final report or working papers or not, each official contact during the course of a fraud examination should be recorded on a "memorandum of interview" on a timely basis. Some guidelines for properly handling the memorandum of interview follow.

- Include all facts of possible evidence on the memorandum of interview.

- Reconfirm dates and supporting information with the interviewee to ensure their accuracy. Reconfirmation acts as a precautionary measure to make certain all facts are accurate before the report is written, not after.

- Include the quotations of the interviewee in the memorandum of interview.

- Transcribe all interviews in writing as soon as practicable following the interview. The main reason timeliness is so important is to ensure the accuracy of witness testimony. The longer the examiner waits to record the interview, the more will be forgotten.

- Record each witness interviewed on a separate memorandum of interview. Recordings of witnesses should not be mixed, since a request by the courts or others for a particular witness's statement can then be fulfilled without providing the entire report.

The contents of a memorandum of interview for a witness should contain these details:

- Nature of the inquiry

- Nature of the interviewer (e.g., voluntary or not)

- Date the interview was conducted

- Method of conducting the interview (i.e., in person or on the telephone)

- Identity of the interviewer (i.e., fraud examiner, internal or external auditor, investigator, consultant, or detective)

- Each source or informant contact should be documented on a memorandum of interview, but always referring to the source or informant by a symbol number (S-2, I-2). State the reliability of the individual source (e.g., job title, expertise). When a source or informant is paid money for information, ensure that the payment is noted in the body of the memorandum of interview. Do not pay an informant or source without obtaining a receipt of payment.

- The identities of informants or sources should be fully documented and retained in a secure file, available only on a need-to-know basis. The symbol number used in the memorandum of interview should be cross-referenced to the secure file.

(iii) Writing Fraud Reports

Writing a report of a fraud investigation is one of the most demanding and important tasks of a fraud examiner or an auditor. Some reasons why a written report is so important are listed next.

- The report is an evidence of the work performed.

- The report conveys to the litigator all the evidence needed to evaluate the legal status of the case.

- The written report adds credibility to the examination and to the examiner.

- The report forces the fraud examiner to consider his or her actions before and during the interview, so that the objectives of the investigation can be best accomplished.

- The report omits immaterial information so that the facts of the case can be clearly and completely understood.

(iv) Characteristics of Fraud Reports

Important characteristics of good report writing include accuracy, clarity, impartiality, relevance, and timeliness (see Exhibit 6.5).

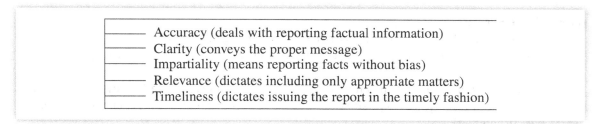

Accuracy (deals with reporting factual information)
Clarity (conveys the proper message)
Impartiality (means reporting facts without bias)
Relevance (dictates including only appropriate matters)
Timeliness (dictates issuing the report in the timely fashion)

EXHIBIT 6.5 Characteristics of Fraud Reports

Accuracy deals with reporting factual information that is correct and that can be verified. There is no room for error. **Clarity** means conveying the proper message in the clearest possible language. If necessary, the interviewed person can be quoted, provided the quotation does not distort the context of the memorandum of interview. Complex terms should be explained since persons who are not familiar with technical terminology might read the report. **Impartiality** means reporting facts without bias. **Relevance** dictates including only matters appropriate to the examination. Irrelevant information confuses and complicates the written report and leaves the examiner open to criticism of his or her methodology. **Timeliness** dictates issuing the draft and the final reports in a timely manner so that they will accomplish their objective(s).

Written Reports

In the absence of an established system of report writing, Wells recommends including five major sections: cover page, witness statements, cover letter, working papers, and index.[16] **The cover page** of a report typically includes all pertinent data gathered during the course of an examination. It includes file number, case description, perpetrator (employee) name, the lead investigator name, date of report, case status (pending, inactive, closed), report number, type of inquiry (civil, criminal, administrative), referrals, synopsis, financial data (all costs incurred, projected losses), final disposition, and predication (basis under which the investigation commenced to establish a reason for investigation).

The final report should include all relevant **witness statements**. Typically a **cover letter** to the requester of the investigation is included with the report. The purpose of the cover letter is to

- Accompany the report.
- Set forth a succinct summary of witness testimony.
- Provide details on the location of potential witnesses.
- Set forth the apparent violation of law, if any, that the report addresses.

---

[16] Ibid.

Summarized **working papers**, when necessary, should be enclosed as attachments to the report. If working papers are enclosed with the report, they should be so described in the cover letter of the report.

If there are a limited number of memorandums of interviews, the **index** may be omitted; otherwise it is a good idea to provide an index. The index should be in chronological order rather than alphabetical, so the reader of the report may easily follow the development of the case.

(vi) Privileged Reports

According to Wells, there is no privilege, per se, for investigative reports and notes, or for any fraud examination, forensic audit, or similar services. However, there are two exceptions.

1. If the examiner is conducting an investigation at the request of an attorney in anticipation of litigation, the report is considered in most courts as an attorney/client work product (i.e., privileged).

2. If a public authority, such as the police, federal agents, the courts or grand jury, or the like, is conducting the investigation, the report can be considered privileged.[17]

If the examination is being conducted under the authority of the lawyer-client-court privilege, each page of the report should be marked "Privileged and Confidential."

Mistakes to Avoid in Writing Fraud Reports

Mistakes are costly, especially in fraud reports. Careless errors should be avoided and are inexcusable. Mistakes and errors can make a report useless. A brief description of areas to be careful about in writing fraud reports, based on Wells, follows.

Conclusions.   One of the most significant mistakes made by fraud examiners and auditors is the statement of conclusions in the written report. Under no circumstances should conclusions be made, as they may come back to haunt the examiner in litigation. The opposing counsel's main tactic is usually to try to impeach whatever testimony is given and to show that the examiner is biased. The conclusions of the investigations should be self-evident and able to stand alone. If not, the report has not been properly prepared.

Opinions.   Like conclusions, opinions have no place in the report. Under no circumstances should an opinion be written concerning the guilt or innocence of any person or party, as this is purview of the courts; it is up to the jury to decide guilt or innocence.

Informant and Source Information.   Under no circumstances whatsoever should the name of a confidential source or informant be disclosed in the report or anywhere else in writing. It is recommended that the source or informant be referred to by symbol number (e.g., S-1, I-1).[18]

More on Discovery Sampling

Discovery sampling is a type of sampling procedure that has a specified probability of including at least one item that occurs very rarely in the population. It is used when there is a possibility of finding such things as fraud and avoidance of internal controls. In discovery sampling, the auditors can specify the probability of including in the sample at least one item with a particular characteristic, if the characteristic occurs at a specified rate in the population. If the sample does

---

[17] Ibid.
[18] Ibid.

not turn up an item with this characteristic, the auditors can make a probability statement that the characteristic's rate of occurrence is less than that specified.

Discovery sampling can be regarded as a special case of attribute sampling. However, in its usual applications, it does not yield an estimated rate of occurrence, and usually it is used only if the particular characteristic's rate of occurrence is thought to be very small—that is, close to zero. For example, discovery sampling is usually used in financial audits to guard against an intolerable rate of fraud.

An auditor could use attribute sampling to estimate the percentage of checks that have problem endorsements. Attribute sampling can be used to determine the deviation rate. Variable sampling could help an auditor determine if a subunit manager of a large company had overstated an asset to increase net income and his bonus.

Discovery sampling, a special kind of attribute sampling, is very useful to fraud examiners when trying to determine whether critical errors exist. Discovery sampling allows examiners to conclude with a certain percentage confidence level whether any problem endorsements or similar critical errors exist in a population. Discovery sampling is attribute sampling with a zero expected-error rate.

> **Attribute Sampling versus Variable Sampling**
>
> Attribute sampling is more useful than variable sampling in fraud examination sampling. Discovery sampling, an extension of attribute sampling, is primarily an investigative technique.

6.7 Integrating Analytical Relationships to Detect Fraud

Topics such as the need to integrate analytical relationships, types of analytical procedures, and the need to prove illicit financial transactions in order to detect fraud are presented in this section.

(a) Major Impetus

The major impetus for the need to integrate analytical relationships in detecting fraud was the recommendation of the Treadway Commission that analytical procedures should be used more extensively to identify areas with a high risk of fraudulent financial reporting.

The results of a research study sponsored by the Institute of Management Accountants (IMA) entitled *The Role of Analytical Procedures in Detecting Management Fraud* indicated that analytical procedures can be an effective supplement to an overall program to detect and prevent fraud.[19] However, the IMA study also says that a question remains unresolved as to exactly what types of errors (unintentional mistakes) or irregularities (fraudulent financial reporting or defalcation) are detected effectively through the use of analytical procedure.

The participants in the IMA study included internal auditors, controllers, and external auditors, and the findings showed that analytical procedures are not being used effectively to detect management fraud due to differing views concerning the participants' responsibility to use the

---

[19]Edward Blocher, *The Role of Analytical Procedures in Detecting Management Fraud* (Montvale, NJ: IMA, 1993).

procedures and lack of specific guidance and training in fraud detection methods. When fraud is detected, it is usually through other audit procedures, although commonly it is revealed by informal disclosures rather than detected.

Treadway Commission: Recommendation about Analytical Review Procedures

Recommendation for the Independent Public Accountant

The Auditing Standards Board should establish standards which require independent public accountants to perform analytical review procedures in all audit engagements and which provide improved guidance on the appropriate use of these procedures.

The public accounting profession widely recognizes the usefulness of analytical review procedures, and auditors perform such procedures in many audits today. Analytical review procedures can encompass a broad range of audit steps. Usually involving comparisons of relationships among data, they range from relatively simple comparisons of ratios and trends to sophisticated statistical modeling techniques. Regardless of specific form, they focus on the overall reasonableness of a reported amount in relation to the surrounding circumstances.

The potential of analytical review procedures for detecting fraudulent financial reporting has not been fully realized. Unusual year-end transactions, deliberate manipulation of estimates or reserves, and misstatements of revenues and assets often introduce aberrations in otherwise predictable amounts, ratios, or trends that will stand out to a skeptical auditor. The Commission observed a number of cases where performing analytical review procedures would have increased the likelihood of the auditor's detecting fraudulent financial reporting.

Existing auditing standards allow, but do not require, analytical review procedures. The Commission recommends that auditing standards be revised to require the use of analytical review procedures on all audit engagements. The revised standards should require auditors to use analytical review procedures throughout the audit, including at the planning phase.

Source: Report of the National Commission on Fraudulent Financial Reporting (October 1987): 52.

Further, the Commission recommends that the public accounting profession provide greater guidance on the application of analytical review procedures. Executive-level auditors should be required to participate in selecting the analytical review procedures to be performed and evaluating the results. Meaningful audit evidence from these procedures depends on the seasoned judgment of executive-level professionals, who should have a greater understanding than the nonexecutives of the company's industry as well as the environmental, institutional, and individual factors that increase the risk of fraudulent financial reporting.

The Treadway Commission defined fraudulent financial reporting as intentional or reckless conduct, whether by act or omission, that results in materially misleading financial statements. Fraudulent financial reporting can involve many factors and take many forms. It may entail gross and deliberate distortion of corporate records, such as inventory count tags, or falsified transactions, such as fictitious sales or orders. It may entail the misapplication of accounting principles. Company employees at any level may be involved, from top to middle management to lower-level personnel. If the conduct is intentional, or so reckless that it is the legal equivalent of intentional conduct, and results in fraudulent financial statements, it comes within the Commission's operating definition of the term "fraudulent financial reporting."

Fraudulent financial reporting differs from other causes of materially misleading financial statements such as unintentional errors. The Commission also distinguished fraudulent financial reporting from other corporate improprieties, such as employee embezzlements, violation of environmental or product safety regulations, and tax fraud, which do not necessarily cause the financial statements to be materially inaccurate.

(b) Types of Analytical Procedures

The IMA research study investigated the use and effectiveness of analytical procedures in the possible link between different types of analytical procedures and the detection of management fraud.[20] The three principal types of analytical procedures are trend analysis, ratio analysis, and modeling techniques (see Exhibit 6.6).

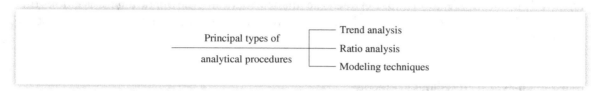

EXHIBIT 6.6 Principal Types of Analytical Procedures

Trend analysis examines the trend of the account balances as a basis for determining whether the current period data potentially are misstated—that is, whether they depart significantly from the trend of the prior data. Trend analysis techniques vary from the simplest two-period comparisons to statistically based time-series models. Trend analysis is the most commonly employed analytical procedure.

Ratio analysis refers to procedures that involve the simultaneous analysis of two or more financial statement accounts. The value in using ratios is that often the relationship between the two (or more) accounts in the ratio is relatively stable over time, so that a variation in a ratio is a direct and clear signal of an underlying unusual condition: It can be a fraud, a simple error, or simply an unusual combination of environmental events. Ratio analysis is potentially a far more useful method for detecting error and fraud than trend analysis because ratio analysis uses the assumed stable relationship between accounts while trend analysis looks at the behavior of only a single account. The behavior of a ratio is expected to be stable while a single account balance can change for a number of reasons related to normal operating factors that do not reflect error or fraud.

A third type of analytical procedure, based on **modeling techniques**, can be more effective than either ratio analysis or trend analysis. The modeling approach is distinguished by the attempt to identify meaningful, stable relationships between financial and operating data.

A common type of modeling approach is the reasonableness test. This procedure involves the use of selected operating data, associated financial data, and external data to predict an account balance.

Reasonableness tests of the expense accounts are common. Two examples are when the auditor or analyst estimates a value for utilities expense based on average temperature and hours of operation and when the auditor estimates payroll expense from operating data on the number of employees, the average pay rates, and the number of days of applicable operations.

---

[20] Ibid.

The reasonableness test can be particularly effective because it links the financial data directly to relevant operating data. When variations in operations are the principal cause for variations in the related accounts (especially the expense accounts), as is often the case, reasonableness tests provide a relatively precise means of detecting errors and frauds affecting these accounts; when a fraud is committed, it is likely that the reported financial and operating facts will not agree. That is, the perpetrator will find it difficult to disguise both the financial data and the related operating data.

For example, a reasonableness test of payroll expense can be an effective means of detecting fraud if there are phony employees or excess time is charged, because personnel records also must be manipulated fraudulently in the same pattern to prevent detection. Because reasonableness tests effectively model the relationships between the financial data and the operating transactions that are the basis for the recorded financial data, these tests are potentially the most effective of the analytical procedures.

(i) Use of Analytical Procedures in Practice

Analytical procedures are a substantive audit procedure and oriented to detecting rather than preventing management fraud. The participants in the research study have a different perspective about their role in management fraud, as indicated next.

IMA Research Findings

- Internal auditors saw their role as preventing fraud or investigating a fraud that had already been revealed. They tended not to use analytical procedures.

- External auditors saw their role as detecting fraud within the context of developing an opinion on the financial statements. They tended to use analytical procedures extensively.

- Controllers saw their role similar to internal auditors in both preventing and detecting fraud. They were found to be the best-trained and most extensive users of analytical procedures.

According to the IMA research study, internal auditors should take a more proactive role in the detection of management fraud.[21] The current IIA *Standards* provide necessary guidance in this area. The key point is that internal auditors should take greater responsibility in the detection of management fraud.

(ii) Implications for Internal Auditors

A pervasive finding in the IMA research study is that there are significant differences among the three participant groups. Internal auditors took a prevention-oriented and control-based approach to fraud. External auditors and controllers tended to take a detection-oriented and analytical approach to fraud. The respective approaches were found to be effective.

In view of the Treadway Commission's recommendation for greater use of analytical procedures by external auditors, the IMA research study findings suggest these points:

- Controllers, internal auditors, and others might employ analytical procedures more effectively as well.

---

[21] Ibid.

- The analytical procedures now being done by controllers to explain changes in account balances need to be redirected in part to looking for potential management fraud.

- As directed in the IIA's *Standards*, the control-based approach of the internal auditors needs to be augmented by analytical procedures to improve the overall effectiveness of the auditors in detecting fraud

(iii) More Examples of Analytical Procedures

Joseph Wells recommends financial statement analysis (ratio analysis, trend analysis, net worth method), statistical sampling, and flowcharting techniques to detect fraud (see Exhibit 6.7).[22] Each of these techniques is explained in the sections that follow.

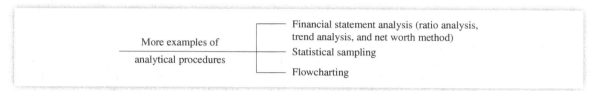

More examples of analytical procedures
- Financial statement analysis (ratio analysis, trend analysis, and net worth method)
- Statistical sampling
- Flowcharting

EXHIBIT 6.7 Examples of Analytical Procedures

(A) Financial Statement Analysis. If financial statements are prepared with integrity, changes in account balances from one period to another should have logical explanations. Manipulating financial statements to hide missing assets or other problems sometimes hides frauds. Using ratios and trend analysis, fraud examiners or auditors can identify unusual relationships suggesting errors or irregularities. The discussion of financial statement analysis includes two elements: (1) analysis of the balance sheet and income statement using ratios and trends, and (2) analysis of changes in cash balances from period to period using a statement of cash flows.

Analyzing the Balance Sheet and Income Statement. The balance sheet and income statement can be analyzed three ways to reveal fraud and other types of errors. First, financial statement data from the current period can be compared with results from prior periods to look for unusual relationships. Second, financial statement data can be compared with similar information from other companies, or with industry statistics to look for unusual relationships. Because comparisons between similar companies are so valuable, industry-wide financial statements are distributed widely by several publishing companies.

Third, financial statements data can be associated with nonfinancial data to see if the numbers on the statements make sense. When searching for fraud, examiners should be inquisitive and challenge things that appear out of order or out of sequence. There should always be analytical relationships between representation in financial statements and physical goods or movements of assets.

KEY CONCEPTS TO REMEMBER: Plausible Relationships

- If sales are increasing, examiners would see buildup of inventory.

- If sales are increasing, examiners would see accounts receivable increasing.

---

[22] Wells, *Fraud Examination.*

- If sales are increasing, examiners would see the cost of outbound freight increasing.

- If purchases are increasing, examiners would see the cost of inbound freight increasing.

- If inventory is increasing, examiners would see increases in the costs of warehousing, storage, and handling activities.

- If manufacturing volume is increasing, examiners would expect the per-unit cost of labor and material to be decreasing.

- If manufacturing volume is going up, examiners would see increases in the dollar amount of scrap sales and discounts on purchases.

- If profits are increasing, examiners would see increases in cash flows from operations.

Examining financial statement data to see if they make sense with respect to nonfinancial statement data is one of the best ways to detect fraud. Examiners who ask themselves if reported amounts are too small, too large, too early, too late, too often, and too rare or who look for things that are reported at odd times, by odd people, and using odd procedures are much more likely to detect fraud than those who view the financial statement without sufficient professional skepticism.

Three techniques can be helpful in comparing financial statement data from period to period: ratio analysis, vertical analysis, and horizontal analysis (see Exhibit 6.8).

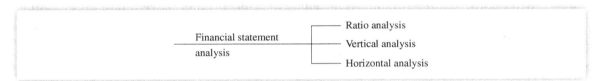

EXHIBIT 6.8 Financial Statement Analysis

Ratio analysis involves computing key ratios to compare significant financial statement relationships from period to period. The most helpful ratios in detecting whether financial statements are reasonable include current ratio, quick ratio, and cash ratio.

Scope of Internal Fraud

Much of internal fraud involves the theft of cash or inventory or the manipulation of receivables—major components of current assets.

These ratios only suggest potential problem areas. By themselves, they do not incriminate anyone or prove conclusively that fraud exists. When the current ratios, quick ratios, or cash ratios suggest a potential problem in either receivables or inventory, five additional ratios can be useful:

1. Accounts receivable turnover

2. Days to collect receivables

3. Inventory turnover

4. Days to sell inventory

5. Days to convert inventory to cash

The examiner's responsibility is to use these ratios to identify significant, unexplained fluctuations and then determine if those fluctuations have logical explanations. If they do not, someone may be overstating or understating current assets or liabilities to conceal dishonest acts. Unexplained changes in the ratios can signal problems.

Vertical analysis is a technique for analyzing the relationships between line items on an income statement or balance sheet by expressing components as percentages. In vertical analysis of an income statement, net sales are assigned 100%. For a balance sheet, total assets are assigned 100%. All other items on the statements are then expressed as a percentage of these two numbers.

Horizontal analysis is a technique for analyzing the percentage change in individual income statements or balance sheet items from one year to the next. Horizontal analysis supplements ratio and vertical analysis and allows an examiner to determine whether any particular item has changed in an unusual way in relation to the change in net sales or total assets from one period to the next.

(B) Statement of Cash Flows. The statement of cash flows identifies sources and uses of cash during a period. The statement is extremely useful for identifying how an entity is funding its operation—whether from investments, earnings, or borrowing; and what it is doing with its money—whether it is being distributed to the principals, used to make additional investments, or used in operations.

Because cash is the asset most often misappropriated, the statement of cash flows is useful for identifying potential fraudulent acts.

The statement of cash flows can be very helpful when detecting fraud, especially for small businesses. In one fraud case, an accountant was stealing money instead of paying payroll taxes and other bills. The statement of cash flows highlighted the significant increase in payables. In another fraud case, cash receipts were stolen over a period of six years. The statement of cash flows showed significant increases in receivables. The discrepancies went unnoticed.

"Red Flags" to Look for in the Statement of Cash Flows

- When sales are increasing, accounts receivable is decreasing.
- Inventory could be overstated to make net income look better.
- Cash could be stolen when accounts payable balance is increasing and delayed payment is occurring.
- Accounts payable balance increases when raw material inventory purchases are decreased.

The examiner or auditor should convert the traditional net income from operations reported in the income statement to obtain the net amount of cash from operation. This conversion helps in understanding the relationships of various components of cash flows.

KEY CONCEPTS TO REMEMBER: Formula for Determining Net Amount of Cash from Operations

Net income from operations
+   Depreciation
−   Increase in accounts receivable
+   Decrease in inventory
+   Increase in accounts payable
=   NET AMOUNT OF CASH FROM OPERATIONS

(v) Flowcharting Techniques

Flowcharting techniques are useful in detecting fraud. The flowcharting method, despite its indirect approach, can prove money-laundering activities. Enterprises used to launder funds will generally have common ownership or other connections, usually under the control of the targets. Therefore, corporate and other business filings and records showing the principals in the suspect business should be obtained and patterns of ownership noted. Financial and bank records can then be subpoenaed to trace the flow of funds between the enterprises. Other charting techniques that were explained earlier include link network diagrams, time-flow diagrams, and matrices to show the relationships between persons, organizations, and events.

(c) Proving Illicit Financial Transactions

This section describes various audit and examination techniques to identify and track the secret movement of funds in fraud, corruption, and money-laundering schemes. Joseph Wells collected many examples, of which a few are briefly presented here.[23] In all these cases, the illegal objectives may differ, but the means are the same, and the means are relatively limited in number.

- Company funds can be used to purchase expensive personal items as a form of embezzlement as well as for corrupt gifts.

- Money can be siphoned from a company account by cash or check for the benefit of the owners as well as to bribe another.

- Hidden interests can be taken in related transactions to earn fraudulent profits or can be given as a means of a payoff.

Typical schemes and devices that are utilized to conceal embezzlement, corrupt payments, and other illicit transfers fall into two categories: on-book and off-book schemes.

(i) On-Book and Off-Book Schemes

On-book schemes occur after the point of receipt of funds. Here illicit funds are drawn from the regular bank accounts and recorded on books, disguised as a legitimate trade payable, salary payment, or other business expense. Such payments are often made by regular business check, often payable to a sham business, through an intermediary. The payer may also cash the check, with the currency given to the recipient or used to create a slush fund for illegal purposes. Direct cash withdrawals are difficult to explain and deduce, if in significant amounts. Relatively small amounts of cash are often generated by fictitious charges to travel, entertainment, or miscellaneous accounts.

Off-book schemes refer to those schemes in which the funds used for illegal payments or transfers are not drawn from regular, known bank accounts. The payments do not appear anywhere on the books and records. In relatively small amounts, such payments may come directly from other ventures. In larger schemes, the funds are usually generated by unrecorded sales or by failing to record legitimate rebates from suppliers. Off-book schemes are often employed by businesses with significant cash sales (e.g., restaurants, bars, and retail shops).

The net worth method or comparative net worth analysis is used to prove illicit income circumstantially by showing that the suspect's assets or expenditures for a given period exceed that

---

[23] Ibid.

which can be accounted for from admitted sources of income. The technique is most useful when the recipient is taking currency or other payments that cannot be traced directly, and when the amount of illicit income generally exceeds the recipient's legitimate income. Net worth evidence is also useful to corroborate testimony of hidden illicit payments.

(ii) Net Worth Computation Methods

According to Joseph Wells, there are two basic methods of net worth computation: the asset method and the expenditures method (sources and application of funds method) (see Exhibit 6.9).[24]

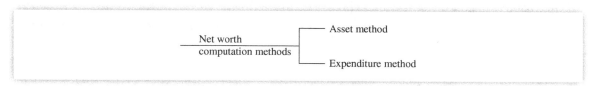

EXHIBIT 6.9 Net Worth Computation Methods

The **asset method** should be used when the suspect has invested illegal funds to accumulate wealth and acquire assets, causing net worth (value of assets over liabilities) to increase year to year. The **expenditure method** is best used when the suspect spends ill-gotten gains on lavish living, travel, and entertainment, which would not be reflected in an increase in net worth.

Asset Method Formula

ASSETS
− Liabilities
= NET WORTH
− Prior year's net worth
= NET WORTH INCREASE
+ Living expenses
= INCOME (or EXPENDITURES)
− Funds from known sources
= FUNDS FROM UNKNOWN SOURCES

Three steps should be analyzed for the asset method.

1. Value all assets at cost, not fair market value. Ignore subsequent appreciation or depreciation of assets.
2. Estimate or compute generously the amount of funds available to the suspect from legitimate sources. Resolve any doubts in favor of the suspect.
3. Attempt to interview the suspect, in order to identify all alleged sources of funds and to negate defenses that he or she may raise later.

---

[24] Ibid.

Expenditures Method Formula

EXPENDITURES (APPLICATION OF FUNDS)
- Known sources of funds
= FUNDS FROM UNKNOWN SOURCES

These steps should be undertaken for the expenditure method.

1. Establish the suspect's known expenditures for the relevant year. Expenditures include the use or application of funds for any purpose, including deposits to bank accounts, purchase of major assets, travel and entertainment expenses, and payment of loan and credit card debts.

2. Identify all sources of funds available to the suspect, including loans and gifts as well as cash on hand from previous years.

3. Attribute to unknown sources the difference between the amount of the suspect's expenditures and known income.

(iii) Money Laundering

An examiner tracing illicit funds may find an apparently legitimate source at the end of the trail: a prosperous cash retail business, a profitable real estate transaction, or offshore "loans" or investments. This is the realm of money laundering. Although money laundering itself is a crime (as a result of the Money Laundering Act of 1986), it is usually detected as a result of the investigation of the underlying offenses. Effective investigation measures have included visual and electronic surveillance and sting and undercover operations.

Laundering schemes conducted through a front business are best proven through the cooperation of an insider, such as the business's accountant or tax preparer, or by infiltrating an agent.

Indirect methods of proving laundering activity include these two techniques.

1. **Ratio analysis and sampling techniques**—Overreporting revenues of a front business to launder funds may result in an imbalance of the normal ratio of costs to sales: Cost will appear unduly low compared to reported revenues. (This is why the ideal laundering operation would have relatively low fixed costs against sales.) Surveillance of the suspect enterprise may provide additional evidence that revenues are being underreported, by showing low customer traffic. Surveillance may also permit sampling procedures wherein a count of the number of customers or sales during a given period is used to extrapolate total sales.

2. **Flowcharting technique**—A laundering operation may also be revealed by the flowcharting technique, which was presented earlier.

(iv) Federal Sentencing Guidelines for Organizational Defendants

Federal sentencing guidelines for organizational defendants became effective in November of 1991. These guidelines provide judges with a concrete formula for sentencing business organizations for various **white-collar crimes**. Included are federal securities, employment and contract laws, as well as the crimes of mail and wire fraud, kickbacks and bribery, and money laundering.

These guidelines represent a unique carrot-and-stick approach calling for business organizations found guilty of crimes to face sanctions reaching potentially hundreds of millions of dollars (the "stick"). Organizations may be given offsetting credits against these penalties if they can demonstrate that they exercised **due diligence** prior to the offense, the wrongdoing was investigated, and they cooperated with government investigators (the "carrot").

An organization is well advised to be able to demonstrate, prior to the accusation of any offense, that it exercised due diligence in seeking to prevent and detect criminal conduct by its agents. Due diligence requires that the organization has taken, at a minimum, seven steps:

1. Established compliance policies that define standards and procedures

2. Assigned specific high-level responsibility to ensure compliance with these standards and procedures

3. Used due care in not delegating substantial discretionary authority to individuals who could engage in illegal activities

4. Communicated standards and procedures to all employees (by requiring participation in training programs and disseminating publications)

5. Taken reasonable steps to achieve compliance with standards (by utilizing monitoring and auditing systems including a system for employees to report violations without fear of reprisal)

6. Consistently enforced standards through appropriate disciplinary mechanisms

7. Taken all reasonable steps to prevent future similar offenses

Internal auditors should play an active role in educating management about the importance of the federal sentencing guidelines and assist in the development of new or expanded programs to address their requirements.

6.8 Interrogation or Investigative Techniques

This section discusses interrogation techniques, including verbal and nonverbal behavior; the role of interviewer and interrogator; the difference between interviewing and interrogation; and the difference between interview and investigation. In addition, investigative techniques, including their processes and phases, team composition, target attacks such as objects and subjects, and search and seizure are presented.

(a) Interrogation Techniques

The objectives of fraud investigation are to determine whom, why, and how. Possible approaches include:

- Testimonial evidence, documentary evidence, physical evidence (forensic analysis), and personal observation

- Theft act investigative methods, such as surveillance and covert operations, invigilation (close supervision of suspects)

- Concealment investigative methods, such as document examination, audits, computer searches, and physical asset counts

- Conversion investigative methods, such as public record searches and net worth analysis
- Inquiry investigative methods, such as interviewing and interrogation[25]

The latter approach is presented in detail.

(i) Interviewing and Interrogating in Fraud Investigations

Auditors will encounter situations where they must interview employees who are suspected of fraudulent activities. Handling a fraud situation is a very delicate matter with associated financial and legal risks. Knowing what questions to ask and how to ask them of suspects and knowing the difference between interviewing and interrogating would help auditors immensely from being exposed to legal and financial risks. These risks arise simply because of the auditors' lack of technical knowledge in the subject area.

Auditors meet many parties during the interviewing and interrogating process, including security staff, prosecutors, and other law enforcement officials. Auditors should clearly understand their own role and the role of others in this process.

During evidence collection activities, the investigative team interviews and interrogates many individuals. The interviewing and interrogation processes are quite different in terms of objectives, techniques, and timing. The goal of the interview is obtaining information about the incident. Here the intent is finding the answers to the five Ws: *who, what, when, where,* and *why.* This requires talking to as many witnesses as possible. The goal of interrogation, however, is to establish enough evidence to consider the subject a suspect.

Interviewing versus Interrogation

- When gathering evidence, use the interview process: Individuals become witnesses.
- When an interviewee becomes a suspect, use the interrogation process: Witnesses become suspects.

Interrogation should be left to experienced investigators since they need to balance between the accused's privacy rights and their own job duties. Investigators must be soft-spoken with clear communications skills and must have incontrovertible facts. Making a false accusation that results in embarrassment or damage to the suspect can cost the organization significantly if the person wrongly accused decides to take legal action against the organization.

(A) Interpretation of Behavior. Interviewers/interrogators should remember that extremes in a suspect's behavior often indicate deception.[26] At least, they should recognize that the stress of not telling the truth often causes changes in attitudes and verbal and nonverbal behavior. These changes should be compared with what is normal for the individual and the population in general. A profile of the truthful and untruthful suspect follows.

(B) Verbal Behavior. Truthful individuals are generally calm, relaxed, and cooperative while being interviewed. As suspects become more comfortable with the situation, they become more relaxed. Overall, truthful individuals are cordial, friendly, and relatively easy to handle.

---

[25] W. Steve Albrecht, Gerald W. Wernz, and Timothy L. Williams, *Fraud: Bringing Light to the Dark Side of Business* (Burr Ridge, IL: Irwin Professional Publishing, 1995).

[26] David E. Zulawski and Douglas E. Wicklander, *Practical Aspects of Interview and Interrogation* (Boca Raton, FL: CRC Press, 1993).

The attitude displayed by untruthful suspects is usually impatience, both in word and action. They are tense and defensive while questioning, look at their watch, and suggest that they need to be somewhere else.

Truthful individuals generally respond to questions and make timely responses. Untruthful suspects are usually vague and stammering in their responses. There may be long pauses when speaking or answers that are too quick, too short, too long, or too elaborate. The guilty talk softly, mumble, and in many cases talk through their hand.

Guilty suspects often attempt to take an overly friendly, polite, or cooperative attitude toward the interviewers/interrogators. Guilty suspects use this tactic in an attempt to make the interviewer into a friend rather than an enemy. Guilty people hope this cooperative attitude will get them a break or even that they will be overlooked as a suspect. Excessive friendliness and politeness by a suspect should immediately alert the interviewer to the suspect's probable deception. This politeness often seems quite out of place.

Verbal Behavior

The ultimate goal of verbal behavior is to elicit the truth from the reluctant suspect. The difficulty in assessing verbal behavior is that both truthful and untruthful suspects may use exactly the same words to the interviewer. Only differences in nonverbal behavior, tone of voice, loudness, and speed of delivery may differentiate truth from deception.

A delay in response to an interviewer's question is a good indicator of a suspect's guilt. Innocent individuals rarely need to think about a response. They simply answer the question posed directly and promptly. The guilty, however, often pause or delay a response while they think. Inappropriate laughter by a suspect is an attempt to make the interviewer's question seem petty. Deceptive suspects can use laughter to cover their delay.

Truthful suspects respond directly and deny the allegation, saying, for example, "I did not steal any money." The guilty respond by denying specifically, "I did not steal that $300." The qualified response is an indication of a deceptive individual.

Some guilty suspects will attempt to take the offensive by presenting a surly, nasty, aggressive attitude toward interviewers. This attitude is designed to put interviewers on the defense and cause them to back off from the confrontation with suspects.

(C) Nonverbal Behavior. Interviewers should remember that the entire body must be considered when observing nonverbal behavior. Also, both verbal and nonverbal behavior must be considered together.

- Guilty people may perspire excessively, particularly on the trunk of the body. However, perspiration may not be a relevant clue if the suspect has engaged in strenuous activity or comes from an extremely hot environment just prior to the meeting.

- The hands and the arms may provide guilty persons with a barrier to protect the abdominal cavity and relieve the stress of sitting across from an interviewer/interrogator. Guilty persons use the hands and the arms to perform created jobs or grooming gestures.

Nonverbal Behavior

The interviewer should attempt to establish a behavioral norm for the suspect. Consideration should be given to the suspect's voice pattern, word choice, eye movement, attitude, and physical behavior.

- Scratching the nose, rubbing the brow, or adjusting the glasses could be used as a ruse to cover the actual purpose of the hand movement.

- The drumming of fingers indicates a suspect's impatience. Clenched fists may show a suspect's frustration or a negative attitude toward the discussion or interviewer.

- Many guilty individuals begin to itch and scratch immediately after the introduction of a stressful topic.

- Suspects may use the thumbs to indicate a defensive or superior attitude. They will lean back in the chair, arms crossed and fingers tucked underneath the armpits with the thumbs extended upward.

- Crossed arms often indicate negative thoughts or displeasure with the conversation. They may also be used in situations where an individual feels uncertain or insecure. Individuals also cross their arms when they feel cold.

- Crossing the ankles or legs typically provides a defensive barrier against the interviewer. As a general rule, the more defensive an individual becomes, the higher the knee rise to protect the abdominal region.

- Truthful individuals will generally have good eye contact with the interviewer. Often the deceptive individual's eyes will be cold and hostile. They have a flat look to them that does not allow the interviewer to see beneath the surface of the eyes.

- To reduce the suspect's level of defensiveness, position chairs directly across from each other or slightly off to one side, which will lessen the confrontational feel of the meeting.

(ii) Role of Interviewer/Interrogator

Interviewers blame denials only on the suspect's fear of consequences. Interviewers can also cause denials because of strategies or tactics employed during the interrogation. The suspect's perception of the interviewer and/or the interviewer's strategy often dictates whether the suspect will deny.

Interrogators who are overbearing, aggressive, or nonempathic toward a suspect often increase the suspect's defensiveness, resulting in denial. When a suspect dislikes an interviewer, the dislike often turns into distrust and denial. Interrogators' attitude should be that of mediator seeking the truth rather than that of dominant, authoritative figure. They should display professionalism.

When interviewers attempt to rush the suspect into a confession due to lack of time or other, the suspect may elect to deny simply because he or she believes the interviewers' hurried demeanor is a weakness to be exploited. By making denials and waiting interviewers out, the suspect believes that he or she can win the encounter.

The verbal and physical behavior displayed by interviewers/interrogators during the interrogation can also directly affect a suspect's decision to deny. If interviewers are perceived as unsure, inconsistent, or weak, the suspect will make a denial to test the interviewer's assertions.

If interviewers are uncertain of the case facts, misquote commonly known facts, or seem unprepared, suspects are encouraged to deny. The suspect's decision to deny is based on a belief that he or she has not been clearly identified with the case. The suspect is taking a chance that the interviewer's bumbling of the facts is directly related to the competency of the investigation. *Most suspects recognize that an incompetent investigation will be unlikely to result in their being proved guilty of the offense.*

Interrogators' word choices may cause denials, as might long pauses or silence. The use of silence by interviewers rarely enhances the likelihood of a confession. To the contrary, it allows the suspect an opportunity to think and assess other possibilities that might convince the interrogator of his or her innocence. In an interrogation, silence invites the suspect to join the conversation. Long pauses by the interrogator invite a denial from the suspect.

> ### Role of Silence in Interviews and Interrogations
>
> ■ Silence in an interview is an effective strategy since it can be filled with more conversation. Remember that in an interview, the interviewee (suspect) does all the talking.
>
> ■ Silence in an interrogation is not an effective strategy since the suspect can deny. Remember that in interrogation, the interviewer (auditor or investigator) does all the talking.

(A) Interviewing versus Interrogation. An interview is a fact-gathering process that attempts to answer the six journalistic (investigative) questions: who, what, when, where, how, and why. The suspect who responds to questions posed by the interviewer dominates talking during the interview. During the interview, the interviewer may ask the suspect behavior-provoking questions to determine the suspect's truthfulness. The setting of an interview also tends to be much less formal than that of interrogation. In an interview, the interviewer often picks a time and location convenient for the person being interviewed. In the earliest stages of investigation, the interview is broad-based, with the interviewer attempting to give direction to the investigation.

An interview can turn into an investigation at any time. The change in the process from nonaccusatory to accusatory can be very direct or very subtle. In either case, the amount of talking done by the interviewee and suspect changes dramatically. During the interview process, the investigator has made the majority of questions broad and open-ended to elicit a narrative response from the suspect. To clarify specific points, the interviewer may have used closed-end questions. However, once the interviewer has elected to confront the suspect, the interviewer begins to do all the talking and offers face-saving rationalizations that minimize the seriousness of the suspect's involvement.

By contrast, an interrogation is designed to obtain information that might be incriminatory from a suspect who may be reluctant to give the information. The purpose of interrogation is to overcome the suspect's initial resistance and open a dialogue that will encourage the suspect to give information against his or her interests. An interrogator is still attempting to answer the six investigative questions (who, what, when, where, how, and why), but there are two basic differences between an interview and interrogation.

1. In interrogation, the suspect talks only when he or she is confessing.
2. The suspect resists telling the truth until he or she is convinced of the need to do otherwise.

Victims and witnesses typically are interviewed at a time and place convenient to them. If the interviewer/interrogator believes that the individual might ultimately be the suspect, an interrogation could follow. In such a case, the interviewer/interrogator should ask the suspect come to his or her office or at a location where a more formal setting can be arranged. Regardless of whether the interviewer plans a nonaccusatory interview or an interrogation of a suspect, the interviewer's behavior should seem reasonable and fair.

There is never room for mistreatment of a witness or suspect by an interviewer. Yelling, screaming, or pounding fists on the table to obtain information from a reluctant witness have no place in either an interview or an interrogation.

INTERVIEW VERSUS INVESTIGATION

An interview is a noncustody and nonaccusatory situation. An investigation is quite the opposite.

In the interview, the interviewer should open the lines of communication so that the victim, witness, or suspect will begin to talk about the incident under investigation. It may be worthwhile to prepare specific written questions to ensure the accuracy of the way that they were asked. The key questions need to be camouflaged during the interview so that the interviewer does not highlight their importance. For example, when conducting a kickback investigation, an investigator may look at a buyer's phone records for investigative leads, but the interviewer does not request the buyer's phone number alone. To conceal the target of the investigation, phone records (landline and mobile/cell) from the entire buying department may be requested. Although investigators may not be able to conceal the fact that they are looking at telephone records, at least they can conceal whom they are looking at.

Rapport is needed both in normal interviewing and in investigative situations. Rapport is more than just smiling. Even the most cooperative, agreeable witness can be turned off by an interviewer who fails to establish rapport. Interviewers who are too blunt and to the point, who attempt to obtain information without establishing rapport, are often faced with witnesses who are cold and uncooperative.

How is rapport established? The interviewer should attempt to establish rapport by finding some common ground or interest about which to speak to the individual. People tend to like people who have similar interests and personalities. The interrogator should avoid using the words *steal*, *embezzle*, or *fraud* when talking to the suspect. People who have a genuine smile are judged to be more honest and trustworthy than those who have cold, expressionless faces. *The kind of words used and the facial expressions displayed lead to good rapport.*

Words alone are not enough to build good rapport between the interviewer and the suspect. Interviewers should practice other techniques, such as mirroring. People who have a high level of rapport tend to mirror each other's behavior. **Mirroring** includes modeling the speech patterns, speed of delivery, breathing, posture, and gestures of the individual to whom the interviewer is speaking. This mirroring shows up as similar body positioning, physiology, tone of voice, and even choice of words used between the two parties. When interviewers mirror an individual's posture, gestures, and physiology, they can create within themselves the same emotions that the suspect is feeling.

TRUTH VERSUS UNTRUTH IN INTERVIEWS AND INTERROGATIONS

- Individuals who are telling the truth about the issue under investigation are more likely to give direct answers during the interview. In addition, they are often helpful and cooperative in their responses.

- Individuals who are not telling the truth are not as specific, direct, or helpful. In many cases, their responses are vague, too elaborate, short, or evasive.

Awareness of Common Law Causes of Action

Employers or interviewers must be aware of these common law causes of action before conducting any interviews. Even though the employee has common law rights, the public or private employer has the right to investigate and to expect loyalty from the employee.

False Imprisonment

This cause of action generally requires that an employee be detained without his or her consent or a legal justification to restrain the employee. False imprisonment is a detention where no arrest warrant has been issued, or if one has been issued, it is void. For an employee to prove a case of false imprisonment, he or she must prove that:

- An arrest or forcible detention took place.

- The arrest or imprisonment was caused by the company.

- The detention was unlawful or made without a warrant.

- There was malice on the part of the company.

An employer is entitled to interview an employee on company premises about violations of company policy without liability for false imprisonment. In a number of cases where false imprisonment was found to have occurred, the employee was physically restrained from leaving.

Defamation

Defamation of character is the most often occurring allegation made by a suspect regarding an incident of misconduct. The defamation of character may occur in the form of a slander or libelous statement. *Slander* is a false statement that was not written down but was spoken to one or more individuals. *Libel* is an untrue statement that was written down and was communicated to others.

In order for employees to establish that they have suffered a defamation of character, they must prove four things.

1. They must prove that particular words were actually spoken, including proving both the time and the place that the activity took place.

2. They must also prove that these words were spoken or published to third persons.

3. They must show that the words written or spoken were actually false.

4. They must also show other facts that prove that the words are libelous or slanderous. This would include that there was malice on the part of the company or investigator and that the libel or slander was not privileged in any way.

An employer has a qualified privilege to communicate allegations during an investigation. However, this qualified privilege is lost if false communication was made out of spite or malice with knowledge that the statements were, in fact, false. In addition, these knowingly false statements must have been communicated to an excessive number of people. During the course of investigative interviews, interviewers should avoid repeating to third parties any information or allegations of which they are uncertain. *As a practical matter, the interview process is one of gathering information rather than giving information to the interviewee.*

An investigator should limit communicating allegations to those who have a need to know as part of the investigation or decision-making process relating to the consequences of the suspect's actions. An investigator can establish the qualified privilege by noting on investigative reports that the document is privileged for counsel. This establishes an attorney-client privilege and protects many documents during an investigation.

The interviewer/interrogator should understand that a qualified privilege exists to express oral charges to superiors, police, prosecutors, or other persons having a need to know within the company. Care

Awareness of Common Law Causes of Action *(continued)*

should be taken that the report of what happened during the investigation, interview, or interrogation is fair and that statements made are fair and done without malice to the suspect.

Malicious Prosecution

Companies investigating employee theft, illegal drug use, or other illegal activities within a company must decide whether it is in their best interest to contact a law enforcement agency. Certain businesses, such as financial institutions, are required to report thefts to the Federal Bureau of Investigation. Illegal activities, such as the theft of firearms or controlled substances, are also closely monitored by federal and state agencies. Since most companies do not have a requirement to notify public law enforcement of internal problems, they generally do not do so because of the cost of prosecution and the difficulty of proving circumstantial cases. A corporation's bonding company may also need to be made aware of loss to keep the insurance contract in force.

Once the company has decided to prosecute an employee, the company can be opening the door to potential liability for an allegation of malicious prosecution and false arrest. For an employee to establish a malicious prosecution claim against the company, the employee must prove that:

- The employer instituted or continued a criminal proceeding.

- The proceeding was terminated in the employee's favor.

- No probable cause existed for initiating a proceeding.

- The employer's motive in initiating the proceeding was malice or some purpose other than bringing the employee to justice.

Private-sector investigators can limit their and the company's potential liability for a malicious prosecution allegation by allowing the prosecution or police officer to make the decision to prosecute. Malice on the part of the company or an employer may be shown through personal animosity between the person making the accusation and the accused employee. It can also be inferred from the lack of a complete investigation on the part of the company. Furthermore, the company may show the element of malice if it conveys facts that are untrue or withholds facts that might mitigate the conclusion reached by police investigators.

Assault and Battery

Although assault and battery are related, they are fundamentally different. Battery is bodily contact that either causes harm or is offensive to a reasonable person's sense of dignity; assault is words or actions that place the employee in fear of receiving a battery. Actual physical contact is not an element of assault, but violence, either threatened or offered, is required. An assault can occur when the person uses threatening words or gestures and has the ability to commit the battery.

Source: David E. Zulawski and Douglas E. Wicklander, *Practical Aspects of Interview and Interrogation* (Boca Raton, FL: CRC Press, 1993).

(b) Investigative Techniques

(i) Investigative Process

The investigative process for a fraud incident can be divided into three phases.

1. **Initiating the investigation.** This phase includes securing the crime scene, collecting evidence, developing an incident hypothesis, and investigating alternative explanations.

2. **Analyzing the incident.** This phase covers analysis of the evidence collected in the first phase along with alternative explanations to determine whether a crime has occurred.

3. **Analyzing the evidence.** This phase involves preparing to present the incident with findings and recommendations to management or law enforcement authorities.

The *order* of investigation is:

1. Gather facts.

2. Interview witnesses.

3. Develop an incident hypothesis.

4. Test the hypothesis.

5. Report to management and others.

(ii) Team Composition

Investigating a fraud or computer-related crime requires a team approach with many participants, where the talent and skills of each participant are required. Each participant has a specific task to complete, consistent with his or her skills and experience. These participants (specialists) can include representatives from corporate investigations, law enforcement officials, system auditors, corporate counsel, consultants, information technology (IT) security management, and functional user management. The objectives of the system auditor and the IT security management are similar during a computer crime investigation. Although the duties of the manager of the crime team are clear, the duties of team participants may not be clear due to overlapping functions and responsibilities.

(iii) Target

A victim organization should practice a delay technique when its computer system is attacked. If a system perpetrator can be delayed longer while attacking, investigative authorities can trace the perpetrator's origins and location.

It is important for the investigative team to know what the intruder is targeting for an attack. Although there are many targets, Peter Stephenson describes these targets as part of denial-of-service attacks.

- **Hard disks.** An attacker can fill up the hard disk to overload it in order to make it inoperable.

- **Bandwidth.** An attacker can fill up the bandwidth so that the network becomes useless.

- **Caches.** An attacker can block the cache or bypass it for further use.

- **Swap space.** An attacker can fill up the swap space so that it cannot be used.

- **Random access memory (RAM).** An attacker can allocate a large amount of RAM. Some system resources, such as mail servers, will become sensitive to too much RAM because they do not need much RAM to begin with. Users can notice that RAM is missing in a personal computer (PC) during a system BIOS boot-up.

- **Kernel tables.** Attackers try to overflow the kernel tables, causing serious problems on the system. Systems with write-through caches and small write buffers are sensitive to this type of attack.[27]

---

[27] Peter Stephenson, *Investigating Computer-Related Crime* (Boca Raton, FL: CRC Press, Florida, 2000).

(iv) Objects/Subjects

An investigation revolves around two things: objects and subjects. Examples of **objects** include computers, networks, switches, processes, data, and programs. **Subjects** include employees (former and current) and outsiders (hackers, intruders, adversaries, crackers, virus writers, cloners, and phrackers).

(v) Search and Seizure

Ownership, occupancy, and possession are three influencing factors in a crime warrant search. A search warrant or court order is necessary to use the "trap and trace" technique, which involves the telephone company and Internet Service Provider in finding the intruder. Traps can be placed on in-circuit emulators, network protocol analyzers, and hardware analyzers.

If computer equipment involved in a computer crime is not covered by a search warrant, the investigator should leave it alone until a warrant can be obtained. A court order is also required to access the evidence and to conduct surveillance techniques. To get a court-ordered search, one has to show that there is probable cause to believe that the suspect is committing an offense and that normal procedures have failed or are unlikely to work or are dangerous to health and life. An independent judge must issue the court order, not a police officer, security investigator, law enforcement agent, or prosecutor.

6.9 Forensic Auditing and Computer Forensics

Auditing for fraud is called forensic auditing. The purpose of forensic auditing or examination is to establish whether a fraud has occurred. One of the major purposes of financial auditing is to attest the financial statements of an organization. Unlike financial auditing, forensic auditing has no generally accepted auditing standards. In fact, most self-proclaimed forensic auditors are certified public accountants or internal auditors specializing in fraud detection. Basically, forensic auditors or investigators conduct interviews, make onsite and offsite inspections, and perform document analysis during their work. Topics such as forensic auditing, computer forensics, and digital forensic analysis methodology are discussed in this section.

(a) Forensic Auditing

According to Joseph Wells[28], forensic auditing can be divided into four phases: (1) problem recognition and planning, (2) evidence collection, (3) evidence evaluation, and (4) communication of results (see Exhibit 6.10).

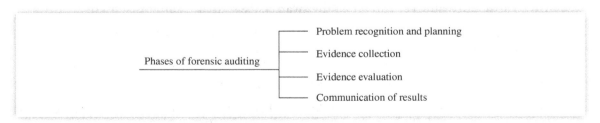

Phases of forensic auditing
- Problem recognition and planning
- Evidence collection
- Evidence evaluation
- Communication of results

EXHIBIT 6.10 Phases of Forensic Auditing

---

[28] Joseph Wells, *Fraud Examination: Investigative and Audit Procedures* (New York: Quorum Books, 1992).

(a) Phase 1: Problem Recognition and Planning

In the problem recognition and planning phase, the pertinent facts and circumstances regarding fraud are gathered. Here fraud examiners learn as much about the potential fraud as possible, without actually gathering evidence. There must be some indication of fraud for an examiner to become involved. The suspected fraud may have become known because of an anonymous tip, a fraud symptom such as a questionable document, suspicion on the part of an employee, or an unusual event or relationship.

The important point is that there must be a legitimate reason to believe that fraud exists. Background checks into the suspects, the environment, and other conditions are conducted. Possible explanations for the potential problem are explored. The problem could be a mistake or unintentional error rather than a fraud. At this stage, no one is convicted or incriminated. Indeed, evidence has not yet been gathered.

(b) Phase 2: Evidence Collection

The purpose of the evidence collection phase is twofold: to determine whether (1) the initial evidence of suspected fraud is misleading, and (2) if further action is recommended to gather sufficient, competent, and relevant evidence to resolve the fraud.

Several rules must be remembered in the evidence-gathering stage. To be effective in detecting fraud, the auditor or the examiner must attempt to identify the three elements of fraud—act, concealment, and conversion—and work on the easiest element first. Most frauds can be resolved by concentrating on the most obvious solutions and the weakest point in the fraud. If someone has an opportunity to commit fraud and/or appears suspicious, he or she probably is the perpetrator.

Another method of obtaining evidence is to search for fraud opportunities by using vulnerability charts and internal control critical combination charts. Fraud cannot occur unless there is an opportunity. The greater or more accessible the opportunity, the more often it is likely to be exploited. Vulnerability charts and critical combinations of controls help examiners arrange risks in the order of their probabilities.

Timely Resolution of a Fraud

In determining when the examination will take place, it should always be remembered that delaying an investigation can lead to destroyed or lost evidence. Early resolution of a fraud case protects both the victim and the perpetrator.

These charts involve correlating stolen assets with potential thieves, possible methods of fraud, effectiveness of controls around the fraud, possible concealment courses, and possibilities of conversion. These charts are objective ways of focusing on the most likely fraud perpetrators. Document examination is another technique to uncover concealment efforts.

Sometimes the gathering of evidence involves using employee searches. This detection technique involves examining employees' desks, lockers, lunchboxes, and other personal effects. When searching, it is important not to violate personal rights. If a search is conducted in an improper way, it can lead to allegations of invasion of privacy, false imprisonment, defamation of character, assault, and/or battery against the examiner. Evidence can be declared inadmissible if obtained illegally.

A seldom-used but powerful method of obtaining evidence is invigilation. Invigilation is the close supervision of suspects during an examination period. It involves imposing such strict temporary controls that during the period of supervision, fraud is almost impossible to commit. Invigilation requires top-management support, as it is expensive and time-consuming. It should be applicable only in high-risk areas. Invigilation has been successfully used to catch fraud committed by suppliers, night watchmen, and warehouse employees.

(c) Phases 3 and 4: Evidence Evaluation and Communication of Results.

After evidence for fraud is properly evaluated, the auditor or the examiner needs to communicate the results of the work to the interested parties. The written report is the only evidence of the work performed and is the best vehicle to communicate results of the examination work. Fraud cases are frequently won or lost on the strength of the report.

(b) Computer Forensics

Forensics is the process of using scientific knowledge for collecting, analyzing, and presenting evidence to the courts. Forensics deals primarily with the recovery and analysis of latent (hidden) evidence. Computer forensics is defined as the discipline that combines elements of law and computer science to collect and analyze data from computer systems, wired networks, wireless communications, mobile devices, and storage devices in a way that is admissible as evidence in a court of law. The admissibility of evidence is one of the requirements of the U.S. Federal Rules of Evidence, consisting of relevant evidence, authenticating or identifying evidence, hearsay evidence, and other types of evidence.

An organization is said to possess a solid computer forensic capability when it develops a robust cyber incident response plan; uses security monitoring tools; conducts vulnerability assessment exercises periodically; deploys intrusion prevention software (IPS); deploys intrusion detection software (IDS); uses web application proxies; places firewalls at multiple levels for a stronger protection; uses web content filtering software to block unwanted website traffic; rotates regular data backup files between onsite and offsite, and hires competent staff. All these combined capabilities are aimed at reporting on the security status of an organization's computer systems and networks with a defense-in-depth protection strategy.

An organization with having a computer forensics capability can accrue several benefits, such as (1) It provides a defense-in-depth approach to network and computer security in that it provides multiple layers of different types of protection from different computer vendors, thus giving a substantially better protection, (2) should a computer intrusion or security incident lead to a court case, the organization with computer forensics capability will be at a distinct advantage because it followed the "due care" legal principle and safeguarded the security and privacy of company's data, (3) it is a proof of complying with computer security best practices and sound security policies, (4) It can potentially avoid lawsuits by customers and employees or regulatory audits by government agencies, resulting from negligence; and (5) It is complying with laws that hold businesses liable for breaches in the security or integrity of computer systems and networks, resulting in data theft, data loss, and data destruction. Examples of these federal laws include SOX, HIPAA, GLB, and Privacy Act. Simply stated, the court system prefers to see that organizations take a proactive role in establishing and monitoring strong security control mechanisms to handle computer incidents.

Two basic types of data are collected in computer forensics such as persistent data and volatile data. *Persistent data* is the data that is stored on a local hard drive or cloud storage and is preserved when the computer is tuned off. *Volatile data* is any data that is stored in computer memory, or exists in transit, that will be lost when the computer loses power or is turned off. Volatile data resides in computer registers, cache, and random- access-memory (RAM). Since volatile data is temporary, it is essential that an investigator knows reliable ways to capture it for evidence before it disappears. In addition, it is important that system administrators, security analysts, and network administrators must understand the computer forensic process and methods to recover data from backup files, computer hard drives, and mobile devices so it can help identify and analyze a security incident.

In a computer crime—for that matter in any crime—successful prosecution depends heavily on presenting good evidence to the court. Computer forensics is used to provide that good evidence. Computer forensics is the art of retrieving computer data in such a way that will make it admissible in court. Computer forensics can be used to convict a computer criminal.

Safeguards to Protect Evidence

- Regular backups
- Offsite storage of backups
- Transaction logging
- Data storage on disks
- Chain-of-custody rules

The victim organization should be able to know who used a computer system and why, trace the criminal's activity through transaction logs, and protect the evidence. From a court's viewpoint, the evidence needs to be (1) understandable to a judge and jury; (2) credible; and (3) defensible. This requires the forensic auditor to think like a lawyer, investigator, and criminal.

(c) Guidelines to a Successful Computer Forensics

This list provides guidelines to a successful computer forensics.

- If one suspects that a computer system has been used in a crime, he should cut off its links to the network immediately.
- When evidence is found, it should be left untouched. This requires freezing or taking a snapshot of the computer records and data.
- Don't create a "reasonable doubt" situation to a judge or jury.
- Prove when each transaction has occurred with time and date stamp.
- Protect the evidential matter (e.g., programs, data, and hardware) in such a way that it will not be modified, tainted, or fabricated. This is very important to the court.
- Store that evidential matter (e.g., data and programs) in an immutable form (e.g., disks) so that it is inexpensive, defensible in a court, and easy to handle, present, and protect.

Digital Forensics Analysis Methodology

Forensically needed data whether it is residing on computers (e.g., files on a hard drive of desktop, laptop, or notebook computers) or on mobile devices (e.g., smartphones, digital tablets, and flash drives) requires a systematic and structured methodology to collect, extract, and analyze such data so that a forensic report can be issued to the interested parties showing the legal evidence. This methodology can take five specific steps in the following order:

Step 1: Collect imaging forensic data

Step 2: Extract the required data

Step 3: Identify relevant data

Step 4: Analyze the relevant data

Step 5: Issue a forensic report

Each step is explained next.

Collect imaging forensic data means receiving an exact, sector-by-sector copy of a hard disk. Software capable of creating such copies of hard drives preserves deleted files, slack space, system files, and executable files (program files), which can be critical for later analysis of a security incident.

Extract the required data means the verification of the integrity of forensic data, selecting forensic tools, and extracting the requested data. Examples of forensic tools include virus and spyware detection software; login scripts; sinkhole routers; IPS and IDS software; packet sniffers; host and file scans; file sharing tools; antivirus and antispyware software; network device logs; protocol analyzers; audit software, password cracking programs, disk imaging software, auditing tools, operating system file utility programs, file zip and unzip utility programs, cable testers, and network line monitors. These and other tools can help investigators identify deleted files, infected files, damaged files, or encrypted files where the latter can represent ransomware attacks.

Identify relevant data requires deciding whether the data is relevant to the forensic request and making a relevant data list with all the associated metadata elements with their attributes.

Analyze the relevant data asks a basic question whether the collected and current data is enough to proceed further or whether more data is needed. If more data is needed, relevant questions include "what", "where", "when", "who", and "how" to get the more data. At this time, the data is analyzed and findings are documented.

Issue a forensic report to all the interested parties based on the findings noted.

Relatively speaking, extracting data from computers could be easier than extracting data from mobile devices due to (1) difficulty in knowing what data to collect with so many smaller and novelty devices on the market, (2) difficulty in knowing where the data is located (i.e., local on the device or remote in the cloud), and (3) difficulty in differentiating between employee-owned mobile devices (BYOD) and company-owned mobile devices. Investigators need to find out the number of web-based email accounts, text messages, social media accounts, apps, and file storage locations to allow them to take an inventory of all the data needed in order to preserve and perform data extraction and recovery efforts.

Investigators can collect the following data from mobile devices, including (1) stand-alone data files such as audio, graphic, and video files, (2) phone call logs showing incoming, outgoing, and missed calls, (3) text messages such as short message service (SMS) and enhanced message service (EMS) messages, (4) multi-media message service (MMS) messages showing audio, graphic, and video files without a text message, (5) browser and email data, (6) social media data containing user profiles with or without pictures, video, or audio files, (7) data on subscriber identity module (SIM) card on a smartphone, and (8) other data of interest include equipment and subscriber data; digital wallet data; and data in personal notes and calendars.

6.10 Use of Computers in Analyzing Data for Fraud and Crime

Topics covered in this section include collection and preservation of computer evidence, chain of computer evidence, and computer fraud and crime examples.

(a) Collection and Preservation of Computer Evidence

(i) Guidelines for the Care and Handling of Computer Evidence

Investigation of computer-related crimes more often than not involves highly technical matters, making it imperative during a search that appropriate steps are taken to ensure both the proper handling and preservation of evidence. There are seven recognized considerations involved in the care and handling of evidence.

1. Discovery and recognition

2. Protection

3. Recording

4. Collection

5. Identification

6. Preservation

7. Transportation

(A) *Discovery and recognition.* The investigator's capability to discover and to recognize the potential source of evidence is vital. When a computer is involved, the evidence is probably not apparent or visible. Nevertheless, the investigator must recognize that computer storage devices are nothing more than electronic or magnetic file cabinets and should be searched if it would normally be reasonable to search a file cabinet.

(B) *Protection.* The physical condition of evidence collected and seized is a major concern. Care should be taken to protect the area where evidence is located. Documents should be handled so as not to destroy latent prints or identifying characteristics. Computer-related evidence is sensitive to heat and humidity and should not be stored in the back seat or trunk of a car without special precautions.

(C) *Recording.* The alleged crime scene should be properly recorded. The use of a video camera to videotape computer equipment, workstations, and so on, and related written documentation at the crime scene is highly encouraged. Examiners should remember to photograph the rear side of the computer (particularly the cable connections).

(D) *Collection.* Collecting computer-related evidence is somewhat different from collecting other forms of evidence. When collecting evidence, examiners should take these precautions:

- When collecting evidence, go after original books, records, magnetic storage media, or printouts where possible.

- Be aware of degaussing equipment. A degausser is an electronic appliance that creates a strong magnetic field used to effectively erase a magnetic tape or disk. When collecting this type of evidence, ensure that any degaussing equipment is secured or rendered inoperative.

- Documents and paper should be handled with cloth gloves, placed in an evidence container, and sealed.

- It is vital to seize all storage media, even ones that purportedly have been erased. Technical personnel may still be able to capture data thought to have been erased or determine that erasures never occurred. (Disk-operating system "delete" commands do not actually erase disk sectors but merely make them available to magnetically write new information over existing information).

Care and Handling of Computer Evidence

Considerations involved in the care and handling of computer evidence include discovery and recognition, protection, recording, collection, identification, preservation, and transportation.

(E) *Identification.* It is usually more difficult to identify computer evidence than other forms of evidence; special knowledge of the thing being marked is required. A list of things to look for during the gathering of computer evidence follows:

- Information on the evidence tag should include the hardware identification and operating system used to produce disks, printouts, and labels.

- All storage media is labeled.

- Printouts should be marked with permanent marking pens.

(F) *Preservation.* Computer evidence can be very volatile. For example, turning the computer's power off prematurely can lose evidence. A list of things to preserve computer evidence follows:

- Remove evidence as soon as possible to prevent tampering. Disks can be erased or damaged quickly and easily.

- Store backup media in a proper temperature (40 to 90°F) and humidity (20 to 80%) in a dust-free environment. Tobacco smoke is also damaging. Avoid placing near strong magnetic fields (e.g., telephones, radio transmitters, photocopiers, or degaussers).

(G) *Transportation.* Particular care should be taken in the handling of computer evidence while in transit. A list of things to do during transportation of computer evidence follows:

- Transport electronic media at the proper temperature and humidity.

- Label the wires connecting various devices at both ends to aid in system reassembly at a later time.

- Photograph the labeled equipment and wires before disconnecting.

- Disassemble, tag, and inventory the equipment.

- Carefully pack seized devices in suitable containers for transport.

- Transport magnetic media in dust-free, climate-controlled environments. Temperature extremes may render magnetically stored evidence unreadable, and various types of contamination can damage electronic equipment.

- Do not take magnetic media through metal detectors, conveyor belts, or X-ray machines. This equipment generates strong magnetic fields that could destroy computer evidence.

(b) Chain of Computer Evidence

This section addresses various aspects of properly maintaining computer-related evidence. These procedures are important in avoiding problems of proof caused by improper care and handling of such evidence.

- Maintaining evidence in the form of computer storage media presents problems that differ from handling other types of evidence. Because they are subject to erasure and easily damaged, magnetic or electronic storage devices must be carefully guarded and kept under controlled temperature and humidity to avoid deterioration.

- In investigating and prosecuting a case involving such evidence, one of the early steps a prosecutor should take is to retain an appropriate computer expert or technical assistance. This can be critical in avoiding problems resulting from inept maintenance procedures or inadvertent loss of key information.

- Sometimes the contents of dozens or even hundreds of computer disks must be copied to allow the business to continue operating while the case is being prosecuted. This must be done under the close supervision of an expert who not only can ensure that it is done right but can also determine the least costly procedure.

- Initials of the seizing agent and the date should be placed on each storage media container, and a **chain-of-custody** sheet or log should be made for every container. The log should show, at a minimum, the date, place, and specific location of the seizure and the name of the agent making the seizure.

The agents investigating the case are likely to have considerable expertise in maintaining computer evidence, gained from training and experience. Their advice and assistance can be invaluable to the prosecutor in minimizing problems of proof inherent in computer-related crimes.

(c) Computer Fraud and Crime Examples

(i) Military and Intelligence Attacks

Espionage can take three forms such as industrial espionage, economic espionage, and foreign government espionage. **Industrial espionage** is the act of gathering proprietary data from private companies or the government for the purpose of aiding another company. Industrial espionage can be perpetrated either by companies seeking to improve their competitive advantage or by governments seeking to aid their domestic industries. The three most damaging types of industrial espionage include pricing data, manufacturing process information, and product development/specification information (trade secrets).

Foreign industrial espionage carried out by a government is often referred to as **economic espionage**. Information related to technology, information on commodities, interest rates, and contract data are the targets of economic espionage. In addition to possible economic espionage, **foreign intelligence services** may target unclassified systems to further their intelligence acts. Some unclassified information that may be of interest includes: travel plans of senior officials; civil defense and emergency preparedness; satellite data; personnel and payroll data; and law enforcement, investigative, and security files. **Countermeasures** against intelligence attacks include implementing user awareness, education, and training programs.

Wiretapping (electronic eavesdropping) is listening in on another's communication during transmission of messages and information. It also occurs when data flowing over cables is intercepted. **Countermeasures** include: locking up the cable closet, using traffic padding technique to confuse the eavesdropper, and implementing voice encryption techniques with (SSL) Security Socket Layer protocol.

Data leakage is removal of data from a computer system by covert means. It might be possible to examine computer operating system usage journals to determine if and when data files may have been accessed. Data leakage attacks might be conducted through the use of Trojan horse, logic bomb, or scavenging methods. **Countermeasures** include encryption, access controls, and cryptographic techniques.

(ii) Business Attacks

Employee sabotage is the most common business attack. The number of incidents of employee sabotage is much *smaller* than instances of employee theft, but the cost of such incidents can be quite high. Common examples of computer-related employee sabotage include: destroying hardware or facilities, planting logic bombs that destroy programs or data, "crashing" computer systems, and entering data incorrectly, deleting data, or changing data (data diddling).

Data diddling involves changing data before or during input to computers or during output from a computer system. The changing can be done by anybody associated with or having access to the process of creating, recording, transporting, encoding, examining, checking, converting, and transforming data that ultimately enter a computer. Examples include: forging or counterfeiting documents; exchanging valid computer magnetic media with prepared replacements; source document entry violations; and neutralizing, bypassing, or avoiding manual controls. *Manipulating input is the most common method of perpetrating fraud using a computer. Data diddling attacks can be prevented with access controls, program change controls, and integrity checking software.*

Super zapping, an example of a business attack, it involves unauthorized use of a computer utility program to modify, destroy, copy, disclose, insert, use, or deny use of data stored in a computer system or computer media. This powerful utility program bypasses operating system security controls and even the access control security software controls. By definition, super zapping is not a computer crime by itself. *A reliable way to detect super zapping work is by comparing current data files with previous data files.*

Simply **writing computer virus programs** is not a criminal activity. However, using, releasing, and spreading a virus with bad intentions of destroying computer resources are the basis for criminal activity.

(iii) Financial Attacks

The **salami technique** of financial attacks involves theft of small amounts of assets (primarily money) from a number of sources. For example, the perpetrator steals a few cents from each customer account on a large number of bank accounts, theft that is unnoticed by most customers. However, the account totals will be kept in balance with double-entry recordkeeping system. The salami technique can also be affected by "round-down" fractions of money, which can be moved into the perpetrator's bank account.

Collecting customers' credit card information through websites and unauthorized access to **wire transfer fund** accounts in a financial institution are other examples of financial attacks. Transfer of money between two parties without a financial institution's involvement is another example of a financial attack.

Toll fraud through telephone cloning is another example of a financial attack; this type of fraud costs telephone company's significant amounts of money.

(iv) Hacker Attacks
Hackers can hold data hostage, or they can demand ransom money for data and programs stolen as in ransomware attacks. They can do data hijacking.

(v) Grudge Attacks
Employees who were fired may have a grudge against the organization where they have worked. The general public may have a grudge against an organization where they do not like what the organization is doing or has done.

(vi) "Fun" attacks.
People can target organizations for fun and challenge to get publicity and to satisfy their intellectual curiosity. Their goal is not to make money.

> **Related Concepts in Computer Crime**
>
> - A person must have a motive, the opportunity, and the means to commit a crime.
> - Computer crime is possible when controls are predictable and avoidable (bypassable).
> - System predictability is a key to a successful computer crime; that is, users and attackers know how the system reacts to a given condition.
> - Computer crime can be minimized with dynamic controls and variable features.
> - White-collar crimes tend to be situation-oriented, meaning that a change in a person's lifestyle and job situations can make the person commit crime.
> - Unknown misbehavior of unknown perpetrators is the major reason for the inability to calculate the risk resulting from computer crime.

6.11 GAO's Framework for Managing Fraud Risks

The U.S. General Accountability Office (GAO) has issued *A Framework for Managing Fraud Risks in Federal Programs* as guidance to prevent, detect, and respond to fraud situations.[29]

---

[29] *A Framework for Managing Fraud Risks in Federal Programs* (July 2015), GAO-15-593SP, www.gao.gov.

(a) Fraud Defined

Fraud is defined as obtaining something of value through a willful misrepresentation. Fraud can take place in several ways, such as improper payments, illegal activities, and collusion. An improper payment is defined as any payment that should not have been made or that was made in an incorrect amount, including overpayments and underpayments.

A pay-and-chase model refers to the practice of detecting fraudulent transactions and attempting to recover funds after payments have been made. This is an example of a reactive practice. Organizations should change the reactive pay-and-chase model to a proactive match-and-pay model, where fraud is identified before payments are made. This model improvement is made possible with data-mapping, data-matching, and data-mining techniques.

Before: Reactive practice = Pay-and-chase model = Detective control

After: Proactive practice = Match-and-pay model = Preventive control

One of the major goals of this framework is to reduce false positives during fraud audit and investigations. A high proportion of false positives can be reduced with this framework because a false positive shows an improper identification of suspect individuals who were not engaged in fraud. Use of multiple analytical tools and techniques (e.g., text mining, web scraping, data mapping, data matching, data mining, data visualization, data dashboards, fraud-data analytics, and statistical analyses) can reduce the occurrence of false positives, which in turn can increase the fraud detection rates.

(b) Control Activities and Components

The GAO's Framework presents three control activities and five components for effectively managing fraud-related risks. The three control activities are prevention, detection, and response controls, which can recover fraudulent payments and delinquent debts. The five components are commit, assess, design and implement, evaluate and adapt, and monitoring and feedback.

Control activities for managing fraud risks include the policies, procedures, techniques, and mechanisms related to three categories of control activities that are interdependent and mutually reinforcing: prevention, detection, and response.

Fraud Risks = Prevention Controls + Detection Controls + Response Controls

Prevention controls mitigate the risk of fraud occurring and include antifraud strategy, employee background checks, fraud-awareness trainings, system-based edit checks, data matching to verify eligibility prior to payment, predictive analytics, segregation of duties, standards of conduct, and transaction limits.

Detection controls discover potential fraud that has already occurred and include internal and external assurance audits to detect fraud, data matching after payments have been made, data-mining applications, document reviews, hotlines and whistleblower reporting mechanisms, and surprise physical site visits and inspections.

Response controls investigate potential fraud, take corrective actions, and remedy the harm caused by fraud. They include investigations, prosecutions, disciplinary actions, suspensions, debarments, and payment recoveries.

The **five components** for effectively managing fraud-related risks are described next. **Commit** requires a commitment to combating fraud by creating an organizational culture and structure conducive to fraud risk management. **Assess** requires a plan to assess risks in a regular fraud situation and to determine a fraud risk profile. **Design and implement** requires a strategy with specific control activities to mitigate assessed fraud risks and collaborate to help ensure effective implementation. **Evaluate and adapt** requires evaluating outcomes using a risk-based approach and adapting activities to improve fraud risk management. **Monitoring and feedback** mechanisms include ongoing practices that apply to the other four components. These mechanisms allow managers to continually incorporate new information, such as changing risks or the effects of actions taken to mitigate risks. Incorporating feedback to continually adapt fraud risk management activities requires constant data collecting, analyzing, and adapting processes.

(c) Data Analytics for Fraud

A risk-based approach to data analytics for fraud is recommended that considers both costs and benefits. Here, costs include the cost of investing in specific data-analytics technologies (e.g., software, hardware, and staff costs) and benefits include reduced improper payments and fraud.

The most commonly used data-analytics tools and techniques in fraud prevention and detection are listed next.

- **Data mapping**—Requires linking or tracing audit tests to the corresponding data elements in order to evaluate the test results and to determine whether the test results achieve the defined objectives.

- **Data matching**—A computer matching process in which information from one source is compared with information from other sources to identify any inconsistencies in the data. These sources can be either a single file or multiple files and can be of any computer data file or database, either internal or external to a company.

- **Data mining**—Analyzes data for relationships that have not been discovered previously. It identifies suspicious activity or transactions, including anomalies, outliers, and other red flags in the data. To this end, it applies data filters, log filters, fraud filters, and data rules that can help identify transactions that exhibit signs of fraud.

- **System-based edit checks**—Help ensure that data meets requirements before it is accepted into computer systems and before payments are made. These edit checks are instructions programmed into a computer system to help ensure data quality (i.e., data are complete, accurate, valid, and recorded in the proper format). These checks identify missing, incorrect, or miscoded data.

- **Predictive analytics**—Includes a variety of automated systems and tools that can be used to identify particular types of human behavior, including fraud, before transactions are completed. Three models exist: rules-based models, anomaly-detection models, and predictive models.

  - **Rules-based models**—Filter claims and behaviors that an individual submitted for an unreasonable number of services. These are the simplest types of models since the analysis conducted using them only involves counting or identifying types of claims and comparing the results to an established threshold of rules.

  - **Anomaly-detection models**—Identify abnormal patterns of an individual relative to the patterns of peers. These models generate analyses that are more complex than rules-based models because they require identification of patterns of behavior based on data collected over a period of time. Then actual patterns are compared to the established patterns that have been determined to be reasonable.

☐ **Predictive models**—Use historical data to identify patterns associated with fraud and then use these historical data to identify certain potentially fraudulent behaviors when applied to current claims data. Predictive models are the most complex type of model because they not only require analysis of large amounts of data but they also may require detection of several patterns of behavior that individually may not be suspicious but, when conducted together, can indicate fraudulent activity. Link analysis is a part of predictive models because it discovers knowledge about an individual who is linked to known bad individuals through addresses or phone numbers.

(d) Success of Data Analytics in Fraud

Measuring the success of data analytics programs to prevent fraud, waste, and abuse is not easy due to difficulties in estimating the savings associated with funds that were never stolen or wasted. However, data analytics can be used to analyze trends over time:

- How much fraud money was recovered?

- How many suspected individuals were arrested?

- How much reduction was noticed in fraudulent activities?

6.12 COSO's Framework for Fraud Risk Management

The U.S. Committee of Sponsoring Organizations of the Treadway Commission (COSO) has issued a fraud risk management guide to prevent, detect, and respond to fraud situations.[30]

(a) Fraud Defined

Fraud is defined as any intentional act or omission designed to deceive others, resulting in the victim suffering a loss and/or the perpetrator or fraudster achieving a gain.

Fraud ⟶ Victim ⟶ Loss

Fraud ⟶ Fraudster ⟶ Gain

A potential for fraud risk exists in all functions of a business, not just in accounting and finance. For example, the procurement function has a great potential for heavy fraud risk because it handles huge amounts of money. Simply stated, fraud can exist wherever and whenever money changes hands.

(b) Fraud Risk Management Program

COSO's Framework for fraud risk management provides guidance on:

- Establishing fraud risk governance policies where they are a part of corporate governance and internal control environment. Here, corporate governance addresses fiduciary

---

[30] COSO, *Fraud Risk Management Guide*, Executive Summary (September 2016), www.coso.org.

responsibilities of the board of directors and the internal control environment creates the discipline supporting the assessment of risks.

- Performing a fraud risk assessment where its scope includes fraudulent financial reporting, fraudulent nonfinancial reporting, asset misappropriation, and illegal acts (including corruption).

- Designing and deploying fraud preventive and detective control activities. Here, preventive controls are designed to avoid a fraudulent event or transaction at the time of initial occurrence. Detective controls are designed to discover a fraudulent event or transaction after the initial processing has occurred.

- Conducting fraud investigations where the framework develops and implements a system for prompt, competent, and confidential review, investigation, and resolution of instances of noncompliance and allegations involving fraud and misconduct.

- Monitoring and evaluating the total fraud risk management program where it requires that ongoing evaluations are built into an organization's business processes at varying levels of details to provide timely information. A not-so-good alternative to ongoing evaluations is periodically conducting separate evaluations with varying degrees of scope and time of work.

(c) Fraud Risk Management Process

An ongoing and comprehensive fraud risk management process consists of five steps, discussed next.

> **Step 1: Policy**—Establish a fraud risk management policy as part of organizational governance.
>
> **Step 2: Risk assessment**—Perform a comprehensive fraud risk assessment.
>
> **Step 3: Fraud-related controls**—Select, develop, and deploy preventive and detective fraud control activities.
>
> **Step 4: Report and correct**—Establish a fraud reporting process and coordinated approach to investigation and corrective action.
>
> **Step 5: Monitor and improve**—Monitor the fraud risk management process, report results, and improve the process.

This comprehensive approach recognizes and emphasizes the fundamental difference between internal control weaknesses resulting in **errors** (i.e., errors could be due to unintentional human mistakes and/or poorly designed system-related problems) and internal control weaknesses resulting in **fraud**. This fundamental difference is i**ntent**.

> Errors have *no* intent.
>
> Fraud *has* intent.

An organization that simply adds a fraud risk assessment to the existing internal control assessment may not thoroughly examine and identify possibilities for intentional acts designed to misstate financial or nonfinancial information, misappropriate assets, or perpetrate illegal acts or corruption.

Implementing a specific and more focused fraud risk assessment as a separate or stand-alone fraud risk management process provides greater assurance that the assessment's focus remains on intentional acts.

Total risk assessment = Fraud risk assessment + Internal control assessment
(Two exercises)   (Separate exercise)   (Separate exercise)

COSO's Framework recommends ways in which governing boards, senior management, staff at all levels, and internal auditors together can deter fraud in their organization. Fraud deterrence is a process of eliminating factors that may cause fraud to occur. Applying fraud data analytics can play an important role in fraud deterrence. Deterrence is achieved when an organization implements a fraud risk management process that

- Establishes a visible and rigorous fraud risk governance process where it is a part of corporate governance and internal control environment. Here, the internal control environment creates the discipline supporting the assessment of risks.

- Creates a transparent and sound antifraud culture.

- Periodically performs a thorough fraud risk assessment.

- Designs, implements, and maintains preventive and detective fraud-related control processes and procedures.

- Takes swift action in response to allegations of fraud including, where appropriate, actions against those involved in wrongdoing.

The focus of fraud data analytics is on fraud prevention, detection, and response (correction). It uses tools such as data mapping, data matching, data mining, data visualization, text mining, web scraping, data dashboards, statistical analyses (e.g., discovery sampling), link analysis, and social media platforms. These tools are in addition to the traditional tools of inspecting, tracing, observing, counting, reconciling, comparing, and contrasting.

6.13 Fraud Analytics

Data analytics is applying quantitative and qualitative tools and techniques to big data in order to gain new insights and new opportunities. Analytics help either individually or collectively in detecting and preventing fraudulent activities. Various types of data analytics are listed next.

- Predictive analytics
- Embedded data analytics
- Forensic data analytics
- Streaming data analytics
- Social media data analytics
- Web-based data analytics
- Text-based data analytics
- Open-source data analytics
- Data modeling analytics
- Visual analytics
- Descriptive analytics

- Prescriptive analytics
- First-digit tests

(a) Predictive Analytics

Predictive analytics is the process of estimating future outcomes based on the analysis of past data and/or current data. It describes what could happen.

For example, the U.S. Department of Health and Human Services has applied the following analytic techniques to identify improper payments and fraudulent activities perpetrated by healthcare providers (bad actors) in its Centers for Medicare and Medicaid Services.

- A rules-based technique filters fraudulent claims and associated behaviors with predefined rules. It identified providers that bill using a Medicare identification number that was previously stolen and used improperly.
- An anomaly-based technique detects individual and aggregated abnormal patients versus a peer group. It identified providers that bill for more services in a single day than the number of services that 99% of similar providers bill in a single day.
- A predictive-based technique assesses against known fraud cases. It identified providers that have characteristics similar to those of known bad actors.
- A network-based technique discovers knowledge with associative link analysis. It identified providers that are linked to known bad actors through addresses or phone numbers.

For example, the retail industry can use these predictive analytics:

- Estimating what customers will buy what products and from what markets
- Store customer foot traffic analysis through sensors and cameras
- Customer orders online
- Actual sales transactions
- Customer merchandise returns
- Online shopping cart abandonment
- Customer financial chargebacks
- New store location
- Cross-store merchandise locator
- Endless aisles of inventory
- Estimating customer retention rates and defection rates

The next predictive analytics can be applied to any industry:

- Identifying new revenue opportunities by products or by markets
- Forecasting workforce requirements by type and skill
- Identifying the factors leading to employee satisfaction and productivity

- Identifying factors for customers' filing a fraudulent claim
- Discovering the underlying reasons for employees' attrition rates
- Predicting what types of customers will default on a loan payment or credit card payment
- Predicting employee turnover rates
- Predicting equipment breakdowns before they disrupt operations

(b) Embedded Data Analytics

Many organizations are using embedded data analytics, such as data visualization tools, reporting routines and methods, and data dashboards, in their business-oriented application systems, providing a real value to end users of such systems. Embedded analytics is a part of predictive analytics and predicts future events and outcomes. Compare the embedded data analytics to the traditional data analytics where the latter presents past events and outcomes and the former presents future events and outcomes.

(c) Forensic Data Analytics

The focus of fraud-related forensic data analytics is on fraud prevention, detection, and response (correction). It uses tools such as data visualization, text mining, web-scraping tools, data dashboards, statistical analysis (e.g., discovery sampling), link analysis, and social media. These tools are in addition to the traditional tools of inspecting, tracing, observing, counting, reconciling, comparing, and contrasting. Usually business rules, such as a dollar amount of claims or the frequency of claims, are used to detect fraud.

(d) Streaming Data Analytics

Streaming data analytics is performed in real time and in memory where it collects data from electronic sensors to produce time-series data. The use of streaming analytics increases as machine-generated data sources increase. Temporal analysis, which is based on the concept of time and which is a part of streaming data analytics, helps to understand the different scenarios that are based on changing times. For example, a retail store selling, activating, or redeeming thousands of gift cards within a short period of time (e.g., three to four hours) can be an indication of fraud, or a sudden surge in activity is an application streaming data analytics.

Data stream processing presents current events as they are occurring. Compare the streaming data analytics to the traditional data analytics and embedded data analytics where the traditional data analytics present past events and where the embedded data analytics predict future events.

Traditional Data Analytics ⟶ Shows Past Events

Streaming Data Analytics ⟶ Shows Current Events

Embedded Data Analytics ⟶ Shows Future Events

(e) Social Media Data Analytics

Social media analytics takes thousands and thousands of data items from online posts, followers, fans, page views, reviews, comments, pins, and mentions in various social media websites to evaluate marketing campaigns, advertisements, and promotions and to conclude what marketing efforts worked and what did not work.

(f) Web-Based Data Analytics

Web scraping is a web-based data extraction and data mining approach. For example, it can search Twitter, a social media network, for keywords relating to fraud.

(g) Text-Based Data Analytics

Text analytics focus on prescriptive and descriptive analytics, where they focus much on written materials and mobile text messages using short message service (SMS) and multimedia messaging service (MMS). Text analytics also include information from web call-center notes, comment fields posted on social media platforms, traditional reports, customer inquiries, web chats, and print books. Text-based data are unstructured data and are useful as a text-mining tool to detect fraud-related words on various data sources.

(h) Open-Source Data Analytics

Open-source analytical tools and techniques are available, including open-source software, interoperable systems, and data-sharing facilities, at low cost or no cost. The open-source algorithms can be consolidated in a central location to allow for ease of access across several organizations to identify fraud, waste, and abuse. Moreover, the use of open-source tools could lessen the challenge of developing licensing agreements for proprietary software tools. Open-source data libraries could help in audits, inspections, and investigations.

(i) Data Modeling Analytics

Data modeling analytics means building data models, using simulation models, and testing them with what-if questions to see their answers in the form of changing outputs (outcomes) when inputs to the model change.

(j) Visual Analytics

Visual analytics use data visualization tools, such as line, bar, scatter, bubble, and pie charts, to present relationships among big data in an easy-to-understand format. Senior managers prefer visual analytics, similar to data dashboards.

(k) Descriptive Analytics

Descriptive analytics describes what already happened and includes content analysis and context analysis.

Content analysis is a set of procedures for transforming unstructured written material into a format for analysis. It is a methodology for structuring and analyzing unstructured written material in documents and reports. For example, two or more documents can be analyzed to discover a fraud-related content using specific words, symbols, names, events, outcomes, and addresses.

Examples of Content Analysis

Using text-data analytics, governmental agencies are looking at social media platforms for specific words posted or comments to identify terrorist activities; to discover fraudulent activities in the food stamp program; and to pinpoint fraud, waste, and abuse in healthcare payments.

Context analysis is possible because because data can be contextual, meaning some data is related to a specific context (in context). Hence, to analyze data trends and patterns, a pool of data must be separated into in-context data and out-of-context data.

Examples of Context Analysis

Insurance companies can analyze claims data during natural disasters; retail companies can analyze sales data during holiday shopping seasons, such as Thanksgiving, Christmas, and New Year's Eve; retail companies can analyze sales data during special promotions lasting one week (e.g., blast sales, flash sales, or tent sales); and retailers can analyze sales data during a season (in context) and nonseason (out of context) if the focus is on seasonal sales.

(l) Prescriptive Analytics

Prescriptive analytics helps decide what should happen and thrives on big data. When faced with a number of potential decisions, it analyzes for the best possible outcome.

Examples of Prescriptive Analytics

- Optimal allocation of a company's stock market portfolio after considering expected returns and dividends

- Airline companies determining ticket prices after considering travel variables, such as customer demand, travel timings, travel locations, and holidays (e.g., ticket prices are higher during holidays)

(m) First-Digit Tests

As part of fraud investigations, internal auditors can apply the **Benford's law** or the first-digit test to detect unusual data patterns arising from human errors, data manipulations, or fraudulent transactions. If the first digit is 1 in a financial account number or business transaction number, chances are good that it is a naturally occurring number (i.e., fraud-free). If the first digit is 9, chances are good that it might be a purposefully assigned number (i.e., fraudulent) to perpetrate fraud. The test looks at the first digit of account numbers to see if it is 1 or 9 because the digit 1 occurs in that location 30% of the time while the digit 9 occurs in that location only 5% of the time. In general, lower numbers (1–5) are known to be fraud-free than the higher numbers (6–9), which are known to be fraudulent on the scale of 1 to 9 as the first digit. The following conditions apply:

The number is fraud-free if digits 1, 2, 3, 4, and 5 appear. They occur in combination 78% of the time.

The number is fraudulent if digits 6, 7, 8, and 9 appear. They occur in combination 22% of the time.

If first-digit analysis indicates that digits 6 through 9 are occurring more often than their expected frequency, it is an indication of fraud or other irregularities, and further investigation is required.

6.14 Fraud and the Internal Auditor

The roles and responsibilities of internal auditors in fraud prevention and detection are often filled with confusion and controversy due to misconceptions and incorrect expectations. The roles and responsibilities of an organization's internal auditors and management are listed next.

- Auditors need to be familiar with how fraud is initiated and committed in her organization.

- An organization's internal control system provides the primary assurance with respect to fraud prevention and detection, not the internal audit function, not an individual auditor, and not a group of auditors.

- An organization's management is fully responsible for fraud prevention and detection because management planned, designed, developed, tested, and implemented the entire internal control system, whether it is a manual system or an automated system.

- Auditors have the professional responsibility to evaluate fraud exposures and to evaluate the capability of the internal control system to prevent and detect fraud.

- Auditors must accept responsibility for those irregularities resulting from their failure to report known weaknesses in the system of internal control.

- Auditors cannot detect fraud when (1) irregular transactions were not recorded and no evidence of traceability and accountability exists; (2) isolated transactions occurred infrequently; and (3) irregular transactions were concealed by collusion.

- Auditors have the professional responsibility to report to the company's audit management, senior management, board of directors, and the audit committee when a fraud is suspected during the course of their routine and regular audit work.

- Auditors have the professional responsibility to exercise due professional care by considering the probability of significant errors, irregularities, fraud, or noncompliance issues.

- When in doubt, auditors have the responsibility to apply additional audit tests and reviews to determine if fraud has actually occurred.

- Auditors have the responsibility to remember the principle of relative risk, meaning that costs to detect fraud should not exceed the benefits from detecting fraud.

- In summary, internal auditors cannot guarantee the prevention and detection of fraud, just as the board of directors cannot guarantee the effective and efficient functioning of corporate governance processes and mechanisms.

6.15 Sample Practice Questions

In the actual CIA Exam for Part 1, 125 multiple-choice (M/C) test questions appear. This book contains 125 M/C sample practice questions divided into syllabus-based domains using the approximate domain weight given in the exam. These questions are added at the end of each applicable domain of this book to show the flavor and structure of the exam questions and to create a self-quiz experience. The answers and explanations for these questions are shown at the end of this book, in a section titled "Sample Practice Questions, Answers, and Explanations." If CIA Exam candidates need to practice more sample questions to obtain a higher level of confidence, Wiley offers a separate online test bank software product with hundreds of similar sample practice questions.

1. Internal auditors would be more likely to detect fraud if they developed/strengthened their ability to:
   a. Recognize and question changes which occur in organizations.
   b. Interrogate fraud perpetrators to discover why the fraud was committed.
   c. Develop internal controls to prevent the occurrence of fraud.
   d. Document computerized operating system programs.

2. According to the IIA *Standards*, which of the following best describes the two general categories or types of fraud that concern most internal auditors?
   a. Improper payments (i.e., bribes and kickbacks) and tax fraud
   b. Fraud designed to benefit the organization and fraud perpetrated to the detriment of the organization
   c. Acceptance of bribes or kickbacks and improper related-party transactions
   d. Acceptance of kickbacks or embezzlement and misappropriation of assets

3. A company hired a highly qualified accounts payable manager who had been terminated from another company for alleged wrongdoing. Six months later, the manager diverted $12,000 by sending duplicate payments of invoices to a relative. A control that might have prevented this situation would be to:
   a. Adequately check prior employment backgrounds for all new employees.
   b. Not hire individuals who appear overqualified for a job.
   c. Verify educational background for all new employees.
   d. Check to see if close relatives work for payable vendors.

4. Red flags are conditions that indicate a higher likelihood of fraud. Which of the following would **not** be considered a red flag?
   a. Management has delegated to subordinates the authority to make purchases under a certain dollar limit.
   b. An individual has held the same cash-handling job for an extended period without any rotation of duties.
   c. An individual handling marketable securities is responsible for making the purchases, recording the purchases, and reporting any discrepancies and gains/losses to senior management.
   d. The assignment of responsibility and accountability in the accounts receivable department is not clear.

5. Internal auditors and management have become increasingly concerned about computer fraud. Which of the following control procedures would be **least** important in preventing computer fraud?
   a. Program change control that requires a distinction between production programs and test programs
   b. Testing of new applications by users during the systems development process
   c. Segregation of duties between the applications programmer and the program librarian function
   d. Segregation of duties between the programmer and systems analyst

6. What is a data diddling technique?

a. Changing data before input to a computer system

b. Changing data during input to a computer system

c. Changing data during output from a computer system

d. All of the above

7. What is a salami technique?

a. Taking small amounts of assets

b. Using the rounding-down concept

c. Stealing small amounts of money from bank accounts

d. All of the above

8. With respect to computer security and fraud, a legal liability exists to an organization under which of the following conditions?

a. When estimated security costs are greater than estimated losses

b. When estimated security costs are equal to estimated losses

c. When estimated security costs are less than estimated losses.

d. When actual security costs are equal to actual losses

9. Which of the following security techniques allows time for response by investigative authorities?

a. Deter

b. Detect

c. Delay

d. Deny

10. Most of the evidence submitted in a computer crime case is:

a. Legal evidence.

b. Documentary evidence.

c. Secondary evidence.

d. Admissible evidence.

11. When computers and peripheral equipment are seized in relation to a computer crime, it is an example of:

a. Duplicate evidence.

b. Physical evidence.

c. Best evidence.

d. Collateral evidence.

12. From a computer security viewpoint, courts expect what amount of care from organizations?

a. Super care

b. Due care

c. Extraordinary care

d. Great care

13. Which of the following is **not** a computer criminal activity in **most** jurisdictions?

a. Writing a computer virus program

b. Using a computer virus program

c. Releasing a computer virus program

d. Spreading a computer virus program

14. Once evidence is seized in a computer crime case, a law enforcement officer should follow which of the following?

a. Chain of logs

b. Chain of events

c. Chain of custody

d. Chain of computers

15. The concept of admissibility of evidence does **not** include which of the following?

a. Relevance

b. Competence

c. Materiality

d. Sufficiency

16. Evidence is needed in a computer crime case to do which of the following?

a. Charge a case.

b. Classify a case.

c. Make a case.

d. Prove a case.

17. What determines whether a computer crime has been committed?

a. When the crime is reported

b. When a computer expert has completed his or her work

c. When the allegation has been substantiated

d. When the investigation is completed

18. The correct sequence of preliminary investigation in a computer fraud is:

  I.   Consult with a computer expert.

  II. Prepare an investigative plan.

  III. Consult with a prosecutor.

  IV. Substantiate the allegation.

  a. IV, I, II, and III

  b. III, I, II, and IV

  c. IV, II, III, and I

  d. I, IV, II, and III

19. A search warrant is required in a computer-related crime:

  a. Before the allegation has been substantiated.

  b. After establishing the probable cause(s).

  c. Before identifying the number of investigators needed.

  d. After seizing the computer and related equipment.

20. If a computer or peripheral equipment involved in a computer crime is **not** covered by a search warrant, what should the investigator do?

  a. Seize it before someone takes it away.

  b. Leave it alone until a warrant can be obtained.

  c. Analyze the equipment or its contents and record it.

  d. Store it in a locked cabinet in a secure warehouse.

21. Computer fraud is increased when:

  a. Employees are not trained.

  b. Documentation is not available.

  c. Audit trails are not available.

  d. Employee performance appraisals are not given.

Sample Practice Questions, Answers, and Explanations

Domain 1: Foundations of Internal Auditing

1. What is the key word in the Institute of Internal Auditors (IIA) mission Statement of internal audit?

   a. Assurance

   Incorrect. Assurance is a part of the internal audit's mission, not the key word.

   b. Advice

   Incorrect. Advice is a part of the internal audit's mission, not the key word.

   c. Value

   Correct. The mission of internal audit is to enhance and protect organizational value by providing risk-based and objective assurance, advice, and insight. Here, value is the key word because it drives the other words.

   d. Insight

   Incorrect. Insight is a part of the internal audit's mission, not the key word.

2. The new International Professional Practices Framework (IPPF) effective from 2017 contains which of the following that was **not** a part of the previous IPPF?

   a. Mission and Core Principles

   Correct. Mission and Core Principles were added to the new IPPF effective 2017.

   b. Definition of Internal Auditing and Practice Guides

   Incorrect. Definition of Internal Auditing and Practice Guides were in the previous IPPF. They are not new.

   c. Code of Ethics and Glossary

   Incorrect. The Code of Ethics and Glossary were in the previous IPPF. They are not new.

   d. International Standards and local standards for internal auditing

   Incorrect. The International Standards and local standards for internal auditing were in the previous IPPF. They are not new.

3. Which of the following adds value to the others?

   a. Governance processes

   Incorrect. See correct answer (c).

   b. Risk management processes

   Incorrect. See correct answer (c).

   c. Internal audit activities

   Correct. Internal audit activities add value to the organization (and its stakeholders) when they provide objective and relevant assurance and contribute to the effectiveness and efficiency of governance, risk management, and control processes.

   d. Control processes

   Incorrect. See correct answer (c).

4. The IIA's definition of internal auditing emphasizes the effectiveness of which of the following?

  a. Value, cost, and benefit propositions

    Incorrect. See correct answer (c).

  b. Inherent risk, residual risk, and total risk

    Incorrect. See correct answer (c).

  c. Risk management, control, and governance processes

    Correct. The definition of internal auditing states the fundamental purpose, nature, and scope of internal auditing. Internal auditing is an independent, objective assurance and consulting activity designed to add value and improve an organization's operations. It helps an organization accomplish its objectives by bringing a systematic, disciplined approach to evaluate and improve the effectiveness of risk management, control, and governance processes.

  d. Purpose, nature, and scope of work

    Incorrect. See correct answer (c).

5. The internal audit activity's Core Principles can be used as which of the following?

  a. Metrics

    Incorrect. Metrics are qualitative and quantitative measurements of an activity.

  b. Benchmarks

    Correct. The Core Principles can be used as a benchmark against which to gauge the effectiveness of an internal audit activity.

  c. Key performance indicators

    Incorrect. Key performance indicators are similar to metrics for measuring an activity.

  d. Dashboards

    Incorrect. Dashboards are presentation tools to show progress of an activity.

6. The internal audit activity's Core Principles describe which of the following?

  a. Efficiency

    Incorrect. Efficiency is not described in the Core Principles.

  b. Resources

    Incorrect. Resources are not described in the Core Principles.

  c. Plans

    Incorrect. Plans are not described in the Core Principles.

  d. Effectiveness

    Correct. The Core Principles are the key elements that describe an internal audit activity's effectiveness.

7. The internal audit activity's Core Principles underpin which of the following?

  a. Code of Ethics and Standards

    Correct. The Core Principles are the foundational underpinnings of the Code of Ethics and the Standards.

  b. Efficiency and effectiveness

    Incorrect. See correct answer (a).

  c. Metrics and key performance indicators

    Incorrect. See correct answer (a).

  d. Resources and skills

    Incorrect. See correct answer (a).

8. The audit committee of an organization has charged the chief audit executive (CAE) with bringing the department into full compliance with the IIA Standards. The CAE's first task is to develop a charter. Identify the item that should be included in the statement of objectives.

   a. Report all audit findings to the audit committee every quarter.

   Incorrect. Only significant audit findings should be discussed with the audit committee.

   b. Notify governmental regulatory agencies of unethical business practices by organization management.

   Incorrect. Internal auditors are not required to report deficiencies in regulatory compliance to the appropriate agencies. However, Institute members and Certified Internal Auditors may not knowingly be involved in illegal acts.

   c. Determine the adequacy and effectiveness of the organization's systems of internal controls.

   Correct. This is a primary function of any internal auditing department.

   d. Submit departmental budget variance reports to management every month.

   Incorrect. This choice is not a primary objective of the internal auditing department. It is a budgetary control that management may require on a periodic basis.

9. The internal audit charter normally requires the internal audit activity to focus on areas consisting of which of the following?

   a. High inherent risk and high residual risk

   Correct. The internal audit charter normally requires the internal audit activity to focus on areas of high risk, including both inherent and residual risk. The internal audit activity needs to identify areas of high inherent risk, high residual risks, and the key control systems upon which the organization is most reliant.

   b. High audit risk and high current risk

   Incorrect. See correct answer (a).

   c. Low inherent risk and low audit risk

   Incorrect. See correct answer (a).

   d. Low inherent risk and high outstanding risk

   Incorrect. See correct answer (a).

10. Consulting engagement objectives must be consistent with all of the following **except**:

    a. Organization's goals.

    Correct. Goals are short term in nature while objectives are long term in nature. Hence, consulting engagement objectives must be consistent with the organization's values, strategies, and objectives.

    b. Organization's values.

    Incorrect. See correct answer (a).

    c. Organization's strategies.

    Incorrect. See correct answer (a)

    d. Organization's objectives.

    Incorrect. See correct answer (a).

11. All of the following are examples of assurance services **except**:

    a. Financial engagement.

    Incorrect. Financial engagement is part of assurance services.

    b. Compliance engagement.

    Incorrect. Compliance engagement is part of assurance services.

    c. Due diligence engagement.

    Incorrect. Due diligence engagement is part of assurance services.

    d. Training engagement.

    Correct. Training engagement is a part of consulting. The IIA's Glossary defines assurance services as "objective examination[s] of evidence for the purpose of providing an independent assessment on governance, risk management, and control processes for the organization. Examples may include financial, performance, compliance, system security, and due diligence engagements."

12. All of the following are examples of consulting services **except**:

a. Legal counsel engagement.

Incorrect. Legal counsel engagement is an example of consulting services.

b. **System security engagement.**

Correct. System security engagement is a part of assurance services. The IIA's Glossary defines consulting services as "advisory and related client service activities, the nature and scope of which are agreed with the client and are intended to add value and improve an organization's governance, risk management, and control processes without the internal auditor assuming management responsibility. Examples include counsel, advice, facilitation, and training."

c. Advice engagement.

Incorrect. Advice engagement is an example of consulting services.

d. Facilitation engagement.

Incorrect. Facilitation engagement is an example of consulting services.

13. The IIA's Code of Ethics includes which of the following two essential components?

a. Definition of internal auditing and administrative directives.

Incorrect. See correct answer (b).

b. **Principles and Rules of Conduct.**

Correct. The IIA's Code of Ethics extends beyond the definition of internal auditing to include two essential components:

1. **Principles that are relevant to the profession and practice of internal auditing.**

2. **Rules of Conduct that describe behavior norms expected of internal auditors. These rules are an aid to interpreting the Principles in practical applications and are intended to guide the ethical conduct of internal auditors.**

Note that the IIA's Bylaws and Administrative Directives are applicable to IIA members and Certified Internal Auditor designation holders. Integrity, objectivity, confidentiality, and competency are part of the Principles and the Rules of Conduct.

c. Integrity and objectivity.

Incorrect. See correct answer (b).

d. Confidentiality and competency.

Incorrect. See correct answer (b).

14. A certified internal auditor (CIA) is working in a non–internal audit position as the director of purchasing. The CIA signs a contract to procure a large order from the supplier with the best price, quality, and performance. Shortly after signing the contract, the supplier presents the CIA with a gift of significant monetary value. Which of the following statements regarding the acceptance of the gift is correct?

a. Acceptance of the gift would be prohibited only if it were noncustomary.

Incorrect. Acceptance of the gift could easily be presumed to have impaired independence and thus would not be acceptable.

b. **Acceptance of the gift would violate the IIA Code of Ethics and would be prohibited for a CIA.**

Correct. As long as an individual is a CIA, he or she should be guided by the profession's Code of Ethics in addition to the organization's code of conduct. Objectivity (Rules of Conduct) of the Code of Ethics would preclude such a gift because it could be presumed to have influenced the individual's decision.

c. Since the CIA is no longer acting as an internal auditor, acceptance of the gift would be governed only by the organization's code of conduct.

Incorrect. Sufficient information is not given to judge possible violations of the organization's code of conduct. However, the action could easily be perceived as a kickback.

d. Since the contract was signed before the gift was offered, acceptance of the gift would not violate either the IIA Code of Ethics or the organization's code of conduct.

Incorrect. Sufficient information is not given to judge possible violations of the organization's code of conduct. However, the action could easily be perceived as a kickback.

15. An auditor, nearly finished with an audit, discovers that the director of marketing has a gambling habit. The gambling issue is not directly related to the existing audit, and there is pressure to complete the current audit. The auditor notes the problem and passes the information on to the chief audit executive (CAE) but does no further follow-up. The auditor's actions would:

a. Be in violation of the IIA Code of Ethics for withholding meaningful information.

Incorrect. The auditor is not withholding information because he or she has passed the information along to the CAE. The information may be useful in a subsequent audit in the marketing area.

b. Be in violation of the Standards because the auditor did not properly follow-up on a red flag that might indicate the existence of fraud.

Incorrect. The auditor has documented a red flag that may be important in a subsequent audit. This does not violate the Standards.

c. Not be in violation of either the IIA Code of Ethics or the Standards.

Correct. There is no violation of either the Code of Ethics or the Standards.

d. Both a and b.

Incorrect. See correct answer (c).

16. As used by the internal auditing profession, the IIA Standards refer to all of the following **except**:

a. Criteria by which the operations of an internal audit department are evaluated and measured.

Incorrect. This is the definition of the IIA Standards.

b. Criteria that dictate the minimum level of ethical actions to be taken by internal auditors.

Correct. The IIA's Code of Ethics defines the minimum ethical standards for the internal auditor.

c. Statements intended to represent the practice of internal auditing as it should be.

Incorrect. The Standards define the practice of internal auditing "as it should be."

d. Criteria that are applicable to all types of internal audit departments.

Incorrect. The IIA Standards are equally applicable across all industries and all types of internal audit organizations globally.

17. Which of the following situations would be a violation of the IIA Code of Ethics?

a. An auditor was subpoenaed in a court case in which a merger partner claimed to have been defrauded by the auditor's company. The auditor divulged confidential audit information to the court.

Incorrect. Article II prohibits members and Certified Internal Auditors from being party to illegal activities. Failure to comply with a subpoena would be illegal.

b. An auditor for a manufacturer of office products recently completed an audit of the corporate marketing function. Based on this experience, the auditor spent several hours one Saturday working as a paid consultant to a hospital in the local area, which intended to conduct an audit of its marketing function.

Incorrect. A part-time job would not be a problem since it was not with a competitor or supplier.

c. An auditor gave a speech at a local IIA chapter meeting outlining the contents of a program the auditor had developed for auditing electronic data interchange connections. Several auditors from major competitors were in the audience.

Incorrect. Giving a speech is not a violation of the Code of Ethics. In fact, the IIA's motto is "progress through sharing."

d. During an audit, an auditor learned that the company was about to introduce a new product that would revolutionize the industry. Because of the probable success of the new product, the product manager suggested that the auditor buy additional stock in the company, which the auditor did.

Correct. Confidentiality (Rules of Conduct) of the IIA's Code of Ethics states that members and Certified Internal Auditors shall not use confidential information for any personal gain.

18. In applying the standards of conduct set forth in the Code of Ethics, internal auditors are expected to:

a. Exercise their individual judgment.

Correct. The IIA's Code of Ethics contains basic principles, such as integrity, which require individual judgment to apply.

b. Compare them to standards in other professions.

Incorrect. While the comparison might be interesting, it would not help determine how to apply the Code.

c. Be guided by the desires of the auditee.

Incorrect. Application might not be in the best interest of the auditee.

d. Use discretion in deciding whether to use them or not.

Incorrect. Judgment may be applied to the use of the Code in all audit matters. But, when comes to auditors' personal involvement in independence and objectivity issues, they have no choice except to apply the Code.

19. Reinforcing the Code of Conduct and ethical behavior standards for all internal auditors can protect which of the following?

a. Business risk

Incorrect. See correct answer (d).

b. Audit failures

Incorrect. See correct answer (d).

c. Audit false assurance

Incorrect. See correct answer (d).

d. Audit reputation risk

Correct. A leading practice to protect the reputation of internal audit's "brand" name is to reinforce the Code of Conduct and ethical behavior standards for all internal auditors.

Domain 2: Independence and Objectivity

1. Which of the following is **not** compromised when an internal auditor has compromised her independence of mind?

a. Integrity

Incorrect. When independence is compromised, the auditor cannot act with integrity.

b. Objectivity

Incorrect. When independence is compromised, the auditor cannot exercise objectivity.

c. Continuing education

Correct. An internal auditor receives continuing education whether she has independence of mind or not because they are two separate and unconnected activities and events.

d. Professional skepticism

Incorrect. When independence is compromised, the auditor cannot demonstrate professional skepticism.

2. When internal audit work is performed based on facts, it is referring to which of the following ethical principles?

a. Integrity

Correct. Integrity refers to auditors performing their work with an attitude that is objective, fact-based, nonpartisan, and nonideological with regard to audit clients and users of the audit reports.

b. Objectivity

Incorrect. Objectivity is based on performing credible audit work.

c. Resource utilization

Incorrect. Resource utilization deals with handling sensitive and confidential information.

d. Professional behavior

Incorrect. Professional behavior deals with putting forth an honest effort in performing audit duties.

3. Organizational politics is a part of which of the following threats to independence of internal audit organization and to an individual internal auditor?

a. Bias threat

Incorrect. See correct answer (c).

b. Familiarity threat

Incorrect. See correct answer (c).

c. Undue influence threat

Correct. Organizational politics is a major challenge in maintaining independence due to its undue influence. Extreme and unnecessary playing of organizational politics can slowly lead to an organization's failure or decline.

d. Management participation threat

Incorrect. See correct answer (c).

4. A peer review can help in mitigating which of the following threats to an auditor's objectivity?

a. Target fixation trap

Incorrect. See correct answer (b).

b. Mirror-imaging trap

Correct. Mirror-imaging trap is an auditor's false assumption that his/her followers and others think exactly like him-/herself. With this trap, auditors are unwilling to examine or analyze other views, variations, or alternatives of the subject matter at hand.

c. Analogy trap

Incorrect. See correct answer (b).

d. Projection trap

Incorrect. See correct answer (b).

5. The silo trap, which is a threat to an auditor's objectivity, belongs to the:

a. Stereotyping trap.

Incorrect. See correct answer (c).

b. Culture trap.

Incorrect. See correct answer (c).

c. Stovepiping trap.

Correct. The stovepiping trap means acknowledging only one source of information or knowledge base as the official source and disregarding other sources of information or knowledge bases as unofficial sources. This trap is similar to a silo trap or legacy trap.

d. Conflicts-of-interest trap.

Incorrect. See correct answer (c).

6. Which of the following will **not** help in identifying the overall risks to the internal audit function?

a. Barrier analysis

Correct. Barrier analysis, as it relates to business activity of organizational change, identifies key determinants (barriers) of human behavioral change in employees to help focus on their behaviors that have not changed, despite repeated efforts by management to change those behaviors. The four key determinants of human behavior are self-efficacy, social norms, positive consequences, and negative consequences. Hence, barrier analysis will not help in identifying the overall risks to the internal audit function.

b. Root-cause analysis

Incorrect. Root-cause analysis identifies the real reasons and specific situations leading to overall risks to the internal audit function. Based on this analysis, changes can be made either in the internal audit process or in the control environment of the organization or both. Hence, the root-cause analysis will help in identifying the overall risks to the internal audit function.

c. Assurance maps

Incorrect. Assurance maps are organization-wide and coordinated exercises involving mapping assurance coverage provided by multiple parties against the key risks facing the organization so that duplicate efforts, missed risks, and potential gaps can be identified and monitored. Hence, assurance maps will help in identifying overall risks to the internal audit function.

d. Risk maps

Incorrect. Risk maps involve profiling risk events to their sources (i.e., threats and vulnerabilities), determining their impact levels (i.e., low, medium, or high), and evaluating the presence of or lack of effective controls to mitigate risks. Hence, risk maps will help in identifying overall risks to the internal audit function.

7. In which of the following situations does the auditor potentially lack objectivity?

   a. An auditor reviews the procedures for a new electronic data interchange connection to a major customer before it is implemented.

      Incorrect. The IIA Standards says that the internal auditor's objectivity is not adversely affected when the auditor reviews procedures before they are implemented.

   b. **A former purchasing assistant performs a review of internal controls over purchasing four months after being transferred to the internal auditing department.**

      Correct. The IIA Standards says that persons transferred to the internal auditing department should not be assigned to audit those activities they previously performed until a reasonable period of time has elapsed.

   c. An auditor recommends standards of control and performance measures for a contract with a service organization for the processing of payroll and employee benefits.

      Incorrect. The IIA Standards say that the internal auditor's objectivity is not adversely affected when the auditor recommends standards of control for systems before they are implemented.

   d. A payroll accounting employee assists an auditor in verifying the physical inventory of small motors.

      Incorrect. Use of staff from other areas to assist the internal auditor does not impair objectivity, especially when the staff is from outside of the area being audited.

8. Which of the following actions would be a violation of auditor independence?

   a. **Continuing on an audit assignment at a division for which the auditor will soon be responsible as the result of a promotion.**

      Correct. The IIA Standard 1130—Impairment to Independence or Objectivity specifies that an auditor who has been promoted to an operating department should not continue on an audit of the new department.

   b. Reducing the scope of an audit due to budget restrictions.

      Incorrect. The IIA Standard 1130—Impairment to Independence or Objectivity states that budget restrictions do not constitute a violation of an auditor's independence.

   c. Participating on a task force which recommends standards for control of a new distribution system.

      Incorrect. The IIA Standard 1130—Impairment to Independence or Objectivity states that an auditor may participate on a task force that recommends new systems. However, designing, installing, or operating such systems might impair objectivity.

   d. Reviewing a purchasing agent's contract drafts prior to their execution.

      Incorrect. The IIA Standard 1130—Impairment to Independence or Objectivity states that an auditor may review contracts prior to their execution.

9. According to the IIA Standard 1130—Impairment to Independence or Objectivity, which of the following is **not** a part of functional reporting to the board?

a. Audit charter

Incorrect. See correct answer (c).

b. Audit risk assessment

Incorrect. See correct answer (c).

c. Audit budgets

Correct. The chief audit executive, reporting functionally to the board and administratively to the organization's chief executive officer, facilitates organizational independence. Functional reporting to the board typically involves the board approving the internal audit activity's overall charter and approving the internal audit risk assessment and related audit plan. Administrative reporting is the reporting relationship within the organization's management structure that facilitates the day-to-day operations of the internal audit activity. Administrative reporting typically includes audit budgets among other things.

d. Audit plan

Incorrect. See correct answer (c).

Domain 3: Proficiency and Due Professional Care

1. The relationship between proficiency and competency is:

a. Direct

Correct. Proficiency is defined as the ability to apply knowledge to situations likely to be faced and to deal with them without extensive recourse to technical research and assistance. There is a built-in and direct relationship between a person's proficiency and competency. One needs to be fully proficient first to become a fully competent person.

b. Indirect

Incorrect. See correct answer (a).

c. Not tested

Incorrect. See correct answer (a).

d. Not observed

Incorrect. See correct answer (a).

2. A person's competency can be derived from which of the following?

a. Knowledge, skills, and abilities

Incorrect. See correct answer (c).

b. More theory and less practice

Incorrect. See correct answer (c).

c. Education and experience

Correct. Competency of a person is derived from a combination of that person's education and experience.

d. Less theory and more practice

Incorrect. See correct answer (c).

3. Regarding competency levels, staff auditors belong to which of the following?

a. Entry level

Correct. In the audit management hierarchy, staff auditors are at the low competency level; they are in their first jobs or new jobs with little or no work experience.

b. Journeyman level

Incorrect. See correct answer (a).

c. Functional level

Incorrect. See correct answer (a).

d. Expert level

Incorrect. See correct answer (a).

4. Regarding competency levels, audit consultants belong to which of the following?

a. Entry level

Incorrect. See correct answer (d).

b. Journeyman level

Incorrect. See correct answer (d).

c. Functional level

Incorrect. See correct answer (d).

d. Expert level

Correct. By definition, audit consultants are at a very high competency level, supposed to be subject matter experts.

5. Regarding competency levels, audit supervisors belong to which of the following?

a. Entry level

Incorrect. See correct answer (c).

b. Journeyman level

Incorrect. See correct answer (c).

c. Functional level

Correct. Audit supervisors are knowledgeable in audit function and other business functions, such as operations, marketing, and finance.

d. Expert level

Incorrect. See correct answer (c).

6. Regarding competency levels, senior auditors belong to which of the following?

a. Entry level

Incorrect. See correct answer (b).

b. Journeyman level

Correct. Senior auditors have more work experience than staff auditors and are at a medium competency level, which is the journeyman level.

c. Functional level

Incorrect. See correct answer (b).

d. Expert level

Incorrect. See correct answer (b).

7. Due professional care for internal auditors is derived from which of the following?

a. Internal audit manual

Correct. Due professional care refers to understanding the systematic and disciplined approach to internal auditing, which is derived from an internal audit's policies and procedures manual (i.e., audit manual).

b. Internal auditor education

Incorrect. See correct answer (a).

c. Internal auditor experience

Incorrect. See correct answer (a).

d. Internal auditor professional certification

Incorrect. See correct answer (a).

8. Internal audit management should perform annually which of the following?

a. Education gap assessment

Incorrect. See correct answer (b). Answer (a) is a part of (b).

b. Competency gap assessment

Correct. Core competencies are defined as the unique and collective capabilities (training and know-how) and specific competencies (skills, experience, and education) that a company has and its competitors do not have. Therefore, internal audit management should perform a competency gap assessment every year.

c. Talent gap assessment

Incorrect. See correct answer (b). Answer (c) is a part of (b).

d. Skill gap assessment

Incorrect. See correct answer (b). Answer (d) is a part of (b).

9. Auditors' professional judgment does not mean:

a. Eliminating all possible limitations.

Correct. Professional judgment does not mean eliminating all possible limitations or weaknesses associated with a specific audit engagement but rather identifying, assessing, mitigating, and concluding on them.

b. Identifying all possible limitations.

Incorrect. See correct answer (a).

c. Mitigating all possible limitations.

Incorrect. See correct answer (a).

d. Assessing all possible limitations.

Incorrect. See correct answer (a).

10. Due professional care for internal auditors does not mean:

a. Developing a systematic approach to audits.

Incorrect. A systematic approach improves due professional care. See correct answer (b).

b. Attending audit-related professional seminars.

Correct. Attending audit-related professional seminars enhances proficiency. It does not improve due professional care.

c. Adhering to a disciplined approach to audits.

Incorrect. A disciplined approach improves due professional care. See correct answer (b).

d. Developing a structured approach to audits.

Incorrect. A structured approach improves due professional care. See correct answer (b).

11. Due professional care is not exercised when:

a. The internal audit work is planned.

Incorrect. Due professional care is fully exercised.

b. The internal audit work is supervised.

Incorrect. Due professional care is fully exercised.

c. The internal audit reports are objective and clear.

Incorrect. Due professional care is fully exercised.

d. Internal auditors fail to follow up on repeated audit findings.

Correct. Due professional care is not exercised when internal auditors fail to follow up on repeated audit findings.

12. Professional judgment for internal auditors includes which of the following?

a. Professional skills and professional work

Incorrect. See correct answer (c).

b. Strong evidence and documented procedures

Incorrect. See correct answer (c).

c. Reasonable care and professional skepticism

Correct. By definition, professional judgment includes exercising reasonable care and professional skepticism.

d. Sufficient evidence and appropriate evidence

Incorrect. See correct answer (c).

13. Regarding professional judgment, internal auditors cannot attain:

a. Absolute assurance.

Correct. Auditors must use professional judgment in planning and conducting the audit engagement and in reporting the audit results. In doing so, auditors cannot provide absolute assurance because so many things could go wrong.

b. Reasonable assurance.

Incorrect. Reasonable assurance can be provided, not absolute assurance. Reasonable assurance includes acting diligently in accordance with applicable professional standards and ethical principles.

c. Possible assurance.

Incorrect. Possible assurance, similar to reasonable assurance, can be provided, not absolute assurance.

d. Expected assurance.

Incorrect. Expected assurance, like reasonable assurance, can be provided, not absolute assurance.

14. Which of the following is the highest-ranked skill required at all levels of internal auditors?

a. Assertion skills

Incorrect. See correct answer (d).

b. Career skills

Incorrect. See correct answer (d).

c. Persuasion skills

Incorrect. See correct answer (d).

d. Communication skills

Correct. Communication, whether it is written or oral, is ranked as the number 1 requirement at all levels of internal auditors.

15. Which of the following can help clear up major sources of conflict between internal auditors and their audit clients?

    a. Assertion skills and listening skills

    Correct. Both assertion skills and listening skills help to clear up two major sources of conflict: errors and lack of information.

    b. Leadership skills and managing skills

    Incorrect. See correct answer (a).

    c. Problem-solving skills and decision-making skills

    Incorrect. See correct answer (a).

    d. Social skills and teamwork skills

    Incorrect. See correct answer (a).

16. Audit teams need more of which of the following?

    a. Collaboration skills

    Correct. Audit teams and other types of teams need collaboration skills because they work in cooperation and coordination with each team member. In collaboration, face-to-face interaction is better than human-to-machine interaction.

    b. Communication skills

    Incorrect. See correct answer (a).

    c. Critical thinking skills

    Incorrect. See correct answer (a).

    d. Creativity skills

    Incorrect. See correct answer (a).

17. Internal auditors ranging from staff auditor to audit director need which of the listed skills?

    a. Technical skills

    Incorrect. See correct answer (b).

    b. Business acumen skills

    Correct. Business acumen skills involve possessing knowledge of core business functions, such as operations, marketing, and finance (functional skills); being committed to mission and vision; and having the ability to develop a grand strategy for the entire business and substrategies for each business line; and more. Since internal auditors audit business functions and operations, they need more business acumen skills.

    c. Social skills

    Incorrect. See correct answer (b).

    d. Motivation skills

    Incorrect. See correct answer (b).

18. Ensuring internal audit teams have the right competencies with right level of work experience and designing effective internal audit procedures can reduce the risk of which of the following?

    a. Business risk

    Incorrect. Business risk is not applicable here.

    b. Audit failures

    Correct. Audit failures result when there is a (1) failure to evaluate both the design adequacy and the control effectiveness as part of internal audit procedures and (2) use of audit teams that do not have the appropriate level of competence based on experience or knowledge of high-risk areas.

    c. Audit false assurance

    Incorrect. Audit false assurance is not applicable here.

    d. Audit reputation risk

    Incorrect. Audit reputation risk is not applicable here.

19. Which of the following differs between assurance services and consulting services when exercising due professional care?

    a. Costs and benefits

    Incorrect. Costs and benefits are the same when exercising due professional care in assurance services and consulting services.

    b. Complexity of work

    Incorrect. Complexity of work is the same when exercising due professional care in assurance services and consulting services.

    c. Extent of work

    Incorrect. Extent of work is the same when exercising due professional care in assurance services and consulting services.

    d. Materiality

    Correct. Materiality is considered in assurance services and procedures but is not relevant to consulting services.

Domain 4: Quality Assurance and Improvement Program

1. When selecting people to work in the internal audit department, the vetting process does **not** apply to which of the following?

   a. External assessors

   Incorrect. External assessors are outsiders who are carefully screened, selected, and hired (vetted) for specific audit work to ensure that they are qualified to do the audit work.

   b. Audit contractors

   Incorrect. Audit contractors are outsiders who are carefully screened, selected, and hired (vetted) for specific audit work to ensure that they are qualified to do the audit work.

   c. Guest auditors

   Correct. Guest auditors are insiders, borrowed from nonaudit departments for temporary work in the audit department, and they go back to their departments after completing work in the audit department. Hence, guest auditors do not need a vetting process because they have already gone through an internal hiring and screening process.

   d. External service providers

   Incorrect. External service providers are outsiders who are carefully screened, selected, and hired (vetted) for specific audit work to ensure that they are qualified to do the audit work.

2. Which of the following is the key performance indicator for an internal audit activity?

   a. Number of audit clients satisfied

   Correct. As in any other business function or activity, customer satisfaction is the key performance indicator, and the internal audit activity is no different. Audit clients are the customers of internal audit activity. The more audit clients who are satisfied, the better it is for the internal audit activity.

   b. Number of audit recommendations made

   Incorrect. Audit recommendations may or may not be useful to audit clients. See correct answer (a).

   c. Number of audit recommendations accepted

   Incorrect. Audit recommendations may or may not be accepted by audit clients. See correct answer (a).

   d. Number of audit recommendations implemented

   Incorrect. Audit recommendations may or may not be implemented by audit clients. See correct answer (a).

3. Which of the following provides assurance as the first line of defense over risks and exposures facing an organization?

   a. Internal auditors

   Incorrect. Internal auditors act as risk evaluators and provide the third line of defense. See correct answer (d).

   b. Senior managers

   Incorrect. Senior managers act as executives and provide the second line of defense. See correct answer (d).

   c. Risk managers

   Incorrect. Risk managers act as a staff function and provide the second line of defense. See correct answer (d).

   d. Operations managers

   Correct. Managers and employees working in operations departments or functions are responsible for providing assurance as the first line of defense over risks and exposures. They work in a line function or frontline operation.

4. The scope of work in developing and maintaining a quality assurance and improvement program (QAIP) includes which of the following processes?

   I. Supervision
   II. Internal assessment
   III. Ongoing monitoring
   IV. External assessment

   a. I only

   Incorrect. This is not the most complete answer. See correct answer (d).

   b. I and II

   Incorrect. This is not the most complete answer. See correct answer (d).

   c. I, II, and III

   Incorrect. This is not the most complete answer. See correct answer (d).

   d. I, II, III, and IV

   Correct. The chief audit executive is accountable for implementing audit processes and the QAIP program is designed to provide reasonable assurance to the various stakeholders that the internal audit activity is properly implementing such processes. These processes include appropriate supervision, periodic internal assessments and ongoing monitoring of quality assurance, and periodic external assessments.

5. Which of the following is **not** included in the ongoing and periodic assessment dealing with measurements and analyses of performance metrics with respect to internal audit's quality assurance and improvement program (QAIP)?

    a. **Money saved from the audit work**

    Correct. A QAIP is an ongoing and periodic assessment of the entire spectrum of audit and consulting work performed by the internal audit activity. This periodic assessment includes ongoing measurements and analyses of performance metrics (e.g., internal audit plan accomplishment, cycle time, recommendations accepted, and customer satisfaction). Although money saved from audit work is an objective measure, it is not a useful and practical measure due to difficulties in quantifying savings and problems in agreement with auditees and the organization's management.

    b. Number of recommendations accepted

    Incorrect. See correct answer (a).

    c. Customer satisfaction

    Incorrect. See correct answer (a).

    d. Audit cycle time

    Incorrect. See correct answer (a).

6. If the results of the assessment of the internal audit's quality assurance and improvement program (QAIP) indicate areas for improvement, which of the following will implement such improvements?

    a. Audit committee of the board

    Incorrect. See correct answer (b).

    b. **Chief audit executive**

    Correct. A QAIP is an ongoing and periodic assessment of the entire spectrum of audit and consulting work performed by the internal audit activity. If results of this assessments indicate areas for improvement of the internal audit activity, the chief audit executive will implement the improvements through the QAIP.

    c. Chief executive officer

    Incorrect. See correct answer (b).

    d. External auditor

    Incorrect. See correct answer (b).

7. All of the following stakeholders receive the results of internal and external quality program assessments of internal audit's activity from the chief audit executive (CAE) **except**:

    a. **Functional managers.**

    Correct. Functional managers do not need to know these results because there are too many functional managers to distribute material to and because the scope of the quality program affects the entire organization, not just managers' individual business function. To provide accountability and transparency, the CAE communicates the results of external and, as appropriate, internal quality program assessments to the various stakeholders of the activity (such as senior management, the board, and external auditors).

    b. Senior managers.

    Incorrect. At least annually, the CAE reports to senior management on the quality program efforts and results. See correct answer (a).

    c. Board of directors.

    Incorrect. At least annually, the CAE reports to the board of directors on the quality program efforts and results. See correct answer (a).

    d. External auditor.

    Incorrect. See correct answer (a).

8. Which of the following is unique to the external assessment of an internal audit's activity when compared to internal assessment?

    a. Findings

    Incorrect. Findings are common with internal assessments.

    b. Conclusions

    Incorrect. Conclusions are common with internal assessments.

    c. Recommendations

    Incorrect. Recommendations are common with internal assessments.

    d. **Overall opinion**

    Correct. External assessments of an internal audit activity contain an expressed opinion as to the entire spectrum of assurance and consulting work performed (or that should have been performed based on the internal audit charter) by the internal audit activity, including its conformance with the definition of internal auditing, the Code of Ethics, and Standards. As appropriate, these assessments include recommendations for improvement.

9. Which of the following facilitates and reduces the cost of the external assessment of an internal audit's activity?

a. A periodic internal assessment performed within a short time before an external assessment

Correct. A periodic internal assessment performed within a short time before an external assessment can serve to facilitate and reduce the cost of the external assessment.

b. A periodic internal assessment performed in parallel with an external assessment

Incorrect. See correct answer (a).

c. A periodic internal assessment performed a long time before an external assessment

Incorrect. See correct answer (a).

d. A periodic internal assessment performed a short time after an external assessment

Incorrect. See correct answer (a).

10. Which of the following is unique to external assessment of an internal audit's activity?

a. Best practices

Incorrect. Best practices are common to both internal and external assessments.

b. Cost recoveries

Incorrect. Cost recoveries are used in internal assessments.

c. Benchmarking

Incorrect. Benchmarking is common to both internal and external assessments.

d. Expected deliverables

Correct. The chief audit executive is to ensure the scope clearly states the expected deliverables of the external assessment in each case.

11. Which of the following is common between internal assessment and external assessment of an internal audit's activity?

a. Audit standards

Correct. By definition, the scope of external assessment is broader than that of internal assessment. However, audit standards are common to both of them.

b. Audit charter

Incorrect. Review of the audit charter is part of the external assessment, not part of the internal assessment.

c. Code of ethics

Incorrect. Review of the code of ethics is part of the external assessment, not part of the internal assessment.

d. Definition of internal auditing

Incorrect. The definition of internal auditing is part of the external assessment, not part of the internal assessment.

12. The scope of external assessment of an internal audit's activity should **not** be limited to which of the following?

a. Assurance services

Incorrect. See correct answer (d).

b. Consulting services

Incorrect. See correct answer (d).

c. Leading practices

Incorrect. See correct answer (d).

d. Quality assurance and improvement program

Correct. External assessments cover the entire spectrum of audit and consulting work performed by the internal audit activity and should not be limited to assessing its quality assurance and improvement program. To achieve optimum benefits from an external assessment, the scope of work should include benchmarking, identification, and reporting of leading practices that could assist the internal audit activity in becoming more efficient and/or effective.

Domain 5: Governance, Risk Management, and Control

1. Internal controls are:
   a. Open systems.

   Incorrect. Open systems do not have a feedback mechanism. See correct answer (b).

   b. Closed systems.

   Correct. Closed systems are much stronger than the open systems due to the former's feedback mechanism. In a feedback mechanism, actual outputs are fed back to the input end for comparison with the desired output. Hence, internal controls are closed systems.

   c. Standalone systems.

   Incorrect. Standalone systems do not have a feedback mechanism. See correct answer (b).

   d. Ad hoc systems.

   Incorrect. Ad hoc systems do not have a feedback mechanism. See correct answer (b).

2. Regarding compliance management, compliance costs are **not**:
   a. Data collection costs.

   Incorrect. Data collection costs are compliance costs.

   b. Data analysis costs.

   Incorrect. Data analysis costs are compliance costs.

   c. Data reporting costs.

   Incorrect. Data reporting costs are compliance costs.

   d. Data evidence costs.

   Correct. Data evidence costs are noncompliance costs, meaning organizations show the data to regulatory authorities as a proof of evidence when regulators allege the organization has not complied with laws, rules, and regulations.

3. Regarding corporate social responsibility, which of the following should be the ultimate goal of corporations?
   a. Social goal

   Incorrect. See correct choice (c).

   b. Environmental goal

   Incorrect. See correct choice (c).

   c. Sustainability goal

   Correct. A sustainability goal refers to a corporation's strategies that allow it to thrive and sustain for a long time in business after considering economic, environmental, social, and governance requirements. Sustainability responsibility goes much beyond the normal corporate social responsibility consisting of legal, ethical, economic, and philanthropic requirements.

   d. Philanthropic goal

   Incorrect. See correct answer (c).

4. Regarding risk management, derisking does not mean:
   a. Risk elimination.

   Correct. Derisking means risk lessening, not risk elimination, because risks cannot be eliminated completely. There will always be some residual risks left over in life and business.

   b. Risk mitigation.

   Incorrect. Risk mitigation facilitates derisking.

   c. Risk management.

   Incorrect. Risk management facilitates derisking.

   d. Risk–return balancing.

   Incorrect. Risk–return balancing facilitates derisking.

5. Control self-assessments are done better when they are:

a. Auditor controlled.

Incorrect. Internal auditors do not control self-assessment exercises. Nonauditors control these exercises. See correct answer (b).

b. Auditor facilitated.

Correct. Internal auditors simply act as facilitators in control self-assessment exercises; they wear a different hat from the regular auditors. This is done to keep the auditor independence and objectivity in place.

c. Auditor planned.

Incorrect. Internal auditors do not plan the self-assessment exercises. Nonauditors plan these exercises. See correct answer (b).

d. Auditor designed.

Incorrect. Internal auditors do not design the self-assessment exercises. Nonauditors design these exercises. See correct answer (b).

6. Which of the following establishes a corporation's governance mechanism?

a. Stockholders

Incorrect. Stockholders' rights and obligations are described in bylaws.

b. Corporate bylaws

Correct. A corporation's governance mechanism is established by a firm's bylaws, which are a set of internal rules or policies. Bylaws describe the powers of the corporation and the duties and responsibilities of the board of directors and officers, and how to treat stockholders.

c. Board of directors

Incorrect. The board of director's duties and responsibilities are described in bylaws.

d. Corporate officers

Incorrect. Corporate officers' duties and responsibilities are described in bylaws.

7. A corporation must be managed on which of the following principles?

a. Corporate governance

Correct. For a corporation to be legitimate, its governance principles must correspond to the will of the general public. Therefore, a corporation must be managed on the principles of corporate governance, which define the roles of shareholders, directors, and officers/mangers in corporate decision making and accountability. Corporate control, law, and ethics become a part of corporate governance.

b. Corporate control

Incorrect. Corporate control deals with acquiring and managing resources to operate the corporation in an efficient and effective manner.

c. Corporate law

Incorrect. Corporate laws deal with complying with laws and regulations and knowing what activities are legal and illegal.

d. Corporate ethics

Incorrect. Corporate ethics deals with understanding what is right or good for employees and knowing what activities are ethical and unethical.

8. The major issue embedded in the structure of modern corporations that has contributed to the corporate governance problem has been:

a. Separation of purchase from lease.

Incorrect. This is not a major issue compared to the separation of ownership from control.

b. Separation of suppliers from producers.

Incorrect. This is not a major issue compared to the separation of ownership from control.

c. Separation of ownership from control.

Correct. This is the major issue embedded in the structure of modern corporations that has contributed to the corporate governance problem. Stockholders are owners, and the board of directors, officers, and managers control the corporation on a day-to-day basis. This means no one shareholder or group of shareholders owns enough shares to exercise control; so, shareholders perceive themselves to be investors rather than owners.

d. Separation of employees from independent contractors.

Incorrect. This is not a major issue compared to the separation of ownership from control.

9. Which of the following is the major reason for agency problems to exist?

a. Owner interest

Incorrect. This has no influence on agency problems.

b. Self-interest

Correct. Agency problems develop when the interests of shareholders are not aligned with the interests of managers, and managers (who are simply hired agents with the responsibility of representing the owner's [principal's] best interest) begin to pursue self-interest instead.

c. Community interest

Incorrect. This has no influence on agency problems.

d. Corporate interest

Incorrect. This has no influence on agency problems.

10. The practice of obtaining critical information from a company in good faith and then using that information for one's own personal financial gain is called:

a. Financial trading.

Incorrect. This choice can result from insider trading as outcomes or tools.

b. Insider trading.

Correct. Insider trading is the practice of obtaining critical information from inside a company and then using that information for one's own personal financial gain. Insider trading perpetrated by corporate executives and managers should be prohibited and reported to the board through whistleblowing activity.

c. Shareholder trading.

Incorrect. This choice can result from insider trading as outcomes or tools.

d. Investor trading.

Incorrect. This choice can result from insider trading as outcomes or tools.

11. Which of the following is **not** an example of ethical dilemma facing a business manager involving a conflict between the:

a. Part versus whole.

Incorrect. See correct answer (d).

b. Individual versus organization.

Incorrect. See correct answer (d).

c. Organization versus society.

Incorrect. See correct answer (d).

d. Individual versus family.

Correct. Ethics deals with deciding and acting on what is right or wrong in a particular situation. Basically, ethics is concerned with knowing what is good and bad and separating them in one's mind. Most ethical dilemmas involve a conflict between the needs of the part and those of the whole—the individual versus the organization or the organization versus society as a whole. The ethical dilemma between an individual and his or her family is outside of a business situation.

12. Abusive acts can be:

a. Legal but unethical.

Correct. Abuse occurs when the conduct of an activity or function falls short of expectations for prudent behavior. Abuse is distinguished from noncompliance in that abusive conditions may not directly violate laws or regulations. Abusive activities may be within the letter of the laws and regulations but violate their spirit or the more general standards of impartial behavior and, more specifically, ethical behavior. This means that abusive acts can be legal but unethical.

b. Ethical but illegal.

Incorrect. See correct answer (a).

c. Legal and ethical.

Incorrect. See correct answer (a).

d. Illegal and unethical.

Incorrect. See correct answer (a).

13. Which of the following statement is not true about ethics and law?

   a. Ethical behavior resides above legal behavior.

     Incorrect. See correct answer (c).

   b. Law embodies notions of ethics.

     Incorrect. See correct answer (c).

   c. Law addresses all ethical questions.

     Correct. The generally accepted view of ethics is that ethical behavior resides above legal behavior. Note that in many respects, the law and ethics overlap because the law embodies notions of ethics. That is, the law may be seen as a reflection of what society thinks are minimal standards of conduct and behavior. It is important to note that the law does not address all realms in which ethical questions might be raised. Thus, there are clear roles for both law and ethics to play in the society. To rephrase, not all unethical actions are illegal and not all illegal actions are unethical, depending on local cultures and legal jurisdictions.

   d. Law and ethics have clear roles to play in the society.

     Incorrect. See correct answer (c).

14. Which type of social responsibility embraces those activities and practices that are expected or prohibited by societal members even though they are not codified into law?

   a. Ethical responsibilities

     Correct. Because laws are important but not adequate, ethical responsibilities embrace those activities and practices that are expected or prohibited by societal members even though they are not codified into law. Ethical responsibilities embody the full scope of norms, standards, and expectations that reflect a belief of what consumers, employees, shareholders, and the community regard as fair, just, and in keeping with the respect for or protection of stakeholders' moral rights. Philanthropic responsibilities include donating money and property to social programs

   b. Legal responsibilities

     Incorrect. See correct answer (a).

   c. Philanthropic responsibilities

     Incorrect. See correct answer (a).

   d. Economic responsibilities

     Incorrect. See correct answer (a).

15. Which of the following refers to the corporate behavior in response to market forces or legal constraints?

   a. Social obligation.

     Correct. Social obligation is corporate behavior in response to market forces or legal constraints. Social obligation, social responsibility, and social responsiveness are examples of corporate behavior in responding to social or societal needs.

   b. Social responsibility

     Incorrect. See correct answer (a).

   c. Social responsiveness

     Incorrect. See correct answer (a).

   d. Social attitude

     Incorrect. See correct answer (a).

16. All of the following provide effective relationships in the organization's governance framework except:

   a. Organizational processes.

     Correct. Governance does not exist as a set of distinct and separate organizational processes and structures. Rather, there are effective relationships among governance, risk management, and internal controls.

   b. Governance.

     Incorrect. Governance provides effective relationships in the organization's governance framework.

   c. Risk management.

     Incorrect. Risk management provides effective relationships in the organization's governance framework.

   d. Internal controls.

     Incorrect. Internal controls provide effective relationships in the organization's governance framework.

17. Which of the following internal audit assessments belong to specific governance processes?

a. Whistleblower processes.

Correct. Internal audit assessments regarding governance processes are likely to be based on information obtained from numerous audit assignments over time. Internal auditors should consider (1) the results of audits of specific governance processes (e.g., the whistleblower process, the strategy management process) and (2) governance issues arising from audits that are not specifically focused on governance (e.g., audits of the risk management process, internal control over financial reporting, and fraud risks).

b. Risk management audit process.

Incorrect. See correct answer (a).

c. Internal control over financial reporting.

Incorrect. See correct answer (a).

d. Fraud risks.

Incorrect. See correct answer (a).

18. Risk registers describe direct links between which of the following?

a. Risk acceptance and risk avoidance.

Incorrect. Risk acceptance and risk avoidance are not related to risk registers.

b. Risk categories and risk aspects.

Correct. Risk registers provide direct links among risk categories, risk aspects, the audit universe, and internal controls.

c. Risk assignment and risk sharing.

Incorrect. Risk assignment and risk sharing are not related to risk registers.

d. Risk limitation and risk spreading.

Incorrect. Risk limitation and risk spreading are not related to risk registers.

19. Risk can be categorized as:

a. Objective-subjective and perils-hazards.

Incorrect. This is a partial answer.

b. Objective-subjective, physical-moral-morale, and pure-speculative.

Incorrect. This is a partial answer.

c. Static-dynamic, subjective-objective, and pure-speculative.

Correct. Risks can be classified into three types: static versus dynamic, subjective versus objective, and pure versus speculative.

d. Objective-subjective, physical-moral-morale, pure-speculative, and perils-hazards.

Incorrect. This is a partial answer. Pure risk is a condition in which there is the possibility of loss or no loss only. Peril is the cause of possible loss. Hazard is a condition that creates or increases the probability of loss.

20. The three most commonly used methods of loss control are:

a. Risk retention, risk avoidance, and risk transfer.

Incorrect. Risk retention, risk avoidance, and risk transfer are risk management techniques focusing on risk financing methods. Risk avoidance is different from loss control, because the firm or individual is still engaging in operations that gave rise to particular risks.

b. Self-insurance, diversification, and risk transfer.

Incorrect. Self-insurance, diversification, and risk transfer are not loss control methods. Instead, they are risk financing methods.

c. Frequency reduction, severity reduction, and cost reduction.

Correct. Common methods of loss control include reducing the probability of losses or decreasing the cost of losses that do occur. Probability of losses is related to frequency and severity. Cost reduction is also a method of controlling losses.

d. Insurance transfers, frequency reduction, and severity reduction.

Incorrect. This answer mixes both correct and incorrect answers.

21. Self-insurance differs from the establishment of a reserve fund in that:

a. Establishing a reserve fund is a form of risk retention.

Incorrect. A reserve fund may not be enough for large losses.

b. Self-insurance involves prefunding of expected losses through a fund specifically designed for that purpose.

Incorrect. This is a necessary element of self-insurance.

c. Self-insurance requires the existence of a group of exposure units large enough to allow accurate loss prediction.

Correct. Self-insurance by a firm is possible and feasible when the firm has accurate records or has access to satisfactory statistics to enable it to make good estimate of expected losses. The general financial condition of the firm should be satisfactory, and the firm's management must be willing and able to deal with large and unusual losses.

d. Self-insurance requires the formation of a subsidiary company.

Incorrect. Self-insurance does not require the creation of a subsidiary company.

22. The purchase of insurance is a common form of:

a. Risk retention.

Incorrect. Risk retention is a technique for managing risk and does not involve insurance.

b. Risk transfer.

Correct. The most widely used form of risk transfer is insurance.

c. Risk avoidance.

Incorrect. Risk avoidance is best if it can be done and does not involve insurance.

d. Loss control.

Incorrect. Loss control involves risk reduction or risk mitigation and does not involve insurance.

23. Which of the following best represents the fit-gap analysis as a risk management tool?

a. This analysis determines the difference between the actual outcome and the expected outcome.

Correct. This choice compares the actual outcomes with the expected outcomes and determines whether these outcomes fit with each other or any gap left in between them.

b. This analysis is used for managing uncertainty as it may be subdivided into sequential decision analysis and irreversible investment theory.

Incorrect. This choice defines option analysis.

c. This analysis deals with quantitative data in terms of dollars and ratios.

Incorrect. This choice defines economic analysis (e.g., return on investment, net present value, internal rate of return, return on sales, and return on equity).

d. This analysis involves assigning weights to responses to questions addressing areas that may introduce elements of risk.

Incorrect. This choice defines subjective scoring analysis.

24. Which of the following financial and accounting practices is not a risk for public corporations?

a. Financial engineering

Correct. The scope of financial engineering involves creating new financial instruments (e.g., derivative securities) or combining existing derivatives to accomplish specific hedging goals (i.e., to reduce financial risk).

b. Earnings management

Incorrect. This is a risk to a public corporation.

c. Creative accounting

Incorrect. This is a risk to a public corporation.

d. Off-the-books accounts

Incorrect. This is a risk to a public corporation.

25. Which of the following has been determined to be a reasonable level of risk?

a. Minimum risk

Incorrect. Minimum risk is the reduction in the total risk that results from the impact of in-place safeguards or controls.

b. Acceptable risk

Correct. Acceptable risk is the level of residual risk that has been determined to be a reasonable level of potential loss or disruption for a specific computer system.

c. Residual risk

Incorrect. Residual risk results from the occurrence of an adverse event after adjusting for the impact of all safeguards in place.

d. Total risk

Incorrect. Total risk is the potential for the occurrence of an adverse event if no mitigating action is taken (i.e., the potential for any applicable threat to exploit system vulnerability).

26. Which of the following enterprise risk management (ERM) frameworks addresses market risk?

a. Strategic risks

Incorrect. Strategic risks include political risk, regulatory risk, reputation risk, leadership risk, and market brand risk.

b. Operational risks

Incorrect. Operational risks include an organization's systems, technology, and people.

c. Financial risks

Correct. Financial risk includes risks from volatility in foreign currencies, interest rates, and commodities. It also includes credit risk, liquidity risk, and market risk.

d. Hazard risks

Incorrect. Hazard risks include natural disasters, impairment of physical assets, and terrorism.

27. The scope of enterprise risk management (ERM) should encompass which of the following?

I. Hazards

II. Opportunities

III. Strengths

IV. Weaknesses

a. I only

Incorrect. See correct answer (c).

b. II only

Incorrect. See correct answer (c).

c. I and II.

Correct. It is important to emphasize that the uncertainties could have a potential upside or downside so that the scope of ERM encompasses the more traditional view of potential hazards as well as opportunities. Hazard risks include both insurable and uninsurable risks.

d. III and IV

Incorrect. See correct answer (c).

28. Which of the following is best qualified to manage the enterprise-wide risk management program?

a. Chief risk officer

Incorrect. See correct answer (b).

b. Board of directors

Correct. Risk is pervasive throughout an organization as it can arise from any business function or process at any time without warning. Because of this widespread exposure, no single functional department management, other than the board of directors, can oversee the enterprise-wide risk management program. This approach also supports the idea that risks cannot be identified, measured, and monitored on a piecemeal basis. A holistic approach is needed.

c. Chief financial officer

Incorrect. See correct answer (b).

d. Chief governance officer

Incorrect. See correct answer (b).

29. An exception report for management is an example of which type of control?

a. Preventive control

Incorrect. See correct answer (c).

b. Detective control

Incorrect. See correct answer (c).

c. Corrective control

Correct. Detecting an exception in a business transaction or process is detective in nature, but reporting it is an example of a corrective control. Both preventive and directive controls do not detect or correct an error; they simply stop the error, if possible.

d. Directive control.

Incorrect. See correct answer (c).

30. Organizational procedures allow employees to anticipate problems. This type of control is known as:

a. Feedback control.

Incorrect. This is a retrospective control based on the outcome of a completed activity.

b. Strategic control.

Incorrect. This is a broader-based control that should go hand in hand with strategic planning.

c. Feedforward control.

Correct. Procedures provide guidance on how tasks should be accomplished.

d. Performance appraisal.

Incorrect. This is a retrospective control.

31. As part of a total quality control program, a firm not only inspects finished goods but also monitors product returns and customer complaints. Which type of control best describes these efforts?

a. Feedback control

Correct. Feedback control ensures that past mistakes are not repeated.

b. Feedforward control

Incorrect. The controls mentioned occur after processing and therefore cannot provide feedforward control.

c. Production control

Incorrect. Complaints are not part of production control.

d. Inventory control

Incorrect. The question is not limited to inventory.

32. To be successful, large companies must develop means to keep the organization focused in the proper direction. Organization control systems help keep companies focused. These control systems consist of which of the following components?

a. Budgeting, financial ratio analysis, and cash management

Incorrect. These are means of financial control.

b. Objectives, standards, and an evaluation-reward system

Correct. These items are the basic components of complex organizational control systems in large companies.

c. Role analysis, team building, and survey feedback

Incorrect. These are several types of organizational development interventions.

d. Coaching, protection, and challenging assignments

Incorrect. Mentoring fulfills several types of career enhancement functions, including these.

33. Closed control systems consist of six elements. Identify one of the six elements.

a. Transforming inputs to outputs and setting performance standards

Correct. This is one of the six elements of the closed control systems, known as a process element, which transforms inputs to outputs and sets performance standards. Other elements to operate include measurement element, comparison element, error element, control element, and correction element.

b. Adequately securing data files

Incorrect. This choice is not an element of a closed control system. See correct answer (a).

c. Approval of audit charter

Incorrect. This choice is not an element of a closed control system. See correct answer (a).

d. Establishment of independent audit function

Incorrect. This choice is not an element of a closed control system. See correct answer (a).

34. The three basic components of all organizational control systems are:

   a. Objectives, standards, and an evaluation-reward system.

   Correct. These are the three basic components of a control system.

   b. Plans, budgets, and organizational policies and procedures.

   Incorrect. These three terms are all used to describe subsystems of a control system.

   c. Statistical reports, audits, and financial controls.

   Incorrect. These three terms are used to describe either a subsystem of a control process or a tool used in a control system.

   d. Inputs, objectives, and an appraisal system.

   Incorrect. While "objectives" is a correct answer, the other two terms are incorrect. "Inputs" is a good distracter because it is part of the "input-process-output" relationship used to describe a system.

35. Which of the following management control systems measures performance in terms of operating profits minus the cost of capital invested in tangible assets?

   a. Open-book management system

   Incorrect. The open-book management system focuses on sharing company's financial information to all employees.

   b. Economic value-added system

   Correct. The economic value-added system is a proven system to measure corporate performance.

   c. Activity-based costing system

   Incorrect. Activity-based costing systems identify various activities needed to produce a product or service and determine the cost of those activities.

   d. Market value-added system

   Incorrect. The market value-added system determines the market value of a firm based on its market capitalization rate.

36. A comprehensive management control system that considers both financial and nonfinancial measures relating to a company's critical success factors is called a(n):

   a. Balanced scorecard system.

   Correct. The balanced scorecard system is a comprehensive management control system that balances the traditional accounting (financial) measures with the operational (nonfinancial) measures.

   b. Economic value-added system.

   Incorrect. See correct answer (a).

   c. Activity-based costing system.

   Incorrect. See correct answer (a).

   d. Market value-added system.

   Incorrect. See correct answer (a).

37. The term "risk appetite" means which of the following?

   a. Risk avoidance

   Incorrect. Risk avoidance is eliminating the risk cause and/or consequence.

   b. Risk limitation

   Incorrect. Risk limitation implements controls to minimize the adverse impact of a threat.

   c. Risk acceptance

   Correct. Risk acceptance is the level of risk that an organization is willing to accept, and it is referred to as risk appetite.

   d. Risk spreading

   Incorrect. Risk spreading is sharing the risk with other divisions or business units of the same organization.

38. Residual risk is also known as which of the following?

a. Audit risk

Incorrect. Audit risk results when an auditor fails to detect a material error or event, and an auditor may fail to detect significant error or weakness during an examination.

b. Pure risk

Incorrect. Pure risks are those in which there is a chance of loss or no loss only.

c. Current risk

Correct. Residual risk is current risk, which is the risk remaining after management takes action to reduce the impact and likelihood of an adverse event, including control activities in responding to a risk. Current risk is often defined as the risk managed within existing controls or control systems. Current risk cannot be ignored; instead, it should be managed well so it can become a managed risk.

d. Inherent risk

Incorrect. Inherent risk is a built-in risk; an example is the susceptibility of information or data to a material misstatement.

39. Residual risk is calculated as which of the following?

a. Known risks minus unknown risks

Incorrect. See correct answer (d).

b. Actual risks minus probable risks

Incorrect. See correct answer (d).

c. Probable risks minus possible risks

Incorrect. See correct answer (d).

d. Potential risks minus covered risks

Correct. Potential risks include all possible and probable risks. Countermeasures cover some but not all risks. Therefore, the residual risk is potential risks minus covered risks.

40. Which of the following is closely linked to risk acceptance?

a. Risk detection

Incorrect. See correct answer (c).

b. Risk prevention

Incorrect. See correct answer (c).

c. Risk tolerance

Correct. Risk tolerance is the level of risk that an entity or a manager is willing to assume or accept in order to achieve a potential desired result. Some managers accept more risk than others do because of their personal affinity to risk.

d. Risk correction

Incorrect. See correct answer (c).

41. Which of the following risk concepts can be assumed to have no mitigating controls?

a. Business risk

Incorrect. Business risk is total risk facing an organization.

b. Residual risk

Incorrect. Residual risk is current risk.

c. Inherent risk

Correct. Two fundamental risk concepts are inherent risk and residual risk (also known as current risk). Inherent risk is a built-in risk. To financial/external auditors, inherent risk can be summarized as the susceptibility of information or data to a material misstatement, assuming that there are no related mitigating controls.

d. Current risk

Incorrect. Inherent risk is the susceptibility of a management assertion to a material misstatement.

42 When dealing with employees, which of the following is not an example of possible management's negative actions if whistleblowing employees report misconduct of management?

a. Reduced duties

   Incorrect. See correct answer (b).

b. Coercion of political activity

   Correct. Coercion of political activity is one of the prohibited personnel practices. The other three answer choices are examples of management's negative actions if whistleblowing employees report misconduct of management.

c. Reassignment of work location

   Incorrect. See correct answer (b).

d. Reshuffling of work schedules

   Incorrect. See correct answer (b).

43. Which of the following was not a major shareholder initiative?

a. Rise of shareholder activist groups

   Incorrect. The rise of shareholder activist groups is a major initiative to express shareholders' concerns about how a corporation operates.

b. Shareholder-initiated golden parachutes

   Correct. Shareholders do not initiate golden parachutes; management does. A golden parachute is a contract in which a corporation agrees to make payments to key management and senior officers in the event of a change in the control of the corporation.

c. Shareholder resolutions and annual meetings

   Incorrect. The filing of shareholder resolutions and activism at annual meetings is a major initiative to document the shareholders' issues raised and solutions reached.

d. Shareholder lawsuits

   Incorrect. The filing of shareholder lawsuits is becoming a common way for shareholders to express disappointment and frustration with management of a corporation.

44. When dealing with stakeholders, which of the following ethical and legal principles is not applicable?

a. Due process

   Incorrect. The due process principle applies to stakeholders, who are owners, investors, and employees. Due process means following rules and principles so that an individual is treated fairly and uniformly at all times with basic rights protected (e.g., life, liberty, and property). It also means fair and equitable treatment to all concerned parties so that no person is deprived of life, liberty, or property without due process of the law, which is the right to notice and a hearing. Due process requires due care and due diligence in fulfilling the right to notice and for a fair hearing. Basically, due process largely applies to governmental agencies in their operations when dealing with citizens and non-citizens.

b. Due diligence

   Incorrect. The due diligence principle applies to stakeholders, who are owners, investors, and employees. Due diligence requires organizations to develop and implement an effective system of controls, policies, and procedures to prevent and detect violation of policies and laws.

c. Due care

   Incorrect. The due care principle applies to stakeholders, who are owners, investors, and employees. Due care means reasonable care that promotes the common good. It involves maintaining minimal and customary practices.

d. Duty of loyalty

   Correct. Duty of loyalty is expected of board of directors and officers of a corporation in that they have a duty not to act adversely to the interests of the corporation and not to subordinate their professional interests to those of the corporation and its shareholders. Therefore, duty of loyalty does not apply to stakeholders.

45. Which of the following is the ultimate goal of shareholder and investor communications?

a. Honesty

Correct. Honesty of management is the ultimate goal of shareholder and investor communications, although the communication should provide consistency, clarity, candor, and effectiveness. Corporations should consider candor, need for timely disclosure, and effective use of technology. However, the ultimate goal of shareholder and investor communications is honest, intelligible, meaningful, and timely and broadly disseminated information.

b. Consistency

Incorrect. See correct answer (a).

c. Clarity

Incorrect. See correct answer (a).

d. Effectiveness

Incorrect. See correct answer (a).

Domain 6: Fraud Risks

1. Internal auditors would be more likely to detect fraud if they developed/strengthened their ability to:

a. Recognize and question changes which occur in organizations.

Correct. The recognition and questioning of change is critical to the detection of fraud.

b. Interrogate fraud perpetrators to discover why the fraud was committed.

Incorrect. Interrogation of fraud perpetrators occurs after detection.

c. Develop internal controls to prevent the occurrence of fraud.

Incorrect. The controls mentioned are preventive, not detective.

d. Document computerized operating system programs.

Incorrect. Documentation of operating systems is not within the scope of internal auditing and would do little to enhance fraud detection skills.

2. According to the *IIA Standards*, which of the following best describes the two general categories or types of fraud that concern most internal auditors?

a. Improper payments (i.e., bribes and kickbacks) and tax fraud

Incorrect. These are examples of kinds of fraud within the two general categories or types given in the Standards.

b. Fraud designed to benefit the organization and fraud perpetrated to the detriment of the organization

Correct. These are the two overall categories or types of fraud given in the IIA Standards.

c. Acceptance of bribes or kickbacks and improper related-party transactions

Incorrect. These are examples of kinds of fraud within the two general categories or types given in the Standards.

d. Acceptance of kickbacks or embezzlement and misappropriation of assets

Incorrect. These are examples of kinds of fraud within the two general categories or types given in the Standards.

3. A company hired a highly qualified accounts payable manager who had been terminated from another company for alleged wrongdoing. Six months later, the manager diverted $12,000 by sending duplicate payments of invoices to a relative. A control that might have prevented this situation would be to:

a. Adequately check prior employment backgrounds for all new employees.

Correct. This practice might give some leads to previous shortcomings.

b. Not hire individuals who appear overqualified for a job.

Incorrect. This does not include checking prior employment.

c. Verify educational background for all new employees.

Incorrect. This does not include checking prior employment.

d. Check to see if close relatives work for payable vendors.

Incorrect. This is not an adequate control in this scenario.

4. Red flags are conditions that indicate a higher likelihood of fraud. Which of the following would **not** be considered a red flag?

   a. Management has delegated to subordinates the authority to make purchases under a certain dollar limit.

   Correct. This is an acceptable control procedure aimed at limiting risk while promoting efficiency. It is not, by itself, considered a red flag.

   b. An individual has held the same cash-handling job for an extended period without any rotation of duties.

   Incorrect. Lack of rotation of duties or cross-training for sensitive jobs is one factor on the red-flag list.

   c. An individual handling marketable securities is responsible for making the purchases, recording the purchases, and reporting any discrepancies and gains/losses to senior management.

   Incorrect. This would be an example of an inappropriate segregation of duties, which is an identified red flag.

   d. The assignment of responsibility and accountability in the accounts receivable department is not clear.

   Incorrect. This is an identified red flag.

5. Internal auditors and management have become increasingly concerned about computer fraud. Which of the following control procedures would be **least** important in preventing computer fraud?

   a. Program change control that requires a distinction between production programs and test programs

   Incorrect. This is one of the elements of good program change control.

   b. Testing of new applications by users during the systems development process

   Incorrect. Testing of new applications by users is one of the most important controls to help prevent computer fraud.

   c. Segregation of duties between the applications programmer and the program librarian function

   Incorrect. An adequate control structure over program changes is one of the most important control procedures in a computerized environment.

   d. Segregation of duties between the programmer and systems analyst

   Correct. This would be the least important control procedure. The analyst is responsible for communicating the nature of the design to the programmer. There is no control reason not to combine these functions.

6. What is a data diddling technique?

   a. Changing data before input to a computer system

   Incorrect. Although this is one data diddling technique, it is not the most complete answer.

   b. Changing data during input to a computer system

   Incorrect. Although this is one data diddling technique, it is not the most complete answer.

   c. Changing data during output from a computer system

   Incorrect. Although this is one data diddling technique, it is not the most complete answer.

   d. All of the above

   Correct. The data diddling technique involves changing data before or during input to computers or during output from a computer system. Data diddling can be prevented by limiting access to data and programs and limiting the methods used to perform modification to such data and programs. Integrity checking also helps in prevention. Rapid detection is needed—the sooner the better—because correcting data diddling is expensive.

7. What is a salami technique?

   a. Taking small amounts of assets

   Incorrect. Although this is one salami technique, it is not the most complete answer.

   b. Using the rounding-down concept

   Incorrect. Although this is one salami technique, it is not the most complete answer.

   c. Stealing small amounts of money from bank accounts

   Incorrect. Although this is one salami technique, it is not the most complete answer.

   d. All of the above

   Correct. A salami technique is a theft of small amounts of assets or money from a number of sources (e.g., bank accounts, inventory accounts, and accounts payable and receivable). It is also using the rounding-down concept, where a fraction of money is taken from bank accounts.

8. With respect to computer security and fraud, a legal liability exists to an organization under which of the following conditions?

    a. When estimated security costs are greater than estimated losses

        Incorrect. This choice poses no legal liability because costs are greater than losses.

    b. When estimated security costs are equal to estimated losses

        Incorrect. This choice requires judgment and qualitative considerations because costs are equal to losses.

    c. When estimated security costs are less than estimated losses.

        Correct. Courts do not expect organizations to spend more money than losses resulting from a security flaw, threat, risk, or vulnerability. Implementing countermeasures and safeguards to protect information system assets costs money. Losses can result from risks (i.e., exploitation of vulnerabilities). When estimated costs are less than estimated losses, then a legal liability exists. Courts can argue that the organization's management should have installed safeguards but did not and that management did not exercise due care and due diligence.

    d. When actual security costs are equal to actual losses

        Incorrect. This choice is not applicable because actual costs and losses are not known at the time safeguards are implemented.

9. Which of the following security techniques allows time for response by investigative authorities?

    a. Deter.

        Incorrect. This choice would not allow such a trap.

    b. Detect.

        Incorrect. This choice would not allow such a trap.

    c. Delay.

        Correct. If a system perpetrator can be delayed longer while attacking a computer system, investigative authorities can trace his or her origins and location.

    d. Deny.

        Incorrect. This choice would not allow such a trap.

10. Most of the evidence submitted in a computer crime case is:

    a. Legal evidence.

        Incorrect. "Legal evidence" is a broad term and is not useful here.

    b. Documentary evidence.

        Correct. Documentary evidence is created information, such as letters, contracts, accounting records, invoices, and management information reports on performance and production.

    c. Secondary evidence.

        Incorrect. Secondary evidence is any evidence offered to prove the writing other than the writing itself and is a part of the best evidence rule. The best evidence is original.

    d. Admissible evidence.

        Incorrect. Admissible evidence is evidence that is revealed to the jury or other trier of fact with express or implied permission to use it in deciding disputed issues of fact.

11. When computers and peripheral equipment are seized in relation to a computer crime, it is an example of:

    a. Duplicate evidence.

        Incorrect. Duplicate evidence is a document produced by some mechanical process that makes it more reliable evidence of the contents of the original than other forms of secondary evidence (e.g., a photocopy of the original). Modern statutes make duplicates easily substitutable for originals. Duplicate evidence is a part of the best evidence rule.

    b. Physical evidence.

        Correct. Physical evidence is obtained via direct inspection or observation of people, property, or events.

    c. Best evidence.

        Incorrect. Best evidence is evidence that is the most natural and reliable. The best evidence is primary.

    d. Collateral evidence.

        Incorrect. Collateral evidence is evidence relevant only to some evidential fact. By itself, it is not relevant to a consequential fact.

12. From a computer security viewpoint, courts expect what amount of care from organizations?

a. Super care

Incorrect. See correct answer (b).

b. Due care

Correct. Courts will find computer owners responsible for their insecure systems. Courts will not find liability every time a computer is hijacked. Rather, courts will expect organizations to become reasonably prudent computer owners taking due care (reasonable care) to ensure adequate security. The term "due care" means having the right policies and procedures, access controls, firewalls, and other reasonable security measures in place. Computer owners need not take super care, extraordinary care, or great care, just due care.

c. Extraordinary care

Incorrect. See correct answer (b).

d. Great care

Incorrect. See correct answer (b).

13. Which of the following is **not** a computer criminal activity in **most** jurisdictions?

a. Writing a computer virus program

Correct. The intentions of the developer of a computer virus program matter the most in deciding what is a criminal activity. Simply writing a virus program is not a criminal activity.

b. Using a computer virus program

Incorrect. Using a virus with intentions of destroying computer resources is a criminal activity.

c. Releasing a computer virus program

Incorrect. Releasing a virus with intentions of destroying computer resources is a criminal activity.

d. Spreading a computer virus program

Incorrect. Spreading a virus with intentions of destroying computer resources is a criminal activity.

14. Once evidence is seized in a computer crime case, a law enforcement officer should follow which of the following?

a. Chain of logs

Incorrect. This choice is indirectly related to the chain of custody.

b. Chain of events

Incorrect. This choice is indirectly related to the chain of custody.

c. Chain of custody

Correct. The chain of custody or the chain of evidence is a method of authenticating an object by the testimony of witnesses who can trace possession of the object from hand to hand and from the beginning to the end. It is required when evidence is collected and handled so that there is no dispute about it. It deals with who collected, stored, and controlled the evidence and does not ask who damaged the evidence. It looks at the positive side of the evidence. If the evidence is damaged, there is nothing to show in the court.

d. Chain of computers

Incorrect. This choice is indirectly related to the chain of custody.

15. The concept of admissibility of evidence does **not** include which of the following?

a. Relevance

Incorrect. Relevant evidence is evidence that had some logical tendency to prove or disprove a disputed consequential fact.

b. Competence

Incorrect. Competent evidence (i.e., admissible evidence) is evidence that satisfied all the rules of evidence except those dealing with relevance.

c. Materiality

Incorrect. Materiality is the notion that evidence must be relevant to a fact that is in dispute between the parties

d. Sufficiency

Correct. Laying a proper foundation for evidence is "the practice or requirement of introducing evidence of things necessary to make further evidence relevant, material, or competent." Sufficiency is not part of the concept of admissibility of evidence.

16. Evidence is needed in a computer crime case to do which of the following?

a. Charge a case.

Incorrect. See correct answer (d).

b. Classify a case.

Incorrect. See correct answer (d).

c. Make a case.

Incorrect. See correct answer (d).

d. Prove a case.

Correct. Proper elements of proof and correct types of evidence are needed to prove a computer crime case. It is proper to maintain computer-related evidence. Special procedures are needed to avoid problems of proof caused by improper care and handling of such evidence.

17. What determines whether a computer crime has been committed?

a. When the crime is reported

Incorrect. See correct answer (c).

b. When a computer expert has completed his or her work

Incorrect. See correct answer (c).

c. When the allegation has been substantiated

Correct. A computer crime is committed when the allegation is substantiated with proper evidence that is relevant, competent, and material.

d. When the investigation is completed

Incorrect. See correct answer (c).

18. The correct sequence of preliminary investigation in a computer fraud is:

I. Consult with a computer expert.

II. Prepare an investigative plan.

III. Consult with a prosecutor.

IV. Substantiate the allegation.

a. IV, I, II, and III

Correct. Step 1 is substantiating the allegation. Step 2 is consulting with a computer expert, as appropriate. Step 3 is preparing an investigation plan that sets forth the scope of the investigation and serves as a guide in determining how much technical assistance will be needed. Step 4 is consulting with a prosecutor, depending on the nature of the allegation and scope of the investigation. Items to discuss with the prosecutor may include the elements of proof, evidence required, and parameters of a prospective search.

b. III, I, II, and IV

Incorrect. See correct answer (a).

c. IV, II, III, and I

Incorrect. See correct answer (a).

d. I, IV, II, and III

Incorrect. See correct answer (a).

19. A search warrant is required in a computer-related crime:

a. Before the allegation has been substantiated.

Incorrect. See correct answer (b).

b. After establishing the probable cause(s).

Correct. Once the allegation has been substantiated, the prosecutor should be contacted to determine if there is probable cause for a search. Because of the technical nature of a computer-related crime investigation, presenting a proper technical perspective in establishing probable cause becomes crucial to securing a search warrant.

c. Before identifying the number of investigators needed.

Incorrect. See correct answer (b).

d. After seizing the computer and related equipment.

Incorrect. See correct answer (b).

20. If a computer or peripheral equipment involved in a computer crime is **not** covered by a search warrant, what should the investigator do?

  a. Seize it before someone takes it away.

  Incorrect. See correct answer (b).

  b. Leave it alone until a warrant can be obtained.

  Correct. If a computer or peripheral equipment involved in a computer crime is not covered by a search warrant, the investigator should leave it alone until a warrant can be obtained. The investigator needs a warrant to collect anything.

  c. Analyze the equipment or its contents and record it.

  Incorrect. See correct answer (b).

  d. Store it in a locked cabinet in a secure warehouse.

  Incorrect. See correct answer (b).

21. Computer fraud is increased when:

  a. Employees are not trained.

  Incorrect. There is no direct correlation between computer fraud and this choice.

  b. Documentation is not available.

  Incorrect. There is no direct correlation between computer fraud and this choice.

  c. Audit trails are not available.

  Correct. Audit trails indicate what actions are taken by the system. The fact that the system has adequate and clear audit trails will deter fraud perpetrators because they fear getting caught.

  d. Employee performance appraisals are not given.

  Incorrect. There is no direct correlation between computer fraud and this choice.

Characteristics of Effective Auditors and Audit Function

In general, effectiveness means achieving the stated mission, vision, goals, objectives, plans, programs, or activities in the most economical manner after considering their costs and benefits. In this section, we present characteristics that define internal auditors as effective and the internal audit function as effective because the characteristics are not the same. This appendix is tested at the proficient cognitive level in Parts 1 and 2 of the CIA Exam.

Characteristics of Effective Auditors

The following is a list of characteristics that can define internal auditors as effective, although the list is not inclusive.

- Effective auditors can make an audit function effective due to their professionalism and competency levels.
- Effective auditors possess several competencies and skills in these areas:

  1. Business acumen
  2. Critical thinking
  3. Communications
  4. Basic legal and ethical principles
  5. Audit and legal evidence
  6. Forensics and investigations
  7. Analytical and functional knowledge
  8. Assurance services and consulting services
  9. Risk management and insurance
  10. Sampling and statistics
  11. Information technology in systems development and systems security
  12. Big-data analytics and data mining
  13. Industry knowledge

■ Effective auditors acquire the core knowledge of the business or industry they work in. This means possessing:

1. Business acumen when working for business organizations.

2. Core knowledge about how a government operates when working for governmental agencies.

3. Core knowledge about the academic world (e.g., schools, colleges, and universities) when working in educational institutions.

4. Core knowledge about how hospitals and medical research institutions operate when working in healthcare industry.

5. Core knowledge about how nongovernmental organizations (NGOs) operate when working for NGOs.

   It is very difficult to understand, operate, and contribute to organizations when auditors do not have the required core knowledge for their work, resulting in a disconnection of auditors with their jobs.

■ Effective auditors adhere to professional standards and possess the required core business knowledge combined with the right mix of business skills (hard skills and soft skills) to implement such professional standards. Up-skilling auditors is the major focus here (i.e., deskilled auditors must be up-skilled, reskilled, and cross-skilled).

■ Effective auditors play several roles, such as trusted advisers, control assessors, control evaluators, cyber-advisers, and internal business consultants/partners to the board of directors (board) and senior management consisting of executives and officers of a company. Auditors earn their trust through demonstrating professionalism and competency.

■ During their work in providing assurance and consulting services, effective auditors can link:

1. Audit strategy to business strategy.

2. Audit objectives to business objectives.

3. Audit risks to business risks.

4. Audit value to business value during their work in providing assurance and consulting services.

■ Effective internal auditors can work with external auditors in coordinating and communicating during standard assurance services (e.g., financial audit) and special services (e.g., governance, risk, and control [GRC] reviews).

■ Effective auditors pay equal attention to financial reporting (revenues, costs, and profits) and nonfinancial reporting (e.g., operations, marketing, legal, ethical, and social improvements and issues).

■ Effective auditors are independent in appearance and action, and they are objective in mind and in reporting their work results.

■ Effective auditors can use data analytics techniques and data mining software tools to assess data integrity and security controls over databases, data warehouses, and data marts.

■ Effective auditors can use statistical analyses. such as regression analysis, factor analysis, cluster analysis, link analysis, and correlation analysis, to detect fraudulent transactions.

- Effective auditors can use data analytics and data mining software tools to assess the overall control environment after identifying systemic breakdowns in controls.

- Effective auditors can use big data analytics as a part of their analytical reviews conducted during audit planning and engagement work.

- Effective auditors apply critical thinking skills and possess the right judgment when collecting and analyzing audit evidence and when reaching audit conclusions and recommendations. They know the difference between:

  1. Strong evidence and weak evidence.

  2. False evidence and true evidence.

  3. Good conclusions and bad conclusions.

  4. Big recommendations (vital few) and small recommendations (trivial many).

  5. Value-creating opportunities and value-destroying events.

     An auditor's recommendations must be big in scope, size, and significance.

- Effective auditors are good in identifying or differentiating between value-creating and value-destroying plans, programs, policies, procedures, and practices. This critical thinking can save an organization's resources from undertaking value-destroying plans. The same thing applies to value-adding tasks and activities and non-value-adding tasks and activities.

- The chief audit executive (CAE) wears several hats, such as supervisor, manager, leader, change agent, coach, mentor, delegator, motivator, inspirer, agile performer, and above all futurist.

- Internal auditors are effective when they treat audit clients and outside auditors with respect, dignity, and humility during their interactions with several parties either in audit work or non-audit work.

- **In summary,** effective auditors are value creators, value enhancers, change agents, team players, agile performers who are resourceful and competent, and business partners with other members of the organization while maintaining their independence and objectivity standards.

Characteristics of Effective Audit Function

The following is a list of characteristics that can define an internal audit function as effective, although the list is not inclusive.

- An audit function is effective only when its auditors are effective. This means auditors must be effective first in order for the audit function to be effective.

- An effective audit function follows and encourages adherence to professional standards to conduct audit work. Any deviations from standards are explained or permissions to exceptions are obtained.

- An effective audit function:

  1. Continuously plans audit work.

  2. Schedules audit resources for audit engagements.

3. Supervises or manages audit engagements.

4. Conducts auditor's performance appraisals.

5. Provides continuing education programs to auditors.

6. Conducts succession planning moves for senior audit management.

7. Coaches audit supervisors, senior auditors, and staff auditors about their career plans and paths.

- Effective audit planning focuses on:

    1. The traditional assurance services (e.g., reviewing policies, procedures, and systems for compliance).

    2. Consulting services (e.g., consulting auditors lend advice and insights in reviewing business processes and practices to improve their performance, productivity, and progress).

    3. Value-for-money (VFM) audits (e.g., focusing on three Es—economy, efficiency, and effectiveness—to ensure maximum utilization of resources and to prevent and detect fraud, abuse, and waste of resources).

    4. Agile audits (e.g., small-size, short-time, target-based, and focus-based reviews with quick results on critical issues).

        VFM audits require auditors to wear an industrial engineer's hat and focus on the 4Ms—men, machines, money, and materials. Industrial engineers are often called efficiency experts. Expertise drives the three Es.

- An internal audit function is effective when it develops yearly audit plans with a major focus on target-based audits (agile audits), strategy-based audits, and risk-based audits in addition to cycle-based audits, operational-based audits, compliance-based audits, performance-based audits, or scheduled-based audits (repeat/routine audits).

- An effective audit function manages audit resources through budgeting, reporting, monitoring, and feedback.

- An effective audit function supports and strengthens the core business functions, such as operations, marketing, and finance, through its audit work, analysis, findings, conclusions, and recommendations for improvements. It provides outside-in views and perspectives to a business function with a fresh mind and new outlook as if it manages that function.

- An effective audit function acquires the required audit talent through a combination of insourcing, co-sourcing, and outsourcing methods as needed to complete an audit engagement. For example, not every auditor needs the same technical and complex skills (e.g., information technology, engineering, actuarial science, and statistical knowledge) as long as the audit team as a whole possesses such skills. Audit talent is needed in cybersecurity (e.g., data breaches and ransomware attacks) and emerging technologies (e.g., bitcoins, artificial intelligence [machine learning], robotics, business analytics with big data, business intelligence, and data mining).

- An effective audit function is an internal business partner with other functions of a business in terms of:

    1. Focusing on value-creating tasks and separating non-value-added activities from value-adding activities.

2. Focusing on risk-identification methods and risk-mitigation efforts.

3. Implementing best practices or meta-practices in governance, risk management, and control.

4. Recommending implementation of cost-effective and time-sensitive continuous controls (automated and manual).

- An effective audit function obtains a 360-degree feedback from audit clients or audit stakeholders such as internal customers (e.g., audit committee members, senior managers, and functional managers) and external customers (e.g., external auditors, bank examiners, and regulatory auditors). Kano principles can be applied by audit stakeholders to this feedback process using three rating scales, such as satisfied, neutral, and dissatisfied for measuring the effectiveness of internal audit. Each rating must give reasons and explanations. In a way, the Kano principles validate what the audit stakeholders value the most.

- The internal audit function is effective when outside auditors (e.g., external auditors, bank examiners, and regulatory auditors) and inside non-auditors (e.g., risk officer, compliance officer, quality auditor, environmental auditor, and control assessor) rely on the work performed by the internal auditors. This reliance can be achieved through coordination and cooperation efforts between these outside and inside parties and due to the effect of economies of scope and size, resulting from working together. Reliance leads to assurance, as shown:

Low reliance = Low assurance

High reliance = High assurance

- Effective and efficient internal audit function establishes a quality assurance and improvement program (QAIP) to add value, improve an audit organization's internal operations, and gain credibility in the eyes of third parties and outsiders.

- The audit function is effective when it is performing value-adding audits with great depth and breadth, not nitpicking audits, fault-blaming audits, superficial audits, checklist audits, surface audits, or error-seeking audits. This new approach requires conducting audits outside of typical accounting and financial areas, such as:

  □ Sales and marketing

  □ Human resources

  □ Capital planning and budgeting projects

  □ Business process improvement projects

  □ Production and supply chain operations

  □ New product/service development projects

  □ New systems development projects

  □ New contract development projects, including outsourcing contracts

  □ Merger, acquisition, and divestiture projects

- The CAE in partnership with legal counsel, the ethics officer, compliance officer, and risk officer must:

  1. Conduct governance audits to ensure that the board addresses long-term strategy with goals and objectives.

  2. Review the compensation and benefit programs to the CEO and other officers and executives.

  3. Focus on the board's reputation.

  4. Look into succession planning for key officers and executives.

  5. Identify separation of duties problems between the chief executive officer and the board chairperson.

  6. Focus on the board's composition (i.e., inside directors, outside directors, and shadow directors).

  7. Recognize conflict-of-interest situations (i.e., abuse of insider information and management scandals).

  8. Review risk management, control, and compliance matters.

- **Reputation management** deals with risks and exposures facing the board resulting from the board's own practices, philosophies, operating styles, litigations, and public statements. It deals with the board's overall image in the eyes of the company's senior management, company stakeholders, affected regulators and bankers, and the public at large (e.g., strong board or weak board, ethical board or unethical board, effective board or ineffective board, or good reputation or bad reputation).

- The audit committee and CAE of the outsourcing organization should conduct cost-benefit analysis, reputation risk analysis, and T-account analysis (i.e., listing the pros on one side of T and the cons on the other side of T) of outsourcing the internal audit function prior to making the actual decision.

- The entire internal audit function will be effective when its internal policies, procedures, practices, processes, and operations are streamlined, simplified, and standardized to provide quick responses and faster results to management with agility to increase its performance and productivity and to show its progress.

- An effective audit function develops and maintains an audit test model or audit test lab to use repeatedly in audits as a template to gain the benefits of economies of scale. This model contains audit test scripts, test beds, test data, test cases, and test results for use in various audit test scenarios. This model saves time, energy, and frustration because auditors do not have to repeat or start all over again for each audit (i.e., benefits). The best candidates for the application of this audit test model are one-time audits, routine audits, ad hoc audits, special audits, continuous audits, and agile audits.

- An effective audit function develops and maintains an audit dashboard tool (i.e., audit reporting tool) to show various items of interest to management, including audit progress reports, actual versus budget spending, and actual audit plan completion versus estimated audit plan.

- An internal audit function is effective when it establishes **escalation procedures** for resolving any differences of opinion between audit staff/management and organization management (audit clients) concerning reported audit findings and recommendations.

- An internal audit function is effective when it establishes a **tracking system** to track and monitor all open audit issues accompanied by an aging analysis showing the number of days the audit issues are open that are not addressed or not implemented to show the status of open audit issues.

- **In summary,** an effective audit function will always look for continuous improvement regarding its scorecard or metrics reporting to the board and senior management (i.e., audit clients and audit stakeholders).

Big Data and Data Mining

This appendix discusses four major topics: big data, data counting methods, data analytics, and data mining.

Big Data

Simply stated, the term "big data" means vast amounts of data collected from a variety of sources. It is big in terms of many data volumes, several data sets, and many data types. Data volumes are related to data files stored in databases and mass storage devices; data sets include several data elements, such as customer name and account number. Data types mean alphabetic, numeric, alphanumeric, and special characters. The term "big data" is subjective, depending on the size and complexity of an organization. New and actionable insights can be deduced from big data. Here, data analytics is the major topic and focus in data analysis and extraction methods as shown in the next table:

Big Data ⟶	Data Analysis and Extraction Methods ⟶	New Knowledge
Structured data	Data analytics	New information
Unstructured data	Statistical analyses	Actionable insights and inferences
Semistructured data	Data mining methods	Meaningful actions
Sanitized data	Simulation techniques	New results and decisions
Data patterns and trends	Forecasting methods	New value uncovered/created

Data Life Cycle

Similar to a product life cycle, data has its own life cycle showing how data is discovered, created, generated, deployed, and used from beginning to the end.

> Data life cycle = Discover + Deploy

Here, "Discover" focuses on tasks such as prepare, explore, and model, and "Deploy" focuses on tasks such as implement, act, and evaluate.

Another way of viewing the data life cycle is to see how data turns into results and decisions. This is shown next.

$$\text{Data} \longrightarrow \text{Analytics} \longrightarrow \text{Insights} \longrightarrow \text{Results} \longrightarrow \text{Decisions}$$

Data is subjected to analysis to yield new insights, results, and decisions. Here, the term "data" refers to collecting or generating data in a form that can be processed. "Analytics" means cleansing, normalizing, aggregating, extracting, and analyzing the data. "Results" means improving decisions, actions, and outcomes to realize new benefits. "Decisions" means (1) acquiring new customers, suppliers, and vendors; (2) increasing sales, revenues, and profits; (3) decreasing costs; (4) signing new business contracts; (5) developing new business partners and strategic alliances; and (6) above all, gaining a competitive edge.

Big data does not necessarily mean good data; it could be bad data. Consequences are:

$$\text{Good Data} \longrightarrow \text{Good Results, Outcomes, and Decisions}$$

$$\text{Bad Data} \longrightarrow \text{Bad Results, Outcomes, and Decisions}$$

What makes data good data or bad data is related to data quality, data security, and data privacy. Data owners and data stewards within an organization manage and control the data quality, security, and privacy.

Data Owners and Stewards

Big data needs owners and stewards to manage and control the data assets on an ongoing basis to reduce risks facing data.

A **data owner** is a person or department responsible for safeguarding or securing data with security controls, classifying data (sensitive or not sensitive), and defining data access rules (grant or deny).

A **data steward or data custodian** is a person or department delegated the responsibility for managing a specific set of data resources (e.g., data volumes, files, and elements). This person defines, specifies, and standardizes the data assets of an organization within and across all functional areas. There can be several data owners and data custodians protecting data assets. Data owners and stewards establish acceptable use policies and access rules because data usage rules stem from data usage policies.

Acceptable use policies require that a system user, an end user, or an administrator (e.g., system, security, and network administrator) agrees to comply with such policies prior to accessing computer systems, internal networks, and external networks (the Internet). Acceptable use is based on authorized access.

For example, in a cloud computing environment, subscribers ensure that all subscriber personnel read and understand the provider's acceptable use policy and negotiate an agreement for resolution of agreed-on policy violations in advance with the provider. The agreement also includes a process for resolving disputes over possible policy violations.

Two concepts related to acceptable use policies and access rules are *rules of behavior and rules of engagement.*

Access rules are clear action statements dealing with expected user behavior in a computer system. Access rules reflect security policies and practices, business rules, information ethics, system functions and features, and individual roles and responsibilities, which collectively form access restrictions.

Rules of behavior are conditions established and implemented concerning use of, security in, and acceptable level of risk of the system. Rules will clearly delineate responsibilities and expected behavior of all individuals with access to the system. The organization establishes and makes readily available to all information system users a set of rules that describes their responsibilities and expected behavior with regard to information system usage. Rules of behavior are established to control the behavior of employees on computer systems.

Rules of engagement are detailed guidelines and constraints regarding the execution of information security testing. These rules are established before the start of a security test. The rules give the test team authority to conduct the defined activities without the need for additional permissions. Rules of engagement are established to control the behavior of contractors, vendors, and suppliers during their work for an organization.

Data Analytics Process

A structured and standard methodology is needed for performing data analysis to yield consistent results and insights. A five-step analytical procedure is suggested here:

1. Define the question and hypothesis.
2. Obtain relevant data from known data sources.
3. Clean and normalize the selected data.
4. Conduct data analysis.
5. Communicate analytical results and outcomes.

Step 1: Define the Question and Hypothesis
This step requires formulating a basic question and its associated hypothesis that can be tested by data analysis. For example, a retailer might put a question as follows: Does the merchandise return policy affect current and future sales? The corresponding hypothesis might look like this: A rigid return policy with a shorter period could decrease sales while a flexible return policy with a longer period could increase sales.

Step 2: Obtain Relevant Data from Known Data Sources
This step requires identifying relevant data needed from all data sources to test the hypothesis. For example, retailers can look at their past sales and past return policies and can gather similar information from other retailers to study.

Step 3: Clean and Normalize the Selected Data

Before data mining software tools are applied, one needs to clean and normalize the target raw datasets to remove missing, erroneous, or inappropriate data. **Data cleansing methods** purify data or filter inappropriate data and include log management functions such as log filtering, log correlations, and log analysis. One reason to perform data cleansing is due to data mingling. In data mingling, data related to some event, incident, or activity is mixed with data unrelated to that event, incident, or activity, thus making these two data types often indistinguishable. Data mingling can be attributed to inadequate labeling and limited memory storage. The comingling of data will make the task of an auditor, analyst, or investigator more challenging because which data caused an event or incident is not known. Thus, data mingling problems make the data unclean.

Data normalization methods convert the clean data into a standardized format and label it consistently. One of the most common uses of normalization is storing computer transaction dates and times (system clocks) in a single format (e.g., synchronizing timestamps of 12-hour format or 24-hour format with different time zones in a country or continent). Converting data to consistent formats and labels makes data analysis and reporting much easier.

Data wrangling software also cleans and normalizes raw data because it refines and reshapes raw data into actionable and usable data.

In summary, the data cleansing and data normalizations actions are performed in a preprocessing prior to data mining step as shown:

Preprocessing →	Data Mining →	Postprocessing
Raw data	Software tools	Insights and decisions
Data cleansing	Data analytics	Results and reports
Data normalization		

Step 4: Conduct Data Analysis

After raw data is cleansed and normalized, the data analyst can analyze the data to test different hypotheses by developing different data models to identify retail sales patterns and to show how they are correlated with the merchandise return policy. For example, a retailer found out that a rigid return policy (e.g., 15 days are allowed to return merchandise after purchase) decreased sales while a flexible return policy (e.g., 30 days are allowed to return merchandise after purchase) increased sales. This is because customers want a longer period to determine whether to keep or return a product based on how it works. So, customers want to buy from a retailer with a flexible return policy, resulting in increased sales, and customers do not want to buy from a retailer with a rigid return policy, resulting in decreased sales. The same thing can be said about shipping terms for merchandise where free shipping increases sales and no free shipping decreases sales.

Step 5: Communicate Analytical Results and Outcomes

The last step is to convert the discovered data analytical results and outcomes into the retailer's strategy and put it into operational use. The retailer changed its merchandise return policy to a flexible policy of 30 days. These results can be communicated to management through the use of data visualization tools such as charts, graphs, tables, or exhibits.

Data Analysis and Internal Auditors

Data analysis can help internal auditors meet their auditing objectives, such as detecting changes or vulnerabilities in business processes that could expose an organization to undue and unplanned risks. The data sources can include fully manual, semiautomated or semimanual, and fully automated. A specific audit objective in analyzing data is to identify fraud, errors, inefficiencies, or noncompliance.[1]

Examples of analytical tests to find patterns and trends in data include:

- Calculation of basic statistical parameters (e.g., averages, standard deviations, variance, highest and lowest values [ranges], excessively high values or low values, and control totals) to identify outlying transactions.

- Numeric digit testing using Benford's Law to identify statistically unlikely occurrences of specific digits in naturally occurring datasets. Benford's Law gives the expected frequencies of the first digits in tabulated data and finds that the first digits are not all equally likely. There is a biased skewness in favor of the lower digits. This means that the digit 1 has a higher likelihood of occurring as the first digit than the digit 9.

- Data match testing of names, addresses, and account numbers in disparate systems and locations.

- Data duplicate testing of payments, payroll, customer claims, or expense reports line items.

- Data gap testing to identify missing numbers in sequential data.

- Date checking tests where timestamps are used to identify transaction posting times or data entry times to determine their appropriateness and correctness.

Data Mapping and Data Matching Tools

Data mapping involves laying out a clear data path containing related data elements of interest to achieve an end goal of identifying data relationships.

Data matching is a computer matching technique that can prevent improper payments and detect fraudulent activities by comparing data from several, related computer systems. Here data from several different data files (i.e., internal and external) are matched to verify the eligibility prior to payment; improper payments are stopped when they happen. Hence, data matching is both a preventive control and a detective control. The goal is to identify data inconsistencies across several computer data files.

Applications of data mapping and matching tools in government include stop payments of:

- Social Security benefits to dead people.
- Maternity benefits to a male employee.
- Overtime hours to a terminated employee.
- Weekly wages to an imposter employee.
- Invoices of a phony vendor.

---

[1]*IPPF—Practice Guide, GTAG-16, Data Analysis* (Altamonte Springs, FL: Institute of Internal Auditors, August 2011); www.theiia.org.

Why Use Big Data?

Traditionally, organizations relied heavily on internal data for decision-making purposes but soon found out that these internal sources are too limited to grow their businesses. Later, organizations realized that they can discover and explore vast amounts of external data that allow them to gain additional insights to grow their businesses. This so-called big data came from internal and external sources. Other names given for big data are data mart, data mall, data highway, data lakes, data hounds, data bazaar, data stash, and data tsunami.

> Big Data = Internal Data + External Data = New Opportunities
>
> Big Data $\longrightarrow$ Big Decisions
>
> Big Data $\longrightarrow$ New Insights $\longrightarrow$ New Strategies $\longrightarrow$ New Decisions $\longrightarrow$ New Actions
>
> Big Data = New Data Asset = New Strategic Asset
>
> Big Data $\longrightarrow$ Assurance Procedures and Consulting Services

For internal auditors, utilizing big data can reveal new insights, which in turn will allow them to make new recommendations to management that will result in new improvements for the organization, resulting in an additional or incremental value.

Nature and Types of Big Data. Big data can be structured and well organized or it can be unstructured and very disorganized. Whether data is organized or disorganized is attributed to its source. However, valid and useful data can be found in both structured data and unstructured data; the only question is how much and where. In comparison, one can say internal data is structured data and external data is unstructured data. Big data can also come in a semistructured format from external sources. It has been said that more than 80% of business data is unstructured data.

> Big Data = Structured Data + Unstructured Data + Semistructured Data
>
> Internal Data = Structured Data
>
> External Data = Unstructured Data + Semistructured Data

Structured data: Structured data consists of internal data sources with fixed-form format; data warehouses; traditional and fixed data structures; database files (e.g., relational or hierarchical); flat data files; interconnected computer systems and data sources; data that is easy to manage and control; validated data; data that uses a standard data structure; data owners and data stewards who are known; and data that uses incompatible data file formats.

Unstructured data: Unstructured data consists of external data sources with free-form format; nontraditional data structures; nonfixed data structures; disconnected computer systems and data sources; data that is not easy to manage and control; nonvalidated data; data that does not use a standard data structure; data owners and data stewards who are unknown; and data that uses incompatible data file formats.

Semistructured data: Semistructured data conists of external data sources with fixed-form format; Extensible Markup Language (XML), Hypertext Markup Language (HTML), and Extended Hypertext Markup Language (XHTML). XML is a metalanguage with a flexible text format designed to describe data for electronic publishing. The web browser interprets the XML, and the

XML takes over the HTML for creating dynamic web documents. HTML is a markup language that is a subset of standard generalized markup language (SGML). It is used to create hypertext and hypermedia documents on the web that incorporate text, graphics, sound, video, and hyperlinks. HTML is a mechanism used to create dynamic web pages on the Internet. XHTML is a unifying standard that brings the benefits of XML to HTML. XHTML is the new web standard and should be used for all new web pages to achieve maximum portability across platforms and browsers.

Sources of Big Data. In comparison of data sources, one can say internal data sources provide structured data and external data sources provide unstructured and semistructured data.

Structured data sources include internal source documents, such as sales orders and invoices; purchase requests and orders (procurement records); operating expenses; production and service records; materials and labor records; finished goods inventory records; payments to employees and vendors (employee payroll and vendor invoices); charge card transactions; cash receipts; payments from customers (receivable receipts); operating budget and capital budget records; contracts; and customer merchandise returns.

Unstructured data sources include external sources, such as public online websites, search engine websites, private online websites, and research websites; public libraries; governmental agency's websites, social media websites, website blogs, online chats, publicly posted videos and audios, electronic mail, office memos, reports, and notes; whitepapers and research studies; text messages (SMS and MMS); and human language, audio, and video. Specifically, unstructured data consists of multimedia files, image files, sound files, and unstructured text files.

Semistructured data sources include web documents and web pages. Another way of classifying big data is by where it is found, such as government data (more reliable), proprietary data (a company's internal data, which is more reliable), open-source data (i.e., Internet-based, which is not reliable), research data (more reliable), industry data (more reliable), and anonymous data (less reliable).

In summary:

- Structured data is found in data tables, data records, and computer flat files.
- Unstructured data is found in human languages, audio, and video.
- Semistructured data is found in XML and HTML web languages.
- Raw data is found in customer orders and point-of-sale terminals.
- Complex data is found in databases (e.g., relational or hierarchical) and legacy systems.
- Social media data is found in blogs, tweets, and posts.
- Machine-generated data is found in electronic sensors, retail merchandise (RFID) tags, mobile devices, and Internet of Things (IoT) technologies.

Characteristics of Big Data

According to the IIA's Global Technology Audit Guide, big data can have seven dimensions, characteristics, or attributes, which are discussed next.[2]

Seven *Vs* of Big Data

1. **Volume** is the amount of data being created, which is vast compared to traditional data sources.

2. **Variety** of data comes from all types of formats. This can include data generated within an organization as well as data created from external sources, including publicly available data.

3. **Velocity** means data is being generated extremely quickly and continuously.

4. **Veracity** means data must be able to be verified based on both accuracy and context.

5. **Variability** means big data is extremely variable and always changing.

6. **Visualization** means translating vast amounts of data into readily presentable graphics and charts that are easy to understand and are critical to end user satisfaction where these graphs and charts may highlight additional insights. Data visualization software tools are available to bring out these insights in the form of pictures, graphs, exhibits, tables, and storyboards because raw analytic results from big data are often hard to read and interpret. Datafication, the process of putting information in an easily searchable and analyzable format, is a prerequisite to data visualization. Examples of datafication efforts include turning paper documents into electronic health and medical records to allow searches, electronically indexing paper documents to allow searches, and electronically indexing websites to allow searches. The idea is that when data is put in a searchable and analyzable format, it can be presented easily.

7. **Value** means organizations, societies, and consumers can all benefit from big data. Value is generated when new insights are translated into actions that create positive outcomes.

In summary, business insight (value of data) and speed (velocity of data) are the main business drivers of investment in big data. Variety of data continues to outweigh volume and velocity as the technical drivers behind big data investment.

Virtual Data Tsunami

According to the United States Government Accountability Office, big data is a "virtual data tsunami." It is a twenty-first-century development consisting of volume, variety, and velocity characteristics that allow performing new analytics, improving cognitive computing systems, and building advanced machine-learning technologies.[3]

New analytics are tools for examining large amounts of varied data to uncover subtle or hidden patterns, correlations, and other insights, such as market trends and customer purchasing preferences.

Cognitive computing systems represent the ability of computing systems to perform human cognitive functions like memory, recall, judgment, inference, and learning.

---

[2]IIA's Global Technology Audit Guide, *Understanding and Auditing Big Data* (2017), www.theiia.org.
[3]*Data and Analytics Innovation*, GAO-16-659SP (Washington, DC: GAO, September 2016), www.gao.gov.

Advanced machine learning technology is an artificial intelligence discipline that allows computers to handle new situations via analysis, self-training, observation, and experience, all with minimal "supervision" by humans.

Return on Data

The real value of big data does not come from a mere collection of data from several sources. Instead, the real value comes from data usage and application, which can lead to major insights and better decisions. Because big data (data asset or strategic asset) is put to so many good uses and with so many benefits, a return on data (ROD) metric can be calculated for value-measuring purposes. ROD indicates how data assets of an organization are utilized effectively and efficiently (i.e., 10% or 40%). ROD is calculated as follows.

$$\text{ROD} = (\text{Dollar benefits from big data}) / (\text{Dollar investment in big data}) \times 100$$

Technologies in Big Data

Big data requires deployment of new technologies that are different from traditional technologies used to simply process day-to-day business transactional, financial, and operational data. New technologies require new software (either developed in house or acquired from outside), new hardware, and new employees with new technical skills. The reason for deploying new technologies to process and handle big data is that big data comes from disparate and disconnected systems from inside and outside of an organization. A proof of concept is required to illustrate the value of deploying a new technology and to obtain management commitment, support, and funding.

Examples of technologies used in big data are listed next.

- Company's online websites
- Company's databases, data warehouses, and data marts
- Data mining software tools to identify patterns and trends in big data
- Data visualization software
- Data dashboard software
- Search engine websites (e.g., Google, Yahoo, and Bing)
- Mobile website operating systems (Apple's iOS and Google's Android)
- Text messaging services (e.g., short message service (SMS) and multimedia messaging service (MMS))
- Electronic mail services (e.g., individual or group)
- Mobile device technologies (e.g., smartphones and digital tablets)
- Social media websites (e.g., Facebook and Twitter)
- Government websites (e.g., U.S. Bureau of Labor Statistics, U.S. Bureau of Economic Analysis, U.S. Department of Labor, and U.S. Census Bureau)
- General research websites (e.g., Pew Research Center, Forrester, Aberdeen, and Gartner)
- Cloud-based data storage
- Active data backup storage

- Inactive data archived storage

- Advanced technologies (e.g., sensors and cameras in retail, radio frequency identification tags, tags on products in manufacturing and retail, the Internet of Things, machine learning, artificial intelligence, cognitive computing systems that learn by themselves, augmented reality, virtual reality, and robots

Risks in Big Data

Like other types of internal data, such as financial data or operational data, big data is not immune to risk. In fact, risks in big data are magnified due to its combination of internal sources and external sources and when the big data is compared to internal sources alone. General risks in big data are data quality, data security, data privacy, and data governance.

Examples of specific risks in big data are listed next.

- Discovering wrong data and bad data, leading to wrong and bad decisions

- Digging deeper into data, thus creating an "analysis paralysis" situation, leading to analytics rich but information poor

- Proceeding with invalid data patterns and trends, assuming that they are valid patterns and trends, thus wasting resources

- Lack of data governance standards, leading to poor-quality data and information

- Lack of data quality standards, leading to wrong decisions

- Lack of information quality standards, leading to bad decisions

- Lack of data security and privacy control guidelines, leading to data breaches

- Inability to apply the right technology to big data, thus wasting resources and missing opportunities

Other Topics Related to Big Data

Next, we focus on several topics related to big data, including data governance standards, data reliability standards, data quality standards, information quality standards, and data security policies and controls due to their relative importance to management.

Data Governance Standards. Data governance standards address several oversight-related issues, such as data ownership and usage policies; data classification and declassification schemes; data cleansing, separation, and normalization; data security policies and controls; and data backup, retention, and recovery methods. Data governance standards include data access, data separation, data integrity, data regulations, data cleansing and disposition, and data recovery.

Data Reliability Standards. Data reliability, especially as it relates to computer-processed data, means that data is reasonably complete, accurate (consistent), and valid. Complete refers to the extent that relevant data records are present and the data fields in each record are populated appropriately. **Accurate** refers to the extent that recorded data reflects the actual underlying information, **Consistent**, a subcategory of accurate, refers to the need to obtain and use data that is clear and well defined enough to yield similar results in similar analyses. For example, if data is entered at multiple sites, inconsistent interpretation of data entry rules can lead to data that, taken as a whole, is unreliable. **Valid** refers to whether the data actually represents what is being measured. So, the analysts must consider risks associated with the possibility of using insufficiently reliable data.

Data Quality Standards. **Data** is a collection of facts and figures, and it is raw. Data is transformed into information in the course of data processing activities. The perception of quality depends on the purpose for which data or information is to be used. For information to be useful, it should be available where, when, and in the form it is needed, and with costs equal to or less than the benefits to be derived from it. The concept of *information economics* with costs and benefits should be used here.

For data or information to be of any use to management, it should possess certain data quality dimensions and information quality elements and standards, which are described next.

Achieving a **data excellence goal** must be the top priority of a business data analyst who collects, compiles, interprets, and presents data results to business managers and executives. The data excellence goal needs to be applied to regular business data as well as statistical data, whether it is generated internally or externally.

Achieving the goal of data excellence is not a one-time task; instead, it must be an ongoing task where it is continuously and constantly monitored and improved in all seven dimensions of quality: relevance, accuracy, credibility, timeliness, accessibility, interpretability, and coherence. (Source: www.oecd.org)

1. The **relevance** of data reflects its ability to satisfy the needs of users. This depends on its utility in adding to the users' knowledge with regard to the topics of greatest importance to them. The evaluation of relevance is subjective and varies according to users' needs. The basic question here is: Is the data what the user expects?

2. **Accuracy** represents the level at which the data or information correctly describes the phenomenon it has been developed to measure. It is normally expressed in terms of the "error" in the statistical data, which can in turn be broken down into different components. The basic question here is: Is the data reliable?

3. The **credibility** of data or information refers to the confidence level that users have in the analyst or entity producing the data or statistic. It is normally based on the reputation of the producer as demonstrated over time, which in turn relates to factors such as the objectivity, technical independence, professionalism, and transparency shown by the producer during the course of analytical activities. Its basic question is: Is the data producer trustworthy?

4. The **timeliness** of data refers to the time it takes to disseminate the data with regard to the reference period, requiring a timetable for releasing data and measuring performance. The timelines of data have a significance impact on its relevance, meaning late presentation of data may not be relevant. In addition, there is a clear trade-off between the timeliness and the accuracy of data. The basic question here is: Does the user receive the data in time and on schedule?

5. The **accessibility** of data reflects the ease with which it can be identified and utilized by a user.

   Accessibility therefore depends on the means with which the data is made available to the user, either on paper medium or electronic medium; the search procedures required, whether they are too long and convoluted; the user's ability to make use of the data in meeting needs; the existence of barriers to access (approvals, cost, and time); and the availability of user support services (hourly, daily, or weekly). The basic question here is: Is the data reachable?

6. **Interpretability** reflects the ease with which the users can understand the basic characteristics of the data and thereby evaluate its utility for their own needs. Some fundamental factors of interpretability include the adequacy of data provided within the coverage limits, the comparability of data over time, the methods used to collect and generate data, and the accuracy of data. The basic question here is: Is the data understandable?

7. **Coherence** relates to the degree to which a particular data item is logically connected and mutually consistent with other related data. It implies that the same term should not be used without explanation for different data items in that different terms should not be used without explanation for the same data item and in that variations in methodology that might affect data values should not be made without explanation. The use of standard concepts, definitions, and classifications increases the coherence of the data or information supplied by various sources while changes in methodology can impede the comparability of the same parameter over time. The basic question here is: Is the data consistent and reconcilable with other data?

Information Quality Standards

Information quality is composed of three elements: utility, integrity, and objectivity. Quality will be ensured and established at levels appropriate to the nature and timeliness of the information to be disseminated. (Source: www.omb.org)

Information quality = Utility + Integrity + Objectivity

Utility means that disseminated information is useful to its intended users. "Useful" means that the content of the information is helpful, beneficial, or serviceable to its intended users, or that the information supports the usefulness of other disseminated information by making it more accessible or easier to read, see, understand, obtain, or use. Where the usefulness of information will be enhanced by greater transparency, care is taken that sufficient background and detail is available to maximize the usefulness of the information.

Integrity refers to security, which is the protection of information from unauthorized access or revision, to ensure that the information is not compromised through corruption or falsification. Integrity also means information is safeguarded from improper access, modification, or destruction, to a degree commensurate with the risk and magnitude of harm that could result from the loss, misuse, or unauthorized access to or modification of such information.

Objectivity consists of two distinct elements: presentation and substance. The presentation element includes whether disseminated information is presented in an accurate, clear, complete, and unbiased manner and in a proper context. The substance element involves a focus on ensuring accurate, reliable, and unbiased information. In a scientific, financial, or statistical context, the original and supporting data will be generated, and the analytic results will be developed, using sound statistical and research methods.

Two standards or concepts related to information quality include reproducibility and transparency. **Reproducibility** means that the information is capable of being substantially reproduced, subject to an acceptable degree of imprecision. For information judged to have more (less) important impacts, the degree of imprecision that is tolerated is reduced (increased).

Transparency is at the heart of the reproducibility standard in that transparency provides information in sufficient background and detail to maximize the usefulness of such information. The level of such background and detail is commensurate with the importance of the particular information, balanced against the resources required (i.e., cost, time, people, hardware, software, tools, and techniques), and is appropriate to the nature and timeliness of the information to be disseminated.

In summary:

- Data quality dimensions include relevance, accuracy, credibility, timeliness, accessibility, interpretability, and coherence.

- Information quality elements and standards include utility, integrity, objectivity, reproducibility, and transparency.

Data Security Policies and Controls

Data security policies and controls address various issues such as rules of behavior, rules of enforcement, access rules, acceptable use policies, rules of engagement, and access agreements for employees and nonemployees (e.g., vendors, consultants, contractors, and third parties). Here, the common issues include (1) controlling an individual's behavior, whether this individual is internal or external to an organization; (2) describing consequences for noncompliance with rules; and (3) making these rules official through issuing policy documents. The goal is to reduce the potential damage to computer systems and property and minimize harm to people.

Data Insurance Policies

Unfortunately, several organizations in the public and private sectors have experienced data security breaches and cyberattacks (e.g., ransomware) by hackers. The average total cost of a data security breach has been estimated at $4 million, and only 15% of organizations have purchased commercial insurance to protect against data security breaches and cyberattacks.

Because data is a strategic asset and a valuable commodity, it should be protected with an insurance policy covering data security breaches, cyberattacks, data losses, data stealing, and protection of customers' personal data.

Data Counting Methods

Raw data has value in providing actionable insights and inferences that can be turned into meaningful actions in terms of new decisions and results in achieving a competitive advantage. After raw data under consideration is sanitized or cleaned and before data mining techniques are applied to big data, such data must be organized and counted for its intended purposes. According to the Stevens power law developed by Stanley Stevens, four types of scales can be used to define how data or things can be coded, scaled, ordered, measured, ranked, arranged, grouped, organized, or otherwise counted. These four data scales are the nominal, ordinal, interval, and ratio scales. Moreover, organized data can be converted into indices, quartiles, percentiles, and outliers, which have several applications in business. Each type of data scale is discussed next.

Nominal Scales

Nominal scales are easy to understand, are nonnumeric, and are mutually exclusive (i.e., no overlap) as they are used to label, name, or code variables such as data or things. They have no inherent order to data values. Nominal scales can be expressed in a dichotomous manner, such as male or female, yes or no, true or false, or accept or reject. Here, either "true" or "false" can be labeled as "1" or "2," indicating that there is no order to the data values.

Example: A human resources department can determine the number of female employees and the number of male employees in a company's workforce. These gender numbers can be tracked over a time period to see if one gender is increasing or decreasing in numbers over the other gender.

Ordinal Scales

Ordinal scales are nonnumeric, have inherent order to data values, and the difference between each value is unknown. A disadvantage of ordinal ranking is that it does not show quantities.

Examples: The marketing department can conduct customer surveys to determine the number of customers who are very unsatisfied (1) or very satisfied (5) or very unhappy (1) or very happy (5). Here the scale is from 1 through 5, implying an order to data values. Ordinal scales are also used to rank first, second, or third place in student grades, games, sports, and competitive awards.

Interval Scales

Interval scales are numeric values with an order and a space (gap) values where the difference between each value is known. Statistical analysis (e.g., computing mean, mode, median, standard deviation, and variance) can be conducted with interval scale data.

Example: Interval scales are used to measure temperature either in Celsius (C) or Fahrenheit (F) degrees. Because temperatures do not have a "true zero" value, ratios cannot be computed.

Ratio Scales

Ratio scales are the ultimate goal of data because they are numeric, show the order of values and data relationships, the difference between data units is known, and they have "true zero" values. Hence, they are good for applying descriptive statistics (e.g., computing mode, median, quartiles, and outliers) and inferential statistics (e.g., testing hypotheses, deriving estimates, and drawing inferences). Ratio variables can be subject to basic mathematical calculations, such as adding, subtracting, multiplying, and dividing. Height and weight measurements can be done with ratios. In addition, ratios can be used to measure length, mass, energy, and statistical data.

Examples: Popular ratios in business include return on investment, return on sales, return on assets, and return on equity. Popular ratios in economic statistics shown as indices are consumer price index, producer price index, and wholesale price index.

Indices, Quartiles, Percentiles, and Outliers

Indices are index numbers where they compare two specific measurements in two time periods, such as current period and base period, and the result is expressed as a ratio. A simple index number represents an individual product. The consumer price index (CPI) data and the population census data are the two most watched, measured, and monitored economic statistics in any country. For example, the CPI is computed as follows:

CPI = (Current price / Base price) × 100

Current price per item = (Base-year price) × (Current CPI / Base CPI)

Examples: Several indices are given as examples next:

- The annual percentage change in a CPI is used as a measure of inflation. CPI is a price index at the retail store level.

- The index of industrial production represents an aggregate of a quantity index.

- A composite index number or an aggregate index number represents a group of products.

- The producer price index represents price changes to acquire raw materials, intermediate materials, and finished goods. Here, the producer can be a farmer or manufacturer, or simply a processor.

- The wholesale price index represents the price index for finished goods at the wholesale level.

Quartiles are three data points that divide the data into four equal groups where each group consists of a quarter of the data. Next the three quartiles are further defined and the interquartile range (IQR) is introduced.

- The first quartile (lowest quartile) is defined as the middle number between the smallest number and the median of the data. It is called the 25th percentile because it splits off the lowest 25% of data from the highest 75% of data.

- The second quartile is defined as the median of the data. It is called the 50th percentile because it cuts the data in half.

- The third quartile (upper quartile) is defined as the middle value between the median and the highest value of the data. It is called the 75th percentile because it splits off the highest 25% of data from the lowest 75% of data.

- The IQR shows extreme values (outliers) that can skew the data and is a relatively robust statistic compared to the traditional range and standard deviation. The IQR helps to establish boundaries with lower fence (bounds) and upper fence levels. Any data falling outside these defined bounds is considered an outlier.

Example: Quartiles are used to express wages, salaries, income levels, tax payments, and student grades (i.e., grade point average). A median salary of $100,000 for a highly technical employee can be said to fall in the second quartile.

Percentiles simply divide the data into 100 pieces; they are not dependent on the distribution of the data. Percentiles are a measure of data dispersion similar to standard deviation and range. Usually percentiles are expressed as 25, 50, 75, 90, or 95. When we say 70th percentile, we mean 70% of data is below the mean and 30% of data is above the mean. Percentiles use quartiles, but they are not the same. Quartile 1 means the 25th percentile; quartile 2 means the 50th percentile (median).

Outliers are data points that are outside of the expected point estimates or range estimates. They can be abnormal data points that should be looked at for further analysis to determine causes or origins.

Example: If a monthly utility bill for natural gas usage is expected to fall within a range of $100 and $150 based on historical data, an actual gas bill of $400 for a month can be called as an outlier.

In summary:

- Nominal, ordinal, interval, and ratio scales all count the frequency of occurrence of data or things.
- Nominal scales are qualitative variables with no inherent order to data or things.
- Ordinal, interval, and ratio scales have an inherent order to data or things.
- Nominal variables are used to name, code, or label data or things.
- A nominal variable is a qualitative variable where data attributes have no inherent order.
- An ordinal variable is a qualitative variable where data attributes are ordered and the difference between adjacent attributes is unknown or unequal.
- An interval variable is a quantitative variable where data attributes are ordered but for which the numerical difference between adjacent attributes is interpreted as known or equal.
- Interval variables provide the order of values plus the ability to quantify the difference between variables. They do not have "true zero" values.
- A ratio variable is a quantitative variable where data attributes are ordered, spaced equally, and with a true zero point.
- Ratio variables provide the order of values plus interval values plus the ability to calculate ratios. They do have "true zero" values.
- Indices, quartiles, percentiles, outliers, and interquartile rages are examples of descriptive statistics.

Data Analytics

Data analytics involves applying quantitative and qualitative tools and techniques to big data in order to gain new insights and new opportunities. Several types of data analytics exist, including these:

- Predictive analytics
- Embedded data analytics

- Fraud data analytics

- Streaming data analytics

- Social media data analytics

- Web-based data analytics

- Text-based data analytics

- Open-source data analytics

- Data modeling analytics

- Visual analytics

- Descriptive analytics

- Prescriptive analytics

- Benford's Law of First-Digit Test

Predictive Analytics

Predictive analytics is the process of estimating future outcomes based on the analysis of past data and/or current data. They describe what could happen.

For example, the U.S. Department of Health and Human Services has applied the following analytic techniques to identify improper payments and fraudulent activities perpetrated by healthcare providers (bad actors) in its Centers for Medicare & Medicaid Services:

- A rules-based technique filters fraudulent claims and associated behaviors with rules. It identifies providers that bill using a Medicare identification number that was previously stolen and used improperly.

- An anomaly-based technique detects individual and aggregated abnormal patients versus a peer group. It identifies providers that bill for more services in a single day than the number of services that 99% of similar providers bill in a single day.

- A predictive-based technique assesses against known fraud cases. It identifies providers that have characteristics similar to those of known bad actors.

- A network-based technique discovers knowledge using associative link analysis. It identifies providers that are linked to known bad actors through addresses or phone numbers.

For example, retail industry can use these predictive analytics:

- Estimating what customers will buy what products and from what markets

- Store customer foot traffic analysis through sensors and cameras

- Customer orders online

- Actual sales transactions

- Customer merchandise returns

- Online shopping cart abandonment

- Customer financial chargebacks

- New store location
- Cross-store merchandise locator
- Endless aisles of inventory
- Estimating customer retention rates and defection rates

These predictive analytics can be applied to any industry:

- Identifying new revenue opportunities by products or by markets
- Forecasting workforce requirements by type and skill
- Identifying the factors leading to employee satisfaction and productivity
- Identifying factors for customers filing a fraudulent claim
- Discovering the underlying reasons for employees' attrition rates
- Predicting what type of customers will default on a loan payment or credit card payment
- Predicting employee turnover rates
- Predicting equipment breakdowns before they disrupt operations

Embedded Data Analytics

Many organizations use embedded data analytics, such as data visualization tools, reporting routines and methods, and data dashboards, in their business-oriented application systems. The embedded analytics provide a real value to end users of such systems. Embedded analytics are a part of predictive analytics as they predict future events and outcomes. In contrast, traditional data analytics present past events and outcomes.

Forensic Data Analytics

The focus of fraud-related forensic data analytics is on fraud prevention, detection, and response (correction). It uses tools such as data visualization, text mining, web-scraping tools, data dashboards, statistical analysis (e.g., discovery sampling), link analysis, and social media. These tools are in addition to the older, traditional tools of inspecting, tracing, observing, counting, reconciling, comparing, and contrasting. Usually business rules, such as a dollar amount of claims or frequency of claims, are used to detect fraud.

Streaming Data Analytics

Streaming data analytics are performed in real time and in memory where they collect data from electronic sensors to produce time-series data. The use of streaming analytics increases as machine-generated data sources increase. Temporal analysis, which is based on the concept of time and which is a part of streaming data analytics, helps to understand different scenarios that are based on changing times. For example, a retail store selling, activating, or redeeming thousands of gift cards within a short period of time (e.g., three to four hours) can be an indication of fraud, or a sudden surge. This unusual activity in gift cards is a red flag.

Data stream processing presents current events as they are occurring. In contrast, traditional data analytics present past events and embedded data analytics predict future events.

Traditional Data Analytics $\longrightarrow$ Show Past Events

Streaming Data Analytics $\longrightarrow$ Show Current Events

Embedded Data Analytics $\longrightarrow$ Show Future events

Social Media Data Analytics

Social media analytics takes thousands and thousands of data items from online posts, followers, fans, page views, reviews, comments, pins, and mentions in various social media websites to evaluate marketing campaigns, advertisements, and promotions and to conclude what marketing efforts worked and what did not work.

Web-Based Data Analytics

Web scraping is a web-based data extraction and data mining approach. For example, it can search Twitter, a social media network, for keywords relating to fraud.

Text-Based Data Analytics

Text analytics focus on prescriptive analytics and descriptive analytics where they focus much on written materials and mobile text messages using SMS and MMS. Text analytics also include information from web call-center notes, comment fields posted on social media platforms, traditional reports, customer inquiries, web chats, and regular books. Text-based data are unstructured data and are useful to mine for fraud-related words on various data sources.

Open-Source Data Analytics

Open-source analytical tools and techniques are available, including open-source software, interoperable systems, and data-sharing facilities at low or no cost. The open-source algorithms can be consolidated in a central location to allow ease of access across several organizations to identify fraud, waste, and abuse. Moreover, the use of open-source tools could lessen the challenge of developing licensing agreements for proprietary software tools. Open-source data libraries can help in audits, inspections, and investigations.

Data Modeling Analytics

Data modeling analytics involve building data models, using simulation models, and testing them with what-if questions to see their answers in the form of changing outputs (outcomes) when inputs to the model change.

Visual Analytics

Visual analytics use data visualization tools, such as line charts, bar charts, scatter charts, bubble charts, and pie charts, to present relationships among big data in an easy-to-understand format. Senior managers prefer visual analytics, similar to data dashboards.

Descriptive Analytics

Descriptive analytics describe what already happened and include content analysis and context analysis.

Content analysis is a set of procedures for transforming unstructured written material into a format for analysis. It is a methodology for structuring and analyzing unstructured written material in documents and reports. For example, two or more documents can be analyzed to discover fraud-related content using specific words, symbols, names, events, outcomes, and addresses.

Example: Using text-data analytics, governmental agencies are looking at social media platforms for specific words or comments to: (1) identify terrorist activities; (2) discover fraudulent activities in food stamp programs; and (3) pinpoint fraud, waste, and abuse in healthcare payments.

Context analysis is useful because data can be contextual, meaning some data is related to a specific context (in context). Hence, a pool of data must be separated between in-context data and out-of-context data to analyze data trends and patterns. Examples of in-context data involve (1) insurance companies analyzing claims data during natural disasters; (2) retail companies analyzing sales data during holiday shopping seasons; (3) retail companies analyzing sales data during special weeklong promotions (e.g., blast sales, flash sales, or tent sales); and (4) retailers analyzing sales data during a season (in-context) and outside of the season (out of context) if the focus is on seasonal sales.

Prescriptive Analytics

Prescriptive analytics helps decide what should happen and thrives on big data. When faced with a number of potential decisions, it analyzes for the best possible outcome.

Examples:

- Optimal allocation of a company's stock market portfolio after considering expected returns and dividends
- Airline companies determining ticket prices after considering travel variables, such as customer demand, travel timings, travel locations, and holidays (For example, ticket prices are higher during holidays.)

Benford's Law of First-Digit Test

As part of fraud investigations, internal auditors can apply Benford's law of first-digit test to detect unusual data patterns arising from human errors, data manipulations, or fraudulent transactions. If the first digit in a financial account number or business transaction number is 1, chances are that it is a naturally occurring number (i.e., fraud-free). If the first digit is 9, good chances are that it might be a purposefully assigned number (i.e., fraudulent) to perpetrate fraud. The law looks to see whether the first digit is 1 or 9 because the digit 1 occurs 30% of the time and the digit 9 occurs only 5% of the time. In general, lower numbers (1 to 5) are usually freer of fraud than higher numbers (6 to 9), which are known to be fraudulent on the scale of 1 to 9. The following conditions apply:

The number is fraud-free if digits 1, 2, 3, 4, and 5 happen. They occur in combination 78% of the time.

It is fraudulent if digits 6, 7, 8, and 9 happen. They occur in combination 22% of the time.

If actual first-digit analysis indicates that digits 6 through 9 occur more often than their expected frequency, it is an indication of fraud or other irregularities, and further investigation as to their causes is required.

Data Mining

Data Mining Defined

Data mining is the application of database technologies and advanced data analytics to uncover hidden patterns, trends, correlations, outliers, anomalies, and subtle relationships in data and to infer rules that allow for the prediction of future results and outcomes. Data mining analyzes data for relationships that have not been discovered previously and other insights not suggested by a priori hypotheses or explicit assumptions. For example, these insights might apply to retail market trends in terms of customer buying preferences and customer shopping behaviors.[4]

Today, mining can be performed on many types of data, including in structured, unstructured, textual, Web, multimedia, and semistructured data (e.g., XML and HTML). Data mining overlaps with a wide range of analytical activities, including data profiling, databases, data warehouses, data marts, virtual databases, online analytical processing (OLAP), structured query language (SQL), statistical analyses, data modeling, and predictive data analytics.

Both private sector and public sector organizations are increasingly using data mining applications to achieve their purposes.

Data Mining in Private Sector

Private sector organizations are using data mining applications to explore new business opportunities with the sole goal of growing their business. A list of major purposes follows.

- Improving service or performance in increasing sales, revenues, and profits (major purpose)
- Detecting fraud, waste, and abuse
- Analyzing intelligence and detecting terrorist activities
- Analyzing scientific and research information
- Detecting criminal activities and patterns

A minor purpose of data mining is to improve employee, customer, and vendor safety.

Broadly speaking, private sector applications of data mining include customer relationship management, market research, retail, supply chain, medical analysis and diagnostics, financial analysis, and fraud detection.

---

[4]Adapted from *Data Mining: Federal Efforts Cover a Wide Range of Uses* (May 2004), GAO-04-548, www.gao.gov.

Data Mining in Public Sector

Public sector organizations are using data mining applications for a variety of purposes ranging from improving service or performance to analyzing and detecting terrorists' patterns and activities. A list of major purposes follows.

- Improving service or performance levels to citizens (major purpose)
- Detecting fraud, waste, and abuse, such as improper payments
- Analyzing scientific and research information for new drugs and new medical treatments
- Managing human resources for promotions, pay scales, pay grades, contractor security clearances, and employee background checks
- Detecting criminal activities or patterns, such as identity theft cases

A minor purpose is analyzing intelligence and detecting terrorist activities using Internet sources.

Broadly speaking, public sector applications of data mining focus on detecting financial fraud and abuse in procurement card and credit card programs and analyzing intelligence and detecting terrorist activities.

Privacy Concerns over Data Mining

A number of privacy concerns about mined or analyzed personal data exist, including worries about:

- The quality and accuracy of the mined data.
- The use of the data for other than the original purpose for which the data were collected without consent of the individual.
- The protection of the data against unauthorized access, modification, or disclosure.
- The right of individuals to know about the collection of personal information, how to access that information, and how to request a correction of inaccurate information.

Technologies in Data Mining

Six technical topics presented in this section include databases, virtual databases, data warehouses, data marts, online analytical processing (OLAP), structured query language (SQL), artificial intelligence and machine learning, and miscellaneous tools and techniques.

Databases

A database contains files with facts and figures on various types of information, such as sales, costs, and personnel. These files are collectively called the firm's database. A database is a collection of related data about an organization, intended for sharing of this data by multiple users. A database management system (DBMS) is comprised of software, hardware, and procedures. The DBMS acts as a software controller enabling different application systems to access large numbers of distinct data records stored on direct access storage devices (e.g., disks).

The DBMS handles complex data structures and should be compatible with the operating system environment. Unauthorized access to data elements is a major concern in a database system due to concentration of data. The DBMS provides a user interface with the application system through increased accessibility and flexibility by means of data views.

A data model describes relationships between the data elements and is used as a tool to represent the conceptual organization of data. A relationship within a data model can be one to one (e.g., between patient and bed in a hospital environment—at any given time, one bed is assigned to one patient), one to many (e.g., between hospital room and patients—one hospital room accommodates more than one patient), and many to many (e.g., between patient and surgeon—one surgeon may attend to many patients and a patient may be attended by more than one surgeon).

The primary purpose of any data model is to provide a formal means of representing information and of manipulating the representation. A good data model can help describe and model the application effectively. A DBMS uses one or more data models, such as relational, hierarchical, network, object, or distributed.

Virtual Databases

A virtual database is created when data from multiple database sources is integrated to provide a total perspective on a specific topic. It is virtual in that such database does not exist physically but is created on demand. For example, an auditor comparing performance of a multiplant organization can use virtual database technology to view key operating and financial ratios of each plant side by side.

Data Warehouses

Data warehouses have several definitions and purposes. The purpose of a data warehouse is information retrieval and data analysis. It stores precomputed, historical, descriptive, and numerical data. It is the process of extracting and transferring operational data into informational data and loading it into a central data store or "warehouse." Once loaded, users can access the warehouse through query and analysis tools. The data warehouse can be housed on a computer different from the production computer.

A data warehouse is a storage facility where data from heterogeneous databases is brought together so that users can make queries against the warehouse instead of against several databases. The warehouse is like a big database. Redundant and inconsistent data is removed from the databases, and subsets of data are selected from them prior to placing them in a data warehouse. Usually, summary data, correlated data, or data that is otherwise massaged is contained in the data warehouse.

Data integrity and security issues are as applicable to warehouses as they are to databases. An issue is: What happens to the warehouse when the individual databases are updated?

Data modeling is an essential task for building a data warehouse along with access methods, index strategies, and query language. For example, if the data model is relational, then an SQL-based language is used. If the data model is object-oriented, an object-based language may be appropriate.

Metadata management is another critical technology for data warehousing. Metadata includes the mapping between the data sources (databases) and the warehouse. Another issue is whether the warehouse can be centralized or distributed.

Data Marts

A data mart is a subset of a data warehouse (i.e., a mini-data warehouse). It brings the data from transaction processing systems to functional departments (i.e., finance, manufacturing, and human resources) or business units or divisions. Data marts are scaled-down data warehouses. Data marts place targeted business information is into the hands of more decision makers.

Online Analytical Processing

Online analytical processing (OLAP) programs are available to store and deliver data warehouse information from multidimensional databases. These programs allow users to explore corporate data from a number of different perspectives, such as product, geography, time, and salesperson.

OLAP servers and desktop tools support high-speed analysis of data involving complex relationships, such as combinations of a company's products, regions, channels of distribution, reporting units, and time periods. Access to data in multidimensional databases can be very quick because they store the data in structures optimized for speed, and they avoid using SQL and index processing techniques. In other words, multidimensional databases have greater retrieval speed and longer update times.

Consumer goods companies (e.g., retail) use OLAP to analyze the millions of consumer purchase records and transactions captured by electronic scanners at the checkout stand. This data is used to spot trends in purchases and to relate sales volume to store promotions (coupons) and store conditions (displays). The data in OLAP is generally aggregated, giving information such as total or average sales in dollars or units. Users can examine the OLAP's hierarchical data in the time dimension, such as sales by year, by quarter, by month, by week, or by day.

Structured Query Language

The primary components of a structured query language (SQL) database are schemas, tables, and views, parser, optimizer, executor, access rights checker, and access rights grantor or revoker. A schema describes the structure of related tables and views. Tables, which consist of rows and columns, hold the actual data in the database. Each row is a set of columns; each column is a single data element. Views are derived tables and may be composed of a subset of a table or the result of table operations (e.g., a join of different tables). A parser is a program that breaks input into smaller chunks so that a program can act on the information.

SQL is a standard query language for a relational database management system (DBMS) that is also used to query and update the data managed by the DBMS. The SQL standard, which is used by most commercial DBMSs, includes specific requirements for enforcing discretionary access controls.

Artificial Intelligence and Machine Learning Technology

Artificial intelligence (AI) is the simulation of human intelligence processing by machines and computer software. These processes contain learning rules, logical reasoning, and self-correction methods. For example, AI uses natural-language processing technology so it will process a retail shopper's questions and requests and provide answers. Other applications can be found in expert systems and speech recognition systems.

Machine learning (ML) is a type of AI that provides computers with the ability to learn without being explicitly programmed. ML focuses on the development of computer programs that can change their behavior when exposed to new data. Computers can handle new situations through analysis, self-training, observation, and experience, all with minimal supervision and involvement by people. ML is a part of predictive analytics and is related to cognitive computing.

Example 1: Macy's is testing the AI technology to improve sales. Customers can ask the Macy's mobile tool designed with the AI technology to receive answers related to the visited store such as where a particular brand is located or what is in stock. Normally, customers would ask a sales associate about these questions face-to-face.

Example 2: Retailers such as North Face and 1-800-Flowers are using the AI technology so customers can receive answers to their questions on the retailer's websites, not face-to-face.

Example 3: Transportation and package delivery companies can use AI-based chatbots to track packages by internal employees and external customers.

Miscellaneous Tools and Techniques

Miscellaneous tools and techniques include neural networks and text-mining. Neural networks learn by training where they can be used or reused in reviewing credit card transactions to detect anomalies and fraudulent activities. Text-mining tools are used to scan unstructured documents such as emails, web pages, and audio/video files and to scan structured data found in databases or data warehouses.

Summary of Technologies Used in Data Mining with Their Purposes

- A database contains raw data collected from daily business transactions.
- A data warehouse contains massaged, cleansed, and normalized data.
- End users query many points with heterogeneous databases.
- End users query only a single point with homogeneous data warehouses.
- A data warehouse provides summary data for the entire business.
- A data mart provides detailed data for a specific function of a business (a mini-data warehouse).
- Data mining is an end user tool to select information from a data warehouse.
- Data mining is an auditing tool to detect fraud, intrusion incidents, and security problems in a data warehouse.
- Advanced technologies are used, including artificial intelligence, machine learning, and neural networks to perform sophisticated analysis

Applications in Data Mining

Data mining is the process of asking (posing) a series of questions (queries) against a database or data warehouse containing large amounts of data to extract some meaningful, relevant, and useful information to perform management analysis. A data warehouse or data mart itself does not attempt to extract information from the data it contains. A data mining tool is needed to extract data.

Data mining applications are best suited to data-intense organizations with millions of customers' data collected in their databases or data warehouses. Examples of data-intense organizations include retailers, market research firms, governmental agencies, online order takers, casinos, travel agencies, vacation cruise line firms, hotels, rental car companies, and airline companies. There is no end to the data mining applications; the imagination of the person requesting the data analysis work is the only limit.

Data mining applications software is available from a number of vendors. Off-the-shelf software generally makes these applications easier to use and less expensive than custom-built software.

Data mining is data analysis, data fishing, data snooping, and data drilling in order to get to the bottom of the vast amounts of data (big data) collected by organizations during their business operations. Another name for data mining is data analytics.

To analyze data, find relationships between data elements, and draw meaningful conclusions that can be incorporated into its decision-making process, management uses various quantitative techniques, such as regression analysis, factor analysis, cluster analysis, sampling, and other statistical methods. The ultimate goal of data mining is to improve business operations and increase profits.

Data mining can be applied to databases as well as to data warehouses and data marts. A warehouse structures the data in such a way as to facilitate query processing. Data mining is a set of automated tools that convert the data in the warehouse into some useful information. It selects and reports information deemed significant from a data warehouse or database.

Before data mining software tools are applied, the target data (raw datasets) must be cleansed (sanitized) and normalized to remove missing data, erroneous data, or inappropriate data. Here, data mining tools can discover data relationships and data clusters; (i.e., groupings of similar data items). Data mining also uncovers patterns and trends in data.

There are several types of data mining applications, including data classifications, data sequencing, data dependencies, and deviation analysis. Data records can be grouped into clusters or classes so that patterns in the data can be found. Data sequencing can be determined from the data. Data dependencies, such as relationships or associations between the data items, can be detected. Deviation analysis can be performed on data. Fuzzy logic, neural networks, and set theory are some techniques used in data mining tools.

Data mining techniques can also be used for intrusion and fraud detection and to audit the databases. Data mining tools can be used to detect abnormal patterns in data, which can provide clues to fraud. A security problem can be created when a user poses queries and infers sensitive hypotheses. That is, the inference problem occurs via the data mining tool. A data mining tool can be applied to see if sensitive information can be deduced from unclassified information legitimately obtained. If so, then there is an inference problem. An inference controller can be built and placed between the data mining tool and the database to detect user motives and prevent the inference problem from occurring. Since data mining tools are computationally intensive, parallel processing computers are used to carry out the data mining activities.

Harrah's Casino and Hotel in Las Vegas, an entertainment company, is a big user of data mining applications. Interested customers (guests) are given an electronic card before gambling. This card collects data on guests' gambling actions in terms of what games they play, how much time they spend on each type of game, what games they lose or win, how many times they visit the casino in a year, how many days they stay in the hotel for each visit, whether they come alone or with family, and their personal income. For example, if a guest's personal income is very high, this application recommends that the guest play high-stakes games with very attractive incentives and rewards. Different incentive and reward programs are available for guests with more typical personal income. This application is a win-win situation in that the casino makes additional profit on the guest and the guest enjoys extra perks (royal treatment) that he or she would not have received otherwise.

Other examples of application of data mining are listed next.

- Market segmentation, where data mining identifies the common characteristics of customers who buy the same products

- Customer defection, where data mining predicts which customers are likely to leave the company

- Fraud detection, where data mining identifies which transactions are most likely to be fraudulent

- Direct marketing, where data mining identifies which prospects are the target for mailing

- Market basket analysis, where data mining identifies what products or services are commonly purchased together

- Trend analysis, where data mining reveals the difference between a typical customer this month versus last month.

About the Author

S. RAO VALLABHANENI is an educator, author, publisher, consultant, and practitioner in business with more than 30 years of management and teaching experience in auditing, accounting, manufacturing, and IT consulting in both the public and the private sector. He is the author of more than 60 trade books, study guides, review books, monographs, audit guides, and articles in auditing and IT, mostly to prepare for professional certification exams in business. He holds 24 professional certifications in business management in the fields of General Management, Accounting, Auditing, Finance, Information Technology, Manufacturing, Quality, and Human Resource. He taught several undergraduate and graduate courses in business administration and management programs at the university level for many years. He earned four master's degrees in Management, Accounting, Industrial Engineering, and Chemical Engineering.

Index